Integral Research and Innovation

Transformation and Innovation Series

Series Editors:
Ronnie Lessem, University of Buckingham, UK
Alexander Schieffer, University of St. Gallen, Switzerland

This series on business transformation and social innovation comprises a range of books informing practitioners, consultants, organization developers, and academics how businesses and other organizations can and will have to be transformed into viable 21st Century enterprises. A new kind of R&D, involving social, as well as technological innovation, needs to be supported by integrated, active and participative research in the social sciences. Focusing on new, emerging kinds of public, social and sustainable entrepreneurship originating from all corners of the world and from different cultures, books in this series will help those operating in the area of interface between business and society to mediate between the two in the way that business schools once did until, as is now argued, they lost their way and business leaders came, in many cases, to be seen as at best incompetent and at worst venal and untrustworthy.

Integral Research and Innovation

Transforming Enterprise and Society

RONNIE LESSEM AND
ALEXANDER SCHIEFFER

GOWER

Gower Applied Business Research
Our programme provides leaders, practitioners, scholars and researchers with thought provoking, cutting edge books that combine conceptual insights, interdisciplinary rigour and practical relevance in key areas of business and management.

Published by
Gower Publishing Limited
Wey Court East
Union Road
Farnham
Surrey, GU9 7PT
England

Ashgate Publishing Company
Suite 420
101 Cherry Street
Burlington,
VT 05401-4405
USA

www.gowerpublishing.com

British Library Cataloguing in Publication Data
Lessem, Ronnie.
  Integral research and innovation : transforming enterprise
  and society. -- (Transformation and innovation)
  1. Social responsibility of business. 2. Organizational
  change--Social aspects.
  I. Title II. Series III. Schieffer, Alexander.
  658.4'08-dc22

  ISBN: 978-0-566-08918-3 (hbk)
  ISBN: 978-0-566-08919-0 (ebk)

Library of Congress Cataloging-in-Publication Data
Lessem, Ronnie.
  Integral research and innovation : transforming enterprise and society / by Ronnie Lessem
  and Alexander Schieffer.
    p. cm. -- (Transformation and innovation)
  Includes bibliographical references and index.
  ISBN 978-0-566-08918-3 (hardback) -- ISBN 978-0-566-08919-0
  (ebook) 1. Organizational change--Social aspects. 2. Organizational sociology. 3. Personality.
  I. Schieffer, Alexander. II. Title.
  HD58.8.L4734 2010
  302.3'5--dc22

                                                                              2009029712

Mixed Sources
Product group from well-managed forests and other controlled sources
www.fsc.org Cert no. SA-COC-1565
© 1996 Forest Stewardship Council

Printed and bound in Great Britain by
MPG Books Group, UK

Contents

List of Figures

About Integral Research and Innovation

'The authors Lessem and Schieffer have written this remarkable book on 'Research Methodology' which is responsive to all relevant stakeholders. Researchers from the North, the South, the East and the West are now able to draw on their own roots to turn social research into social innovation. A major achievement!'

Prof. Dr. Martin Hilb, Managing Director of the Institute for Leadership and Human Resource Management,University of St. Gallen, Switzerland

'A landmark contribution of social and management research scholarship conceptually and methodologically. A readable and rigorous book, which is characterised by comprehensiveness, insights, structure and clarity; and which is aided by informative executive summaries, figures and illustrations. The book represents a coherent interpretation and a reliable reference of key and diverse classical and contemporary schools of research philosophy and methodology. It is a timely and pioneering book which successfully demonstrates the intellectual and the practical grounds of 'social innovation' and which convincingly argues for the beneficial employment of the so long neglected philosophical and conceptual contributions of South and East in social and management research scholarship. I strongly believe that the book's provocative, grounded and convincing arguments will extend the horizons of prevailing research thoughts and practices and would leave a positive impact on social and management research scholarships and students.'

Prof. Adel Rasheed, Professor of Management, Yarmouk University, Irbid, Jordan

'Ronnie Lessem and Alexander Schieffer have developed a bold new way of framing transformation processes that crosses the boundaries of several disciplines. Their 'integral approach' offers a novel analysis that cleverly bridges research and social innovation. Their way of generating innovation provides a valuable road map that enables change agents to creatively synthesize local identities and global context.'

Prof. Dr. Raoul C. D. Nacamulli, Università di Milano-Bicocca, Italy

In love and gratefulness:
From Ronnie, to Joey and his mother Edith
From Alexander, to Rama and his mother Anemone

1 *Orientation to Social Innovation*

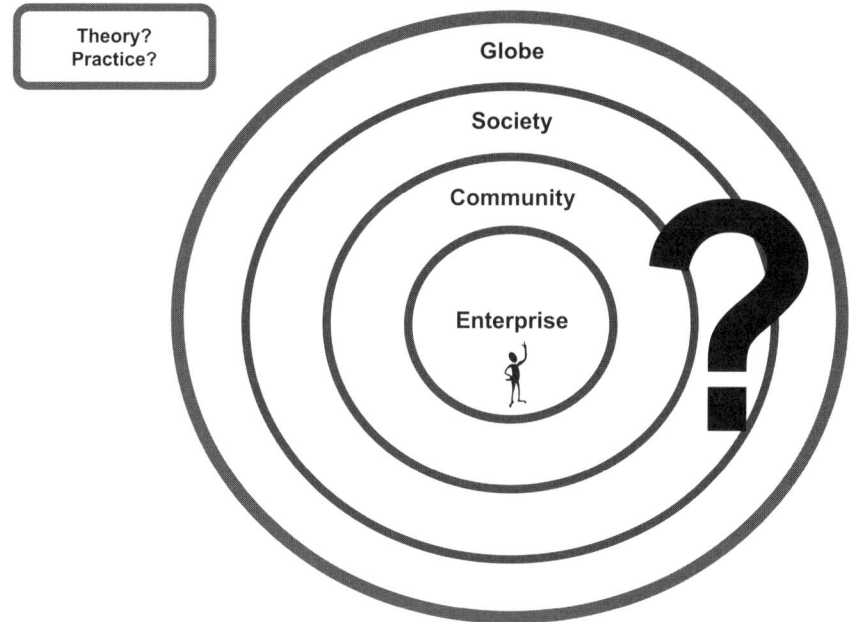

1 *Towards A New Research and University Paradigm*

Introducing Integral Research and Integral University

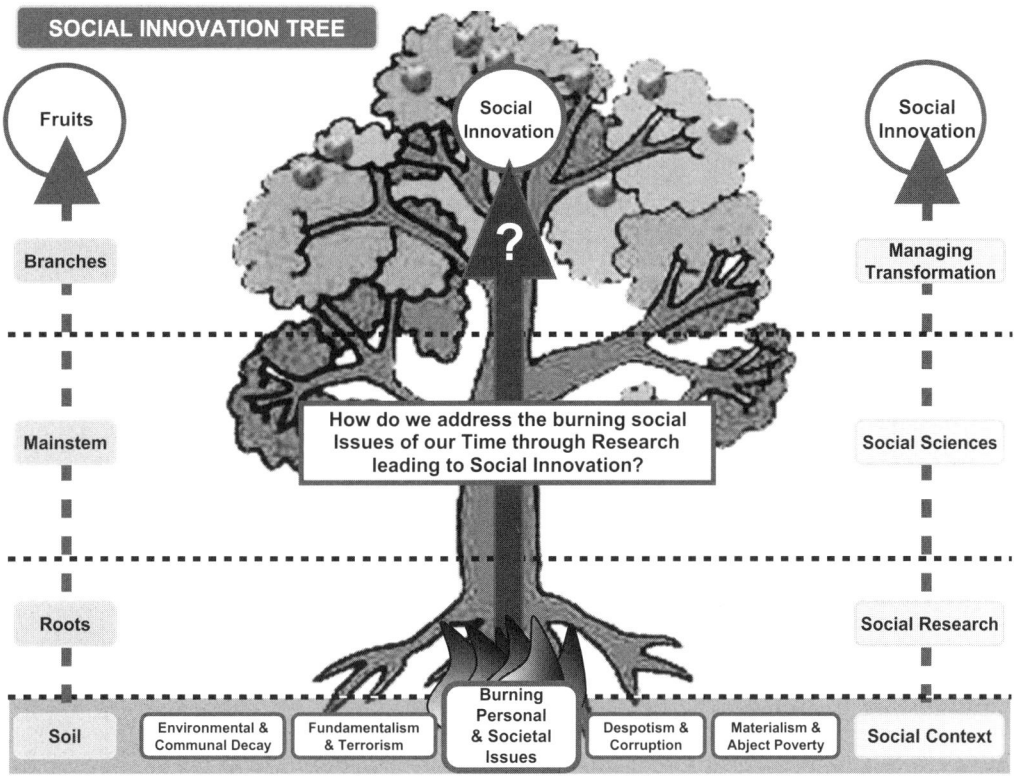

Figure 1.1   Can Research lead to Social Innovation?

Summary: Towards a New Research and University Paradigm

- The core question underlying this book is: 'How can social research be turned into social or indeed "integral" innovation?' We ask this question because there is a distinct lack of social innovation coming out of social research, on the one hand, and a desperate need for innovation in most sectors of society, on the other.
- In this book, therefore, we address social scientists, students and practitioners who want to become innovators in the social and economic arena by applying Integral Research and innovation to their research and development work.
- We believe that if this takes place, university social sciences departments around the world will regain their rightful place as sources of knowledge creation, and ultimately social innovation, dealing with burning issues that are particular to their society, rather than delegating that role to corporate research and development (R&D) departments on the one hand and the natural sciences on the other.
- In research terms, as in 'real life', it is the Western and the Northern approaches that dominate (with some exceptions), while the Southern and Eastern ones have been left out. One of our core arguments is that this is the reason why most research fails to lead to innovation.
- We also reconnect with the social philosophies which are vital for all research. All too often we fail to recognize the philosophical foundations of research methodologies, which in most social science research are disconnected from the research content.
- In the rare cases where philosophies *are* recognized, it is mostly those representing the North and West; philosophers from the East and South, whose methodological approaches are more closely linked to their culture and its issues, are left out.
- The story of one of us (Ronnie Lessem) serves as a representative tale of a social researcher who initially involved himself in the Western and Northern worlds, while bypassing (for a while) his own southern (African) home ground, even though it was in desperate need of social innovation.
- In this one researcher's lifetime is embodied the global phenomenon, which many of you might be experiencing, of a left-out South and East. Now Ronnie, together with fellow author Alexander, is seeking to make up for it.
- The route we take towards Integral Research and innovation is a fourfold one, encompassing Southern and Eastern, as well as Northern and Western, paths, each of which has a fourfold, and double layered, static as well as research-to-innovation trajectory.
- Such an approach to Integral Research is potentially embodied in an Integral University, lodged within a particular culture and society, and inherently transdisciplinary in its approach to social science and the humanities.

1.1 The Quest for Social Innovation

INNOVATION: BUZZWORD OF OUR TIMES

'Innovation' is the buzzword of our times. Each business is concerned with it and claims that it will soon be 'out of the market' if it loses its power to innovate. Entire societies, governments and political parties nail their colours to the innovation mast, and thereby claim to be doing everything in order to promote it. They are committing themselves to developing a legal, financial, educational and communicational infrastructure for innovation, with business being inevitably expected to take the lead.

But what do we really mean by innovation?

Invariably the term innovation is used to represent 'technical and technological innovation'. It reflects advancement in core industries (from automotive to communications, from information technology to chemistry and biotechnology, from solar energy to medical science, from the financial industry to logistics, from airline to space technology). Billions of dollars are pumped into research and development to enable technological innovation to take place in those sectors. Of course all of such is important. But, while parts of the world have become highly innovative in technological terms, what we term 'social innovation' lags way behind.

The world increasingly suffers from the downsides of such technological, and now also financial, innovation. Now we are faced with environmental destruction and economic crises, all too often serving to increase the gaps between wealth and poverty, and social injustice, health and security problems, as well as so-called clashes between civilizations. As materialism advances, there is an increasing sense of unrest, insecurity and lack of rootedness, psychologically and spiritually. And then we turn again to technology to find the solutions for such problems. We want our industries to become more environmentally friendly, we want our pharmaceutical companies and global health initiatives to solve our health problems, we want technology to be developed to resolve the digital divide, and so on. Moreover, we in the West and North believe that once poor countries have developed economies, with technology thereby playing a major part, many of the current problems will be solved automatically.

RE-SEARCHING THE ROLE OF RESEARCH AND UNIVERSITY

We, the authors of this book, believe, in fact, otherwise. After all, the might of technology, aligned with economics, has not so far proven able to solve these problems, nor to significantly reduce them. Our claim therefore is not that we should abandon innovation, but that we are seeing innovation in far too one-dimensional terms. There is more to life, and work, than technological and economic innovation. There is social innovation, and in this book we are going to demonstrate why social innovation is equally important and how it can be achieved by drawing upon a new approach towards research. Such a new approach towards research is lodged in specific cultural soils, intimately connected with the social sciences, addressing burning issues of our day. In the process, we also draw upon a new approach towards university education as a whole to promote such. In this book we coin these new approaches *Integral Research* and *Integral University*.

We will explore the scope of social innovation and will demonstrate how different cultures have developed over time different ways to generate knowledge and to become socially innovative. We argue that the roots as well as the main stem of being and becoming socially innovative need to be re-discovered, and, moreover, that such a dual process can only be undertaken in relation to the particular cultural context, explicitly drawing upon social science content. The ultimate objective we are trying to achieve with our new Integral Research design is to reformulate research in the social sciences in a way that leads to social innovation.

While technological innovation focuses on the natural sciences, we focus on the social sciences. This book is therefore for social scientists, ranging from economists to political scientists, from geographers to historians, from anthropologists to sociologists, from psychologists to students of religious, environmental and of course business studies and management. But it is particularly for those social scientists who aim to become social innovators. Our approach to uncovering the roots of social innovation (see Figure 1.1) is not merely an intellectual exercise. It is much more than that. It requires a deep understanding of the roots of social innovation in your own specific society.

In that context we need to understand why research in the social sciences does not lead to social innovation, and, later in this chapter, why most universities are ignoring what for us is their birthright: that is, to be a hub for social innovation.

1.2 Why Social Innovation Falls Behind Technological Innovation

ENTERPRISE, UNIVERSITY AND HUMANITY

When we ask many of our business or academic colleagues how they are advancing the lot of mankind through their commercial activities or the 'research' papers they write, we get incredulous looks. Similarly, when we ask clients in the corporate world how their research and development activities are contributing to resolving our pensions crisis, social injustice, human poverty around the globe, the problem of world climate change, or, more recently, the global financial crisis, we get similarly blank looks. 'That's all very well', the academics say, 'our students just want to get a degree', or 'I have a PhD to complete'. Alternately, for business or management practitioners, 'I have targets to meet', or, 'It's up to the government, not us'.

The idea that they might be advancing the lot of mankind, purposefully through social innovations, as opposed to pragmatically and rationally getting on with things that concern themselves, is left way out in the cold. In fact, and this was very true of the 2008 financial crisis, it is amazing that nobody seems to look towards universities for either the source of a problem or as the source of its solution. That is why – in Amy Chua's[1] words – the world is on fire! Enterprise, university and humanity don't meet.

Three decades ago, then, one of us (Ronnie Lessem) set out on a research journey to re-create 'business as an extension of the human being', as a potential social innovation. Having been involved in a large and commercially successful family business in the former Rhodesia, now Zimbabwe, he had the nagging feeling that, for all its material benefit, business was failing his people spiritually. For while his company would readily adopt and adapt the latest fashions from Europe, and materials from the Far East, the spirit of Africa seemed to be missing from both the factory floor and from the clothing designs. In other words, the company, a thousand strong, was technically and economically highly efficient, and was commercially very profitable, but there was no indigenous artistic impulse or overall spiritual uplift to behold.

Moreover, when he first studied 'Principles of Economics' at the University of Rhodesia and Nyasaland – as it was called in the early 1960s – the 'Western' free market subject matter was alien to his 'Southern' soul. Most certainly it was not invented there, in Rhodesia-becoming-Zimbabwe, and the social sciences he studied, ranging from political science to economics theory, political philosophy to economic history, had no intrinsic connection with the culture and nature of Africa! Actually, it was just the opposite. 'Free market Rhodesia' into Zimbabwe did not altogether go, and many a tragedy was to unfold out of that particular impasse.

So Ronnie embarked in the 1970s on a journey around what he conceived as a more *Global Business*...[2] Soon afterwards, as politics and economics came to blows with each other, Rhodesia in becoming Zimbabwe began to 'catch fire', firstly through the liberation war in the 1970s, and secondly through the land crisis and Mugabe's response to it in the 1980s and 1990s. In fact, the classical economic concept of private property and economically laden free markets, as Ronnie came to discover, sat uncomfortably with the anthropologically oriented 'natural man'. The gap between the two concepts, the global, propertied rich and the local, landless poor, remains just as great to this day, now visible around the world.

FIDDLING AWAY FROM HOME WHILE THE HOME FIRES BURNED

It was in the 1970s and 1980s, now based in the UK, that Ronnie completed his own PhD on 'Action Learning for Business Development', focused on the development of entrepreneurs in London's inner cities. It feels to him now, looking back, that he was fiddling away from home, while the world of his birth burned. He was not the only one. How many Africans, Indians and others had proceeded onto greener pastures?

His doctoral research seemed to have no relevance (in the 1970s) to his cause: that of linking African as well as Arab, Chinese or Indian spirits to global technique, and there was certainly nothing co-creative about him pursuing his individual cause. Indeed no social innovation was in the immediate offing. That having been said, his focus was on 'action learning', something he would revisit later in now 'action research' guise (see Chapter 16). Moreover, it was the originator of such action learning, the English management philosopher Reg Revans, who proclaimed:

> the salvation of individual countries and their enterprises is not to be found by observers scouring the world in the hope of turning up some miracle there. Their salvation rather, their 'Kingdom of God' is to be found within their own shores, and within the wills of their own people. At the level of the individual enterprise, it is not unreasonable to suggest that an essential part of any research and development policy is the study of the human effort, out of which the saleable products of the enterprise are largely created ... Learning as such must demand not only research and analysis. It must demand power to get the knowledge needed to see one's part in what is going on. In particular one needs to know the effect of one's behaviour upon those with whom one works ... best achieved within small action learning groups...[3]

It was indeed in the context of such small action learning groups, together engaged with individual business start-ups in the UK, that Ronnie pursued his doctoral studies. They were duly inspired by Revans' action learning approach, which also served to underpin the project-based Masters which he subsequently evolved at City University, in the financial heartlands of London. In fact, as a graduate of the 'Western' Harvard Business School, he had found its allegedly practical 'case study' approach distinctly lacking in genuinely experiential Anglo-Saxon foundations. Whether for a Masters or a doctorate, one simply 'had to do' research. Further, no distinction was made between method and methodology, not to mention the critical emancipatory or action research orientations Ronnie would discover 20 years later. In fact, it was as far removed at the time from any social innovation as planet Earth is from Mars. It had no meaning in relation to his personal, professional or societal origins, as Ronnie Lessem, as an economist, or as a Rhodesian/Zimbabwean, and offered his society no potential for innovation.

So when Ronnie returned periodically to a newly independent Zimbabwe as a management educator and researcher in the 1980s, he tried to make up for lost time, to rediscover the lost spirit of the 'South' in a business context. The specific cause he was seeking to advance, that of business as grounded in human *being*, rather than in purely commercial *doing*, only seemed to take off when he assumed authorship of his life through his work as a management researcher and would-be social innovator in the latter part of the 1980s. Unwittingly, he was beginning to uncover a new approach to research that was genuinely 'out of this whole world' and that could lead to authentic social innovation. Initially it drew upon 'global',[4] and subsequently upon African[5] – as well as European, Arab and Chinese – management styles. How so?

SOCIAL RESEARCH IS DISCONNECTED FROM PHILOSOPHIES

Business enterprise in the European Community, Ronnie wrote in the early 1990s – together with his co-author Franz Neubauer[6] – has not emerged in a vacuum. In effect it has evolved in significant part, notwithstanding the ever-increasing influence of America and Japan, out of the European continent's particular set of cultural heritages. These distinct heritages are reflected in art, religion, philosophies and ideologies, duly manifested in the approaches to anthropology and sociology, politics and psychology, that have developed over the past three millennia in Europe. At the same time the continent has evolved its diverse people and communities, its multifaceted sciences and institutions, as well as its specific attitudes and behaviours. Yet none of these institutions 'speaks for themselves' as its seminal ideas, that is its diverse European philosophies:

> *Philosophy brings clarity and meaning into careers of individuals, nations, civilisations. Such is the strength of tradition that men have always tended to accept the particular philosophy or religion prevailing in the group into which they were born. Human beings, primitive or civilised, educated or uneducated, cannot escape from philosophy. Philosophy is everybody's business.*[7]

The importance of philosophy for research is well illustrated by the example of Orlando Fals Borda in the 1970s. Spearheaded by Fals Borda, the Colombian professor of economics who had become disenchanted with conventional 'Northern' European academe, 'Western' (capitalist) and 'Eastern' (socialist) economics, a new research methodology was devised which was called 'participative action research' (PAR). PAR (see Chapter 7) was not only an intriguing 'southern' counterpart to Revans' 'Western' orientation to action learning and action research, it was also a new philosophical fusion of action and knowledge.

Philosophers like Fals Borda are supposed to be our experts in integration; they form a general staff for coping with the increasing fragmentation of our culture:

> *They are the liaison officers among the many different and often isolated branches of knowledge; between the civilizations of the past and present; between the great living systems of belief that move the various nations of our day. Philosophers are always reminding people of the interrelatedness of things, bringing together what has been torn apart and disunited...*[8]

What we did not realise in the 1990s is that philosophy is indeed the foundation of research, as shall be explained later in this chapter and in full detail in Chapter 3.

The origination of a new research methodology has always been connected to philosophy, more precisely, to a fundamental philosophical critique of the societal status quo. This is true, as we shall see, for empiricism and critical rationalism, as much as for phenomenology, feminism and postmodernism. It is also true in the case of PAR. The problem, as we see it, is that this fundamental connection is often not made, and, because of that, not actively taken forward. For example, even to this day – in the emerging knowledge era – neither socialists nor capitalists have yet purposefully drawn upon PAR. For Bangladesh's Muhammad Anisur Rahman, who was formerly based at the International Labour Organization (ILO) and is, together with Fals Borda, a seminal figure in PAR:

> Historical experience calls for rethinking the meaning of social transformation for people's liberation. The dominant view of such has been preoccupied with the need for changing the oppressive structures of relations in material production – certainly a necessary task. But, and this is the distinctive view of PAR, domination of elites is also rooted in control over social power to determine what is useful knowledge, the one (knowledgeable) then reinforcing the other (material). In fact existence of the gap in knowledge relations can offset the advantages of reducing the gap in relations of physical production ... People then cannot be liberated by a consciousness and knowledge other than their own. It is therefore essential that they develop their own endogenous consciousness-raising and knowledge generation abilities. This requires the social power to assert this vis-à-vis elite consciousness and knowledge.[9]

These participatory action researchers were effective Southern forerunners of the knowledge revolution, which was to ensue in the West, North and East 20 years later. However, they virtually got lost in the process.

SOCIAL RESEARCH FAILS TO INTEGRATE DIFFERENT EPISTEMOLOGIES

As Ronnie and his German colleague Franz Neubauer – both then based at the Institute for Management Development (IMD) in Switzerland – wrote in the early 1990s, as Europe develops its knowledge-based economy so the need to replace the materially based factors of production – land, labour and capital – with knowledge-based ones becomes paramount.[10] *The four most pervasive sources of knowledge, or philosophies, from our point of view, are pragmatism, rationalism, holism and humanism.* What would take us long years is to realize that these philosophies (or 'ontologies') spawn in turn different 'epistemologies', which give rise to the diverse 'methodologies' with which our new approach to research is concerned. Moreover, and of particular significance for us as researchers and developers, *each of these philosophies has different political and economic implications.*

These generic philosophies have, at a micro level, spawned diverse concepts and applications that at least partly precondition European as well as American business and economic activity. However, at a macro level only one of these, that of the pragmatically based market economy (and its derivative business practice of free enterprise), has yet seen the full light of our economic day. As for the other three philosophies, their time is still to come, both in business theory and in practice. Now that Marxism has suffered its demise, as Fals Borda and Rahman were already recognizing in the 1970s when PAR first began to emerge, we are left with the limiting prospect of only one sociopolitical ideology

– capitalism – dominating the macro economic scene. We hence felt the need to deepen and extend our business and economic foundations, on the one hand, and our research methodologies, on the other. In so doing we were following in PAR's emancipatory footsteps, while also recognizing that we needed the altogether integral impetus from the West, North, East and South. Such an integral approach serves to enliven and transcend both capitalism and socialism, by fusing together pragmatism and rationalism, holism and humanism.

In the course of uncovering *'European Management Systems'* we probed into the philosophies of Bacon, Locke and Mill in England; Descartes, Diderot and Montesquieu in France; Leibniz, Goethe and Kant in Germany; as well as Vico and Croce in Italy. At that time, in the early 1990s, despite having successfully completed his PhD some ten years before, Ronnie was blissfully unaware of the fact that these philosophers had any influence whatsoever on the research method he had deployed in his thesis. In fact, he was ignorant of the link when he wrote a subsequent work, *The Light and the Shadow: How Breakthrough Innovation is Shaping European Business*[11] (cited in *Managing in Four Worlds*).[12] Whereas we are now able to connect Ikijiro Nonaka's knowledge creating cycle of socialization and externalization, combination and internalization, with the Four Worlds of humanism (Southern) and holism (Eastern), rationalism (Northern) and pragmatism (Western), research methodology has remained totally disconnected from such. In effect, John Heron's action research oriented process of co-operative inquiry (see Chapter 10), not to mention David Kolb's[13] famous learning cycle (concrete experience – reflective observation – abstract conceptualization – active experimentation), and indeed Revans' process of action learning (audit – survey – hypothesize – act), are similarly aligned. However, altogether lacking in such an integral learning and research process, social innovation has been stultified.

SOCIAL RESEARCH AND INNOVATION ARE A MILLION MILES APART

Ronnie's wake-up call came when he established a global doctoral programme at the University of Buckingham in the UK. It was then, and only then, that the proverbial penny began to drop. *Not only was research methodology an extension of philosophy, but the philosophers that had spawned such methodologies were all, yes all, social innovators of the day.* This indeed applies as much to Africa and the Middle East today, for example, as it did in the Europe of yesterday.

Even the standard 'Western' pragmatism, or more specifically the empiricism and 'positivism' that characterizes such European-based research philosophy and methodology, originally emerged in the Enlightenment as a reaction against religious and political dogmatism. Indeed Morton Schlick, a key member of the Vienna Circle of 'logical positivists'[14] in the 1920s and 1930s, was shot by the Nazis, because of his anti-fascist beliefs. When Ronnie compared these original philosophies, which he had now systematically begun to absorb from all parts of Europe, with the anodyne way in which they were conventionally described in the academic research texts, he was shocked. In fact, his colleague John Heron, then based at the Centre for Human Potential at the University of Surrey, put it very well in his seminal work on 'co-operative inquiry':

> *Research in the human sciences is very much an academic pursuit, based in and originating from universities. They are committed to the intellect as the controlling force in individual and*

social life, and to the pre-eminence of 'propositional' knowledge, a set of intellectual statements published in systematic form. Staff, as such, unilaterally make decisions on behalf of students. They decide what the students should learn, how and when, and assess such according to their own criteria. Academics do not need to acquire the kind of emotional and interpersonal competence to empower students to learn more holistically and participate in educational decisions to enable them to become progressively more self-determining ... Such authoritarian control, moreover, is transferred from teaching to research. While we consider that the 18 year old has the right to vote, he or she has no right to participate in educational decision-making. We consider that a person has the choice whether to take part in a research program, but has no right to have a say in what it is about...[15]

So what we began to realize, firstly, was not only that these quintessentially European philosophies were sources of knowledge creation, but also that they potentially fuelled social innovation. Secondly, such philosophies and derivative methodologies were almost all European – as much as the corresponding research methods were American – so that Asia, the Middle East, Latin America and Africa did not get a look in. Thirdly, the very reason that such methodologies were not explicit sources of social innovation was their lack of global reach. For example, while empirical and experimental research had led to technological innovation in the physical sciences, this was less apparent in the social sciences. Similarly, as far as participatory action research was concerned, its social activism all too often has fallen short of social innovation. That hurt. Where, then, could we go from here, being confronted, as we illustrate in Figure 1.2, with dysfunctional social research?

Figure 1.2   Dysfunctional Research

1.3 A New Research Paradigm: Towards Integral Research

THE FIRST WAKE-UP CALL: SOCIAL RESEARCH CAN LEAD TO SOCIAL INNOVATION!

Method and Methodology are Part of an Integral Whole

It had taken him, as we have now intimated, some 40-odd years of wandering, like Moses, in the research desert as a management academic, before Ronnie saw gradually emerging pictures of the Promised Land. These involved, firstly, an integral perspective on research (leading to social innovation), out of which *research method and methodology were each parts of a more integral whole*. For he had been absolutely put off for those four long decades by an initially tedious, stand alone undergraduate course on 'statistical research methods'. The other author, Alexander Schieffer, had developed the same aversion during various doctoral seminars on research methodologies at the University of St Gallen in Switzerland, and he was fortunate to have met Ronnie at an earlier stage of his life, enabling him to reconnect to this matter.

Ronnie laments that it took him those long years of travelling through such an educational, managerial and research desert, across four continents, to ultimately transform, with the help of the oases of leading lights he periodically discovered, such prosaic methods into formative grounds, building blocks or sources of origination for social innovation. The key that opened such a transformative door was his discovery that differentiated research paths could not only be horizontally aligned with the Four Worlds, but that each of them led from research origination to transformative innovation.

Ronnie had been supervising doctoral and Masters students as an academic, within his transcultural field, for some 25 years, that is since the 1980s, and Alexander had been doing so since 2002. While the topics of doctoral research that we have supervised had been wide-ranging, the research methods remained pretty standard, and duly isolated from any developing whole. While the use of case studies has recently predominated, historically speaking survey methodologies generally, and questionnaires and interviews specifically, have been the order of the undergraduate and postgraduate day. The approach has been invariably pragmatic and rational, bereft of humanity and holism, invariably combining the use of questionnaires with a statistical analysis of the results.

As far as our practical and project-based Masters programme in transformation management had been concerned, which had been developed before our doctoral programme, first at City University in London and subsequently at the University of Buckingham, we had fought shy of incorporating research method or methodology because, for all that we were aware, it would take the managers involved straight down a classically analytically, and thus exclusively rational, research track, rather than furthering the practice of transformation. In fact, for the first time in 2007, after the project-based Masters had been running for almost two decades, we felt ready to incorporate research methodology, because of its transformative, action-centred orientation, building upon the informative methods, methodologies and critiques that come before.

The Disintegrated Conventional Wisdom Ignored the Integral Whole

As far as the doctoral students were concerned, each research project would include an overarching methodological chapter, which would differentiate between 'positivist' and 'interpretivist' approaches. Due heed would be paid to inductively oriented Bacon and Mill, and to deductively oriented Popper if not also Hempel. Robert Yin was invariably referred to for his case study method, and, on occasion, Glazer and Strauss for their 'grounded theory'. Ultimately, there would be an extensive reliance on interviews, questionnaires and statistical analysis of results. Above all, what would characterize the vast majority of the research, altogether at undergraduate and postgraduate – Masters and doctoral – levels, was the *extraordinary lack of originality*.

At no point, for Ronnie, were either the postgraduate students or he himself aware that such methods or methodologies had anything to do with something as grand as such 'Integral Research', or indeed – even more distant from our conventional research horizons – social innovation. They were merely required to, in our terms, follow the paths of reason and realization, that is pursuing academically respectable, rational and empirical research, whether in Belgium or Bermuda, Switzerland or Senegal, England or Ecuador. There was no reference, in southern Africa for example, to any possible difference between the basic influence of a 'black' or 'white' consciousness, vital force or *élan vitale* on the research and development horizons.

THE SECOND WAKE-UP CALL: THE NORTH AND THE WEST ARE POLES APART!

Research Method and Methodology Fail to Meet

Now we come to the second overwhelming discovery. There was a vast gulf between methodology (incorporating philosophy) and method (incorporating technique) of which only the enlightened few had become aware. We had discovered that, amongst colleagues and students alike, *reference to method and methodology tended to be intertwined rather than clearly differentiated*. This mix of terms was replicated in much of the literature. We had found it virtually impossible to discover any research texts that dealt, sequentially and complementarily, with methodology philosophy and method technique. Critical realism for example, which had recently become ever more credible as a methodology, prided itself on its pluralism of 'method'. That for us seemed to be a bit of a cop out!

Such pluralism may appear to welcome flexibility, but it all too often leaves researchers confused. Methodology, or philosophy, remains disconnected from method or practicality, not to mention the fact that action research is all too often left out of the picture altogether, and hence innovation is curbed. As such the corrosive gap between the research ivory tower (methodology and philosophy) and the research muck and brass (method and action) is reinforced. Research methodologies were often profound in scope, but they were all too often very difficult to follow, or indeed apply. However, while methods may have been easier to comprehend, it was difficult to decide what method applied to which methodology.

In summary, there were virtually no attempts to bridge the gap between methodology, as research philosophy, and method, as research activity. Each stood in splendid isolation from the other, so that ultimately social innovation, which needed methodology and method, was inhibited.

North–Western Dominance: Colonization of the Minds

As our journey of discovery accelerated, moreover, Ronnie came to the next revealing realization that, whereas methodology was predominantly European in origin, and method was more likely to be American, the rest of the world really did not get a look-in at all. In other words, whether our research students came from South Africa or the Middle East, China or India, Europe or the US, their methodological orientation would invariably be European or American. Somehow that did not make sense to us. No wonder the world was on fire. Furthermore, the very fact that the philosophical 'Northern' Europeans predominated methodologically, and the practical 'Western' Americans prevailed where method was concerned, meant that there was bound to be gap in the mid Atlantic!

Academe has Given up its Knowledge Birthright

Furthermore, we found ourselves confused by two knowledge domains with very different 'rules of the game'. For, on the one hand, there was the field of business administration where knowledge management, or indeed knowledge creation, had recently become the order of the day. Therein, as was the case for the 'knowledge-creating company', popularized by the two Japanese organizational sociologists, Nonaka and Takeuchi, it was the norm to integrate diverse knowledge perspectives...

This, for example, involved – in the case of their well-known 'knowledge spiral' – the linking of the so-called 'socialization' (our Southern and relational) and 'externalization' (our Eastern and developmental), 'combination' (our Northern and reason-able) and 'internalization' (our Western and realizable) of knowledge. However, *when it came to academic research in the social sciences, the norm was to specialize in one knowledge domain or research methodology*. So it seemed, as least in Nonaka's knowledge-creating terms, that four into one won't go.

Moreover, while Nonaka's approach to knowledge creation was exclusively organizational, no such approach, which we in fact had come to identify as social innovation, existed at the societal level. In fact where there is, increasingly, reference to such entrepreneurship and innovation, there is no connection with academically based research in the social sciences. Unlike the case, as we indicated in Chapter 2 of the natural sciences, social research and social – as opposed to technological – innovation, are completely split apart.

But we had one more fundamental discovery to make before finally putting together our thoughts on Integral Research. In fact, with the third wake-up call we would come back full circle to where we had started as undergraduates in Switzerland and what was then Rhodesia, at the University of St Gallen in the 1980s, and the then University of Rhodesia and Nyasaland in the 1960s, with research methods.

THE THIRD WAKE-UP CALL: RESEARCH NEEDS INTEGRATION!

Origination Precedes Foundation

Our third wake-up call, had several connected parts to it, paving the way for Integral Research. Firstly, now that we had discovered the fact that research methodology was indeed philosophy, we were duly uplifted, but too much so. Our feet had left the ground, so that we, and also our research students, were up in the clouds. Phenomenology and critical rationalism, postmodernism and critical realism, for example, were truly revolutionary in nature and scope, particularly when we were able to touch base with their founding fathers, such as:

- *Moravia's Edmund Husserl:* the founder of phenomenology, who heralded, in the 1930s, a crisis in the European sciences.
- *Austria's Karl Popper:* the founder of critical rationalism, a refugee from Nazism, who, in the 1940s, made his specific call for an open society, against its enemies.
- *France's Michel Foucault:* founder of postmodernism, who was a leading light in the 1960s in the radical, anti-capitalist student movement of the time.
- *Anglo-Indian Roy Bhaskar:* founder of critical realism, an ex-Marxist, who saw his critical realism as an antidote to an empirically based free-market society.

However, there was a twist in the revolutionary tale. For these research philosophies were difficult for your normal research mortal to grasp, from the ground up. Then it came to us: research method had to be reconceived as a form of origination, or a point of access, prior to what then became a research foundation. For example, the source of origination, or point of access, for phenomenology, was descriptive method, whereas for critical rationalism it was grounded theory. These methods, because they were more 'hands on', as we shall see in Chapter 4, were the place to start. So was research methodology the end, given that our ultimate aim was to promote social innovation? Absolutely not!

Emancipation Succeeds Foundation

What we simultaneously discovered, with a little help from Australian research philosopher Norman Blaikie, in his *Approaches to Social Inquiry*,[16] was that what he termed 'classical' and 'contemporary' research methodologies were qualitatively different from each other. Whereas the *classical* ones – empiricism, critical rationalism, hermeneutics and phenomenology – were implicitly revolutionary, at least when originally conceived, the so-called *critical emancipatory* ones – critical realism, postmodernism, critical theory and feminism, were explicitly radical. So we decided not only to differentiate method (origination) from methodology (classical foundation), but also contemporary critique (emancipation) from the other two. So the overall rhythm, or what we now termed a *research trajectory,* went from origination to foundation to emancipation.

As we can see, such a trajectory laid a path, as it were, from research towards innovation. However, we were not quite there. For although the emancipatory approaches were more radical and transformative in intent than what came before, they still were primarily means of reflection rather than action.

Integrating Research and Action

Ironically, Ronnie's own doctoral thesis, completed in the mid-1980s, was based on Reg Revan's original approach to *Action Learning*,[17] applied to entrepreneurship development. Such an action learning approach, combining thought with action, theory with practice, was very closely connected with so-called 'action research'. Interestingly enough, through, the two closely connected from of, respectively, learning and research, have become disconnected from each other.

As a great advocate of such action learning, Ronnie was naturally drawn to action research, though, at the time, in the 1980s, he saw it in very instrumental, what we would subsequently identify as Western, terms. Action research, like action learning, meant continually cycling between action and reflection, as a means of problem solving. It was only when the authors rediscovered the work of John Heron on *Co-operative Inquiry*,[18] that they realized that there was much more to action research than initially met the proverbial Western eye.

Kurt Lewin, who founded action research in the 1950s, and was a refugee to the UK from Nazi Germany, claimed that research in the social sciences lacked authenticity, if it did not involve action, to test out the otherwise inauthentic theory. Moreover, we were soon to discover, now in the new millennium, that there were four fundamentally different, albeit related, approaches to action research: generic action research (AR), socio-technical design (STD), co-operative inquiry (CI), and participatory action research (PAR). Lo and behold, we then concluded, each embodied, in particular, one or other our Four Worlds: Western (AR), Northern (STD), Eastern (CI) and Southern (PAR). That, in turn, lead to our final, and perhaps most fundamental, breakthrough, as far as Integral Research leading to social innovation was concerned.

Four Research Paths, each one with a Dual Analytical-Transformative Trajectory

Double Layered Trajectory – Method to Action, Origination to Transformation: One of the major stumbling blocks to assimilating the wide range of research methodologies is that there are too many of them for the mind to absorb. In fact none of the texts on research methodology help in that respect. As a result, all too often, researchers go for the lowest common denominator, that is research method and an empirically based, often quantitative approach. This is most especially the case in developing countries. In developed countries, particularly for sociologists, the alternative is to plump for one particular methodology, say feminism or postmodernism, which happens to be a favourite in a particular department.

Our means of resolving this problem was twofold. First, we have developed a double-layered research trajectory. The first, *analytic research* oriented trajectory, serves to differentiate research *method* from *methodology*, methodological *critique* from *action* research. The second *transformative innovation* oriented trajectory starts with social *origination* (linked to research method), building up towards social *foundation* (linked to research methodology), onto social *emancipation* (linked to research critique), and ultimately social *transformation* (linked to action research).

Readers of our book on *Transformation Management*[19] will recognize that this trajectory draws upon our transformative orientation, which is called the GENE. The GENE represents the transformative spiral of grounding (method and origination), emergence (methodology and foundation), navigation (critique and emancipation) and effect (action and transformation). This dual logic will be explained later in this chapter, and again, more fully, in Chapter 4 .

Four Research Paths – Relational to Realization: The second thing we have done, to make thoroughgoing research more accessible, and indeed more feasible with a view to social innovation, is to divide it up into four overall paths: relational, renewal, reason and realization. Each of these paths not only has its double-layered fourfold trajectory, from method (origination) to action (transformation), but, between then, they span the Four Worlds, which are generic to our transcultural approach. Specifically then, as will be explained in much more detail in Chapter 3 , we distinguish the:

- *relational path*, which is intrinsically Southern, aligned with humanism;
- *path of renewal*, which is inherently Eastern, aligned with holism;
- *path of reason*, which is innately Northern, aligned with rationalism;
- *path of realization*, which is quintessentially Western, aligned with pragmatism.

In fact our Masters and doctoral students, particularly in the most marginalized part of the world, the South, feel a sense of pride and relief when they find that there is a legitimate research path, the relational one, that is attuned to their own world. But that relief of having found an authentic path for doing your research is only the starting point. Equally important is the sense of empowerment that any Integral Researcher experiences, when you discover that each path is designed to bring about social innovation, and thereby, through addressing a burning issue, brings relief to society itself. The following table presents an example of one of the research path's movement through the fourfold trajectory to social innovation.

The Integral Research to social innovation trajectory unfolds, as we can see, from the ground up, analytically (method to action) and transformatively (originate to transform) encompasses method (origination) and methodology (foundation), emancipation (critique) and ultimately transformation (action research), for each of the four research paths in turn. So the South and the North, the East and the West, each has its own intrinsic path to social innovation, each path has four levels to it, and, finally, each such trajectory is double layered – analytical and transformative. The example in the table illustrates the Northern path of reason. In fact, the Northern and Western paths of what we have termed 'reason' and 'realization' have taken worldwide precedence over the, for us, Southern and Eastern 'relational' and 'renewal' paths, with very damaging regional effects.

Having taken you through our own journey of discovery towards an integral approach to research and to social innovation, we now move on to a critique of current-day universities. We feel inclined to present this critique, over and over again, because universities are not fulfilling their unique roles as hubs of social innovation, in a particular context, and as centres for societal renewal. This critique is further relevant, for us, as such innovative research needs to occur on a large scale, with integral universities to house such. How does such an Integral University look? Once we have presented our critique of the status quo, we shall introduce the conceptual framework of an Integral University.

The Double-Layered Integral Research/Social Innovation Trajectory		
Integral Research Trajectory	**Example** of the application of the double-layered trajectory: **for example, the Northern path of reason**	**Social Innovation** *Trajectory*
Action *Research*	Action research, in this Integral Research design, does not stand in analytical isolation. At this ultimate level the researcher or research community effectively engages with society in order to transform the originally identified burning issue into a full-fledged social innovation and, at the same time, develops a new kind of organization. **For example, socio-technical design**	**Transformation** *Towards Innovation*
Research **Critique**	At this third level you become a philosopher yourself. You engage in a fundamental critique of the contemporary paradigm, with a view to moving towards an emancipated state. You do so in analytical relation to the underlying theory base as well in transformative relation to promoting social betterment, with a view to bringing about social innovation. **For example, postmodernism**	**Emancipation** *towards Innovation*
Research **Methodology**	Theory-based methodology serves as classical research foundation, philosophy or paradigm for you, on the one hand, to develop an analytical knowledge base to substantiate the chosen method; on the other hand it serves, transformatively, to provide a base from which to address your/a burning issue. **For example, critical rationalism**	**Innovation** *Foundation*
Research **Method**	Method serves to ground your research, analytically and reflectively; it is also an active source of origination of a particular social innovation, aiming to resolve a burning issue in your cultural and social context. **For Example, theorizing**	**Origination** *of a Social Innovation*

1.4 Why Universities Fail to be Unique as Social Innovation Hubs

UNIVERSITY – QUO VADIS?

As we have indicated so far, whether it's the current energy or financial crisis, the environmental crisis or the so-called clash of civilizations, universities have a central role to play, through both their research and now also, as we shall argue, their education – the two of which should be mutually supporting – in dealing with these.

Unfortunately this is not normally the case, because our universities have been established as rational (Northern), and sometimes pragmatic (Western) institutions, without any distinctly humanistic (Southern) or holistic (Eastern) foundations. That may be an extreme statement, and many an individual academic, be it a Foucault in France, a Chomsky in the USA, or indeed you the reader, might radically defy that norm. But these, and you, are individuals, and the university is an institution that needs to transcend you as an individual or even as part of a department.

Naturally there are exceptions, such as the New School for Social Research in New York, which emerged out of the radically based Frankfurt School of critical theorists in Germany in the 1930s, philosopher Herbert Marcuse and psychotherapist Erich Fromm being perhaps the best known of these theorists. Another example of a university research department that was radically concerned with the lot of humanity was Wallerstein's World Systems Analysis Group at Fernand Braudel Center for the Study of Economies, Historical Systems and Civilization, based at Suny University in upstate New York, from the 1970s until 2005. But these are very rare exceptions to the university norm. In fact, the very fact that we, the authors, hold the views we do is because we consider ourselves to be strongly Southern (humanistic) and Eastern (holistic) in outlook, while also having some leanings towards the rational (Northern) and pragmatic (Western) worlds.

Moreover, one of us (Ronnie), born and brought up in southern Africa, finds his country, Zimbabwe, today, in a state of total crisis. Moreover, he regards the academic world, specifically the former University of Rhodesia and Nyasaland, to be, at least partly, responsible, on three counts. Firstly, while the likes of a Robert Mugabe may have seemingly gone completely off the rails in recent years, with a devastating effect on his country, he was the prior victim of a psychic and economic split between an errant capitalism and a failed socialism.

In other words, alongside whatever personal failings he has, Mugabe was left with 'nowhere to go', most especially in the 1990s, because of the poverty of modern-day economics. Specifically, so the conventional argument goes, there is no alternative to capitalism, even though such Western capitalism was something Mugabe absolutely despised. So what could he do when the Berlin Wall came down? In fact, Ronnie was personally a victim of such poverty-stricken academe when he studied Anglo-Saxon economic principles at the University of Rhodesia and Nyasaland, finding them totally irrelevant to the needs of his country.

Finally, and thirdly, the didactic teaching methods that were used then, and are still popular today, alongside the sterile research methods we were taught and still are taught today, were alienating to the extreme. This applied to a sensitive soul like Ronnie not only individually, but also as a member of a family business in Rhodesia: he could not see what relevance the economics he was studying, then, or thereafter at the London School of Economics or at Harvard, had to his family business as a Southern enterprise, for a humanist like himself.

In fact, it was all these academic shortfalls that led us, to where we are now, with Integral Research, leading to social innovation.

WHAT'S WRONG WITH THE CONVENTIONAL UNIVERSITY?

Transformational Myopia: Individual, Organizational, Societal Issues Bypassed!

Up to this point, then, we have discovered two major anomalies. First, university-based education, if not also research in the social sciences and in management, is directed at individuals, despite leading-edge academic thinking in management and cutting-edge research in the natural sciences, both of which are much to the contrary. In other words, seminal ideas and practices on organizational if not also societal learning and knowledge creation, and on communities of practice, prevalent in management, are ignored in universities. Second, for all the talk about the shift in the world's overall power base, from America and Europe to India and China, Western and Northern academic approaches dominate, even in the now economically ascendant East, and most certainly in the economically depressed South. What effect does this have on our Integral Research case?

One core effect, that of predominating individualism, is that our own tendency to favour organizational and communal as well as individual approaches to learning and knowledge creation are continually marginalized by the prevailing educational establishment. Interestingly enough, such individualism, at least in research terms, is much more evident in the social sciences and the humanities, than it is in the natural sciences, where large-scale research projects may be the norm.

The implication of such excessive individualism, in the social and economic arena, is that addressing burning issues by the groups needed to do so is massively inhibited. Moreover, the overall accreditation system, whereby individuals are awarded degrees, rather than groups of academic researchers being rewarded, is a major deterrent to progress towards social innovation. Ironically, as a result, the whole field of organizational knowledge creation, as we have intimated, pioneered by Japan's Nonaka and Takeuchi, has completely bypassed the universities, despite the fact that the two Japanese researchers themselves are gifted organizational sociologists. Moreover, the very much watered-down and duly Westernized field of 'knowledge management', so popular in organizational and management circles today, indeed all over the world, has absolutely nothing to do with academe, supposedly the traditional repository of knowledge. That brings us to the second major critique.

Transcultural Myopia: Where are the South, East and Middle East?

Even more damaging than the prevalence of individualism and lack of transformational impulse is the predominance of Europe and America (totally dominant in the field of business and management), in university-based research and education at large. This has several damaging effects. First, curricula and concepts, in the sciences if not also in the humanities, are developed in very few parts of the world, that is predominantly in western Europe and America. The Anglo-Saxons in economics, the French and the

Germans in philosophy, and the Americans in business and management, rule the roost. With few exceptions then, Africa, Latin America, the Middle East, even the Near and Far East, hardly get a look-in. This is catastrophic for the knowledge base of the world as a whole.

Interestingly enough, there are specific areas where knowledge is much more widely spread, for example in philosophy where Africa has made its mark; in anthropology and religious studies where many different parts of the world have their own unique sets of beliefs and practices; and in the humanities, in art and in music, in literature and in drama, where richly comparative studies prevail. However, these subject areas are invariably isolated, one from the other, and when it comes to overall community development and institution building all the humanities, social sciences and even natural sciences need to be brought together, and this is absolutely not happening. In fact the one example of their having been combined, that of so-called *area studies*, is again America, and used by the US to further its strategic interests in particular parts of the world.

Further, the West and the North are particularly well bestowed with analytical as well as practical, that is rational as well as pragmatic, inclinations. The East and the South, comparatively speaking, are more richly endowed with intuitive as well as experientially based orientations. Yet it is the former, predominantly analytic, rather than the latter, more transformative, orientations which prevail in university settings. What often happens, particularly in the South, is that students end up with the worst of all worlds. In other words, they are precluded from exercising their naturally experiential and imaginative talents, and, in mimicking the practical and conceptual West and North, they come off second best. Meanwhile students and researchers from the East, especially from India and China, may well excel in a Western and Northern environment, performing even better than we in the North and West do, because such Easterners are very adept at imitation and at adaptation. As a result they fail to make their own unique contribution to our world.

Perhaps even most devastating, there are fields of educational activity where the marginalized do excel, but they are not, formally at least, part of education. In the East, ranging from China and Japan, to Korea and India, martial arts and meditation, tai chi and yoga, are all tried and tested means of attaining self-mastery, but they have nothing to do with conventional education. They are indeed extra-curricular. The result is that such elevated practices are isolated from conventional academe, rather than being creatively merged with such. The same applies, in the South, to music, dance and even sporting activity. Such rhythmical and kinaesthetic pursuits again take place outside the formal curriculum. The effect of all this is not merely damaging to the self-esteem of those, most especially from the South. For there is another, more subtle and ultimately more damaging point. For the arts, nature and the humanities, as we shall see in Chapter 2, are the primary locus for our human being, in the same way as spirituality and psychology, philosophy and history, are essential constituents of our becoming. By segregating off nature and the community, as well as culture and spirituality, from science and technology, as well as ultimately politics and economics, we cut ourselves, and our societies, into pieces.

Finally, in predominantly Southern, as well as in some Eastern, societies, nature, culture and the humanities are their primary source of pride and joy, given that science and technology, politics and the economy, all too often lag behind the West and the North, in terms of their development. For example, for Africans, music is in their soul. Unless such a soul force can be tapped, individually and institutionally, the student or researcher will invariably be half a person, recognizing, at the same time, that music, for the Southerner, is a communal activity.

Transdisciplinary Myopia: Social Sciences and Humanities Don't Meet!

Modern universities were invented in the North, that is in Europe, most particularly in Italy, France, the UK and Germany, and were established along the path of reason. Curricula were developed in particular disciplines, at first within the natural sciences. In the 15th to 19th centuries, as they evolved, physics and chemistry were pre-eminent, alongside the lesser-regarded humanities, and seldom the twain did meet. What predominated was the establishment of a well-thought-out, self-contained, rationally coherent curriculum.

In the 20th century, especially in the latter part of it, we saw the emergence of the social sciences, trying to establish themselves in the image of physics and chemistry, if not also biology, with rationalism and empiricism occupying pride of place. In fact a continuum was established, in the social sciences, between the pragmatic Anglo-Saxons, oriented towards economics and behavioural psychology, and the more rational French and Germans, who were more focused towards the systematic pursuit of sociology, political science, and a more institutionally based (German) and mathematically based (French) economics.

Furthermore, and in the context of business and management studies, which rose to prominence in the second half of the 20th century particularly in America, the comparison conventionally made was between Chicago Business School, with its rationally based (Northern) business disciplines, and the pragmatically based (Western) Harvard Business School, with its case study orientation. What becomes overwhelmingly apparent, then, is the historical and contemporary predominance of the North and the West in both universities generally and business schools specifically. This applied both to research and to education. Ironically then, the East and the South, in our terms, ranging from China and India to Latin America and Africa, merely mimicked the North or the West.

Overall then, each one of the social sciences, ranging from economics to anthropology, and from political sciences to sociology, is taught in isolation, one from the other. So-called 'joint majors', say in psychology and sociology, may be offered, by the individual subjects will be taught in isolation. Moreover, when it comes to management, the field in which both authors teach, not only is one so-called specialism, be it marketing or finance, taught in isolation of the other, but business schools are all too often isolated from the university as a whole. One of the authors, Ronnie Lessem, can vividly remember studying 'The Politics of Modernity' as an allowable second-year elective at Harvard Business School. What was taught had absolutely nothing to do with the business of business and with the lot of Rhodesia becoming Zimbabwe.

Transpersonal Myopia: No Reach into Organizations, Communities and Society!

Let us consider a little more the natural lie of the Western and Northern academic land, at least as far as the educational and research body is concerned. Educationally, to begin with, universities, like schools in the West and the South, educate individuals. This may seem obvious, at first, but at second glance perhaps not so. After all, any academic with their salt as we indicated previously, at least in the business and management field we are in, would be familiar with Peter Senge's notion of the *learning organization*,[20] if not also

Etienne Wenger's[21] *communities of practice*, and indeed Nonaka and Takeuchi's[22] *knowledge-creating company*. While Senge is an American, influenced by Eastern philosophy, and Nonaka and Takeuchi are Japanese, influenced by the West, Wenger is of Swiss origin, though resident in California. For all of these progressive educators, and researchers, it is organizational and communal learning and innovation that occupies pride of place, rather than individual education and research.

Yet outside of this very specific, indeed rarified managerial, educational and research context, it is the individual that stands tall, whether we are at universities in America or India, China or South Africa. This has struck us, for a long time, as very odd. In fact, if anything, *individual* education and training at universities and colleges, is, in practice, even more of a preoccupation in the South (southern Africa) and the Middle East (Egypt, Jordan and Oman, from our personal experience), than it is in the North and West. In parts of the world then, where, traditionally at least, 'it takes a village to educate a child' (African proverb), or where family and community occupy pride of social and psychological space (Arab world), why is education restricted to individuals?

Of course, when we move from education to research, then, at least in the natural sciences, institutions occupy pride of place, rather than individuals. Research groups in the best universities, in Europe and America, characteristically work alongside renowned business corporations, in pharmaceuticals or biotechnology, aerospace or microelectronics, to promote fundamental as well as applied research. Interestingly enough such institutionally based research is restricted to the natural, as opposed to the social, sciences as well as the humanities, where the individual researcher is still, lamentably for us, pre-eminent. That is a core reason, as we have already intimated, why technological races ahead of social innovation.

So where do we go from here? We now provide an outline of the Integral University needed to ultimately accommodate Integral Research, alongside integral education, thereby addressing the kinds of issues we have identified. Such a university is transformational, transcultural, transdisciplinary and ultimately transpersonal in its educational and research orientations.

1.5 A New University Paradigm: Towards the Integral University

AN INTEGRAL UNIVERSITY IS TRANSFORMATIONAL: TOWARDS SOCIETAL RENEWAL

Earlier on in this chapter we established our newly Integral Research paradigm, aligned with social innovation. The overall approach underlying this, as outlined in our companion volume on *Transformation Management: Towards the Integral Enterprise*,[23] is simultaneously transformational and transcultural, transdiciplinary and transpersonal.

Addressed at resolving burning issues, the transformation we seek through such social innovation is from the ground up, lodged in specifically local natural and cultural soils, at the same time reaching out, politically and economically, to the globe as a whole. What then becomes evident, from the outset, at this initial stage of our research journey, is that Integral Research needs to be lodged within a particular kind of university, which we term an *Integral University*. Why do we say that?

An Integral University is firstly, through its educational and research activities, concerned with societal renewal, or indeed transformation, at a particular time and place, albeit that this cannot occur apart from individual and organizational renewal. Its primary concern, as such, is with a particular *nature and community*, that is the one where it is located locally, as well as with nature and community in the societies in which its students are located, globally. The particular subjects of concern in relation to nature and community, therefore, are ecology, anthropology and geography.

AN INTEGRAL UNIVERSITY IS TRANSCULTURAL: WORKING WITH CULTURAL DYNAMICS

An Integral University secondly, through again its educational and research activities, works with cultural dynamics, involving diverse local and national communities and ethnicities, involving also interpersonal and institutional dynamics. Its primary concern, as such, is with *culture and spirituality*. The major academic disciplines involved are philosophy, psychology (depth psychology), theology and history, alongside reconciliation, conflict and peace studies.

As such, the whole of the curriculum is infused with transcultural diversity. Moreover, the entire university becomes a transcultural embodiment of such, with a view to becoming a knowledge-creating community. The overarching academic discipline is conscious evolution. We now turn from the transcultural to the transdisciplinary.

AN INTEGRAL UNIVERSITY IS TRANSDISCIPLINARY: PROMOTING SOCIAL INNOVATION

An Integral University thirdly, through its educational and Integral Research activities, works with a multiplicity of disciplines, in the social sciences and in the humanities: it spans sociology and psychology, political science and economics. Building on the transcultural orientation that came before, in many of these cases there would be a comparative approach adopted.

The transdisciplinary means to that end, as we have seen, involves for each of the four research paths – relational and renewal, reason and realization – a full trajectory from research origination (method) to research foundation (methodology), and thereafter from emancipation (critique) to transformation (action research). This trajectory from fundamental research to transformative action serves to bring about social innovation. The integral and overarching academic discipline involved is that of knowledge creation, involving individual, organization and society.

We finally turn to the transformed educational curriculum.

AN INTEGRAL UNIVERSITY IS TRANSPERSONAL: TRANSFORMED EDUCATION

An Integral University finally, through its ultimately transformed education, serves to develop individual, organization and society within a particular cultural context. The transformed education that results is therefore contextualized for each person, enterprise and community/society involved. In our tree of knowledge and social innovation (see Figure 1.1 and 1.3) these three levels are symbolized by the branches of the tree.

Each of the four research paths, moreover, has a specific connection with each of the educational meta-disciplines. Specifically the relational path is connected with community building; the path of renewal is aligned with conscious evolution; the path of reason is connected with knowledge creation; and finally the path of realization is aligned with sustainable development.

1.6 Conclusion: Integral Research Needs an Integral University

We started this chapter with asking whether and how research in the social sciences can be turned into social innovation. We have been working with this question for many years now, trying to address the burning issues we, our organizations and societies are facing. Working with Masters students and doctoral researchers from all over the world, we have developed a fundamentally new approach towards research in the social sciences, designed to bring about social innovation. We call this approach Integral Research.

By applying Integral Research, you, individually or preferably as a research group, engage with particular burning issues in your specific contexts, also pursuing a double-layered trajectory, along a specific research path, towards social innovation. In the second part of the book we will lay out in detail the full architecture of Integral Research; we will then guide you through each of the four paths and trajectories, and shall come, in the final chapter of this book, back to the notion of the Integral University. Ultimately, in our experience, Integral Research needs, in order to fully flourish, a fundamental revision of the university in, or alongside, which it is housed. We introduced in this chapter our notion of the Integral University, which we have, in theory and practice, started to build. This will be spelt out more specifically in our final chapter. At this stage, we summarize our conceptual overview on Integral Research and the Integral University in Figure 1.3. The figure illustrates how aligned both conceptual frameworks are, and how, together, they embody the process towards (Integral Research) as well as the structure of (Integral University) social innovation.

We close this chapter by citing Wallerstein, one of the most prolific contemporary advocates of a new approach to knowledge creation, an approach that allows for reuniting the social sciences with the humanities:

Can we tear down the old structure of social science while simultaneously constructing new pillars for some kind of roof? And will the roof be limited to just social science or rather encompass a reunited single world of knowledge that knows no division between humans and nature, no divorce between philosophy and science, no separation of the search for the true and the search for the good. Can we unthink social science while reconstructing the structure of knowledge?[24]

By introducing Integral Research, we echo Wallerstein's claim. In the next chapter we introduce the natural and cultural foundations for our integral orientation towards research and knowledge creation, promoting a fundamentally new approach towards the social sciences. We start with a tour de world, researching different approaches to knowledge creation and social innovation from the four corners of the globe.

Figure 1.3   Integral Research and Integral University

References

1.   Chua, A. (2003). *The World on Fire*. London: Heinemann.
2.   Lessem, R. (1987). *Global Business*. New York: Prentice Hall.
3.   Revans, R. (1999). *ABC of Action Learning*. Rochester: Mike Pedlar Library.
4.   Lessem, R. (1999). *Global Management Principles*. New York: Prentice Hall.
5.   Christie, P., Lessem, R. and Mbigi, L. (eds) (1993). *African Management*. Johannesburg: Knowledge Resources.
6.   Lessem, R. and Neubauer, F. (1993). *European Management Systems*. London: McGraw Hill.
7.   *Ibid*.
8.   Fals Borda, O. and Rahman, M. (1991). *Knowledge and Action*. New York and London: Apex Press.
9.   *Ibid*.
10.   Lessem and Neubauer, *European Management Systems*.
11.   Kalthoff, O., Nonaka, I. and Nueno, P. (1997). *The Light and the Shadow: How Breakthrough Innovation is shaping European Business*. Oxford: Capstone.
12.   Lessem, R. and Palsule, S. (1997). *Managing in Four Worlds*. Cambridge, MA: Blackwell.
13.   Kolb, D. (1991). *Experiential Learning*. New York: Prentice Hall.
14.   Smith, M. (2002). *Social Science in Question*. London, Thousand Oaks, CA, and New Delhi: Open University Press.
15.   Heron, J. (1993). *Co-operative Inquiry*. London: Sage.
16.   Blaikie, N. (1994). *Approaches to Social Inquiry*. Cambridge: Polity Press.
17.   Revans, R.W. (1998). *ABC of Action Learning*. London: Lemos and Crane.

18. Heron, J. (1997). *Co-operative Inquiry*. London: Sage.
19. Lessem, R. and Schieffer, A. (2009). *Transformation Management: Towards the Integral Enterprise*. Farnham: Gower.
20. Senge, P. (1992). *The Fifth Discipline*. New York: Doubleday.
21. Wenger, E. (2006). *Cultivating Communities of Practice*. Boston, MA: HBS Press.
22. Nonaka, I. and Takeuchi, H. (1995). *The Knowledge Creating Company*. Oxford: Oxford University Press.
23. Lessem and Schieffer, *Transformation Management*.
24. Wallerstein, I. (1999). *The End of the World as We Know It: Social Science for the 21st Century*. Minneapolis, MN: University of Minnesota Press.

2 *Design for Social Innovation*

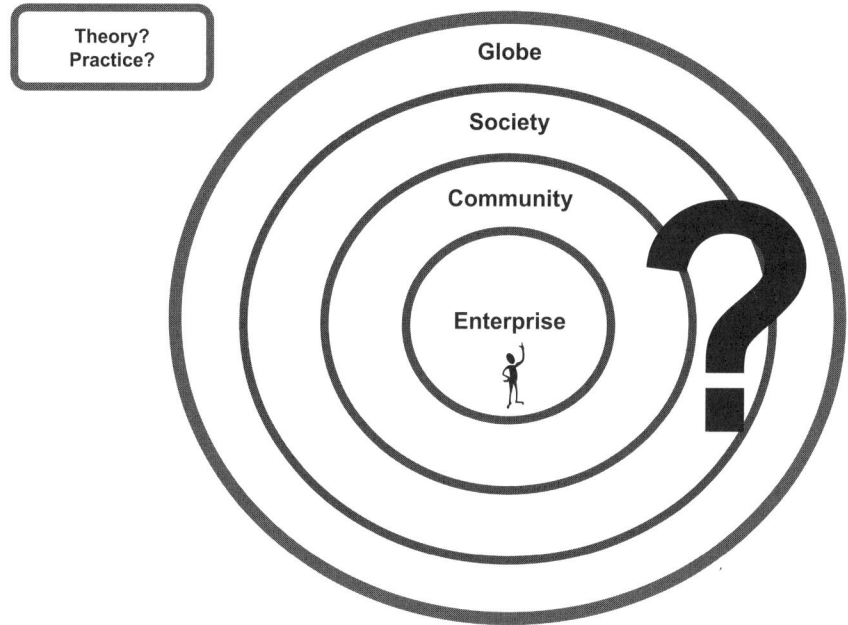

2 The Four Innovation Paths of Integral Research

From the Relational Path to the Path of Realization

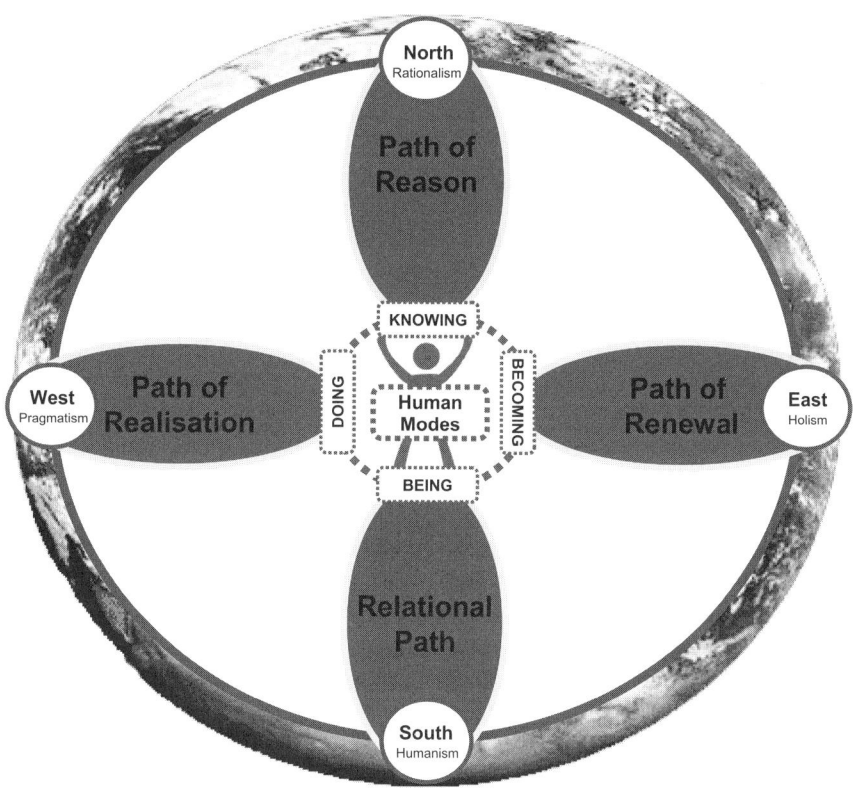

Figure 2.1   Paths of Integral Research

Summary: The Four Innovation Paths of Integral Research

- In order to achieve true social innovation the social researcher needs to (a) connect with the creativity (historic creative achievements) of the culture it is applied to, hence rooting it organically in a specific cultural soil (how else can it be of use for a particular environment and context?) and (b) support the further evolution and sustainability of a culture as a whole.
- We demonstrate with a large number of examples that societies all over the world have, in particular times, developed a perspective about the nature of the diverse elements, which formed their particular cosmos, and how these elements could be held in a dynamic balance. Such modes of being and becoming, knowing and doing, found their way into the social design of those societies, and thereby provided an orientation for a particular civilization.
- In our tour of the world we shall make another remarkable discovery: while each society embodies the above-mentioned modes, there are regions in the world that have over time developed a particular strength in one particular field as opposed to the others. In research or knowledge-generation terms we found that there is a Southern 'relational path' (linked to the human mode of being), an Eastern 'path of renewal' (becoming), a Northern 'path of reason' (knowing) and a Western 'path of realization' (doing). Our Four World Model that we rooted in this research suggests that in order to have a dynamic balance on a global level, each world needs to contribute its unique path of knowledge generation into the whole in order to ensure 'unity in diversity'.
- We recognize that when a society is at its peak, it manages to keep a kind of dynamic balance between its various parts and modes. It practises 'unity in variety', both internally, through interconnecting its different societal functions, and externally by interacting, on equal terms, with different cultures. This is also a time when there is a relatively free flow of knowledge and innovation in that society, and in interaction with other societies. It was the renowned African-Muslim philosopher Ali Mazrui who saw in the creative synthesis between cultures the roots for any civilization to come about and to flourish.
- You, as the Integral Researcher, start by immersing yourself in the very soils of the creative source of your society, as well as those of others, before entering a particular research path authentic to you, leading ultimately to social innovation.

2.1 Origins of Social Innovation

ROOTED IN IMAGES: BEYOND 'JOE THE PLUMBER'

In Chapter 1 we highlighted the need for social, as opposed to merely technological, innovation, and the kind of Integral University that would be required to promote it. In this chapter we explore the roots of such social innovation, particularly in relation to the large variety of major cultures around the world. For unlike technological innovation, which, like the European Enlightenment, emerged out of an emerging 'age of reason', social innovation has a fourfold heritage: building equally on the four human modes we shall outline – being, becoming, knowing, doing – as well as on the Four Worlds of the South, East, North and West.

In other words, such *social* innovation is as much to do with being and becoming, as with knowing and doing. It addresses and builds on all these four human modes.

Moreover, it needs to build upon the roots of a particular society, that is on a society in each of the four corners of our world. As such, whereas the original Industrial Revolution emerged out of uniquely English soils, its subsequent impact around the world has been all too often to displace, rather than build upon, indigenous knowledge.

The process of uncovering and releasing a particular society's nature and culture, or being, so that, through such subsequent cultural emergence, or becoming, it can thereafter activate, and articulate, its own innate process of knowing, is a very particular one. It involves, in our terms, releasing your 'GENE-ius', individually, organizationally and societally, from the bottom up. Such a bottom-up, for us though, does not mean starting from 'Joe the Plumber', as John McCain tended to do in the 2008 US election, but from the 'image of America', as the land of the free, which was Barack Obama's starting point.

RELEASING YOUR GENE-IUS

Your tasks as a social innovator, then, are to:

- connect to the creativity (historic creative achievements) of the culture with which you are concerned, being rooted organically in a specific cultural soil;
- transformationally combine this locally indigenous with globally exogenous knowledge, to support the further evolution and sustainability of your society;
- purposefully engage in (fundamental as well as applied) research and development, within and across the social sciences, to promote fully fledged social innovation.

It is the creative interaction of diverse elements that is needed for innovation. But such social innovation can only take place if a dynamic balance between the interacting elements is retained, including the balance between being and becoming, knowing and doing. As we have indicated such being is connected with our *relational* grounding, becoming with emerging or *renewal*, navigating with *reasoned* knowing or, and doing with *realizing* or effecting. It is in that transformational respect, overall, that we talk of releasing your GENE-ius.

All societies have developed over time their own kind of knowledge about the design of their social and material creations and how to maintain a healthily dynamic balance with creation, or indeed co-creation (cultural synthesis) itself. Again and again, (wo)man has also tested the limits of this balance, which – in its worst cases – led to wars, to destruction and extinction. Often, those were the times where a particular society became out of touch with its knowledge of how to continually re-create its genius. That leads us to the responsibility of the social innovator.

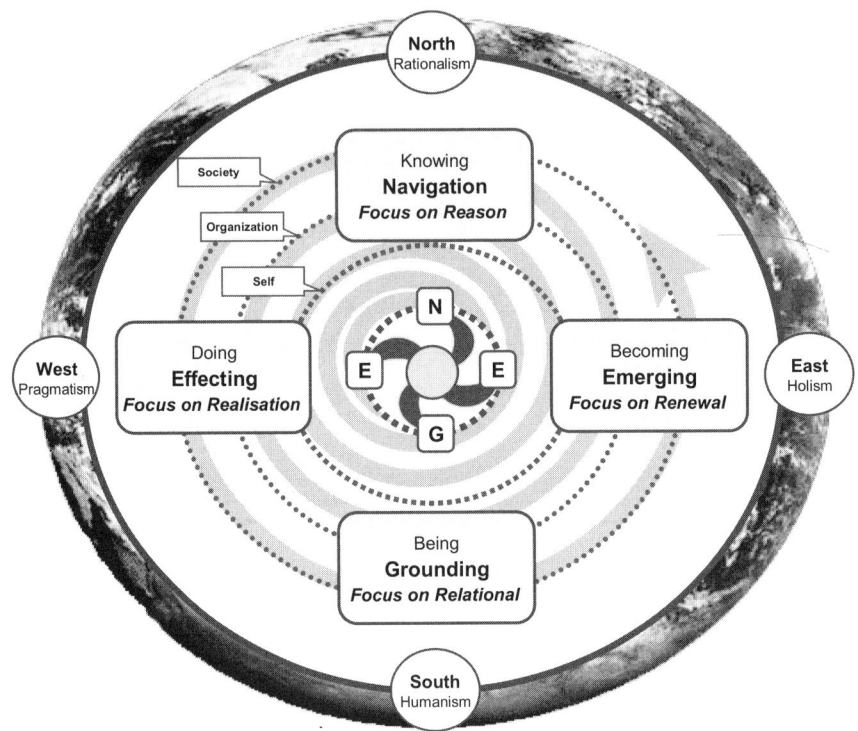

Figure 2.2   Becoming a Social Innovator – Releasing Your GENE-ius

THE RESPONSIBILITY OF THE SOCIAL INNOVATOR

Your responsibility then as a social innovator, invariably together with others, is to contribute to improving human well-being and livelihood. As Nobel Laureate Amartya Sen writes:

> *poverty is seen as a deprivation of capabilities ... by focussing on developing capabilities, rather than on, for example, income, enhancement of various social aspects of life can contribute to general development. Understanding and using social design processes can contribute to the improvement of livelihood.*[1]

As such, and for us, a social innovation serving to bring about a particular and unique social improvement by drawing explicitly on the social sciences, needs to bring dynamic balance to the four factors which together form the underlying and integral social design, that we have developed, based on our Four World Model:[2]

- nature and community;
- culture and spirituality;
- science and technology;
- politics and economics.

We now turn to such cultural design behind social innovation in more detail.

2.2 Designs Behind Social Innovation

CYCLE, FOURFOLD AND CENTRE

You may have noticed that the model we have presented of social design and social innovation has been presented in circular fashion, containing an outer fourfoldness and an inner centre. These serve to express a specifically and dynamically balanced interaction of particularly diverse factors.

In our transcultural research around the world we have discovered that the core visual design, or indeed guiding metaphor, of many cultures is expressed either in a cycle (or, as a variation, in a spiral) or a fourfold or a combination of both. All of them embodied a philosophical and/or spiritual understanding of a dynamically balanced order of communities, societies, and individuals in relation to nature and their particular version of God. Most of these designs have differentiated the core defining forces within a particular worldview and illustrate the relation among them.

The cycle, as we shall later see, is perhaps the single most distinct visual design that can be found, in one form or the other, at the core of the self-perspective of many cultures. So, for examples, in various cultures the cycle was a symbol for the absolute as well as for unity. It has been used as a symbol of the sky (the limitless), again, for absolute beauty (Platonic interpretation) and for emptiness (Hinduism). The cycle embodies harmony of all spiritual forces (Zen), and it is a symbol of time and eternity.

According to mythological interpretation, the four is one of the core order-giving principles (four directions, four elements, four seasons, four temperaments, and currently our four research paths). The most elemental visual expressions of the fourfold is the geometric form of the square. On a symbolic level, the square was a symbol for the earth and for the co-operation of the four elements. It stood for absolute beauty (Platonic interpretation); in Islam it represented the heart (as per four sources of inspiration). And in China it stood for the Cosmos as a whole.

THE PROCESS ELEMENT

The designs that various cultures created over time often include a process element – in addition to the cycle or the square (or a combination of both of them). While the fourfold cycle could be interpreted as an embodiment of an ongoing process, or dynamic, the form in itself does not express a lot of vitality, but is rather static, or indeed a stabilizing entity.

Such designs were always an expression of a 'balanced order' or unity between diverse elements. On a societal level, for us here, the core defining elements can be understood as firstly nature and community, secondly culture and spirituality, thirdly science and technology and fourthly politics and economics (see Figure 2.3). On a personal level, such defining elements can be viewed as being, becoming, knowing and doing. These dimensions can be found in each personality and civilization. And each of these two, in order to survive on a long-term basis, needed then, and needs now, a kind of healthy and dynamically evolving balance between these core elements.

In our studies, we have made another (for us remarkable) discovery.[3] While each society embodies the Four Worlds of nature/community, culture/spirituality, science/technology and politics/economics, there are regions in the world that have over time developed a particular strength in one particular field, as opposed to the others. Figure 2.3 illustrates this finding.

This pattern suggests that in order to have a dynamic balance on a global level, each part needs to bring its unique contribution – that is when it is functioning at its 'functional' best – into the whole in order to ensure 'unity in diversity'. Figure 2.3 shows which particular element each world does contribute. Moreover, as we shall see later, the four research paths each represent a part of an integral whole.

Of course, you find these 'archetypal features' in every society, in every organization, in every individual. We are not saying that, for example, humanism or being is only rooted in the South (hence in Africa), or that holism or becoming is only rooted in the East (hence in countries like Japan and China). We argue that each world region has evolved over time one inner dimension (interior design) that seems to be more strongly developed than the others. However, what we are saying is that while each region of the world, potentially, has all Four Worlds embodied within it, actually one or other world predominates, so that each part of the world needs to consciously seek after what we term 'global integrity' by recognizing and evolving, rather than bypassing or enclosing itself within its local identity.

Figure 2.3   Integral Societal Design – Orientations of the Four Worlds Model

The East has arguably the longest and deepest tradition in the area of holism, spirituality and non-material aspects, as we shall see for our path of renewal, while, for example, the West has developed an enormous capacity for the pragmatic and material self-expression, our path of realization. And it is the centre (countries in the Middle East) that has historically been, more so than any other world region, a crossroads for the most diverse cultures and that has also experienced various epochs, most notably in the 9th to 14th centuries AD, when a 'creative synthesis' between different cultures and religions did prolifically happen. Even Islam itself could be seen as 'creative synthesis' and further evolution of Judaism and Christianity – and has in itself been a major social innovation for the region, and ultimately for the world. At its best, the Middle East and Islam have demonstrated an enormous ability to generate a dynamic balance between most diverse parts. That's why we see the integrative ability of 'creative synthesis' as the particular contribution of the centre, including our own ability to 'centre' ourselves, when at our integrative best as opposed to dissipative worst.

You could say that what we can observe on a global level also mirrors the inner designs, images, worldviews or archetypes of each individual and society. Each of us has our potential South, its East, its North, its West and centre. At the same time each of us has developed a particular strength in one or two areas, and only a few individuals, organizations and societies 'manage' to keep a harmonic, yet dynamic balance between the four elements. Yet all four elements – the relational circle and spiral of renewal, a line of reason and points of realization – are required.

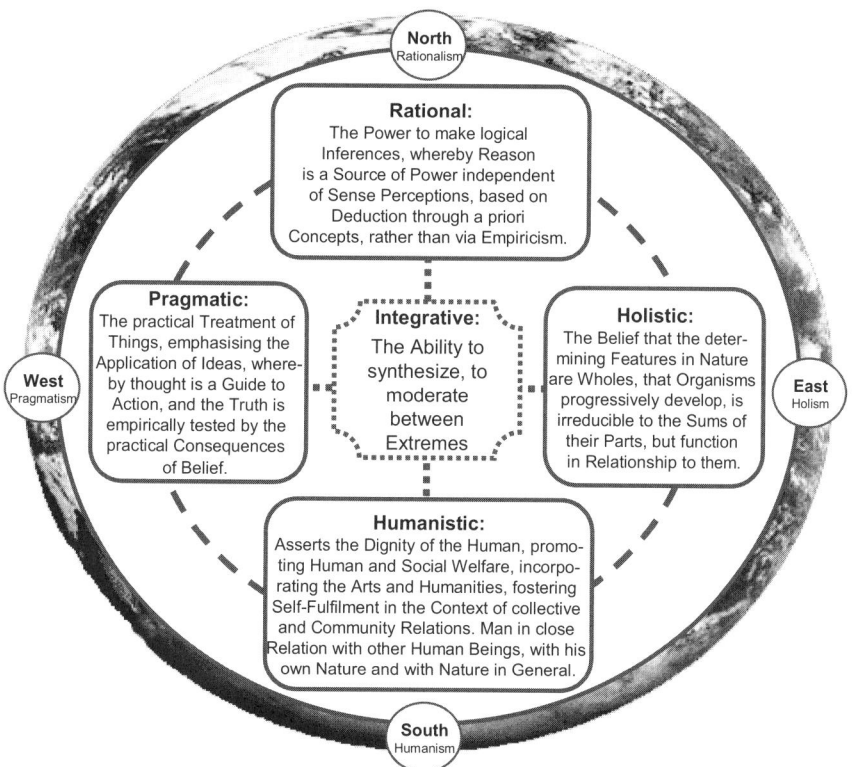

Figure 2.4   Contribution of the Four Worlds and the Centre

This archetypal social and psychological design is a distillation of our research and observations in different cultures and personalities. It is also a design that resonates with core cultural and artistic artefacts (visual designs) that occur in most societies. We shall demonstrate that outer design in its more explicit visual expression is implicitly linked with the inner design of a culture or psyche as a whole, thus such a psychic design can be regarded as the underlying spirit of its material expression. It is hence important to understand this deeper layer, and we shall now explore it and its inner and outer expressions in various cultures.

2.3 Images Behind the Innovation Paths

PATHS OF CREATIVE SYNTHESIS

We shall start by exploring what kind of 'inherently sustainable and dynamically balanced social designs' have been developed over time by different cultures and how that has been expressed inwardly (design) as well as outwardly (symbol). In the case of each of our Four Worlds, mediated by our 'centre', we shall find an all-encompassing design, in each case with a particular orientation, towards, a path of realization (Western), renewal (Eastern), reason (Northern) and relation (Southern), as well as an ultimately integral one. The outer symbol representing the cosmology of a particular society has an explicit, static outer structure, in which is represented, in turn and at a deeper level, an implicit, dynamic inner or process dimension. These archetypal and relational *images* moreover, as we have discussed in *Transformation Management*,[4] in terms of a *transformational topography,* need to be manifested as societal *ideologies*, organizational *institutions* and individual *inclinations* that are resonant with one another.

When each of our world civilizations were at their peak, the process dimension was at its most active, becoming a field of force if you like, leading to a fruitful exchange amongst its diverse elements: being (relational), becoming (renewal), knowing (reason), doing (realization). The same of course applies to an individual or an organization. At such a time, each such entity was able to keep its unity and to orchestrate its diversity in a way that it was fertile for all its parts. Indeed, the great African Muslim philosopher Ali Mazrui defines a civilization as a 'creative synthesis' of diverse parts, related not only to the combination of the rich 'interior design' of a society, but also bearing upon the civilization's interaction with other civilizations, thereby embodying unity-in-diversity. When 'creative synthesis' was at its best, so was the inner process of innovation. We will need to bear this in mind when we start to discuss *Integral* Research methodology and our four research paths: relational, renewal, reason and realization.

When societies lose their power to socially innovate, through following these research paths as it were, thereby interlinking the explicit structural form (outer design) with the implicit dynamic process (inner design) neither the deeper meaning of the symbol, nor its power to connect, is any longer present. So the symbol of the cross, for example, as a bridge between reason (lines of reasoning) and faith (*religere* as renewal), loses its fusion power. To take another example, in the Arab world, buildings, both inside and out, are still richly laden with Arabesque forms, but few people know what these structurally symbolize, or indeed the force field which they dynamically represent.

Many of us, therefore, enjoy visits to museums, where the static artefacts of civilizations are aesthetically displayed for us to get to know. We admire the artefacts that ancient generations of our own and other cultures have created, from a distance, even how innovative they had been. But we make no conscious connection between material or practical innovations of the past, and the spiritual or mental process that allowed these to come into being, thereby taking into conscious account the current ability of a society to be creative.

We now start with an exploration of social innovation in the *relational* South, in fact from the neglected grounds of indigenous African civilization. Thereafter we reach out to the other polarities, that is the East, North and West, before we turn towards the centre.

SOUTHERN IMAGINATION: THE RELATIONAL PATH

Obtala: Benefactor of Humanity

In the South, to begin with, the relational thrives, but renewal, reason and realization have been thwarted by influences from both within and without. The spiritual worldview of Nigeria's Yoruba people, for example, influenced a large number of African religious traditions, which nowadays are practised, aside from Nigeria itself, in a number of Latin American countries as well as North American states. The core cosmology is rooted in an inseparable cosmos, in which the conscious and the unconscious are held together in a kind of relational balance through the life energy called Ashé. There is no polarization of good and bad.

Within this cosmos, Yoruba religion speaks about a fourfold activation within the human being. This fourfold is represented by Orishas: these divinities are contained not outside the individual but deep within; and the individual possesses the gods and goddesses as a way of repossessing those divine aspects of the self. Obtala, as such, is creative, compassionate, and patient, one prepared to accept his lot; benefactor of humanity; dedicated to friendship and the maintenance of the social fabric. Eshu is the inner guide – that part of ourselves leading us to life-changing and life-sustaining insights and revelations. Shango was famous as a king passionately devoted to war and a master magician. He presents us with the tenacious aspect of the human personality – will, determination, commitment. Ogun, finally, is the dynamic centre of the psyche capable of containing, integrating, synthesizing and even transcending the many opposing forces that operate within us.[5] At the heart of this fourfold system is a cross – uniting a horizontal axis known as the 'chief way' with a vertical axis, the 'secondary way'.

Life Emerges from Divinity

For the West African Bambara people, the centre of the cross is symbolically the *kuru* or God Point; here, the Bambara say, life emerges from divinity through birth and merges back into divinity through death, and through this notably cyclical transformation immortality is achieved.[6]

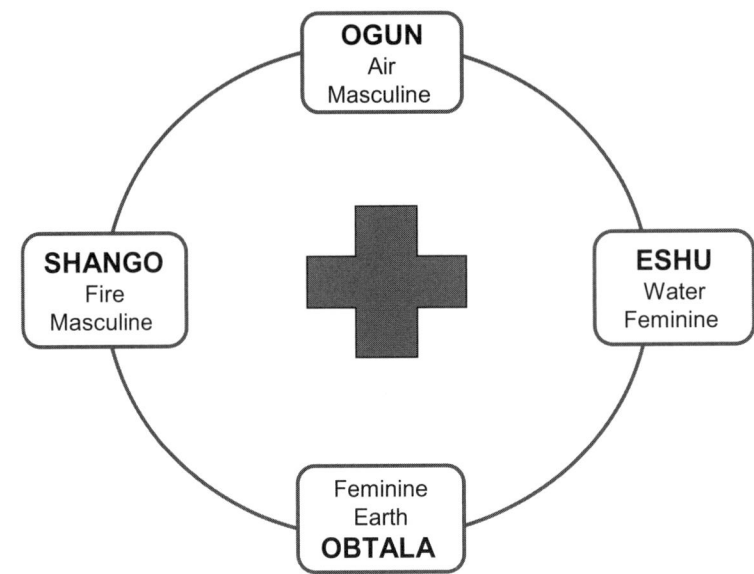

Figure 2.5   Fourfold 'Inner World' of the Yoruba (according to Frobenius)

Using Sound for Bringing New Things into Creation

If you take a look at the human cosmos of the Cree and Objiway peoples from Northern America (shown later in this chapter in Figure 2.9), you will notice that they link sound (music and rhythm) to the 'people of black colour' and describe them as people 'using sound for bringing new things into creation'. Indeed, music, dance and rhythm are still today core expressions of African culture and there is hardly any other form of art that has such an immediate relational power as music and dance. For Africans it is indeed a way of knowing; knowing the rhythm of the eternal dance called life. Such a way of knowing, though, has yet to become institutionalized, other than in African religion.

We now turn from the Southern relational to Eastern renewal.

EASTERN IMAGINATION: THE PATH OF RENEWAL

Continual Becoming

The quest for knowledge in the East was oriented, more than in other parts of the world, towards a path of ongoing renewal, rooted in dynamic forces within nature and culture, such as, for the ancient Chinese, the forces of yin (feminine-responsive) and yang (masculine-assertive). You could reason things out, or realize the truth, but only if you renewed your connection with the grounds of your being. The truth, moreover, was not what could be seen and touched, but rather somewhere 'in between'. In fact, notably today in China, especially from an economic point of view, renewal is lodged somewhere in between the East and the West, as was the case in Japan in the second half of the last century. Dialogue, as such, means 'between the words'; it is about knowledge that is 'flowing through' past, present and future, in a process of continual becoming. Hence, it needs to be continuously re-acquired, as the entire cosmos itself underlies continuous change and transformation. The path of renewal is a spiralling one, continually reaching back, to ever present origins, and then forward again. Two core visualizations of this are the wheel of life and the mandala.

The Way of the East

In Buddhism, which emerged from ancient India, the wheel of life is a symbol for the Eightfolded Way, aiming for freedom from reincarnation or rebirth. It is also found in Indian Hinduism, Jainism, Sikhism and other related religions.

Mandala (Sanskrit for 'circle', 'completion') is a term used to refer to various objects. It is of Hindu origin, but is also used in other Dharmic religions, such as Buddhism. In the Tibetan branch of Vajrayana Buddhism, they have been developed into sandpainting, expressing the belief that knowledge cannot be fixed, but needs to be regenerated again and again. In practice, mandala has become a generic term for any plan, chart or geometric pattern that represents the cosmos metaphysically or symbolically, a microcosm of the universe from the human perspective.

A mandala, especially its centre, can be used during meditation as an object for focusing attention. The symmetrical geometric shapes tend to draw the attention towards their centre. The Swiss Psychologist Carl Gustav Jung saw the mandala as 'a representation of the unconscious self', and believed his paintings of mandalas enabled him to identify emotional disorders and work towards wholeness and integration in personality.[7]

Figure 2.6   Wheel of Life (Centre, Outer Cycle plus a Double Fourfold) (left) and a Tibetan Mandala (Fourfold in a Cycle) (right)

Sources: Image 1: Source: Library of Congress http://www.loc.gov. Image 2: Wikimedia Commons http:// commons.wikimedia.org/

Holistic Design: Existence and Non-Existence

Taoism, for the ancient Chinese, represents the force behind all natural order. Tao can be roughly stated to be the flow of the universe.[8] It is believed to be the influence that keeps the universe balanced and ordered. Tao is associated with nature, due to a belief that nature demonstrates the Tao.[9] The flow of *qi*, as the essential energy of action and existence, is compared to the universal order of Tao. It is often considered to be the source of both existence and non-existence. And hence, it does not search for knowledge and enhanced awareness through distinction and differentiation (either/or) but embodies the ability of embracing paradox (and holding opposites as equal forces, not valuing them as good or bad).

Taoists believe that man is a microcosm for the universe.[10] The body ties directly into the Chinese five elements. The five organs correlate with the five elements, the five directions (including our Four Worlds and a centre) and the seasons.[11] Akin to the 'neoplatonic maxim' of 'as above, so below', Taoism posits that by understanding himself, and in particular his path of becoming, man may gain knowledge of the universe. The Taijitu (yin and yang) symbol is a keynote of Taoist symbolism. While almost all Taoist philosophies make use of the yin and yang symbol, one could also call it Confucian, Neo-Confucian or pan-Chinese.[12]

The five directions as conceived by the ancient Chinese (east, south, west, north, centre) can be linked to the yin and yang symbols; each have their own attributes, as follows in the chart below. [13] As we can see, flow and interconnectivity is a feature of the east, and renewal, linking past, present and future, goes together with it.

The Cyclical Yin–Yang in Relation to the Fourfold (Four Elements/Four Seasons) and the Centre		
Element	**Season**	**Force**
Wood	Spring	Yang
Fire	Summer	Yang
Metal	Autumn	Yin
Water	Winter	Yin
Earth	None	Neutral

We now turn from the relational cycle in the South, and the perennial flow of renewal in the East, to the path of reason in the North that is within Europe. Moreover, it is important to realize that, from an integral perspective, one path needs to build on another. In this case, the force of renewal (development spiral) is much more powerful if it builds on the prior relational force (circle of communion). When Northern reason is added, to complement rather than supplant what has come before, such potency increases ever more.

NORTHERN IMAGINATION: THE PATH OF REASON

Europe's civilization has been influenced mostly by two major sources: Judaeo-Christianity and its Greek heritage.

The Cross: A Means of Connection

The single strongest symbol in Christianity is the cross and its variations, including the monogram of Christ. On a superficially explicit level it is a static, structural symbol of a torture instrument, which led to the death of Jesus. However, in its deeper implicit, dynamic meaning the cross could be understood as a symbol that holds opposites together, that incorporates the ability of embracing paradoxes. As such, it is a means of connection not only between earth (matter/mother) and heaven (spirit/father), but also between the past and the future (embracing eternity). These are also implicit aspects of 'creative synthesis', here with a stronger emphasis on the metaphysical world. In addition, on such a process-oriented level, the cross (see Figure 2.7) stands for horizontal and vertical connections, and, in contemporary management consultancy terms, for graphs, for matrices, self-assessment inventories, and other such analytical devices for gauging your business or management performance and prospects. On the other hand, if taken out of its dynamic context, a cross is simply a static form. Every time an athlete or other performer crosses him- or herself such a static form is reinforced.

For a certain period Christianity was indeed the cultural driving force in western Europe not only in religious and spiritual matters, but also in the arts and the sciences. A number of monasteries became true centres of civilization; they emerged as showcases of social and economic transformation, where communities based on brotherhood enhanced not only the Christian spiritual tradition, but also fostered the arts and sciences, cultivated the land and even became economically successful.

However, at a certain stage the church used its enormous influence on politics and economics, on culture and nature, for domination rather than for liberation.

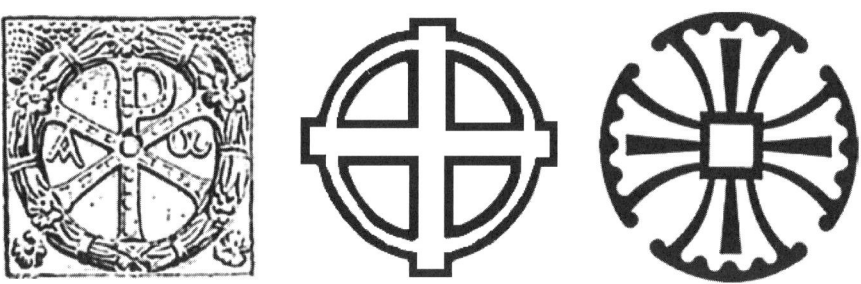

Figure 2.7   Monogram of Christ/Representations Christian Crosses

Sources: Image 1: Saint Leon the Great http://www.st-leothegreatw-s.org/. Image 2: losterkirche Lippoldsberg http://www.klosterkirche.de. Image 3: Kent and Canterbury Hospital http://www.kent-and-canterbury-nurse.co.uk/

Renaissance Man: Focusing on the Power of Reason

The Enlightenment period, from the 14th century onwards, was of particular importance for the birth of a modern society in Europe and it freed the continent from the oppressive medieval form of Christianity. Now man, not god, was in the centre of the universe. Now, so it was believed, it was man who kept the world going (see da Vinci's Vitruvian Man), not Christ. Man could do it with the power of his mind and his own imagination. While in the symbol of the 'fourfold' cross the centre is where the two lines meet (many paintings place here the 'eye of god'), da Vinci's expression of the Renaissance Man, moves the 'centre of power to the mind of the human being'. Since then, for Europe (in our archetypal representation: the North), reason and rationalism, or indeed the *path of reason,* that is the 'northern' mind rather than the heart, spirit or soul, becomes the main source of progress.

In fact, da Vinci himself became the embodiment of imagination, science and innovation. Some claim da Vinci was one of the last men in European history to embody universal knowledge, linking science and arts in a most innovative manner.

The period of the Enlightenment, which in arts and design was called the 'Renaissance' (rebirth), reanimated the second pillar of European civilization: the Greek tradition. It was the Greek philosophers and their focus on reasoning and democratic interaction of minds who enabled one of the most innovative periods within Europe to take place: when Greek civilization was at its peak, so was their innovative power with regard to politics, arts and science. Interestingly enough it was the Middle *Eastern* Arabs who played a major part in recovering the classical Greek tradition. The *Odyssey* and the *Iliad*, as the two core myths of that time, tell stories about the intelligence of man, which helped him, especially in the case of Odysseus, to triumph even over the gods.

Figure 2.8　Leonardo da Vinci's Vitruvian Man (The Mind on Top of the Hierarchy)

Sources: Image 1: Source: Chaim Zins http://www.success.co.il/. Image 2: 2012 Forum http://2012forum.com/

Lacking Paths towards an Integrated Future

However, the sole focus on the power of human reasoning has led to a new kind of distortion. For decades now, Europe has been suffering from a spiritual vacuum. The 'more than human' world[14] is evidently missing. Many analysts claim that Christianity has failed to renew itself and to refill this spiritual gap. In contrast, a growing number of the western European (and US) population have taken their spiritual journey in their own hands and are looking for alternative offerings; often trying to 're-root' themselves in other belief systems, such as Buddhism and Islam, rather than renew their own Northern path, as indeed, as we shall see, the postmodernists have attempted to do. Furthermore, the sole focus on rationality and mind has increasingly created work and communication processes that are not in synch with nature in general and with human nature specifically. Technology and economics as a single North-Western world or dimension has taken precedence over all other worlds, and is often out of touch with nature, culture, politics and social sciences. The awareness of this misfit is gradually increasing throughout the globe. Yet we lack social designs for a more integrated future. In effect the North (reason) and the West (action) dominate the rest, and, at least for the time being, the 'middle' ground has lost its way.

There are however amazing examples of social innovators, from Austrian polymath Rudolf Steiner to Swiss German psychotherapist C.G. Jung (both influenced by the East if not also the South), who started to pave the way towards more integrated perspectives of the various dimensions of human psyche and society. In our work, we concertedly build on them, acknowledging that they are very much the Northern and integral exception, rather than the rule. We now turn from the South (relational), East (renewal) and North (reason), to the West, starting with the original Native Americans.

WESTERN IMAGINATION: THE PATH OF REALIZATION

Specific Directions: Healer, Visionary, Warrior, Teacher

The West today, our ultimate point of realization, is most vividly embodied in the United States of America. From the outset historically, however, it missed its opportunity to build on its indigenous South. In fact we identified some astonishing examples of balanced fourfold designs in a number of indigenous (what we term Southern) societies from North America. They are, if you like, deep expressions of the original Southern and also Eastern dimension of what we now call the West or North America. As such we begin with the 'original' West, as opposed to the 'derivative' Western frontier spirit, as exhibited historically, and still to this day, by the American 'cowboy' and footloose 'get up and go'.

Native Americans bear a strong relation to mother nature, embodying balanced ways of portraying how man interacts with nature in general, with his or her own inner nature, and with the nature of other human beings. Such a rich source of imagery has been patently ignored by social researchers in the USA, who thereby cut themselves off from their original cultural and psychic birthright. The cosmos of the Cree and Objiway people (native American tribes), for example, includes all of the knowledge required to live in harmony with creation; that is the knowledge of body and mind and the ability to disseminate knowledge through communication. All those attributes are, according to this perspective, necessary to form a holistic (nature) and humanistic (culture) worldview. These Native Americans recognized particular strengths in specific ethnic groups, who together, once again, constitute a 'creative synthesis'. It is interesting now to see how they were able to recognize the unique contribution of the 'white (wo)man', who, after all, until this day, did not embrace the Native American heritage in his or her own cosmos.

In ancient medicine wheels attributed to Native American civilizations, it is often different personality types that form a fourfold. In one example,[15] each of the four types in the human spectrum, the healer, the visionary, the warrior and the teacher is connected to a specific direction, element, season and human resource (HR): love, vision, power and wisdom. Individuals represent a certain type or a combination of two or more types, and their individual developmental path is influenced by that type. Each type, according to the medicine wheel, is also represented by a particular instrument, emphasizing the strong connection the 'human south' has to music and rhythm. Indeed, music may even be seen as a way of knowing and a way to know oneself and the other in a deeper way. An outstanding record of the wisdom behind the Native American medicine wheel, representing the very way of life of Native American Indians, is Hyemeyohsts Storm's *Seven Arrows*.[16]

Figure 2.9   Fourfold Design of the Human Cosmos of Cree and Objiway People (left) Fourfold of an Ancient Medicine Wheel (Native American Origin) (right)

Sources: Healer: Testedich.de http://www.testedich.de/. Visionary: The Lyons Den http://www. lyonsdenbooks.com/. Warrior: Source: Native Americans @ Buffalo Trails http://native-americans.org/. Teacher: Dunywood http://www.dunywood.de/

Oriented Towards what is Materially Realisable

North America today is a 'melting pot' of all kinds of cultures and personalities, ironically exclusive – rather than inclusive – of the native Indian, who is shut off within a native reserve. In a most fascinating way, the 'United States' has managed to develop out of this enormously diverse cultural amalgam, a society whose economic and technological forces come to the fore. It is active, future-oriented and pragmatic like no other country; and it has quite obviously enabled lots of technologically and economically laden creative synthesis within the country, focusing on what is materially *realizable*. However, it is also increasingly evident that the US has lost its ability to engage in such creative synthesis, both within its own psychic being, and also together with other countries and civilizations. It still interacts most easily with those countries and personalities which are most comparable to the US – Western style economies and democracies, and similar behavioural orientations towards work and life. But it seems to be unable to embrace diversity on a global level, especially when it comes to other religious and cultural, individual and institutional forms and outlooks that do not want to follow the 'American Way'.

It may be worthwhile to explore to what extent this 'out of balance' perspective is also a manifestation of North America's inability to embrace the cultural and spiritual heritage and knowledge that the indigenous Native American cultures had to offer. Such an exploration is such an obvious one, when we recognize that among the greatest of problems that the US faces is its difficulty in engaging with other cultures, including its indigenous own, as well as with nature and environment. America, overall then, is much more at home in exercising reason and in the process realizing its material objectives, than at socially relating and spiritually renewing itself. The inability to integrally engage with the Afro-American, if not also Hispanic Southern, may be somewhat redressed with Barack Obama as US president.

There are, however, very promising Western exceptions. There is an increasing number of social scientists trying to reconcile the primary focus on economics, politics and natural science, with culture, community and nature. Paul Hawken's, Amory and Hunter Lovins' *Natural Capitalism*[17] and David Peak's *Blackfoot Physics*[18] are just two recent expressions of this.

From Realizable to Relational

These examples of 'reflecting back' ('re-ligio') to identify the deep cultural knowledge of a society are becoming more prolific, especially in those countries where the original indigenous culture has been neglected. Like North America, Australia is a Western country, in our terms, which has hitherto been disconnected from its indigenous roots, as recently revealed by the Swedish and aboriginal 'knowledge management' duo Karl-Erik Sveiby's and Tex Skuthorpe's *Treading Lightly – Uncovering the Wisdom of the Australian Aborigines*.[19]

Yet another strong voice is that of the Israeli peace activist Jesaiah Ben-Aharon who, in outlining *America's Global Responsibility*, argues that an evolving Western culture must rather serve to integrate than to isolate or dominate the South, East, North and centre. He argues that the major destabilizing power in the modern era is the modern economy. For Ben-Aharon, globalization has the capacity to tear away from the state its economic, political and cultural (and natural) assets. Only therefore a clear relational understanding and thereby practical and social implementation of the human interactions and relationships among the various sectors of society will yield the power to replace the pure focus on the economy with more adequate modern social design.[20]

We now turn, finally, to the centre of the Four Worlds, represented by the most 'synthetic' or integral form of monotheist religion, Islam; albeit that voices from both within and without have served to distort such an integral orientation.

CENTRED IMAGINATION: CONNECTING PATHS

Infinity, Balance and Architectural Beauty in the Islamic World

The interaction between self and the other generally, or between Muslim, Roman, Persian and Byzantine architecture specifically, as an evolutionary catalyst for creation and innovation, is evident in the most important architectural expression of the Islamic world: the mosque.

The mosque is the sacred architecture of Islam *par excellence*. It is but a re-creation of the harmony, order and peace inherent in nature. The specifically recognizable Islamic architectural style developed soon after the time of the Prophet Mohammed, evolved as a creative synthesis of Roman, Egyptian, Persian/Sassanid and Byzantine models. An early example may be identified as early as 691 with the completion of the Dome of the Rock (Qubbat al Sakkrah) in Jerusalem. It featured a circular dome and the use of stylized repeating decorative patterns (arabesques). The Hagia Sophia in Istanbul also influenced Islamic architecture. When the Ottomans captured the city from the Byzantines, they converted the Christian basilica to a mosque and incorporated a Byzantine architectural element into their own work.

Distinguishing motifs of Islamic architecture have always been ordered repetition, radiating structures and rhythmic, metric patterns. In this respect, fractal geometry has been a key feature, especially for mosques and palaces. Many argue that Islamic architecture also borrows heavily from the Persian and in many ways can be called an extension and further evolution of it. Many cities such as Baghdad, for example, were based on precedents such as Firouzabad in Persia. In fact, it is known, that the two designers who were hired by al-Mansur to design the city were Naubakht, a former Persian Zoroastrian, and Mashallah, a former Jew from Khorasan, Iran.

A Meeting of Islamic and Judaeo-Christian Cultures

Moorish architecture (to be found mainly in North Africa and on the Iberian Peninsula) is another example of when a civilization reaches its peak by predominantly peaceful and constructive interactions with others. The Moorish period in Spain is indeed famous for the atmosphere of peaceful co-existence and creative interaction between Muslims, Christians and Jews. Core examples are the Great Mosque of Cordoba (the Mezquita) and the Alhambra, the magnificent palace-fortress of Granada.

The Alhambra most especially embodies the perfect harmony of manmade architecture and nature, interconnected by the most sophisticated watering and fountain systems that underscore the dynamic, organic and flow-oriented nature of creation. Even after the completion of the so-called 'Requoncista', Islamic influence had a lasting impact on the architecture of Spain. In particular, medieval Spaniards used the Mudéjar style, an imitation of Islamic design. One of the best examples of the Moors' lasting impact is the Alcázar of Seville.

From Egyptian Mamluk to Turkish Ottoman

For many, the Ottomans achieved the highest level in architecture of mosque-building. They mastered the technique of building vast inner spaces confined by seemingly weightless yet massive domes, and of achieving perfect harmony between inner and outer spaces, as well as light and shadow. At that stage the mosque was transformed into a sanctuary of aesthetic and technical balance, refined elegance and a hint of heavenly transcendence.

The reign of the Mamluks (1250 to 1517) marked a breathtaking flowering of Islamic art, which is most visible in old Cairo. Mamluk decorative arts were prized around the Mediterranean as well as in Europe, where they had a profound impact on the local production. The influence of Mamluk glassware on the Venetian glass industry is only one such example.

Taj Mahal: Mughal Fusion of Muslim, Persian and Indian

Another distinctive sub-style is the architecture of the Mughal Empire in India in the 16th century: here a fusion of Persian and Hindu elements can be found. The most famous example of Mughal architecture is the Taj Mahal, the 'teardrop on eternity', completed in 1648 by the Mughal emperor Shah Jahan. The Taj Mahal is completely symmetrical.

From India we could go on to Sino-Islamic architecture. The first Chinese mosque was already established in the 7th century. An important feature in Chinese architecture in general is its emphasis on symmetry.

If we take a closer look at most mosques, we immediately find evidence of the interaction of the fourfold (squares, rectangles), the cycle (domes) as well as flow and process-oriented designs (arabesques) and natural elements (water, plants).

Distilling the meaning behind the predominant design of most mosques, we conclude that key conceptual and aesthetic elements are those of:

- *Infinity:* Designs with repeating themes suggest infinity and evoke the concept of Allah's infinite power.
- *Balance:* The balance of vast inner spaces confined by seemingly weightless domes, the perfect harmony between inner and outer spaces, as well as light and shadow is a reflection of the perfection of the creation. That also links to balance (justice) as one of the core tenets of Islam.
- *Beauty:* Islam's architecture has been called the 'architecture of the veil' because the beauty lies in the inner spaces (courtyards and rooms), which are not visible from the outside.

These three aspects can also be found in the single most prominent ornamental feature in mosques specifically, but in Islamic design generally: the arabesque.

The Arabesque: Displaying Unity in Diversity

The arabesque is an elaborate application of repeating geometric forms. Geometric artwork was not widely used in the Islamic world until the golden age of Islam came into full bloom. During this time, ancient texts were translated from their original Greek and Latin into Arabic at the House of Wisdom, an academic research institution in Baghdad. Like the Renaissance in Europe that followed much later, mathematics, science, literature and history were infused into the Islamic world with mostly positive repercussions. The works of Plato and especially of Euclid became popular among the literate. In fact, it was Euclid's geometry along with the foundations of trigonometry codified by Pythagoras that were expounded on by Al-Jawhari (*c.* 800 to 860) whose *Commentary on Euclid's Elements*[21] became the impetus of the art for that was to become the arabesque. Plato's idea about the existence of a separate reality that was perfect in form and function and crystalline in character also would contribute to the development of the arabesque.

Hence the arabesque is a symbol of the particular worldview that Islam developed.

There are two modes to arabesque art: the first reflects the principles that govern the order of the world. These principles included the bare basics of what makes objects structurally sound, and, by extension, beautiful. In this first mode, each repeating geometric form has a built-in symbolism ascribed to it. For example, the square, with its four equilateral sides, is symbolic of the equally important elements of nature: earth, air, fire and water. If any one of the four were missing, the physical world, represented by a circle that inscribes the square, would collapse and cease to exist. The second mode is based upon the flowing nature of plant forms. This mode recalls the feminine nature of life giving. In addition, upon inspection of many examples of arabesque art, some would argue that there is in fact a third mode, the mode of Arabic calligraphy.

As figurative art was considered to be idolatrous and was forbidden (*haram*) in mosques, calligraphy and abstract figures became the main methods of artistic expression in Islamic cultures. Arabic, Persian and Ottoman Turkish calligraphy is associated with geometric Islamic art on the walls and ceilings of mosques as wells as in books. Contemporary artists in the Islamic world draw on the heritage of calligraphy. The guiding principles of infinity, balance and beauty can also easily be found in Islamic calligrams.

Knowledge as a Historic Driving Force in Muslim Culture

For the Muslim calligraphy is a visible expression of the highest art of all: the art of the spoken word (the transmittal of thoughts and of history) – in short: knowledge. In Islam, the most important document to be transmitted orally is, of course, the Qur'an. Proverbs and complete passages from the Qur'an can be seen in arabesque art. The coming together of these three forms creates the arabesque, and this is a reflection of unity arising from diversity, which is another basic tenet of Islam.

Knowledge is indeed the major driving force of Islamic culture. Its Islamic translation, *ilm*, is one of the most frequently occurring terms in the Qur'an; indeed, only two other words appear more frequently: *Allah* (God) and *Rabb* (Creator or Sustainer). One may claim, that without this inner urge to know, without this dedication towards knowledge, an Islamic civilization would not have been possible. At the same time, if the flow of knowledge is interrupted, for example, because it is dominated by one societal group, then the civilization declines. That is, one could argue, what we sadly see in much of the Muslim world today. For seven centuries now, it has been the religious authorities in the Muslim *ummah* who have suppressed the free flow of knowledge.

It is interesting that the written word (expressing knowledge) had such a major influence in the development of the arabesque. The way in which calligraphy finds its way into this Islamic design form is always in a flow form. The flow form is beautifully interwoven in the geometric balance that all arabesques display. Hence it is the flow of knowledge that keeps the more static and abstract geometrical forms in a dynamic balance.

This very brief review of Islamic design has served to make it obvious that its development has been continuously furthered and stimulated by the 'productive interaction' of various cultural heritages (Arabic, Persian, Turkish and more). At the peak of Muslim civilization creative synthesis worked at its best: knowledge was able to flow. This same flow of knowledge is characteristic of our integral approach to research.

Figure 2.10 Arabesques (Fourfold, Circular and Process Elements, Centre)

Source: Peacay's Blog http://peacay.vox.com/

Figure 2.11 Examples of Islamic Calligraphy

Sources: Image 1: V-Arabic http://varabic.wordpress.com/. Image 2: Exotic India http://www. exoticindiaart.com/. Image 3: Middle East Blog http://internetservices.readingeagle.com/blog/syria/

2.4 Conclusion: Four Worlds and Four Paths – An Integral Research Design

In our tour of the world we have introduced core social designs and the visual manifestations of these, both static (explicit structure) and dynamic (implicit process) of many societies. We have recognized that when a civilization is at its peak, it has managed to keep a kind of dynamic balance between its various parts. It practises unity-in-diversity both internally, through interconnecting its different functions, and externally by interacting, on equal terms, with different cultures. This is also a time when there is a relatively free flow of knowledge. As such the knowledge-creating power of the civilization is at its height and its artistic expressions (or visual designs) most evolved.

Social innovation for us means the purposeful development of social images, ideologies, institutions and inclinations, originating and developing a creative synthesis of the diverse elements within a society's soils (and of a society with other societies). In order to be socially innovative on a sustainable basis, a social organism needs an effective inner process that allows the diverse worlds to interact and to stay in a dynamic balance; such balanced interaction, for us, occurs when each worldview is enabled to fully express itself.

We have demonstrated with a number of examples that societies all over the world have, in particular times, developed a perspective about the nature of the diverse elements, which formed their particular cosmos, and how these elements could be held in a dynamic balance. Such modes of being (relational) and becoming (renewal), knowing (reason) and doing (realization), found their way into visual images that embodied them, and thereby provided the potential for a particular civilization to evolve, which we have now turned into four paths of ultimately Integral Research. Based on this we have developed an Integral Research design that leads towards social innovation and which simultaneously embodies our Four Worlds.

We have attributed to each path a particular symbol, which most evidently represents its particular quality:

- *Southern Relational Path:* symbolized by a cycle, representing wholeness in nature (full moon, sun, and so on.) and community (family and community cycles).
- *Eastern Path of Renewal:* symbolized by a spiral, representing continuous, interconnected cycles of renewal, as well as continuous storylines, interconnecting past, present and future (civilizational spiral).
- *Northern Path of Reason:* symbolized by a line or matrix, representing lines of reasoning, order within manmade social systems (institutions, enterprises, and so on) or constitutions (for example, laws).
- *Western Path of Realization:* symbolized by a point, representing the focus on personal, organizational and community goals, realizing the material potential and culminating point of a social system, if it builds on the primary relational quality.

From an innovation perspective, circle, spiral, line and point need to mutually reinforce one another, not only visually but also viscerally, so to speak. Furthermore, it is no accident that we talk in terms of a 'line of reasoning', and the 'point of an argument'. Each symbolizes a particular, cultural or individual mentality. Interestingly enough, in English at least, we have no such positive colloquialisms for the other two archetypal forms: cycle and spiral. In fact, we allude negatively to someone 'going around in circles', and 'getting nowhere' as a result. Spirals, proverbially as such, are not even on our radar screens.

As we come to a detailed analysis of research method, the starting and originating point of our research journey towards social innovation, you will see even more clearly, how well these symbols represent the four paths. The Southern path starts with the descriptive methods which are about encircling a particular research phenomenon. The Eastern path starts with narrative methods, where the researcher seeks for the unfolding and evolving narrative of the research object. The Northern path starts with methods of theorizing, in search for a linear relation between various aspects researched. And the Western path commences with experiments and survey methods, going straight towards a pointed direction.

Figure 2.12 summarizes the four core research paths in relation with the human modes and depicts the symbols chosen for each path.

Integral Research, based on a representation of the Four Worlds, does not only link the various ways in which knowledge has been generated, it also aims to uncover the inner rhythm of knowledge creation. Thus we seek a coherent link between outer design (social innovation) and inner process (Integral Research).

As researcher-innovator you start with your own life world, thereby reviewing the history of your society to uncover what structures and processes the society had previously developed, which allowed it to become a dynamic civilization. From there you take this story forward and work yourself through the Integral Research process, progressively leading towards social innovation that can ultimately have a true impact on your society.

Figure 2.12 Integral Research – The Four Core Research Paths

The core defining factors of Integral Research are summarized as follows:

- *Building on Local Roots:* reconnecting the researcher with the innovative power of their own civilization as a starting point for their research path; ensuring that the researcher/innovator is true to their own culture.
- *Integrating Knowledge Paths:* integrating and equally valuing different worlds, and hence different approaches to research methodology and knowledge creation.
- *Enabling Creative Synthesis:* enabling creative synthesis of diverse dimensions within a social organism (self, organization, society) and between social organisms (between organization, between societies) interconnecting different knowledge paths.
- *From Local Roots to Global Reach:* through the integration of knowledge paths and the enabling of creative synthesis, Integral Research fosters a gradual evolution from local roots (local identity) to global reach (contributing to an integrated, balanced perspective on a global level). The connection of the local and global also helps to enable forms of social innovation that, while reaching globally, stay true and authentic to the local context where they are ultimately applied.

The illustration of our social innovation tree in Figure 2.13 translates once more our core architecture into an organic picture. While the Four World illustration highlights the cultural morphology of each world, the tree illustration highlights the organic process underlying social innovation. Hence we link such cultural and the natural perspectives together, emphasizing the combined significance of culture and nature as a starting point for any social innovation.

Figure 2.13 The Social Innovation Tree and the Four Paths of Integral Research

Altogether, we have seen how particular societies and civilizations have developed knowledge about maintaining a healthy and dynamic balance. To the extent that such healthy balance turned to be a dynamic and creative synthesis, so the society developed its power to innovate. Such an innovation power was born out of the interaction between cultures, what we term transcultural, as was the case for the Muslim world at its height (in the 9th to 14th centuries), and for America in the 19th and first half of the 20th centuries.

Integral Research is an approach that weaves major approaches or paths towards research and knowledge creation that have been developed all over the world into a coherent framework, or living organism. In the next chapter we shall map out the entire architecture of Integral Research. Thereby we illustrate how each of the four paths follows a fourfold trajectory towards social innovation.

References

1. Sen, A. (2000). *Development as Freedom*. New York: Anchor Books.
2. Lessem, R. and Schieffer, A. (2009). *Transformation Management: Towards the Integral Enterprise*. Farnham: Gower.
3. Lessem, R. and Palsule, S. (1996). *Managing in Four Worlds*. Oxford: Blackwell.
4. Lessem and Schieffer, *Transformation Management*.
5. Ford, C. (2000). *The Hero with an African Face – The Mystic Wisdom of Traditional Africa*. New York: Bantam. (citing: anthropologist Leo Frobenius)
6. Ford, C. (2000). *The Hero with an African Face – The Mystic Wisdom of Traditional Africa*. New York: Bantam.
7. Jaffé, A. (2001). *Erinnerung, Träume, Gedanken von C.G. Jung*. Zürich: Walter.
8. Cane, E.P. (2002). *Harmony: Radical Taoism Gently Applied*. Victoria: Trafford Publishing.
9. Martinson, P.V. (1987). *A Theology Of World Religions: Interpreting God, Self, and World in Semitic, Indian, and Chinese Thought*. Augsburg: Augsburg Publishing House.
10. Robinet, I. (1997). *Taoism: Growth of a Religion*. Stanford CA: Stanford University Press.
11. Kohn, L. (ed.) (2000). *Daoism Handbook*. Leiden: Brill.
12. Little, S., with Eichman, S. *et al.* (2000). *Taoism and the Arts of China*. Chicago IL: Art Institute of Chicago.
13. Little, S., with Eichman, S. *et al.* (2000). *Taoism and the Arts of China*. Chicago IL: Art Institute of Chicago.
14. Abram, D. (1997). *The Spell of the Sensuous*. New York: Random House.
15. Arrien, A. (1993). *The Four-Fold Way – Walking the Paths of the Warrior, Teacher, Healer and Visionary*. San Francisco, CA: Harper.
16. Storm, H. (1972). *Seven Arrows*. New York: Ballantine
17. Hawken, P., Lovins, A. and Lovins, H.L. (1999). *Natural Capitalism – Creating the Next Industrial Revolution*. Boston, MA: Little, Brown.
18. Peak, F.D. (2005). *Blackfoot Physics. A Journey into the Native American Universe*. York Beach, ME: Red Whell/Weiser.
19. Sveiby, K.E. and Skuthorpe, T. (2006). *Treading Lightly – The Hidden Wisdom of the World's Oldest People*. Crows Nest: Allen and Unwin.
20. Ben-Aharon, J. (2002). *America's Global Responsibility*. Herdon: Lindisfarne.
21. De Young, Gregg (1997). 'Al-Jawhari's Additions to Book V of Euclid's Elements.' *Zeitschrift für Geschichte der Arabisch-Islamischen Wissenschaften*, 11 (10): 153–78.

3 The Integral Research Trajectory

From Method to Action, From Origination to Transformation

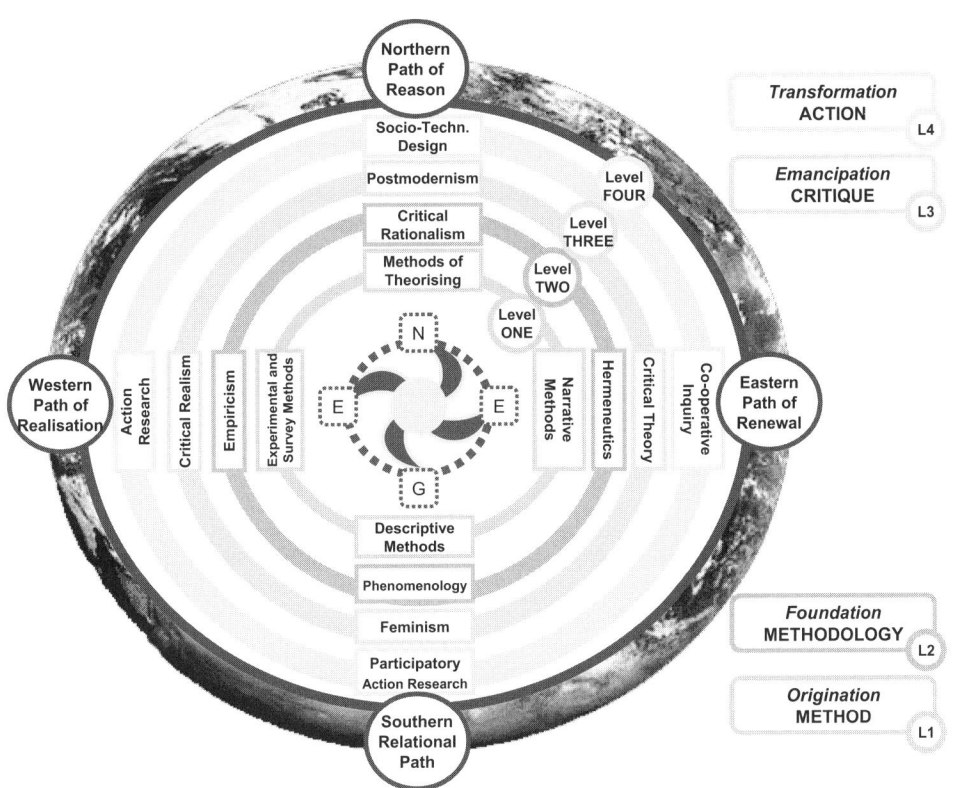

Figure 3.1   Overview Chapter 3 – Integral Research (Full Architecture)

Summary: The Integral Research Trajectory

- In this chapter we set out the four paths to Integral Research that you are able to follow: the Southern and humanistic relational path; the Eastern and holistic path of renewal; the Northern and rational path of reason; and the Western and pragmatic path of realization.
- These four discrete paths serve to make up the Integral Research GENE, a term we have created in previous work. The GENE stands for grounding, emerging, navigation and effecting, and is the generic trajectory that releases the full GENEius of a person, a community or a society. In this case, it releases the GENEius of your research, turning it into social innovation.
- Within Integral Research the GENE can be found in two forms: Four World and fourfold. First, each research path represents one part of a Four World GENE. Within our architecture the relational South is strongest on grounding; Eastern renewal places the greatest emphasis on emergence; the Northern path of reason is predisposed towards conceptual navigation, and that of realization towards practical effect. We call this GENE the Four World GENE constituting Integral Research.
- Secondly, each path holds its own fourfold. This is comprised of the four research levels. Each of the four research paths enables you to move through those four research levels: from originating research method to transformative action research: by starting out (1) with research method (the origination of innovation and grounding of your research), followed by (2) methodology (the emerging innovation foundation of your research), onto (3) critique (your emancipation towards innovation, based on your own knowledge navigation), culminating (4) in the particular action (effective transformation) that leads to your social innovation. The Path GENE complements for each path the overall Four World GENE.
- What does that mean for you? Firstly and most important, once you have identified your specific path, you immerse yourself into a GENE trajectory. For example, if your research path is the Southern relational path, you would move from description (grounding), to phenomenology (emerging), feminism (navigating) and ultimately participatory action research (effecting). However, from the very beginning, you would see your research in the light of the whole, being fully aware of your particular path, but also of the overall knowledge- and value-creating process you are ultimately contributing to.
- Each level is differentiated for each of the four research paths. The first level, in terms of each respective path, of method (origination) is differentiated into descriptive methods (Southern relational path) and narrative methods (path of renewal), methods of theorizing (Northern path of reason) and experimental and survey methods (Western path of realization).
- The second level of methodology (foundation) consists of phenomenology (relational) and hermeneutics (renewal), followed by critical rationalism (reason) and empiricism (realization). Each of them is building upon the research method that came before.
- The third level of critique (emancipation) builds in turn on method and methodology, and is constituted of feminism (relational), critical theory (renewal), postmodernism (reason) and critical realism (realization). Each of these critiques tends to be relatively more rounded than the methodologies that came before. They thereby serve to connect different research paths.
- The fourth level of ultimate action (transformation), which is the most integral, thereby serving most concertedly to turn social research into social innovation, is comprised of participatory action research (relational), co-operative inquiry (renewal), socio-technical design (reason) and overall action research (realization).
- Now you, the researcher, are ready to immerse yourself in the roots of knowledge and value creation, whichever of the four research paths you pursue. In each case you move from method (origination) to methodology (foundation), to critique (emancipation) and finally, to action (transformation). The ultimate goal is a social, or, as we call it, an Integral Innovation.

3.1 Introduction: A Double-Layered Trajectory

Within this chapter we shall lay out in detail the paths and trajectories of Integral Research, both analytical and transformative. They are, as we shall see, 'growing' out of the particular underlying soil (culture and nature), and linked with a specific main stem (social science). We build progressively on the four research paths that we introduced in Chapter 2. These paths represent different approaches to Integral Research, analytically based research and transformatively oriented innovation, which have been developed over time in different parts of the world.

These four paths within the Four World framework each follow a double-layered Integral Research trajectory that combines an analytical orientation towards research with a transformative orientation towards innovation. Once you have chosen your particular research path, you work yourself through the four levels specific to that path, though, as we have seen in our research programmes, there is some flexibility to move between paths. Altogether, the interaction between the two kinds of trajectory serve to 'dynamize' your research, and to keep you in constant contact with the burning issue you choose to address and with what we have termed the integral, transformative innovation you are destined to bring about. In other words, the innovation trajectory serves to infuse your research with dynamism, purpose, relevance and direction. Overall then you progressively and cumulatively advance through the following four levels:

- *Level 1:* Research *method* linked with *origination* of an innovation.
- *Level 2:* Research *methodology* aligned with a philosophical and paradigmatic *foundation* for that innovation.
- *Level 3:* Research *critique* linked with a philosophical and socio-political sources of *emancipation* behind innovation.
- *Level 4: Action research,* building on all previous levels, serving to realize the necessary *transformation,* to bring about a full-fledged integral innovation.

To make this overall process of Integral Research more clear, we now guide you through the two, aligned trajectories. Have in mind, that at each level you simultaneously engage with both trajectories. Integral Research is then an interactive journey between a more analytical (research) and a more transformative (innovation) trajectory, leading towards an integral social innovation. We now examine the four levels, both analytical and transformative in each of the four cases, in turn.

LEVEL 1: METHOD AND ORIGINATION

Method: Research Method

You engage in a particular research method or technique, which is, as we shall show, closely related to underlying human modes of being and becoming, knowing and doing. We start with method, as this brings you in the most direct contact with your own 'natural' way of being a researcher (your own origin), but also with your social context. Hence, you start (see Figure 3.1) through your chosen path, with descriptive methods (relational path), narrative methods (path of renewal), methods of theorizing (path of reason) or experimental and survey methods (path of realization).

Origination: Origination of Your Innovation

Closely aligned with analytical method is the transformatively oriented origination, in this case of your innovation. You identify and address a personal and/or societal burning issue, lodged in the soil of your particular social context. You thereby not only uncover the origins and root causes of your burning issues, but you also tap into the origins and originality of your own culture and community, activating its particular local wisdom and problem-solving potential.

LEVEL 2: METHODOLOGY AND FOUNDATION

Methodology: Research Methodology

You engage methodologically and philosophically with existing theories, which have been built up over time to establish a solid analytical basis or paradigm for your research. Here you choose, according to your path, between phenomenology (relational path), hermeneutics (path of renewal), critical rationalism (path of reason) or empiricism (path of realization).

Foundation: Innovation Foundation

You develop a philosophical and methodological foundation for your envisioned innovation, lodged in one or other of the social sciences. You learn to see that the research methodology you are engaging with at this level is, in its very essence, a fundamental critique of society or response to fundamental flaw in the prevailing epistemological tradition (for example, phenomenology has been a critical response to the overwhelming dominance of empiricism). By seeing this, you start to see that each social innovation needs a solid theoretical and philosophical basis.

LEVEL 3: CRITIQUE AND EMANCIPATION

Critique: Research Critique

You now start to engage with a core contemporary critique within research methodology, further evolving, analytically, your philosophical and methodological position. Here you choose, according to your path, between feminism (relational path), critical theory (path of renewal), postmodernism (path of reason) or critical realism (path of realization). These critiques are notably more transdisciplinary than the original methodology/philosophy/social science considered on level 2. Your analytical perspective broadens, and you engage more intensely with co-researchers to evolve your own position.

Emancipation: Emancipation for Innovation

You evolve the foundation to innovation further, now specifically with a view to promoting human flourishing. You also immerse yourself deeper, and indeed developmentally, in the specific societal and cultural context in which your burning issue is lodged. You emancipate yourself as a potential agent of transformation, now developing your own philosophical fundamentals, building a new theoretical foundation for your envisioned innovation. Operating on level 3 you are no longer a researcher outside the burning issue, but you critically engage with it. You take a transformative stance. This level is far more dynamic than level 2, and you start moving from social philosophy to social movement. Indeed, you thereby follow the critical philosophies with which you have been engaging (feminism, postmodernism, and so on.). All, at least to some extent, also represent a social movement.

LEVEL 4: ACTION AND TRANSFORMATION

Action: Action Research

Finally, having worked yourself through levels 1, 2 and 3, you are ready for action. You have built up sufficient experience, theory and critical understanding of your burning issue, to develop your own knowledge base. You are now ready to apply this knowledge and engage with the institution, community or society at hand, in action research. On this ultimate level 4 you choose, according to your path, between participatory action research (relational path), co-operative inquiry (path of renewal), socio-technical design (path of reason) or generic action research (path of realization).

Transformation: Transformation for Innovation

Your action research is transformatively directed to bringing about an integral innovation addressing the original burning issue. Based on your emancipated philosophical perspective, you engage in actively realizing a transformation within your social context, contributing a significant, both theoretical and practical, contribution to the organization, community or society with which you are engaging.

The social innovation tree (see Figure 3.2) summarizes the fourfold Integral Research journey leading to an ultimately integral social innovation. According to the burning issue chosen and the path taken your innovation would contribute to (or have generated fruit in) one of the four core fields of burning issues. In very general terms, in each case you seek to overcome one or other of the core distortions of our Four World out of balance:

- *Healing the Planet:* overcoming environmental and communal decay.
- *Promoting the Peaceful Co-Evolution of Peoples:* overcoming fundamentalism and terrorism.
- *Building Open Societies:* overcoming corruption and despotism.
- *Creating Economic Opportunities:* overcoming materialism and abject poverty.

We will now start to build systematically from this basis. While the detailed Integral Research framework is presented in linear terms, Integral Research is quintessentially a back and forth cyclical, spiralling and ultimately original and organic living process, where the end of 'doing well' is created out of the beginning, 'doing good'. But let us move forward step by step. So get ready fo(u)r Integral Research and Innovation, get ready to release your GENE-ius as an analytical researcher and transformative innovator. Note, that in this book, we use both terms, 'social' and 'integral' innovation, simultaneously. We do so to highlight, that our particular approach towards social innovation is an integral one, spanning origination, in particular soils; foundation in social research methodology; emancipation through a transdisciplinary orientation to the social sciences; and ultimate social and economic transformation. We believe that this is key, not only to coming up with truly original and authentic social innovations, but also to gradually building a new knowledge base, which leads to a transformation through and of the social sciences as well as to new educational curricula, enabling future social, and thereby also integral, innovators. We thereby distinguish ourselves clearly from the generally very loose use of the term 'social innovation'. Integral Research and integral innovation are the two analytical and transformative sides of the same coin.

3.2 The Fourfold GENEtic Code to Social Innovation

Integral Research is both analytical and transformative, stabilizing and dynamic. The paths illustrated here may generate the illusion of a purely linear movement. But they are also expressions of archetypal patterns of creation. You will remember from Chapter 2 that the visual social design (like the illustration of the four research paths) is only the outer expression of an inner dynamic process. It is this creative inner process alongside an analytical, stabilizing structure that combine to form Integral Research, and we shall turn to uncover this innermost 'vital force'.

Figure 3.2   The Social Innovation Tree – Four Paths, Four Levels

If you review the examples of dynamically balanced social designs in different civilizations (see Chapter 2) and the implicit meaning as well as explicit form of them, you can say, that – without exception – all of them were designed as orientations for knowledge seekers, on a path to social innovation that has emerged in a particular culture and society.

In all cases these designs are invitations to raise consciousness and to engage in a knowledge-creating journey. Many of them refer at some point or another directly to nature itself and build on the wisdom of how nature continuously innovates by developing higher, more suitable forms (outcomes of a 'creative synthesis').

We have analysed the knowledge-generating (consciousness-raising) patterns underlying such diverse social designs. We found that each design has its particular inner process, or vital force, allowing for the creative synthesis of and between its parts, also serving to promote a productive interaction with other social organisms (communities or societies). This process is a kind of 'vital force' or 'attractor' that attracts individuals, organizations and societies towards knowledge creation. We have called this process the GENE, an acronym that stands for grounding, emerging, navigating and effecting, and have described it in detailed in our work on *Transformation Management*.[1] The table introduces the transformative rhythm of the GENE, adapted already to the particular needs of the Integral Researcher.

| **The GENE** |
| *Vital Force in Transformation Processes in Living Systems* |
| **Grounding:**
In the grounding phase, you as an integral researcher/innovator build reconnect with the grounds of your own individual and collective life world. |
| **Emerging:**
The phase of emergence allows you to understand the core social need that emerges within this context and to understand how a solution of this problematic situation may contribute to the whole. |
| **Navigating:**
The navigation phase brings you in contact with the social sciences, from anthropology to economics, geography to history, sociology to psychology, from all over the world, and enables you to link it with existing local knowledge to prepare for a true synthesis. |
| **Effecting:**
the phase of effecting allows you to finally develop a social innovation, drawn from a burning issue lodged in the grounds for your life world, which is applicable and a true contribution to your own context. |

In the context of Integral Research, and distilling our findings in various cultures, we identified two GENE rhythms, both differentiating and integrating, which we call the Four World GENE and the Path GENE. Altogether they ensure dynamic and ongoing interaction between the four Paths of Integral Research as well as between the four levels of each path. Figure 3.3 illustrates the functioning of these two GENE rhythms.

The following labels appear within the figure:

Northern Path of Reason

Four World Model

Builds the Global Framework of Integral Research.

Represents archetypally the four core Domains of Man (Being, Becoming, Knowing, Doing), the four core cultural Morphologies in the World (Humanism, Holism, Rationalism, Pragmatism) and the four core Paths of Knowledge Creation (Relational, Renewal, Reason and Realisation), all following the same South to East to North to West - Rhythm

Level FOUR
Level THREE
Level TWO
Level ONE

Navigating

Western Path of Realisation

Effecting

Emerging

Eastern Path of Renewal

Path GENE

Example for a Path GENE. (Southern Path).

The Path GENE spirals in each Path from Origination (L1) to Innovation (L4). The Spiral is sourced in the (local) Centre, and its growing Dimension symbolises the increasing Interrelatedness and Integration between the 4 Paths the more the outer (global) Level is approached.

Grounding

Descriptive Methods

Phenomenology

Feminism

Participatory Action Research

Southern Relational Path

Four World GENE

Represents the inner Innovation Cycle ('Engine') of Integral Research.

The Four World Gene links the different Elements of four Research Paths in a cyclical ongoing Process, continuously striving for Balance and Integration between them.

Figure 3.3   The GENEs

Based on our argument so far, it is obvious that the grounding phase is the first step into Integral Research. The 'effecting' step is the final one, and for once it is the South that leads the process, followed by the East and the North. The archetypal West, so our argument posits, becomes only truly effective if it builds on the other worlds. In other words, you need to uncover the South, East, North and West, metaphorically, not geographically, of your society, while also, and in the process, drawing from these worlds.

The Four World GENE distinguishes between the relational path of research, as well as the research paths of renewal, of reason and of realization. As mentioned hitherto in this chapter, as an Integral Researcher you opt for one of the four specific research paths, one that is authentic to yourself and your society.

3.3 The Four Level Research-to-Innovation Journey

OVERVIEW: INTEGRAL RESEARCH LEADING TO INTEGRAL INNOVATION

Integral Research

By now you have received a first introduction to Integral Research and Innovation. Our intention was to give you an initial understanding of the two, respectively analytical (research) and transformative (innovation) approaches. Integral Research distinguishes between four discrete research paths – relational to renewal, reason to realization – and within each one, between four levels in a research trajectory – research method and research methodology, research critique and action research. These differentiations constitute an analytical device whereby we help you make sense of what is otherwise a very confusing body of literature, spanning research method and methodology. In fact the conventional division between qualitative and quantitative method, for us, is singularly unhelpful.

Instead, we have come up with four mutually exclusive and collectively exhaustive research paths, each with a similar fourfold trajectory, from research method to action research. Moreover, while each of the four paths can be aligned with one or other of our four worlds, each trajectory, as we have demonstrated, follows the course of our GENE, from grounding (method) and emergence (methodology) to navigation (critique) and effect (action). Integral Research therefore provides a coherent set of categories for you to work with and select from in undertaking your research, alongside the literature you search through and the fieldwork you undertake. As such, it is also an *integral* approach to research method and methodology. How then does social innovation compare and contrast with the integral approach to research?

Integral Innovation

While research is analytical, innovation is transformative. While research is exclusive and self-contained, innovation is inclusive of, and interconnected with, the burning issue you address, the culture with which you engage, and the social sciences which you deploy. The link between the burning issue that you are addressing and the innovation that you are destined to bring about serves to enfold one level of the trajectory into the other. In that unfolding and progressively transformative respect, research method becomes origination; methodology, becomes a new foundation or research paradigm; research critique heralds social emancipation; finally, and for each of the four paths, action becomes transformation. What then actually turns research into innovation, analysis into transformation?

On the one hand, as we have already intimated, we now focus on the developmental connection as opposed to analytical separation between each level. On the other hand, and even more significantly, the following connections are inclusively made:

- *Transformational Origination:* The origination of the innovation takes place within the underlying social context (nature and community within a particular society), identifying the burning issue, setting the transformational course for the research-to-innovation journey.
- *Transcultural Foundation:* The innovative foundation is formed out of the relevant philosophical foundation (for example, critical rationalism) and/or a particular core discipline (for example, management or sociology). You seek to include solid philosophical foundations related to the issue at hand, including such from your own culture that critically engages with the local context. It is here, where you fully engage with one of the four transculturally oriented paths – relational, renewal, reason or realization – to innovation, while also, progressively, reaching out to other cultures.
- *Transdisciplinary Emancipation:* The existing theoretical basis is to be further evolved through critical reflection and through transdisciplinary interaction with a variety of social sciences and humanities. It is at this highly dynamic third level that the combination of a socially and economically critical stance, with a strong urge to improve the lot of humankind, leads to an inner and outer mobilization of the

researcher, potentially linked with a socioeconomic movement, such as feminism, of his or her time.

- *Transpersonal Transformation:* At this culminating level you actively engage with a particular enterprise, community or society. Thereby the personal realm of the individual researcher is transcended. It is here where the full-fledged integral innovation is to be achieved.

Drawing on the same logic that John Heron[2] uses in his approach to action research, that is co-operative inquiry (see Chapter 10), we argue that origination, foundation, emancipation and transformation form the full transformational trajectory. It is for that reason that we take into account all four. We are responding thereby to a call of our time, which accuses social innovation, as we mentioned in Chapter 1, of failing to match technological innovation. We have particularly emphasized that this thwarted development has much to do with a domination of Western and Northern ways of knowledge generation, on the one hand, and the overtly analytical (as opposed to action-centred and transformative) approach to the social sciences, on the other. We therefore need to ultimately come to an integral perspective of the different ways, illustrating the specific contributions which each world or research-to-innovation path represents, each of which is needed in order to enable creative synthesis, resulting out of the constructive transcultural interaction within and between the various worlds.

As all truly innovative social scientists have done, we intend to make a contribution to the particular context we are currently living in – a world where social innovations are too rare to significantly improve the world in which we live. So let us start to uncover now the various layers of Integral Research, with which, when understood and acted upon, will enable you to pursue the full transformational trajectory.

METHOD TO ACTION – ORIGINATION TO TRANSFORMATION

We start out with research method (level 1) from an analytical research perspective, and of *origination*, from a transformative and innovative perspective, altogether constituting the grounding of your endeavours.

Level 1: Research Method (*Origination of Innovation*)	
Descriptive Methods	Describe phenomena (relational path) in intimate detail: *root yourself in a particular life world.*
Narrative Methods	Narrate unfolding storylines (path of renewal): *immerse yourself in a particular culture's origins.*
Methods of Theorising	Conjecture (path of reason) and form research hypotheses: *uncover the value base of a particular culture.*
Experimental and Survey Methods	Survey and experimentation (path of realization): *observe the way people behave around here.*

Level 2 is comprised of more sophisticated but still conventional wisdom, for the analytical research trajectory is serving to locate yourself in one or other of four respectively phenomenological or hermeneutic (interpretive), rational and empirical (positivist) methodologies. In parallel, the transformative innovation trajectory is serving to form the emerging paradigm or research *foundation* for your ultimate innovation.

Level 2: Research Methodology (*Innovation Foundation*)	
Phenomenology	A radical inquiry into the inner quality of a world: *immerse a world in yourself and yourself in a world, ecologically, anthropologically, and psychologically.*
Hermeneutics	Interpret the past in terms of the present: *review your individual and communal origins, historically, spiritually and culturally, fusing past and present, self and other.*
Critical Rationalism	Deduce relevant theories on your subject of concern: *apply sociological, political and systems theory in order to provide relevant explanations.*
Empiricism	Apply empirically based inductive analysis: *apply observations in the present and from the past to provide reliable and verifiable economic and behavioural analysis.*

Level 3 encompasses the more contemporary, unconventional wisdom, spanning so-called 'critical methodologies', which serve to provide an overtly transformative and sociopolitical outlook upon your research. In addition, from an innovation perspective, they serve as a basis for social and economic emancipation, building upon a major social movement of your time and place.

Level 3: Research Critique (*Emancipation towards Innovation*)	
Feminism	Feminism promoting knowledge as personal liberation: *build upon the wisdom inherent in nature, and on the growing respect for indigenous knowledge systems.*
Critical Theory	Critical theory as emancipatory dialectic: *build upon the systemic breakdown in historical capitalism to evolve new potential social orders.*
Postmodernism	Postmodernism as alternative discourses: *build a knowledge creating, post-industrial community, draw on diverse knowledge sources.*
Critical Realism	Critical realism as stratified knowledge: *uncover the generative forces that underlie the prevailing events and observations of our day and age.*

Level 4, for the first time, involves *action* research; it serves to ultimately bring about social *innovation* through a combined process of action and reflection:

Level 4: Action Research (*Transformation for Innovation*)	
Participatory Action Research	Communal problem solving to promote self-reliance: *alleviate communal and environmental decay; serve, locally, to heal the planet, globally.*
Co-operative Inquiry	A democratic process of inquiry, using diverse knowledge modes: *serve to democratise education and research, and to root processes of learning in communal grounds, while creating newly imagined futures.*
Socio-Technical Design	Co-generating democratic workplaces: *build non-hierarchical, networked communities and societies.*
Action Research	Continual cycling between action and reflection: *promote social change and challenging and overturning existing power bases.*

At this ultimately integral point, the individual and the communal need to be mutually aligned to promote social innovation. For Integral Research is immediately communal, in that you as an individual researcher need to align your activities with the group. Formally speaking, the process of 'research supervision' needs to be a simultaneously personal and collective process.

This is realized by an interactive and dialogical approach, which continually invites a comparing and contrasting between the research issue, research question, research hypothesis and research fieldwork, as well as critique of the individual's research, vis-à-vis the group, always and ultimately with a view to social innovation.

We now turn from this analytical structure of Integral Research to its more dynamic orientation, as Integral Innovation.

WALKING THE FOURFOLD PATHS TO INNOVATION

South to West: Four Innovation Narratives

To provide you with a better sense of how the journey along your paths towards a particular innovation may look and feel, we have translated each fourfold path into an innovation narrative. Such a narrative, following the transformative trajectory, is to be read alongside, and in continuous interaction with, the more analytical research trajectory.

The Southern Relational Path

- *Origination of your Innovation (Research Method):* Engaging your total self in passionate involvement with a phenomenon, you undertake careful, comprehensive descriptions, vivid and accurate renderings of your and others' experiences, rather than conducting measurements or ratings.

- *Innovation Foundation (Research Methodology):* Immersing yourself in a life world of immediately lived experiences, you concentrate on illuminating the nature of your 'inner self', and that of self and other, locating every unique case of your individual, communal and natural history as an episode in a larger societal story.
- *Emancipation leading to Innovation (Research Critique):* Aiming to create social change, you see knowledge that leads to such as a means of liberation not domination, of physical and human nature. You strive to represent diversity.
- *Transformation for Innovation (Action Research):* Fully and actively participating in and through the community, aiming at the exploited, the poor, the oppressed, the marginal, serving to create awareness of their own resources, mobilizing for self-reliant development, with you as committed participant.

The Eastern Path or Renewal

- *Origination of your Innovation (Research Method):* Tying together potentials and possibilities of individual, organizational or societal beginnings; no struggle, no story, no trouble, no tale, no ill, no thrill. The narrative is like a plot shaped by many of the larger stories in which it is set.
- *Innovation Foundation (Research Methodology):* Reconnecting with a historical, cultural and spiritual source. You understand how the world with which you are dealing, including yours, is constructed. You give relevant others a voice in it.
- *Emancipation for Innovation (Research Critique):* Your social construction arises out of the problems of everyday life. Through critical theory you uncover power relations. You analyse specifically the suffering of people and are explicitly focused on promoting liberation of self and others.
- *Transformation for Innovation (Action Research):* You finally engage in a politically oriented process. You do so in a participative form of inquiry, and you are also involved in a Four World knowledge-oriented process. You engage in an alternating current of informative and transformative inquiry, in action-reflection cycles. The validity you seek for your research-and-transformation is goodness, trustworthiness and authenticity.

The Northern Path of Reason

- *Origination of your Innovation (Research Method):* Observations you undertake make sense when organized by some 'conception', an organizing idea. You apply hypotheses (theories) to bring some order to data. In your search for the truth, you cannot establish it, only eliminate what is false.
- *Innovation Foundation (Research Methodology):* Deriving theories from tentative conjectures, you falsify rather than verify. You know that strong theory drives out the weak. The natural and, more especially, the social sciences you engage with – sociology or psychology, political science or economic – you perceive as value neutral.
- *Emancipation for Innovation (Research Critique):* You pursue multiple discourses, or worldviews, focusing on meanings as multiple and shifting. You construct your own

unfolding meaning, using language purposefully as a means of cultural representation, reviewing history as potentially transformative.

- *Transformation for Innovation (Action Research):* You adopt a problem-solving orientation. Your research is inevitably linked to action and geared towards social betterment. You use a co-generative approach to organization development, acting as a 'friendly outsider'.

The Western Path of Realization

- *Origination of your Innovation (Research Method):* Able to ask good questions, you are a good listener and not trapped by your own ideologies and preconceptions. You are adaptable so that newly encountered situations can be seen as opportunities. You are unbiased by preconceived notions, and you are responsive to contradictory evidence.
- *Innovation Foundation (Research Methodology):* In the search for the truth you seek after the 'positive facts', separating facts from values. You collect observational data and build theories from them. You control the results of any experimental research through 'closed systems', excluding unwanted variables.
- *Emancipation for Innovation (Research Critique):* Critical of the status quo, you become involved with a stratified or layered reality. You view such a layered perspective on reality as fallible, knowing that there is an interpretive as well as an empirical side to the research critique at hand, critical realism.
- *Transformation for Innovation (Action Research):* Starting out, transformatively, with appreciative enquiry, you also challenge power relations. You diverge and also converge, undertaking social research for social change. Knowing how is more important than knowing that, and finally action research, for you, incorporates action learning.
- By now you have a clear understanding of the double-layered research-to-innovation trajectory, and, before we conclude this chapter, it is time for a brief reflection on the journey towards integral innovation.

3.4 Responding to a Crisis: A Fourfold Reflection on the Research-to-Innovation Journey

RETRACING STEPS THROUGH THE RESEARCH JUNGLE

Now you have a bird's eye view of the four levels, almost as if you had cast your eyes upon all of them, in the course of a picturesque journey. As we have mentioned before the research-and-innovation process is a non-linear one, and you are likely to move back and forth between levels, while cycling and recycling across each of the elements within each level, as well as connecting such roots of your research with the underlying soils, the main stem of your research-and-innovation tree, the branches and ultimate fruits: healing the planet, promoting peaceful co-evolution, building up an open society and creating economic opportunity.

Before we move on we invite you to undertake a brief reflection on the four research levels just presented to you. Review, for a moment, the overall 'landscape of qualitative research', at least as seen by those doyens of qualitative research, Denzin and Lincoln.

We shall then retrace our own steps through the methodological jungle, which hopefully will serve to give you fresh insight into your own journey, so that you can trace a path of your own.

This book is being written for social or 'integral' innovators around the world. As researchers, educators and practitioners in the social sciences, conventionally on Masters and doctoral programmes, many of you want to find a way of transforming public, private or civic organizations in your society.[3] As such you are required to become philosophers as well as practitioners, individual social scientists as well as co-operative inquirers, and, most importantly, integral innovators as well as researchers. While this has opened up the 'qualitative' research field, it has simultaneously filled us with booming, buzzing confusion, as American psychologist William James used to say!

Faced with such a daunting prospect, researchers and practitioners alike, as we have seen from our own experience, all too often retreat into a self-protective shell. Therein a rigid pursuit of method-laden form (research method) overtakes the supposed emphasis on original, substantive form-and-content (social innovation). At the same time, because of the linear pursuit of an analytically based research project, devoid as such of origination, and lacking the iterative approach we are recommending here, what results is paralysis through analysis. How many research projects then, most particularly doctoral theses, have we seen, where, at the end of the day, the research has nothing original to say, and certainly has not made any active contribution to social innovation? The fault, as is so often the case with any science or religion, lies not with the research methodologies themselves, but with the way in which they have been interpreted and disseminated by the 'research powers' that be to you 'lesser mortals'. Moreover, those integral approaches to research, which serve to ultimately and actively promote such integral innovation, those related to action research, have typically stood out on a limb, rather than serving as means of innovation.

In addition, in our own case as aspiring citizens of the globe, we have been alarmed by the narrowness of the cultural context of conventional research activity. How then, as academics, researchers, management consultants and aspiring innovators, have we come to these conclusions, and what specific implications do they have for the 21st century? For having previously dedicated our thoughts and actions to culture and management, we are now embarking with you on a combined integral 'research to social innovation' path. What then, in a mainstream context, is the qualitative research tradition on which we stand? How does our own evolving work relate to the establishment view of qualitative research?

FOUR RESEARCH MOMENTS

Norman Denzin and Yvonne Lincoln,[4, 5] based at the Universities of Illinois and Texas in the United States, are probably the pre-eminent authorities on qualitative research in the world. For them there have been, historically speaking, seven critical moments in its recent development. However, the last three of these moments appear so recent, and thereby tenuous, that they hardly seem worth taking seriously. It is the first four such moments which are critical for our purposes:

1. *Positivist-quantitative Paradigm:* The traditional quantitative period (our first level) is associated with the foundational 'positivist' paradigm, which still exercises a strong

empirical influence to this day, and in which basic research methods, quantitative and qualitative, still predominate.

2. *Modernist Quantitative-qualitative Era:* The modernist quantitative-qualitative conventional era comes second (our level 2): the quantitative positivist orientation is now split between the former empirical and the latter rational approach, the one being inductive and the other deductive; at the same time the newly 'interpretevist' approach becomes clearly distinguishable in its own right. It is at this point that Husserl heralds the phenomenological 'Crisis in European Sciences', and joins hands with the prior hermeneutic influence to make a qualitative stand on research methodology.

3. *Interpretative Qualitative Perspectives:* In the 'blurred genres' contemporary era (our level 3), new, interpretative and qualitative perspectives are vigorously taken up. Examples of this include, for Denzin and Lincoln, not only hermeneutics and phenomenology, but also structuralism, semiotics, cultural studies, and for us feminism, critical theory, postmodernism (discursive) and critical realism (stratified), as duly reformative.

4. *Crisis of Representation:* In the fourth era (our level 4), the so-called 'crisis of representation' emerges. It becomes apparent that only a very small part of the world, geographically and philosophically, is represented in the overall methodological story.

Transcending this crisis of representation, our Integral Research and innovation evolves a co-creative approach that is ultimately transformative, thereby resolving the crisis through its cultural spread.

3.5 Conclusion: Which Path is for You?

In contrast to the traditional research approach, our integral one requires you to take account of the full range of methods and methodologies, critiques and actions, to some degree or another, though you will inevitably specialize. The choice for a particular research path is made based on the individual and societal background and context of the researcher. It is important that the research path is authentic to yourself and your cultural context. Each path ultimately reaches into the fourth action centred or transformative level, and the strong co-creative nature and scope of it (just listen to the rhythm of terms like, for example, participatory action research and co-operative inquiry) enables each of you who decided for one of the paths to ultimately encompass its full trajectory, analytically and transformatively. However, you approach the fourth and ultimately transformative level from your own particular perspective, represented by one of the paths: relational (Southern), renewal (Eastern), reason (Northern), realization (Western).

We mentioned that each of the paths is ultimately an archetypal construction which represents a particular way of doing research, a particular way of knowledge generation, a particular, integral approach to innovation. We demonstrated earlier that – archetypally – each of the Four Worlds (South, East, North and West) has evolved over time through a particular preference for one way. In our Integral Research and innovation framework we build on these preferences and particular strengths to enable each of you to contribute your strength to the whole.

In our doctoral programme, for example, different people naturally choose different paths. Due to our ever-growing communal orientation we ensure that through interaction with other research colleagues, participants continuously reflect their own path and reach out to others. That is practically how we reinforce the principle of creative synthesis in our groups.

While you choose one particular path, the spiralling Four World GENE 'pulls' you to engage with your 'inner Four Worlds' by guiding you continuously through your own south, east, north, and west. Following such rhythm – that of our four Rs – you avoid getting stuck in a particular world. We have demonstrated in Chapter 1 the danger of such stuckness.

As such, the you as an analytically based Integral Researcher gravitates towards transformative innovation, which is rooted in a local context but contributes to the global perspective. Let us sum up the core elements of our Integral Research-and-Innovation architecture, comprising of four research paths and a fourfold double-layered research-to-innovation trajectory.

In conclusion, through Integral Research you start with reflection: firstly, reflection on your own self/organization and society/culture in order to reconnect with the innermost strengths of both in relation to knowledge generation and integral innovation; secondly, reflection on yourself in relation to your society and your own research preferences and strengths; and, thirdly, reflection on the Integral Research landscape designed to provide orientation for your own research-and-innovation. For our research programmes we have developed an Integral Research inventory, helping each participant to identify his or her own path.

In the next chapter we enter the first prospectively integral level of research method (analytical) and innovation (transformative). It is a chapter on method, particularly crafted to enhance your reflection and to further help you to identify the research-and-innovation path, which is truly authentic to you. But in addition, the following chapter contains another wake-up call to alert you to the historic and conventional blindfolds that conventional research method has put upon us. 'Method' – the first level – will tell you more about yourself then you had thought before – and indeed, the entire integral process introduced in this book is ultimately a journey to progressively heightened energy and consciousness – and far more exciting than the traditional 'dry and boring reputation' of research in the social sciences has ever promised.

References

1. Lessem, R. and Schieffer, A. (2009). *Transformation Management: Towards the Integral Enterprise*. Farnham: Gower.
2. Heron, J. (1994). *Co-operative Inquiry*. London: Sage.
3. Lessem and Schieffer, *Transformation Management*.
4. Denzin, N. and Lincoln, Y. (eds) (1994). *Handbook of Qualitative Research*. London: Sage.
5. Denzin, N. and Lincoln, Y. (eds) (2003). *Landscape of Qualitative Research*, 2nd edition. London: Sage.

3 *Paths Towards Social Innovation*

4 *Originating Integral Research*

Method Matters!

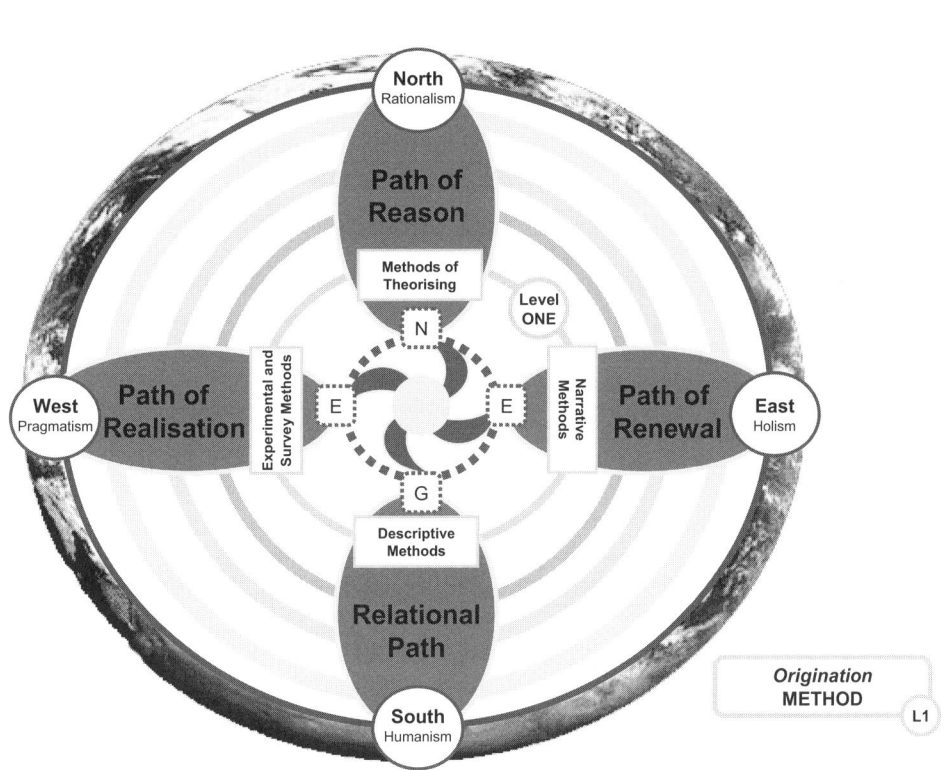

Figure 4.1   Overview Chapter 4 – Method

Summary: Originating Integral Research

- *Originating Integral Research*: We start with integral method (analytical) and origination (transformative). We introduce, as such, the research methods that go with it, and that form the basic building blocks of our Integral Research. We illustrate why 'method matters', serving as the grounding for a successful research-to-innovation journey.
- *Origins*: Research method, as a force of origination, provides direct experiential access to the origins and originality of a particular cultural/personal context, also with a view to addressing a burning issue. It is in this cultural originality or creativity that we see the seed for the particular emerging social innovation.
- *Methods*: Overall human integrity is comprised of four modes: being, becoming, knowing, doing. Directly linked to them are four integral methods, that constitute the source of origination for our four research paths: descriptive methods for the Southern relational path, narrative methods for the Eastern path of renewal, methods of theorizing for the Northern path of reason and experimental and survey methods for the Western path of realization.
- *Descriptive Methods*: Description requires you to engage with yourself and another being similar to the way in which an artist, or an empathetic counsellor might do. Being 'scientific' in that descriptive sense involves opening yourself up to a phenomenon, without pride or prejudice, premise or preconception.
- *Narrative Methods*: Whereas description is overwhelmingly concerned with locational space and place, in narrative methods you are more concerned with historical time, that is with becoming. Here you become a 'narrator' of the 'stories we are', drawing upon the specific technique of 'storytelling'.
- *Methods of Theorizing*: From narrative methods we enter the mode of knowing. This – in research terms – is the world of theory building. Here we draw on Karl Popper's deductive method of hypothesis building (the method of the formulation of hypotheses), and on Glazer, Strauss and Corbin's grounded theory, whereby theory is generated inductively from data.
- *Experimental and Survey Methods*: We finally introduce the fourth and by far the most prolific of the research building blocks: experimental and survey methods. The specific technique we are focusing on is the case study. Case studies have a particular richness, serving as a bridge between the more passive 'survey' and more active 'experimentation', and thereby naturally close the 'method cycle' of describing, narrating and theorizing, and ultimately acting, experimenting, doing.

4.1 Introduction: Origins of Your Research-and-Innovation

METHOD: THE BUILDING BLOCKS OF RESEARCH MATTER

We start then with integral method, recast as orientation (analytical) or origination (transformative). Why then do we recast research method as a source of origination, as opposed to a technique for data processing, as it is more conventionally conceived? Let us take you four years back to make the case.

In the autumn of 2005 we established our transformation programme on the African continent, in conjunction with CIDA (Community and Individual Development Association), South Africa's newest and seemingly most innovative university. Several of the participants from CIDA on our Masters programme were tutors at the university, many of them recent graduates. What astounded us was that in their research proposal for their first transformation project on our part-time Masters, every student followed the same basic Western approach to research method, as a crudely conceived, or indeed copied, 'technique' for data collection, questionnaires and the like, each of which pointed towards specific kinds of empirical data. After that awful experience one of the authors (Ronnie Lessem) began to see the light.

First, the very fact that these otherwise highly creative students who were doing amazing things in their local communities, some even as potential social innovators, started with such an arid approach to individual research, to which they were obviously paying mere lip service, meant that we had to try all the more to help them evolve their own approach by building on their home African grounds. It then dawned upon us, that, potentially if not actually, *such individual research origination lay not in the erudite methodologies, but in the formative methods, which could be deeply connected with the grounds of human being and becoming, knowing and doing.*

The trouble was, that the students focused on using exclusively survey (and partly experimental) methods, while totally ignoring theory formation, descriptive and narrative approaches. Further, they were totally oblivious, in this research context, to the grounds of their own Southern (relational) being. In other words, they were all focused on Western doing, largely to the exclusion of Northern knowing, Eastern becoming and their ultimately Southern being. In that respect they were out of touch with their local grounds. Their very *being* was out of touch with the very soil in which they intended to plant their integral innovation tree.

METHOD: ACTIVATING THE VITAL FORCE OF THE GENE

In terms of our GENE (see previous chapter), our South African students were aiming to be effective, while lacking appropriate grounding, emergence and, to a large extent, navigation. This way, the Southern GENE-ius of these would-be-social-innovators was circumvented by a Western bypass. First, for us then, the grounds for social innovation needed to be prepared, and that's where our recast method (our level 1) comes in play. Research method, as we are going to show, does not only provide the analytic grounding of each of the four research-to-innovation paths, it also plays an initially transformative role, in that it is through method that you originally tap into the grounds or origins of your particular nature and culture.

By doing so, you not only get – through direct and personal experience – in touch with the origins of the burning personal or social issues you feel inclined to address, you can also reach into the origins and originality of the particular cultural context, within which lies the very seed for a successful social innovation to flourish. For us, this was a major discovery. Method, if seen in this original light, has the potential to bring the transformative force of the GENE into motion. That is the reason why we combine analytical research method with transformative origination. Let us probe into this now more deeply.

Analytical Method and Transformative Origination

As an Integral Researcher – from an original perspective – you start your research by reconnecting with the creative source of your self, organization and society, that is your individual, institutional, communal, professional nature and culture. Here, as close as possible to yourself (to home), you find the original seed (or the origin) for your research. You review your own personal and collective centre, before entering a particular research path that is altogether authentic for you, your institution and your society. That is why we call the first level of Integral Research 'origination', closely aligned with method. It is through method – describing or narrating, theorizing or experimenting – that you experience, most directly, which research path is most authentic to you and to your culture.

Method is then linked to soil and origins of a person/culture/society, embodied in your nature, art, religion, music, dance and so on. Origination (as level 1), however, not only alludes to the starting point of the social innovation journey; the success of such a journey is also dependent on your capacity to connect with and activate the origins and originality of your particular individual and social as well as cultural context.

Integral Method, Origination and Culture

In Chapter 2 we introduced cultural images from the Four Words and illustrated how those distinct images helped us to distinguish culturally different paths to knowledge generation and innovation. Research methods, for us, are indicators of the kind of personal and cultural mode, out of which the origination of a social innovation is to come. We recognized that the:

- Southern circular mode would be best embodied in rich *description*;
- Eastern spiraling mode would be best represented by a *narrative*;
- Northern linear mode would be best embodied in cause-effect *theorizing*;
- Western point mode would be best represented in *experimentation*.

More specifically, these methods are reflected in, and for us recast as, particular research techniques (see Figure 4.2), such as, for example, empirical phenomenology (descriptive), storytelling (narrative), grounded theory (theorizing) and case methods (survey and experimentation). Another strong reason, why we place research method at the beginning of the research to innovation journey, is that this basic level allows you to get in initial touch with self-and-society more concretely than the immersion in theory-based research methodology could ever do. Indeed, each passionate quest or re-search, for us, must be intimately connected with your personal life story and the mode of being or becoming, knowing or doing, which comes most naturally to you.

Integral Method and Human Integrity

We realized that, whether we were dealing with undergraduates or management practitioners, Masters or doctoral students, we had to start with your all-round human integrity. The equivalent to what we term a Western (predominantly American) 'survey' or 'experimental' method, which our students at CIDA had reacted to mechanically, is the 'descriptive' or ultimately more Southern relational research path. Such a relational path, then, of which description-origination is an integral part, emerges out of the humanistic mode of *being*. Ironically, our African students were psychologically much closer to such a descriptive life world, and yet academically totally disconnected from such.

Figure 4.2   Human and Research Foundations – Following the Same Rhythm

We now delve into such a descriptive method of origination and so-called 'empirical phenomenology' as a derivative technique in a little more depth, before working through the other three methods, or sources of origin, as well.

4.2 Origins of the Southern Relational Path: Descriptive Methods and Empirical Phenomenology

DESCRIPTIVE METHOD: 'BEING' INTEGRAL

We now turn to each of the four methods of origination in turn, in each case also relating them to the learning and knowledge creating approaches that generally apply to each one, before subsequently focusing on a specific method.

Starting out with such richly a descriptive, generally Southern mode of *being*, we find that identity, to begin with, is originally rooted in the 'life world' of or indeed circle or 'life cycle' of local people, as much for the Bedouin or the Bantu as for the Belgians or the Burmese.

Such an indigenous world is lodged in nature and religion (from *'re-ligere'* meaning linking back). We refer to this circle of origination as Southern, though it is to be found all over the world, because of its deep roots in mankind's place of origin, where nature and religion continue to exercise a major influence.

THE SPELL OF THE SENSUOUS – DAVID ABRAM

Example of Rich Description

The living world – this ambiguous realm that we experience in anger and joy, in grief and in love – is both the soil in which all our sciences are rooted and the rich humus into which their results ultimately return, whether as nutrients or poisons. Phenomenology, by thus returning to the taken-for-granted realm of subjective experience, not to explain it but simply to pay attention to its rhythms and textures, not to capture or control it but simply to become familiar with its diverse modes of appearance – and ultimately to give voice to its shifting and enigmatic patterns – would articulate the grounds of the other sciences.

The human mind, then, is not some otherworldly essence that comes to house itself inside our physiology. Rather, it is instilled and provoked by the sensorial field itself, induced by the tensions and participations between the human body and the animate earth. By acknowledging such links between the inner, psychological world and the perceptual terrain that surrounds us, we begin to turn inside-out, loosening the psyche from its confinement within a strictly human sphere. Intelligence is no longer ours alone but is a property of the earth; we are in it, immersed in its depths. And indeed each terrain, each ecology, seems to have its own particular intelligence, its unique vernacular of soil and leaf and sky. Each place has its own mind, its own psyche, a place-specific intelligence shared by all the humans that dwell within, in fact by all beings in that zone. Each place is its own psyche. Language, for oral peoples, is not a human invention but the gift of the land itself. By denying that birds and animals have their own form of language, we cut ourselves off from such deep meanings, severing language from that which supports it. We then wonder why we are unable to communicate even amongst ourselves.

In contrast to the apparently unlimited, global character of the technologically mediated world, the sensuous world – the world of our direct, unmediated interactions – is always local. The sensuous world is the particular ground on which we walk, the air we breathe. Human persons, too, are shaped by the places they inhabit, both individually and collectively. Our bodily rhythms, our cycles of creativity and stillness, and even our thoughts are influenced by shifting patterns of the land. It is surely not a matter of 'going back' but of coming full circle, uniting our capacity for cool reason with those more sensorial and mimetic ways of knowing, letting the vision of a common world root itself in our direct participatory engagement with the local. Sooner or later, technological civilization must accept the invitation of gravity and settle back into the land, its political and economic structures diversifying into the varied contours and rhythms of a more-than-human-earth. Our task is that of taking up the written word, with all its potency, and writing language back into the land. Our craft is that of releasing the budded, earthly intelligence of our words, freeing them to respond to the green uttering-forth of leaves from the spring branches. It is the practice of spinning stories that have the rhythm and lilt of the local sound-scape, slipping off the lettered page to inhabit coastal forests or desert canyons, letting language, once again, take root in the earthen silence of leaf and shadow and bone.[1]

In knowledge-creating terms, this is the realm of socialization. It is identified with community building, with nature, with the animate and with the environment. Therein lie the very grounds of our being. This is the home or *oikos* of our vital, individual, organizational and societal being. In terms of Integral Research method and origination, this is an intimately descriptive arena. We turn from being to learning.

LEARN FROM EXPERIENCES

Experiential reality moreover, as an integral expression of human being, is the indigenous lived experience or the mutual and reciprocal co-determination of person and world. Positioned in a learning or development cycle this provides firstly, a strong emotional base – in the individual case, confidence, fulfilment and positive arousal; in the societal case a well-developed, positively functional, open and formative indigenous 'local identity'. This yields the hypothesis that emotional confidence, fulfilment and positive arousal are the most important for effective individual learning; while a strong local identity, a richly imaginative national culture, an intellectual and institutional capacity to deal with complexity, and an altogether open society constitute its formative, societal potential.

Individual people and whole societies learn and develop more effectively when they are enjoying themselves and what they are doing; when they are satisfying some felt need or interest, and are emotionally involved in what has personal and societal relevance to them; when they feel good about the whole idea of learning and development as well as the exercise of their learning competence; when they feel confident, secure and in a low-threat, co-operative, non-competitive position. We now turn from learning to descriptive method of origination, and from such a research method (and orientation to learning and knowledge creation) to the descriptive technique: empirical phenomenology.

RELATIONAL ORIGINATION: DESCRIPTION

The aim of so-called 'empirical phenomenology'[2] is to *produce an exhaustive description of the phenomena of everyday experience.* Typically in phenomenological investigation, the long interview is the method of fieldwork. Within our Integral Research framework, such a descriptive immersion of subject in object also provides the source of origination, as we shall see in Chapters 5 to 7, for the Southern research path, phenomenological methodology and a subsequently feminist critique, using a relational perspective with a view to human emancipation. This is followed by participatory action research, as the relational orientation to transformation.

ORIGINATION GROWS OUT OF IMMERSION

The challenge you face in preparing to ground such descriptive origination is to focus on an integral issue that has both social meaning and personal significance. The desire for origination grows out of an intense interest in a particular area. But what exactly means 'immersion' for you as an Integral Researcher and innovator?

Descriptive Methods and Origination
Towards an Original Description through Empirical Phenomenology

- You seek to reveal more fully the essences and origins of human experience.
- You uncover qualitative and quantitative factors in these essences and origins.
- You engage your total self as participant, in a state of passionate involvement.
- You do not seek to predict or to determine causal relationships.
- You rather illuminate them through careful, comprehensive descriptions, vivid and accurate renderings of experience, rather than measurements or ratings.

The people who have done most to uncover this so called empirical-phenomenological approach as a specific descriptive method are the Duquesne School of empirical phenomenology in the United States.

We now conclude our humanistic orientation to this originative and integral, descriptive method, as the source of origin of the Southern relational path, and to the process for evoking it through empirical phenomenology. If you choose to engage fully in the Southern relational path, a deep understanding of phenomenology would be the next foundational step, involving a thorough immersion in a particular 'life world'. Our symbol for the relational path is the circle. Before we move from descriptive to narrative method and origination, we shall lay out the overall, double-layered relational path, from the method and origination covered in this chapter, to methodology and foundation, critique and emancipation, action and transformation, covered in subsequent chapters.

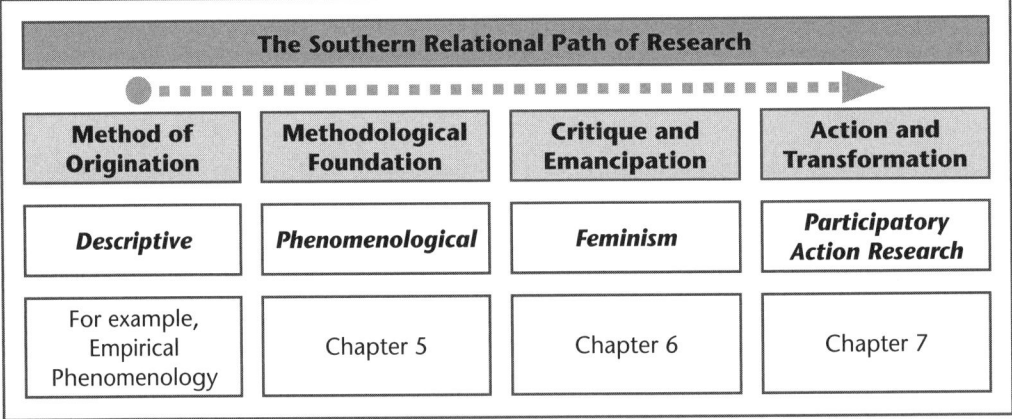

4.3 Origins of the Eastern Path of Renewal: Narrative Methods and Storytelling

NARRATIVE METHODS AND 'BECOMING' INTEGRAL

We now turn from the origins of the relational path to the origins of renewal, that is from descriptive to narrative method, from being to becoming integral. In the process of such narrative becoming you enter, individually and/or collectively, into that no-man's land between the familiar (self) and the unfamiliar other. This is initiated through the unfolding of narrative, through the pursuit of meaning, referred to as the 'fusion of horizons'. In that emergent world, of loss of identity, of letting go of the old with a view to becoming the new, the power of imagination becomes all-important. Such an aesthetic sensitivity is necessary to make the strange 'other' familiar and the familiar 'self' strange.

BANKER FOR THE POOR – MUHAMMAD YUNUS

Example of Narrative

The Grameen Bank based in Bangladesh has come a long way in twenty-five years, when it was founded by a Bangladeshi professor of economics, Muhammad Yunus, now world famous as the latest laureate of the Peace Nobel Price. From $27 lent to fifty-two people in 1976 to $2.3 billion lent to 2.3 million families in 1998, Grameen programmes now stretch around the world, from Ecuador to Eritrea, from the Norwegian Arctic Circle to Papua New Guinea, from Chicago's inner city ghettos to remote mountain communities in Nepal – by the new millennium fifty-eight countries had become Grameen clones. Unlike other banking establishments, the object of the financial exercise is not, primarily, to earn a good commercial return but, rather as an instrument of cultural production, to enhance people's liberty, their equality and their fraternity. For Muhammad Yunus, the objective is to enable people to make the most of their lives, so that they become authors of their own destiny.

For Yunus then: 'when the borrower finally receives her loan, she is literally trembling, shaking. The money is burning in her fingers. Tears roll down her eyes because she has never received so much money in her life. She carries it as she would a delicate bird, until someone tells her to put it away in a safe place. She cannot believe such a treasure has been put in her hands. All of her life she has been told that she was no good, that, being a woman, she only brought misery to her family, because they now had to pay for a dowry, which they could not afford. But today, for the first time, an institution had trusted her with all this money. She is stunned. She promises herself she will never let down this institution, which has trusted her so much. She will struggle to make sure every penny is paid back. And she does it'. Grameen then is a self-help organization. It wants to liberate the genius of individuals to create a better life for themselves. For Yunus, there was never a doubt about their commitment to break away from poverty, which leads us to tell one more of the many Grameen stories, that of Jorimon (in Yunus' words):

'Jorimon was born around 1952, suffered a terrible skin rash that almost killed her at the age of 6 and which still scars her today; as a child she also suffered terribly from ringworm. At the age of 10, she was married off to a poorhouse worker 12 years her elder. She had two sons and a daughter. During the famine of 1974 she and her children spent the year in near starvation. Her husband used to beat her up on the slightest pretext and he was always threatening to divorce her. In spite of working non-stop she and her husband knew nothing but suffering, hunger and sorrow. On December 29th, 1979, she and four other women joined the Grameen bank project and in January, her group received its first loan for 600 taka. With the paddy-husking business that she started Jorimon was able to repay her first loan by January, 1981. During this first year she and her family never went hungry thanks to the earnings generated by the Grameen loan. She also had enough money to buy clothes for her family, and had some profit left over. At first her husband was very worried about her joining the group, but once it worked out without problems, he accepted. She went on to buy a cow and to build a house with her profits. In her words 'previously we went hungry for days on end; I worked like a slave in other people's houses; I walked from village to village with a heavy load of firewood on my head, trying to get some money in return. We had no home of our own. People used to ignore us all the time. No one ever looked. But today God has shown us the path to happiness through a bank loan'. [3]

ENGAGE YOUR IMAGINATION

Underlying narrative imagination, and thereafter such narratively based research and origination, is a preconceptual form of learning. Specifically, the material to be learnt is presented so that its preconceptual form can be directly grasped by the imaginal mind prior to explicit verbal and intellectual understanding. Such material can also be presented in visual forms incorporating colours and graphic designs that relate to the meaning of the images portrayed, as well as in a 'colourful' form of rich, and textured, metaphorically laden narrative. It can also be shown in mobile and dramatic form. Narrative, moreover, can be elaborated through the imaginative use of metaphor and analogy. Where possible and relevant, the material in all these presentations tells a story, also giving a coherent, global overview of the subject matter, so that the basic 'patterning' of its central concepts and principles stands out.

UNFOLD YOUR BURNING ISSUE

As you turn from describing the phenomenon with which you are originally engaged, to imagining your unfolding burning issue, so you move from being to becoming, from empirical phenomenology to 'the stories we are'. It is in that evolving context, that the character of your integral research and innovation assumes developmental, emergent proportions. Such a narrative then spans the transformative emergence of yourself, your organization or profession and your society. In other words, starting out with your research question, the research narrative and origination and ultimate creation continually unfold.

Your storyline underpins both your action and reflection on such.[4] As your storyline is transplanted from individual to organization and to society, so the interpretive and the hermeneutic as well as critical theory, and ultimately co-operative inquiry, as we shall see later, come into play. In the case of critical theory, the dialectical interplay between plot and counter-plot, the conflict and tension between one force and another, exercise their dynamic influence. For us, the best guide to such a research method is that of William Randall, who has developed a particular method of uncovering *The Stories We Are*.[5]

STORYING AND RE-STORYING

For Canadian professor of English literature and developmental psychologist, William Randall, the object of narrative method is not to survey (through pre-structured interviews or formalised questionnaires) or experiment, to hypothesize or to theorize. Rather, the aim is to uncover 'the stories we are', individually, as well as, for us, organizationally and societally.

The title *The Stories We Are* implies, moreover, that your personal, institutional and societal stories are incomplete: that your individual and collective lives are still unfolding, mysteries yet unresolved, open books for whose endings you can but wait and see. This implies that each one of you, personally and collectively, is legendary. This could involve, for example in South Africa, the unfolding narrative of an individual researcher, Tommy Mkanzi, that of the South African Truth and Reconciliation Commission (TRC) or of South Africa altogether. *Reality itself – at least human reality – is inherently storied, that all events constitute one grand, unfolding story*. This is the story between the world and its

Creator, understood as a 'cosmic artist'. Each event in your individual and institutional lives is therefore emergent and novel, charged actually or potentially with significance.

Your author-ity, with respect to your unfolding story, lies somewhere in between you and it. *You co-author your story in partnership with some authoritative agent, whether nature, society, fate, God, ultimate reality, or whatever your philosophical propensities lead you to call it.* You are in a position to reconstruct – not so much the events or idea within your research and development story – but the plots whereby you make them into your own. A new plot means a new story, and a new story leads to a new construction.

Thus, over the course of originating your path of renewal you critique the old plots by which your story has previously been lived and told, and experiment with new ones, and you thereby assume authority over your work and your life, together with a cast of co-creators. Naturally people and communities vary in that respect. Some are passive in the matter of self-creation; others active. Some are less inclined to compose their own life-plot than to adopt one of the packaged ones proffered them by their family or clan, profession or culture, religion or cult, industry or society. Others reject such patterns passionately, preferring to do it their way, in stages.

> *Stage 1 = Narrating:* According to Randall, the first stage within your research is that of a research protagonist; in this stage you are narrating the 'origin story' of your individual, professional or societal life with a new intensity and honesty to your research colleagues. At this stage the guiding question is simply what is your individual and collective story, at a particular point of time, and how do both serve to address your research question, or the grounds of your prospective innovation? The research supervisor's role, together with that of the research community as a whole, is primarily that of a listener, affirming your emerging novelty.

> *Stage 2 = Re-Storying:* The second stage in re-storying is that of reading the story, that is studying, evaluating and critiquing it as it unfolds. Here the key question is what kind of story is the story – its themes, conflicts, characters, author-ity, plot line, genre? It can also mean inquiring into the themes and characters of the larger stories that envelop your individual and organizational life – impersonal, institutional, ideological – whereby the personal and institutional can lead to the political and societal. The research supervisor's and research community's role is to expand and deepen your story, thus releasing the energy bound within it.

> *Stage 3 = 'Re-genre-ate'/Re-author:* Through both the narrating and the reading, another key question comes – how can we 're-genre-ate', re-author the story? How can you find a research story big enough to accommodate the whole of an individual/organizational/societal life as a coherent whole, with a view to ultimately actualising social innovation?

In summary then, and in narrative terms:

Narrative Methods and Origination
Towards an Original Narrative through Storytelling

- Your individual and communal stories are still unfolding.
- Each one of you, personally and collectively, is legendary.
- Each event in your individual and communal lives is therefore novel.
- The narrative mode leads to gripping drama and to creative origination.
- You are tying together potentials and possibilities of your respective beginnings.
- No struggle, no story; no trouble, no tale; no ill, no thrill!
- Your narrative is a plot shaped by many of the larger strategy-stories in which it is set.

We now conclude narrative method and origination through 'the stories we are'. You have become aware of their link to the methodology of hermeneutics. If you choose to engage fully in the Eastern relational path, a deep understanding of hermeneutics and interpretivism would be the next step. Typical for the path of renewal is a thorough understanding of the 'stories we are', and the capacity to engage in an ongoing dialogical process of revealing or 'unfolding' meaning. Hence, our symbol for the path of renewal is the spiral. A continuous (spiralling) reflective process will lead you from hermeneutics to critical theory, and ultimately to co-operative inquiry. It is here that your Integral Research and integral innovation will become effective. Before we move from narrative method to the theoretical method of hypothesis building, we shall lay out once more the path of renewal before you:

The Eastern Research Path of Renewal			
Method and Origination	**Methodological Foundation**	**Critique and Emancipation**	**Action and Transformation**
Narrative Methods	*Hermeneutics/ Interpretivism*	*Critical Theory*	*Co-operative Inquiry*
For example, Storytelling	Chapter 8	Chapter 9	Chapter 10

We now turn from being and becoming to knowing, from description and narrative to theorizing, both as an analytical method and as transformative origination, initiating the path of reason.

4.4 Origins of the Northern Path of Reason: Methods of Theorizing and Grounded Theory

METHODS OF THEORIZING AND INTEGRAL 'KNOWING'

The purposeful navigation of the 'renewed' self, organization or society that we are seeking to establish represents the knowing consolidation of the prior process of becoming. As such, transformatively, the fully fledged new concept, as a product or entity, is established out of the prior fusion of horizons. In fact the success of the 'North–West' in business, in Europe and America, is born out of just such a 'global' fusion. This has recently been the case 'East–West' for Japan, and perhaps also now is becoming so, though to a lesser 'global' as opposed to 'globalizing' effect for China. Moreover, the emerging 'network society', born out of the critical rationalism embedded into an open society (see Chapter 11), is reflected here.

In all these cases, there is a genuine combination between *being* and *becoming*, of different cultures and societies, though it is only in the Japanese case, in business interestingly enough, that this has been made explicit. In fact the Japanese knowledge-creating company explicitly builds in such an 'East–West' linkage. Conversely, in many a developing society, one local identity dominates or distorts the other, rather than serving to establish a transnational entity.

We now turn from becoming and imaginal to knowing and conceptual learning. Thereafter, we shall focus on the specific research technique 'grounded theory'.

ENGAGE IN CONCEPTUAL LEARNING

In knowledge-creating terms, this is the realm of combination or of explicit knowledge. Herein lies the process of theorizing underlying knowing. In terms of integral research method and origination this is the realm of theorizing and of hypothesis formation, and of the linear determination of cause–effect. Ultimately, and in human terms, this is the secondary realm of knowing, after primary human being and becoming.

In other words, this is the conceptual realm of statements, made in words or numbers, theories or mental models, which yield the explicit intellectual, conceptual content of the material to be learnt. Hitherto this has been regarded as the central and only medium of learning if not also research, and the policy base for development. In our integral scheme of things it is only third in importance and order, and tends to become alienated and desiccated if made the sole medium.

We now turn, more particularly, from learning and knowledge creation to research and innovation.

THEORIZE AND BUILD HYPOTHESES

When the Anglo-Austrian philosopher Karl Popper,[6] and originator of so-called 'critical rationalism' speaks of theory building, as a rationalist you value the intellectual independence of others too highly to want to convince them in important matters. You seek not to convince but to arouse. Free opinion formation is precious to you: not only because this brings you closer to the truth but also because you respect free opinion formation as such. We now turn specifically to what Popper called 'hypothetico-deductivism'– the formulation of hypotheses.

ENDOGENOUS KNOWLEDGE – PAULIN HOUNTONDJI

Example of Theorizing

A standard feature of economic activity in colonial territories was the practical absence of industry. An equally standard feature of scientific activity was a howling absence of theoretical work. Just as there were no colonial factories, there were no colonial laboratories or think tanks. Now generally speaking advances in all branches of knowledge, whether they belong to the natural sciences, the social sciences or the humanities, necessarily begin in laboratories, broadly defined as venues for the systematic processing of intellectual and scientific knowledge. In fact, the two forms of extraction – material and intellectual – are not discrete realities but two sides of the same coin. The name of that coin is accumulation on a grand scale.

It was altogether natural, given such a perspective, for the physical, geographical annexation of the Third World and its integration into the world capitalist system through the slave trade and colonialism to go hand-in-hand with the intellectual annexation and integration. The vocation of neo-colonial industry, meanwhile, is to turn out luxury consumer items for privileged minorities. It does not care about producing consumer goods for the masses. It is therefore incapable of serving the social advancement of the majority of the population. Yet that service is the core of real development. Hountondji then refers to Third World countries as typically *extroverted*:

- Scientific work depends largely on the use of apparatus imported from the centre.
- Intellectual work is to a large extent dependent on journals, libraries, archives, publishing houses and other support facilities in the North.
- Scholars and intellectuals are better known and read in the North than in the South
- Research in the peripheral countries is trapped in particularistic details, unable and unambitious to break through to the levels of the universal.
- The much discussed brain drain that takes Southern intellectuals Northwards is a specific expression of the extroversion of intellectual life.
- European or American scientists go to Zaire or the Sahara not in search of paradigms or methodological and theoretical models; rather, they go hunting for information and new facts that are likely to enrich their paradigms.

To break that logic at source, to recover individual and collective initiative, to become ourselves again, as societies in transition, is one of the major tasks prescribed by history. That task, within the specific field of knowledge, amounts to taking an informed enough view of current practices in order to work out other possible modalities of producing knowledge, other possible forms of technological and scientific production relationships, first between the South and North, but also in the South itself, and inside each and every country.[7]

For Popper, theories can only be tentative conjectures about the world, which are ultimately unverifiable by empirical evidence. Their discovery involves imaginative leaps, which are the forerunners of scientific activity. The process whereby predictive and thereby testable hypotheses are deduced from theoretical conjectures and subjected to confrontation with an intellectually accessible world is the distinctive attribute of a critically rational science, subject to falsification rather than verification. According to him, science advances through the detection and elimination of error as falsified theories fall away leaving a core of theory not yet disproved. So such science can only ever be piecemeal and incomplete. Social engineering as a result should involve 'piecemeal tinkering', which, combined with critical analysis is the way to achieve practical results in the social as well as natural sciences.

In essence, Popper's falsification leads to a situation where the strong theories drive out the weak. Empirical data are not the final arbiter of the truth of theory. Finding theories which are better approximations to the truth is what the scientist aims at. This involves the growth of the content of our theories for the development of our knowledge of the world. You learn, in Popper's view, *only through trial and error. Your trials, however, are always your hypotheses.* They stem from you and the concepts that you have inherited, not from your external empirical world. All you learn from the external world is that some of your efforts are mistaken. You are active; you are constantly testing things out, constantly working with the method of trial and error. In this research world you are guided by the following attitude:

- We know nothing – that is the first point.
- Therefore we should be very modest – that is the second.
- We should not claim to know when we do not know – that is the third.

According to Popper, the following assumptions guide theorizing:

| **Methods of Theorizing and Origination** |
| *Towards an Original Theory* |
| • Nature and social life consist of essential uniformities – patterns of events.
 • It is the aim of science to discover these uniformities to find universal statements, which are true because they correspond to the forces of nature.
 • Sensory experience is rejected as a secure foundation for scientific theories.
 • Observations do not make much sense until they have been organized by some 'conception', an organizing idea; hypotheses formulated bring order to data.
 • As a process of conjecture and refutation, we can never hope to actually establish a truth; we can only eliminate those theories which are false. |

We now turn from theorizing and the process of hypothesis formation associated with it to the more specific technique of 'grounded theory'.

ENGAGE IN SYSTEMATIC THEORY DEVELOPMENT: GROUNDED THEORY

Grounded Theory as a Comparative Method

We now turn to grounded theory as perhaps the best-known approach to systematically developing theory from the bottom up as it were. Its American founders, Glazer and Strauss, were both social scientists, the one (Glazer) a social psychologist and statistician, and the other (Strauss) a social anthropologist and sociologist. Grounded theory is a comparative method, as is our own Four World approach. For the constant comparison of many groups draws attention to their many similarities and differences. Considering such leads to the generation of abstract categories and their properties, which, since they emerge from the data, will be an important part of an explanatory theory.

Lower-level categories emerge rather quickly during the early phases of data collection. Higher-level, overriding and integrating conceptualizations – and the properties that elaborate them – tend to come later during coding and analysis. Although categories can be borrowed from existing theory, generating theory does put a premium on emergent conceptualizations. As they are emerging, their fullest possible generality and meaning are continually being developed and checked for relevance. Conversely, *forcing data to apply to pre-existing theories is sure to arouse the disbelief* of colleagues and laymen from the start. Similarities and convergences with the literature can be established after the analytical core of categories has emerged.

Integration of the theory is best when it emerges, like the concepts. In other words, Glazer and Strauss have a similar notion of experiential Grounding, imaginative Emergence and conceptual Navigation to ours, except for the fact that their experiential ground is empirically rather than phenomenologically formed. It is thereby *rooted in externally observable data, rather than in the internal life world of an individual or community*. The theory, for them as for us, should never just be put together, abstracted from the underlying grounds, nor should a formal theory be applied unless we are sure it will fit the data (them), and the context (us). The possible use of a formal model of integration can be determined only after a substantive model has sufficiently emerged. The *truly emergent integrating framework, which encompasses the fullest possible diversity of categories and properties, becomes an open-ended scheme*. In working towards such it is critical that collection, coding and analysis of data are done together.[8]

Strauss and Corbin then turn in great detail to what they term 'coding'. The particular focus of grounded theory, and its real strength (albeit that such coding imposes enormous demands on you as a researcher), is its 'coding procedures'. There are three types of coding procedures: open, axial and selective. Coding represents the operations by which data are broken down, conceptualized, and put back together in new ways. It is the central process from which theories are built from data.[9]

Start Theorizing with Open Coding

Open coding pertains to the naming and categorizing of phenomena. During open coding the data are broken down into discrete parts, closely examined, compared for similarities and dissimilarities. Through this process your own assumptions about phenomena are questioned or explored, leading to new discoveries. In our own case, for example, early in our qualitative research, we established the codes Southern and Northern, Eastern and

Western, to describe different societal and managerial orientations. More recently we have identified the GENE, in terms of grounding, emergence, navigation and effect.

Grounded Theory: 1st Coding Procedure

Open Coding: Establishing Categories and Subcategories

- Break data down into discrete parts, compare for similarities and dissimilarities, given each a name and a category.
- Concepts are then identified and developed in terms of their properties and dimensions.
- Two analytical procedures prevail: making comparisons and asking questions.

We now turn from such open coding to so-called 'axial' coding.

From Open Coding to Axial Coding

Open coding fractures the data and allows you to identify some categories, their properties and dimensional locations. So, for example, 'Westerners' were identified by us as practical, empirical, individualistic and pragmatic. *Axial coding puts those data back together in new ways by making connections between a category and its subcategories.* Individualism, to take our example further, incorporates masculinity, atomization, competitiveness and assertiveness.

In axial coding, your focus is on specifying a category – phenomenon – in terms of the conditions that gave rise to it, the context in which it is embedded, the action/interactional strategies by which it is handled, managed, carried out, and, finally, the consequences of these strategies.

Grounded Theory: 2nd Coding Procedure

Axial Coding: Identifying Intervening Conditions

- Identify causal conditions – events or incidents that led to the occurrence/ development.
- Recognize the central idea, theme, event, happening.
- Identify intervening conditions – the broad and general constraining and enabling conditions.
- Recognize consequences – outcomes of actions and interactions.

We now finally turn from open and axial to 'selective' coding.

Conclude with Selective Coding

You now have categories worked out in terms of their salient properties, dimensions and associated relationships, giving the categories richness and density. You should also have begun to note possible relationships between major categories along the lines of their properties and dimensions. Furthermore, you have probably begun to formulate some conception of what your research is about.

The question is how do you take that – which is in a rough form, in your diagrams and memos – systematically forward and turn it into a picture of reality that is conceptual, comprehensible? For Strauss and Corbin there are 10 steps, which we have distilled down to four, through which such selective coding is accomplished:

Grounded Theory: 3rd Coding Procedure

Selective Coding: Storyline to Review

Step 1: A storyline – a descriptive story about the central phenomenon under study – can be aligned with both the phenomenological and interpretive approaches we have seen.

Step 2: From description to conceptualization – telling the story analytically. The central phenomenon has to be given a name: this becomes the core category.

Step 3: Relate subsidiary categories around the core category.

Step 4: Revisit the story, arranging and re-arranging the categories and subcategories accordingly.

We now conclude the methods of theorizing. You have become aware of its link to the methodology of rationalism, particularly of Popper's critical rationalism. If you choose to engage fully in the Northern path of reason, a deep understanding of that methodology would be the next step. Typical for the path of reason is a thorough understanding of the positivist facts of life; it requires the ability to reason and to build strong hypotheses which are able to drive out formerly existing weaker ones. You strive to uncover patterns and to codify knowledge. The symbol for the systematic path of reason is the Line. From critical rationalism you will move on to postmodernism, where you uncover the matrix of different discourses and learn to engage in them. Ultimately, out of this third critical stage you emerge towards socio-technical design where you engage in the systematic evolution of democratic processes. Before we move from the methods of theorising to experimental and survey methods, we shall lay out once more the path of reason before you:

We now turn from being, becoming and knowing to doing, and from description, narrative and theorizing, to survey and experimentation.

4.5 Origination of the Western Path of Realization: Experimental and Survey Methods Embodied in Case Study

EXPERIMENTAL UND SURVEY METHODS AND INTEGRAL 'DOING'

The realm of doing represents the practical culmination of our research journey, at least insofar as it is revealed in linear terms. The term 'excellence' has evolved from the Greek *arête*, which originally stood for virtue. Such excellence involves purposefully incorporating all three other worlds into your own. Ideally, this would mean standing at the centre of all of them. Such a practical and empirically based realization of a global perspective, as you enter into a unique world of your own, makes for a kind of 'global integrity' which is still connected with your local ground. In addition, we need to recognize the following:

- Each world is incomplete and imbalanced in itself and needs the other three to become fully operational.
- Each of the Four Worlds has its under-developed or dysfunctional manifestation, and its developed, or functional, one.
- Each world is divided into topographical layers, from surface inclinations to depth images. Global integrity in one world is potentially a condition reached when one world is able to engage with the other three worlds and with its own depths – inclinations, institutions, ideologies and images.

ENGAGE WITH PRACTICAL LEARNING

Practice, ultimately, can be written, graphic, spoken or alternatively sung, physically active, interpersonal, as we see today in Southern Africa. It can involve extensive collaboration in peer groups, in which much co-operative and self-directed learning goes on. As such the principle overall working hypothesis remains learning through activity, based on prior conceptual discrimination within material which is first of all presented in imaginal form, the whole being grounded on a positive emotional foundation. Whereas what we have indicated, so far, applies to specific learning situations, individually or collectively, how more generally does it apply to the development of a society as a whole? We now turn to such.

In knowledge creating terms, this is the realm of internalization, that is moving from explicit to tacit knowledge. In terms of research method this is the realm of survey methods and of experimentation.

THE END OF POVERTY – JEFFREY SACHS

Survey Example

Jeffrey Sachs, the Columbia University academic economist closely involved with both the World Bank and also the UN Millennium Development Goals, cites empirically identifiable reasons why some countries fail to materially thrive. Of the world's population of 6.3 billion, roughly 5 billion have reached at least the first rung of economic development. In actual economies, for Sachs, a rise in gross domestic product is typically the result of four factors simultaneously at work: saving and capital accumulation, increasing specialization and trade, technological advance and greater natural resources.[10]

The key problem for the poorest countries is that poverty itself can be a trap. When poverty is very extreme, the poor do not have the ability – by themselves – to get out of the mess. Even if such a notion of a 'poverty trap' is the right diagnosis, it does not explain why some countries are trapped and others not. The answer, Sachs believes, lies in the frequently overlooked, and easily visible, problems of physical geography. Governments, moreover, are critical to investing in public goods and services, such as primary health care, power grids, roads and the like. The government may lack the financial means to provide these public goods, however, for at least three reasons. First, the population itself may be impoverished, so taxation is not feasible. Second, the government may be inept, corrupt or incapacitated, and thereby unable to collect tax revenue. Third, the government may already be carrying a tremendous load of debt. What then are the measurable goals that the world community has set to alleviate poverty and suffering around the 'developing' world?

- *Eradicate Extreme Hunger and Poverty:* Halve, between 1990 and 2015, the proportion of people on one dollar a day; and halve the number of people who suffer from hunger.
- *Achieve Universal Primary Education:* Ensure that by 2015 children everywhere will be able to complete a full course of primary schooling.
- *Promote Gender Equality and Empower Women:* Eliminate gender inequality in primary and secondary education by 2005, and for all levels of education, by 2015.
- *Reduce Child Mortality:* Reduce it by two thirds between 1990 and 2015.
- *Improve Maternal Health:* Reduce maternal mortality rates by three quarters between 1990 and 2015.
- *Combat HIV/AIDS, Malaria and Other Diseases:* Begin to reverse, by 2015, the spread of HIV/AIDS, as well as malaria and other diseases.
- *Ensure Environmental Sustainability:* Integrate the principles sustainable development into country policies; halve the proportion of people without access to drinking water by 2015.
- *Develop a Global Partnership for Development:* Commit to good governance, development and poverty reduction; address special needs of developing countries; deal comprehensively with debt problems; provide access to essential drugs, in co-operation with drug companies and the private sector, make available benefits of new technologies.

ENGAGE IN SURVEY, EXPERIMENTATION AND CASE STUDY METHOD

We now consider the final and by far the most prolific of the research building blocks: that of experimental and survey methods. For unlike descriptive, narrative and theorizing methods, each of which has gained relatively scarce attention in the social sciences (with psychology being to some extent an exception) hundreds of books and billions of dollars have been devoted to such experimental and survey methods of research. Every minute in the day and all over the world undergraduate and postgraduate students will be attending classes on survey methods, ranging from interview methods and questionnaire design to focus groups and to statistical methods. For that reason, we are going to omit these from this particular book, while we recommend, for example, Martin Denscombe's[11] excellent recent work *The Good Research Guide* to cover such conventional ground.

What we want to focus on here is the case study, as a specific technique that provides a source of origination for the research path of realization. Such a case study method has in fact only secured intensive coverage from one researcher, inevitably an American, Robert Yin.[12]

We first turn briefly to experimentation, and then more specifically to the case study. When researchers around the world, particularly in developing societies, engage in social 'research', they tend to focus on the more passive aspect of empirical method; that is survey method, questionnaire design and distribution and statistical analysis. What ares left out of account are the more active elements, which we discuss here.

Experimentation, of course, is in the purist sense difficult to achieve within the social sciences. Yet the basic approach underlying experimentation is very much in tune with an inductive, positivist methodology, and also with liberal-empiricist ontology. *Experimentation then involves the manipulation of circumstances.* You need to identify factors which are significant and then introduce them or exclude them from the situation so their effect can be observed. *The introduction or exclusion of factors to or from the situation enables you as a researcher to pinpoint which factor actually causes the observed outcome to occur.*

Experiments rely on precise and detailed observation of outcomes and changes that occur following the introduction or exclusion of potentially relevant factors. In experiments, you attempt to control the situation in a way that manipulates the range of variables that might have an impact, so that it will be possible to ultimately eliminate interference in the cause–effect chain by any other factor. The aim is to control variables, all at once or in a sequence of experiments, so that only the one factor at the end remains a viable cause of the observed change. As such a factor may be deliberately excluded, or may be held constant, the use of control groups is the most established way of exercising control over significant variables: introducing two matched groups, adding a new factor to one group and not the other, and watching for the difference over time.

The *focus in the experiment is on discovering the dependent and independent variables.* The size, number, structure or volume of the independent variable is autonomous, owing nothing to any other – a change in the independent variable affects the dependent. Experiments normally take place in laboratories because they are purpose-built for research. Such experiments are normally relatively short in duration, and are on site rather than in the field, involving close control of variables to isolate causal factors with meticulous observation. The use of tests to measure things like knowledge and ability is commonplace. These tests do have a place in research through first the application of a uniform procedure; second an emphasis on measuring a specific unit; and third a comparison with some universal standard, through 'standardized' tests.

Closely aligned with such experimentation in the social sciences is systematic observation. This has its origins in social psychology – particularly studies of classroom interaction – and is normally quantitative and statistical. It needs to involve measurable behaviours that are obvious, require minimum interpretation and that are not context dependent, while being relevant to what is studied, complete as a category, precise as well as easy to record.

Such a 'closed' laboratory-based approach is very difficult to align with the descriptive and narrative methods we have described before. So we need to exercise some artistic licence as Integral Researchers. The case study method, then, is a more feasible and versatile means of conducting empirically based, qualitative research. Of course, such a method is likely to incorporate survey elements, like interviewing, as part of a more integral empirical whole.

For Robert Yin, the doyen of the case-study-based approach to empirical research, such a study is an empirical inquiry that investigates a contemporary phenomenon within its real life context, especially when the boundaries between phenomenon and context are not clearly evident. In other words, you would use the case study method because you deliberately wanted to cover contextual conditions, believing that they might be highly pertinent to your phenomenon of study. An experiment, by way of contrast, deliberately divorces a phenomenon from its context, so that attention can be focused on a few controlled variables. A history, in comparison, does deal with the entangled situation between phenomenon and context, but usually with non-contemporary events.

For case study analysis three points related to research design are important:

1. *Study Questions:* in terms of 'who, what, where, how and why'.
2. *Study Propositions:* each proposition directs attention to something that should be examined in the scope of a study, for example, 'organizations collaborate because they derive mutual benefits'. At the same time, in the context of an exploratory case study, there may be no such definitive propositions, but, in their stead, an overall statement of purpose – like 'I want to uncover the constituents of "quality control" that can be identified with Islamic principles and practices' – together with criteria for success.
3. *Unit of Analysis:* once the general definition of the case has been established, clarifications regarding the unit of analysis become important. If the unit is a small group, for example, those within must be distinguished from those without (the context). Moreover, boundaries of time and place are all important.

For Robert Yin, the demands of a case study on a person's intellect, ego and emotions are far greater than those of any other research strategy. This is because the data collection procedures are not routine. So what are the desired skills?

Experimental and Survey Methods
Towards an Original Case Study

- You are able to ask good questions – and to interpret the answers.
- You are a good listener – not trapped by your own ideologies and preconceptions.
- You are adaptable so that new situations can be seen as opportunities.
- You have a firm grasp of issues being studied, theoretically or policy oriented.
- You are unbiased by preconceived notions, responsive to contradictory evidence.

Intentional action then is at the apex of the supportive pyramid of fourfold being, becoming, knowing and doing, actualizes all of these dimensions and brings it to an integrated focal point. Undertaken by a learning or knowledge-creating community, for us embodied in the Four Worlds, it becomes a concerted and congruent set of behaviours that is honed through cyclical integration of all four modes, and includes a centred integration, as a necessary condition of its continuing practice. Practice as such, then, as the outcome of an inquiry, fulfils all other modes. It fulfils them because it involves them all, integrates them, gives them human purpose, imbuing them with intentionality and completes them by manifesting them. Furthermore, it *celebrates* them by showing the reality that they articulate manifests an ultimate effect. It is a declaration by concerted doing.

We are now ready to conclude our discussion of the experimental and survey methods. You have become aware of its link to the methodology of pragmatic empiricism. If you choose to engage fully in the Western path of realization, you would need to be equipped with strong investigative skills and an open experimental mind, driven by systematic observation and committed to analytically uncover within an experiment the variables and their relationship towards each other. In order to move out of the originally narrow frame of empiricism, which you would need to understand that as a following step, you would engage with the critical emancipatory position of critical realism. Here you gain a widened perspective, which allows you then to finally enter in action research where you are supposed to realize your social innovation. The symbol of this path is the arrow pointing to the centre, underscoring your commitment to social innovation through action. Before you move on to fully engage with the various paths or research, we shall lay out, once more, the path of realization, before you:

The Western Research Path of Realization			
Method and Origination	**Methodological Foundation**	**Critique and Emancipation**	**Action and Transformation**
Survey and Experimental Method	*Empiricism*	*Critical Realism*	*Action Research*
For example, Case Study	Chapter 14	Chapter 15	Chapter 16

4.6 Conclusion: Beyond Origination – Onto Your Path

Figure 4.3 distils the core relationships between research methods and techniques, our GENE and core human modes and life stages, emphasizing once more the importance of going back to the origins of social science research. You, as the Integral Researcher, are now about to choose, according to your path, with which specific method or technique you are engaging yourself. Within this book we highlight one specific technique for each method group.

The four research method groups, serve, in their turn, as building blocks for the four research paths: the relational path (describe), the path of renewal (narrate), the path of reason (theorize) and the path of realization (experiment/survey). As illustrated, for us, a research method is more than a technique. It is an originating and culturally laden – Southern cycling, Eastern spiralling, Northern linear and Western pointed – building block for a particular research path. It is like the 'overture to a symphony', or the foreword to a book. It sets the analytical and transformative tone for what is still to come.

By now, you as the Integral Researcher have tapped deeply into research methods and the corresponding human and cultural modes. You have probed, through analytical research methods and transformative origination, into the soil of your particular cultural and societal context. You have not only been in touch with your own origins and those of our community and society, but also with the burning issue that is personally pressing upon you or your society. And, finally, you now have a clear sense of the integral innovation you want to bring about but also for the innovation path, which is most authentic to you.

Groups of Research Methods	Overview on Specific Research Methods (Techniques)	GENE Analogy	Human Analogies Essential Modes
Descriptive Methods (S)	• **Empirical Phenomenology** • Explorative Interview • Participating Observation • And so on.	Grounding	BEING
Narrative Methods (E)	• **Storytelling** • Narrative Interview • World Café • And so on.	Emerging	BECOMING
Methods of Theorising (N)	• **Grounded Theory** • Hypothesis Formation • Discourse Analysis • Document Analysis • And so on.	Navigating	KNOWING
Experimental and Survey Methods (W)	• **Case Study** • Survey • Qualitative Experiment • And so on.	Effecting	DOING

Core Methods used within Integral Research Architecture

Figure 4.3   Research Methods – Human Modes

We now turn from method and origination, spanning all four research paths, to each of these four paths in turn. We start with the Southern relational path, which is closely linked with anthropology and sociology.

References

1. Abram, D. (1997). *The Spell of the Sensuous*. New York: Vintage Books.
2. Moustakas, C. (1994). *Phenomenological Research Methods*. London: Sage.
3. Yunus, M. (1999). *Banker for the Poor*. London: Aurum Press.
4. Polkinghorne, D. (1988). *Narrative Knowing and the Human Sciences*. New York: State University of New York.
5. Randall, W. (1995). *The Stories We Are*. Toronto: Toronto University Press.
6. Popper, K. (1999). *On Problem Solving*. London: Routledge Classics.
7. Hountondji, P. (ed.) (1997). *Endogenous Knowledge*. Dakar: Codesria.
8. Glazer, B. and Strauss, A. (1967). *The Discovery of Grounded Theory: Strategies for Qualitative Research*. New York: De Gruyter.
9. Strauss, A. and Corbin, J. (1990). *Basics of Qualitative Research: Grounded Theory Procedures and Techniques*. London: Sage.
10. Sachs, J. (2005). *The End of Poverty*. Harmondsworth: Penguin.
11. Denscombe, M. (2002). *The Good Research Guide*. London: Sage.
12. Yin, R. (1989). *Case Study Research: Design and Methods*. London: Sage.

5 *From Descriptive Methods to Phenomenology*

Engage with Your Life World

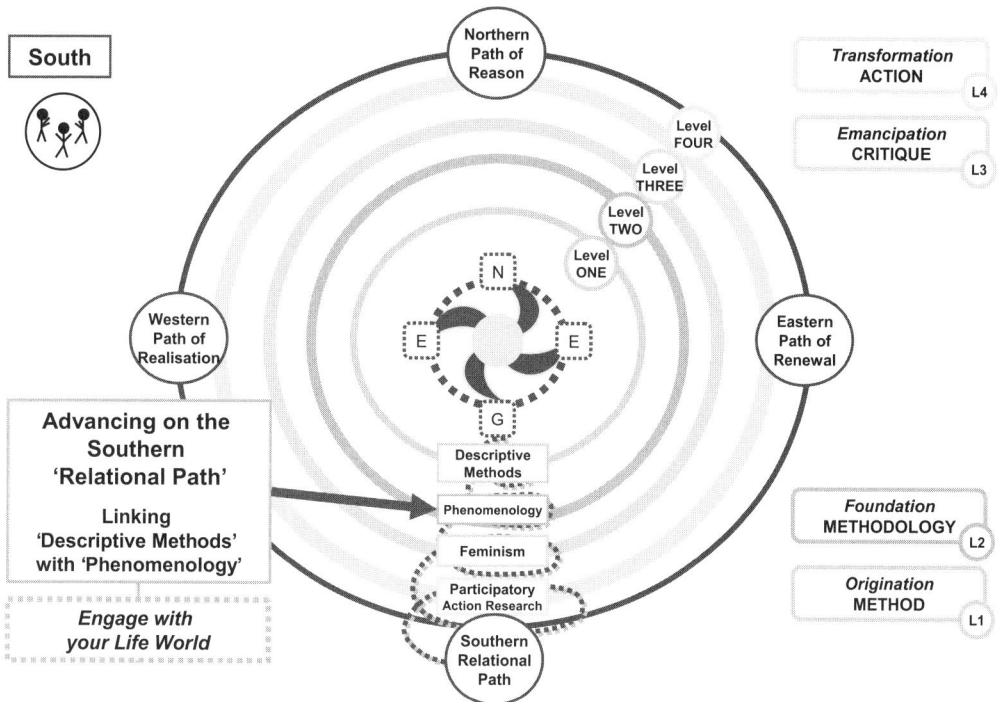

Figure 5.1   Overview Chapter 5 – Level 1/South

Summary: Phenomenology

- Advancing firstly on the Southern relational path, we now turn from method to methodology. In other words, we turn from descriptive methods and the origination of your research to phenomenology, where you lay the methodological foundation of your work.
- A core claim of phenomenology is that explanations are not to be imposed before the phenomena have been understood from within. Hence, Husserl, the 'father of phenomenology', sees this methodology also as putting the study of culture or 'spirit' on a proper scientific footing.
- He saw the life world (*Lebenswelt*) as the universal framework of human endeavour. For him, there is not one single life world, but a set of overlapping worlds, beginning from the world, which is the 'home-world', and extending to other world farther away, the worlds of other cultures.
- He criticizes traditional empiricism for naively dictating that all judgements be legitimized by 'experience', instead of realizing that many different forms of intuition underlie our judgements and our reasoning process. We overcome the subject–object divide only by finding a deeper meaning within subjectivity itself. This constitutes the 'qualitative' character of research.
- For Heidegger, who profoundly altered Husserl's phenomenology, the great threat to human existence is that thinking has become a kind of technical information processing. This leads to a fundamental homelessness and rootlessness (and in such a case to inauthentic research).
- To be authentic – for Sartre the existentialist (existentialism is an evolution of phenomenology) – is to grasp one's freedom and recognize it. Being inauthentic means being in flight from one's freedom, attempting to cover it by clinging to a persona, or indeed adopting one research methodology or another, because that is 'what you are supposed to do'. Social innovation, in such terms, is a process of authentic engagement with the world, grasping one's freedom by enabling others to realize theirs.
- Rudolf Steiner's anthroposophy is also closely aligned with the emerging phenomenology. Steiner's idea of philosophy was as liberation from limiting forms of thought, rather than as a wagging moral finger or an intellectual programme. Instead of a desperate search for objective foundations, knowledge might emerge from the growing and changing being of man, in a continually developing society.
- From this perspective knowledge ceases to be a mirroring, passive affair and becomes a process whereby we insert ourselves actively in the given setting of our lives. Hence, we need to accept the responsibility that as knowers we change the potential and actual course of the world. In other words, research and innovation are the two sides of the same coin.
- Finally we turn from philosophical thought to sociopolitical practice, from Husserl's phenomenological 'life world' to the Czech Republic's Velvet Revolution and Havel's 'living in truth'. Here we demonstrate that phenomenology also constitutes a basis for sociopolitical and economic transformation.

5.1 Orientation to Phenomenology

We now turn on our relational Southern research path from method to methodology, in this case from descriptive methods to phenomenology. For each of the methodologies, critiques and action research orientations that follow, within each one of the four respective paths, we shall incorporate, systematically:

- an overall orientation to phenomenology (5.1);
- the key tenets of phenomenology (5.2);
- an orientation to phenomenology in depth (5.3);
- a re-orientation: a global expression of Husserl's methodology (5.4);
- a practical and sociopolitical example of phenomenology being applied (5.5).

From a phenomenological perspective, all too often in the social sciences, when a researcher refers to him- or herself conducting themselves 'scientifically', they have in mind an exclusively empirical model of research. It is worth noting that Edmund Husserl, the father of phenomenology, as is the case for innumerable others cited in this book, radically parted company from this model in the 1930s.

ORIGINS: A TOTAL TRANSFORMATION OF THE TASK OF KNOWLEDGE

Phenomenology was initially developed by Edmund Husserl, a mathematician and philosopher, known as the 'father of phenomenology'. His work broke away from the purely positivist orientation of the science and philosophy of his day, giving weight to subjective experience as the source of all of our knowledge of objective phenomena.

Husserl was born 1859 into a Jewish family in Prost jov (Prossnitz), Moravia, in the Czech Republic (then part of the Austrian Empire). He was a disciple of the Czech philosopher and psychologist Franz Brentano, who influenced him greatly, and Carl Stumpf.

Husserl felt that the objectivism of science precluded an adequate apprehension of the world.[1] He presented various philosophical conceptualizations and techniques designed to locate the sources or essences of reality in the human consciousness.

Husserl proposed a radical new phenomenological way of looking at objects by examining how we, in our many ways of being intentionally directed toward them, actually 'constitute' them. In order to better understand the world of appearances and objects, phenomenology attempts to identify the invariant features of how objects are perceived and pushes attributions of reality into their role as an attribution about the things we perceive (or an assumption underlying how we perceive objects).

Franz Brentano
(1838 to 1917)

Edmund G.A. Husserl
(1859 to 1938)

Martin Heidegger
(1889 to 1976)

Figure 5.2   Phenomenology – Core Thinkers

Sources: Image 1: University of Wuerzburg http://www.philosophie.uni-wuerzburg.de. Image 2: Boston University http://people.bu.edu/. Image 3: Philosophische Schriften / Falsafeh http://www.falsafeh.com/

In a later period, Husserl began to wrestle with the complicated issues of intersubjectivity (specifically, how communication about an object can be assumed to refer to the same ideal entity) and tried new methods of bringing his readers to understand the importance of phenomenology to scientific inquiry (and specifically to psychology). *The Crisis of the European Sciences*[2] is Husserl's unfinished work that deals most directly with these issues. In it, Husserl for the first time attempts a historical overview of the development of Western philosophy and science, emphasizing the challenges presented by their increasingly empirical and naturalistic orientation. Husserl declares that mental and spiritual reality possess their own reality independent of any physical basis, and that a science of the spirit (*Geisteswissenschaft*) must be established on as scientific a foundation as the natural sciences have managed: 'It is my conviction that intentional phenomenology has for the first time made spirit as spirit the field of systematic scientific experience, thus effecting a total transformation of the task of knowledge.'

HOW PHENOMENOLOGY OPERATES

Phenomenology operates rather differently from the way social science was formerly conducted. While it is a theoretical orientation, it does not generate deductions from propositions that can be empirically tested. It operates more on a meta-sociological level, demonstrating its premises through descriptive analyses of the procedures of self, situational and social constitution. Through its demonstrations, audiences apprehend the means by which phenomena, originating in human consciousness, come to be experienced as features of the world.

Phenomenological tools include the use of introspective and understanding (*Verstehen*) laden methods to offer a detailed description of how consciousness itself operates.[3] Introspection requires the phenomenologist to use his or her own subjective process as a resource for study, while *Verstehen* requires an empathic effort to move into the mind of the other.[4, 5] Not only are introspection and *Verstehen* tools of phenomenological analysis, but they are procedures used by ordinary individuals to carry out their projects. Thus, the phenomenologist as analyst might study himself or herself as an ordinary subject dissecting his or her own self-consciousness and action schemes.[6] In this technique, an analytic attitude toward the role of consciousness in designing everyday life is developed. Phenomenologists use the term 'reflexivity' to characterize the way in which constituent dimensions serve as both foundation and consequence of all human projects. The task of phenomenology is to make manifest the incessant tangle or reflexivity of action, situation and reality in the various modes of being in the world.

What does this suggest regarding humanity and sociology? Phenomenology advances the notion that humans are creative agents in the construction of social worlds.[7] It is from their consciousness that all being emerges. The alternative to their creative work is meaninglessness and chaos: a world of dumb puppets, in which each is disconnected from the other and where life is formless.[8] This is the nightmare of phenomenology. Its practitioners fear that positivist sociologists actually theorize about such a world.[9]

Phenomenology itself is politically neutral. Inherently, it promotes neither transformative projects nor stabilization. In the work of a conservatively inclined practitioner, the legitimation process might be supported, while the liberative and transformative practitioner might seek to puncture or debunk the legitimations.[10]

> **Example for Phenomenological Research**
>
> Phenomenological work with young children examines how both family interactions and the practices of everyday life are related to the construction of childhood. It is revealed how the children's illustration of family life and common sense are actualized through ordinary interaction. Penetrating the inner world of children requires that the phenomenological practitioner view the subjects in their own terms, from the level and viewpoints of children. Such investigation shuns adult authoritative and particularly scientific perspectives and seeks to give voice to the children's experience of their own worlds. Infants' and children's communicative and interactive competencies are respected and are not diminished by the drive toward higher-level functioning.[11]

HEIDEGGER'S CRITIQUE

While the Moravian Husserl thought philosophy to be a scientific discipline that had to be founded on a phenomenology understood as epistemology, the German Heidegger, however, held a radically different view. According to him philosophy was not at all a scientific discipline, but more fundamental than science itself. He saw science as only one way of knowing the world with no specialized access to truth. Furthermore, the scientific mindset itself is built on a much more 'primordial' foundation of practical, everyday knowledge. Martin Heidegger believed that Husserl's approach overlooked basic structural features of both the subject and object of experience – what he called their 'being'. He expanded phenomenological inquiry to encompass our understanding and experience of Being itself, thus making phenomenology the method (in the first phase of his career at least) of the study of being: ontology. Husserl was sceptical of this approach, which he regarded as quasi-mystical, and it contributed to the divergence between their thinking.

INFLUENCE OF PHENOMENOLOGY ON SOCIAL SCIENCES

Phenomenology is an influential and complex philosophic tradition that has given rise to various related philosophical movements such as existentialism, poststructuralism, postmodernism, feminism, culture critique and various forms of analytical and new theory. Major contemporary figures such as the Frenchmen Foucault and Derrida, and America's Rorty, find the impetus and sources of their writings in earlier phenomenological works by Husserl and Heidegger;,the French philosophers Blanchot and Levinas; and others.

The phenomenological influence upon contemporary sociology can be seen in the increased humanization of theoretical works, research methods, educational assessment procedures and instructional modes.[12] Phenomenological thought has influenced the work of postmodernism, poststructuralism, critical theory and constructionism.

Hence, phenomenology, while remaining an identifiable movement within the discipline of sociology, has influenced mainstream research a lot. Inclusion of qualitative research approaches in conventional research generally expresses this accommodation.[13] The greater acceptance of intensive interviewing, participant observation and focus groups reflect the willingness of non-phenomenological sociologists to integrate subjectivist approaches into their work.

FURTHER INFLUENCE

Phenomenology also influenced the arts, for example architecture. Here, phenomenology is seen as a philosophical design and refers to the physical and haptic experience of building materials and their sensory properties. Phenomenology in architecture favoured an approach to design that was highly personal and inward looking.[14, 15]

We now turn from our overall orientation to the key tenets of phenomenology.

5.2 Phenomenology – Key Tenets: Radical Inquiry Beyond Reductive Empiricism

There are six key tenets of phenomenology, laying out as such the conventional grounds for a relational path to research. These are the following:

Phenomenology – Key Tenets
①   Engage in a process of radical inquiry.
②   Immerse yourself in a life world of immediately lived experiences.
③   Concentrate on illuminating the nature of the 'inner self'.
④   Focus on the subjective view of experience.
⑤   Locate every unique cultural history as an episode in the larger story.
⑥   Go beyond reductive positivism and naïve empiricism.

① ENGAGE IN A PROCESS OF RADICAL INQUIRY

Most of the founding figures of phenomenology emphasized the need for a renewal of philosophy as a process of radical inquiry. Above all else, phenomenology must pay attention to the nature of consciousness as actually experienced, not as pictured by commonsense or philosophical tradition; it must make a fresh interpretation of phenomena, 'bracketed off' from customary outlooks and conventional assumptions.

② IMMERSE YOURSELF IN A LIFE WORLD OF IMMEDIATELY LIVED EXPERIENCES

Phenomenology, for Husserl, has as its exclusive concern experiences intuitively seizable in their essence, not empirically perceived and treated as empirical facts. Further, it seeks to avoid all impositions placed on experience in advance, whether these are drawn from religious or cultural traditions, from everyday common sense, or indeed from science itself. Explanations are not to be imposed before the phenomena have been understood from within.

③ CONCENTRATE ON ILLUMINATING THE NATURE OF THE 'INNER SELF'

Husserl sees phenomenology as putting the study of culture or 'spirit' on a proper scientific footing. In that context your 'life world' underlies your intentional experiences. He saw such a life world as the universal framework of human endeavour – including our scientific endeavours. It is the ultimate horizon of all human achievement.

④ FOCUS ON THE SUBJECTIVE VIEW OF EXPERIENCE

In its time, when the advance of 'outer-directed', objectively cast science and technology was rampant, phenomenology steadfastly protected the subjective view of experience as a necessary part of any full understanding of the nature of knowledge. In its profound critique of naturalism as a philosophical programme, Husserl and his followers saw this scientific approach as self-defeating because it consciously excluded consciousness, the very source of all knowledge and value of all creativity and innovation.

⑤ LOCATE EVERY UNIQUE CULTURAL HISTORY AS AN EPISODE IN THE LARGER STORY

Husserl's *Crisis of the European Sciences*[16] is an attempt to alert the world to the increasing danger of the collapse of a genuinely scientific and philosophical outlook, which had marked out the progress of the West since the time of the Greeks. 'Given-ness', as such, sums up his view that all experience is experience to someone, according to a particular manner of experiencing. In that context, you will need to attend through your research to your particular approach to experiencing the world. It is also critical in that respect that you are aware of what kind of individual and societal essential 'intentionality' you together bring to it.

⑥ GO BEYOND REDUCTIVE POSITIVISM AND NAÏVE EMPIRICISM

Science, for Husserl, comes from a very special theoretical attitude, one of detached playfulness and curiosity. Galileo, for example, had displaced our immediate forms of lived experience with forms of objects as dictated by these qualities. If the objects produced in this play are then uncritically asserted, without reference to their subjective intent, to be the real objects of our experience in the life world, then serious problems will arise.

We now turn from these key tenets of phenomenology to its deeper and broader connotations, starting out with the insights of American cultural anthropologist David Abram.

5.3 Phenomenological Methodology in Depth

THE MORE THAN HUMAN WORLD

The crisis in the sciences was mirrored by a crisis in the social and natural world. One of the most eloquent contemporary exponents of this is the American anthropologist and phenomenologist David Abram, who has spent much of his life in Asia and Africa. We shall now consider Abram's current phenomenological perspective, before returning to Husserl.

Our 'life world', for Abram, is both the soil in which all our sciences and institutions are rooted and the rich humus into which their results ultimately return, whether as nutrients or poisons. Our spontaneous experience of the world, charged with subjective, emotional and intuitive content, remains the vital and dark ground of our objectivity. *'Phenomenology' returns to the taken-for-granted realm of subjective experience, not to explain it but simply to pay attention to its rhythms and textures.* For Abram, such a phenomenal life world has various layers: underneath the surface layer of a cultural world there reposes a deeper, more unitary life world. It is always already there beneath all our cultural acquisitions: a vast and continually overlooked dimension of experience that nevertheless supports and sustains all our diverse and discontinuous worldviews.[17]

The true task of phenomenology then lies in its careful demonstration of the way in which every theoretical and scientific practice grows out of, and remains supported by, the forgotten ground of our directly felt and lived experience, and has value and meaning only in reference to this primordial and open realm. European civilization's neglect of the natural world and its needs, as Afrikaaner novelist and adventurer Laurens Van der Post[18] has highlighted in an African context, has clearly been encouraged by a style of awareness that disparages sensorial reality. For it denigrates the visible and tangible order of things on behalf of some absolute source assumed to exist entirely beyond or outside of the bodily world. The Jewish and Christian traditions have followed in the footsteps of Plato's philosophical derogation of sensible and changing forms. Indeed both traditions, for Abram, made use of the strange and potent technology we call 'the alphabet'.

These letters printed across the page are hardly different from the footprints of prey left in the snow. We read these traces with organs honed over millennia by our tribal ancestors. In fact, the Chinese word for writing, *wen*, signifies a conglomeration of marks. It applies to the veins in stones and wood, to constellations, to the tracks of birds. The term *wen* has designated, by extension, literature. With the advent of the Hebrew *aleph-beth*, a new distance is opened between human culture and the rest of nature. The larger, more-than-human world is no longer a part of the system. But not quite. For example, the Hebrew word for *aleph* comes from 'ox' – an ox head with horns became our letter A. As the Hebrew *aleph* became the Greek *alpha* the sensorial reference to the concrete phenomenon was completely lost.

To members of a non-writing culture, places are never just passive settings. In oral cultures the human eyes and ears have not yet shifted their participation from the animate surroundings, or the beating rhythm of the drums to the written word. Particular mountains, canyons, streams or grove trees have not yet lost the expressive potency and dynamism with which they spontaneously present themselves to the senses. Indeed, by virtue of its underlying and enveloping presence, the place may even be felt to be the source, the primary power that expresses itself through the various events that unfold there. To an oral culture, experiences and events remain rooted in the particular soils, the particular ecologies, the particular places, and the particular life rhythms that give rise to them. This brings us to Husserl's life world.

HUSSERL'S LIFE WORLD: LEBENSWELT

The Primacy of Intentionality

Every act of knowledge, for Husserl, is to be legitimized by 'ordinary intuition', which lies at the core of his philosophy. He criticizes traditional empiricism for naïvely dictating that all judgements be legitimized by 'experience', instead of realizing that many different forms of intuition underlie our judgements and our reasoning process. 'Given-ness' sums up his view that all experience is experience to someone, according to a particular manner of experiencing. In that context, you will need to attend through your research to your particular approach to experiencing the world. It is also critical in that respect that you are aware of what kind of individual and essential 'intentionality' you bring to it.

Husserl sees phenomenology as putting the study of culture or 'spirit' on a proper scientific footing. In that context your 'life world' underlies your intentional experiences. He saw such a life world as the universal framework of human endeavour – including our scientific endeavours. It is the ultimate horizon of all human achievement. As conscious human beings, we always inhabit the life world. It is pre-given in advance and experienced as a unity. The life world is the general structure, which allows objectivity and thing-hood to emerge in the different ways in which they do emerge in different cultures. There is not one single life world, for Husserl, but a set of overlapping worlds: this set begins from the world which is the 'home-world', and extends to other world farther away, the worlds of other cultures.

Practical concerns, culturally laden assumptions and smatterings of scientific knowledge, however, all get in the way of a pure consideration of experience. What Husserl termed 'bracketing' meant that all scientific, philosophical, cultural and everyday assumptions had to be put aside. Returning to examine this pre-given world is a return to the so-called *Lebenswelt* (life world). Phenomenology has to interrogate the supposedly objective view of the sciences, what has been termed the 'God's eye perspective', or the 'view from nowhere'. Husserlian phenomenology did not dispute the possibility of our gaining a 'view from nowhere' understood as the 'objective' view of things. This indeed accorded with Popper's rationalist perspective. Husserl was anxious to give full credit to this view, but he saw it as an idealization, one remote from everyday experience.

Besides rejecting such supposedly rationalist and idealist accounts of reality (see Chapter 11) phenomenologists were also critical of the narrow reductionist models of human experience found in various 19th century versions of empiricism (see Chapter 14). Phenomenology claimed to have overcome the basis of the opposition between rationalism and empiricism and indeed to have rejected the subject–object distinction altogether. Husserl saw intentionality as a way of reviving the central discovery of Descartes' *cogito ergo sum* ('I think therefore I am'). We overcome the subject–object divide only by finding a deeper meaning within subjectivity itself. This constitutes the 'qualitative' character of your research.

Subjectivity and Consciousness

In common with many researchers working at the end of the 19th century, such as America's William James and France's Henri Bergson, Husserl was fascinated both by the ever-changing stream of conscious experience and by its apparent seamless unity. For Husserl, objectivity was always a particular achievement of such consciousness. Furthermore, consciousness was always particularized as someone's consciousness. Husserl's central concern then, in his 'Logical Investigations', was how such objective knowledge can be possible for a knowing subject? His investigations are concerned with analysing the most basic elements which were required for any form of knowledge. These experiences were to be studied not as factually occurring psychological entities, but in terms of their necessary structure as acts of their kind. In other words, Husserl was asking: what is the essence of an act of perception, an act of thinking, and so on. Essences, for him, are the web of ideal possibilities and relationships that constitute a particular domain of experience.

Hence, phenomenology is a science of pure essences. It must abstract from the purely contingent, factual features of your experience in order to isolate what is essential to all experiences of that kind. And it must overcome contingency, factuality or factualness. In that context, phenomenology is stripped of all empirical content, thereby providing essential knowledge, irrespective of what goes on in the actual world. Husserl believed in what he termed 'eidetic seeing', that it was possible to have an insight into the essential nature of things, that these could be 'seen' in a manner analogous to the perceptual seeing of a physical object. Such essential seeing was then 'eidetic'. For him, traditional empiricism had allowed itself to be blinded by its faith in a narrow empiricism that ignored the fact that the sciences operated with such essences. Hence the importance of moving from the merely factual to the level of essential truths.

In contrast to the positivistic outlook of naturalism, Husserl believed that all knowledge, all science, all rationality depended on conscious acts, acts which cannot be properly understood from within the 'natural' scientific outlook at all. Consciousness should not be viewed naturalistically as part of the world, since consciousness is precisely the reason there was a world there for us in the first place. For Husserl it is not that consciousness creates the world – this would be subjective idealism – but rather that the world is opened up or disclosed through consciousness. Our genuinely natural life, he maintained, is in community, living in a world of shared objects, shared environment, shared meanings, shared language. His treatment of 'inter-subjectivity' employed a conception of empathy with others.

We now turn to Martin Heidegger who, unlike his teacher Husserl, believed that it was necessary to link phenomenology with hermeneutics.

Linking Phenomenology with Hermeneutics

Phenomenology, for Germany's Martin Heidegger, is transformed into hermeneutical or existential phenomenology. For him the phenomena of existence always require interpretation, and hermeneutics is the art of interpretation. So an interpretation of human existence cannot be a neutral, dispassionate, theoretical contemplation, but must take into account the *involvement* of the inquirer. *Heidegger's ultimate aim is to understand the meaning of being in relation to time* (see also Chapter 9). For this purpose he draws heavily on the German historical tradition of Hegel and Dilthey.

According to Heidegger's analysis, the basic structure of 'factical' life is 'caring' which involves 'circumspection'. Mostly humans are drawn into the world in a way he characterizes as 'falling'. In falling, humans live their concrete lives as 'bogged down in inauthentic tradition and habituation'. Heidegger profoundly alters Husserl's phenomenology. He does not refer to natural attitude. He remains more faithful to the *historical, lived*, practical nature of human experience. *Dasein* ('being'), is not an entity that stands on its own, like a stone or chair; it is always caught up in a world. 'World' here means a context, an environment, a set of references and assignments within which any meaning is located. All neutral understanding of things, for example scientific understanding, presupposes our 'existential' encounter (Heidegger is actually an early existentialist) with things and our original interpretation of them in the light of our concerns and dealings with the world.

The Existential Nature of Dasein

Your life, for Heidegger, presents itself in terms of the set of possibilities that you are. Of course, a lot of the way your life presents itself is given by the culture you have grown up in, or is simply carried along by a kind of unquestioned horizon of acceptance. But, as Heidegger indicates, *you can choose certain possibilities for* yourself. This part of his analysis was seized on by the existentialists, especially by the French 20th-century existentialist Jean Paul Sartre, who took from Heidegger the view that humans can make themselves who they are by seizing their possibilities. Sartre's account, however, is much more action oriented than that of Heidegger, who is really giving a phenomenological description of how we encounter ourselves in our lives.

For Heidegger 'authentic moments' are those in which we are most at home with ourselves, at one with ourselves. You may initiate or take up possibilities as your own; you have a deep, concrete experience of what is 'yours'. This 'authentic' orientation can be compared and contrasted with your more usual, normal, everyday moments, where you do not treat things as affecting you deeply in your 'own-most' being. Heidegger therefore thinks we live in an inauthentic way most of the time. Anxiety is the recognition of a certain nothingness, a groundlessness in our existence. As Sartre was to describe it, anxiety leads us into a kind of vertigo where we literally have no ground beneath our feet. Fear is always fear of *something*, and for the sake of something. Anxiety, on the other hand, is a rather shapeless mood, which does not have a precise object. Anxiety reveals to us a certain homelessness – we are not at home in the world. The world faces us as something weird.

Thrown into Inauthenticity

In our ordinary everydayness, we simply pass information along, not getting wrapped up in it, and our speech (if not also our research) is merely 'idle talk' or 'passive information gathering'. This is for Heidegger an inauthentic state. In our everyday mood we are absorbed in the world, caught up in our tasks; we don't reflect on who we are, we are 'thrown'. We are also peculiarly constructed so that we actually run away from facing up to aspects of our existence. This structural feature of running away Heidegger calls 'falling'. Falling means getting caught up in the public self, so that we no longer have proper access to our authentic sense of our lives. We are thrown into history and can experience this as a kind of fateful acceptance, repeating what is handed down through tradition, or we can try and achieve a moment of resoluteness, in your case through your research, projecting yourselves into possibilities.

For Heidegger, the great threat to human existence (and specifically here in our research programme) is that thinking has become a kind of technical information processing. This leads to a fundamental homelessness and rootlessness (and in such a case to inauthentic research). Against this account of transcendental homelessness stands genuine philosophy as a kind of homecoming, a thinking-back from our current displaced sense back to finding our place and preserving what we have found. Heidegger's later writings develop his thinking on the nature of genuine dwelling and the global homelessness of humanity. His account of the technological framework bounding the modern world expands to such a degree that even the early Greeks are seen as having cast the metaphysical fate of the West to be technological. This is through the Greeks' earliest thinking about *techne* and *episteme*, skill and knowledge. Technology is a form of revealing. However, it is a form, which also uses up the material, which it is setting forth. It turns nature into a mere stockpile of coal, iron, water, and so on. For Heidegger, the nature of this technological revealing is such that it obscures and does not reveal its own essence. Furthermore, it transforms the humans involved in technology. Human beings have been caught up in this mode of revealing.

The influence of Heidegger on 20th-century philosophy has been huge. The Canadian philosopher Charles Taylor has said that Heidegger's importance lies in the fact that he is one of the few contemporary philosophers who has helped to free us from the grip of rationalism. Among his own students were Gadamer (hermeneutics) and Marcuse (critical theorist). In Germany he influenced the Frankfurt School of Social Research, from whence came critical theory. Adorno, a founder of the Frankfurt School, juxtaposed the young Marx's view of human alienation and domination by ideology against Heidegger's account of man and the domination of technicity. For Marcuse, Heidegger had articulated the principles of human historicity, a necessary part of the Marxist attempt to explain man with reference to historical movement. Finally, his philosophy was absorbed by French existentialism and by Derrida's deconstruction and Foucault's anti-Enlightenment humanism (see Chapter 12 on postmodernism).

Being and Nothingness

Jean Paul Sartre, in the middle of the last century, embraced phenomenology as a way of overcoming 'idealism'. For him, idealism is the view that reality is apprehended only indirectly through mental representations of ideas. There was now a way to discuss the manner in which consciousness was immediately in the presence of things. The real merit of *Being and Nothingness*, his most famous philosophical work, is the manner in which it provides close descriptions of various human situations, which are rich in phenomenological and philosophical insight. Chief amongst these are descriptions of what it is to be 'in bad faith', to adopt a 'persona'. In such bad faith a person is denied their true choice.

Human consciousness, for Sartre, is truly free in this existential and phenomenological context. It can be anything. It is pure possibility, and hence ripe for innovation. Yet, on the other hand, at every moment we are embedded in the historical situation. Human nature is caught up in facticity, in what Sartre calls 'the situation'. Authenticity is how we respond to the situation in a manner, which acknowledges and preserves our freedom. Husserl had characterized the situation as 'mine-ness', which Heidegger had analysed in terms of the basis of possibility that may appropriate one's life either in an 'authentic' or an 'inauthentic' way. *Being and Nothingness* is an extended meditation on these notions. To be authentic is to grasp one's freedom and recognize it. Being inauthentic means being in flight from one's freedom, attempting to cover it by clinging to a persona, or indeed adopting one research methodology or another, because that is 'what you are supposed to do'. Social innovation, in such terms, is a process of authentic engagement with the world, grasping one's freedom by enabling others to realise theirs.

We now turn from phenomenology's most well-known heritage (with Husserl, Heidegger and Sartre being amongst its best-known representatives) to some of its globally dispersed representatives, starting with Rudolf Steiner in Austria.

5.4 Global Variations of Phenomenology

FROM PHENOMENOLOGY TO ANTHROPOSOPHY

The Philosophy of Freedom

Rudolf Steiner, an Austrian who lived at the turn of the last century, was a philosopher and educator, architect and agronomist, historian and musician, economist and political scientist, amongst other things. Because of the esoteric nature of some of his anthroposophical work he became disconnected from the philosophical and methodological mainstream. Andrew Welburn, a Fellow of New College, Oxford, has done us a real service by linking Rudolf Steiner's work into the phenomenological establishment.[19]

Actually, Steiner was a leading exemplar of a researcher and innovator in the social realm. For not only did he conceive of anthroposophy as a philosophical movement, but, through it, he pioneered innovative approaches to art and architecture, medicine and agriculture, education and economics, some of which – particularly in education (Waldorf Schools) and agriculture (biodynamic farming) – have spread throughout the world.

Steiner's idea of philosophy was as liberation from limiting forms of thought, rather than as a wagging moral finger or an intellectual programme. Such liberation enables us to grasp other possibilities, taking place in the thick of life, and coinciding with the freedom to see things anew. Such a concept of freedom is precisely one that may be embodied in the form of a building or a room, in a gesture or in a painting or in a new approach to economics, for him based on fraternity rather than liberty. Scientific knowing is the way in which we can relate to the world through developing our inner activity. Scientific activity does not reveal our passivity before fixed facts of nature, but our own living process of knowledge, the free development of the self. For example, his concept of 'associative' economics was based on what he reckoned to be the phenomenological and concrete 'reality' of economic life, rather than the liberal and abstract 'ideal' of it embodied in the free-market approach.

In view of the economic reforms that took place in Eastern Europe in the 1990s, Steiner's recognition of the need for these to be based on an absolute respect for freethinking individuals is highly germane. For him the individual was a creative force in society, an agent of necessary change, and a constant test of the validity of social forms. Now that, for Steiner, the myths of West and East have played out their extraordinary history on the capitalist-communist stage of the 20th century, it may be that the signs of a more balanced reappraisal of their respective values may also draw inspiration from Steiner's proposals. Steiner suggested a more dynamically conceived 'threefold social order' than capitalism versus communism, designed to obviate the unproductive dualistic tensions built into such assumptions of individual-versus-state. Such an order was comprised of the political, economic and cultural spheres. Steiner saw them as the respective homes of political equality, economic fraternity and cultural liberty – or indeed freedom.

Phenomenology as the Bridge between East and West

The polarizations of the modern world, according to Steiner, were rooted in assumptions that reach back to the beginnings of the 19th century and indeed before then. The one side of the polarity, an idealistic philosophy, traced its origin back to Immanuel Kant. The other, an embodiment of a materialistic worldview, had come down from Jeremy Bentham and was influenced by J.S. Mill. There was apparently no middle way. Their clash in the 19th century prefigures some of the terrible struggles subsequently enacted in the 20th. The struggles above all were concerned with the value of the individual. For Steiner, neither dominant tradition assigns value to the individual as such. Idealist Kant held that moral imperatives come to us with blinding force as 'categorical imperatives'. The knowing individual has only the function of recognizing the necessary laws of existence. The realist Bentham felt that fulfilment lies in the value of the whole society, tribe or race.

Steiner's philosophical approach, in contrast with realism and idealism, is closely aligned with the emerging phenomenology. Instead of a desperate search for objective foundations, knowledge might emerge from the growing and changing being of man, in a continually developing society. That would mean abandoning the notion of the impassive onlooker, and including the seeking, striving human self in the picture we form of the cognitive process. As such we arrive at a picture which is neither the blank sheet of empiricism, nor the mind locked up in its own categories as for Kant. What we know of the world depends on the fact that we are part of the world and have been shaped by it, so that from the beginning our nature and organization become not a limit, but the actual key to the nature of the universe to which we belong and which brought us into being.

From this perspective knowledge ceases to be a mirroring, passive affair and becomes a process whereby we insert ourselves actively in the given setting of our lives, which therefore always carries a moral significance (for ourselves and, of course, for our research). Steiner's view is that we need to accept the responsibility that as knowers we change the potential and actual course of the world. In other words, research and innovation are the two sides of the same coin. His view of knowledge as relationship stresses our own need to be transformed, to learn and grow through cognitive encounter and allow reality to reveal itself in ever-new aspects. The task of knowledge is not to recapitulate in the form of concepts what is given to us in some other way. It is rather to create an entirely new domain which, when taken together with the world presented through sense perception, yields for the first time full reality. The human being is not an idle onlooker before the pageant of the world; he is an active participant in a cosmic creative process. That, for us, is the essence of social research and its counterpart social innovation.

We now turn from European phenomenological ontology and epistemology to its more widely dispersed (but still relational) global expressions.

DISPERSED PHENOMENOLOGY: FROM LOCKE AND HUME TO BUDDHA AND BIKO VIA IQBAL

Locke's and Hume's Radical Empiricism and Radical Doubt

Husserl, through his focus on individual freedom and intentionality, had something in common with the Western Locke and Hume, even though he rejected Locke's exclusive focus on objective reality. He also shared with the Anglo-Saxon empiricists an orientation towards the concrete and 'real', as opposed to the ideal. This he termed the 'life world', albeit that it was full of subjectivity as well as objectivity. At the same time Husserl was a rationalist, who drew inspiration from 'Northerner' Descartes, through the latter's sense of 'radical doubt', although he disagreed with Descartes' separation of body and mind. In Husserl's words:

> the European world was born out of reason, that is, out of the spirit of philosophy. The European crisis should therefore not be interpreted as the failure of rationalism ... an impoverished rationalism has become entangled in 'naturalism' and 'objectivism'.[20]

Buddha's Radical Detachment

Even more interesting is the resonance between phenomenology and Buddhism, involving self-detachment, alongside self-interest (intentionality) and self-knowledge (rationality). Caroline Brazier, in her book *Buddhist Psychology*, makes the point that Buddhist psychology is sometimes described as a 'non-self' psychology. The self is a defensive structure built in response to affliction. This is what is referred to in Buddhism as ignorance or *avidya*.[21] We ignore much that is going on around us and limit our behaviour and interest to things that relate to our self-view. In the process, we initially grasp for something we can hold on to that seems permanent; we call this 'me' or self. The self is the fortress we create to protect ourselves from experiencing loss and impermanence. It is our greatest defence mechanism. It is also our prison. Keeping the fortress in place becomes our life project, and consumes large amounts of energy. This constituted, for the Buddha, greed and attachment.

So what has this all got to do with phenomenology? If Buddhist psychology is a psychology of addiction, then it is also a psychology of encounter. Encounter is the antidote to those addictive patterns that holds us trapped. By encountering the world beyond the walls of self, we break through to freedom. The path to health is in encountering that which is not self. In other words, we need to encounter that which is other. To break out of self-absorption we have to allow ourselves to be touched by something beyond ourselves.

Biko's Radical Consciousness

Interestingly enough, such self-detachment with its characteristically Eastern self-effacing connotations, is expressed in both similar and different terms within the self-expressive Southern context of *ubuntu*. The attitude of seeing people not as themselves but as agents for some particular function either to one's advantage or disadvantage is, for the late Steve Biko (a key figure in South Africa's 'Black Consciousness' movement), foreign to the African. We are not, he says, a suspicious race:

> *We believe in the inherent goodness of man. We enjoy man for himself. We regard our living together not as an unfortunate mishap warranting endless competition amongst us but as a deliberate act of God to make us a community of brothers and sisters jointly involved in the quest for a composite answer to the varied problems of life. Hence in all we do we always place man first and therefore all our action is usually joint and community oriented.*[22]

Nothing then dramatizes the eagerness of the African to communicate with each other more than their love for song and rhythm. Music in the African culture features in all emotional states, for South Africa's Steve Biko as for Senegal's former philosopher-president Leopold Senghor:

When we go to work we share the burdens and pleasures of the work we are doing through music. In other words, for Africans, music and rhythm are not luxuries but part and parcel of our way of communicating. Any suffering we experienced was made more real by song and rhythm. There is no doubt that the so-called 'Negro spirituals' sung by black slaves in the States as they toiled under oppression were indicative of the African heritage. The major thing to note about our songs is that they were never songs for individuals. All African songs are group songs.[23]

Biko adds that Africans, being a pre-scientific people, do not recognize any conceptual cleavage between the natural and the supernatural. They experience a situation rather than face a problem. By this is meant that they allow both the rational and the non-rational elements to make an impact upon them. Hence, any action they may take could be described more as a response of the total personality to the situation than the result of some mental exercise.

We believed that God was always in communication with us and therefore merited attention everywhere and anywhere. In rejecting Western values, therefore, we are rejecting those things that are not only foreign to us but that seek to destroy the most cherished of our beliefs – that the cornerstone of society is man himself – not just his welfare, not his material being, but just man himself with all his ramifications. We reject the power-based society of the Westerner that seems to be ever concerned with perfecting their technological know how while losing out on their spiritual dimension. We believe that in the long run the special contribution from Africa will be in the field of human relationships. The great powers of the world may have done wonders in giving the world an industrial and military look. But the great gift still has to come from Africa – giving the world a human face.[24]

That is not a million miles away from where Edmund Husserl was coming from, philosophically in entering wholeheartedly into the life world of self and other, even though he and Biko were far apart in place and time. Husserl states in such *ubuntu*-like terms:

Personal life means living communalised as 'I' and 'we', within a community horizon, and this in communities of various forms – family, nation, supra-national community. It involves purposeful life, the term life in this context not having a physiological sense, but in the broadest sense creating culture in the unity of a historical development.[25]

Most *ubuntu* thinkers in an African philosophical context formulate their views in terms of 'a person is a person through other persons', or, 'I am because you are'. In this way human dignity gains a central place and seems to be related to both morality and nationality. There is no dualism in this position because rationality and morality are required from community life and do not follow from so-called universal categories or fixed ideologies.

Sharing, for Zimbabwe's management philosopher and consultant Lovemore Mbigi,[26] means participation in the context of business management. In the final analysis, he bases his *ubuntu* model on four principles: 'morality', which involves trust and credibility; 'interdependence', which concerns the sharing and caring aspect of relationships, that is co-operation and participation; 'spirit of man', which refers to human dignity and mutual respect, implying that activities should be person-driven and humanness should be central; and lastly 'totality', which pertains to the continuous improvement of everything in the organization by every member of it.

Reconstructing Islam

We finally turn to the phenomenology of religion. In this case, we do so via the 20th-century Pakistani poet-philosopher, Muhammad Iqbal, and his *Reconstruction of the Islamic Religion.*

Interestingly enough, Iqbal positions Islam, as does Husserl phenomenology, in between the ideal and the real, emphasizing the relatively concrete nature of Islam vis-à-vis classical Greek philosophy:

The failure of Cartesian ontological and teleological arguments is that they look upon 'thought' as an agency working on things from without. This creates an unbridgeable gap between the real and the ideal. It is, however, possible to take thought not as a principle that organizes its material from the outside, but as a potency, which is formative of the very being of its material. Thus regarded thought or idea is not akin to the original nature of things; it is their ultimate ground and constitutes the essence of their beings, inspiring their onward march to a self-determined end. But our present situation necessitates the dualism between thought and being.[27]

Iqbal argues that the radical doubt, that Husserl evolved from Descartes, was anticipated by an Islamic 11th-century philosopher. Iqbal sees Islam as a bridge between the ancient and modern worlds. As such, he also sees Islam as the origin of empirically based scientific method, as we know it today:

The Prophet of Islam seems to stand between the ancient and modern worlds. In so far as the source of his revelation is concerned, he belongs to the ancient world. At the same time the birth of Islam is the birth of the modern, inductive intellect. In Islam, prophecy reaches its perfection in discovering the need of its own abolition – in order to achieve full self-consciousness man must be thrown inductively back on his own resources. The abolition of the kingship and hereditary priesthood in Islam, the constant appeal to reason and experience in the Qur'an, and the emphasis that it lays on Nature and History as sources of human knowledge, are all different aspects of the same idea of finality. As such the Qur'an regards both 'Anfus' (self) and 'Afaq' (world) as sources of knowledge. Inner experience is one source of human knowledge; the external sources are Nature and History.[28]

Ultimately, for Iqbal and for many Islamic scholars, Islam is rooted not only in concreteness, as opposed to abstraction, but also in a concept of 'inner freedom' that anticipates not only phenomenology as a whole, but also and particularly existential phenomenology, as reflected in the work of Heidegger and Sartre:

The Qur'an has no liking for abstract universals. It always fixes its gaze on the concrete, which the theory of relativity has only recently taught science to do. Omniscience, abstractly conceived, is merely a blind, capricious power without limits. The Qur'anic legend of the Fall has, in fact, nothing to do with the first appearance of man on the planet. Its purpose is rather to indicate man's rise from a primitive, instinctive state to the conscious possession of a free self, capable of doubt and disobedience. The Fall does not mean moral depravity; it is man's transition from simple consciousness to the first flash of self-consciousness, a kind of awakening from the dream of nature to a throb of causality in one's own being. Man's first act of disobedience was his first act of free choice. Freedom is thus a condition of goodness. But to permit the emergence of a finite ego who has the power to choose, after considering the relative values of several actions open to him, is really to take a great risk. For the freedom to choose good also involves its opposite.[29]

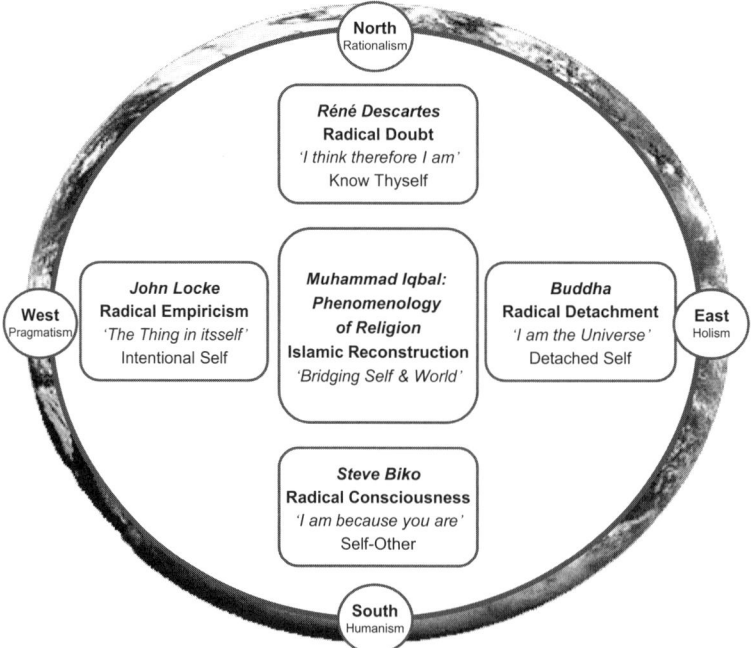

Figure 5.3   A Phenomenal Field of Force

We now turn from theory to practice, from methodology to application. We now return to Europe, in fact to the Czech Republic where Husserl himself was born. Thereby we turn from philosophical (and religious) thought to sociopolitical practice, from Husserl's phenomenological life world to Havel's 'living in truth'.

5.5 Phenomenology in Practice: The 'Czechoslovakia-Case'

FROM SCIENTIFIC TO VELVET REVOLUTION: SOCIAL SCIENCE TO SOCIAL ACTIVISM

Phenomenology also constitutes a basis for sociopolitical and economic transformation, as has been illustrated over the past few decades in the former Czechoslovakia. Unlike Locke and Adam Smith, Rousseau and Marx, Husserl was not conventionally seen to exercise direct social and political influence. Yet his philosophical revolution, transforming a 'free world' into a 'life world', unbeknown to most of us, preceded the 'Velvet Revolution' in which Vaclav Havel, the poet-playwright who later became Czech president, played a central role.

It all started at the turn of the last century, though antecedents date back 600 years. A prominent background presence for Havel is Thomas Masaryk, a philosopher who served for 14 years as a member of the Austrian Parliament at the turn of last century. Opposed to Germany's nationalism in Austria and Austria's adventurous policies in the Balkans, Masaryk became convinced that Austro-Hungary could no longer serve as the common homeland for the small nations of Central Europe. Thus, following the outbreak of World War I, Masaryk became the champion of an independent Czechoslovakia, leading troops who fought successfully alongside Allied forces. At the end of the war, Masaryk became president of the first Czechoslovakian Republic, from 1919 to 1938.

Primarily a philosopher, Masaryk had come under the influence of Franz von Brentano during his studies in Vienna. Subsequently, Masaryk developed a friendship with Husserl and was instrumental in convincing him to switch from the study of mathematics to philosophy. And from Masaryk, Husserl acquired a heightened sense of the crisis of the European sciences. *Alarmed that increased scientific sophistication did not bring moral progress, he feared that modern reason had become detached from the world of good and evil, which for him was the foundation of lived reality*. In addition, Masaryk affirmed that Czech national consciousness had been grounded and shaped by the Hussite movement. Through Masaryk's testimony, the national martyr Jan Hus (1370–1415), gained fresh place in contemporary Czech thinking. So when Jan Palach burned himself after the Soviets invaded Czechoslovakia, it was appropriate for Czech patriots to assign Hussite martyr symbolism to the event. We must also cite the strong influence of the philosopher Jan Patocka, who studied under Husserl, taught Vaclav Havel and subsequently was instrumental in publishing Charter 77. In this statement of resistance to Soviet occupation and communist ideology, Patocka drew upon the thought of his significant predecessors. He studied under Husserl, and he also devoted a good portion of his graduate work to a systematic study of Masaryk's thought.

CHARTER 77

Patocka initially drew up the so-called Charter 77 texts, prompted by the 1977 Helsinki Agreement on human rights. These rights affirmed that human beings are obliged to discover and protect a valid moral foundation, since there can be no rightful expectation that salvation will be provided by the state, or that it can be effected by any combination of social powers and forces. In a message to the Czech people, Patocka explained Charter 77 as follows: *a moral system does not exist in order to help society function but simply so that man can be human. It is not man who defines a moral order according to the arbitrary nature of his needs, wishes, tendencies, and desires, but morality defines man.*[30]

Havel himself was arrested and jailed for four months for his part in Charter 77 activities. In 1979 he was convicted again, this time sentenced to four-and-a-half years in prison, but received a suspended sentence because of poor health and an international protest campaign.

Already in the 1950s, while the Czech Communist Party was terrorizing the Czechoslovak people, the young Havel drew together a remarkable circle of friends and acquaintances who were all 36, and whom he soon began to call the Thirty-Sixers. His circle was preoccupied with literature, and they learned as teenagers the art of criticizing and being criticized in turn – to concede that it was finally necessary to disclose, to reveal oneself and to look at oneself as well through the eyes of others.

By the early 1960s, it is estimated that nearly half a million men and women of the communist 'nomenklatura' occupied key decision-making positions, particularly in the management of enterprises, for which they were formally unqualified. The combined consequences of these various structural problems of the socialist state – unqualified leadership, administrative bottlenecks, economic stagnation, the absence of social 'shock-absorbers' – was to encourage a faction of the ruling oligarchy, headed by Dubcek, to go on a dangerous journey called liberalization. He therefore enabled the growth out from underneath the edifices of state power, of the first tender shoots of social life. In the end though, Dubcek proved a poor match for the political and social forces that he helped to unleash; and in August 1968, when the Soviets invaded, he fell victim to his own success.

LIVING IN TRUTH

Almost a decade later dissident intellectuals, including Havel himself, signed the famed Charter 77. The centre of gravity of potential resistance is what he called 'the existential dimension of the world'. That's what Husserl, as we have seen, coined *Lebenswelt*: here a different life – what Havel called 'living in truth' – can be lived. This system serves people only to the extent that people will serve it.

Havel's thesis necessarily involved something of a Copernican Revolution – following from where Husserl left off – in the way power was conceived. The powerless, then, have within themselves the power to obstruct normality, to embarrass the authorities, to point to the possibility of living life differently – according to values like trust, openness, responsibility, solidarity and love.

Living in truth requires the cultivation of individuation, self-protection and co-operation. The empowerment of the powerless first and foremost requires individuals to build open, flexible structures of resistance that run parallel to and underneath the late socialist state. There is a fundamental contrast for me and my philosophical predecessors between the world that can be constructed out of some presumed ideological viewpoint and the world that is rooted in trustworthy lived-experience; impersonal, mechanistic, manipulative force can be effectively resisted only by the one true power that all persons have at their disposal, their humanity.[31]

System, ideology and apparat – for Havel as for Husserl – have deprived human beings of rulers, as well as the ruled of their conscience, of their common sense and natural speech and thereby also of their actual humanity. States grow ever more machine-like and totalitarian; men are transformed into statistical choruses of voters, producers, consumers, patients, tourists or soldiers. In politics, good and evil, categories of the natural world and therefore obsolete remnants of the past lose all absolute meaning; the sole method of politics is quantifiable success. This absolute power achieved its most complete expression in the totalitarian systems. And these systems, for Havel, are none other than a convex mirror of all modern civilization.

The question about capitalism and socialism in the context of such modernization seems to emerge from the depths of the last century. It seems to Havel that these highly ideological and semantically confused categories (isms) have since long been beside the point. *The question for him is wholly other, deeper and equally relevant to all; whether we shall, by whatever means, succeed in reconstituting the natural and human world, phenomenologically, as the true terrain of politics, rehabilitating the personal experience of human beings as the initial measure of all things, placing morality above politics and responsibility above our desires.*

The task therefore is that of resisting vigilantly, thoughtfully and attentively, but at the same time with total dedication, the irrational momentum of anonymous, impersonal and inhuman power: the power of ideology, systems, bureaucracy, artificial languages and political slogans. We must trust the voice of our conscience more than that of all abstract speculations and not invent other responsibilities than the one to which the voice calls us. We must not be ashamed that we are capable of love, friendship, solidarity, sympathy and tolerance, but just the opposite; we must set these fundamental dimensions of our humanity free from their private exile and accept them as the only genuine starting point of meaningful human community. We must be guided by our own reason and serve the truth under all circumstances as our own essential experience.

How then, in the wider context of the Velvet Revolution and its aftermath did phenomenology become a sociopolitical force?

UNLEASHING VELVET POWER – RELEASING THE LIFE WORLD

The Velvet Revolution flung everybody temporarily into an everyday world marked by flux, ambiguity and contingency. On board the revolution roller coaster, Havel worked hard through what had now become known as the Civic Forum, both to ensure its survival and to guarantee its role as the beating heart of the emerging opposition body. With his support the Civic Forum dispatched delegates all over the country with the aim of establishing brother and sister chapters. Meanwhile the revolution itself was proving to be a great spectacle. It enchanted observers and participants alike, and Havel, a master dramatist and compulsive planner of his and others' moves, climbed eagerly onto a stage already clotted with other actors. His public quest to confirm his leadership began at the famous Prague Theatre Laterna Magica. Havel chose that as the site to base the headquarters of the Civic Forum, whose inner circles began to function quickly as a government in waiting.

From the first day of assuming his presidency, Havel began experimenting with his new role as 'King of the Castle' – the presidential home was in Prague castle! He tried to transform the castle into a giant stage. From there he tried to direct a new performance – the biggest so far in his life. The play served as the supreme expression of the revolution. It displayed the newfound sense of collective awareness and solidarity, a blending of the self with the other. There was a cast of thousands of people, some famous and others previously unknown, whose performances would for a time win the hearts of the country's citizenry and attract the attention of the whole world.

Havel therefore emphasized the need to cultivate a tolerant and open civil society, in the process doing battle with the free marketer Vaclav Klaus. The latter was to significantly inhibit phenomenal transformation. So, on the one hand, Havel began to develop a brilliant modern idea: that economic actors always and everywhere go about their business and do their work only insofar as they tap into and cultivate sources of 'social capital'. A market economy, he insisted, can only function if its members are 'embedded' in a wider civil society that harbours social interaction based on such norms as trust, reliability, punctuality, honesty, friendship, resolution, the capacity for group commitment, humility and mutual recognition. Yet, on the other hand, there was no dialectical force to ultimately transcend the Havel–Klaus divide. Havel was also opposing the Klausite effects of the obsession with state-backed privatization, which were antithetical to civil society. He criticized it especially for its blindness towards the way markets tend to 'fail', in the process weakening or destroying the structures of civil society upon which they otherwise depend for their survival and growth. Meanwhile in 1992, the peaceful co-existence of two close nations, Czech and Slovak, ended. Czechoslovakia is now the name of a country from the past.

THESIS AND ANTITHESIS WITHOUT SYNTHESIS

Not only then were Havel's hopes dashed, as far as keeping Czechoslovakia together was concerned, but he was also to face stiff opposition within the Czech Republic, to 'living in the truth' in the face of global market forces. These forces were welcomed in by that other Vaclav, Vaclav Klaus, a Thatcherite, neoliberal economist who became prime minister in the 1990s. At the end of the day, the philosophical and sociopolitical impulse provided first by Husserl and Masaryk, and subsequently by Patocka and Havel, fell upon the free market economic sword. The conventionally liberal powers that be, and the overarching influence of the West, served to overpower this force from the centre.

5.6 Conclusion

The philosophy of phenomenology emerged out of the 'crisis of the European sciences' early in the 20th century. When it began to be reduced to a discrete method by the Duquesne School in America, almost a century later, it inevitably lost some of its radical socio-political character. What Husserl, Heidegger and Steiner were talking about ontologically and epistemologically has only been somewhat digested. In fact, when we come to participatory action research (see Chapter 7), we shall find a more thoroughgoing attempt to position phenomenology in the context of social innovation.

In grounding your research, you identify and immerse yourselves into a questioned phenomenon. It is one with which you want to engage because it disturbs you, moves you, calls upon you and ultimately motivates you to both investigate it further; one that stimulates you to think, feel and act upon it.

ENTERING INTO A LIFE WORLD

As a conscious human being, you always inhabit a life world; it is given in advance and experienced as a unity. The life world is the general structure, which allows objectivity and thing-hood to emerge in the different ways in which they do emerge in different cultures. There is not one single life world, but a set of overlapping worlds, beginning from the world, which is the 'home-world', and extending to other world farther away, the worlds of other cultures.

What does that mean for you as researcher? At the outset of your research you enter into your own problematic life world. You have chosen such, because you feel impelled to, because you feel called to, because the world around you is incomplete without what your research will offer.

ENGAGING WITH REALITY

The task of pursuing knowledge is not to recapitulate in the form of concepts what is given to you in some other way. It is rather to create an entirely new domain, which yields for the first time full reality. The human being is not an idle onlooker, before the pageant of the world; he is an active participant in a cosmic creative process.

As a researcher and innovator, you not only want to uncover and engage with what is really going on, beneath the surface – internally within yourself and externally in the world around you – but you want to transform it. You have come to recognize your real intentions. At this opening point in your thesis, you are called upon to describe such intentions, richly and intricately, qualitatively and poignantly, in relation to the field into which those intentions are implanted. In other words, you are called upon to lay aside your prejudices, your preconceptions and your analytical frameworks; then you enter into that world and immerse yourself in the phenomenon.

OVERLAID WITH PERSONAL MEANING AND SOCIAL SIGNIFICANCE

For you as a researcher, the challenge you ultimately face is to conduct such a phenomenological investigation in a way that has both social meaning and personal significance. The topic grows out of an intense interest in a particular area, close to your nature and culture, while also reaching out to others. That interest is provoked, outside in, by the unfilled needs that you see around you; it is also provoked inside out, by your own will and intent at this particular point of time.

To the extent that such an interest is situated in a particular time and place, as well as within you and your profession or institution, so the relational path of research takes us on to feminism.

References

1. Husserl, E. (1931). *Ideas: General Introduction to Pure Phenomenology*. W.R. Boyce Gibson, trans. New York: Humanities Press.
2. Husserl, E. (1970). *The Crisis of the European Sciences*. Evanston, IL: Northwestern University.
3. Hitzler, R. and Keller, R. (1989). 'On Sociological and Common-Sense Verstehen', *Current Sociology*, 37: 91–101.
4. Helle, H. J. (ed.) (1991). *Verstehen and Pragmatism: Essays in Interpretative Sociology*. Frankfurt: Peter Lang.
5. Truzzi, M. (1974). *Verstehen: Subjective Understanding in the Social Sciences*. Reading: Addison-Wesley.
6. Bleicher, J. (1982). *The Hermeneutic Imagination: Outline of a Positive Critique of Scientism and Sociology*. London: Routledge and Kegan Paul.
7. Ainlay, S.C. (1986). 'The Encounter with Phenomenology.' In Hunter, J.D. and Ainlay, S.C. (eds). *Making Sense of Modern Times: Peter L. Berger and the Vision of Interpretive Sociology*. London: Routledge and Kegan Paul.
8. Abercrombie, N. (1980). *Class, Structure and Knowledge*. New York: New York University Press.
9. Phillipson, M. (1972). 'Phenomenological Philosophy and Sociology.' In Filmer, P., Phillipson, M., Silverman, D. and Walsh, D. (eds). *New Directions in Sociological Theory*. Cambridge, MA: MIT Press.
10. Morris, M.B. (1975). 'Creative Sociology: Conservative or Revolutionary?' *American Sociologist*, 10: 168–78.
11. Sheets-Johnstone, M. (1996). 'An Empirical-Phenomenological Critique of the Social Construction of Infancy', *Human Studies*, 19: 1–16.
12. Darroch, V. and Silvers, R.J. (eds) (1982). *Interpretive Human Studies: An Introduction to Phenomenological Research*. Washington, DC: University Press.
13. Bentz, V.M. and Shapiro, J.J. (1998). *Mindful Inquiry in Social Research*. London: Sage.
14. Norberg-Schulz, C. (1980). *Genius Loci: Towards a Phenomenology of Architecture*. New York: Rizzoli.
15. Norberg-Schulz, C. (1963). *Intentions in Architecture*. New York: Rizzoli.
16. Husserl, *The Crisis of the European Sciences*.
17. Abram, D. (1966). *The Spell of the Sensuous*. New York: Random.
18. Van der Post, L. (1954). *The Dark Eye of Africa*. Cape Town: Lowery Press.
19. Welburn, A. (2004). *Rudolph Steiner's Philosophy and the Crisis of Contemporary Thought*. Edinburgh: Floris.
20. Husserl, *The Crisis of the European Sciences*.
21. Brazier, C. (2003). *Buddhist Psychology*. London: Constable and Robinson.
22. Biko, S. (2004). *On Steve Biko*. Cape Town: Picador.
23. Senghor, L. (1964). *African Socialism*. London: Pall Mall Press.
24. Biko, *On Steve Biko*.
25. Husserl, *The Crisis of the European Sciences*.
26. Mbigi, L. (2000). *Ubuntu*. Johannesburg: Knowledge Resources.
27. Iqbal, M. (2000). *The Reconstruction of Religious Thought in Islam*. New Delhi: Kitab Bhavan.
28. *Ibid.*
29. *Ibid.*
30. Keane, R. (1999). *Vaclav Havel*. London: Bloomsbury.
31. Havel, V. (1987). *Living in Truth*. London/Boston: Faber and Faber.

6 *From Phenomenology to Feminism*

Uncover Indigenous Knowledge

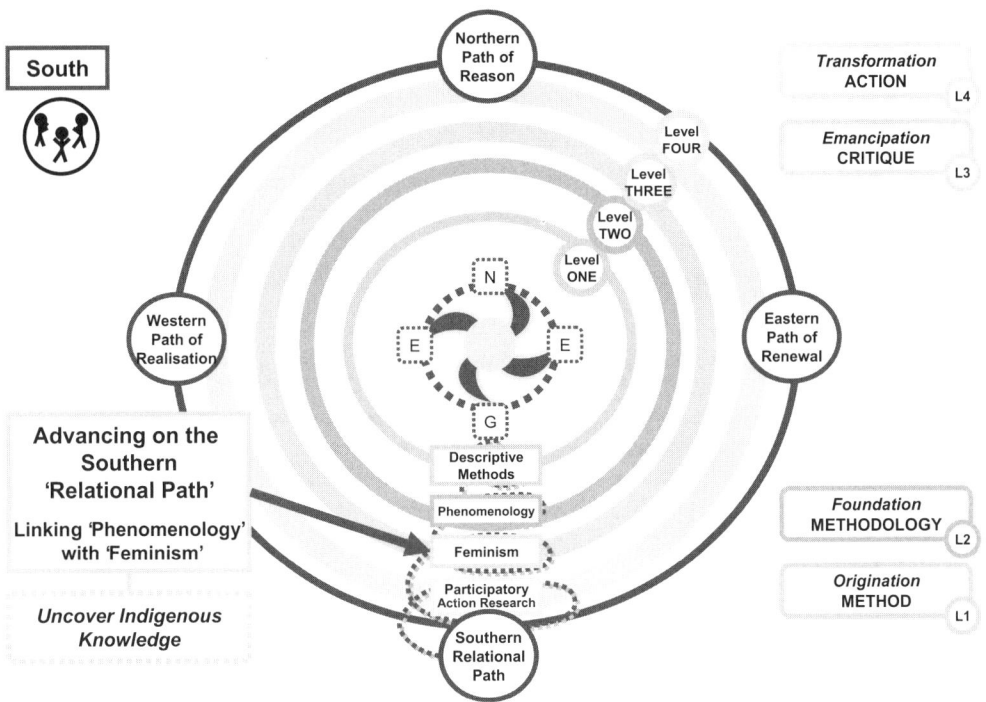

Figure 6.1   Overview Chapter 6 – Level 3/South

Summary: Feminism

- Advancing along the Southern path, we are now entering its critical realm (level 3), where we meet feminism. Feminism, originating in Europe and America in the 1950s and 1960s, could be considered as a further development of Husserl's phenomenology. Both methodologies take 'personal experience' as a starting point. However, some researchers claim that feminism takes a more realistic position towards the researched 'life world'.

- Feminism emerged as an organized movement of social theories, moral philosophies and economic and political thought, all focused on the liberation of women from a perceived subordination to men. With an increasingly broadening focus, feminism can now be regarded as a grassroots movement that does not only focus on gender issues, but seeks to cross boundaries based on social class, race, culture and religion, recently championing the cause of indigenous peoples.

- Feminist epistemology and philosophy of science studies the ways in which gender does and ought to influence our conceptions of knowledge, the knowing subject and practices of inquiry and justification. It identifies ways in which dominant conceptions and practices of knowledge systematically disadvantage women and other subordinated groups, and strives to reform these conceptions and practices so that they serve the interests of these groups.

- The central concept of feminist epistemology is that of a situated knower, and hence of situated knowledge: knowledge that reflects the particular perspectives of the subject. Further key tenets of feminist research are that it aims to create social change, that it sees knowledge as a tool for liberation (not domination), that it strives to represent human diversity and sees itself as complementary to an androcentric perspective.

- The ontological claims of feminism are that both the natural and social worlds are socially constructed, and that these worlds are constructed differently by people who, in different locations, have different life experiences, for example men and women. Conventional dualisms such as fact/value, objective/subjective, reason/emotion and the separation of the knower and the known are rejected as part of androcentric epistemology.

- Introducing global variations of feminism, we focus in this chapter on Catherine Hoppers' *Indigenous Knowledge Systems*. For Hoppers, any dynamic knowledge system has to evolve through the continuance of traditional knowledge and contemporary innovations, and this should be pursued by individuals as well as communities. The present knowledge framework, however, lets knowledge flow in one direction only and excludes indigenous knowledge.

- Hoppers' proposal that we legitimize diverse and, especially, indigenous knowledge systems and the one we connect with the feminist case, introduced at the end of this chapter, is the story of the Australian aborigines. Often called 'the oldest people of the world', they managed to build the world's longest-lasting sustainable society, even while, in modern times, they were persecuted by immigrant white populations. Anthropologists and contemporary investigators of indigenous knowledge systems acknowledge their ability to keep knowledge alive through a strong network of relationships (within their community, among communities, to ancestors, nature and animals) and a simultaneous focus on the outer, material (masculine) and the inner, immaterial (feminine) world.

6.1 Orientation to Feminism

ENTERING THE THIRD LEVEL OF THE SOUTHERN RELATIONAL PATH

We now turn from the first and second to the third level of our Integral Research framework, from descriptive methods and methodology ('phenomenology') to critique ('feminism'). As we thereby progressively broaden our research base, so our research points ever more towards social innovation. What exactly happens in this process?

If you engage in feminism, you build on prior foundations. As such you have (in the first level) grounded your research in a descriptive approach to a problematic life world. There, you have described a qualitative phenomenon with which you have chosen to engage, including your relationship with it.

Subsequently (in level two), you drew on phenomenology as a distinct methodology. You deepened and broadened your involvement with the questioned phenomenon, now more purposefully articulating the qualitative character of your research. As such you have covered the first two levels of the Southern relational path of your research project.

However, as a would-be social innovator, you will need to span the third level, and you now move into critical terrain. The major critical methodologies, representing together the field of emancipation, are:

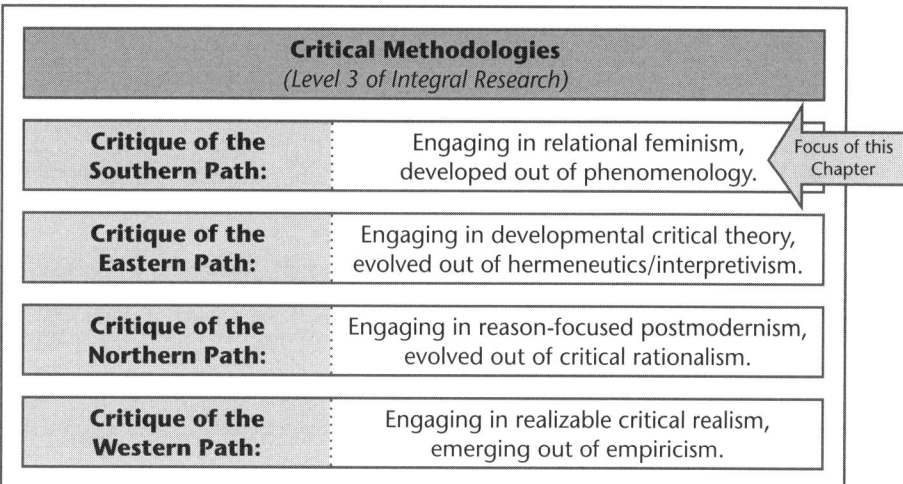

The path of this chapter is the Southern one; hence we are now engaging with feminism. Let us first retrace what feminism is all about.

ORIGINS OF FEMINISM

Josephine Donovan identifies early liberal feminism as a daughter of the Enlightenment. Thinkers like Mary Wollstonecraft and Sarah Grimké provided an 'image of a woman as a rational, responsible agent; one who is able, if given a chance to take care of herself, to further her own possibilities.'[1]

These early thinkers shared a belief in a combination of relationality and rationality; a belief that both genders are ontologically the same; the belief that critical thinking is an effective way to transform society; the view that an individual is an isolated entity who operates as a rational independent agent.[2]

Those were the early thinkers. Feminism can now be described as an organized movement of social theories, moral philosophies, economic and political thought, all focused on the liberation of women from a perceived subordination to men. Many feminists are concerned with practices and social, political and economic inequalities that discriminate against women. Some have argued that gendered and sexed identities, even 'man' and 'woman', are socially constructed.

Feminists may disagree over the sources of inequality, how to attain equality, and the extent to which gender and gender-based identities should be questioned and critiqued. Liberal feminists believe the women's liberation movement revolves around the equality of sexes, and that biological sex should not be the only factor in shaping a person's social identity, sociopolitical or economic rights. Radical feminists would also argue that feminism is about ending domination or elitism in society. Modern feminist political activists commonly campaign for women's human right to bodily integrity and autonomy on matters such as reproductive rights, including the right to abortion, access to contraception and quality prenatal care; for protection from violence within a domestic partnership.

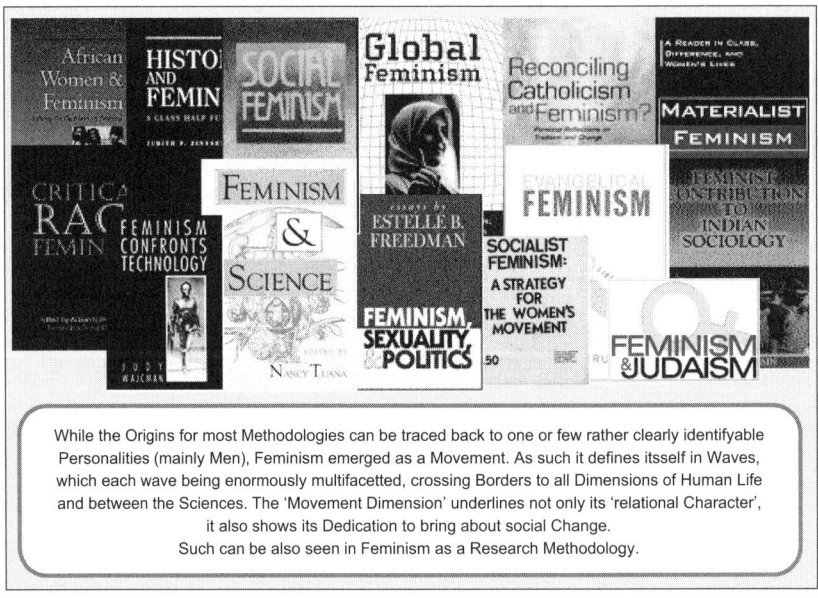

Figure 6.2 Multifaceted Feminism

Sources: Image 1: Frauensolidaritaet.org http://www.frauensolidaritaet.org/. Image 2: Language in India http://www.languageinindia.com/. Image 3: Penn State Press http://www.psupress.org/. Image 4: Faith and Gender http://faithandgender.wordpress.com/. Image 5: Shakespeare and Sons http://www.shakes.cz/. Image 6: Source: NYU Press http://www.nyupress.org/. Image 7: Amazon http://www.amazon.com. Image 8: Africa world Press http://www.africaworldpressbooks.com. Image 9: Amazon http://www.amazon.com. Image 10: Aish.com http://www.aish.com/. Image 11: Amazon http://www.amazon.com. Image 12: Campus Bookstore http://www.campusbookstore.com/. Image 13: Duke University http://library.duke.edu/

Many feminists today regard feminism as a grassroots movement that seeks to cross boundaries based on social class, race, culture and religion. They also argue that an effective feminist movement should address both universal issues, such as rape, incest, and prostitution, and culturally specific issues relevant to the women of the society in question, such as female genital cutting in some parts of Africa and the Middle East and 'glass ceiling' practices that impede women's advancement in developed economies. Feminism also explores subjects including patriarchy, stereotyping, sexual objectification and oppression.

FEMINISM'S MANY FORMS

A variety of different feminist ideologies have emerged, in waves over the latter part of the 20th century. While the first wave were deeply engaged with women's issues per se, the second and third waves became more concerned with marginalized groups in general.

THE INFLUENCE OF GENDER ON KNOWLEDGE AND KNOWLEDGE CREATION

Feminist epistemology and philosophy of science studies the ways in which gender does and ought to influence our conceptions of knowledge, the knowing subject, and practices of inquiry and justification. It identifies ways in which dominant conceptions and practices of knowledge attribution, acquisition and justification systematically disadvantage women and other subordinated groups, and strives to reform these conceptions and practices so that they serve the interests of these groups. Various practitioners of feminist epistemology and philosophy of science argue that dominant knowledge practices disadvantage women in the following ways:

- by excluding them from inquiry;
- by denying them epistemic authority;
- by denigrating their 'feminine' cognitive styles and modes of knowledge;
- by producing theories of women that represent them as inferior, deviant, or significant only in the ways they serve male interests;
- by producing theories of social phenomena that render women's activities and interests, or gendered power relations, invisible;
- by producing knowledge that is not useful for people in subordinate positions, or that reinforces gender and other social hierarchies.

Feminist epistemologists trace these failures to flawed conceptions of knowledge, knowers, objectivity and scientific methodology. They offer diverse accounts of how to overcome these failures. They also aim to explain why the entry of women and feminist scholars into different academic disciplines, especially in biology and the social sciences, has generated new questions, theories and methods, show how gender has played a causal role in these transformations, and defend these changes as cognitive, not just social, advances.

In summary, the central concept of feminist epistemology is that of a situated knower, and hence of situated knowledge: knowledge that reflects the particular perspectives of the subject. Feminist philosophers are interested in how gender situates knowing subjects.

Based on that introduction, let us look at the key tenets of feminism.

6.2 Feminism – Key Tenets: From Social Change to Natural Inclusiveness

Feminism – Key Tenets	
①	You aim to create social change.
②	You see knowledge as a tool for liberation not domination.
③	Feminist research strives to represent human diversity.
④	Feminist research complements the androcentric (masculine) perspective.
⑤	As a researcher you as a person are included …
⑥	… and so is nature.

① YOU AIM TO CREATE SOCIAL CHANGE

At the heart of much feminist research is the goal, even the obligation, of bringing about change in the condition of women. Even those feminists who don't directly speak of change in the condition of women have social change at the foundation of their goals as researchers. By and large, the international feminist community is committed to the dual vision of research as firstly benefiting the welfare of women and secondly furthering social science knowledge. For example, in delving into the life of an African-American female teacher, feminist researcher Maenette Nee Benham advocates a researcher's role in 'giving voice' to ethnic minority women through narrative or a retelling of their stories, both to empower them and to learn from their experiences. Whether a researcher recommends explicit policy recommendations or less overtly offers social implications of his or her findings, this focus on creating social change appears to be a theme across much of feminist thought.

② YOU SEE KNOWLEDGE AS A TOOL FOR LIBERATION NOT DOMINATION

Feminism takes a close look at language, gender and power. Language is the medium in which we conduct our social lives and create our symbolic existence; gender is the fundamental dichotomous figure of thought characterizing our public as well as private lives; power entangles all of us in its constantly reinvented ruses and snares, which some scientists regard as the fine-grained structure that holds society together. The feminists add the gender dimension to considering the impact of power relations. They regard gender relations as problematic since they are associated with conditions of dominance, inequality, stress and conflict and argue that gender relations are socially constructed, which means they are not given by nature, nor are they inevitable; rather they are the result of sociocultural and historical conditions and can be radically altered by human action.

③ FEMINIST RESEARCH STRIVES TO REPRESENT HUMAN DIVERSITY

Feminism offers new ways of viewing human values, decision-making and the very nature of human experience – beginning with fundamental differences between men and women. For instance, Frances K. Stage, professor of higher education from the University of New York, asserts that scholars have noted that women's judgement and orientation to work differ from those of men. For example, research on gender differences that contrasts the male and female normative ways of 'seeing' and 'knowing' has come (for example, in the case of research professor Mary Field Belenky from the University of Vermont) to the following conclusion:

- *Men*: the individual is positioned in a hierarchical social order, seeking power and accomplishment (status); independence is a priority value; the male perspective on self and others is: 'we are separate and different'.
- *Women*: the individual situated in a network of connections, seeking friendship; intimacy and interdependence are priority values; central to the female perspective is the idea that 'we're close and the same'.

Another feminist criticism of mainstream androcentric research is that, when it does attempt to include women as important and unique from men, they are viewed as a homogeneous group. Across the works of many researchers, *feminism* focuses on differences within the community of women. Within the feminist paradigm, there exists a broad diversity of points of view, based on individual and group experiences in society as members of different racial, cultural, and economic groups.

In struggling with this goal of representing human diversity, some contemporary feminist researchers have come to view diversity as a 'new criterion for feminist research excellence' and advocate for the inclusion of diversified samples (by race, economic class, sexual preference) in all studies. Others assert that feminist researchers can neither ethically nor successfully study women whose racial, cultural or social background is different from their own.

④ FEMINIST RESEARCH COMPLEMENTS THE ANDROCENTRIC (MASCULINE) PERSPECTIVE

Something that sets feminist research apart from other approaches to social inquiry is its ontological claim that the reality depicted by much of social science knowledge is incomplete and fundamentally distorted. The world described by many studies of human and organizational behaviour is dominated by an androcentric worldview: that means that it communicates the male experience and is based on male assumptions and perspectives. Females – their experience, assumptions, and perspectives – often have been excluded as subjects of study, as researchers and as interpreters of results.

The androcentric perspective in and of itself is not a problem when the researcher acknowledges that women are missing in the study and, thus, in the interpretation of results. The problem is significant, however, when androcentric research is described as representative of the universe under study and when findings are presented as universally true. Many feminist researchers propose that social science dominated by theories and concepts emerging solely from a male consciousness may be irrelevant for the female experience and inadequate for explaining female behaviour.

At the most basic level, then, feminist research simply attempts to incorporate into social reality the female perspective. Further, feminist criticism of established research often stems from a distrust of the power and perspective of androcentrism in research and society, not from a rejection of traditional methods of inquiry. As such, some argue that *feminism* is a perspective rather than a method in itself .

⑤ AS A RESEARCHER YOU AS A PERSON ARE INCLUDED …

Feminism is seen as a science in which no rigid boundary separates the subject of knowledge (the knower) and the natural object of that knowledge. In contrast to much of mainstream research, which generally seeks to attain value neutrality, feminism proposes often a 'metabolism of subject and field', seeing researcher and researched as one organism. Feminist researchers will often integrate personal experiences into their research. Personal experiences are not perceived as tainting the methods and results of research. Rather, many feminists, such as Shulamit Reinharz, professor of sociology and founder of the Women's Studies Research Center at the University of Brandeis University in the US, view it as serving to validate their research. Reinharz quotes her colleague Marie Mies: 'Feminist women must deliberately … integrate their repressed, unconscious female subjectivity, that is, their own experience of oppression and discrimination into the research process.'[3]

For example, one of America's leading black feminists, sociology professor Patricia Hill Collins, describes her position in her research as very personal: 'I often use the pronoun "our" instead of "their" when referring to African-American women, a choice that embeds me in the group I am studying instead of distancing me from it. In addition, I occasionally place my own concrete experiences in the text.'[4]

Feminist researchers may use these personal experiences to inform their research questions, to guide their involvement in the research process. However, while the subjective–objective relational character of the research becomes more distinct, the close relationship this establishes between the researcher and the subject of the research has also led to ongoing discussion in the feminist research community about how to walk that fine line and work out the tension between objectivity and subjectivity.

⑥ … AND SO IS NATURE

Feminism can finally be understood as a science where the subject–object split is not used to legitimize the domination of nature. Nature itself is conceptualized as active rather than passive, a dynamic complex totality requiring human co-operation and understanding, rather than a dead mechanism requiring only manipulation and control.

That links with US cultural anthropologist Riane Eisler's latest work *The Real Wealth of Nations*,[5] where she proposes a new caring economics that takes into account the full spectrum of economic activities – from the life-sustaining activities of the household to the life enriching activities of carers and communities, to the life-supporting process of nature. Eisler demonstrates how our values are distorted by the economic double standard that devalues anything stereotypically associated with women and femininity; reveals how current economic models are based on a deep-seated culture of domination; and shows how human needs would be better served by economic models based on caring.

For American developmental economist and social activist David Korten the defining choice we have is between two contrasting models of organizing human affairs: empire and earth community.[6] Empire features 'organization by domination', which has been a feature of male-dominated societies for some 5,000 years. Racism, sexism and classicism, for him, have been characteristics of such empire. Earth community, which features 'organization by partnership', a more feminine approach, unleashes the potential for human co-operation and allocates the productive surplus of society to growing the generative potential of the whole.

We now turn to feminist methodology in depth.

6.3 Feminist Methodology in Depth

PHENOMENOLOGICAL TO FEMINIST ONTOLOGY AND EPISTEMOLOGY

As we start to have a closer look at feminism as a research methodology, we remain aware of its close alignment with phenomenology. This is generally true, when we look at feminism from a historical perspective and particularly when we see how this historical dimension has been reanimated within our integral research framework.

You may recall that for Husserl, phenomenology was born out of a 'crisis of the European sciences'. He saw in the 1930s that the positivist approach to science could be linked to the totalitarianism that he saw breaking out around him. Husserl was diagnosing what he considered to be the disastrous social consequences of a science, which espoused reductive positivism and naïve empiricism. He also opposed what he regarded as the misguided, deformed rationalism as a consequence of the Enlightenment, which settled for a naïve objectivism, and did not notice the very subjectivity which made genuine rational objectivity and creativity.

The wave of feminism then, emerging in Europe and America in the 1950s and 1960s, could be considered as a further, reformative development of Husserl's phenomenology. Both methodologies take 'personal experience' as a starting point. However, some researchers claim, that in phenomenology, the experience is more important than the external happening that is experienced. A phenomenologist gets therefore sometimes criticized as idealist, where the internal experience is the matter of contemplation. Feminism, on the other hand, focuses on what happens external to the impacted entity: it can hence be called a more realistic position than phenomenology.[7]

Feminism also gained power and influence by being more closely aligned with the environmental movement, as David Abram's 'eco-feminism' (see Chapter 5) has indicated. As described by the social philosopher Richard Tarnas, in his *Passion of the Western Mind*, feminism heralds a complete ground-shift in our societal consciousness. For Tarnas, feminism is the most important movement of our times.

The Western intellectual tradition has been produced and canonized almost entirely by men, and informed mainly by male perspectives. The 'man' of the Western tradition has been a questing masculine hero, a Promethean biological and metaphysical rebel who has constantly sought freedom and progress for himself, and who has constantly striven to differentiate himself from and control the matrix out of which he emerged. This masculine proposition in the evolution of the Western mind, though largely unconscious, has been not only characteristic of that evolution, but essential to it. For the evolution of the Western mind has been driven by a heroic impulse to forge an autonomous rational human self by separating it from the primordial unity of nature. The fundamental religious, scientific, and philosophical perspectives of Western culture have all been affected by this decisive masculinity – beginning four millennia ago with the great patriarchal nomadic conquests in Greece and the Levant over the ancient matriarchal structures, and visible in the West's patriarchal religion from Judaism, its rationalist philosophy from Greece, its objectivist science from modern Europe. All of these have served the cause of evolving the autonomous human will and intellect; the transcendent self, the independent individual ego, the self-determining human being in its uniqueness, separateness, and freedom. But to do this the masculine mind has repressed the feminine.

This separation calls forth a longing for a reunion with that which has been lost – especially after the masculine heroic quest has been pressed to its utmost one-sided extreme in the consciousness of the modern mind.

Man now faces the existential crisis of being a solitary ego thrown into an ultimately unknowable universe. And he faces the psychological and biological crisis of living in a world that has come to be shaped in such a way that it precisely matches his world view – in a man made environment that is increasingly mechanistic, atomized, soulless, and self destructive. The crisis of modern man is an essentially masculine crisis, and I believe that the resolution is already now occurring in the tremendous emergence of the feminine in our culture: visible not only in the rise of feminism, the growing empowerment of women, and the widespread opening up to feminine values by both men and women, but also in the increasing sense of unity with the planet and all forms of nature on it, in the increasing awareness of the ecological, in the growing embrace of the human community, in the accelerating collapse of long standing ideological and political barriers separating the world's peoples, in the deepening recognition of the value and necessity of partnership, pluralism and the interplay of many perspectives.[8]

As Carl-Gustav Jung[9] prophesised, an epochal shift is taking place in the contemporary psyche. This shift is about a reconciliation between the two great polarities, between the long-dominant but now alienated masculine and the long-suppressed but now ascending feminine. And this dramatic development is not just compensation, not just a return of the repressed. The driving impulse of the West's masculine consciousness has been its dialectic quest not only to realize itself, to forge its own autonomy, but also finally to recover its connection with the whole, to come to terms with the great feminine principle in life, with the mystery of life, of nature, of soul. But to achieve this reintegration of the repressed feminine, the masculine must undergo a sacrifice, an ego death. The Western mind must be willing to open itself to a reality, the nature of which could shatter its more established beliefs about itself and the world. This is where the real act of heroism is going to be. A threshold must now be crossed, a threshold demanding a courageous act of faith, of imagination, of trust in a larger and more complex reality; a threshold, moreover, demanding an act of unflinching self-discernment. And this is the great challenge of our time, the evolutionary imperative for the masculine to see through and overcome its hubris and one-sidedness, to own its unconscious shadow, to choose to enter into a fundamentally different relationship of mutuality with the feminine.

We seem to be witnessing the labour pains of a new reality being born, a new form of human existence, a 'child' that would be the fruit of this great archetypal marriage, and that would bear within itself all its antecedents in a new form. Tarnas therefore would affirm those indispensable ideals expressed by the supporters of the feminist, ecological, archaic and other counter-cultural and multicultural perspectives. But he would also wish to affirm all those who have valued and sustained the central Western tradition, for he believes that this tradition – the entire trajectory from the Greek epic poets and Hebrew prophets on, the long and intellectual struggle from Socrates and Plato and Paul and Augustine to Galileo and Descartes and Kant and Feud – that this stupendous Western project should be seen as a necessary and noble part of a great dialectic, and not simply rejected as an imperialist-chauvinist plot. Not only has this tradition achieved that fundamental differentiation and autonomy of the human which alone could allow the possibility of a larger synthesis, it has also painstakingly prepared the way for its own self-transcendence. Perhaps the end of 'man' himself is at hand. But man is not a goal. Man is something that must be overcome – and fulfilled, in the embrace of the feminine.

We now turn to the more specific attributes of feminism as a research methodology.

FEMINIST RESEARCH EPISTEMOLOGY AND METHODOLOGY

The Natural and Social Worlds are Socially Reconstructed

The ontological claims of feminism are that both the natural and social worlds are socially constructed, and that these worlds are constructed differently by people who, in different locations, have different life experiences, for example men and women. Feminist epistemology, moreover, substitutes women's experiences for men's. Conventional dualisms such as fact/value, objective/subjective, reason/emotion and the separation of the knower and the known are rejected as part of androcentric epistemology.

Many feminist theorists have argued that women have different conceptions of the basic constituents of reality, different assumptions about their own relationships to the natural world, and different views of the importance and connectedness of other people. They are generally more ready to access their own emotions and feelings, and have distinct ways of assessing moral responsibility, based on a context of human relationships rather than abstract rights of isolated individuals.

It has been suggested[10] that the preconditions of a feminist science would be:

Feminist Science: Preconditions
Feminism as a science in which no rigid boundary separates the subject of knowledge (the knower) and the natural object of that knowledge.
Feminism as a science where the subject–object split is not used to legitimize the domination of nature.
Feminism as a science where nature itself is conceptualized as active rather than passive, a dynamic complex totality requiring human co-operation and understanding rather than a dead mechanism, requiring only manipulation and control.

In such feminist imaginings, the scientist is not seen as an impersonal authority outside and above nature and human concerns, but simply as a person whose thoughts and feelings, logical capacities and intuitions are all relevant and involved in the process of discovery. Such scientists would actively seek ways of negotiating the distances now established between knowledge and its uses, between thought and feeling, between objectivity and subjectivity, between expert and expert, and would seek to use knowledge as a tool of liberation rather than domination. As such, two types of objectivity have been distinguished.

Dynamic objectivity aims at a form of knowledge that grants to the world around us its independent integrity but does so in a way that remains cognizant of, and indeed relies on, our connectivity with that world. This dynamic objectivity is – not unlike empathy – a form of knowledge of other persons that draws explicitly on the commonality of feelings and experiences in order to enrich one's understanding of another in his or her own right. By contrast, static objectivity is the pursuit of knowledge that begins with the severance of subject from object rather than aiming at the disentanglement of one from the other.

What is Wrong with Conventional Science?

Feminism has provided a collection of themes about what is wrong with conventional science, and what kind of social science will overcome these difficulties, that can be summed up in the following way:

Feminism – Core Themes	
Metabolism of Subject and Field	Deals with the problem of objectivity, proposing the notion of 'dynamic objectivity' or of the 'metabolism of subject and field' as if they are one organism.
New Materialism	Deals with the 'New Materialism' in which knowledge is to be grounded in personal experience.
Socio-historical Location	Deals with the problem of the socio-historical location of the researcher.
Reflexive Nature of Social Inquiry	Deals with the reflexive nature of social inquiry, whereby the researcher needs to reflect, continually, on him- or herself.
Social Sciences as New Paradigm	Proposes that the social sciences, not physics, should be the paradigm for all sciences.
Nature is Active and Complex	Deals with the recognition that nature is active and complex, adopting an ecological or open systems approach.
Knowledge for Liberation	Knowledge should be used as a tool for liberation not domination.

As we can see, all these themes are couched in critical-emancipatory language, albeit that the particular focus on nature leads to a close affinity between feminism and the environmental movement. Moreover, the focus on gender, sometime alongside of race and class, is particular to feminism, afro-centricism and cultural studies, as radical discourses.

Language, Gender and Power

Three dimensions which are fundamental to all of the above, are language, gender and power. Language is the medium in which we conduct our social lives and create our symbolic existence; gender is the fundamental dichotomous figure of thought characterizing our public as well as private lives; power entangles all of us in its constantly reinvented ruses and snares, which some scientists (for example, Max Weber) regard as the fine-grained structure that holds society together. The feminists add the gender dimension to considering the impact of power relations that is also of central concern to the critical theorists and the postmodernists. Allowing for considerable variations and conflicts within the feminist movement as a whole, three central elements can be said to prevail:

- First, gender represents an essential theme in the attempt to understand virtually all social relations, institutions and processes.
- Secondly, gender relations are seen as problematic since they are associated with conditions of dominance, inequality, stress and conflict.
- Thirdly, gender relations are regarded as socially constructed, which means they are not given by nature, nor are they inevitable; rather they are the result of sociocultural and historical conditions and can be radically altered by human action.

It is felt, that feminism could make a contribution to social science in the shape of a critique and re-evaluation of existing theories, most of which contain gender bias. Another of feminism's contributions has been to indicate neglected areas such as sexual harassment in the workplace, or to show how elusive conditions, such as practices of birth control, can contribute to a great variety of social structures. A third contribution of a more general theoretical kind concerns the development of new ways of theorising. In Richard Tarnas' words:

A new feminist paradigm would place women and their lives, and gender, in a central place in understanding social relations as a whole. Such a paradigm would not only pose new questions about women and gender but also help to create a more complex and adequate account of industrial, capitalist society. A feminist paradigm would also contain a methodology that produces knowledge for, rather than of, women in their many varieties and situations.[11]

FEMINIST RESEARCH METHODOLOGY AND METHOD

Relations Between Researcher and Researched

Feminism involves above all a close and mutual relationship between yourself as researcher and the research subject. That relationship is seen as critically important, and is evoked within research through descriptive methods. Unless a relationship of trust is developed between your self and the other, you can have no confidence that your research on people's lives and consciousness accurately represents what is significant to them in their everyday life worlds, and thus has validity in that sense. Procedures and formal methods are toned down. The research is characterized by an emancipatory knowledge interest, and is often oriented towards everyday life, where there are pronounced interests in ethics and solidarity.

Emotion, in feminist methodology, is the inevitable and important part of the researcher's motivation and choice of orientation, and of the specific way in which your research is handled.

Just as observation directs, shapes, and partially defines emotion, so too emotion shapes, directs and even partially defines observation. Observation is not simply a passive process of absorbing impressions or recording stimuli: it is an activity of selection and interpretation. What is selected and how it is interpreted are influenced by emotional attitudes. On the level of individual observation, this influence has always been apparent to commonsense, which notes that we remark very different features of the world when we are happy, depressed, fearful, or confident.[12]

It follows that self-reflection and the critical self-analysis of feelings are an important part of your research process. It does not mean that emotions should be given a more central position than observation, reason or action; nor should they be second to each of these. Martin Heidegger strongly emphasized the inseparability of reason and emotion. Theodor Adorno, the critical theorist, wrote that the highest objectification of the mind is nurtured by human urges and without these no insight would be produced. Even Karl Popper acknowledged that 'without passion we can achieve nothing – certainly not in science'. What does this imply for a feminist research method?

Descriptive Method to Discourse Analysis

An important research method, which has emerged in recent years, is discourse analysis (DA). As we shall see even more explicitly in Chapter 13 for postmodernism it puts great emphasis on modes of expression. *DA is interested in the discursive level – all forms of writing and speech – as well as the relational, and emphasizes diversity rather than seeking to reduce variations.* Consequently DA, a variation on basic descriptive method, which is as applicable to feminism as to postmodernism, pays less attention to the 'underlying reality' to which critical realism pays so much attention, and pays more attention to describing modes of expression, and indeed discourse, that present themselves to you. To that extent, feminism is influenced not only by phenomenology but also by postmodernism.

Discourse analysis claims that through language people engage in constructing the social world that is establishing a relationship, as subjects, with it, as an object. There are three aspects to this. Firstly, people actively create accounts on a basis of previously existing linguistic resources. Secondly, they are continually and actively involving some of the infinite words and meaning constructions available, and in rejecting others. Thirdly, the chosen construction has its consequences: the mode of expression has an effect, it influences ideas, generates responses. DA starts from the following assumptions then:

Discourse Analysis: Core Assumptions
Language is used for a variety of functions.
Language is both constructive and destructive.
The same phenomenon can be described in different ways.
Consequently there will be considerable variations in accounts.
There is no foolproof way of determining which is accurate.
The constructive and flexible ways in which language is used should be a central object of study.

In the final analysis, interview statements, written documents and spontaneous talk can be described and interpreted at three levels:

1. *Discursive level:* whereby different people, including yourself, in different contexts express themselves.
2. *Ideational level:* at which you speak of your conceptions, values, beliefs, ideas, meanings and fantasies.
3. *Level of action and social conditions:* where your research aims to say something solid about relations, behaviours, social patterns, structures 'out there'.

As you can see, such a feminist, discourse oriented approach, pays much more attention to the subjectivity and inter-subjectivity of your approach to, and interpretation of, say, an interview or case study, than an empirical approach would involve.

We now turn to a global variation of feminism, in this case focusing on indigenous knowledge systems.

6.4 Global Variations of Feminism: The Example of 'Indigenous Knowledge Systems'

For Ugandan-born Swedish-bred Catherine Hoppers, an international educational expert and visiting professor at Stockholm University, any dynamic knowledge system has to evolve through the continuance of traditional knowledge and contemporary innovations, and this should be pursued by individuals as well as communities. The aim is to connect creative people engaged in generating local solutions that are authentic and accountable, thus facilitating people-to-people learning.[13]

Knowledge then is a universal heritage and a universal resource. It is diverse and varied. The acquisition of Western knowledge has been and still is invaluable to all, but, on its own, it has been, for Hoppers, incapable of responding adequately in the face of massive and intensifying disparities, and rapid depletion of the earth's natural resources.

In that context a return to indigenous knowledge, albeit cast in contemporary light, is all-important.

By way of definition, the word 'indigenous' refers to the root, something natural or innate. It is an integral part of culture. The ideal of knowledge as espoused within this framework, for instance, is not just about woven baskets, handicrafts for tourists or traditional dances. Rather it is about excavating the technologies behind these practices and artefacts, recasting the potentialities they represent in a context of democratic, equitable participation for community, national and global development in real time.

The issue of indigenous knowledge systems (IKSs) posits profound challenges to contemporary practice, including:

- knowledge-generation and legitimation processes, such as the type of knowledge being generated in scientific institutions, as well as in corporate research laboratories;
- the social and economic survival of 'resource rich but economically poor' local communities;
- the need to explore deeper the interface between epistemology, diversity and democracy;
- the need to facilitate the active re-appropriation and authentication of IKSs into current, living research work;
- subjecting to direct interrogation the discourses behind the semantic shift that turned the illiterate from someone ignorant of the alphabet to an absolute illiterate;
- realizing the fundamental intolerance of modern science towards the legitimacy of folk or ethnic knowledge, coupled with our inability to develop an ecologically coded society;
- moving the frontiers of discourse and understanding in the sciences as a whole, opening new moral and cognitive spaces within which constructive dialogue and engagement for sustainable development can take place;
- finally developing a clearer sense of the ethical and judicial domain within which science works, and to begin to understand the political economy of 'othering'.

Indigenous knowledge systems are characterized by their embeddedness in the cultural web and history of a people, consisting of tangible and intangible aspects that:

- have exchange value and that, with support, can be transformed into enterprises or industries;
- perpetuate social, cultural, scientific, philosophical and technological knowledge that can provide the basis for an integrated and inclusive knowledge framework.

It is in turn the re-appropriation of this heritage that may provide new clues and directions as to the visions of human society, human relations, sustainable development, poverty reduction and scientific development, all of which cannot be resolved using the existing ethos of the Western framework alone.

The focus on IKSs then aims at fostering understanding of the interface between culture and science, culture and technology, sustainable human development and the comprehensive development of human, material and scientific resources, in a manner that gives cognisance to the wisdom and authenticity of traditional practices, institutions and knowledges.

Moreover, it will provide a new basis for the generation of knowledge and a new consciousness in protecting intellectual property and other rights of those who have been ignored or taken for granted for so long.

TOWARDS A HOLISTIC KNOWLEDGE FRAMEWORK

Hoppers goes in her work beyond the gender issue of feminism. By proposing a holistic knowledge framework, she builds strongly on the female dimension of relating, integrating, caring and love. For her, the challenge of creating an integrated and holistic knowledge framework for societal progress and development is not only real but also urgent, seeking to make whole that which was partial, incomplete, in large measure stunted and therefore also stunting. A dialogic search for integration is incompatible with legacies in which one group consistently deposits ideas into others. Dialogue cannot exist in the absence of profound love of the world and of people. The search therefore is for a framework that will affirm, not deny, the integrity of all human beings; a framework that by underscoring the notion of 'agential citizenry' can posit people not as perpetual victims or pawns, but as knowing subjects, irrespective of the knowledge frameworks within which they are located.

As governments seek to transform their societies and empower local communities, the challenge becomes one of how to 'operationalize empowerment' itself in a context where diverse knowledges are barely tolerated and exist only in sufferance and subjective deference to a mainstream, essentially Western form of knowledge. All in all, for Hoppers, a profound cultural imbalance has resulted in the systems of academic, political and economic institutions we see around us.

Instead the contingence of the social and the historical, as well as the affirmation of the multiplicity of worlds and forms of life, need to be recognized and affirmed. De-centred understanding of knowledge systems and other forms of universal conscience are emerging outside the exclusivist frameworks of Western modernity. The total effect of these trends is to bring to bear a forceful return of philosophy to the social sciences, and to the evolution of emergent 'open' non-linear and flowing spaces of information. Such is the strength of the new demands that it would appear that the legitimacy of the social sciences no longer rests in the obligation to produce objective knowledge alone, but also in the identification of a nexus between the development of knowledge and the transformation of societies.

Rural people's knowledge and modern scientific knowledge can be seen complementary in their strengths and weaknesses. Combined they can achieve what neither would alone. But for this complementarity to occur, outside professionals have to step in humility down off their pedestals and sit down, listen and learn. The present framework in which knowledge flows in one direction only – downwards – is not only disempowering but also demeaning.

Hopper's focus on indigenous knowledge, and the marginalized status of indigenous peoples, and their respective knowledge systems, brings us directly to the following case: the hitherto downtrodden, and knowledge-wise unrecognized Australian aborigines. Often called 'the world's oldest people', their concept of relationality included their own and other communities, the ancestors, the landscape and animals. Their story –

though commonly not very well known – is a remarkable proof for the significance of the relational, feminine dimension for the building of a sustainable community and society, in tune with human nature and with nature in large, and offering a new–old sustainable route for mainstream Western' society to follow.

6.5 Feminism in Practice: The World's Oldest People

RECOGNIZE INTANGIBLE VALUE

Sveiby and Skuthorpe have recently teamed up to explore the potential for modern-day knowledge creation and new-found sustainability of Australian aborigines. For Tex Skuthorpe, an indigenous aborigine: 'Our land is our knowledge, we walk on the knowledge, we dwell in the knowledge, we live in our thesaurus, we walk in our bible every day of our lives. Everything is knowledge. So we don't need a word for it'. In fact, for his colleague, the Swede Karl Sveiby, the Australian aboriginal society's model for sustainability has the longest proven track record on earth.[14]

The most striking feature of the particular Nhunggabarra aboriginal society to which Tex belongs is its *knowledge-based economy*. Because food and handmade tools were the only production scientists and economists have recognized and have been able to measure, they have long dismissed the aboriginal economy of producing very little of value. What they have dismissed is more than half of the aboriginal economy: the very high production of *intangible value,* such as education, knowledge, art, law, entertainment, medicine, spiritual ceremonies, peacekeeping and social welfare. The aboriginal people created the world's first systematic approach to eco-farming, and indeed intangible trade.

The Nhunggabarra did not worship any gods – not even nature spirits. Instead, for them every rock and every landform, every plants and every animal, had its own consciousness, just as people did. Everything was alive. Spiritual life was much more significant than material life for the Australian aboriginal people. Instead of putting their surplus energy into squeezing more food out of the land, aborigines expended it on intangibles: spiritual, intellectual and artistic activities. They carried their palaces on their backs, their cathedrals were built in their minds and they felt no need to glorify human heroes. It is in the mind and the creativity of the spirit – in the intangible rather than the tangible artefacts – that aboriginal society stands out.

The Nhunggabarra and other aboriginal peoples conceived time not as a movement from past to future, but as a continuous channelling of consciousness from an intangible and tacit to a tangible and explicit expression. The rock in the landscape was the ongoing tangible expression of the rock's consciousness in the sky world, as it had been since the time of creation. It was the same with people, animals and vegetation. The Nhunggabarra also did not make a distinction between time and space in their language. The suffix *baa* means both 'space of' and 'time of'. Today of course time is regarded by quantum physicists as part of a space–time continuum, a concept that the West required an Einstein to discover.

SUSTAINING THE EARTH

The mission of the Nhunggabarra people was to sustain the earth, to keep totems alive and to keep themselves alive. The Australian landscape was to a large degree an aboriginal artefact created by thousands of years of sustaining the earth. In that context people and animals were the same. In particular, a person felt responsible for his or her own totem animal. In a hunting ceremony, the aboriginal men internalized the animal so that they became the animal in spirit. In this way the spirit life of the animal was extended in the men in exchange for the animal's physical death.

Children learnt not by formal education, but by participating in life itself, by doing. Stories, songs and dances had a physical connection to the country, animals and vegetation. Aboriginal children were educated, for example, in how to develop awareness during sleep and how to enter meditative states. They learnt the tricks they could use in hunting, and parents encouraged their children to learn all about the behaviour of their totem animals as a way to learn about themselves. Children were taught what was edible and how to locate water. Gradually the person learnt everything there was to learn about the land, so that adults became self-sufficient in terms of food all year round. Learners, meanwhile, were never given a test question or a quiz. It was their own learning journey that they undertook – no one imposed an opinion and the old people never gave them a 'right' or 'wrong' mark.

JOURNEYING TOWARDS THE OTHER

At the age of about 12, the young Nhuggabarra man would embark on a journey, together with his contemporaries, to other communities in his area, and would not return to his community for 14 to 16 years. During this initiation period he visited all the communities in his area and learnt from them, and when he eventually returned he would perform three more ceremonies, lasting altogether six months, before he was considered a man. The girls, meanwhile, learn the neighbouring habits from the women in the community, who came from all the surrounding areas. One of the ceremonies for the girls was to be taken to a neighbouring water hole, where they stayed for three months to observe the 'red fly', from whom they learnt the cycle of life. They also learnt many languages form the women.

The so-called *coroborees* were organized events and performances, involving traditional songs and dances, where the young learnt to regulate social harmony and to connect with the spirit world. Depending on the person's age and experience they would learn at different levels. Trade and trust were similarly interconnected. Characteristically, the Nhunggabarra selected items from their country they had a surplus of and brought it to a designated trading place, placing a message stick therein. Trading parties had to accept all items, even if they did not need them; to leave anything would have shown disrespect. What they did not need they would trade with people further away. In this way a vast trading network was established all across aboriginal Australia. The trade was entirely based on trust. In the 1930s anthropologist McCarthy identified seven different trunk trade routes traversing the whole continent, based on physical exchange – no money was involved. Trade was community to community rather than individual to individual.

The central element was the enjoyment inherent in the process of giving. The preparation for a visit to relatives, the journey, the ritual, the formalities to be observed, were all enjoyable elements of life. The fact that some artefacts were exchanged was the tangible proof that the process had taken place with mutual appreciation, but it was not the main reason for the 'trade'. The Nhunggabarra were keen to exchange dances, songs and ceremonies and probably invested considerable time in this kind of trade. Production primarily fulfilled an intangible demand.

The aboriginal approach to farming was to learn how nature worked and then 'help it on the way' with minimum energy and effort. They knew, for example, that fruit trees grow from the seeds of fruits, so they deliberately spat out fruit tree seeds into the debris of fish remains in refuse heaps at the edge of the camp, which were ideal environments for tree growth. The model was 'knowledge-based eco-farming' – to learn and adapt but not to change. Fire was the most important eco-farming tool, being used to expose or capture a harvest and to generate and regenerate pastures for grazing animals. Fish traps, moreover, constituted an ecological system for catching the maximum number of fish with the minimum effort, while at the same time sustaining the stock. Meanwhile the aborigine's physical fitness was due to their active lifestyle and diet, which consisted mainly of natural and unprocessed food. Their methods secured food species available in the field all year round, which enabled more or less immediate consumption of foods and required only limited storage. And when they needed storage, they preferred storing their food live. They knew what we know today: that fresh food tastes best and contains the most nutrients.

A LEADER ROLE FOR EVERYONE

The image that emerges through stories of the ideal Nhunggabarra was someone who shared generously, who was an active provider of care for children and for the old; a person who fulfilled kinship obligations; and who showed compassion for others and respected integrity, taking responsibility for both one's own people and for other communities. Crimes against the law were recognized as offences; however, the offender would not receive a penalty until they felt guilt, understood what they had done and owned up to that error. A recurring theme of Nhunggabarra law stories is respect: for diversity, for other people and countries, as well as for life itself. At the core of such is respect for knowledge itself. The respect for knowledge gave all knowledgeable people a leadership role. But they had to lead without imposing themselves on others, and without giving outright orders. The ideal leaders respected all people, and encouraged people to learn from different perspectives and from different communities.

Everybody had at least one major role to fill on behalf of the community. And because there were no kings or even chieftains there was no army, nor people who were exclusively warriors or soldiers. Everyone had direct access to the spiritual world so there was no need for intermediaries. The roles they did have were teachers, child minders, story custodians, storytellers, dancers, painters, hunters and gatherers, net and basket makers, spear makers and fishermen, grain grinders and totem minders, medicine men and cooks.

Moreover, these roles evolved. For example, the primary 'carer' was to devote more and more time in service to the community as a whole as she matured. Old people generally functioned as teachers and mentors, knowledge repositories and conflict mediators. The ideal that applies to all larger-scale organized activities is that everyone should know their role and work should be done with as few directives as possible. The law added support and authority to a multiplicity of such roles because there was a need for respect for the person fulfilling the role. A leader was safe in a role – as long as he or she showed respect for the followers. Finally, the stories provided a means of critical self-reflection among the leaders.

Nhunggabarra women, meanwhile, were the principle contributors to the community's economy, responsible for up to 80 per cent of production. They were expected to undergo a full training, including extensive training in paediatrics, medicine, nursing, ecology, biology and spirituality. Women would build up over time an enormous knowledge of the medicinal plants and herbs of their country, and their usage. They were also the teachers of all children until puberty; they conducted their own sacred ceremonies and greeted newcomers to the community. Finally land was inherited via the women. The European immigrants saw none of this, failing to see that women functioned on equal terms to men in aboriginal society. What then, overall, was the recipe that the Nhunggabarra people had for sustainability?

THE NHUNGGABARRA RECIPE FOR SUSTAINABILITY

1. Mission
   - Keep all alive
2. Core belief: all are connected
   - All are connected – ancestors, people, animals, plants, sky and earth
   - Eternal life and reward (when one's mission is accomplished on earth)
   - Individual spiritual relationship with ancestors – no formal religion, or gods
3. Core value: respect
   - For knowledge diversity (learn from foreigners)
   - For the rights of foreign people and countries (no conquests)
   - For the leadership role of other individuals (do not usurp the role of another)
4. Economy: intangible
   - Tools and equipment made of natural materials – recyclable
   - Tightly coupled teams (families) are core production units
   - Intangible processes to keep all alive (stories, ceremonies, dances)
5. Ecosystem: core
   - Ecological farming methods
   - Natural medicine
   - Nomadic life (to reduce human pressure on the ecosystem)
6. Primary resource: knowledge
   - Life-long learner driven education
   - 18-year knowledge journey
   - Status from knowledge – not from material wealth
7. Leadership: all have a role
   - Context-specific leadership – all have a leadership role to play
   - Knowledge based organizing (creating, sharing and maintaining knowledge)
   - Consensus decision-making
8. Society: build community
   - Fuzzy-country borders – country ends where story ends
   - Networking processes for keeping peace (knowledge journeys, marriage rules)
   - Individual career (responsibility for functionality of community)
   - Generosity and sharing (reinforced by kinship rules)

- Custodianship of land and knowledge – no individual ownership
- Collaborative methods for increasing productivity
- Widows, orphans and elderly cared for by community.

Sveiby and Skuthorpe end with a quote from none other than the English explorer James Cooke, from his visit to Australia in 1770:

From what I have said of the Natives of New Holland they may appear to some to be the most wretched people on Earth, but in reality they are far happier than the Europeans. They live in tranquility, which is not disturbed by the Inequality of Condition. They think themselves provided with all the necessaries of life and they have no superfluities.

We do not know whether the Nhunggabarra built the first sustainable society, but we are reasonably sure that they built the longest lasting one.

6.6 Conclusion

In summary, there are three different versions of feminism, the final one being of broadest relevance in our relational, critical emancipatory context:

- *A first approach covers any understanding of economic, social, or psychological phenomena:* such phenomena range from the division of labour, class conditions and wage setting to recruitment and selection as well as political and social mores. This approach starts from the recognition that (among much else) there are possible differences between men and women in terms of situation, experiences, and so on, which must be taken into account.
- *A second approach emphasizes the importance of acquiring a broader and deeper descriptive picture of women's conditions and experiences:* here the ideal is to study various phenomena from the perspective of women or from a feminist point of view. This so-called 'standpoint' research strongly emphasizes political and practical relevance. It is not only a question of looking for the truth in an abstract sense; even more important is to stimulate social change and emancipation.
- *A third approach calls into question the gender categories that the other two approaches regard as given and unproblematic:* the meaning of concepts such as men and women, male and female, is considered uncertain. Such feminists emphasize the temporary and fragile nature of social constructions. Genders as labels and clues to identities are regarded as transient and contradictory. This brand of feminism *shifts the emphasis from gender to an emphasis of diversity.*

The first of the above is strongly influenced by phenomenology, the second by critical theory and the third by postmodernism. In fact, a strong characteristic of the reformative approaches is their mutual interdependence on each other, as well as their prior dependence on one or other method and methodology. So whereas methods are clearly distinct from one another, and conventional methodologies (our level 2) somewhat so, the postconventional methodologies (our level 3) are 'blurred genres'. Why? First, they overlap with each other, and, second, they are as much sociopolitical philosophies as they are research methodologies.

We now turn from feminism to participatory action research, as its next evolutionary step. It is also the final step in the Southern relational path.

References

1. Donovan, J. (2000). *Feminist Theory: The Intellectual Traditions*. London: Continuum.
2. Michael, K. (forthcoming). 'Economics as if South Africans Mattered.' Unpublished dissertation, Buckingham, Buckingham University.
3. Reinharz, S. (1992). *Feminist Method in Social Research*. Oxford: Oxford University Press.
4. Collins, P.H. (1990). *Black Feminist Thought: Knowledge, Consciousness and the Politics of Empowerment*. London: Routledge.
5. Eisler, R. (2007). *The Real Wealth of Nations*. San Francisco, CA: Berrett Koehler.
6. Korten, D. (2006). *The Great Turning – from Empire to Earth Community*. San Francisco, CA: Berrett Koehler.
7. Michael, K. (forthcoming). 'Economics as if South Africans Mattered.'
8. Acker, J. (1994), quoted in: Blaikie, N. (1994). *Approaches to Social Inquiry*. Cambridge: Polity Press.
9. Jagger, A. (2005). *Feminist Ethics*. London: Taylor and Francis.
10. Blaikie, N. (1994). *Approaches to Social Inquiry*. London: Pluto Press.
11. Tarnas, R. (1991). *The Passion of the Western Mind*. New York: Ballantyne Books.
12. Van der Post, L. (1984). *Jung and the Story of Our Time*. Harmondsworth: Penguin.
13. Hoppers, C. (2002). *Indigenous Knowledge Systems*. Cape Town: New Africa Books.
14. Sveiby, K. and Skuthorpe, T. (2006). *Treading Lightly: The Hidden Wisdom of the World's Oldest People*. Sydney: Allen and Unwin.

7 *From Feminism to Participatory Action Research*

Liberate the Oppressed

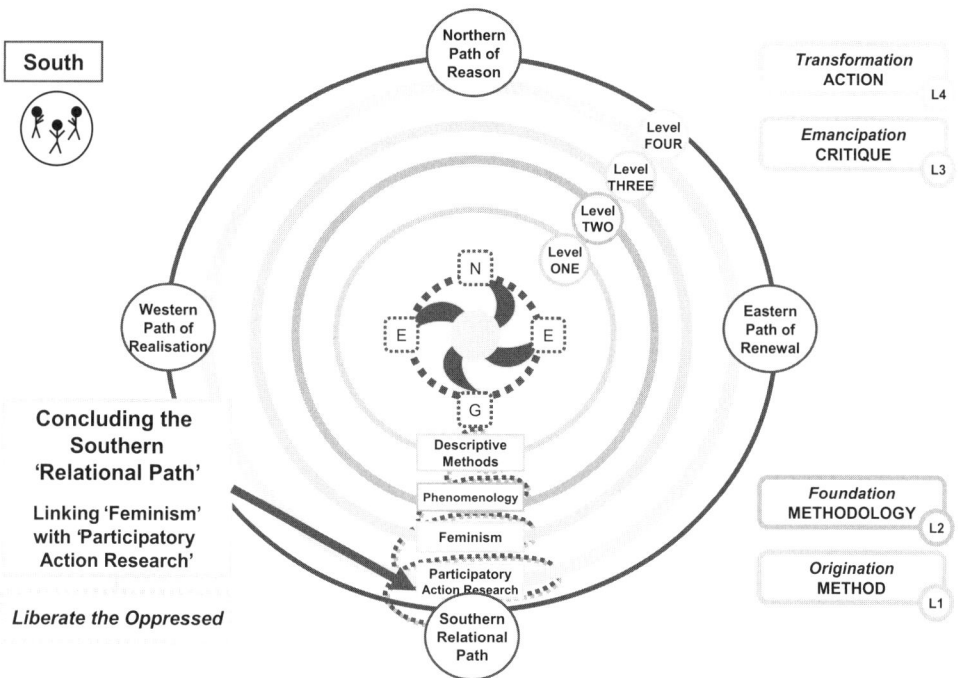

Figure 7.1   Overview Chapter 7 – Level 4/South

Summary: Participatory Action Research

- Transformation – the fourth level of our Integral Research framework – starts out with the community, through so-called participatory action research. As a researcher you now enter, finally, fully fledged social innovation – following upon the original description, phenomenological foundation and feminist emancipation.
- Such participatory research takes integrally on from where descriptive methods, phenomenological methodology and feminist critique leave off, following the Southern relational path.
- Participatory research, as a branch of action research, is unique in its Southern origins, most specifically in Latin America, Africa and the Indian subcontinent, with Columbia's Fals Borda, Ecuador's Daniel Selener and Bangladesh's M.D. Rahman being its leading lights.
- In place of the phenomenological life world or the Germanic *Lebenswelt*, Fals Borda cites the Spanish *vivencia* as a focal point for dialogic research and innovation, oriented toward such questions as 'Why is there poverty?' or 'Why is there oppression and dependence?'.
- Grassroots representatives participate as a reference group in the action-research process, thereby 'popularizing science', transforming the researcher/researched relationship, and pursuing autonomy and identity in the course of exercising people's own countervailing power.
- The action-centred journey for Bangaldeshi academic and social activist M.D. Rahman brings out the dynamic interrelationship between the development of people's consciousness, on the one hand, and the necessary control over the society's resources and social, economic and political institutions, on the other.
- For Selener, such participatory research is intended to empower the powerless groups in society. Practitioners therefore tend to apply conflict-oriented paradigms, seeking after the transformation of oppressive social, economic and political structures in society.
- Finally, specific examples of PAR are introduced: ranging from the monumental efforts of the Six S movement in Burkina Faso to the significant achievements of the fisherfolk communities in Tanzania.

7.1 Orientation to Participatory Action Research (PAR)

THE CULTURAL TURN

As we have already indicated, *all of the methods and methodologies that prevail originate from either America (method) or Europe (methodology)*. The rest of the world hardly gets a look-in. In fact, while we have drawn on African philosophers to provide a non-European developmental context, the underlying methods, methodologies and philosophies have been basically Western or Northern. That has to be problematic, if we are talking of 'integral' research.

At this ultimate stage of the Southern relational path of such Integral Research, we retrace steps to Denzin and Lincoln and their *Landscape of Research*.[1] There they refer to the 'crisis of representation' currently taking place. For them a 'fourth' research moment arising out of a 'cultural turn'. These moments can be described as follows:

Retracing: Four Research Moments	
According to Denzin and Lincoln	
①	The first turn, early on in the 20th century, is quantitative in orientation.
②	The second turn, toward the middle of the 20th century, is qualitative, but still with a quantitative edge to it.
③	The third turn, in the latter part of the century, is characterized by 'blurred genres', that is a mix of qualitative approaches.
④	In the fourth turn, as the 21st century unfurls, there is the 'crisis of representation', when a cross-cultural orientation first becomes apparent.

Interestingly enough, the point at which the rest of the world begins to exert an influence is when we move toward the ultimately transformative approaches. For, as has already been indicated by our African philosophers, most particularly Serequeberhan, *nothing short of transformation will enable such societies in transition to authentically research and develop themselves.* Moreover, the South and the East (culturally and philosophically speaking) are generally less rationally and empirically inclined than the North and West, but have a collective and cultural edge (phenomenologically and interpretively). In other words and in general terms, the North and the West are rational and pragmatic, the South and the East humanistic and holistic.

ORIGINATION TO ACTION

We now have entered into our fourth level from origination onto foundation, and thereafter onto emancipation and finally, now, transformation. This is the complete *integral rhythm,* which culminates in social innovation. For us, the term 'action research', which underlies the participatory approach at this stage, does not carry the full impetus that social innovation does. In the table below we summarize the Southern journey so far, in the context of the other three Eastern, Northern and Western journeys to come. Then we turn to action research in general before introducing PAR specifically.

The Four Paths and Levels of Integral Research				
	Origination Level 1	**Foundation** Level 2	**Emancipation** Level 3	**Transformation** Level 4
Southern Relational Path	Description	Phenomenology	Feminism	Participatory Action Research
Eastern Path of Renewal	Narrative	Hermeneutics	Critical Theory	Co-operative Inquiry
Northern Path of Reason	Theory (Hypothesis)	Critical Rationalism	Post-Modernism	Socio-technical Design
Western Path of Realization	Survey/ Experiment	Empiricism	Critical Realism	Action Research
	Method	Methodology	Critique	Action

INTRODUCING ACTION RESEARCH AS A WHOLE

The founding fathers of action research are the American pragmatic philosopher and educator, John Dewey, and the Jewish refugee from Nazi Germany, the social psychologist Kurt Lewin, who developed it in the middle of the last century. Action research – for one of its contemporary co-creators Peter Reason at the University of Bath in England, together with a follower of his, Hilary Bradbury, based in California – is:

> a participatory, democratic process concerned with developing practical knowing in the pursuit of worthwhile human purposes, grounded in a participatory worldview which is believed to be emerging at this historical moment. It seeks to bring together action and reflection, theory and practice, in participation with others, in the pursuit of practical solutions to issues of pressing concern to people, and more generally the flourishing of individual persons and their communities.[2]

Figure 7.2 illustrates action research's core components.

We now turn specifically to participative action research and to three of its primary instigators.

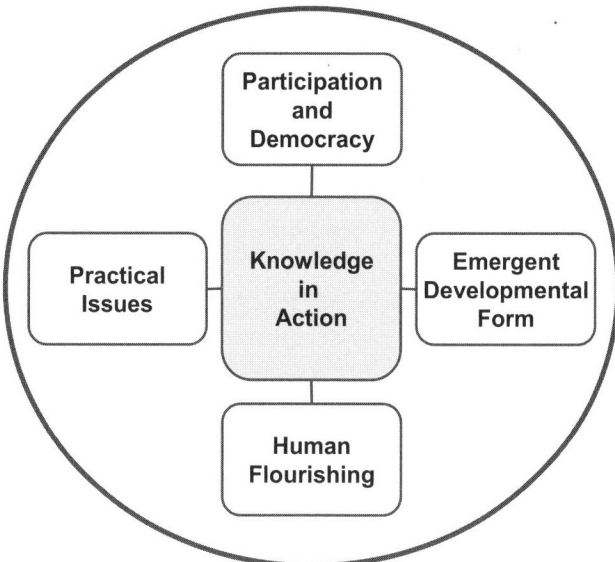

Figure 7.2 Knowledge in Action

PARTICIPATORY ORIENTATION ALONG THE RELATIONAL PATH

Research Method to Action Research; Origination to Transformation

We now set the stage for the ultimately transformative and thereby innovatory effect of the humanistic, relational path to individuation, or indeed social innovation: that of participatory action research.

While the overall orientation for participative research is humanistic, there is, to some extent at least, an orientation toward all four paths of development. It is for this reason that action research is the most fully integral of our research approaches. So, as we shall see with PAR, while the phenomenological orientation toward a community's life world is pre-eminent, there is reference to other critical emancipatory antecedents, most especially to feminism. However, what stands out about PAR is its strong rootedness in the development world, with its founding fathers being a Colombian, Fals Borda and a Bangladeshi, M.D. Rahman, who originally drew their inspiration from Julius Nyerere, the first Tanzanian president.

Founding Mothers and Fathers of PAR

In 1975, a young Canadian adult educator named Budd Hall, at that time temporarily based in Sussex, UK, compiled a special issue of the journal *Convergence* on the topic of participatory research. Beyond Hall's expectations, this issue sparked an international network of educators, academics and activists interested in this area, the International Participatory Research Network, which would grow stronger and larger over the next decades.

Figure 7.3 Towards Participatory Research

The beginning of this story can be traced to Tanzania, where Hall worked from 1970 to 1974. At that time, under the leadership of President Julius Nyerere, Tanzania had launched an experiment in what is known as 'ujamaa socialism'. In Tanzania, Hall (who would later become Chair of Adult Education and Community Development at OISE/ University of Toronto and Dean of Education at the University of Victoria) had the fortune of learning from many inspiring adult educators. Among them were Finland's Marja Liisa Swantz, Brazil's Paulo Freire and the Tanzanian president himself Julius Nyerere, probably the only adult educator in the world who has become president of a country.

Through these experiences, Hall became acquainted with approaches to education based on the principles of self-reliance, active participation and dialogue. He also became interested in the potential of research to promote transformative learning, local development and progressive social change, and in research models that departed from the traditional positivist approach to social research based on the natural sciences. In 1974/1975 Budd Hall was a visiting fellow at the Institute of Development Studies at the University of Sussex, where he met people from many other countries who were thinking along similar lines to him and his Tanzanian colleagues, seeking a connection between education, research, politics and action. Among them were Francisco Vio Grossi from Chile and Rajesh Tandon from India.

From his experiences in Tanzania and England, Hall noticed that many educators, researchers and activists from different countries were exploring similar paths through independent avenues, in most cases without being aware of related work done by others. At that time they did not constitute yet a community or even a loose network. Moreover, their approaches did not have yet an encompassing name that would capture its essence. The major impetus for the development of a network (and later an international community) came from that special journal of *Convergence* edited by Hall in 1975. In naming the theme of the issue, Hall labelled this approach 'participatory research'.

That term was used because it seemed to be the best common description of the various approaches that were described within the issue. While Hall had begun to learn about the long traditions in Europe of action research, and Maria Liisa Swantz had been using 'participant research' to describe this approach for several years, the choice of the term 'participatory research' was simply made as a descriptive term for a collection of varied approaches which shared a participatory ethos.

The topic of participatory research struck a chord among adult educators and community development practitioners around the world, and soon after its publication all the copies of the issue were sold out, a first in the history of *Convergence*. Moreover, requests for copies were sent from all regions of the world, and a comment in Hall's article inviting people to exchange information on the topic provided the needed driving force to create a community of practice. This massive response made Hall realize that many people in the world were actively pursuing alternative research avenues that were ignored by most universities, and that these people needed some spaces to establish connections among them in order to share their experiences. That issue of *Convergence*, and the active networking of Hall, helped to generate those spaces, which in turn helped to consolidate a vibrant tradition in the field of adult education that would grow year after year for the decades to come. It seems that the time was ripe for an international network on participatory research, but a catalyst was needed.

A few months later, another important catalyst for the development of an international participatory research network came forth when the First World Assembly of the International Council for Adult Education was held in Dar es Salaam, Tanzania, in 1976. Again, Hall played a key role, acting as conference secretary. One of the recommendations of the Dar es Salaam conference was that 'adult educators should be given the opportunity to learn about and share their experiences in participatory research.' The following year, a conference on action research took place in Cartagena, Colombia. Interestingly enough, the co-ordinator of this conference was the Colombian sociologist Orlando Fals Borda, who has since become a leading light in the PAR movement. He was working on the same alternative approach to social research but without being aware of the international initiatives that took place in the previous years. Thanks to Paz Buttedahl, the Latin American programme officer for the International Council of Adult Education (ICAE), a connection was made between the Colombian group and the international network spearheaded by Hall during the planning stages of the conference. Hence, the April 1977 Cartagena conference provided a third key moment for the expansion the participatory research network, building on the 1975 issue of *Convergence* and the 1976 conference in Dar Es Salaam.

Orlando Fals Borda and his colleagues were using the term 'action research', a concept that had been used in the 1940s by Kurt Lewin (see Chapter 16). Lewin argued that research that produced nothing but books was not sufficient, and that a new type of research for social practice was needed. Thus, he called for 'a type of action research on the conditions and effects of various forms of social action, and research leading to social action'. At the 1977 Cartagena conference the concept of 'action research' used by Fals Borda met the concept of 'participatory research' coined by Hall, and the concept of 'participatory action research' was later born. The term was used for the first time by

Orlando Fals Borda to name a new paradigm in social research. Several decades later, the concept became popularized and known by its initials PAR.

We now turn to its key tenets.

7.2 Participatory Action Research – Key Tenets: From Community Problem Solving to Committed Participation

Participatory Action Research (PAR) – Key Tenets
①   The problem is defined, analysed and solved by the community.
②   As a scientific methodology, PAR facilitates an authentic analysis of social reality.
③   PAR involves the full and active participation of the community.
④   PAR is aimed at the exploited, the poor, the oppressed, the marginal.
⑤   PAR creates awareness of the people's own resources, mobilizing for self-reliant development.
⑥   The ultimate goal of the research-and-innovation is the radical transformation of social reality.
⑦   You as researcher/innovator are a committed participant, facilitator and learner in this transformation.

① THE PROBLEM IS DEFINED, ANALYSED AND SOLVED BY THE COMMUNITY

For Colombia's renegade academic, Fals Borda,[3] learning to interact and organize with PAR is based on the existential concept of experience proposed by the Spanish philosopher Jose Ortega y Gasset. Through the actual experience of something we intuitively apprehend its essence; we feel, enjoy and understand it as a reality, and we thereby place our own being in a wider, more fulfilling context. In PAR such an experience, called *vivencia* (akin to life world and aligned to learning with head and heart) in Spanish, is complemented by another idea, that of authentic commitment. In that context both internal and external animators, or agents of change, have the shared goals of social transformation.

These 'animators' contribute their own knowledge, techniques and experience to the transformation process. A dialectical tension is created between a Cartesian and academic orientation combined with an experiential and practical one, bringing together academic and popular knowledge in shared problem solving. Through participation a subject–subject relationship replaces the hitherto asymmetrical subject/object researcher/researched relationships; thereby it is attuned to feminism. The general concept of authentic participation as defined here is rooted in cultural traditions of the common people and in their real history referring to core values that have survived the destructive impact of foreign invasions. Such resistant values are based on mutual aid, the communal use of the land, forest and water, the extended family and other old social practices, the endogenous experiences of the common people.

② AS A SCIENTIFIC METHODOLOGY, PAR FACILITATES AN AUTHENTIC ANALYSIS OF SOCIAL REALITY

For Fals Borda action and knowledge go hand in hand. Historical experience calls for rethinking the meaning of social transformation for people's liberation. The dominant view of such liberation has been preoccupied with the need for changing the oppressive structures of relations in material production – certainly a necessary task. But, and this is the distinctive view of PAR, domination of elites is also rooted in control over social power to determine what is useful knowledge. In fact, existence of the gap in knowledge relations can offset the advantages of reducing the gap in relations of physical production.

People then cannot be liberated by a consciousness and knowledge other than their own. It is therefore essential that people develop their own indigenous consciousness-raising and knowledge generation, and this requires the social power to assert this. The scientific character or objectivity of knowledge rests on its social verifiability, and this depends on consensus as to the method of verification. All scientific knowledge is relative to the paradigm to which it belongs, and the verification system to which it is submitted. An immediate objective of PAR is to return to the people the control over their own verification systems.

③ PAR INVOLVES THE FULL AND ACTIVE PARTICIPATION OF THE COMMUNITY

This altogether implies a specific mode of interaction with the people, the essence of which could be summarized as the break-up of the classical dichotomy between 'subject' and 'object' (manipulation and dominance) and its replacement by a humanistic mode of equal relation between two subjects (animation and facilitation). The essential differences between the latter approach and that typically undertaken by a political party or conventional development practitioner are:

- Starting from where people are – their perceptions, knowledge, experiences and rhythm of work and thoughts, as opposed to preconceived agendas.
- Stimulating people (animation) to undertake self-analysis of their life situations, and helping them to derive from such self-inquiry into the political-economic-cultural environment an intellectual base for initiating changes.
- Assisting people to organize themselves into People's Organizations (POs) which are non-hierarchical in structure and democratic in operations.
- Facilitating the actions for change, with the external catalyst paving the way for internal self-reliance.
- Stimulating the POs to carry out regular self-reviews, to assess and learn from success and failure.

④ PAR IS AIMED AT THE EXPLOITED, THE POOR, THE OPPRESSED, THE MARGINAL

Stimulation of the poor and deprived to undertake self-reliant initiatives requires two essential steps. The first is the development of an awareness about the reality in which they live. In particular, they need to understand that poverty and deprivation are the result of specific social forces rather than an outcome of some inherent deficiency on their part or even 'fate'. Second, based on such critical awareness, they need to gain confidence in their collective abilities to bring about positive changes in their life situations and organize themselves for that purpose.

⑤ PAR CREATES AWARENESS OF THE PEOPLE'S OWN RESOURCES, MOBILIZING FOR SELF-RELIANT DEVELOPMENT

A typical PAR programme stimulates direct social analysis by the landless. In many places this has led to intense and sustained pressure-group action to confront social injustice and oppression by rural elites. In other areas, confrontational activity to resist social oppression by rural elites has been particularly intense for several years and has led to many forms of harassment, of both the landless leaders and NGO (non-governmental organization) workers:

- What was their experience?
- What did they learn themselves from this?
- What would they, with their past experience, advise the landless in other villages who might want to get organized?
- What was the relation of their present activities with past ones?
- Would they like to document their story, draw its lessons more systematically after thorough discussion in the base of the organization, and
- Disseminate them so that fellow landless in other villages would not need to start from zero and could benefit from their experience?

⑥ THE ULTIMATE GOAL OF THE RESEARCH-AND-INNOVATION IS THE RADICAL TRANSFORMATION OF SOCIAL REALITY

For Orlando Fals Borda, those involved in PAR start with the thesis that science does not have absolute or pure value, but is simply a useful form of knowledge for specific purposes and based on relative truths. Any science as a cultural product carries those biases and values, which scientists hold as a group. It therefore favours those who produce and control it. A people's science may hence serve as a corrective.

Ingredients and Techniques of a People's Science	
Collective Research	Obtained from groups through dialogue, discussion, argument and consensus in the investigation of social realities.
Critical Recovery of History	To discover, selectively through collective memory, those elements of the past which have proved useful in the increase of conscientization, using popular stories and oral traditions 'fleshed out'.
Valuing and Applying Folk Culture	Account is taken of art, music, drama, sports, story-telling and other expressions related to human sentiment and imagination.
Production and Diffusion of new Knowledge	different levels of communication are developed for people ranging from pre-literate to intellectual, using image, sound, painting, mime, photograph, theatre, poetry, music, puppetry and exhibitions. The groups involved include co-operatives, trade unions, cultural centres and so on.

Ideally, in the process, the grassroots are able to participate in the research process from the beginning: that is from the moment it is decided what the subject of the research should be, to the time it is completed. Its essence is the proposition that more is to be gained by using the affective logic of the heart than the cold-headed analyses that come from laboratories.

⑦ YOU AS RESEARCHER/INNOVATOR ARE A COMMITTED PARTICIPANT, FACILITATOR AND LEARNER IN THIS TRANSFORMATION

Finally, at the micro level, PAR is a philosophy and style of work with the people to promote their empowerment for changing their immediate environment, through socioeconomic initiatives. These often confront state bureaucracies and technocracies that seek to impose their ideas of 'development' or modernization. The people's own initiatives seek to promote their authentic self-development which takes off from their traditional culture and seeks to preserve the physical environment with which they have an organic association. Two elements which have PAR priority are, first, democratic people's organizations and, second, the restoration of the status of popular knowledge and its promotion. Both are fostered by a process of awareness raising through a series of social inquiries. These range from dialogue sessions to full-scale historical and socioeconomic investigations. Transforming the relations of knowledge, overall then, has centrality.

7.3 Participatory Action Research in Depth

ACTION AND KNOWLEDGE: ORLANDO FALS BORDA

Remaking Knowledge

Doing Research with and for People: Building up people's self-awareness, for Fals Borda, has been an ever-present preoccupation of participatory action researchers – an extremely important task in order for their actions to be effective if they want to avoid the betrayal of ideals. For this purpose Fals Borda places the interplay between explicit and implicit science – or between Cartesian and popular knowledge – as a fact, which has to be taken into account since it involves dialectical encounters, which are inevitably part of day-to-day living. His central concern has been to direct this interplay to allow the common people to have sufficient control over the generation of new knowledge, thereby 'remaking science' for the benefit of the masses victimized by power.

The developing world, he says, of course, is too small for this tremendous task: the victims of poverty constitute the majority of the earth's inhabitants and the effort has many detractors. But a hopeful methodological start has been made with participatory action research. In adopting a marginal and even subversive role, following the likes of Ghandi, Luther King and Mandela, PAR is not denying the merits of science; without the scientific bearings they would have felt as if moving in a void. Ways of building connections between different scientific traditions are then sought while doing research with and for people, and not on them, duly combining the role of activist and researcher.

Fals Borda asserts, at the same time, that PAR applies rigour and responsibility in observation-inference or in carefully handling data just as positivists do. But it has had to remake other aspects of their scholarship so as to relate it to ordinary people's way of interpreting reality. In a similar manner it had to discover and apply its half-hidden science – 'people's knowledge' – for the people's benefit. For this purpose, a series of procedures have been developed in which theory and practice, conventional learning and implicit knowledge could be combined in special *vivencias*.

From Life World to Vivencia: The reconstruction of knowledge for the purpose of furthering social progress and increasing people's self-awareness with PAR *vivencias* takes dialogue as its point of insertion in the social process. It is dialogic research, oriented to the social situation in which people live. PAR starts by asking such questions as 'Why is there poverty?' or 'Why is there oppression and dependence?'. As such the grassroots representatives should be able to participate as reference group in the action research process from the very beginning that is from the moment it is decided what the subject of research will be. And they should be involved at every step in the process.

Autonomy and Collective Research: Popular knowledge does not come as isolated facts known by specific individuals, but as packets of cultural data generated by social groups. PAR as an autonomous collective investigation is quite different from the detached individual observer undertaking his or her doctoral thesis, advancing science or gaining personal prestige or financial gain. The task now becomes a communal in which social validation of knowledge is obtained not only by confronting previous ideas but also through the people's own processes of verification.

Three theoretical elements – not usually included in dominant paradigms, are included:

1. the ontological possibility of *a real popular science*;
2. the existential possibility of *transforming the researcher/researched relationship*;
3. the need of autonomy and identity in *exercising people's own countervailing power*.

People's science does have its own endogenous processes; it is formally constructed on its own terms, with its own practical rationality and empirical systematization and its own way of institutionalizing, accumulating and transmitting knowledge. As such, the wisdom of the sage and the knowhow of the scientist converge and intermingle, as recognized during the lifetimes of Descartes, Kant and Galileo themselves. By giving importance to both, a more useful and complete knowledge for social change can be produced. *Emancipatory collective knowledge and popular science become tools then in the quest for justice, and this is the answer to the perennial question 'knowledge for what?'.*

The second element, transformation of the researcher/researched liaison, leads to an interpretation of participation that is indeed demanding, whereby both parties seek the mutual goal of advancing knowledge in pursuit of justice. They interact, collaborate, reflect and report in collectivities on an equal footing, each one offering in the relationship what he or she knows best. In other words, a meeting of diverse scientific traditions takes place, resulting in an enriched overall knowledge, which is more effective in the struggle for justice and the achievement of social progress and peace. The third element – autonomy and identity in collective research – rests on the observation that progressive social movements cherish and fight for their culture and personality to the last, for their lives depend on it. Stimulating autonomous movements and defending the articulation of local life is a worthy goal for PAR researchers, involving both stripping down the oppressor's power and understanding how to internalize one's own. It also includes the power to speak in the context of establishing a 'knowledge democracy'.

If the 18th century in Europe, then, has been called 'the Enlightenment' for its collective efforts to revamp science and philosophy, the 21st century may be expected to be the 'Century of Awakening'. The common peoples are already awakening to their rights and possibilities for action. They are also responding to the call of their own voices – hitherto half muted – to honour their dignity and the meaning of their own history.

Action, Knowledge and Animation in Participatory Action Research

Ways of Stimulating People: Stimulation of the poor and deprived to undertake self-reliant initiatives requires two essential steps. The first is the development of an awareness about the reality in which they live. In particular, they need to understand that poverty and deprivation are the result of specific social forces rather than an outcome of some inherent deficiency on their part or even 'fate'. Second, based on such critical awareness, they need to gain confidence in their collective abilities to bring about positive changes in their life situations and organize themselves for that purpose.

A stimulation of this sort implies a specific mode of interaction with the people, the essence of which could be summarized as the break-up of the classical dichotomy between 'subject' and 'object' (manipulation and dominance) and its replacement by a humanistic mode of equal relation between two subjects (animation and facilitation).

Creation of Sensitized Agents: A cadre of such sensitized agents will have undergone a process of rigorous learning based on exposure to concrete experience and self-reflection rather than formal training. Potential such persons have generally originated from:

- socially conscious and active segments of the middle class who have had practical experience in such social activities;
- those who had begin to critically reflect on their earlier roles and were looking for more relevant or fulfilling roles for society.

Specifically then:

- the starting point is a *collective reflection* on the experiences such people already have in working with communities, including self criticism and unlearning;
- *exposure to concrete field experiences*, living among selected communities to gather socioeconomic information through informal discussions;
- through interaction with groups in the community, the learner seeks to stimulate them to *identify issues of common concern*, collect and analyse information on such, to enrich their understanding of their life situations;
- while engaged in such fieldwork, meeting regularly as a group amongst themselves as a *collective learning* exercise;
- *identify* those individuals within a community who possess potential *skills in animation*, and assist them in improving their skills.

We now turn from action and knowledge to people's self-development.

PEOPLE'S SELF-DEVELOPMENT: M.D. RAHMAN

Integrating Education with Life Processes

Like many other of his compatriots, M.D. Rahman[4] had been inspired by popular mobilizations for social reconstruction and development in Bangladesh after its independence in 1971. He saw a breakthrough in the development status of the country to be possible only through a national mobilization for popular initiatives; on smaller scale, such initiatives were demonstrating their potential for solving people's problems and for creating a spirit of personal sacrifice for collective outcomes, challenging the premises of received economics and development thinking which were pushing the country towards humiliating dependence on external assistance rather than indicating a viable path for social progress.

As a teacher, Rahman had been stimulated by demands from sections of Bangladesh's student community for radical reform to integrate educational processes with processes of life. Yet most of the popular initiatives in the country faded, died or were repressed as reactionary forces gradually consolidated their hold on society's commanding structures. Joining the ILO (International Labour Organization) in 1977, Rahman was able to pursue the same interest, linking up with significant trends in the grassroots movements in several countries and jointly reflecting on their approaches, experiences and visions; initiating methodological experiments in field 'animation' work (see below) and in the sensitization of animators; linking with intellectual trends; working with popular movements; and in synthesizing and conceptualizing from the ongoing experiences. In his contribution to the faculty seminars, he raised as a basic problem in the transition to socialism the question of a 'consciousness gap' between revolutionary intellectuals who generally provide leadership in socialist transition, and the masses. Socialism would be alienating of this consciousness gap could not be closed. This problem remained one if his central concerns throughout his explorations of participatory or people's self-development, and in his prolific engagement with the NGO movement.

Organizing the Rural Poor

According to Rahman, organizing the rural poor, for an NGO, can have several different objectives:

> *Economic Uplift:* This means raising the incomes of the poor, giving them greater stability of income and some social security or insurance against unforeseen situations, old age, and so on. If this is the only or the principal objective, external delivery of such can be in the form of credit, technology and expertise. But emphasis on external delivery contradicts the other objectives.

> *Human Development:* Creativity is the distinctive human quality, for Rahman, and the human development objective aims to develop creative people. Creation is the product of thinking and action that is *participation*. This consists of investigation, reflection, decision-making and application of decision: reflection upon action gives men and women the sense of creation, of having developed as human beings. Human development is a process of *self*-development – outsiders cannot develop the rural poor. Outsiders can have a role, however, in stimulating and assisting development.

> *Achieving Social and Economic Rights:* The means of elimination of economic and social oppression, and achieving equity in the use of public resources, implies the exercise of collective power of the poor, and often implies *struggle*. The role of outsiders is to help develop a consciousness amongst the poor of short-run failures as a learning process upon which subsequent strategy is to be built.

The above three objectives, moreover, become complementary if they are pursued together. This implies care to pursue the economic uplift objective through primary reliance on the people's own resources and creativity, and channelling their organized efforts towards obtaining their rightful share of normal public resources. In all this, the emphasis must always be on stimulating people's reflection and analysis, assisted but not dominated by external knowledge and intervention. In this way, people's consciousness will keep advancing.

Macro Social Transformation: The above three objectives can be considered to be 'locally progressive' if they are pursued together, that is progressive at a micro level. Their contribution to macro social transformation can be positive, if such micro work spreads on a broad enough scale. Since the great bulk of the flow of external resources is controlled by external forces, interested (according to Rahman) in dominating and exploiting the country rather than in its self-determination and development, a self-reliant development effort is an absolutely necessary element for the country to shape its own destiny and stand up with pride. Self-reliance at the national level cannot be achieved without self-reliance at the grassroots levels – in fact at all levels. This by itself requires primary reliance on people's own effort and creativity rather than on external deliveries.

However, successful social transformation, which includes social reconstruction, is much more than the mere act of formal transfer of political power: it requires a social psychology, culture and the capability of self-reliant economic and social effort. A corollary of self-reliant people's effort is reliance on people's own knowledge. There is no self-reliant way of development without primary reliance on people's resources including their own knowledge, and professional knowledge has to play a complementary but not dominating role in such development. With this perspective in view, work with the poor which seeks to develop their creativity primarily through their own collective effort, giving emphasis to both the people's self-reliant thinking and acting through which collective action and consciousness both keep advancing, would be creating positive assets for the task of social transformation.

Overall then, from an NGO perspective:

- The chosen objectives and their rationale should be discussed with the target groups; they should be asked to *reflect why development effort in the country has been a failure*, notwithstanding so-called 'learned' men being in charge.
- The people should be asked to deliberate *what they want to do in this overall context*, and how the NGO can help them.
- The people should have the opportunity to discuss all of such, and *take action in small groups*.
- The *people must periodically evaluate their own experience* and review their progress collectively, draw lessons from success and failure, formulate a future course of action based on past experience and formulate advice on how to achieve agreed objectives. They should be encouraged to document, store, and disseminate their ongoing experience for progressive advancement of their collective knowledge based on their collective effort.
- In areas where there is a past history of collective effort by the poor, this *history should be collected and discussed, and lessons drawn* from it as a guide to current effort.

We now turn from our in depth analysis of PAR, through the eyes of Fals Bordan and Rahman, to its more global expression. 'Global', for us in this case, does not refer to the geographical spread of PAR, which has been most prolifically evolved in Africa, Latin America and South-East Asia, but do its broader conceptual base. For such we turn to the recent work of Daniel Selener, starting by positioning PAR in its wider, consciousness-raising context, and then continuing by positioning it in a wider conceptual framework.

7.4 Global Variations of PAR

CONSCIOUSNESS RAISING: PAR IN COMMUNITY DEVELOPMENT

For the most recent of PAR's exponents, Ecuador's Daniel Selener,[5] now based at Cornell University in the USA, Paulo Freire is again a major source of inspiration. Freire has been a fundamental influence on the development of participatory research. In his seminal

Pedagogy of the Oppressed he introduced the concepts of conscientization and critical reflection (see Chapter 9 of the present volume). The former means the identification and critical analysis of the social, political and economic contradictions leading to organized action to solve immediate problems and to counter the oppressive aspects of society. As a research approach, Freire proposes thematic investigation through which people identify and analyse their own problems in order to solve them. This implies a change in the traditional role of researcher from that of 'objective' external researcher to 'committed' co-investigator, together with those who are the subjects of the research.

The philosophical origins of participatory research, aside from those already cited, can be traced back to both pragmatism and also historical materialism. Students of pragmatism maintain that knowledge arises from human action. In the view of historical materialists, participatory research is structured by democratic interaction between researcher and the oppressed classes, and takes the form of a dialectical relationship between theory and practice.

The professional origins of participatory research focus on the inability of the dominant, classical positivist paradigm to promote social change. The emphasis on quantitative analysis, critics maintain, reduces the complexity, meaning and richness of social systems. Because survey research oversimplifies social reality, it produces results which are inaccurate in three ways: extracting information from individuals in isolation from one another, diminishing the richness of human feelings and experience; the respondent may be obliged to select a pre-structured response which does not reflect his or her perceptions; survey instruments are ahistorical and lack context, they create a static snapshot of individuals with no past nor future.

Critics further charge that survey research is oppressive and alienating in nature. To maximize objectivity and control over the research process, questionnaires and interview schedules are designed by researchers and analysed by them. This approach does not allow the people being studied to participate in the decision-making stage. People are regarded as mere objects to be studied rather than active participants. In fact the research conducted may be irrelevant to the problems that the subjects perceive to be a priority. The distinctive feature of participatory research is that the group researched participates in the whole research process, and such research is directly related to transformative actions.

A GENERAL FRAMEWORK FOR PAR ANALYSIS: EQUILIBRIUM VERSUS CONFLICT PARADIGMS

Theories of Social Change

Daniel Selener (it is interesting that he now based in the USA; that is, in the developed North-Western world), has taken the most analytical and conceptual approach, to PAR, of the three philosophers of research that we have cited. As such he has located the relevant theories of social change, of which participative research is one, shown overleaf:

Theories of Social Change	
Equilibrium Paradigm	Evolutionary/neo-evolutionary theory Structural-functional theory Systems theory
Conflict Paradigm	Marxist/neo-Marxist theory Cultural revitalization theory Anarchist-utopian theory Participatory research

He then goes on to describe the characteristics of each.

Equilibrium-based Paradigms

Evolutionary and Neo-Evolutionary Theory: Classical evolutionary theories, influenced by Darwin's work on biological evolution, offer sociological analogues to the living organisms. They are based on notions of progress involving stages of development from lower to higher forms. Society, according to evolutionary theorists, is an organism with specialized structures facilitating survival. The purpose of social change is the maintenance of equilibrium in society. As societies progress or become increasingly differentiated, social change efforts should aid individuals in specializing and adapting, altogether leading to 'modernizing' the social, technological and educational sectors of society, modelled on developed societies. Overall then for Selener, *people embracing evolutionary theories focus on adaptation, specialization and experimentation.*

Structural-functional Theory: Structural-functional theory is a 20th-century version of evolutionary theory, the main difference being that the latter focuses on linked stages of socioeconomic and cultural development, whereas the former is concerned with balancing mechanisms whereby societies maintain a 'uniform state'. Theorists in both camps conceive society as complex and differentiated, but essentially balanced. They are therefore in favour of adaptive and incremental adjustments which will restore balance to the system. They view forces for change as external to the system, and major conflicts as a sign of system breakdown. *Structural-functionalists view inequality as necessary and inevitable, leading to the rise of the most capable to important roles.* Change requires fitting into the existing system, as required by the needs of society as a whole. Those constituencies embracing structural-functionalist theory identify disruptions, or weak links in the system, whereby corrective actions ensue.

Systems Theory: From a systems theory perspective, the need for reform arises when the system malfunctions, thus jeopardizing efficiency and endangering 'equilibrium'. Reforms are implemented through innovative problem-solving techniques within existing systems. Inequities and inefficiencies are the result of dysfunctional organizations or ignorant individuals rather than as a consequence of self-interested elites. *Those using systems theory focus on system breakdowns and malfunctions, identifying subsystems requiring change.* Conflict-based paradigms are different.

Conflict-based Paradigms

Marxist and Neo-Marxist Theory: Marxist and neo-Marxist theoreticians focus on issues of power, exploitation and contradictions in society. They view change as structural, taking place at economic, political and social levels. While structural-functionalists attribute problems to malfunctions in the system, Marxists trace them to struggles for power, control and status among powerful elites. Changes that occur in institutions or groups are the result of major structural changes in society as a whole. *For advocates of Marxist theory, the focus is on identifying power relations and subsequently transforming such in favour of the powerless.*

Cultural Revival and Social Movement Theory: Unlike Marxist theory, cultural revitalization theory does not focus on social classes, but, rather, on deliberate, organized, conscious efforts by members of society to construct a more satisfying culture. Such revitalization may be based on mass, ethnic, charismatic or revolutionary movements. *For people embracing cultural revival theory, the research agenda may focus on the unique contributions of different people, that is elements in their knowledge, values, ideologies and experiences that promote social justice.*

Anarchistic and Utopian Theory: Anarchistic and utopian theorists of social change share the goals of radical transformation with Marxists, as well as concerns for cultural revival and for individual renewal. Although their ideas are seldom put into practice, they open up debate. *Utopian theorists, finally, may seek to identify a common vision of what the 'good society' may look like. Change may be oriented to building such a society.*

Selener then turns specifically to the participatory research that is our main concern in this chapter.

Participative versus Action Research: Selener finally compares and contrasts, from his perspective, 'participative', with more conventional 'action' research. *Participatory research* is intended to empower the powerless groups in society. Practitioners therefore tend to apply conflict-oriented paradigms, seeking after the transformation of oppressive social, economic and political structures in society. *Action researchers* work at making organizations more efficient and effective for the purpose of achieving organizational goals. As such they work within the system, making incremental changes and minor reforms.

We will now illustrate the application of PAR with remarkable case stories from Burkina Faso and Tanzania.

7.5 PAR in Practice

BURKINA FASO: THE CASE OF SIX S

PAR as a Cultural Movement

What, then, is the significance of PAR as a macro-level social transformation? Possibly the largest such movement, at least in the early 1990s, was the so-called Six S movement in Burkino Faso, which covered about two-thirds of the country's villages.[6]

Bernard Lédéa Ouédraogo, a core initiator of the Six S movement, was born in Upper Volta (now Burkina Faso) in 1930. He completed his secondary education there and gained numerous diplomas before studying in France, where he obtained a doctorate from the Sorbonne in 1977. After finishing school in 1950, Ouédraogo became a teacher and school director and then turned to agriculture, where his talents as a trainer led him to the top echelons of the civil service. But he found he was unable to help the farmers and village groups whom he was supposed to be training, so he left to find out why.

His first question was whether anything existed in the traditional society of the Mossi (Burkina's largest ethnic group) that resembled village groups. 'We undertook a thorough study of village social organization – the people's thinking and their social and economic structures – and we discovered that the Naam group, a traditional village body composed of young people, had the most highly developed cooperative characteristics. We decided we would attempt to work with the Naam structures.' The result was an initiative unique in Africa. Despite a lot of problems, the Naam groups prospered. By 1978 there were over 2,500 groups in Yatenga province with 160,000 members. Twenty years later this had risen to 6,480 groups all over Burkina Faso – almost half of them women's groups – with a membership of 300,000. The transformation of the traditional Naam groups into modern social structures was a brilliant piece of practical sociology by Ouédraogo.

He gives four reasons for their success: dynamic local leadership and activity; maintenance of traditional values; proscription of any sort of social, ethnic, political or religious discrimination; and training and motivation generated from within the group. The activities of the Naam groups are as broad as life itself. They grow, build, manufacture, trade. As of 1999, they had created 235 cereal banks, 115 mills, 22 dams and about 300 wells. In addition they have established 17 credit banks and constructed six cellars in Yatenga for preserving the 1,000 tons of potatoes they grow each year. The Naam groups are helped with aid funds from French, Swiss, Dutch and German agencies, but they generate their own incomes as well. In 1976 Ouédraogo founded, with the French development expert Bernard Lecomte, the Association Six S (Se Servir de la Saison Sèche en Savane et au Sahel), becoming its executive director two years later. While Naam is a people's movement, Six S is a non-governmental organization. It was dedicated to removing three obstacles to peasant mobilization: the lack of technical knowhow for coping with drought and desertification; the lack of negotiating skills to deal with government and aid agencies; and the lack of funds to implement small projects.

Six S became a federation of peasant organizations like (and including) the Naam from nine countries in the Sahelian zone. By the late 1980s, Six S was reckoned to serve over 2 million people, on the basis of a direct membership of 245,000 farmers. More recently, Six S has undergone some restructuring. In the mid-1990s, Ouédraogo was elected mayor of his hometown, Ouahigouya. Apart from the success of Six S, he is doubtful of the future: 'The danger for many Africans is that the erosion of our ways by the aggressive ways of others, our own values by foreign values, will destroy our sense of responsibility for solving our communities' problems.'

Animating Agency

The enormous scales of activity, described previously, are being attained through two processes of 'multiplication': people engaged in one village animating and assisting another; and specific stimulation of such by an animating agency. In effect PAR at this stage may be seen as a cultural, rather than political, movement. In the context of such, for M.D. Rahman, consciousness is an organic part of one's social existence, which generates its own paradigm for the discovery of the truth. The two truths, between professionals and the people, may only dialogue with each other, and none may claim to be the greater of the two.

There is no assured method of transferring commitment to succeeding generations who have not lived through the struggles from which commitment is socio-historically born. Such a pursuit becomes a happy hunting ground for self-seekers. And genuine accountability to the people is not merely a matter of formal institutional structures, but also, and critically, of people's self-awareness and the confidence to assert such in the affairs of society. The crisis of the left – and for that matter of the right as well – ultimately boils down to this dissociation between the productive forces and the leadership of concerned societies. With such dissociation prevailing, the need is to generate social processes which would promote the possibility of organic leadership. PAR attempts, as has been demonstrated in the Burkina Faso case, just that.

We now turn from Burkina Faso to Tanzania.

TANZANIA: A STORY TO TELL – 'HILI LI MAMA' MEANING 'THIS MAMA …'

Another compelling example of working with PAR is the story of Mwajamah Masaiganah who worked originally with fisherfolk communities in rural Tanzania:

My [Mwajamah Masaiganah] journey takes you back to 1985 when, for the first time, I involved myself in participatory action research (PAR) with fisherfolk communities in Tanzania, focusing specifically on women. Back then, I used to do things the way I was told by higher authorities, taking directions or sending messages to communities, be they right or wrong, no questioning! Using PAR and video as a way of communicating changed my way of looking at things, doing things; created a special interest in me for women and community issues, developed in me a respect for communities and in totality, changed my entire life.

During my work with the communities in Mtwara and Lindi regions as a rural development advisor and then as a facilitator with the fisherfolk communities, we managed to learn from one another, create awareness in communities, create allies (even with politicians). This helped us to integrate with higher government authorities and lobby for policy changes. Our aim was to stop dynamite and other illegal fishing methods, which claimed lives, left people maimed and threatened people's livelihoods. Nobody thought that we were doing the right thing because, to some people, banning dynamite fishing and taking measures to stop it was interfering with their trade. The dynamite traders and illegal fishermen could lose money by stopping the illegal deal.

I will give just part of my life history working with bureaucrats and within bureaucratic systems, the hustles I encountered and how they helped shape my life. I will narrate my story starting in December 1996, when I facilitated a five-day evaluation workshop with a group of fishermen in Sudi, Lindi district, as part of the RIPS1 marine environment project. Our first meeting in Sudi village led to the Sudi declaration, which was made by fishermen and women from 12 coastal villages of Mtwara, Lindi and Kilwa districts. During this meeting they agreed to form a committee, called the Sudi Committee, to oversee the whole issue of marine environment protection in the area and raise awareness in all people in the area and at regional and national levels. This was to be done through mass meetings, leaders' (villagers') meetings, but using video as a medium of communication.

Figure 7.4   Mwajuma's 'Drawing in Action'

This idea of using a video was just to start filming when we started the meeting and show back the video every evening of the day's workshop proceedings. This seemed to work, as people, villagers, came forward and volunteered to talk freely in front of the camera and expressed their concerns on the issue of dynamite fishing. This was because, first, video was new in these areas so it was a proud moment for the people to see themselves talking on film. Secondly, people had built trust in us and they knew that it would help us show their leaders what 'they', the people, say. Previously their fears were that whilst many researchers had been talking to them during the many meetings in their villages, all reports from such discussions were just put on shelves and nothing was done. The people were tired because these meetings benefited researchers and their bosses alone, leaving them with nothing.

So, using this kind of media, we assured them that their leaders would see exactly what they said without filtering the information. Therefore, we agreed with them that the Sudi Committee would use the video in their organized tours to create awareness. When we went back to the office, I happened to come across a report or a personal note written by my chief technical advisor, Lars Johanson. It read '…I have never seen in my life such great facilitation skills as displayed by Mwajuma in this exercise …'

From this, you can imagine how unbelievable it was for me and at the same time how good I felt. I developed and grew even stronger. But, this strength did not take more than four years before landing me into problems and friction with the Regional Authorities.

In January 1997, things started to turn really sour. After an evaluation workshop, the Sudi Committee, formed from the strengthened fisherfolk who had been at the workshop, agreed to meet and draft a constitution to start an NGO called 'Shirikisho' so that they could be independent to do things that concern their lives. In that meeting, one member reported that the situation in the neighbouring region of Kilwa was bad and had reached the extent that illegal fishermen had raised a flag on one of the islands stating, 'Kilwa Hakuna Serikali' meaning 'There is no Government in Kilwa'.

As we were also using media to put pressure on the government to change the policy, I told this story about Kilwa to a newsreader on Radio One. The next morning it was like a hot cake, repeated in the headline news for about a day and a half. After looking for me the whole morning, the Kilwa police left a message that I should report to them. I reported but took along with me the Secretary of Shirikisho. In case something happened to me, then they should know and act quickly.

The police wanted to know why I had made such statements. I said yes, that I had and the reason was that the police were not doing their job. I said that this was highlighted in the evaluation workshop and that in ranking, the police were given zero in efficiency. I explained that I was only telling what people say. After long discussions, they agreed that they are having problems. In a way, it was getting difficult for them to perform their duties because the dynamite problem was an inside job. Then they said that it was the Police Commander that had instructed them to bring me to the police station. I said 'Yes, here I am and if only you put me in now, try it, you'll see what happens. The people will retaliate to your actions'. I told them we knew much more of what was happening than the police knew and if they wanted to get anywhere, they had to work closely with us. The first agony was over, but I knew I was being monitored.

We decided to record the whole process by video, even the follow up of what happened six months after the evaluation workshop. We made a video documentary and organized trips to visit the Regional Commissioners of Lindi and Mtwara; the Ministers of Communication and Works, Natural Resources and Tourism, the Environment (both in the mainland and in the Isles); the Attorney General and Agricultural and Industries Supplies Company Ltd.; and other companies which are directly or indirectly related to the sale or keeping of dynamite and natural resources. During all these trips, we took video as a means of documenting the process. Many trips of the same kind were made to meet leaders like the then Prime Minister and Vice President who visited the area. In both incidences it was hard for us to get a chance to show them our video or talk to them, as nobody took us seriously. But in all occasions we did actually manage to provide these leaders with a video documentary called *Bahari Yetu Hatutaki* – meaning 'Not in Our Ocean'.

In February 1997, during the parliamentary session, four Sudi members, plus myself, travelled to Dodoma to meet the Prime Minister, together with Members of Parliament (MPs) from the southern coastal area. To our amazement, they had talked to other members of parliament from the south and they had agreed that the problem did not concern only the coastal constituencies but the entire southern region, because that was their only source of protein – fish from the sea. So, the MPs received us as a team, and made plans to meet the Prime Minister (PM), Mr. Sumaye, the next day. In the morning we attended the parliament session as guests and in the afternoon, we had a very fruitful meeting. I went with the group from Sudi, not as a member, but to document the process. One of our aims was to document and make a video for the purpose of training and educating the masses and policy makers.

So, our meeting started with the current Minister of Regional Administration and Local Government, an MP from Kilwa, introducing the team to the Prime Minister. He said, 'Mr. PM, in front of you is a team of four members of the Sudi committee and a group of southern MPs who have come to see you on this issue. Seeing us here as a team, you should understand that we are fed up with the situation…'. The PM asked, 'You have said four members, but I can see *there is one other person. Who is she?'. I introduced myself as a facilitator of the process and that I was only there to document what was going on using video and audio on behalf of the communities. During this meeting, the Sudi Committee members gave the Prime Minister their video with documentation of the whole process and argued for him to take action, which he did! During this process we also asked for permission to film the meeting session and he permitted us to do so. We explained to him that it was important for the Association to document and that our final video would provide documentation of the whole process.*

As facilitator of the process, I never contributed to the discussion in any way. I only documented the process. This group was empowered so much that they needed no outsider to speak for them. Generally the video had a big impact on people to come out and speak because holding the microphone was a way of empowering them and giving them a voice. It draws people nearer as they tend to believe more in what they say, rather than in what we say for them. With the experiences above and the many others which I did not give here, I was moved to look critically at the issue of empowerment, participation, rights and what are the processes of government; laws, policies, acts put in place for us (its people). We need to look critically at whether these processes are benefiting the people of Tanzania in a way that protects their livelihoods and empowers them socially and economically. We need to analyse how and whether the current systems have offered women and the poor what they are supposed to offer, according to what is stipulated in government policies and regulations, for the benefit of the people and the country's benefit at large. And we need to always look at whether the voices of the people are heard in the democratic process.

7.6 Conclusion

FURTHER THE PROGRESS OF THE GRASSROOTS – REDISCOVERY OF CULTURAL ROOTS

Reflecting on 'What is Development?'

People's collective self-development initiatives, for Fals Borda, not only point to a way out of the development impasse. They also suggest the need for reflection on the very notion of 'development'. For a long time, development has been associated with the mechanistic notion of the development of physical assets and increasing the flow of economic and social goods and services. Much of the activities articulated here are developmental, but questions remain as to whether the process of people mobilizing themselves is a means of 'development' or an end in itself.

Africa in particular, for Fals Borda writing in the 1990s, is indeed showing evidence of vibrant and assertive people's self-development efforts in rural areas, which are in the frontier of such efforts anywhere and from which inspiration can be gleaned and much learned. Genuine people-oriented activists seldom come from the professional classes. However, people with a powerful societal vision, conception, intellectual ability and methodological skill for translating conception into practice are needed to provide some guidance and perspective for such initiatives, and for these to spread widely with some coherence. People seem to be ready to respond to such 'animation'.

Must this be left to spontaneous historical emergence, or can some method of 'schooling' be devised to promote a greater concern among a nation's potential intellectual leaders to work *with* and not *upon* the people, so that the 'other Africa' could develop faster?

Praxis and the Recovery of History and Culture

Participative action research, in conclusion, has demonstrated in concrete cases its ability to further the progress of the grassroots rather than the vested interests of dominant groups. As such, the rediscovery of cultural roots is an essential element in any effort to improve depressed communities. Recent analysis, moreover, has pointed to the need to distinguish three movements in cultural-historical praxis: investigative, ideological and political. PAR researchers attempt to connect all three in an action-reflection cycle, spiralling towards successively more complex stages of theory and practice. The flavour and ambience of science, then, has changed dramatically in recent times, as witnessed by the seminal work of such scholars as Fritjof Capra (*Tao of Physics*), and the 'chaos' theorists, each of whom emphasize the holistic philosophy, relativist knowledge and interdisciplinary methods. Following Foucault, moreover, the PAR movement may see itself developing hitherto 'subjugated knowledges'.

The more important practical challenge PAR faces, for Fals Borda, is the need of common people to articulate in social movements, along with new knowledge, the necessary political struggles for justice and progress. As such we are discovering once more the pertinence of participatory action research to the transformation of our societies into a more satisfactory and less violent world.

Spell of the Sensuous to Six S

We have travelled a long way along the relational path, leading towards 'healing the planet', both in human and 'more-than-human' terms. In terms of practical cases in point we have journeyed descriptively from David Abram's 'Spell of the Sensuous' towards, participatively, Bernard Ouedraogo's Six S in Burkino Faso. In such a journey from the formative to the transformative, from origination to innovation, we moved from the descriptive to the phenomenological, onto feminism and participatory research. In doing so, we moved progressively through being and becoming, knowing and doing. While Abram's primary concern is with a mode of being, Ouedraogo is primarily motivated by doing, Havel with a process of becoming, and Karl Sveiby and Tex Scuthorpe with the mode of knowing.

TOWARDS COMMUNITY BUILDING AND HEALING THE PLANET

We come to the end of the Southern relational path by revisiting once more the four levels along the research-to-innovation trajectory that you have, by now, progressively built upon. Through such, your integral innovation would have come about, on an organizational and communal level, supporting community building (the Southern function of an enterprise or community) and, on a societal level, contributing to healing the planet. The following table summarizes the entire Southern journey.

While the four-level path to innovation may be presented here in linear from for ease of presentation, a full-fledged integral innovation is by no means a linear, but rather a cycling, spiralling and iterating, process. The organic and natural metaphor of a tree, which needs to be rooted deeply in a particular soil, which grows slowly, and whose bearing of fruits depends on a large number of favourable conditions, is a more authentic representation. After all, a tree supports, metaphorically, the notion that an integral innovator needs to stand up against many storms, preventing him or her from becoming a transformative agent. We therefore feel that it is more appropriate to end the path with our integral innovation tree, also here focusing on the particular theme and social scientific disciplines that are most relevant for this path.

Southern Relational Path	
Community Building – Healing the Planet	
Passion *Originate*	*Passionately and concretely involved with a particular people and environment,* you portray them vitally and intimately, in rich colour and texture, rhythm and form.
Engagement *Found*	You enter philosophically *into the life world and spirit of a culture;* conceiving of their unique time and place, as a local part of a larger story and a wider world.
Liberation *Emancipate*	You reflect critically and contextually on your self and others, ecologically, anthropologically, and sociologically, using *such situated knowledge as a means for liberation.*
Participation *Transform*	Via discussion, consensus building, activity, using popular stories and oral traditions, *you heal environments and build communities,* enhancing human and more-than-human life.

Figure 7.5   The Integral Innovation Tree and the Southern Relational Path

We now turn from the relational path to the research 'path of renewal', starting out with conventional hermeneutics, an interpretive methodology that follows on from narrative methods.

References

1. Denzin, N. and Lincoln, Y. (2004). *Landscape of Qualitative Research*. London: Sage.
2. Reason, P. and Bradbury, H. (2004). *Handbook of Action Research*. London: Sage.
3. Fals Borda, O. (ed.). (1991). *Action and Knowledge*. New York: Apex Publishing.
4. Rahman, M.D. (1993). *Peoples' Self Development*. London: Zed Books.
5. Selener, D. (1997). *Participative Action Research for Social Change*. Ithaca, NY: University of Cornell.
6. Pradervand, P. (1990). *Listening to Africa – Developing Africa from the Grassroots*. New York: Praeger.
7. Masaiganah, M. (2004). *A Story to Tell*. Tanzania: self-published document.

8 *From Narrative Methods to Hermeneutics*

Fuse Horizons

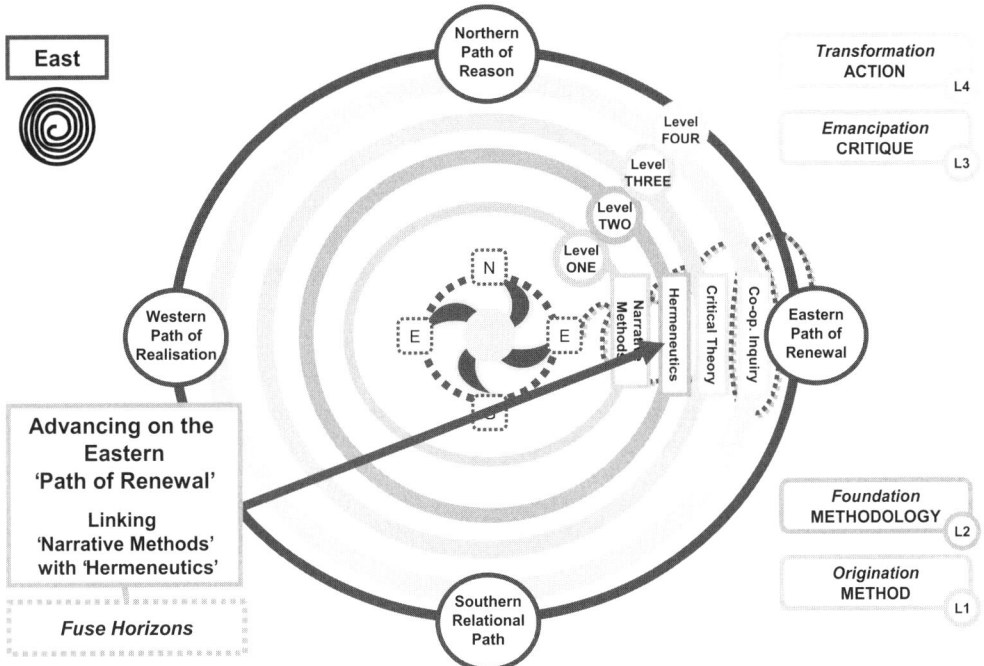

Figure 8.1   Overview Chapter 8 – Level 2/East

Summary: Hermeneutics

- We now immerse you in the Eastern path of renewal, building on the narrative methods that were introduced in Chapter 4. There you were engaged in narrating your own story and that of your life world and society. What then in your research is the emerging storyline that underlies your individual, institutional and societal explorations?
- To discover that, we turn to interpretive hermeneutics: From the hermeneutic perspective, the primary aim of qualitative research is to develop an understanding of how the world is 'constructed'. The notion of a 'constructed' world implies that it is complex, layered and can be viewed from different perspectives. Interpretivism, hence, gives the other a voice, allows their experiences and stories to be documented. This brings us to cultures and to 'multiculturalism'.
- Multiculturalism refers to something crucial in the contemporary world: that people importantly differ from one another, are in contact with and must deal with each other. All multiculturalists focus on understanding and living with cultural and social difference. But such multiculturalism poses an epistemic problem: if others live within their own framework and we live within ours, how can we understand them? That is where hermeneutics comes in.
- Context plays a crucial role: people and things exist only within a certain political and moral context, and they are not understandable outside it. This is where hermeneutics differs from phenomenology. Individuals and their context form a dialogical, interpenetrating unit. By studying one, the researcher inevitably studies the other. Also, in undertaking a research project, the researcher brings his or her own cultural frame of reference into the picture, which continually and unavoidably frames and shapes the process.
- This chapter distinguishes between the traditional hermeneutic position originating from Europe and new forms of hermeneutics emerged in transition countries; in this case we focus on Africa.
- *European (interpretive) hermeneutics:* In the 20th century hermeneutics came to be seen as perhaps *the* methodology of the social sciences. It is an interpretive social science, taking as its goal the achievement of understanding, backed by rich description and unfolding narrative. The aim is not to conform and extend universalized experiences to attain knowledge of a law but to understand how this man, this people or this state is what it has become.
- *African (transformative) hermeneutics:* African and Afro-American philosophers lend a somewhat more transformative edge to 'narrative' interpretive method and to 'hermeneutic' constructivist methodology than their more purely interpretive European counterparts. The fruitful tension between esteem and criticism, tradition and modernity, when properly cultivated, constitutes the critical edge of transformative hermeneutics. Hermeneutics, here, has also the role of reconnecting a people with its own source. Such a 'return' is not a return to tradition or stasis. We as researchers are not engaged in an antiquarian quest for an already existing authentic past tradition. Rather, we are engaged in the affirmation of the historicity of the rural indigenous people.
- In interpretive-hermeneutic terms then, the originating of your research question involves uncovering an original story in each case, a return to source, underlying your research phenomenon.
- In concluding this chapter, we introduce Zahra Al Zeera, an Islamic researcher who discovered hermeneutics as a means of going beyond the positivist and reductionist paradigm in which most education in the Islamic world, in her view, is lodged, to achieve 'wholeness and holiness in education'. After hermeneutics (foundation) we will turn to critical theory (emancipation).

8.1 Orientation to Hermeneutics

Pursuing a research path of renewal, you move from your narrative origination onto an interpretive foundation, before advancing toward emancipatory critique (in this Eastern case, that of critical theory), culminating in co-operative inquiry as your ultimate means of transformation.

You have now the questionable issue that you feel called upon (by your own will and intent) to investigate. Such a question could be, for example: 'What are the constraints and opportunities of banking in and for China, from a cultural as well as economic perspective?', or 'What are the specific needs and opportunities facing social entrepreneurship in South Africa, as a society and economy in transition?' For you as a researcher one or other of these issues is a burning one, of great significance for you and your society. In addition, getting immersed in a particular subjective way needs to fit with your unfolding story.

What then becomes your research question? How might it be arising out of that subjective/objective relationship between you as a researcher and the emergent phenomenon you are researching? What then will constitute your original storyline, one that aligns your own originality with the uniqueness of the particular phenomenon? What in your research is the emerging storyline that underlies your individual, institutional and societal explorations?

We turn now to the interpretive and hermeneutic methodology, which provides the methodological wisdom to build upon the narrative methods that formed an integral part of our flow of innovation in Chapter 4. But let us first retrace our steps and understand hermeneutics' own story.

ORIGINS OF HERMENEUTICS

Hermeneutics may be described as the development and study of theories of the interpretation and understanding of texts. Essentially, it involves cultivating the ability to understand things from somebody else's point of view, and to appreciate the cultural and social forces that may have influenced their outlook.

In contemporary usage, hermeneutics often refers to study of the interpretation of biblical texts. In fact, it was Rabbi Ishmael Ben Elisha (90 to 135 AD) of the Amoraic era of Judaism who interpreted laws from the Torah through 13 hermeneutic principles. This was the first known appearance of hermeneutics in the world.

In the last two centuries of the modern era, the scope of hermeneutics has expanded to include the investigation and interpretation not only of textual and artistic works, but of human behaviour generally, including language and patterns of speech, social institutions and ritual behaviours (such as religious ceremonies, political rallies, football matches, rock concerts, and so on). Hermeneutics interprets or inquires into the meaning and import of these phenomena, through understanding the point of view and 'inner life' of the researcher or of the first-person perspective of an engaged participant in these phenomena.

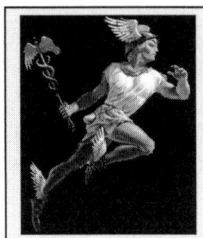

The word 'Hermeneutics' is a Term derived from 'Ἑρμηνεύς', the Greek Word for Iinterpreter. This is related to the Name of the Greek God Hermes in his Role as the Interpreter of the Messages of the Gods. Hermes was believed to play Tricks on those he was supposed to give Messages to, often changing the Messages and influencing the Interpretation thereof. The Greek Word thus has the basic Meaning of 'one who makes the Meaning clear'.

Figure 8.2   Origins of the Hermeneutic Term

Source: Acambiode http://imagenes.acambiode.com/img-bbdd/hermes.jpg

HISTORY OF HERMENEUTICS

Hermeneutics in the Western world, as a general science of text interpretation, can be traced back to two sources. One source was the ancient Greek rhetoricians' study of literature, which came to fruition in Alexandria. The other source has been the Midrashic and Patristic traditions of biblical exegesis, which were contemporary with Hellenistic culture. It was actually Aristotle who struck a chord in his treatise *De Interpretatione* that reverberates through the intervening ages and supplies the key note for many contemporary theories of interpretation.

The early Jewish rabbis and the early Church Fathers deployed similar philological (language-based) tools; their biblical interpretations stressed allegorical readings, frequently at the expense of the texts' literal meaning. They sought deeper meanings below the outward appearance of the text. Examples of such interpretations include the writings of Philo of Alexandria, Origen and the Talmud. Interestingly enough, before the studies of the bible that explicitly gave rise to hermeneutics, innumerable Islamic scholars, from the 9th century onwards, came to study the Qur'an in the same interpretive light.

During the European Renaissance of the 15th century, the discipline of hermeneutics emerged through the new humanist education as a historical and critical methodology for analysing texts. In a triumph of early modern hermeneutics, the Italian humanist Lorenzo Valla proved in 1440 that the *Donation of Constantine* was a forgery, through the intrinsic evidence of the text itself. Thus hermeneutics expanded from its medieval role in purely explaining the correct analysis of the Bible. However, biblical hermeneutics did not die off at the time. For example, the Protestant reformation brought about a renewed interest in the interpretation of the Bible, which took a step away from the interpretive tradition developed during the Middle Ages back to the texts themselves.

MODERN HERMENEUTICS: FROM SCHLEIERMACHER TO DILTHEY ...

Modern hermeneutics started with the German philosopher Friedrich Schleiermacher. He explored the nature of understanding in relation not just to the problem of deciphering sacred texts, but to all human texts and modes of communication. Schleiermacher said that every problem of interpretation is a problem of understanding. He even defined hermeneutics as the art of avoiding misunderstanding. He also provided a solution to the avoidance of misunderstanding: acquiring a knowledge of grammatical and psychological laws in trying to understand the text and the writer. There arose in his time a fundamental shift from understanding not only the exact words and their objective meaning to understanding the individuality of the speaker or author.

With Schleiermacher, hermeneutics begins to stress the importance of the interpreter and his understanding of the text in the process of interpretation. Understanding, for Schleiermacher, does not simply come from reading the text, but involves knowledge of the historical context of the text and the psychology of the author.

The German 19th-century philosopher Wilhelm Dilthey broadened hermeneutics even more by relating interpretation to all historical descriptions. Understanding thereby moves from the outer manifestations of human action and productivity to explore their inner meaning. In his last important essay *The Understanding of Others and their Manifestations of Life*,[1] Dilthey makes it clear that this move from outer to inner, from expression to what is expressed, is not based on empathy. Empathy involves a direct identification with the other. Interpretation involves an indirect or mediated understanding that can only be attained by placing human expressions in their historical context. For Dilthey, understanding is not a process of reconstructing the state of mind of the author, but one of articulating what is expressed in the work, that is specifically by placing it in its historical context.

… TO HEIDEGGER AND GADAMER

Since Dilthey, the discipline of hermeneutics has detached itself from this central task and broadened its spectrum to all texts, including multimedia and to understanding the bases of meaning. In the 20th century, Martin Heidegger's philosophical hermeneutics shifted the focus from interpretation to so-called 'existential' understanding, which was treated more as a direct, non-mediated, thus in a sense more authentic, way of being in the world than simply as a way of knowing.

Hans-Georg Gadamer's hermeneutics is a development of the hermeneutics of his teacher, Heidegger. He describes the process of interpreting a text as the fusion of one's own horizon with the horizon of the text. He defines 'horizon' as 'the totality of all that can be realized or thought about by a person at a given time in history and in a particular culture.'

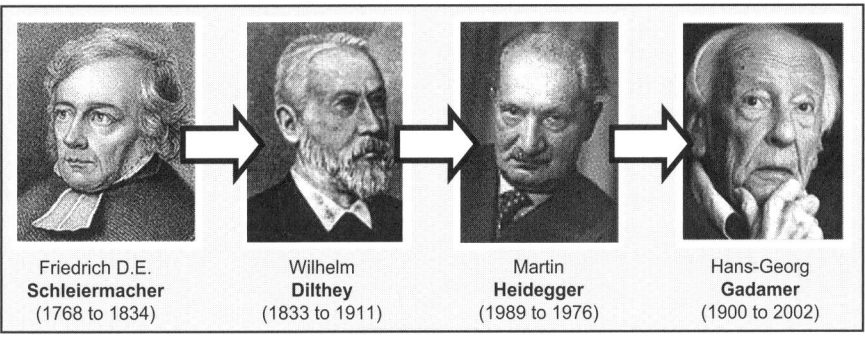

Friedrich D.E.	Wilhelm	Martin	Hans-Georg
Schleiermacher	**Dilthey**	**Heidegger**	**Gadamer**
(1768 to 1834)	(1833 to 1911)	(1989 to 1976)	(1900 to 2002)

Figure 8.3 Hermeneutics – Core Thinkers

Sources: Image 1: Muenchner Uebersetzerforum http://www.muenchner-uebersetzerforum.de/. Image 2: University College Cork http://www.ucc.ie/en/. Image 3: Philosophische Schriften/Falsafeh http://www.falsafeh.com/. Image 4: Philweb http://www.phillwebb.net/

Gadamer's philosophical project, as explained in his magnum opus *Truth and Method*, was to elaborate on the concept of 'philosophical hermeneutics', which Heidegger initiated but never dealt with at length. Gadamer's goal was to uncover the nature of human understanding. In the book Gadamer argued that 'truth' and 'method' were at odds with one another. He was critical of two approaches to the human sciences. On the one hand, he was critical of modern approaches to humanities that modelled themselves on the natural sciences (and thus on rigorous scientific methods). On the other hand, he took issue with the traditional German approach to the humanities, represented for instance by Friedrich Schleiermacher and Wilhelm Dilthey (http://en.wikipedia.org/wiki/Wilhelm_Dilthey) which believed that correctly interpreting a text meant recovering the original intention of the author who wrote it.

In contrast to both of these positions, Gadamer argued that people have a 'historically affected consciousness' (*wirkungsgeschichtliches Bewußtsein*) and that they are embedded in the particular history and culture that shaped them.

In fact history does not belong to us; but we belong to it. Long before we understand ourselves through the process of self-examination, we understand ourselves in a self-evident way in the family, society and state in which we live. The focus of subjectivity is a distorting mirror. The self-awareness of the individual is only a flickering in the closed circuits of historical life. That is why the prejudices of the individual, far more than his judgments, constitute the historical reality of his being.[2]

Thus interpreting a text involves a 'fusion of horizons' where the scholar finds the ways that the text's history articulates with their own background. 'Truth and Method' is not meant to be a programmatic statement about a new 'hermeneutic' method of interpreting texts. Gadamer intended *Truth and Method* to be a description of what we always do when we interpret things (even if we do not know it): 'My real concern was and is philosophic: not what we do or what we ought to do, but what happens to us over and above our wanting and doing.'[3]

We now turn from an overview of hermeneutics to its key tenets.

8.2 Hermeneutics – Key Tenets: From Understanding the World to Reconnecting with Your Source

Hermeneutics – Key Tenets
① Understand how the world is 'constructed'.
② Give 'the other' a voice.
③ Interpret reality indirectly.
④ Reconstruct self and society.
⑤ Move from spectator to active agent.

⑥	Evolve from interpretive to transformative.
⑦	Reconnect with the source.

① UNDERSTAND HOW THE WORLD IS 'CONSTRUCTED'

Hermeneutics is perhaps the most pre-eminent, conventionally 'interpretive' qualitative methodology. Qualitative research is a process of a careful inquiry into the social world, and indeed worlds, serving to newly understand them, and thereby produce knowledge that becomes practically useful.

The primary aim of such an interpretive approach is to develop an understanding of how the world is 'constructed'. The notion of the world being constructed implies that it is complex, layered and can be viewed from different perspectives. We construct the world through talk, action, systems of meaning, rituals and institutions that have been created, as well as through the ways in which the world is physically and materially shaped. In particular, hermeneutic research seeks to uncover historical and cultural horizons of meaning, that is, if you like, story lines, through which a world is experienced.

② GIVE 'THE OTHER' A VOICE

This giving voice to the other is seen as invaluable to the human conduct. Hermeneutic research, hence, serves to expand a practitioner's awareness of the process of management, social work, therapy, social and economic transformation, or whatever, within particular contexts. Such research may cover the historical development of a field, or serve to establish a bridge between one field and another, either in terms of disciplines or in terms of cultures. Hermeneutics is hence 'tradition-informed understanding'. As such, it is especially suited for a transcultural orientation, and for a grounding of self and organization in a particular place and time.

Multiculturalists focus on understanding and living with cultural and social difference. But such multiculturalism poses an epistemic (knowledge-based) problem: if others live within their own framework and we live within ours, how can we understand them? That is where hermeneutics comes in. Hence, the basic question of the philosophy of social science today ought not to be whether social science is 'scientific'. Rather, it ought to be whether understanding others – particularly others who are different – is possible, and if so, what does such understanding involve?

③ INTERPRET REALITY INDIRECTLY

According to so-called 'perspectivism', as an offshoot of hermeneutics, knowers rather approach reality from their own slant, with their own assumptions and preconceptions. Hence, facts are also rooted in such perspectives. In other words, description requires a scheme consisting of terms by means of which facts will be constituted. This is exactly what perspectivism claims: without an organizing conceptual scheme, or overall perspective, no intellectual activity can occur. For a blank slate is incapable of learning anything. Knowers have to bring to their experience, their culture and society, a rich assortment of ideas and conceptual commitments to bear upon people and things, in order even to describe what they see, that is in order to have something about which to theorize. Without basic propositions, knowledge itself would be impossible. All knowledge is therefore a constructive activity in which knowers are active contributors.

④ RECONSTRUCT SELF AND SOCIETY

People and things exist only within a certain political and moral context, and they are not understandable outside of it. This is where hermeneutics, as Heidegger pointed out, differs from phenomenology. Individuals and their context form a dialogical, interpenetrating unit. By studying one, you as researcher inevitably study the other. Also, in undertaking a research project, you bring your own individual (self) as well as cultural (society) frame of reference into the picture, which continually and unavoidably frames and shapes the process. Finally, by reconnecting with your own source, you, as a researcher, fully contextualize your research and become an active participant in a creative process of reconstructing self and society.

⑤ MOVE FROM SPECTATOR TO ACTIVE AGENT

Philosophical schemas, or indeed personal or cultural 'self-constructed' perspectives, serve as important devices for making a world intelligible at a particular period in time, and for one set of people in relation to another, rather than the whole world for all time. As languages of understanding are developed and disseminated, you as research scientist cross the threshold from passive responder or reactor to active constructer of meaning, and enter not as a spectator of the inevitable, but as an active agent. To communicate your understanding is to make a small investment in the creation of the future, and, in the process, to participate in social innovation.

⑥ EVOLVE FROM INTERPRETIVE TO TRANSFORMATIVE

African and Afro-American philosophers lend a somewhat more transformative edge to 'narrative' interpretive method and to 'hermeneutic' constructivist methodology than their more purely interpretive European counterparts. Such a different notion is deeply linked to African history. For Serequeberhan, Africa's core hermeneutic philosopher, it is in the painful gap between the ideal and actuality that the African hermeneutic philosophy finds its source and the locus of its concerns. As such, Africa and other societies in transition including the ex-communist countries of Eastern Europe, China and India need to re-invent themselves to transform themselves, rather than 'be developed' by others. In so doing, the review of an individual's, an institution's or a society's own narrative and destiny, is matched by hermeneutical re-invention or re-construction.

⑦ RECONNECT WITH THE SOURCE

Humans do not have a pure, fundamental human nature that is transhistorical and transcultural; you are incomplete and therefore unable to adequately function unless embedded in a specific cultural matrix. Hence, the cultural matrix 'completes' humans. The material objects we create, the ideas we hold and actions we take are shaped in a fundamental way by the social framework in which we are raised. These cultural artefacts are not only the reflection or expression of an era, they are the immediate stuff of daily life. Your research task is to interpret the multitudinous and conflicting ways in which various worlds are constructed and human meanings developed.

Finally, as a hermeneutic researcher with a view to social innovation, you should not passively adhere to what is given by tradition. Rather the relation to the tradition is an open-ended encounter, between self and other, past and present, in which what is explicitly preserved and implicitly betrayed by tradition is revealed. Historically – a person, organization or community – always becomes what it is by projecting itself out of its past, its lived inheritance. Its 'destiny' is thus always what comes out of itself, its 'has been' out of the prospects of its history and the possibilities of its generation. Hence, in many countries, such a 'return' to its history is a cultural and political recovery of the oppressed historic possibilities in the existence of the colonized. However, the 'return' is not meant to be a return to tradition or stasis. We as researchers-and-innovators are not engaged in an antiquarian quest for an already existing authentic past tradition. Rather, we are engaged in the affirmation of the historicity of the rural indigenous people.

We now turn from the philosophy to the psychology of hermeneutics, and from a Germanic to a more Anglo-Saxon perspective.

8.3 Hermeneutic Methodology in Depth

REFLEXIVE KNOWING

We now consider hermeneutics in more depth, moving from the original German founding fathers – Schleiermacher, Dilthey, Heidegger, Gadamer – to the more contemporary (mostly) Anglo-Saxon interpreters of such a research orientation. In fact, the Scottish researcher, John McLeod, and the American researchers, Fay, Gergen and Cushman, all take a psychological as well as a philosophical approach.

The primary aim of qualitative research is to develop an understanding of how the world is 'constructed'. This at least is what the Scottish researcher and psychologist John McLeod[4] believes, arguing from a constructivist hermeneutic perspective. *The notion of the world being constructed implies that it is complex, layered and can be viewed from different perspectives.* We construct the world through talk, action, systems of meaning, rituals and institutions that have been created, as well as through the ways in which the world is physically and materially shaped. In particular, hermeneutic research seeks to uncover historical and cultural horizons of meaning, that is, if you like, story lines, through which a world is experienced. Why then pursue such qualitative inquiry?

McLeod divides his response, both in relation to phenomenology and also to hermeneutics, between one of knowing and that of becoming a knower. Everyday common-sense knowledge, firstly then, is far from being coherent and consistent. There may have been times in the past when people lived according to fixed rules and axioms, but these days are well gone. New elements of common sense become reworked, appropriated by different groups and ultimately outmoded. *Qualitative research is a process of careful inquiry into the social world, and indeed worlds, serving to newly understand them, and thereby produce knowledge that becomes practically useful.* McLeod divides such careful inquiry into three areas:

1. knowledge of phenomena;
2. knowledge of the other;
3. reflexive knowing.

Interpretivism gives the other a voice, allows their experiences and life stories to be documented, this being seen as invaluable to the human being. Such research, for McLeod, serves to expand a practitioner's awareness of the process of management, social work, therapy, social and economic transformation, or whatever, within particular contexts. Reflexive knowing occurs when you deliberately turn your attention to your own processes of constructing a world, with the goal of saying something new about that personal (or shared) world that you indeed construct. Such research may cover the historical development of a field, or serve to establish a bridge between one field and another, either in terms of disciplines or in terms of cultures. We start with such cultures in particular, then move onto social constructivism in general, ultimately moving onto hermeneutics per se, both in Europe (as a developed society) and also Africa (reflecting societies in transition).

FROM INTERPRETIVISM TO PERSPECTIVISM

Beyond Self versus Other

Multiculturalism, for the American social philosopher Brian Fay, refers to something crucial in the contemporary world: that people importantly differ from one another, are in contact with and must deal with each other. All multiculturalists focus on understanding and living with cultural and social difference. But such multiculturalism poses an epistemic problem: if others live within their own framework and we live within ours, how can we understand them? That is where hermeneutics comes in. For Fay, the basic question of the philosophy of social science today ought not to be whether social science is 'scientific'. Rather, it ought to be whether understanding others – particularly others who are different – is possible, and if so, what does such understanding involve?

Prevailing conceptions of multiculturalism emphasize difference, cultural integrity and resistance to cultural domination. They think in rigidly dualistic categories of 'self' versus 'other'; of 'us' versus 'them'; of 'sameness' versus 'difference'; of 'assimilation' versus 'separatism'; and of 'insider' versus 'outsider'. In place of difference Fay emphasizes interchange; in place of integrity, openness and interaction; in place of resistance he emphasizes learning. Throughout he replaces a dualistic mode of thought with a dialectical one, rooted in a so-called 'perspectivism' aligned with 'interpretivism'.

From Interpretivism to Perspectivism

According to perspectivism, knowers never view reality directly as it is in itself; rather they approach it from their own slant, with their own assumptions and preconceptions. Facts are not just states of affairs, which present themselves immediately sorted out and identified. Without a prior vocabulary, which a describer brings to a situation, there would be no facts whatsoever. Where does this vocabulary come from? Describers must possess some scheme of terms to provide the basic building blocks for their factual descriptions. Put succinctly: facts are rooted in conceptual schemes. So description requires a scheme consisting of terms by means of which facts will be constituted. *This is exactly what perspectivism claims: without an organizing conceptual scheme no intellectual activity can occur.*

Just as descriptive statements are rooted in theories, theories themselves are nested in larger conceptual structures. Science aspires to link individual theories together to form a network of theories. The theories of the unconscious, of dreams, of psychosocial development and repression are all linked together, for example, to form the Freudian theory of the psyche. Science seeks to explain a divergent and extensive range of phenomena in terms of a few basic principles. Theories are also themselves explained by higher level, more general theories. For example, the theory of consumer behaviour in neoclassical economic theory is itself explained by the more abstract theory of consumer preference. All theories, then, presuppose some basic commitments as to the fundamental core of a subject, to the basic concepts by which to identify and describe such, and to basic claims as to the nature of this core.

This is the way perspectivism portrays science. Human knowers cannot look at reality directly in some unmediated manner, no matter how much they try to purge their minds of prior ideas and concepts. It is a good thing that they cannot: for a blank slate is incapable of learning anything. *Without basic propositions, knowledge itself would be impossible. All knowledge is a constructive activity in which knowers are active contributors.*

HERMENEUTICS AND SOCIAL CONSTRUCTIVISM

Philosophical schemas, for a constructivist-interpretevist like American philosopher and psychologist Kenneth Gergen,[5] serve as important devices for making a world intelligible at a particular period in time, and for one set of people in relation to another, rather than the whole world for all time. As languages of understanding are developed and disseminated, the scientist crosses the threshold and enters not as a spectator of the inevitable, but as an active agent. To communicate one's understanding is to make a small investment in the creation of the future.

A theorist is engaged in a form of 'ontological education', like you, who creates a compelling theory. Such generative theory challenges the guiding assumption of a culture, raises fundamental questions regarding contemporary life, fosters reconsideration of existing constructions of reality and, by so doing, furnishes new alternatives of action. When used generatively, theory may increase the adaptive potential of an individual, institution or society, starting indeed for you as a person. However, and in our context here, there is more to social innovation than the construction of theory.

America's Philip Cushman,[6] based at the School of Professional Psychology in California, has acknowledged that our dedication to the philosophical frame of reference of the physical sciences has helped us to develop the power to manipulate the physical world in undreamed of ways. But that same frame of reference has within it a built-in paradox. By conceiving of a world that irrevocably separates 'inner' from 'outer', body from mind, the objectively oriented physical science framework makes it nearly impossible to use traditional ideas, philosophical thinking and a sense of moral authority – and thus to make a subjective moral stand. A society wide consensus, a shared sense of right and good and true, arising out of the interrelatedness of culture, simply does not exist in our time.

To grasp the remarkable interrelatedness of a culture – to sense for an instance how the disparate pieces of the social fabric are woven into a whole, how they politically reinforce, reproduce, collude with, resist and reshape one another, to understand the innocence, the cynicism, the terror and the brave fiction of it all – that is the task of interpretive, hermeneutic, cultural history. People and things exist only within a certain political and moral context, and they are not understandable outside of it. This is where hermeneutics, as Heidegger pointed out, differs from phenomenology.

Studying humans by abstracting them from their cultural context and observing them in a dispassionate, objective manner in a psychological laboratory is more akin, for Cushman, to removing a fish from water than to picking up a rock from its resting place. Studying people in a 'positivistic' way, as we do in Chapter 14, renders them lifeless. Individuals and their context form a dialogical, interpenetrating unit. By studying one, the researcher inevitably studies the other. Also, in undertaking a research project, the researcher brings his or her own cultural frame of reference into the picture, which continually and unavoidably frames and shapes the process.

According to Cushman, the overall social constructionist argument, inclusive of hermeneutics, as initially proposed by Gergen, can be distilled in eight propositions:

1. *Humans do not have a pure, fundamental human nature* that is transhistorical and transcultural; we are incomplete and therefore unable to adequately function unless embedded in a specific cultural matrix composed of language, symbols, moral understandings, rituals, rules, institutional arrangements of power and privilege, origin myths and explanatory stories.

2. *The cultural matrix 'completes' humans*, whereby culture infuses individuals through the social practices of the everyday world, shaping and forming in the most fundamental ways how humans conceive of the world and their place in it, how they see others, and how they engage in a moral framework of mutual obligations and responsibilities.

3. The material objects we create, the ideas we hold, and actions we take are *shaped in a fundamental way by the social framework in which we are raised;* they have been created out of a particular perspective of a specific historical and cultural situation and therefore they express that perspective.

4. These cultural artefacts are not only the reflection or expression of an era, they are *the immediate stuff of daily life*, pertaining to language, clothing, the marking of time and the concept of self, as well as to monetary exchange and eating utensils.

5. Owing to the dual nature of artefacts, whereby they both reflect and produce an era, one task of human science is to discuss the artefact in such a way as to interpret the particular social construction of the era and culture in which it was produced; seen in this way *the research task is to interpret the multitudinous and conflicting ways in which various worlds are constructed* and human meanings developed.

6. Because *cultural artefacts* express aspects of the society from which they were created, they also *reinforce and reproduce the constellations of power*, the wealth and powers that dominate in that society; artefacts are not benign, apolitical coincidences, but are part of the subtle and effective social contrivances that keep human communities surviving and functioning. This is something that will be picked up later by Eritrean philosopher Serequeberhan, in an African context.

7. *The researcher's task is to define in each culture what constitutes the broad cultural framework,* the institutional structures and finally the everyday artefacts that instruct, influence and shape the individual's moment-by-moment perspective and experiences.

8. Because the West's concept of a bounded autonomous self is an expression of the current historical era, that concept *reinforces and reproduces that era*, serving whatever forces may benefit from the current configuration of power and wealth; because the dominant dynamic of our era is consumerism, the pre-eminence of the isolated, autonomous self is both a consequence of that dynamic and means of reproducing it.

We now compare and contrast the European and the African perspective on hermeneutics, to illustrate how culture and context influence methodology. In this case it is about turning hermeneutics from an informative (European) to a transformative (African) orientation. However, what is clearly common to the two approaches is the overtly *developmental* orientation that both adopt. In other words, it is now narratively oriented *becoming* rather than descriptively oriented *being* that occupies pride of place.

8.4 Global Variations of Hermeneutics: European and African Hermeneutics

EUROPEAN HERMENEUTICS: INFORMATIVE AND DEVELOPMENTAL

Original Imagination

What differentiates objective 'methodological sterility' from genuine 'inter-subjective' understanding is original imagination. This is how one of the seminal figures in philosophical hermeneutics, Germany's 20th-century philosopher Hans-Georg Gadamer,[7] sees things. In fact the origins of hermeneutics, reaching back to Schleiermacher and his biblical interpretations in the late 19th century, were entirely German. Such subjectively imaginative (as opposed to objectively analytical) ability, involves seeing what is questionable in any subject and formulating questions to explore the subject further. The precondition of this capacity is that, firstly, one is open to be questioned by the other and willing to be provoked to risk involvement in a dialogue that carries you imaginatively beyond the present position. The real meaning of a research context you are seeking to understand, secondly, is always co-determined by the historical situation of yourself as an original interpreter. Thus understanding is not an objective, analytical, reproductive procedure, but rather always a subjective–objective, imaginative and productive one.

Hermeneutics, as we have seen, was originally concerned in the 19th century with the interpretation of texts, primarily religious scripts. Established in the 19th-century context of scriptural interpretation, in the 20th century it came to be seen as perhaps the quintessential methodology of the social sciences. It is an interpretive social science, taking as its goal the achievement of understanding, backed by rich description and unfolding narrative. This use of interpretivism is compared and contrasted with the positivistic scientific orientation of the natural sciences, duly oriented towards explanation, backed by observation, experimentation and survey.

Whereas interpretive social scientists develop understandings of richly textured phenomena, and of 'the stories we are', natural scientists carry out experiments and test hypotheses that are derived from explanatory models or theories. It can be argued, though, that what is properly meant by hermeneutics goes far beyond interpretation. The argument, for Gadamer, is that any text is created in one cultural-historical context and then interpreted in another. It is the dislocation in time and place that makes interpretation necessary. Our attempt to understand the text is framed by what Gadamer has called 'historical consciousness'. The act of understanding involves the coming together of the historical understanding of the world, of the interpreter and of the text. This fusion of horizons of each may represent a moment of insight, but, more crucially, it signifies an act of continuing and deepening cultural-historical tradition of which the interpreter is a member. Understanding is to be thought of as less a subjective act than as participation in an event of tradition, or indeed in a process of origination.

The Enlightenment promoted rationality and empiricism as antidotes to tradition, constructing a modern world in which social life could be re-invented on rational grounds. But this is impossible if we live in history, and in cultures and communities that perpetuate traditions. As such, hermeneutics is tradition-informed understanding, which is especially suited for a transcultural orientation, and for a grounding of self and organization in a particular place and time. For Gadamer, the experience of the socio-historic world in which your research is lodged, cannot be raised to a science by the inductive procedure of the natural sciences. The aim is not to conform and extend universalized experiences to attain knowledge of a law – for example, how men, people and states evolve – but to understand how this man, this people, or this state is what it has become, or, more generally, how it happened that this is so.

Self-Formation and Bildung

This perspective builds on the prior grounds established by German philosopher Herder covering the historical concept of self-formation, education, or cultivation that is *Bildung*. As we can see, such an approach is very much concerned with both origination and with understanding as well as with contextualization within a particular individual, institution, society.

We now turn from a European and American perspective on social constructivism, interpretivism and narrative method, to what has been identified as 'African hermeneutics'. It is at this juncture (in this chapter and in the next two on methodology) that we bring in the perspective of societies in transition, or what has been termed 'developing' societies. As we will see, that developing perspective has more of a sociopolitical tone to it than its culturally and historically laden Northern and Western counterparts, and therefore is more resonant with societies in transition, as in China or the Middle East, Eastern Europe and South-East Asia.

AFRICAN HERMENEUTICS: TRANSFORMATIVE AND DEVELOPMENTAL

Dialogical Knowing and Human Becoming

African and Afro-American philosophers lend a somewhat more transformative edge to 'narrative' interpretive method and to 'hermeneutic' constructivist methodology than their more purely interpretive European counterparts. For Afro-American philosopher Richard Bell, to begin with, in his *Understanding African Philosophy*:

> *we share in forming and expressing our particular life worlds through stories or narratives. It is through such narratives that we see both the uses and the abuses of power and human identity ... Out of our liberation struggles come the poetry, the stories, the telling of Africa's suffering and indignity. From the cries of injustice, the memory and narration, come a new and broader sense of justice and the hope of the transformation of communal values to engage modernity.*[8]

We immediately see the different 'critical emancipatory' tone when compared, for example, with that of Germany's Gadamer. This 'telling' from these 'texts' is part of the narrative enterprise that is diary of philosophy. *Such 'interpretative' philosophy takes account of the contexts in which the conversations of human life take place.* It is the narrative aspect of philosophy that is to a culture and gives it its existential texture. It is also this aspect, emerging from the local ground, which preserves it from a globalized abstraction. For Bell, this is what is involved in approaching the nature and scope of our understanding from an aesthetic and thereby also hermeneutic point of view. *It is through our aesthetic consciousness that we see the reflexivity of our human being and the dialogical nature of our knowing and understanding of the world, however 'strange' it may seem to us.* In this context, the Nzonzi is a most interesting African figure. For the Congolese philosopher Ernest Wamba-di-Wamba, as cited by Bell, the Nzonzi was a special kind of leader with an aesthetically laden 'mastery of the clarification of speech', whereby he or she:

> *must know how to listen attentively and tirelessly; to pick up the essence of each spoken word, to observe every look, every gesture, every silence, to grasp their respective significance, and to counter unjust positions, while reinforcing just ones.*

We now turn from Afro-American Bell to Africa's Eritrean-born philosopher Tsenay Serequeberhan[9] and his own African interpretation of hermeneutics.

Local Tradition and Destiny

The Congolese philosopher Okonda Okolo proposes a hermeneutical interpretation of two notions of fundamental importance in Africa – tradition and destiny. In Western anthropology a culture based on tradition is frequently portrayed as one devoid of change. Destiny is portrayed as encouraging determinism, and thereby inhibiting the development of individual initiative. For Okolo, tradition in Africa is constantly interpreted and reinterpreted – and therefore always changing – by different individuals in different historical contexts. Tradition therefore does not inhibit invention or change, creation or transformation. Destiny, from the vantage point of African hermeneutics, is not a symbol of determinism, but involves a people's 'vision of the world'. For Sekem's Ibrahim Abouleish in Egypt:

> *I carry a vision deep within myself: in the midst of sand and desert I see myself standing as a well drawing water. Carefully I plant trees, herbs and flowers and wet their roots with the precious drops. The cool well water attracts human beings and animals to refresh and quicken themselves. Trees give shade, the land turns green, fragrant flowers bloom, insects, birds and*

butterflies show their devotion to God, the creator, as if they were citing the first Sura of the Koran. The human, perceiving the hidden praise of God, care for and see all that is created as a reflection of paradise on earth. For me this idea of an oasis in the middle of a hostile environment is like an image of the resurrection at dawn, after a long journey through the nightly desert. I saw it in front of me like a model before the actual work in the desert started. And yet in reality I desired even more: I wanted the whole world to develop.[10]

As such it represents the history of a people – and of Ibrahim Abouleish himself – their past, present and future and whatever sense of identity they can create and re-create for themselves.

Transformative Hermeneutics – Tradition and Modernity

In his book on the *Hermeneutics of African Philosophy*, Serequeberhan is, on the one hand, radically open to that which is preserved in his own Eritrean cultural heritage. On the other hand, he is critical of tradition to the extent that the cultural elements which have been preserved in it have ossified and are a concrete hindrance to the requirements of contemporary, or modern existence. This fruitful tension between esteem and criticism, tradition and modernity, when properly cultivated, constitutes the critical edge of his transformative hermeneutics.

Emergent transformation is thus a grasping and exploring of grounding concerns, aimed at the enhancement, emergence and ultimate transformation of its own lived actuality. In Africa's specific political and historical context (this could equally apply to Latin America, and parts of Asia and the Middle East), the concerns of contemporary philosophy are focused on the possibility of overcoming the misery and political impotence of the continent's postcolonial situation. Hermeneutics in such a context has more of a critical, emancipatory and transformative edge to it than it does in the reflectively European one. Postcolonial Africa then poses the challenge of self-transformation and the concrete actualization of its alleged 'independence'. It does so in view of the suffering millions that have been victimized by the lived actuality as opposed to the hoped-for ideal of an 'independent' Africa. This is indeed the case for much of Latin America and the Arab world as well.

For Serequeberhan, *it is in this painful gap between the ideal and actuality that the hermeneutic philosophy finds its source and the locus of its concerns*, engaged, in the words of the late Franz Fanon – the extraordinary Martiniquan psychiatrist and philosopher – in 'turning over a new leaf and working out new concepts'. As such, Africa and other societies in transition, including the former communist countries of Eastern Europe, China and India, needs to re-invent themselves to transform themselves, rather than 'be developed' by others. In so doing, the review of an individual's, an institution's or a society's own narrative and destiny is matched by hermeneutical re-invention. In fact this is patently not what is happening in China and Eastern Europe today, neither of which is actually drawing on their combined tradition and destiny in the sense that Okolo talks about it.

In other words, the philosopher/interpreter should not passively adhere to what is given by that tradition. Rather the relation to the tradition is an open-ended encounter, between self and other, past and present, in which what is explicitly preserved and implicitly betrayed by tradition is revealed. For example, China would engage with its Taoist, Confucian and Buddhist past, with a view to renewing it in a purposeful and open-ended way. Historically 'being there' – a person, organization or community – always becomes what it is by projecting itself out of its past, its lived inheritance. Its 'destiny' is thus always what comes out of itself, out of the prospects of its history and the possibilities of its generation. For contemporary Africans, what impels them to such is precisely the estranged actuality of the continent's present deriving from the colonial experience, the specific particularity of Africa's history. As Okolo points out:

> Our hermeneutical situation is that of the formerly colonized, the oppressed, that of the underdeveloped, struggling for more justice and equality. Here we affirm the methodological pre-eminence of praxis on hermeneutics, praxis understood in the sense of an action tending toward the qualitative transformation of life.

This applies as much for Ibrahim Abouleish[11] in Egypt, as it does for Okolo in the Congo or for Serequeberhan in Eritrea, as it did for Havel in Czechoslovakia.

Fractured Split and Fusion of Horizons

Insofar as the anti-colonial struggle, for Serequerberhan, is aimed at overcoming colonialism and neo-colonialism, it is an attempt to end the fissure in African existence between exogenous dominance and indigenous tradition. It is in the hope of overcoming this split through a positive union that the counter-force of the colonized acquires a political form and becomes a project for a possible freedom.

In fact, *liberation movements in Africa or in Latin America, in Asia as in the Middle East, are born out of the 'fusion of horizons' of two broad segments of society, the urban and the rural.* Each manifests in itself what the other does not have and is estranged from. The Westernized urbanized native is acquainted with the 'global' world beyond the colony or neo-colony and the struggles of other peoples. The rural non-Westernized native, on the other hand, is steeped in the broken 'local' heritage of his own particular past. In the fusion of these two fractured urban and rural 'worlds' the possibility of African, or indeed of Brazilian or Indonesian, freedom is concretized or made tangible in the form of specific historical movements. In like manner, in a neo-colonial context, it is when the globalized native puts at the local people's disposal the intellectual and technical capital that he or she snatched, that the dialectic force and counter-force is transcended in the reconstitution of a new ethos. This is the process – for Serequeberhan as for us – that appropriates the global possibilities of a specific local tradition from within the lived confines and concrete possibilities of that tradition itself. Again for Abouleish, as he reflected on himself as a young Egyptian doing his doctoral studies in Austria:

> During my studies, I noticed inner changes taking place within me. I became thoroughly involved with European culture, getting to know its music, studying its poetry and philosophy. Somebody looking into my soul would have seen anything 'Egyptian' left completely behind, so I could absorb everything new. Because of my childhood and adolescent grounding in Egyptian culture, I could not leave such entirely behind. I now existed in two worlds, both of which were essentially different: the oriental, spiritual stream I was born into and the European, which I felt was my chosen course. But I was neither Egyptian nor European. I realised this particularly when I was experiencing art. For example I started hearing Händel's Messiah with Muslim ears as praise to Allah. The two differing worlds within me gradually began to dissolve and merge

into a third entity, so I was neither completely one nor the other. What I experienced was not a cheap compromise, but an elevation, a real uniting of the two cultures within me.[11]

This lived self-formative ethos of the liberation struggle becomes the practice of freedom. This is the hermeneutical response to the emergent question: what are the people of Africa, or the Middle or Far East, trying to free themselves from and what are they trying to become? This brings us from Serequeberhan onto the work of the French postmodernist Foucault, about whom we shall here much more in Chapter 12.

The Liberation Struggle: Existence and Historicity

Michel Foucault, in characterizing the focus of his philosophical thought, refers to liberty and liberation as being constituted by the reformative 'practice of the self' on the self:

When a colonial people tries to free itself from the coloniser, that is truly an act of liberation, in the strict sense of the world. But this act is not sufficient to establish the practices of liberty; later on it will be necessary for the people, this society and these individuals to decide upon receivable and acceptable forms of their existence or political society. That is why I insist on the 'practice' of freedom.[12]

As Foucault pointedly observes, *the struggle for freedom is indispensable for the practice of freedom, but it is not sufficient*. The question then is, how can one establish the practice or ethos of freedom in the process of liberating one's existence from external, direct or indirect, domination? The 'practice of freedom' or liberty is grounded on and arises out of the reformative ethos of a people. This presupposes the liberation struggle as it unfolds within the context of specific and particular histories, and with it the concrete implementation, the practice, of liberty, which is the proclaimed *raison d'être* of the struggle in its very inception.

In his *Africa in Modern History*[13] the eminent historian on Africa, Basil Davidson, notes that the African countries that achieved independence in the late 1950s and early 1960s were, paradoxically, wedded to colonial attitudes and values. Old inequalities from the precolonial heritage were enlarged by the new inequalities of the colonial heritage. In contradistinction to the above, starting from the 1970s, a more radically democratic conception of liberation took root. In concrete and practical terms, the new liberation movements emerged out of the contrast between the miserable situation of postcolonial Africa and the empty status of 'political' independence. They were grounded on the lived and stark comparison between unfulfilled ideals and unforgiving realities. In so emerging, in differing ways and out of the lived exigencies of differing African histories and specific contexts, such becoming served to articulate a notion of liberation as a process of reclaiming history. Such a dialectical notion draws as much on critical theory (Chapter 9) as it does on hermeneutics.

Davidson points in this context to the theoretical perspective of Guinea-Bissau's Amilcar Cabral. The political parties initially formed in that country after independence were of and for the urban centre. Their point of reference was European theory and practice. Their basic objective was to transfer power from Europeans to Africans. In the process they were susceptible to the rationality of the colonizer. So, on the one hand, they were the mediating link between colonialism and neo-colonialism; on the other, they abstractly formulated the possibility of African freedom. In the process they suspected indigenous culture as being worthless. It was those who were closest to Europe who became leaders of the pack, and the political parties formed totally disregarded the rural native or indeed the *Lumpenproletariat* – the coolie labour that inhabited the shantytowns.

The Urban–Rural Dynamic Fusion

The urban parties were not inserted in the lived needs and concerns that move and define the life of the rural native. And yet, in the meeting between those who come from the towns as globalized natives and the local country dwellers as peasant or nomads, is the dynamic locus, out of which unfolds self-emancipation.

This approach is instead of a situation where the cities remain the centres of European mimicry and the interior is frozen, mummified and held back in stasis as the enclave of 'ethnic cultures'; that is as wildlife preserves and ethnic 'cultural' exhibitions yielding foreign exchange. The politics and economics that emanate from the centre are then geared towards Europe, cash crops complemented by parliamentary 'procedures' or socialist edicts of a one-party state.

Even the old colonial policy of divide and rule remains in place, for the Guinea-Bissau philosopher and revolutionary Amilcar Cabral, in the 1960s the transfer of power 'does not take place at the level of structures ... since that caste, the Westernised African bourgeois has done nothing more than take over unchanged the legacy of the economy, the thought and the institutions left by the colonialists'

Return to Source

Therefore, for Cabral, there is a need to return to source. Only when a rooting in history becomes a lived actuality at the grassroots level, through the establishment of local mass political institutions of people's power – people's assemblies, village associations and so forth – in which popular democracy is implemented, only in such a context is 'the practice of freedom' possible. The struggle secures the support of the mass to the extent that it concretely involves the common folk at all levels, and in doing so helps them metamorphose themselves from inert, ahistorical beings absent from history into active and emergent protagonists of their own existence. For Fanon: 'Their ears hear the true voice of the country, and their eyes take in the great and infinite poverty of their people.'

This process of becoming does not come out of formal proclamations. It occurs out of cohabiting the same historical, political and existential space. It occurs by osmosis and diffusion. It is in this concrete sense that the struggle at a fundamental level necessitates the radical reformation of traditional society. Colonialism 'globally' petrifies the subjugated culture. This is the 'local' state of affairs that needs to be overcome. To date the African liberation struggle has failed in its promise, for Serequeberhan, to reclaim the historicity of African existence.

Such a 'return' is a cultural and political recovery of the oppressed historic possibilities in the existence of the colonized. The turning toward the 'native mass' is the first moment in the fusion of the rural and the urban. The Westernised urban natives who join the anti-colonial eruption do so by rejecting their assimilation and successfully indigenise themselves into the historicity of their people. It is the moment of a historical and existential decision, at which point the *assimilado* begins the cultural and historical metamorphosis that will positively re-immerse him- or herself into the local historicity of the indigenous folk. The 'return' is not a return to tradition or stasis. We are not engaged in an antiquarian quest for an already existing authentic past tradition. Rather, we are engaged in the affirmation by the exogenized native of the historicity of the rural indigenous mass. For Cabral:

> *Urban working classes discover at the grassroots the richness of their cultural values – philosophical, political, artistic, social and moral – and realise, not without astonishment, the richness of spirit, the capacity for reasoned discussion, the facility for understanding, on the part of population groups who were yesterday forgotten.*

European values and skills are thus absorbed, in management as in agriculture, in development as in ecology, into a new synthesis, through this hermeneutic fusion of horizons, of self and other, of tradition and modernity, of indigenous and exogenous. This is possible because in embracing indigenous historicity the Westernized native purges himself of the Eurocentric frame that structures his consciousness. The 'return' is thus a two-way process of cultural filtration and fertilization. In this dialectic, European culture/history is recognized as a particular and specific disclosure of existence, aspects of which are retained or rejected in terms of the lived historicity and practical requirements of the history being reclaimed. The ossified African past – embodied in the rural native – is thus not preserved intact, but is cut and cast to fit the historic requirements of the struggle:

> *the practice of democracy, of criticism and self-criticism, the increasing responsibility of peoples for the direction of their lives, literacy work, creation of schools and health services, training of cadres from peasant and worker backgrounds, and many other achievements ...*

Overall then, for Cabral:

> *the objectives must be at least the following: development of a popular culture and of all positive indigenous values; development of a national culture based on the history and achievements of the struggle itself; constant promotion of the political and moral awareness of the people to the cause of independence, justice, progress; development of a scientific and technological culture based on a critical assimilation of man's achievement in science, art and literature ...*

Ironically then, for Cabral and for Serequeberhan, a return to phenomenological origins (in Abram's terms) is called for, in the same way as, for your research question, you need to return to your source.

We finally now turn to an example of the deployment of hermeneutics, in this case the example of Zahra Al Zeera, a Muslim scholar.

8.5 Hermeneutics in Practice

WHOLENESS AND HOLINESS IN EDUCATION: AN ISLAMIC PERSPECTIVE

Zahra Al Zeera, an educator and researcher based in Bahrain, who pursued her doctoral studies in Canada, introduces in her book *Wholeness and Holiness in Education*[15] an approach to 'transformative inquiry', as an alternative research method that emerges from the Islamic paradigm and leads, for her, to the creation of Islamic science on the one hand and inner self-transformation on the other.

Owing to the positivist indoctrination at most universities, Muslim students she argues, like their non-Muslim counterparts, are following the mainstream as an easy and safe passage to their graduation. By doing so they waste the most precious years of their life doing research that neither advances Islamic knowledge nor increases self-awareness and the awakening of the soul. So Muslims are torn between the development of mind and soul. They are indirectly made to choose between the sacred that lies inside of them – invisible, silent and profound – and the secular demands of the modern mind. The more they feel fragmented the more they feel the pain of separation from their inner selves. Both positivist (reductionist) and constructivist (relativist) views are fragmentary.

The concept of transformation is not new; what is new for Al Zeera is the role of the sacred and the spiritual in research and inquiry. For her 'social constructivism' is the back door leading to transformative inquiry. Hermeneutics, phenomenology and narrative inquiry can be characterized as such. The transformational perspective is holistic and relational, viewing the world from a complementary perspective that accepts extremes. Reality, as such, is subjective and objective, real and ideal, material and spiritual. Transformation, or indeed renewal, occurs when a system is open and has dissipative structures where ideas, thoughts and feelings flow freely.

RENEWAL AND TRANSFORMATION

Instability is the key to transformation. The dissipation of energy creates the potential for sudden reordering. The greater the instability and variation in the society the more interactions occur. If the research methodologies we use allow for free and open interaction between ourselves and other researchers, as well as the situation we are studying, then transformation is more likely to happen. It embraces individual and society. It touches individual and collective consciousness.

A controlled and manipulative system allows energy to only flow hierarchically and in one direction; this consciously blocks all other directions and prevents a natural flow of energy. Thus transformation is prevented. So transformation is not acknowledged in a positivist paradigm because it causes instability and disturbance. Transformation occurs when elements, ideas, thoughts and feelings flow freely. Relationships suffer when there is fragmentation of knowledge since variables are controlled. However constructivism, for Al Zeera, is too open, allowing for a flow of energy in all directions.

Open systems accept a flow of energy in all directions and at all levels by the interaction between the inquirer and the situation, combining wholeness and relationships. A flow of conversation and open interviews promotes transformation. In constructivism the knower and the known are interactive and inseparable. There are no cause–effect laws but all entities are in a state of mutual simultaneous shaping. Elements interact dialectically.

To have a transformative relationship you must be open and vulnerable. Although, for Al Zeera, the constructivist paradigm and interpretive research methods promote transformation at certain levels, the Islamic paradigm and transformational research methods have the capacity for a more coherent and comprehensive transformation. A holistic worldview must, in the end, draw all levels – personal, social, spiritual – into a coherent whole. This Islamic worldview transcends the dichotomy between mind and body, inner and outer, the creative dialogue ensuing thereby becoming a basis for creativity. She illustrates this through her own case story.

For Al Zeera, narrative inquiry, if practised within the Islamic perspective, can illuminate the soul and awaken the inner self, giving us the courage to create and reconstruct our personal experiences, to go beyond the pain and the hurt and transform them into higher qualities of acceptance, understanding and submission to God's will. Narrative inquiry can be the first step on the long, spiritual journey, where we are in continual dialogue with our inner self, God and the 'other'. Any inquiry, regarded from an Islamic perspective, ought to be multi-levelled and multidimensional. Researchers have to be open and flexible, therefore, to operate within different inquiry methods so as to be able to capture the complexity of the phenomena. Whereas phenomenology deals with personal, subjective experiences, hermeneutics interprets the larger social context in which individual meaning is embedded.

Here is Zahra's story.

ZAHRA'S SELF-TRANSFORMATION

The Starting Point

'Being a graduate student in the Department of Measurement, Evaluation and Computer Applications at the University of Toronto located me at the heart of the empire of figures and numbers. I have always been impressed by Western efficiency, so here I was. Yet what began to trouble me was the paradox in the superficiality of knowledge and the prevailing arrogance of computerized, pre-packaged designs. It is confining rather than liberating thinking.'

The Stirring Point

'What troubled my soul, therefore, was the lack of appreciation for intellectuality, for genuine knowledge. The domination and control of hard data and computerized packages are a reflection of the predominant rule of economics and finance over cultural and liberal education. Educators changed their direction to accommodate the financial, industrial world instead of trying to affect change to make the outside world more humane. The paradoxical effect of disempowerment led me to seek an answer to this confusion. The result was an intellectual crisis and a rebellious researcher. I was led to understand Islamic theories and to try to bring them down from the ivory tower to meet practical educational needs. The first result was a term paper "The Collapse of Westernized Universities in Islamic Societies." It was a turning point in my life, and I got to know many great Muslim philosophers. I was like a wanderer in a desert who, after a long search for a sip of water, found an oasis in the middle of the desert. For the first time I felt united with myself.

The enjoyment came not only from reading the work of those great minds but also from enjoying the richness of the Arabic language.

'The paper cited the causes of the decline of education in Muslim-Arab countries in recent times for external and internal reasons. External factors were colonization and modernization. Internal factors were the incongruity and lack of harmony between the original Islamic philosophies and the political, social and educational practice in Islamic countries. The result has been the disempowerment of countries that are dependent economically, intellectually and even psychologically on their former colonizers. The West has become the standard against which everything is measured. During the summer of 1988 there was great pressure on the volcano inside of me. I was boiling with new ideas and old feelings. After intense reflection I found three landmarks that enriched me then and still now: (1) alternative research paradigms and interpretive research methods; (2) personal practical methods and narrative inquiry; (3) social knowledge and the Frankfurt school.'

The Turning Point

'First, I was exposed to new research paradigms, rather than mere methods, and to the overall democratisation of research and learning. Second, I was introduced to personal practical knowledge, which mirrored my emerging ideas of wholeness, democracy, humanity and morality. Third, I did a course on language, power and learning which introduced me to Foucault, Habermas and others. What I came to realize was that my education in the Middle East and then in the West had caused a split in consciousness. Gradually the idea of wholeness began to take shape. In a letter I wrote to my thesis committee I said:

> *Since I was 17 I have been wandering the world, between the Middle East, Europe and North America, trying to understand myself and the world around me. Different value systems, different lifestyles, different languages … During my journey I suffered severely, from intellectual and spiritual shocks. Between one world and another something was missing, but I was not sure what. At last I came to realize, after a wide range of educational and work experiences, that the whole was missing. Reconciliation between the mind and the soul. Propositional knowledge – explicit – in mind, spiritual knowledge – tacit – in soul.*

'My thesis proposal, then, was about reconciliation between mind and soul. The journey for reconciliation started inside out. Reconciliation on a personal level was the first step. Personal development goes hand in hand with social development. In February, 1999, I wrote, again to the committee:

> *The dilemma of Islamic societies lies partly in the fact they imported secular educational systems and planted them into the heart of Islamic traditional societies. To me it is like planting a palm tree in Alaska and expecting it to grow naturally. The lack of harmony between peoples lives inside the university and out, and the conflict between the two extremes, the secular and the religious, confuses everybody. The materialism of the West pushed spirituality out of the curricula; the denial of freedom of speech in the East was a barrier to intellectual development.*

Going back and forth between the two caused me immense pain. But from pain new branches grow; the confusion of pain caused me to search for the causes.'

Answering Crucial Questions

'In the West I felt my spiritual freedom endangered. In the East my intellectual freedom. Did I have to give one up for the other? Why not keep both? Do we, as a non-Western society have to give up our culture and religion for the sake of economic development?

'Eventually peace and harmony might come through communication, interaction, reflection and understanding. A breakthrough came when I saw myself as microcosm and Bahrain as macrocosm:

My life world is not my private world, but rather it is inter-subjective.

'Many Muslim students I talked to equated Islamic with religious education. I realized I had to find a balance between scientific and religious education. I sought reconciliation rather than compromise, at a deeper level of understanding. Writing a paper in 1989, for the World Congress of Comparative Education, I said:

The goal of locating my study in hermeneutics is to increase the understanding of how the East and the West came to misunderstand each other. Being the child of East and West I had learnt to compare languages and cultures, histories and personalities. My two selves were in continuous dialogue, even conflict. Since hermeneutics involved dialogue, and dialectical interchange, I came to realise that my own dialectic would involve love rather than hate. I realised that my longstanding struggle was rooted in my feelings of insecurity that I might lose my Arabic/Eastern identity in the West ... hermeneutics is concerned with the interpretation of human products and experiences. The goal of such is understanding.

'When the choice is made between two parts of one's being, soul and mind, the spiritual and the intellectual, the struggle is great.'

Creating the Framework

'It was only after reading Balleche's *Dialectical Thinking and Adult Development* that I was able to create a framework for my thesis. I was then able to find a secure home for my dispersed ideas. It was a relief to know that the pain, the conflict, the struggle, were stages in the dialectical thinker's development. The assurance came from Riegel: "Such conflicts and crises are not to be regarded as negative. The discordance and contradiction generated provide the sources of individual and societal change. The synchronous leaps of development are of seminal importance to both."[16] The concept of wholeness itself is dialectical.'

Dialectical Thinking, Multidimensionality and Wholeness

'Three factors contributed to my dialectical thinking: my bicultural upbringing (Arabic and Persian), diverse educational experiences in the East and West, and the interpretive methods of inquiry to which I had been exposed. I discovered gradually that I had an obsession with the idea of multidimensionality. I discovered that the pain of unfulfillment, intellectually and spiritually, was caused by the unidimensional approach to education and to measurement. Overall, moreover, I came to realize that the unidimensional imposition of intellectual and scientific imperialism, as well as political imperialism, imposed on the Middle East, had caused an explosion in my own psyche, as well as in the Muslim world at large. Freedom from intellectual imperialism was the empowerment I had sought and gained. As the Martiniquan poet and statesman Aime Cesaire said: "There are two ways of losing yourself: through fragmentation in the particular, or dilution in the universal".'

8.6 Conclusion

ENTERING THE PATH OF RENEWAL

You have now engaged in the second stage of your path of renewal that is following an interpretive course which unfolds out of your prior narrative. Your research question and the original storyline that follows emerge out of your questioned life world, and that of the other people and things in which you have chosen to immerse yourself through your research. Your own narrative, that of the profession or institution with which you are engaged, and that of your community or society, forms the developmental backdrop for this Eastern journey or research path. Moreover, it is Eastern, not in the literal sense of being lodged in an Asian or even Middle Eastern worldview, but that it lies on the Eastern edge (German) of the western European world from both of which most conventionally research methodologies arise.

In other words, whereas Britain and France, and indeed Austria, have played a major part, as we shall see in later chapters, in the Western and Northern research paths, Germany has played a leading role from both a Northern and indeed also an Eastern perspective. For both hermeneutics, and as will soon become apparent, critical theory, have been strongly influenced by Germany. For it is in Germany that historicism and holism have had a major part to play, in contrast with the empiricism and pragmatism of the West. The fact that Germany also has a strong Northern and rational side to it, not to mention the recent pragmatic influence from the West, does not preclude this otherwise Eastern orientation.

ENGAGING WITH REALITY

The task of the knowledge you pursue is not to recapitulate in the form of concepts that are given to you by the powers that be. It is rather to create an entirely new domain which, when taken together with the world presented through sense perception, yields for the first time full reality. Hence, you are not an idle onlooker before the pageant of the world; you are an active participant in a creative process.

In other words, you not only want to describe and thereby uncover what is really going on, beneath the surface, internally within yourself and externally in the world around you in the interactive field of your concern, but you want to transform it. You have come to recognize (phenomenologically so to speak) your real intentions. At this opening point, in your proposed research activity, you are called upon to describe such intentions, richly and intricately, qualitatively and poignantly, in relation to the field in which those intentions apply, for real. In other words, you are called upon to lay aside your prejudices, your preconceptions, you analytical frameworks, and enter into that world, immerse yourself in the phenomenon.

OVERLAID WITH PERSONAL MEANING AND SOCIAL SIGNIFICANCE

The challenge that you ultimately face is to conduct such an interpretive investigation in a way that has both social and cultural meaning as well as personal and spiritual significance. The topic grows out of an intense interest in a particular area, close to your nature and culture, while also reaching out to others. That interest is provoked, outside in, by the unfilled needs that you see around you, related to yourself, your profession and your society; it is also provoked inside out, by your own will, and intent, at this particular point of time. How then does such narrative 'grounding' relate to what interpretively emerges from it?

RETURNING TO YOUR ORIGINAL STORYLINE: AS A RESEARCHER-AND-INNOVATOR

In interpretive-hermeneutic terms, the originating of your research question involves uncovering an original story in each case, a return to source. Such a story will necessarily be authorized not only by yourself, as researcher, and by the research community around you, including you research supervisor, but also by one or more authoritative agencies – a business, a community, a professional body – with which you are engaging.

To reiterate in Gadamer's philosophical terms: what differentiates objective 'methodological sterility' from genuine 'intersubjective' understanding is your original imagination. Such imaginative, as opposed to merely analytical ability, involves seeing what is questionable and significant, in the state of yourself, your profession, your society, even the world, and formulating questions to pursue, to take the story on to an ultimately satisfactory conclusion. The precondition for such is that you are open to be questioned by the very field with which you are engaged, to be provoked to risk involvement in a dialogue that carries you imaginatively beyond the present position, towards a more desirable one that your research serves to instigate.

TRANSFORMING THE PLOT – AS AN ORIGINAL INTERPRETER

The real meaning of a context you are seeking to evolve is always co-determined by the historical situation of yourself as a shared 'original interpreter'. Thus understanding is not an objective, analytical, reproductive procedure, but rather always a subjective–objective, imaginative and transformative one.

Further, and in the practical terms set by William Randall , Canadian professor of literature and author of *The Stories We Are*, you are in a position to reconstruct not so much the events of your story, but rather the plots that underlie them. A new plot means a new story, and a new story leads to a new construction.

Thus, you critique the old plots by which your story has previously been lived and told, and experiment with new ones, and you thereby assume authority over your work and your life. As such, the originating of your research question, and the grounding of your prospective innovation, is the same thing as uncovering the plot. To begin with, you start out as a narrative researcher … once upon a time … returning to source.

MAKING EFFECTIVE HISTORY – AS A WOULD-BE SOCIAL INNOVATOR

Finally, having then immersed yourself in a significant phenomenon, and having recognized the unfolding plot surrounding it, with a view to changing it, in Serequeberhan's terms:

> the horizon of the past in the form of tradition, that is heritage, is always in motion. It is not historical consciousness that first sets the surrounding horizon in motion. But in this motion it becomes aware of itself. In its lived existence, each generation sees for itself its own-most possibilities out of the concerns of its own horizon. For the 'motion' of a heritage becomes aware of itself only in concrete individuals and out of the horizon of their lives' self-awareness. For it is in the living and thinking of those who embrace it that a heritage – an 'effective history' becomes aware of itself.[17]

You, your organization and your society embody that 'effective history'. To make history, though, you need to move from uncovering the plot, that is your plot and that of such an institution, and the surrounding community, in narrative terms.

We shall now turn from hermeneutics to critical theory, advancing further on the developmental and dialogical Eastern path. For Habermas, the core exponent of critical theory still alive, hermeneutics is only one dimension of critical social theory. He criticized the conservatism of previous hermeneutics, especially Gadamer, because the focus on tradition seemed to undermine possibilities for social criticism and transformation.

Habermas and Gadamer actually engaged in the 1960s in a famous debate over the possibility of transcending history and culture in order to find a truly objective position from which to criticize society. The debate was inconclusive, but marked the beginning of warm relations between the two men. It was Gadamer who secured Habermas's first professorship in Heidelberg. Another attempt to engage the French Jacques Derrida, to whom we shall turn later (Chapter 12), proved less enlightening because the two thinkers had so little in common. After Gadamer's death, Derrida called their failure to find common ground one of the worst debacles of his life. Perhaps, our Integral Research framework serves to make this 'common ground' more visible. We now turn from hermeneutics to critical theory, along the research path of renewal.

References

1. Dilthey, W. (1991). *Selected Works: Volume 1*. Princeton, NJ: Princeton University Press..
2. Gadamer, H.-G. (1989). *Truth and Method*. London: Sheed and Ward.
3. *Ibid.*
4. McLeod, J. (2000). *Qualitative Research in Counselling and Psychotherapy*. London: Sage.
5. Gergen, K. (1994). *Toward Transformation in Social Knowledge*. London: Sage.
6. Cushman, P. (1995). *Reconstructing Self, Reconstructing America*. New York: Da Capo.
7. Gadamer, H. (1976). *Philosophical Hermeneutics*. Berkeley, CA: University of California Press.
8. Bell, R. (2002). *Understanding African Philosophy*. London: Routledge.

9. Serequeberhan, T. (1999). *African Hermeneutics*. London: Routledge.
10. Abouleish, I. (2005). *Sekem – A Sustainable Community in the Desert*. Edinburgh: Floris.
11. *Ibid.*
12. Foucault, M. (2002). *The Archaeology of Knowledge*. London: Routledge.
13. Davidson, B. (2001). *Africa in History*. London: Weidenfeld and Nicolson.
14. Trompenaars, F. and Hampden-Turner, C. (1998). *Riding the Waves of Culture* 2nd edition. New York: McGraw-Hill.
15. Al Zeera, Z. (2001). *Wholeness and Holiness in Education*. Leicester: International Institute of Islamic Thought.
16. *Ibid.*
17. Serequeberhan, T. (2000). *Our Heritage*. Lanham, MD: Rowan and Littlefield.

9 *From Hermeneutics to Critical Theory*

Develop a Dialectical Argument

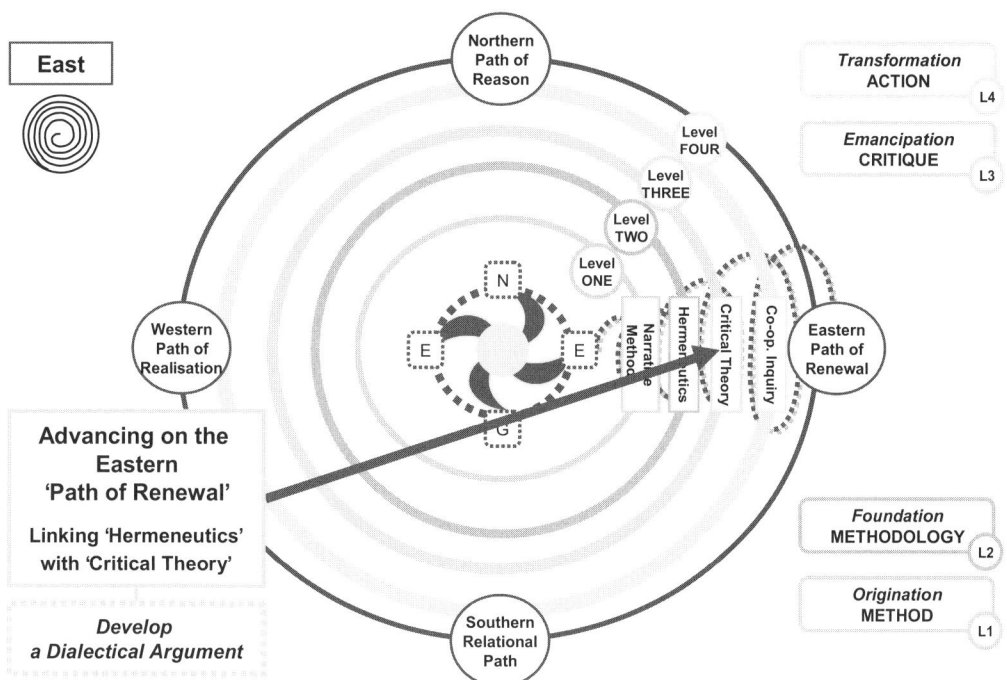

Figure 9.1   Overview Chapter 9 – Level 3/East

Summary: Critical Theory

- We shall now introduce critical theory, as we advance on the Eastern path from foundation (methodology) to emancipation (critique). Criticial theory, in sociology and philosophy, was a label used by the Frankfurt School. As a term 'critical theory' describes their collective work oriented toward radical social change.
- For the core thinkers of critical theory three aspects of their approach stand out: Firstly critical social theory should be directed at society in its historical specificity. Secondly, critical theory should improve understanding of society by integrating all the major social sciences, including economics, sociology, history, political science, anthropology and psychology. Thirdly, it anticipated postmodernity in its orientation toward a post-capitalist, post-industrial but non-communist world.
- Engaging in critical-theory-related research includes the rooting of the researcher in concrete experience, that the research issue arises out of problems of everyday life. Further such research needs to be strongly critical in orientation, uncover power relations, analyse the suffering of people and focusing on promoting 'liberation'.
- The ways in which we analyse and interpret information, for critical theorists, are conditioned both by the way our research is theoretically framed and also by your ideological assumptions as a researcher. Therefore research in the critical tradition takes the form of 'self-conscious criticism' in the sense that you try to become aware of the ideological presuppositions that inform your sense-making.
- Further, facts never stand alone in social contexts; the objects of social science rather express precisely that they are part of such a context and need to be interpreted as such. In order to do so, according to Swedish social researchers Alvesson and Skoldberg, critical research methodology demands at least three sorts of theory, which need, to some extent at least, to be taken into account, which they term a 'triple hermeneutcs', that is (a) a hermeneutic understanding of history, language and meaning, (b) a social theory of society as a totality, and (c) a theory of the unconscious.
- As a result, critical theory should be simultaneously a critical engagement with the contemporary social world, a critical account of the historical and cultural conditions and a continuous critical re-examination of the constitutive categories and conceptual frameworks of your understanding.
- Whereas philosophers and researchers from the developed world, like Jürgen Habermas, tend to be transformative in words, those like Paulo Freire from the developing world tend to be so also in action.
- Freire is also the most prominent thinker within the tradition of critical theory who also applied the approach towards his immediate life world, based on personal experiences. Hence, as a case for this chapter, we introduce the astonishing case of Freire's activism in promoting literacy in Brazil.
- Critical theory provides the grounds for emancipation and thereby paves the way for the final more action oriented step in this Eastern path of renewal: democratically laden, transformatively oriented co-operative inquiry.

9.1 Orientation to Critical Theory

ORIGINS AND MEANING

Critical theory, historically, has begun where hermeneutics left off. Both born and bred in Germany, hermeneutics, through Schleiermacher, originated in the late 19th century, and critical theory in the early 20th. Whereas the former emerged out of tradition, that is through the interpretation of religious texts, the latter heralded, at one and the same time, modernity and postmodernity.

'Critical theory' was a label used by the Frankfurt School. The 'school' consisted of members of the Institute for Social Research of the University of Frankfurt in Germany, including their intellectual and social network. As a term 'critical theory' describes their collective work oriented toward radical social change.

'Critical theory' was for the first time introduced by one of the Frankfurt School's founding members, Max Horkheimer. He defines it as *a social theory oriented toward critiquing and changing society as a whole, in contrast to traditional theory oriented only to understanding or explaining it.* Horkheimer characterized critical theory as a radical, emancipatory form of Marxian theory. As such he critiqued both the model of science put forward by logical positivism and what he and his colleagues saw as the covert positivism and authoritarianism of orthodox Marxism and communism.

THE TERM 'CRITIQUE': ROOTED IN KANT AND MARX

The choice of the term 'critical theory' was also partly influenced by the school's wanting to use a term which sounded less politically controversial than 'Marxism'. However, in an intellectual context defined by dogmatic positivism on the one hand and 'scientific socialism' on the other, critical theory meant to rehabilitate both, through its philosophically critical approach and revolutionary orientation.

Furthermore, critical theorists were explicitly connecting with the 18th-century 'critical philosophy' (*Critique of Pure Reason*) of Immanuel Kant. For Kant the term 'critique' meant philosophical reflection on the limits of claims made for certain kinds of knowledge, a direct connection between such critique and the emphasis on moral autonomy.

We now turn to the core critical thinkers.

CORE THINKERS – CORE CONCEPTS

Max Horkheimer, Theodor Adorno and Herbert Marcuse, all of them German and Jewish, became the most prominent thinkers of the Frankfurt School at its early stage, with Jürgen Habermas being the best-known representative of the second generation. However, there are many other notable, first-generation figures in critical theory, who are globally acclaimed, among them Erich Fromm, Paulo Freire and Walter Benjamin.

For all of these critical thinkers three aspects of their approach stand out. Firstly critical social theory should be directed at *society in its historical specificity* (that is how it came to be configured at a specific point in time). Secondly, critical theory should improve understanding of society by *integrating all the major social sciences*, including economics, sociology, history, political science, anthropology and psychology. Thirdly, it anticipated postmodernity in its *orientation toward a post-capitalist, post-industrial, but non-communist world.* Interestingly enough, virtually all of the critical theorists were Jewish, and victims – hence their familiarity with what it means to be oppressed – from Nazi Germany. The one who is not Jewish and is still alive today is Jürgen Habermas. The other, who recently died, and from whom we shall hear much more, is Brazil's Paulo Freire. That leads to the activist side of critical theory.

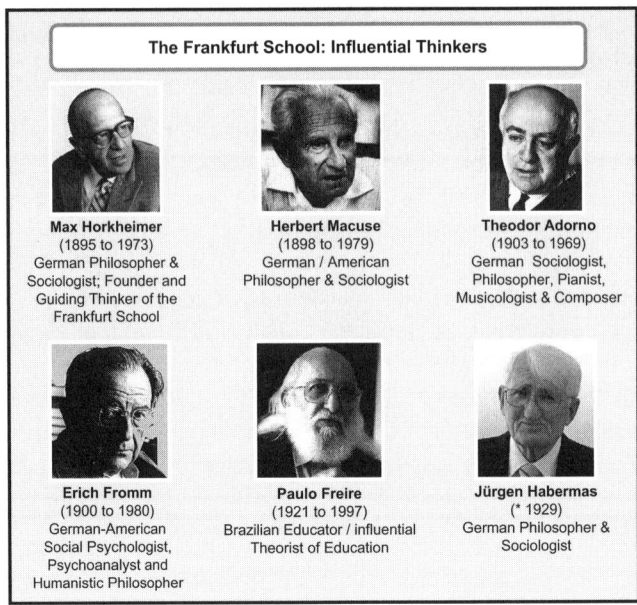

Figure 9.2   Critical Theory – Core Thinkers

Sources: Image 1: Philweb http://www.phillwebb.net/. Image 2: Bundeszentrale fuer Politische Bildung http://www.bpb.de. Image 3: Marcuse.org http://www.marcuse.org/. Image 4: Makara http://www.makara.us/. Image 5: University of KwaZulu Natal http://www.ukzn.ac.za/. Image 6: Spiegel.de http://www.spiegel.de

POLITICAL ACTIVISM: MARCUSE AND HABERMAS

Herbert Marcuse, in escaping from Nazi Germany, emigrated to the United States of America. Marcuse's critiques of capitalist society there (especially his 1955 synthesis of Marx and Freud, *Eros and Civilization* and his 1964-published *One-Dimensional Man*) resonated with the concerns of the leftist student movement in the 1960s. Because of his willingness to speak at student protests, Marcuse soon became known as 'the father of the New Left', a term he disliked and rejected.

Many radical scholars and activists, however, were influenced by him. Marcuse's 1965 essay 'Repressive Tolerance', in which he claimed capitalist democracies can have totalitarian tendencies, has been strongly criticized by conservatives. Marcuse argues that *genuine tolerance does not tolerate support for repression*, since doing so ensures that marginalized voices will remain unheard. He characterizes tolerance of repressive speech as 'inauthentic'. Instead, he advocates a discriminating tolerance that does not allow repressive intolerance to be voiced.

In the 1960s, Habermas's critical theory conceptualized knowledge in terms that enabled human beings to emancipate themselves from forms of domination through self-reflection. As such he considered psychoanalysis, including the psychology of the unconscious mind, as the paradigm of critical knowledge. This expanded considerably the scope of what counted as critical theory within the social sciences. Nowadays, the term 'critical theory', in the sociological sense, is also used to loosely group all sorts of radical thought, including Michel Foucault's theories, feminist theory and so on, that has in common the critique of domination.

CRITICAL THEORY AND LITERARY CRITICISM

It is worth noting, finally, that in literature, literary criticism and so-called cultural studies, 'critical theory' means something quite different. To use an epistemological distinction introduced by Jürgen Habermas in 1968 in his *Erkenntnis und Interesse* ('Knowledge and Human Interests'), critical theory in literary studies is ultimately a form of hermeneutics, with a view to understanding the meaning of human texts and symbolic expressions. Critical social theory in the social sciences is, in contrast, a form of self-reflective knowledge involving both understanding and theoretical explanation to reduce the chance of our being trapped in systems of domination or dependence.

From the 1960s and 1970s onward, language, symbolism, text and meaning became foundational to theory in the humanities and social sciences, through the influences of such leading philosophical lights as Ludwig Wittgenstein, Ferdinand de Saussure, George Herbert Mead, Noam Chomsky, Hans-Georg Gadamer, Jacques Derrida. These also linked up with other thinkers in such emerging disciplines as linguistic and analytic philosophy, structural linguistics, symbolic interactionism, hermeneutics, semiology, linguistically oriented psychoanalysis and deconstruction. When, in the 1970s and 1980s, Jürgen Habermas also redefined critical social theory as a theory of communication, the two versions of critical theory began to overlap or intertwine to a much greater degree than before.

We now introduce, more systematically, seven key tenets of critical theory.

9.2 Critical Theory – Key Tenets: Rooted in Concrete Experience, Promoting Liberation

Critical Theory – Key Tenets
① As a critical theorist, your research is rooted in concrete experience.
② It arises out of the problems of everyday life.
③ Critical theory is strongly emancipatory in orientation.
④ Critical theory uncovers power relations.
⑤ You analyse specifically the suffering of people.
⑥ Reality is regarded as socially constructed and multiple interconnections exist.
⑦ Critical theory is explicitly focused on promoting 'liberation'.

① AS A CRITICAL THEORIST, YOUR RESEARCH IS ROOTED IN CONCRETE EXPERIENCE

Critical theory is clearly rooted in concrete experience, explicitly conceived with the practical intention of overcoming felt dissatisfaction. Words, for Brazil's Paulo Freire, should be laden with the meaning of the people's existential experience, and not of the teacher's experience. Surveying the word 'universe' thus gives us the people's words, pregnant with the world, words from the people's reading of the world. We then give the words back to the people inserted in what Freire calls 'codifications', pictures representing real situations. Decodifying or reading the situations' pictured leads them to a critical perception of the meaning of culture by leading them to understand how human practice or work transforms the world. To sum up, reading always involves critical perception, interpretation and rewriting of what is read.

② IT ARISES OUT OF THE PROBLEMS OF EVERYDAY LIFE

Critical theory arises out of the problems of everyday life, and is constructed with an eye towards solving them. It offers a way out of an untenable situation. To be literate, for Brazil's Paulo Freire, is to be able to name one's experience as part of what it means to 'read' the world and to begin to understand the political nature of the limits and possibilities that make up the larger society. Language is the 'real stuff' of culture, and constitutes both a terrain of domination and a field of possibility. Critical literacy is both a narrative for agency as well as a referent for critique.

Literacy then becomes synonymous with an attempt to rescue history and experience. It means developing the theoretical and practical conditions through which human beings can locate themselves in their own histories, and in doing so make themselves present as agents in the struggle to expand the possibilities of human life and freedom.

③ CRITICAL THEORY IS STRONGLY EMANCIPATORY IN ORIENTATION

Critical theory is ultimately based on an emancipatory interest in achieving rational autonomy of action freed from domination. This orientation includes the conviction that the search for the truth must be tolerant of ambiguity and pluralism. Statements about society cannot be impartial. Rather they tend to confirm or challenge existing social institutions and establish modes of thought. According to the Frankfurt School, social science should strive to develop an independent and critical stance vis-à-vis these institutions and modes of thought, and should call attention to the contradictions in the way society functions. The inherent restrictions and irrationalities that inform modern capitalist societies should be among the major subjects of research. From this perspective, the social sciences are doing the business world, today, a disservice by helping it to enhance its 'bottom line' performance.

④ CRITICAL THEORY UNCOVERS POWER RELATIONS

Uncovering hidden power relations, critical theory engages in the critical interpretation of unconscious processes, ideologies, power relations, and other expressions of dominance of one group of interests over others. There are four types of mechanisms of hegemony identified by critical theorists that form a culture of silence:

1. 'conquest', involving relations of domination and subordination;
2. 'divide and rule', rather than seeing the totality;
3. 'manipulation' through communicative distortions;
4. 'cultural invasion', imposing a view of the world that deprives subordinate groups of any sense of alternative possibilities.

⑤ YOU ANALYSE SPECIFICALLY THE SUFFERING OF PEOPLE

Critical theory names the people for whom it is directed; it analyses their suffering; it offers enlightenment to them about what their real needs and wants are. One of the first kinds of knowledge indispensable to the person who arrives in a ghetto or in a place marked by our betrayal of the right 'to be' is the kind of knowledge that becomes solidarity, becomes a 'being with'. In that context, the future is seen as something not inexorable but as something that is constructed by people engaged together in life, in history. It is knowledge that sees history as possibility, not as determined. The world is not finished. It is always in the process of becoming.

The subjectivity with which I dialectically relate to the world, my role in the world, is not restricted to a process of only observing what happens, but it also involves my intervention as a subject of what happens in the world. My role in the world is not simply that of someone who registers what occurs but of someone who has an input into what happens. I am equally subject and object in the historical process. In the context of history, culture and politics I register events not so as to adapt myself to them but so as to change them.

⑥ REALITY IS REGARDED AS SOCIALLY CONSTRUCTED AND MULTIPLE INTERCONNECTIONS EXIST

Critical theory assumes that social and cultural reality are constructed and already pre-interpreted by the participants, and can be changed over time. The process for understanding this socially constructed reality is dialogic; it allows individuals to communicate about their experience within a shared framework of cultural meanings. As such, critical theory is also a critical and dialectical account of underlying historical and cultural conditions.

⑦ CRITICAL THEORY IS EXPLICITLY FOCUSED ON PROMOTING 'LIBERATION'

Critical theory is partially determined by whether those for whom it is written recognize it as a way out and act on those principles. As a result, critical theory should be seen as an interpenetrating body of work.

Such a critical methodology is initially formed by narrative methods, is ultimately co-operative and in between is oriented towards historical emergence, and, hence, to consciousness raising and to liberation. We can immediately see, retrospectively, that Sereqeberhan's African hermeneutics combines interpretivism with critical theory (compare with Chapter 8). Critical theory is concerned with the analysis of the current situation, which enables us to understand how it has developed; such analysis liberates us from seeing the current order as the natural order of things.

We turn now from these key tenets to a more in depth study of critical theory. We start with critical co-operation and participation, which serves to illustrate how critical methodologies, like critical theory, ultimately serve to connect our separate research paths.

9.3 Critical Theory in Depth

LEADING TO CO-OPERATION AND PARTICIPATION

Two approaches towards ultimately co-operative and participative research are highlighted by critical theorists: co-operative inquiry and participatory action research.

Co-operative and Participative Research (According to Critical Theorists)	
Co-operative Inquiry (see Chapter 10)	Involves you in co-operating in undertaking the research process, and in developing self-awareness in the process.
Participatory Action Research (see Chapter 7)	Has two objectives – one is to produce knowledge and action directly useful to a group, and the second is to empower people through raising consciousness, and self-awareness, over the course of time.

Fundamental to these approaches is that the research makes a difference to individuals' experience and that those who are being researched play an active role in the evolving process, rather than being passive subjects. Critical theory is also explicitly value laden in its approach, and geared towards 'surfacing' such underlying values and ideologies.

AFFIRMING AN EMANCIPATORY ORIENTATION

The ways in which we analyse and interpret information, for critical theorists, are conditioned both by the way our research is theoretically framed and also by your ideological assumptions as a researcher. Therefore *research in the critical tradition takes the form of 'self-conscious criticism'* in the sense that you try to become aware of the ideological presuppositions that inform your sense-making. Such developing self-awareness emerges interpretively with a narrative identification of your unfolding story line, alongside that of your society. Validity, in the context of critical theory is associated with:

- The credibility of *portrayals of constructed realities* whereby constructions are deemed plausible to those who constructed them.
- *Anticipatory accommodation* serving to accommodate the unique aspects of what you perceive in new contexts.

- *Catalytic validity* involving the degree to which research moves those you study to understand the world and the way it is shaped so as to transform it.

Critical theory counteracts empirical research. As a critical theorist you reject the idea of theory-neutral observational language, showing instead that values and interests underpin your knowledge. This will be picked up when we consider co-operative inquiry (Chapter 10) later.

COUNTERACTING EMPIRICAL RESEARCH

Critical theory inspires consideration of a broader context than the more singular, conventional approaches to research methodology, such as empiricism. *The relation between the specific object of cultural critique,* for example the role of capital in business and society, *and the whole historical and social context, is the key issue for critical theory.* It then becomes natural to adopt a freer range in which imagination, creativity and your own evolving insights, together with your analytical and interpretive capabilities, can be called upon.

The focus shifts away from empirical research towards the interpretation and reasoned appraisal of such empirical material. In that respect critical theory is similar to hermeneutics, but it is also further complemented by critical emancipatory observations, as we saw with Serequeberhan, and interpretations of the surrounding societal context. In other words, the storyline that you uncover and evolve has much stronger sociopolitical overtones than in the purely interpretive case.

If the respondents in an in-depth interview on leadership maintain, for instance, that 'leadership is important in the workplace', how do you interpret such a response? Do you infer that leadership is necessarily important, or is it merely important for these respondents? In other words, have they have adopted the 'leadership ideology', that is of the heroic individual leader or entrepreneur, propounded in prodigious amounts of recent popular literature? It may seem interesting enough that people hold this view, but it might be more important to find out what this view means, where it comes from and what the consequences may be? Perhaps it is just a 'semi-deep' notion that could easily change under different circumstances, or is it so deeply rooted in that it has the effect of a quasi-natural position for the people concerned? Perhaps there is a natural law that states that most people are dependent on their leaders?

> *Facts never stand alone in social contexts researched by critical theorists; the objects of social science rather express precisely that they are part of such a context and need to be interpreted as such.*[4]

How then do we probe beneath the surface of such things?

SELF-REFLECTION: TOWARDS A TRIPLE HERMENEUTICS

Critical research methodology, for the Swedish social researchers Alvesson and Skoldberg,[5] demands at least three sorts of theory, which need, to some extent at least, to be taken into account, altogether drawing upon an in-depth, self-reflexive interpretive orientation, which they term a 'triple hermeneutcs', that is:

- a hermeneutic understanding of *history, language and meaning*;
- a social theory of *society as a totality*; and
- a theory of *the unconscious*.

In fact, Eritrea's Serequeberhan, as we have seen in Chapter 8, quotes extensively from Franz Fanon – the Martinique-born activist in Algeria during its liberation war – who was a psychiatrist and thereby active interpreter of the colonizer's unconscious, not to mention that of the colonized. To this may be added an anthropological theory or form of understanding, pointing at the relativity of cultural meanings, something that the Senegalese poet-statesman Leopold Senghor often highlighted.

All of these do not replace the need for specific theories associated with the areas to be researched. Some critical researchers, like the critical realists as we shall discuss in Chapter 15, distinguish between surface and deep structures. Surface structure is where individuals lead their conscious lives, where things are natural and existence is (or can be made to be) rational and comprehensible. Deep structure is here taken to refer to those unquestioned beliefs and values upon which the taken-for-granted surface structure rests.

The aim for the critical emancipatory researcher is to be able to identify this deep structure, and in particular such beliefs and values as give rise to 'frozen' social institutions and 'locked' thought and action. It is in that specific sense, for Alvesson, that critical theory can be described as a kind of 'triple hermeneutics':

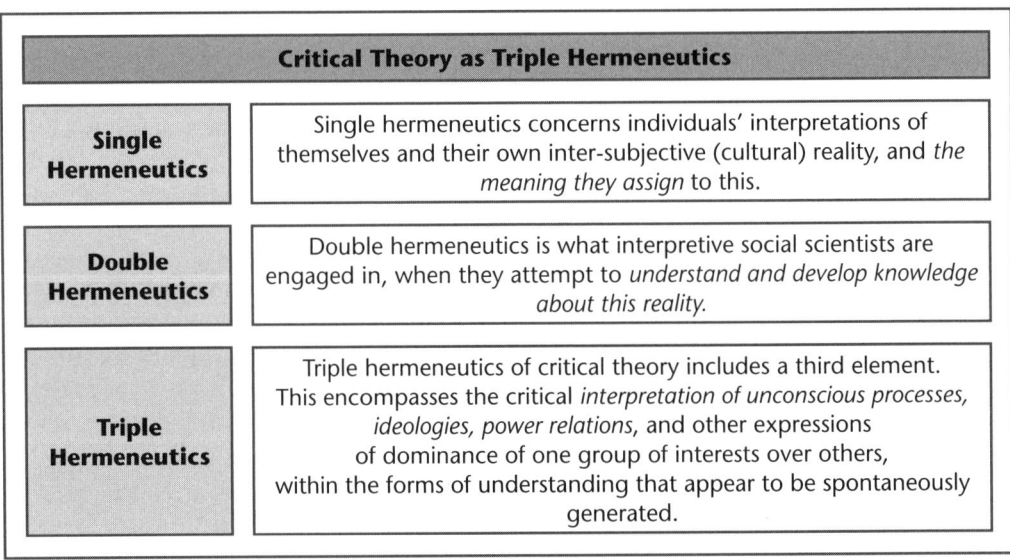

Critical Theory as Triple Hermeneutics	
Single Hermeneutics	Single hermeneutics concerns individuals' interpretations of themselves and their own inter-subjective (cultural) reality, and *the meaning they assign* to this.
Double Hermeneutics	Double hermeneutics is what interpretive social scientists are engaged in, when they attempt to *understand and develop knowledge about this reality.*
Triple Hermeneutics	Triple hermeneutics of critical theory includes a third element. This encompasses the critical *interpretation of unconscious processes, ideologies, power relations,* and other expressions of dominance of one group of interests over others, within the forms of understanding that appear to be spontaneously generated.

Four broad themes are then integral to critical theory:[6]

1. *Social Construction*: an emphasis, as is the case for hermeneutics and phenomenology, on the social construction of reality.
2. *Power and Ideology*: a focus on issues of power and ideology, whereby there is an awareness that social constructions are influenced by these.

3. *Multiple Interconnections*: the need to understand any social or organizational phenomenon in interdisciplinary terms, that is of its multiple interconnections and location within holistic historical contexts.
4. *Social Praxis*: the importance of praxis, that is the ongoing construction of social arrangements that are conducive to the flourishing of the human condition.

As a result, *critical theory should be seen as an interpenetrating body of work*, which demands and produces three particular things:

1. *a critical engagement with your contemporary social world*, recognizing that the existing state of affairs does not exhaust all possibilities and offering positive implications for social action;
2. *a critical account of the historical and cultural conditions* on which your own intellectual activity depends;
3. *a continuous critical re-examination of the constitutive categories and conceptual frameworks* of your understanding, including your historical and dialectical construction of these as a critical confrontation with other works of social explanation.

Where then, in conclusion, does critical theory fit, overall, in our path of renewal?

A DIALECTICAL AND COGNITIVE APPROACH TO INTERDISCIPLINARY DEVELOPMENT

The ontology[7] adopted by critical theory has much in common with phenomenology and interpretivism – in that both natural and social realities are seen to be socially constructed. However, *it places its pre-emphasis on cognitive interests*. Specifically established in Germany in the 1930s, it *builds epistemologically on European intellectual traditions*. This involves the idea that reason is the highest potentiality of human beings and that, through its use, it is possible to criticize and challenge the nature of existing societies.

Knowledge stemming from sociology, psychoanalysis, philosophy, economics and aesthetics has been combined here in a unique social science environment. The early critical theorists who emigrated from Germany to America in the Nazi period regarded capitalist society as fundamentally irrational in that it failed to satisfy existing wants from a humanist perspective, and produced false wants and needs. As such, the critical theorists departed radically from the liberal-market perspective of Locke and Mill, and were also more anti-establishment – in their views – than Popper, with his market-based, democratic 'open society'.

The idea for the critical theorists is that social phenomena are best described as changeable elements in a dialectical social development, and are to be understood as an emergent process of becoming. Statements about society cannot be impartial. Rather they tend to confirm or challenge existing social institutions and establish modes of thought. According to the Frankfurt School, social science should strive to develop an independent and critical stance vis-à-vis these institutions and modes of thought, and should call attention to the contradictions in the way society functions. The inherent restrictions and irrationalities that inform modern capitalist societies should be among the major subjects of research. From this perspective, the social sciences are doing the business world today a disservice by helping it to enhance its 'bottom-line' performance.

Whereas social scientists like Elton Mayo and Chris Argyris in the US, in the 1940s and 1950s, adopted a critical-emancipatory line, their counterparts today tend to tow the conventional party line. Important sources of inspiration for critical theory, meanwhile, had been Germany's Marx, Weber, Kant, Hegel and Austria's Sigmund Freud. At the same time the school was also powerfully affected by the political climate in Germany in the 1920s and 1930s, and the development of authoritarian Stalinism in the Soviet Union. The critical theorist and social psychologist Erich Fromm, for example, emphasized that people's desire to subordinate themselves in authoritarian relationships and ideologies was a mechanism for avoiding the anxiety that freedom and independence can engender.

Now we turn to the overall significance of critical theory in our current day and age, not only in Europe and America (North-West) but also in developing societies (South-East)?

9.4 Global Variations of Critical Theory: Towards Transformative Social Change

COMMUNICATIVE FOUNDATIONS BY GERMANY'S JÜRGEN HABERMAS

From Monologic to Dialogic ...

Critical theory's two leading contemporary exponents are Germany's academic and social philosopher Jürgen Habermas (developed world), and Brazil's pedagogue and policy maker, the late Paulo Freire (developing world). Whereas philosophers and researchers from the developed world, like Habermas, tend to be transformative in words, those like Freire from the developed world tend to be so also in action. Habermas' intellectual roots were in hermeneutics and, like Gadamer, he claimed that the respective subject matters of the natural and social sciences were completely different. He described the natural sciences as using 'sense experience' and the social and cultural or hermeneutic sciences as using 'communicative experience'. Following Husserl, Habermas today accepts the same two central premises as those adopted by phenomenology and hermeneutics:

- Social and cultural reality is already pre-interpreted by the participants as a cultural symbolic meaning system, which can be changed over time.
- The process for understanding this socially constructed reality is dialogic; it allows individuals to communicate about their experience within a shared framework of cultural meanings.

... and from Empirical-Analytical to Critical-Emancipatory

Alternatively, in the natural sciences and in management science, the process is 'monologic'; involving the technical manipulation by the researcher of some aspect of physical or human nature. One of the central concepts in Habermas' understanding of knowledge, is in relation to what he terms *'knowledge-constitutive interests'*. These interests, he argued, *determine what counts as the objects of knowledge*. Habermas therefore classified the processes of scientific enquiry into three categories,[8] the first two, in our terms, being normative and the third transformative in orientation:

Process of Scientifc Inquiry Categories according to Habermas		
①	*The empirical-analytical sciences*, including the natural sciences, economics, sociology and political science, are interested in *technically exploitable knowledge, in prediction and control*, increasing the possibility of human domination over nature and social relations.	**Focus on Work**
②	*The historical-hermeneutical sciences* are based on the practical interest in promoting communicative *understanding between individuals and within and between social groups*, including language and art.	**Focus on Interaction**
③	*Critical theory* involves self-reflection, and is ultimately based on an emancipatory interest in *achieving rational autonomy of action free from domination*.	**Focus on the Exercise and Abuses of Power**

TRANSFORMATIVE FOUNDATIONS BY BRAZIL'S PAULO FREIRE

The Practice of Freedom: Conscientisation

We now turn from the European Habermas to the prominent Latin American critical theorist of our day and age: Paulo Freire. A Brazilian by birth, he spent much of his adult life as an exile from his native land in Chile, and also as a fellow and visiting professor at Harvard. Freire was one of the 20th century's greatest thinkers on education. Overtly transformational in his approach, he operated on one basic assumption:

> *man's ontological vocation is to be a subject who acts upon and transforms the world, and in so doing moves toward ever newer possibilities of fuller and richer life individually and collectively. This 'world' to which he relates is not a static and closed order, a given reality which man must accept and to which he must adjust; rather, it is a problem to be worked on and solved. It is material used by man to create history, a task which he performs as he overcomes that which is dehumanizing at any particular time and place and dares to create the qualitatively new.*[9]

For Freire, the resources for that task at the present time are provided by the advanced technology of the Western world, but the social vision, which impels us to negate the present order and demonstrate that history has not ended, comes primarily from the suffering and struggle of the people of the Third World. Education either functions as an instrument, which is used to facilitate the integration of the younger generation into the logic of the present system and bring about conformity to it, or to become 'the practice of freedom', the means by which men and women deal critically and creatively with reality and discover how to participate in the transformation of their world.

Freire's pedagogical theory and practice – for North and South American educators Morrow and Torres[10] – presupposes something like Habermas' threefold account of knowledge interests, but expresses them in more actively transformational terms:

Core Implications of Freire's Pedagogy
(according to Morrow and Torres)

Technology as a form of empirical-analytical knowledge is indispensable for the purpose of fulfilling basic human needs.

Hermeneutic-historical interpretation is the basis for discovering cultural themes necessary for establishing subject-object communication.

Critical insight is required for the movement toward critical consciousness – conscientization – that transforms reality.

Freire's epistemology, like that of Habermas, is also based on a *distinction between two rationalities of action*: first, 'manipulative strategies' that treat people as objects to be technically controlled; and second, 'dialogical relations' in which there is subject–subject co-participation and mutual learning. In Habermas' work this is elaborated in terms of two forms of rationality: 'strategic rationality and communicative action'.

For Freire and Habermas, human history reveals a constant struggle for democratization and the realization of individual autonomy that is linked to the dialogical and developmental nature of the human subject. For both, however, there is a *problematic relationship between instrumental rationalization, understood as one-sided economic modernization, and social rationalization as manifest in authentic democratization and individuation*. For Freire there is the assumption that within the 'culture of silence' there are accumulated experiences which potentially can take the form of critical knowledge through processes of dialogical learning.

Four types of anti-dialogical actions are identified as mechanisms of hegemony that form a culture of silence:

1. 'conquest', involving relations of domination and subordination;
2. 'divide and rule', based on a 'focalized' view of problems, rather than seeing the totality;
3. 'manipulation' through communicative distortions;
4. 'cultural invasion' by directly penetrating the cultural contexts of groups, imposing a view of the world that deprives subordinate groups of any sense of alternative possibilities.

Conscientizacao and Dialogic Praxis

How then can learners escape the 'culture of silence', take steps towards critical consciousness, and enter into authentic dialogue? The Portuguese word *conscientizacao*, popularized by Freire for educational environments, has been translated into 'conscientization' in English. It is a way of reading how society works. This deeper reading of reality is revealed through praxis, identified with cultural action for freedom, whereby the subject finds the ability to grasp, in critical terms, the dialectical unity between self and object. The crucial psychological process required is that of using new forms of language to get 'distance' from taken-for-granted realities of everyday life. The revelatory processes unleashed through conscientization are not only cognitive, but also ethical, in evaluating the consequences of domination:

> When we live our lives with the authenticity demanded by the practice of teaching that is also learning, and learning that is also teaching, we are participating in a total experience that is simultaneously directive, political, ideological, gnostic, pedagogical, aesthetic, and ethical. In this experience the beautiful, the decent, and the serious form a circle with hands joined. At the same time, in the context of true learning, the learners will be engaged in a continuous transformation through which they become authentic subjects of the construction and reconstruction of what is taught, side by side with the teacher, who is equally subject to the same process ... I believe that all educational practice requires the existence of 'subjects' who, while teaching, learn. And who in learning also teach. The reciprocal learning between teachers and students is what gives educational practice its gnostic character. It is a practice that involves the use of methods, techniques, materials; in its directive character, it implies dreams, utopias, ideas, objectives. Hence we have the political nature of education.[11]

We shall see, later in Chapter 10, the similarities and differences between Brazil's Paulo Freire and the UK's John Heron, both inspired by critical theory in their educational and political orientations. We end with Freire's five principles of moral philosophy:

A Transformative Approach to Research and Education
(based on Freire's Five Principles of Moral Philosophy)

① People ought to pursue their ontological vocation of becoming more fully human, through engaging in critical, dialogical praxis.

② No person or group of people ought to knowingly constrain or prevent another person or group from pursuing their vocation.

③ We ought – collectively and dialogically – to consider what kind of world, including social structures, processes and relationships, would be necessary for all to pursue their humanization.

④ All people ought to act to transform existing structures where critical reflection reveals that these structures serve as impediments.

⑤ Educators and others who assume positions of responsibility in the social sphere ought to side with the oppressed in seeking to promote a better world through their activities.

We now turn, finally, to the practice of critical theory, as illustrated by Paulo Freire.

9.5 Critical Theory in Practice: Paolo Freire's Reflective Activism

Paulo Freire is certainly the most prominent thinker within the tradition of critical theory who also applied the approach towards his immediate life world. In order to understand Freire's work it is important to see him in his own context.

FREIRE'S CONTEXT: PEDAGOGY OF THE OPPRESSED

Born in 1921 to middle-class parents in Recife, Brazil, Freire knew poverty and hunger during the 1929 Great Depression, an experience that would shape his concerns for the poor and would help to construct his particular educational viewpoint.

Freire entered the University of Recife in 1943, enrolling in the Faculty of Law, but also studying philosophy and the psychology of language. Despite his being called to the legal bar, he never actually practised law and instead worked as a teacher in secondary schools teaching Portuguese. In 1944, he married Elza Maia Costa de Oliveira, a fellow teacher. The two had five children and worked together for the rest of her life. In 1946, Freire was appointed Director of the Department of Education and Culture of the Social Service in the State of Pernambuco, the Brazilian state of which Recife is the capital. Working primarily among the illiterate poor, Freire began to embrace a non-orthodox form of what could be considered liberation theology. In Brazil at that time, literacy was a requirement for voting in presidential elections.

In 1961, he was appointed director of the Department of Cultural Extension of Recife University, and in 1962 he had the first opportunity for significant application of his theories, when 300 sugarcane workers were taught to read and write in just 45 days. In response to this experiment, the Brazilian government approved the creation of thousands of cultural circles across the country. In 1964, a military coup put an end to that effort; Freire was imprisoned as a traitor for 70 days. After a brief exile in Bolivia, Freire worked in Chile for five years for the Christian Democratic Agrarian Reform Movement and the Food and Agriculture Organization of the United Nations.

In 1967, Freire published his first book, *Education as the Practice of Freedom*. The book was well received, and Freire was offered a visiting professorship at Harvard University in 1969. The previous year, he wrote his most famous book, *Pedagogy of the Oppressed*, which was published also in Spanish and English in 1970. Because of the political feud between the successive authoritarian military dictatorships and the Christian socialist Freire, it wasn't published in Brazil until 1974, when General Ernesto Geisel took control of Brazil and began his process of cultural liberalization. After a year in Cambridge, USA, Freire moved to Geneva, Switzerland, to work as a special education adviser to the World Council of Churches. During this time Freire acted as an adviser on education reform in former Portuguese colonies in Africa, particularly Guinea-Bissau and Mozambique.

In 1979, he was able to return to Brazil, and moved back in 1980. Freire joined the Workers' Party (PT) in the city of São Paulo, and acted as a supervisor for its adult literacy project from 1980 to 1986. When the PT prevailed in the municipal elections in 1988, Freire was appointed Secretary of Education for São Paulo. Freire died of heart failure in 1997.

The following case describing Freire's work is taken from *Literacy: Reading the Word and the World* by Paulo Freire and Donaldo Macedo.[12]

IMAGINING A CHANGED WORLD

A Dialectical Exchange: Language, for Freire, is not merely a means to a literate end, but it assures the power of envisaging things: because we can name the world and thus hold it in mind, we can reflect on its meaning and imagine a changed world. Language is the means to critical consciousness, which, in turn, is the means of conceiving change and of making choices to bring about further transformations. Thus, naming the world transforms reality from 'things' in the present moment to activities in response to situations, processes, to becoming. Liberation comes only when people reclaim their language and, with it, the power to envision their future, the imagination of a different world to be brought into being.

Instead then of education as extension – a reaching-out to students with valuable ideas we want to share – there must be a dialogue, a dialectical exchange in which ideas take shape and change as the learners in the Culture Circle think about their thinking and interpret their interpretations. The dichotomy of the 'affective' and the 'cognitive' plays no part in Freire's pedagogy, important as it is in American educational theory. He sees thinking and feeling, along with action, as aspects of all that we do in making sense of the world. In summary, the basic themes of Freire's ongoing literacy campaign, over the course of his life, were:

- comprehension of the work process and the productive act in its complexity;
- ways to organize and develop production;
- the need for technical training, though not reduced to narrow specialization;
- comprehension of culture and its role, not only in the process of liberation, but also in national reconstruction;
- problems of cultural identity, whose defence should not mean the ingenious rejection of other cultures' contributions.

What if … the Power to Dream? Criticism for Freire always means interpreting one's interpretations, reconsidering contexts, tolerating ambiguities so that we can learn from the attempt to resolve them. By thus representing the power to envisage – 'What if … How could it be if … – language provides the model of social transformation. Dreams are formed by a critical and inventive imagination, exercised in dialogue, in the naming and renaming of the world, which guides its remaking. The lecture, in that context, is a late medieval invention instituted because books were scarce. In its stead Freire is saying: 'there is no way to transformation, transformation is the way'.

THE PEDAGOGY OF POLITICAL EMPOWERMENT

Language and Transformation: Central to Freire's approach to literacy, is a dialectical relationship between human beings and the world, on the one hand, and language and transformative agency, on the other. Within this perspective, literacy is not merely approached as a technical skill to be acquired, but as a necessary foundation for cultural action for freedom, a central aspect of what it means to be a self and a socially constituted agent. In this sense, literacy is fundamental to aggressively constructing one's voice as part of a wider project of possibility and empowerment.

To be able to name one's experience is part of what it means to 'read' the world and to begin to understand the political nature of the limits and possibilities that make up the larger society. Language is the 'real stuff' of culture, and constitutes both a terrain of domination and a field of possibility. Critical literacy is both a narrative for agency as well as a referent for critique. As a narrative for agency, literacy becomes synonymous with an attempt to rescue history and experience from conventional discourse and dominant social relations. It means developing the theoretical and practical conditions through which human beings can locate themselves in their own histories, and in doing so make themselves present as agents in the struggle to expand the possibilities of human life and freedom.

To be literate is not merely to be free, it is to be present and active in the struggle for reclaiming one's voice, history and future. That includes a view of human agency in which the production of meaning takes place in the dialogue and interaction that mutually constitute the dialectical relationship between human subjectivities and the objective world. Such a pedagogy of empowerment needs to be centred in a social project aimed at the enhancement of human possibility.

Production of Knowledge as a Developmental and Relational Act: Hence, the production of knowledge is both a developmental and a relational act. For teachers this means being sensitive to the actual historical, social and cultural conditions that contribute to the forms of knowledge and meaning the students bring to school. In its more radical sense critical literacy means making one's self present as part of a moral and political project that links the production of meaning to the possibility for human agency, democratic community and transformative social action. As used here, history means recognizing the traces of untapped potentialities as well as sources of suffering that constitute one's past. To define literacy in the Freirean sense as a critical reading of the world and the word is to lay the theoretical groundwork for more fully analyzing how knowledge is produced and subjectivities constructed within relations of interaction. As such teachers and students attempt to make themselves present as active authors of their own worlds.

A curriculum itself represents a narrative or voice, one that is multilayered and often contradictory but also situated within relations of power that more often than not favour white, male, middle-class, English-speaking students. What this suggests for a theory of critical literacy is that curriculum in the most fundamental sense is a battleground over whose form of knowledge, history, vision, culture, language and authority will prevail as a legitimate object of learning and analysis.

The Importance of the Act of Reading: Language and reality are, for Freire, dynamically interconnected. The understanding attained by critical reading of a text implies perceiving the relationships between text and context. Freire describes his birthplace in Recife, Brazil. The trees that surrounded him felt like persons, such was the intimacy established. Animals were equally part of that context – the way the family cats rubbed against his legs, their mewing of entreaty or anger. Part of the context of his immediate world was also the language universe of his elders, expressing their beliefs, tastes, fears and values, which linked his world to a wider one whose existence he could not even suspect. Hence, reading a word, a phrase, a sentence never entailed a break with reading the world. Reading the word meant reading the word-world.

Freire always saw teaching adults to read and write as a political act, an act of knowledge, and therefore a creative act. The student then becomes the subject of a process of learning to read and write, as an act of knowing and creating. Reading the world always precedes reading the word, and reading the word implies continually reading the world. However, we can go further and say that reading the word is not preceded merely by reading the world, but by a certain way of writing or rewriting it, that is of transforming it by means of conscious, practical work.

Words, for Freire, should be laden with the meaning of the people's existential experience, and not of the teacher's experience. Surveying the word universe thus gives us the people's words, pregnant with the world, words from the people's reading of the world. We then give the words back to the people inserted in what Freire calls 'codifications', pictures representing real situations. Decodifying or reading the situations pictured leads them to a critical perception of the meaning of culture by leading them to understand how human practice or work transforms the world. To sum up, reading always involves critical perception, interpretation and rewriting of what is read.

Education Models Souls and Re-creates Hearts as a Fulcrum for Change: To impose on people one's own understanding in the name of their liberation is to accept authoritarian solutions as ways of freedom. But to assume the naïveté of those becoming educated demands from educators a most necessary humility to assume also their ability to criticize, thus overcoming our naïveté as well.

The neutrality of education, which results in being understood as a pure task, to serve in the formation of an ideal type of human being, disembodied from what is real, virtuous and good, is one of the most fundamental connotations of the naïve visions of education. From the point of view of such a vision, the world is reborn in the intimacy of consciences, moved by the goodness of hearts. And since education models souls and re-creates hearts, it is the fulcrum of social change. Conversely from the authoritarian, elitist reactionary point of view, the people's incompetence is almost natural. The people need to be defended because they are incapable of thinking clearly, of abstracting, knowing and creating; they are eternally 'of lesser value' and their ideas are permanently labelled exotic. Popular knowledge does not exist. The notion of emancipatory literacy, for Freire, suggests two dimensions. On the one hand, students have to become literate about their histories, experiences and the culture of their immediate environments. On the other hand, they must also appropriate those codes and cultures of the dominant spheres so they can transcend their own environments. There is often an enormous tension between those two dimensions of literacy.

For Freire, the consciousness of the world is constituted in relation to the world. The world enables you to constitute the self in relation to it. The transformation of objective reality, in other words the 'writing of reality', represents precisely the starting point where the animal that became human began to write history. It started when these animals began to use their hands differently. As this transformation was taking place, the consciousness of the 'touched' world was constituting itself. It is precisely this consciousness, touched and transformed, that bred the consciousness of the self.

For a long time these beings, who were making themselves, wrote the world much more than they spoke it. They directly touched and affected the world before they talked about it. Sometime later, these beings began to speak about their transformed world. After another long period of time they began to register graphically the talk about the transformation. Before learners attempt to learn how to read and write, therefore, they need to read and write the world. They need to comprehend the world that involves talk about the world. The reinvention of power that passes through the reinvention of production, therefore, would entail the reinvention of culture, within which environments would be created to incorporate, in a participatory way, all those discourses that are presently suffocated by the dominant discourse. The legitimation of these different discourses would authenticate the plurality of voices in the reconstruction of a truly democratic society. Human agency, finally, makes sense and flourishes only when subjectivity is understood in its dialectical, contradictory, dynamic relationship with objectivity, from which its derives.

9.6 Conclusion

In concluding this chapter on critical theory, from a dialectical and also developmental perspective, we can see that the perspectives from the developed and the developing worlds are somewhat different. While both have strongly sociopolitical overtones, these are stronger in the developing world's persepective. While Habermas is an academic with strong political views as well as epistemological perspectives, the late Paulo Freire was much more of a political and social activist, his medium for this being education. In that light, we conclude with an appropriate quote from Freire:

> One of the first kinds of knowledge indispensable to the person who arrives in a ghetto, or in a place marked by our betrayal of the right 'to be' is the kind of knowledge that becomes solidarity, becomes a 'being with'. In that context, the future is seen as something not inexorable but as something that is constructed by people engaged together in life, in history. It is knowledge that sees history as possibility, not as determined. The world is not finished. It is always in the process of becoming. The subjectivity with which I dialectically relate to the world, my role in the world, is not restricted to a process of only observing what happens, but it also involves my intervention as a subject of what happens in the world. My role in the world is not simply that of someone who registers what occurs but of someone who has an input into what happens. I am equally subject and object in the historical process. In the context of history, culture and politics I register events not so as to adapt myself to them but so as to change them. [13]

We now turn, along the Eastern path of renewal, from narrative methods, hermeneutics and now critical theory, to co-operative inquiry. John Heron, as we shall see in the next chapter, takes on – politically and epistemically – from where the critical theorists left off.

References

1. Johnson, P. and Duberley, J. (2000). *Understanding Management Research*. London: Sage.
2. Blaikie, N. (1994). *Approaches to Social Inquiry*. London: Pluto Press.
3. Alvesson, M. and Skoldberg, K. (2000). *Reflexive Methodology*. London: Sage.
4. Held, M. (1980). *Introduction to Critical Theory*. London: Routledge.
5. *Ibid.*
6. *Ibid.*
7. *Ibid.*
8. *Ibid.*
9. Freire, P. (1972). *Pedagogy of the Oppressed*. Harmondsworth: Penguin.

10. Morrow, R. and Torres, C. (2002). *Reading Freire and Habermas: Critical Pedagogy and Transformative Social Change*. New York: Teachers College Press.
11. Freire, *Pedagogy of the Oppressed*.
12. Freire, P. and Macedo, D. (1987). *Literacy: Reading The Word And The World*. South Hadley, MA: Bergin and Garvey.
13. Freire, *Pedagogy of the Oppressed*.

10 *From Critical Theory to Co-operative Inquiry*

Uncover Shared Potential

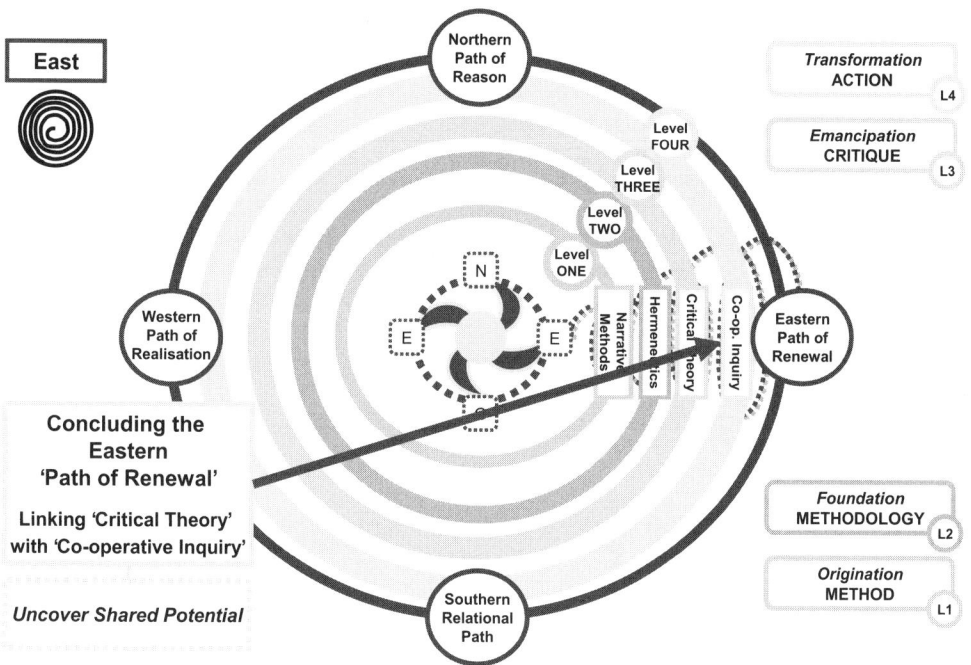

East

Northern Path of Reason

Transformation
ACTION
L4

Emancipation
CRITIQUE
L3

Level FOUR

Level THREE

Level TWO

Level ONE

N

Narrative Methods

Hermeneutics

Critical Theory

Co-op. Inquiry

E

E

Western Path of Realisation

Eastern Path of Renewal

Concluding the Eastern 'Path of Renewal'

Linking 'Critical Theory' with 'Co-operative Inquiry'

Uncover Shared Potential

Foundation
METHODOLOGY
L2

Origination
METHOD
L1

Southern Relational Path

Figure 10.1 Overview Chapter 10 – Level 4/East

| **Summary: Co-operative Inquiry** |

- The culmination of your research path of renewal lies in co-operative inquiry, which most explicitly addresses social innovation in this context.
- Co-operative inquiry, invented mainly by UK action researchers John Heron and Peter Reason, takes on from where narrative methods, interpretive methodology (hermeneutics) and critical theory leave off, giving rise to an ultimately transformative and integral approach.
- Such an approach to co-operative research is both politically integral and transformative, in that it involves co-researchers working together, as fellow subjects rather than as researcher/subject and researched/object, and encompasses experiential, imaginative, conceptual and practical ways of knowing.
- These four ways of knowing or modes of consciousness include altogether the Southern humanistic (experiential) and the Eastern holistic (imaginative), the Northern rational (conceptual) and the Western pragmatic (practical) dimension, albeit that the holistic path to renewal and innovation holds pride of place.
- Overall, the guiding objectives of co-operative inquiry are: political flourishing in individual and social life which includes a process of social participation where there is a balance between autonomy, co-operation and hierarchy; epistemic flourishing in individual and social life which includes a growing participative awareness of social contexts; and a conscious indwelling and resonance with the cultural life of the planet.
- In concluding this chapter with a practical application, we introduce the Japanese concept of Ba. This Eastern concept, adopted by Japan's knowledge management icon, Ikijiro Nonaka, offers remarkable analogies to co-operative inquiry. Ba and its application demonstrate the relevance of Heron's developmental and spiralling rhythm (from the experiential to the practical) in today's organizational practice, particularly for the area of knowledge creation.

10.1 Orientation to Co-operative Inquiry

PAR TO CI

As in the previous case of Southern innovation through participatory action research (PAR), so in this Eastern case, co-operative inquiry is integral, in that it draws to some extent on the three other research paths (or epistemologies), albeit being most firmly lodged within the path of renewal. This is what gives John Heron's work its 'worldly-ness'. However, while participatory research has strongly Southern and relational overtones, co-operative inquiry has more Eastern developmental ones. While participatory research is aligned with rich description, phenomenology and feminism, and also with the human mode of 'being', co-operative inquiry is dialectical and spiritual in orientation. It is therefore more closely aligned with narrative methods, interpretivism, and critical theory, and with a process of 'becoming'. This, altogether, constitutes the holistic path, starting with and unfolding through 'the stories we are'.

Co-operative inquiry is explicitly transformative as well as informative in its approach. Moreover, it deals with such issues as research validity and quality, which adds an orthodox flavour to it. Finally, as was the case for participative research, *while co-operative inquiry has a distinctively holistic feel to it, it also has shades of humanism, rationalism and empiricism.*

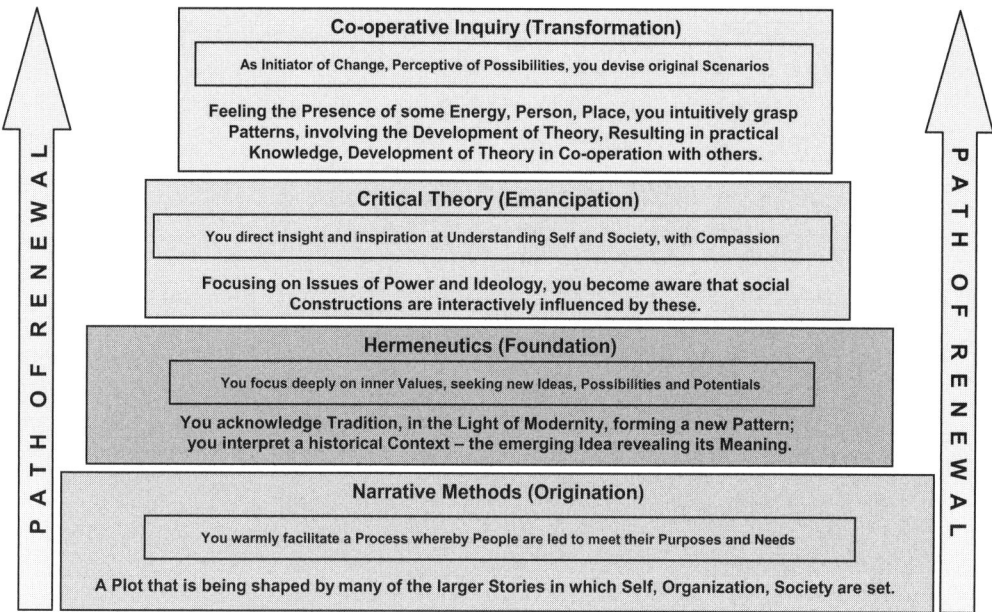

Figure 10.2 Towards Co-operative Inquiry

CO-OPERATIVE INQUIRY IN AN ACTION RESEARCH CONTEXT

A Changing East-West Paradigm

John Heron, while an educator and psychologist at the University of Surrey, together with his close colleague Peter Reason at the University of Bath, were the two leading co-creators of action research in Britain. Later, Reason and Bradbury, in their *Handbook of Action Research*,[1] took on, where Heron and Reason had left off. For them, the idea of a paradigm in science can be transferred to the worldview of a whole culture, and to the notion that the Western worldview may be in evolutionary transition. Research in the West, hitherto, has been associated with a so-called 'positivist' worldview, a view that sees science as separate from everyday life and the researcher as a subject within a world of separate objects. This is part of a worldview based on the metaphor of linear progress, absolute truth and rational planning. Seeking objective truth, this modern worldview makes no connection between knowledge and power.

For Reason, Bradbury and Heron, such a positivist view has outlived its usefulness. For the contemporary German philosopher and critical theorist Habermas, such Western 'modernism' is dead. Against such a historical backdrop, what does action research stand for today, set in the transpersonal and even spiritual Eastern context of this chapter?

Figure 10.3 Co-operative Inquiry – Core Thinkers

Sources: Image 1: Amazon http://astore.amazon.com/. Image 2: South Pacific Centre for Human Inquiry http://www.human-inquiry.com/. Image 3: University of Bath http://www.bath.ac.uk/. Image 4: eFollet http://www.efollett.com/

Contemporary Action Research: Towards a Participatory Worldview

The emergent worldview that action research espouses can be described as systemic, holistic, relational, feminine and experiential, but *its defining characteristic is that it is participatory and developmental*; our world does not consists of separate things but of *relationships which we co-author.*

John Heron was a pioneer in the creation of participatory research methodologies in the social sciences. As such, he was the founder and director of the Human Potential Research Project at the University of Surrey in England from 1970 to 1977, the first university-based centre for humanistic and so-called 'transpersonal' psychology and education in Europe. He was Assistant Director of the British Postgraduate Medical Federation at the University of London from 1977 to 1985, in charge of an innovative programme of personal and professional development for hospital doctors and GPs, including a co-operative inquiry into whole-person medicine, out of which the British Holistic Medical Association was formed. Later, from 1990 to 2000, he became Director of the International Centre for Co-operative Inquiry in Tuscany in Italy, where radical forms of spiritual inquiry were developed. Currently, he is Co-director of the South Pacific Centre for Human Inquiry in Auckland, New Zealand.

Within the context of co-operative inquiry, human persons are linked in a generative web of communion with other humans and the rest of creation. *Human persons do not stand separate from the cosmos; we evolved with it and are an expression of its intelligent and creative force.* As we are part of the whole we are necessarily actors within it, which leads us to consider the fundamental importance of the practical. All ways of knowing, then, support our skilful being-in-the-world from moment to moment, our ability to act intelligently in support of worthwhile purposes. Hence, human inquiry is necessarily practical, and any participatory form of inquiry is for Reason, Bradbury and Heron a 'sacred science'. It is a kind of knowledge, moreover, that one has only from within a social and (in this 'transpersonal' case) within a spiritual situation.

Such a participatory worldview is at the same time a political statement as well as a theory of knowledge. Just as the classical Cartesian worldview emerged out of the political situation of the time, and found its expression in science and technology, so a participatory worldview implies democratic, peer relationships as the political form of inquiry. The political dimension affirms people's right to have a say in decisions that affect them and which claim to generate knowledge about them. It asserts the importance of liberating the muted voices of those held down by class structure and neo-colonialism, by poverty, sexism, racism and homophobia. To paraphrase the 18th-century American revolutionary Tom Paine, the democratic activist in the late 18th century:

It is for people themselves, in their own right, to enter into agreements with each other to discover and create knowledge, and this is the only principle on which research and inquiry has a right to exist.

Healing and Whole Making

A participative worldview invites us to inquire into what we mean by flourishing and into the meaning and purpose of our endeavours. As the contemporary philosopher and priest Thomas Berry has written: 'What is the "great work" of humanity in our time, and how are our individual human projects aligned with it?' For him, sacred experience, like sacred science, is based on reverence, in awe and love for creation.

Given the condition of our times, a primary purpose of human inquiry is not so much to search for the truth but to heal. For Reason and Bradbury then:

To heal means to make whole: we can only understand our world as a whole if we are part of it; as soon as we attempt to stand outside, we divide and separate. In contrast, making whole necessarily implies participation: the individual is restored to a circle or community and the human community to the context of the wider natural world. To make whole also means to make holy: a participatory worldview restores meaning and mystery to human experience, so that the world is experienced as a sacred place.[2]

As we have seen, co-operative inquiry and its creator John Heron have been born and bred in the West. However, Heron is certainly an unusual Westerner, in that he has been heavily exposed to the North, South and, most particularly, the East.[3]

In the latter respect he has been influenced by critical theory in the overtly political and critical emancipatory stance he takes towards both research and also education. The self-generating culture he has sought to promote is a research community whose members are in a continuous process of co-operative participation, learning and development. Its forms are consciously adopted, periodically reviewed and altered in the light of experience, reflection and ever-deepening vision. Its participants continually re-create themselves and their work through cycles of collaborative inquiry in living and working together. At the same time co-operative inquiry has affinities with the more conventionally recognized approach to action research as well as experiential learning, that arose originally from the work of the social scientist Kurt Lewin, and was duly espoused by the critical theorists, whereby:

In action research, all actors involved in the research process are equal participants, and must be involved in every stage of the research process .. Collaborative participation in theoretical, practical and political discourse is a hallmark of action research and the action researcher.[4]

We now turn to the key tenets of co-operative inquiry.

10.2 Co-operative Inquiry – Key Tenets: Participation, Knowledge Creation, Authenticity

Co-operative Inquiry – Key Tenets
① You engage in a politically oriented process, in a participative form of inquiry.
② You are involved in a knowledge-oriented process – epistemic in nature and scope.
③ You engage in an alternating current of informative and transformative inquiry.
④ You undertake your research in successive action-reflection cycles.
⑤ The validity you seek for your research is goodness, trustworthiness and authenticity.

① YOU ENGAGE IN A POLITICALLY ORIENTED PROCESS, IN A PARTICIPATIVE FORM OF INQUIRY

Oriented to Being Values

The co-operative paradigm has two wings, that is political (value based and transformation oriented) and epistemic (knowledge based and informative). *Co-operative inquiry, distinctively speaking, involves research with other people, who are invited to be full co-inquirers with the initiating researcher.* They become involved in operational decision-making, and are then committed to this kind of research design in principle, both politically and epistemologically. We can see already the resonance with critical theory, if not also with feminism.

The political wing of the participative paradigm is formed by a theory of value, oriented for Heron to being values, which holds that:

- *Human flourishing is intrinsically worthwhile;* it is construed as a process of social participation in which there is a mutually enabling balance within and between people, of autonomy, hierarchy and co-operation, and is conceived as interdependent with the flourishing of the planetary system.
- *What is valuable as a means to this end is participative decision- making,* through which people speak on behalf of the wider ecosystem of which they are a part, including the way that integral research is conducted within our research community.

Political Participation

The reasons for political participation are:

- Persons have *a right to participate in research* – or educational – *design*, the purpose of which is to formulate knowledge about, and through them.
- This gives them the opportunity to *identify and express their own preferences and values in the design*, in association with the other members of their research community.
- It *empowers them to flourish* as fully human persons in the research, and to be represented in its conclusion.
- It *avoids their being disempowered*, oppressed and misrepresented by the researcher's implicit values in any unilateral research design.

② YOU ARE INVOLVED IN A KNOWLEDGE-ORIENTED PROCESS – EPISTEMIC IN NATURE AND SCOPE

Focusing on Truth Values

The epistemic wing, formed by truth values, is:

- *An ontology that affirms a mind-shaped reality which is subjective-objective*: it is subjective because it is only known through the form that the mind gives it; and it is objective because the mind interpenetrates the given cosmos it shapes.
- *An epistemology that asserts the participative relation between the knower and the known*, and where the known is also a knower.
- *A methodology that commands the validation of outcomes through the congruence of practical, conceptual, imaginal and empathetic forms of knowing* amongst co-operative knowers, and the cultivation of skills that deepen these forms.

Multiple Ways of Knowing

Co-operative inquiry is ultimately geared towards social innovation, insofar as it evolves from the experiential to the practical. Four ways of knowing are distinguished:

1. *Practical Knowledge:* evident in exercising skill and closely aligned with the empirical and with the path of realization; builds upon the experimental and the real.
2. *Propositional or Conceptual Knowledge:* closely linked with theory and closely aligned with critical rationalism; builds on hypothesis formation and upon multiple discourses.
3. *Presentational or Imaginal Knowledge:* which can be identified with interpretive approaches, evident in the intuitive grasp of the significance of patterns; builds upon the narrative and dialectical.
4. *Experiential (Empathetic) Knowledge:* closely aligned with phenomenology and evident in meeting and feeling the presence of some energy, person, place, process or thing.

As a result, for Heron:

- *experiential* knowing lies at the base of a 'knowledge pyramid', comprising the direct, lived 'being-in-the-world', aligned with your research *grounds;*
- *imaginal* knowing, underlying your interpretive research as it *emerges*, which;
- supports *propositional* or conceptual knowledge, your concepts or *navigation;*
- upholds *practical* knowing, the exercise of your practical research-and-innovation effect.

At the same time, what is above consummates what lies below. Practical knowing, knowhow, research method, is the consummation of the knowledge quest. It is grounded in and empowered by all the prior forms of knowing, and is immediately supported by propositional knowing which it celebrates and affirms at a higher level in its own relatively autonomous way. It affirms what is intrinsically worthwhile, by manifesting it in action.

③ YOU ENGAGE IN AN ALTERNATING CURRENT OF INFORMATIVE AND TRANSFORMATIVE INQUIRY

Uniquely in co-operative inquiry – when compared and contrasted with other research methodologies – there are two distinct forms of inquiry, the first being 'informative':

Informative Inquiry

- Participation in nature: molecules to galactic clusters.
- Participation in art: sculpture to song.
- Participation in intra-psychic life: sensations to ecstasies.
- Participation in interpersonal relations: one to one to large groups.
- Participation in forms of culture: environment, economics, politics, education.
- Participation in altered states of consciousness: especially cosmic consciousness.

The second form covers transformative inquiries or research that have a practical or skill-based outcome. This form is more in line with action research generally, and also with our kind of integral research project.

Transformative Inquiry

- Transformation of the social and economic structure, organization development, economic and political transformation, liberation of the disempowered.
- Transformation of the environment: ecology to architecture.
- Transformation of education: birth to death, self-directed learning.
- Transformation of professionalism: creating a culture of competence, or even de-professionalization.
- Transformation of personhood: personal growth skills, interpersonal skills.
- Transformation of lifestyle: from intimacy and domicile to occupation and recreation.

④ YOU UNDERTAKE YOUR RESEARCH IN SUCCESSIVE ACTION-REFLECTION CYCLES

There are four specific stages of inquiry:

Inquiry Stage 1: The First Reflection Phase

- The focus or topic of inquiry.
- A launching statement of the inquiry topic.
- A plan of action for the first action phase to explore some aspect.
- A method of recording experiences in the first phase.

Inquiry Stage 2: The First Action Phase

- Exploring in action and experience some aspect of the inquiry topic.
- Applying an integrated range of inquiry skills.
- Keeping records of the experiential data gathered.

Inquiry Stage 3: Break through into New Awareness

- Lose your way.
- Transcend the inquiry format.

Inquiry Stage 4: The Second Reflection Stage

- Review and modify the inquiry topic in the light of making sense of the data.
- Choose a plan to explore a different aspect of the inquiry topic.
- Review and amend the systems of recording data.

After the first four stages are completed, the inquiry continues through several more reflection–action–reflection cycles. Positively, such research cycling refines, clarifies, extends and deepens the focus. Negatively, such cycling checks, corrects, amends.

⑤ THE VALIDITY YOU SEEK FOR YOUR RESEARCH IS GOODNESS, TRUSTWORTHINESS AND AUTHENTICITY

Qualitative researchers include all those methods, which have in common the study of people in their own social setting, and the understanding of them in terms of their own categories and constructs. Generally, these methods accept an interpretivist or constructivist view of reality as mind-dependent, especially applied to people's view of their own social situation and context. Validity, for Heron, becomes a matter of quality or goodness or trustworthiness. He further proposes some of such 'authenticity criteria':

The change of criteria, for Heron, is a move from a concern with truth to a concern with goodness, from whether the outcomes are credible to whether they are desirable, from epistemology to axiology. The new criteria are all to do with values, with what states of human affairs are intrinsically worthwhile.

We now turn from the five key tenets of co-operative inquiry to an in-depth investigation of those tenets which are most critical, that is the political/participative, the epistemic/knowledge-oriented, and finally Heron's unique perspective on research validity from a qualitative perspective.

10.3 Co-operative Inquiry in Depth

THE POLITICAL PERSPECTIVE: PARTICIPATION 'WITH' PEOPLE

Beyond the Academic Status Quo

Research in the human sciences is very much an academic pursuit. They are committed to the intellect as the controlling force in individual and social life, and to the pre-eminence of propositional knowledge, a set of intellectual statements published in systematic form. Faculty, as such, unilaterally make decisions on behalf of students. They decide what the students should learn, how and when, and assess such according to their own criteria. Academics, as has also been our experience in the various institutions with which we have been involved, do not need to acquire the kind of emotional and interpersonal competence to empower students to learn more holistically, and participate in educational decisions to enable them to become progressively more self-determining.

For Heron, this model of authoritarian control is transferred from teaching to research. The same kind of authority is exercised over the research subjects, as has taken place amongst teaching their students. While the 18-year-old has the right to vote, he or she has no right to participate in educational decision-making. We consider that a person has the choice whether to take part in a research programme, but has no right to have a say in what it is about. As such, people are surveyed, but not enabled, case studies are drawn up, but the cases in point are not emancipated as a result. As well as universities sustaining a model of seemingly authoritarian intellectual control of students in education and as subjects in research, they are also, as Heron has said, biased in favour of propositional knowledge. Such involves intellectual statements, verbal and numeric, that can be suitably examined and conceptually organized so as not to infringe on rules of logic and evidence. This one-dimensional approach to 'knowing' offends a fundamental principle of systemic logic, that the conceptual part is interdependent with the experiential, imaginal and practical whole.

Beyond Research 'on' People

Co-operative inquiry, hence, favours, as we do, research 'with' over research 'for' people. It is a form of participative, person-centred inquiry, which does research with people and not on them or about them. What then are the defining features of it?

Research with People – Defining Features
All the subjects are involved in decisions about content and method of research.
There is an intentional interplay between reflection and making sense, on the one hand, and experience and action on the other.
There is shared explicit attention to the validity of the inquiry.
It is both informative about and transformative of the issues at hand.

What does this imply, epistemologically and politically?

Research with People – Core Implications
Propositions about human experience that are the outcome of the research are of questionable validity if they are not grounded in your experience as a researcher.
The most rigorous way to do this is for you to ground the statements directly in your experience as a co-subject: this involves a deep kind of participative knowing.
The human condition is one of shared and dialogic embodiment; you can only operate through the full range of your sensibilities, in a relation of reciprocal dialogue.
This enables you as a researcher to come to know not only the external forms (individual and collective) but also the inner apprehension of these.

We now turn from the political to Heron's epistemic perspective, whereby we go into more depth in relation to his distinctive 'ways of knowing'.

THE EPISTEMIC PERSPECTIVE: WAYS OF KNOWING

Four Inquiry Outcomes: Experiential to Practical

For Heron, there are at least four main kinds of inquiry outcomes, corresponding to the four modes of inquiry:

1. Transformations of personal being, for you as a researcher, through engagement with the focus and process of the inquiry.
2. Presentations of insight about the research inquiry, through expressive modes such as your drawing or participation in drama, providing significant patterns in our realities.
3. Propositional reports which are informative about your research inquiry domain, describing and explaining what has been researched, through your research activity.
4. Practical skills you exercise, which are connected with transformative action within the inquiry domain, on the one hand, or are connected with various kinds of participative knowing and collaboration on the other.

Inquiry Outcomes as an Up-Hierarchy

There are two important features of this fourfold epistemology.[3] Firstly, there is a pyramid of support or grounding. Experience of a presence is the ground of having presentational knowledge of significant patterns of imagery. Both these together are the ground of propositions about it. Experiential knowing is the ground of fourfold knowledge, intentional action the consummation of it, and presentational as well as propositional knowing mediates between them. Because of their relatively autonomous form, each of these, except for practical knowing, can function in a limited way without the other three.

There is a fundamental asymmetry in the epistemological pyramid. Thus you can experience a phenomenon with little or no presentational (perceptual) data about it, as with audiovisual images, in the absence of the people being filmed, without propositional information about them and without acting in relation to them. However, you cannot take intentional action in direct relation to something without having some conceptual information about it, without some presentational data and without meeting it.

Intentional action, at the apex of the supportive pyramid of fourfold knowing, consummates it and brings it to an integrated focal point. Undertaken by a group of co-inquirers, it becomes a concerted and congruent set of behaviours that is honed through cyclical integration of all four modes, and includes that integration as a necessary condition of its continuing practice. 'Practice as consummation', in that context, is a way of saying two things.

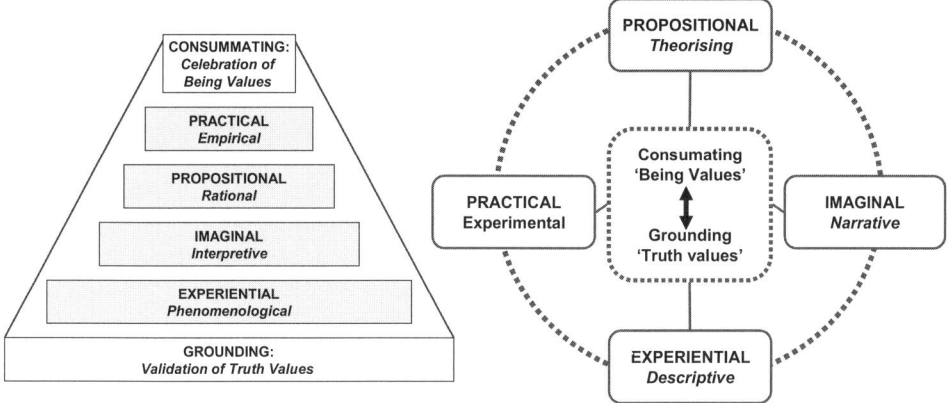

Figure 10.4 Bipolar Convergence (Pyramid) and Bipolar Congruence as a dialectical Process (Cycle)

Grounding and Consummation

What is below, then, grounds and validates what is above, and what is above consummates, celebrates and shows forth what is below. Whether it is illustrated as a pyramid form or a four worldly circular process form (see Figure 10.4), the following is important: at one pole it is the congruence between the four modes of knowing as their grounding in each other, and ultimately in experiential knowing, unrestricted and integral lived experience that makes their expressions valid. At the other pole is their congruence as being consummated in and through excellent and concerted practice, the apex of the pyramid that fulfils them and shows them forth. This crowns their world with the value of human flourishing. Valid outcomes alone are not enough. They need to be self-transcending and metamorphose into exuberant outcomes.

VALIDITY AND CO-OPERATIVE INQUIRY

Validity in General

For Heron, the outcomes of co-operative inquiry are valid only if they are well grounded in all four modes – practical, propositional, imaginal, experiential. While practice is the primary outcome, it is validated by being grounded on criteria of sound practice: so-called 'executive', 'technical', 'psychosocial' and 'value' criteria. This can be compared and contrasted with the more narrowly circumscribed validity criteria in quantitative research, as indicated below.

Validity in Quantitative Research

Traditional positivist research assumes there is one objective reality; hence, the world is empirically perceived by the senses, which is the same for all observers and independent of what they think about it. Research findings are sound if they are accurate, if they match this reality and measure it correctly. This is so-called internal validity and it appeals to a simple correspondence, or dictionary theory of truth. This holds that truth is in conformity with the facts, as if facts are out there, empirically, quite independent of us and waiting to be confirmed.

This in turn dictates criteria for an acceptable methodology. The research must be designed so that its findings are generalizable – so-called external validity – hence, for example, the importance of randomized sampling. It must be designed so that it can be replicated by others with similar results thus establishing the reliability of its findings, their consistency or stability. And it must be designed so that it is free of your bias and distortion, thus ensuring the objectivity of the findings. The collapse of such overt positivism, with the advent of phenomenological, interpretive and critical emancipatory orientations, has led to the collapse of the necessarily objective fact. The well-established counter-positivist view is that every statement of fact is theory, or perspective, laden. It is, for Heron, an interpretation of reality.

Participative Reality

Rejecting outright positivism, Heron's transactional or participative view of reality is seen as subjective-objective, an intermarriage between the creative, construing human mind and what is externally given. *Participative reality is neither wholly subjective nor objective, neither wholly dependent on your mind nor independent of it. It is always subjective–objective, inseparable from the creative, participative, engaged activity of your mind but never reducible to it, always transcending it.*

Truth and Reality

'Valid' then becomes a perfectly healthy word, and in a generic overall sense – applied to the expression of the diverse modes of being, becoming, knowing and doing – simply means sound, well founded, well grounded. 'True' is a closely related and also healthy word as long as it is stripped of any necessary association with objective fact. What is important about it, once the notion of independent fact is taken out of it, is that it implies some validating relationship with reality, other than the mistaken notion of correspondence. Heron uses it then in the generic sense of 'articulating reality', meaning a combination of revealing and shaping. Further he proposes that 'true' is applied not just to propositions but also to the forms of expression of the other three modes. We can hence speak of four 'types' of validity:

So we can say that:

- an interpersonal encounter (experiential being) involves a true meeting of minds;
- a piece of music (imaginal becoming) is true to heartfelt experience; and
- your knowledge of a text (propositional knowing) is accurate;
- a person's action (practical doing) is true to his or her principles.

What makes a subjective–objective reality a reality, for Heron, is a congruence between the four modes. By means of cycles of inquiry, the four ways are brought successively and repeatedly to bear upon each other. Ultimately, though, and this is where Heron remains true to his Anglo-Saxon heritage, the outcome of practical knowing, albeit built upon the other three, is the most critical.

Reality, in terms of each of the four modes, can then be understood as follows:

- *experiential:* reality is the lived experience of the mutual co-determination of person and world;
- *imaginal:* reality is significant form and pattern, in perceptual and other imaging, that interconnects analogically and metaphorically the whole network of other significant forms and patterns;
- *prepositional:* reality is the combined sense and reference of concepts;
- *practical:* reality is excellent practice and its effects.

The Validation of Practice

Practice as the culminating mode has a self-validating criterion internal to it, which is the knack of knowing how to perform it, according to:

Executive Criteria:
- Can you execute the practice?
- Can you do it elegantly, with style and grace?

Technical Criteria:
- Does the practice have the effects claimed for it?
- Is this form of practice the most effective?

Psychosocial Criteria:
- Is the practice relatively free of social pathology – free of distortions caused by personal distress?
- Is the practice relatively free of organizational pathology – the distortion of restrictive and rigid norms and values?

Intentional Criteria:
- Is the practice intentional, not merely ad hoc or reactive?

- Do the inquirers give evidence of creatively sustaining congruence among the components of their practice – its motives, guiding purpose and values, strategy and norms, actual behaviour and effects?

Value Criteria:
- Does the practice contribute to personal and social transformation as to your view of an intrinsically worthwhile way of life for human beings?
- Does the practice support your view of basic human rights?

For any given practice some will be more relevant than others. The value criteria, though, are indispensable for any transformative inquiry. We now turn to the more global expression of what Heron now terms 'participative spirituality'. For it is in relation to such that Heron makes a strong turn toward the East by focusing on what he terms 'sacred' science.

10.4 A Global Variation of Co-operative Inquiry

SACRED SCIENCE DEFINED

Heron in his *Participative Spirituality*[5] defines the 'sacred' as:

- the all inclusive illimitable presence of *what there is;*
- that which calls human beings to *comprehensive flourishing.*

'Science', for him, is an activity, which exercises critical rigour in articulating human experience of what there is. The twin pillars of this are:

1. *Sacred Science – Pillar 1:* discriminating judgement both individually and collectively, involving:
   - personal apprehension and reflection;
   - shared debate and dialogue;
   - apprehending the significance of patterns;
   - understanding the validity of propositions.

2. *Sacred Science – Pillar 2:* being engaged with what there is has a subjective and objective component:
   - in terms of our own sensitivities;
   - relating to what is there, what is cosmically given;
   - meeting what there is;
   - taking action in relation to what there is.

PARTICIPATIVE ONTOLOGY: A VIEW OF PRESENT REALITY

For Heron, present reality is *subjective–intersubjective–objective.* In the very process of meeting what there is, we know there is a cosmic given, which at the same time is given shape by our enacting it, our forming and shaping it, in terms of our own sensitivities. Present reality can then be described as:

- *participative*: we are conjoined with it;
- *incomplete*: it is transient, and contextual;
- *distinctive*: each has its own potential;
- *seamless*: there is no gap between subject and object.

Epistemology: Ways of Knowing

Sacred science involves four ways of knowing which are mutually supportive and correlative with each other. Each of them has a strong resonance with one of the Four Worlds:

The Four Ways of Knowing of Sacred Science		
Sacred science is practical	= Western =	Engaged with the active transformation of the human experience of being, in the interest of comprehensive flourishing
Sacred science is conceptual	= Northern =	Generating language, mental models and maps which symbolize the human experience
Sacred science is aesthetic	= Eastern =	Evokes human experience through visual, auditory and kinaesthetic patterns of vital significance
Sacred science is experiential	= Southern =	Inclusive of the whole range of sensitivities whereby human beings engage with other humans and life forms

In relating to each other, there are two kinds of congruence:

1. *groundedness*: the lower forms validate the higher;
2. *consummation*: the higher forms serve to fulfil the lower.

Altogether leading to a cycle of accumulative flourishing.

PARTICIPATIVE AXIOLOGY: A VIEW ON VALUE

Sacred science presupposes a view that what is intrinsically valuable is comprehensive human flourishing, set within, firstly, individual and social life and, secondly, a planetary and cosmic context. With regard to each there is a political and cosmic dimension:

- *Political Flourishing in Individual and Social Life:* a process of social participation where there is a balance between autonomy, co-operation and hierarchy.
- *Autonomy* (fulfil own true needs) is about deciding for yourself, *co-operation* (mutual aid and support) about deciding with others, and *hierarchy* (taking appropriate responsibility) about deciding for others. Hierarchy therefore has value when it is:
  - manifested by a person well grounded in their own autonomy and co-operation, both rooted in a deeply participative relationship with others;
  - exercised to empower the emergence of autonomy and co-operation with others;
  - reduced as that emergence occurs;
  - abandoned when that emergence has occurred; otherwise it is oppressive.
- *Epistemic Flourishing in Individual and Social Life*: a growing participative awareness of social contexts, from face-to-face to global associations, a conscious indwelling, and resonance with, the cultural life of the planet.
- *Political Flourishing in a Planetary and Cosmic Context:* a process of eco-participation, locally and globally.
- *Epistemic Flourishing in a Planetary and Cosmic Context:* a growing participative awareness of, and felt resonance with, the biosphere, solar systems and galaxy.

We now turn, finally, from the sacred depths of Heron's 'global' reach to the equally spiritual, but at the same time practical, effects of his co-operative inquiry, now linking it to the seminal work on knowledge creation of Japan's Ikijiro Nonaka. In fact, what Nonaka and his colleague at Hitotsubashi University in Japan have done, is to take not only Heron's co-operative approach a step further, into an organization as a whole, but also to turn his modes of knowing, from a linear pyramid into a 'knowledge spiral', thereby making it even more authentically Eastern. In combination, the Japanese 'knowledge creating company' becomes an enriched expression of 'co-operative inquiry', now placing its pre-emphasis on active 'creation', as opposed to more purely reflective 'inquiry'.

10.5 Co-operative Inquiry in Practice: The Spirit of BA

FROM BA TO CO-EXISTENCE

For Ikijiro Nonaka, renowned for his research into the *Knowledge Creating Company*,[6] his Eastern evolutionary spiral is a continuous, self-transcending process through which one transcends the boundary of the old self into a new self by acquiring a new context, a new view of the world. In short, it is a journey 'from being to becoming', and in John Heron's terms from the experiential to the imaginal, onto the conceptual and the practical, via four version of Japanese *Ba* (which signifies a physical or spiritual place). One also transcends the boundary between self and other, through the interactions amongst individuals or between individuals and their environment.

It is important to note that the movement through such modes of development forms a spiral, not a circle or a straight line, as the Westerner Heron had depicted. In such a developmental spiral, the knowing interaction between tacit (subjective knower) and explicit (objective known) is amplified through these four levels of meaning. The spiral becomes larger in scale as it moves up and through these levels, expanding horizontally and vertically across organizations, such as those researched in Japan, including Sharp and Sony, Honda and Toyota.

It is a dynamic process, starting at the individual level and expanding as it moves through communities of interaction that transcend sectional, departmental, divisional and even organizational boundaries. Development is a neverending process that upgrades itself continuously. This interactive spiral process takes place both intra- and inter-organizationally, transferred beyond organizational boundaries. Through dynamic interaction, one organization's development can trigger that of outside constituents such as consumers, affiliated companies, universities or distributors. For example, an innovative new manufacturing process may bring about changes in the suppliers' manufacturing process, which in turn triggers a new round of product and process innovation within the organization. It should be also noted that *development is a self-transcending process, in which one reaches out beyond the boundaries of one's own existence, transcending the boundary between self and other, inside and outside, past and present.*[7]

BA: SHARED CONTEXT IN MOTION

'Ba' in General: Based on the philosophy originally developed by Nishida, and subsequently further developed by Shimizu,[8] 'Ba' is here defined as a shared context in which being and becoming, and thereafter knowing and doing are communicated, created and utilized. In such generation and regeneration Ba is the key, as Ba provides the energy, quality and place to perform the individual conversions, and to move along the evolutionary spiral. Social, cultural and historical contexts are important for individuals; as such contexts provide the basis for them to create meanings. Ba then does not necessarily mean a physical place. The Japanese word means not just a physical space, but a specific time and space. Ba therefore is a time–space nexus or, as Heidegger expressed it, a 'locationality' that simultaneously includes space and time. It is a concept that unifies physical space, virtual space such as e-mail, and mental space such as shared ideals. The key concept in understanding Ba is interaction. Development then is a dynamic and indeed dialectical human process.

Ba can be described as 'shared context in motion'. Ba is the context shared by those who interact with each other, and through such interactions, those who participate in Ba and the context itself, evolve through self-transcendence to evolve. Participants of Ba cannot be mere onlookers, as is so often the case on the objectively oriented, analytical North and West. Instead, *such co-evolvers are committed to socially constructing Ba through action and interaction.*

Ba has a complex and ever-changing nature. It sets a boundary for interactions amongst individuals, and yet its boundary is open. As there are endless possibilities to one's own contexts, a certain boundary is required for a meaningful shared context to emerge. Yet Ba is still an open place where participants with their own contexts can come and go, and the shared context (Ba) can continuously evolve. By providing a shared context in motion, Ba sets binding conditions for the participants by placing certain limits on the way in which the participants view the world. And yet it provides participants with higher viewpoints than their own. Ba lets participants share time and space, and yet it transcends time and space.

Four Types of Ba: There are four types of Ba. In our Four World terms, those are: *originating Ba* (Southern – experiential), *dialoguing Ba* (Eastern – imaginal), *systemizing Ba* (Northern – conceptual), and *exercising Ba* (Western – practical). These, altogether, are defined by two dimensions of interaction. One dimension is the type of interaction; whether the interaction takes place individually or collectively. The other dimension is the media used in such interactions; whether the interaction is through face-to-face contact or virtual media such as books, manuals, memos, e-mails or teleconferences. Each Ba offers a context for a specific step in the evolutionary process, though the respective relationships between each single Ba and conversion modes are by no means exclusive. For us (encompassing the Four Worlds), building, maintaining and utilizing Ba is important to facilitate conscious organizational evolution. Hence, one has to understand the different characteristics of Ba and how they interact with each other. The following paragraphs describe the characteristics of each kind of Ba:

- *Originating Ba is defined by individual and face-to-face interactions.* It is a place where individuals share experiences, feelings, emotions and mental models. Originating Ba then is an existential place in the sense that it is the world where an individual transcends the boundary between self and others, by sympathising or empathising with others. From such originating Ba emerges care, love, trust and commitment (for us characteristics of the archetypal South), the ground for evolution within and among individuals and organizations.
- *Dialoguing Ba is defined by evolving and interactive dialogue.* It is the place where individuals' mental models and skills are shared, converted into common terms, and articulated as concepts. What is articulated is also brought back into each individual, and further articulation occurs through Eastern style self-reflection,and contemplation. Dialoguing Ba is more consciously constructed than originating Ba. It involves the conscious use of metaphor and analogy, as well as negation and affirmation, transforming Eastern non-being into being, to make the tacit explicit.
- *Systemizing Ba is defined by Northern style depersonalised and virtual interactions.* Information technology, through online networks, groupware, documentation and databanks, offers a virtual collaborative environment for the creation of systemizing Ba. Today, many organizations use electronic mailing lists and news groups through which participants can exchange necessary information or answer each other's questions.
- *Exercising Ba is defined by personalised, individual as well as virtual Western style interactions.* Here, individuals embody explicit facts and concepts communicated through virtual media, such as written manuals or simulation programmes. Exercising Ba synthesizes transcendence and reflection through action, while dialoguing Ba achieves this through thought.

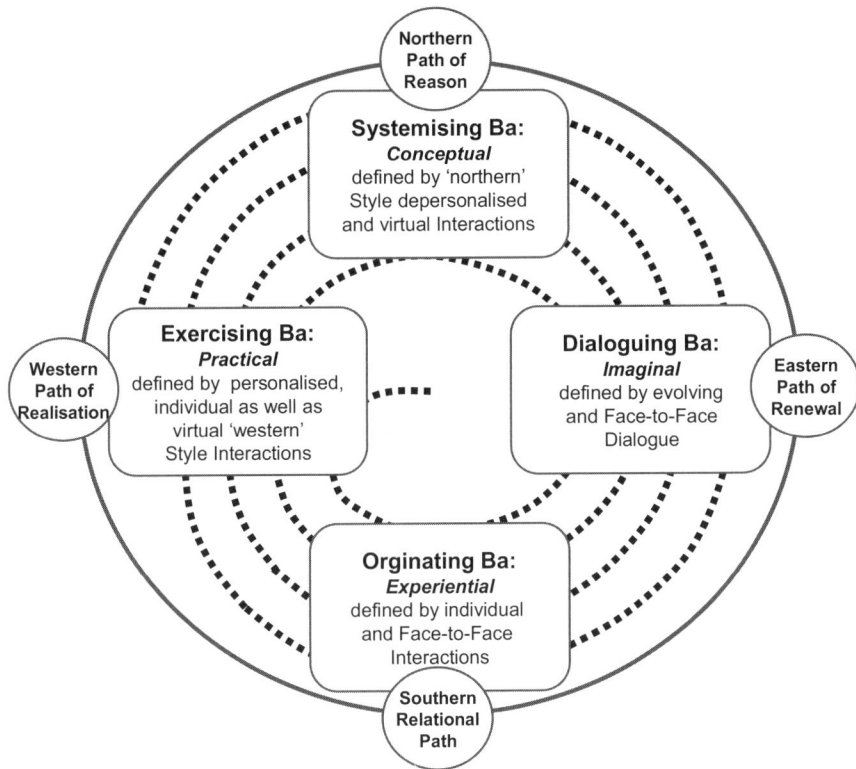

Figure 10.5 Four Types of Ba (Japan)

The emergent, Japanese style evolutionary spiral is arising out of an Eastern, consciousness-based perspective; it mirrors, in its modes of becoming, the process of co-operative inquiry. In fact, both Nonaka and Heron build up from a Southern relational perspective towards an Eastern path of renewal, that is from the experiential to imaginal (Heron) and from socialization to externalization (Nonaka).

10.6 Conclusion

HALFWAY HOUSE BETWEEN SOCIAL RESEARCH AND INNOVATION

In conclusion, co-operative inquiry, as well as participative action research, are humanistic and holistic approaches to research and innovation, albeit that they are generally integral in nature and scope. Co-operative inquiry is actually a halfway house between social research and innovation, information and transformation. For whereas Heron does focus on both, he is still recognized as part of the academic research community. Actually, Denzin and Lincoln, in their *Landscape of Research*, are great supporters of his approach. Although Heron was influenced by the East, he remains true to his Anglo-Saxon pragmatic colours, with practicality as his hallmark. In fact one of the distinguishing features of co-operative inquiry is that, in itself, and through its for modes of 'knowing' – or, as we would describe such, being (experiential) and becoming (imaginal), knowing (conceptual) and doing (practical) – Heron encompasses all four of our worlds, albeit, for us, his major orientation is towards the path of renewal, that is toward co-evolution.

TOWARDS CONSCIOUS EVOLUTION AND PEACEFUL CO-EVOLUTION OF PEOPLES

We hence come to the end of the Eastern path of renewal by revisiting once more the four levels along the research-to-innovation trajectory that you have, by now, progressively built upon. Through this, your integral innovation would have come about, on an organizational and communal level, supporting conscious evolution (the Eastern function of an enterprise or community) and, on a societal level, contributing to the peaceful co-evolution of peoples. The following table summarizes the entire Eastern journey.

Eastern Path of Renewal *Conscious Evolution – Peaceful Co-evolution of Peoples*	
Narrative *Originate*	Each event in the grounding of self, organization and society is novel; no struggle, no story; no trouble, no tale. The overall plot in each case unfolds with a view to continuing development.
Interpretation *Found*	Through a fusion of horizons between tradition and modernity, matter and spirit, self and other, indigenous and exogenous, you *imaginatively re-conceive* of your world.
Dialogue *Emancipate*	Such understanding and co-evolving of reality is dialogic and dialectical – via history, psychology, and spirituality – *promoting a progressively raised consciousness.*
Co-evolution *Transform*	Effectively engaging co-researchers as fellow subjects, you *consciously evolve* self/others via experiential, imaginative, conceptual and practical modes of thought and activity.

Again, we turn finally to the organic and natural metaphor of a tree as an even more authentic representation of your research-to-innovation path. And again, this concluding figure focuses on the particular theme and social scientific disciplines that are most relevant for this path.

We now turn from the path of renewal to the path of reason, and from peaceful co-evolution to the building up of an open society. We are starting out with critical rationalism.

Figure 10.6 The Integral Innovation Tree and the Eastern Path of Renewal

References

1. Reason, P. and Bradbury, H. (2004). *Handbook of Action Research*. London: Sage.
2. Heron, J. (1994). *Co-operative Inquiry*. London: Sage.
3. *Ibid*.
4. Heron, J. (1997). *Feeling and Personhood*. London: Sage.
5. Heron, J. (2006). *Participative Spirituality*. Raleigh, NC: Lulu Press.
6. Nonaka, I. and Takeuchi, H. (1995). *Knowledge Creating Company*. Oxford: Oxford University Press.
7. Nonaka, I. (2000). 'SECI, Ba and Leadership', *Long Range Planning: International Journal of Strategic Management*, 33.
8. Shimizu, H. (1995). 'Ba-principle: New Logic for the Real-time Emergence of Information', *Holonics*, 5 (1).
9. Heron, J. (2005). *The Complete Facilitator's Handbook*. London: Kogan Page.

11 *From Methods of Theorizing to Critical Rationalism*

Build up a Theoretical Perspective

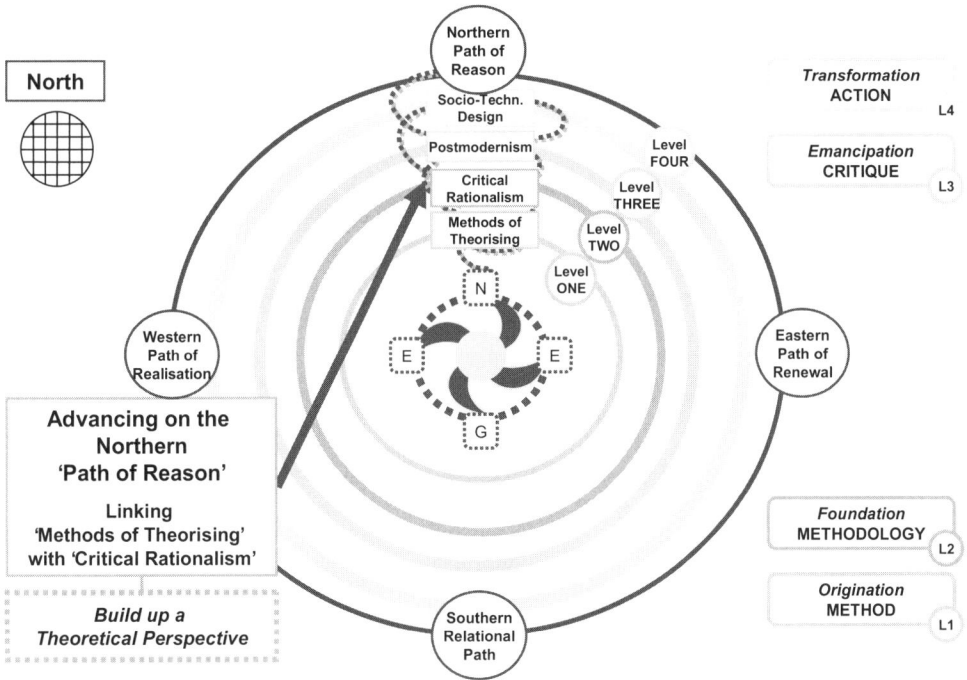

Figure 11.1 Overview Chapter 11 – Level 2/North

Summary: Critical Rationalism

- Having built up your capacity to theorize and to thereby develop theories from the data you have gathered, we now turn to critical rationalism as a means of consolidating upon such theoretical ground, drawing primarily on the work of Karl Popper.
- In Popper's theory of knowledge, hypotheses, theories or conjectures precede all observation. Analytically based concepts, emerging out of your experience and imagination, serve to evolve your original research question into a set of testable hypotheses.
- Popper was also the leading advocate of an 'open society'. For him and for George Soros, an open society is one in which critical thinking and discussion can flourish; the society is open to improvement. The key to progress towards such is the recognition of your fallibility.
- From Popper we turn to Paulin Hountondji, who is considered to be the pre-eminent rationalist amongst African 'professional' (as opposed to 'ethno') philosophers. In turning from Europe to Africa, we take particular account, again, of the research needs of societies in transition.
- There are two currents of 'critical rational' philosophy in the African context: the universalist approach of Kwasi Wiredu, and the dialectical current of Paulin Hountondji. For Hountondji, the universalist approach risks African philosophy being overtaken by a Western bias; a dialectical current is more in tune with the political struggles and recent history of Africa.
- While Africa was for Hountondji phenomenologically and interpretively richly endowed, it lacked critical rational thought where 'professional philosophy' came in. This is not 'scientism': science is not valued for itself, but for its human significance and meaning for life.
- Modern science, hitherto, had been introduced by the colonizer in the overseas territories in the form of an impoverished science, deprived of the theory-building activity that makes integral science. This, in fact, was a side-effect of the same colonizers' launch of so-called 'modern', rational and pragmatic economies in these territories, devoid of holistic and humanistic underpinnings.
- What is needed in Africa today is not just to apply traditional knowledge while continuing to import from the West technologies that are poorly understood and mastered by the local users. What is needed, instead, is to help Africa's peoples and their educated elite to capitalize and master existing indigenous knowledge and develop new knowledge in a continual process of uninterrupted creativity, while applying the findings in a systematic and responsible way to improve their own quality of life.
- For the same reason the notion of philosophy (and research) has to be re-examined. Hountondji deplores Africa's exclusion from science, exclusion being the case for most of the developing world, and its remaining on the margins of the global production of knowledge, and he argues for constructing a new space of theoretical construction.

11.1 Orientation to Critical Rationalism

THEORY-BUILDING TO CRITICAL RATIONALISM

We now turn from the process of theory-building generally, and grounded theory specifically, along the Northern path of reason upon which you have embarked here, to fully fledged critical rationalism. In other words, whereas grounded theory is a very elaborate method or technique for processing data, so as to build up theory from the ground up, critical rationalism is a fully fledged epistemology.

The doyen of such rationality is the late Anglo-Austrian philosopher and leading advocate of 'open society', Karl Popper,[1] in fact a central European neighbour of Moravia's Husserl. After exploring Popper's rich European heritage we shall turn again to an African counterpart of his, the 'professional philosopher' from the Centre for Advanced African Studies in Benin, Paulin Hountondji, for his reformative version of such rationalism in the context of a developing society. As is the case for Eritrean born philosopher Tsenay Serequeberhan (see Chapter 8), such a developmental orientation tends to be lead towards a new version of, in this case, critical rationalism. Interestingly enough, Hountondji was a student of Husserl's, but deliberately put phenomenology on the 'back burner' until he had pursued the rational and professional philosophical course he felt his continent required of him.

Karl Popper was born in Vienna (then in Austria-Hungary) in 1902 to middle-class parents of Jewish origins, who had both converted to Christianity. Popper received a Lutheran upbringing and was educated at the University of Vienna. His father was a bibliophile who was rumoured to have 10,000 volumes in his library at home. He took a PhD in philosophy in 1928. In 1934 Popper published his first book, *The Logic of Scientific Discovery*, in which he criticized the inductive approach to scientific method, and the logical positivism that underlay it. At the same time he put forth his theory of potential falsifiability being the criterion for what should be considered science.

In 1937, the rise of Nazism led Popper to emigrate to New Zealand, where he became lecturer in philosophy at Canterbury University College New Zealand (at Christchurch). In 1946, he moved to England to become reader in logic and scientific method at the London School of Economics, where he was appointed professor in 1949. He was president of the Aristotelian Society from 1958 to 1959. He was knighted by Queen Elizabeth II in 1965, and was elected a Fellow of the Royal Society in 1976. He retired from academic life in 1969, though he remained intellectually active until his death in 1994. Popper was a member of the Academy of Humanism and described himself as an agnostic, showing respect for the moral teachings of Judaism and Christianity.

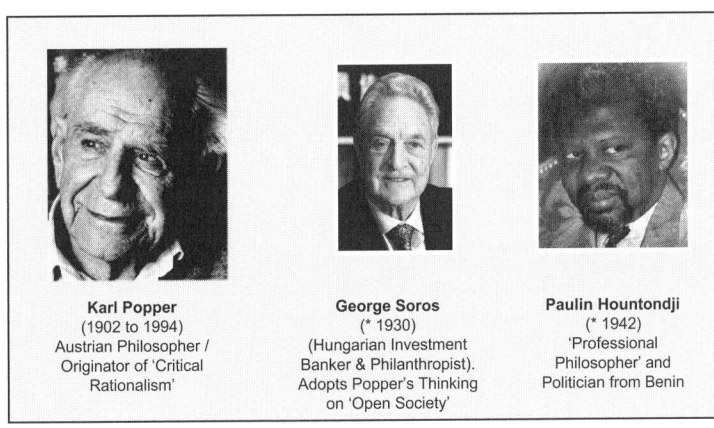

Karl Popper
(1902 to 1994)
Austrian Philosopher /
Originator of 'Critical
Rationalism'

George Soros
(* 1930)
(Hungarian Investment
Banker & Philanthropist).
Adopts Popper's Thinking
on 'Open Society'

Paulin Hountondji
(* 1942)
'Professional
Philosopher' and
Politician from Benin

Figure 11.2 Critical Rationalism – Core Thinkers

Sources: Image 1: Huizen Daxis http://huizen.daxis.nl/~henkt/popper-karl-biography.html. Image 2: daylife http://www.daylife.com/. Image 3: Prince Claus Fund for Culture and Development http://www.princeclausfund.org

POPPER'S PHILOSOPHY OF SCIENCE

Popper coined the term 'critical rationalism' to describe his philosophy. The term indicates his rejection of classical empiricism. Popper held that scientific theories are universal in nature, and can be tested only indirectly, by reference to their implications. He also held that scientific theory, and human knowledge generally, is irreducibly conjectural or hypothetical, and is generated by the creative imagination in order to solve problems that have arisen in specific historico-cultural settings.

Popper's account of the logical asymmetry between verification and falsifiability lies at the heart of his philosophy of science. It also inspired him to take falsifiability as his criterion of demarcation between what is and is not genuinely scientific: a theory should be considered scientific if and only if it is falsifiable. This led him to attack the claims of both psychoanalysis and contemporary Marxism to scientific status, on the basis that the theories enshrined by them are not falsifiable. For Popper, it is in the interplay between the tentative theories (conjectures) and error elimination (refutation) that scientific knowledge advances toward greater and greater problems; in a process very much akin to the interplay between genetic variation and natural selection. Where does 'truth' fit into all this? As early as 1934 Popper wrote of the search for truth as 'one of the strongest motives for scientific discovery'.

We now turn to the key tenets of critical rationalism, starting with Popper's attack on logical positivism, which, as we shall see in Chapter 14, was in fact the Anglo-Austrian school of empirical thinking that came before him.

11.2 Critical Rationalism – Key Tenets: Beyond Empiricism, Strong Theory, Value Neutral

Critical Rationalism – Key Tenets	
①	Empirical science has nothing absolute about it.
②	Derive theories from tentative conjectures.
③	Falsify rather than verify.
④	Strong theory drives out the weak.
⑤	Natural and social sciences are value neutral.
⑥	You ultimately formulate an overall deductive strategy.

① EMPIRICAL SCIENCE HAS NOTHING ABSOLUTE ABOUT IT

The empirical basis of science has nothing absolute about it. Science does not rest on solid bedrock. The underlying idea of Popper's theory of knowledge is that problems and attempts to solve them through hypotheses, theories or conjectures precede all observation. Logically as well as historically, theories come first in our experience of the world.

② DERIVE THEORIES FROM TENTATIVE CONJECTURES

Theories can only be tentative conjectures about the world, which are ultimately unverifiable by empirical evidence. Their discovery involves imaginative leaps, which are the forerunners of scientific activity. The process whereby predictive and thereby testable hypotheses are deduced from theoretical conjectures and subjected to confrontation with a cognitively accessible world is the distinctive attribute of a critically rational science, subject to falsification rather than verification. In effect, science advances through the detection and elimination of error as falsified theories fall away leaving a core of theory, which has not yet been disproved.

③ FALSIFY RATHER THAN VERIFY

Critical rationalism opposes the inductive base of logical positivism because, for Popper, 'it excluded as sheer gibberish metaphysical ideas which were often the predecessors for scientific ones'. The key outcome for the critical rationalist is the replacement of induction and verification with those of deduction and falsification – the hypothetico/deductive method. Through an inductive approach you look for evidence to confirm your generalizations, sometimes referred to as justification. Via deduction you try to refute your hypotheses, to falsify them, whereby you engage in falsification.

④ STRONG THEORY DRIVES OUT THE WEAK

Science can only ever be piecemeal and incomplete. Social engineering, as a result, should involve 'piecemeal tinkering', which, combined with critical analysis is the main way to achieve practical results in the social as well as natural sciences. In essence, such falsification leads to what Popper termed epistemological Darwinism where the strong theories drive out the weak. As such, he still shares with the logical positivists the epistemological commitment to empirical data as the final arbiter of the truth of the original theory.

> *finding theories, which are better approximations to the truth is what the scientist aims at. This involves the growth of the content of our theories, the growth of our knowledge of the world.*

⑤ NATURAL AND SOCIAL SCIENCES ARE VALUE NEUTRAL

As such critical rationalism preserves the unity of the natural and social sciences, only arguing that, in the latter case (social science), causality is contingent whereas in the former (natural science) it is invariable. Critical rationalism, then, revitalizes key aspects of logical positivism; specifically the possibility of a theory-neutral observational language; a modified correspondence theory of truth; sceptical anti-metaphysics; the methodological unity of the sciences; and the utility of science for enabling human intervention into the social and natural worlds.

⑥ YOU ULTIMATELY FORMULATE AN OVERALL DEDUCTIVE STRATEGY

Deductive strategy can be summarized as:

- Begin by putting forward a tentative idea, a conjecture, a hypothesis or set of hypotheses that form a theory.
- With the help of other previously accepted hypotheses, or by specifying conditions under which the hypotheses are expected to hold, deduce a conclusion, or a number of conclusions.
- Examine the conclusions and the logic behind them; compare this argument with existing theories to see if it constitutes an advance in understanding; if so:
- Test the conclusion by gathering appropriate data; make the necessary observations or conduct the necessary experiments.
- If the test fails – if the data are not consistent with the conclusion – the 'theory' must be false; the original conjecture must be rejected.
- If the conclusion passes the test, because the data are consistent with it, the 'theory' is temporarily supported; it is corroborated, not proved to be true.

A deductive theory consists of a set of hypotheses or propositions, which are arranged in such a way that from some of the propositions all other propositions follow. Such a theory has the form of a logical argument that leads to certain conclusions.

11.3 Critical Rationalism in Depth

TOWARDS AN OPEN SOCIETY

For Anglo-Austrian Karl Popper[2] as for Anglo-Hungarian George Soros,[3] an *open society is one in which critical thinking and discussion can flourish.* To be free to hypothesize or conjecture is to be free to construct your own thoughts and to debate these with others. Whereas Popper was a victim of the Nazi regime in Austria and, as a Jew, had to flee from his country, Soros, who is also Jewish, had to flee from a communist and anti-Semitic Soviet Union. They had therefore experienced in their own life worlds (being) the evils of closed societies first hand, so that their evolving stories (becoming) were infused with such.

Both Popper and Soros became avid opponents of 'closed societies', this forming the backdrop to their rational 'knowing'. For Soros, an open society falls short of perfection, but it has the great merit of assuring freedom of thought and of speech, giving ample scope to experimentation and creativity. In partaking of such you must content yourself with a form of social organization that falls short of perfection but holds itself open to improvement. *This is the concept of an open society – a society open to improvement.* Therein lies its superiority over closed society, which seeks to deny its own imperfection even as the world around it changes. *Recognition of your fallibility is the key to progress towards an open society*, in the latter case truly embracing a 'rainbow society', to which Mandela's South Africa aspires.

As had originally been the case for the Anglo-Saxon liberal thinkers in the 18th and 19th centuries, Popper and Soros have also been political radicals in their own right. Critical rationalism, as Popper conceived it in a 'modern' moment, has more to it than first meets the conventional rational eye. Hypothesis setting, he argues, is not entirely the rational-empirical exercise that it is conventionally set up to be. Why is that?

RATIONAL METHODOLOGY AND BEYOND

Worlds within Worlds

Popper was not the 'pure rationalist' he is claimed to be. For he describes three worlds:

*   World 1: the physical cosmos;
*   World 2: the world of conscious human processes;
*   World 3: the world of the objective creations of the human mind.

The worlds of physical and mental events, for Popper, are relatively straightforward. The difficulty begins with World 3. In the broadest sense it is the world of products of the human mind; in the narrow sense it is the world of theories. Moreover, he conjectured, literary and artistic works such as Mozart's operas might even belong to a World 4.

Creative World 3 usually has an indirect effect on physical World 1, via the mental World 2. If a skyscraper or bridge collapses this is sometimes attributable to a World 2 error in thought, or else to a false objective theory or error in World 3. The existence of World 3, and the fact that we can grasp World 3 objects through thought processes in World 2, plays a critical role in accounting for human self-consciousness, for self-awareness and for the human mind, as distinct from the animal mind. Let us return to these rational and deductive as opposed to inductive thought processes.

Underlying Critical Rationalism

The underlying idea of Popper's theory of knowledge is that problems and attempts to solve them through hypotheses, theories or conjectures precede all observation. Logically as well as historically, theories come first in our experience of the world, first both in our personal history and on the history of humanity. What correspond to theories at a pre-human level are dispositions and expectations. Magic and ritual probably have close antecedents in the animal realm. What we humans have in addition is the speech form of storytelling. The novelty in human language is that it can describe and argue. With the problem of whether an account is true or merely wishful boasting, the decisively important problem of truth makes its appearance. At the same time, the telling of fairy tales or stories becomes possible.

Such tales or stories or myths are also the original theoretical explanations: the beginnings of science among the Greeks go back to Homer and Hesiod; the beginnings of art, the prehistoric cave paintings of hunting and animals, are magical stories; Egyptian and Assyrian art largely comprise illustration of contemporary stories and events. This is how World 3 began to develop. Our humanity, for Popper, is rooted in the existence of World 3, if not also a World 4, in the world of creation myths as well as of objective truth. So critical rationalism (or knowing as such) was built on the prior grounds of being and becoming.

For example, as Popper saw it, the reality (World 1) that Kepler sought behind appearances was inspired by the Pythagoreans and Kepler's own interest in music (World 3 or 4). The great astronomer thought that the world was filled with melodious sound, conducted and held together by harmony and resonance, but also by dissonances and their eventual resolution. The world, for him, was a divine symphony, architecture of the divine, and a heavenly beauty. This idea made him a relentless seeker after the truth. The truth, for Popper, must be beautiful; it must reveal a heavenly beauty. *Popper's whole methodology consists in the realization that the natural sciences try to find a reality hidden behind appearances.* To that extent, his conceptual world, aside from seeking empirically based falsification, is founded upon a prior experiential and imaginal world (see John Heron and co-operative inquiry in Chapter 10).

Whenever we know nothing we must guess, just as Kepler did. If we want to subject our testable hypotheses to the strict test of experience, these are no longer metaphysical but scientific ones that enable us to learn from our mistakes. Kepler, like every scientist, was guided by intuition, by trial (hypothesis) and error (empirical refutation). Without intuition and imagination, Popper asserts, we get nowhere, even though most of our intuitions turn out wrong. We need intuitions, ideas, if possible competing ideas; and we need ideas about how those ideas can be criticized, improved and critically tested. So Popper and Husserl had their subjectively intuited similarities as well as their objectively empirical differences.

We now turn to Paulin Hountondji, who is considered to be the pre-eminent rationalist, amongst African 'professional' (as opposed to 'ethno') philosophers. In turning from Europe to Africa, we take particular account of the needs of a society in transition, and one, like most societies in Africa, Asia and Latin America, that has experienced colonization.

11.4 Global Variations of Rationalism

PROFESSIONAL PHILOSOPHY IN AN AFRICAN CONTEXT

Critical Rationalism to Professional Philosophy

Like Popper, the Ghanean philosophers Wiredu and Gyekye and Benin's Hountondji are committed to an open society. At the same time, Hountondji does not entirely part company from the interpretative and phenomenological approaches, which we have investigated so far. There are, then, for Afro-American philosopher Barry Hallen in his *Short History of African Philosophy*,[4] two currents of 'critical rational' philosophy in the African context. These are the universalist approach of Kwasi Wiredu and the dialectical current of Paulin Hountondji. For the universalist, African philosophy must be opposed to traditional cultural beliefs. For Wiredu, the African philosopher must combine insights from the East and West with his own indigenous philosophical resources. The point is to lift the philosophical enterprise to a universal level of discussion, and then turn to the specific existential conditions and priorities of the African social and political context, combining these to seek a truth.

Wiredu rejects an 'objectivist' theory of truth; whatever is called 'truth' is always someone's truth. 'What I mean by opinion is a firm rather than an uncertain thought. I mean what is called a considered opinion.' Moreover, several 'traditional' practices should be carried over into contemporary African politics. Wiredu is sceptical of the Western multi-party system, which serves to heighten social and ethnic tensions in Africa. Affirming and reformulating the traditional consensus-based approach would be preferable. Wiredu's most illustrious philosophical compatriot in this respect is the Ghanean Kwame Gyekye, whose work on tradition and modernity will be reviewed by us later.

Kwame Gyekye[5] also considers how philosophical inferences can be derived from traditional (in his case Akan) cultures. Gyekye criticizes the notion of ethnicity (tribalism) in Africa as a dangerous invention and tool of political ideologies and argues that it must be supplanted by notions of group identity comparable with those found in multicultural societies. His vision of modern African society becomes one which incorporates and interrelates the best elements of other cultures in the 'world' with those aspects of Africa's cultural heritage which deserve to be valued. The transcendent and universal criterion on the basis of which the positive contribution of any of these elements can be rated is humanistic: 'bringing about the kinds of progressive changes in the entire aspects of human culture necessary for the enhancement and fulfilment of human life'.

We now turn to Hountondji, the best-known of the African professional philosophers.

For those of you in China or India, the Middle East or Latin America, it is instructive to note how strong the contemporary African philosophical orientation is, and to perhaps use it as a counter-force to the dominant, European philosophical discourse, so as to develop a healthy dialectic between them.

Hountondji's Pluralism

For Hountondji,[6] the universalist approach risks African philosophy being overtaken by a Western bias. He believes that a dialectical current of critical philosophy would be more in tune with the political struggles and intellectual history of contemporary Africa. As we can see immediately, there is a critical emancipatory, prior foundation to his rationalism. In that sense ethno-philosophy and negritude are philosophies of an earlier age – texts to be taken up dialectically into a new stage of ongoing dialogue.

The present debate on the question of African philosophy, for Hountondji therefore, can be seen to form part of a comprehensive process of reflection by the African intelligentsia upon its historical being: it represents a significant moment in the intellectual response of Africans to the challenge of Western civilisation. In the same vein, such ontology provides for a reformation of Eurocentric research methodology, and we invite the other transitional societies amongst us to take the story on from here.

Hegel's philosophy of history, Houtondji asserts, remains the most exalted statement of European self-affirmation in opposition to other races, the most elaborate rationalization of European ethnocentricism. It provided a powerful philosophical base for the chorus of denigration of the non-white races, which buoyed up the European colonial adventure. The high point of such denigration was attained in the work of French anthropologist

Lévi-Bruhl, who devoted his career to demonstrating the 'primitive mentality' of the non-Western peoples. On the one hand, for him, there were the Western societies that had emerged from the Mediterranean civilization, within which developed rationalist philosophy and positive science, and on the other hand, 'primitive' societies ruled by a mentality to which the Western mode of thought was alien. Such societies, he argued, were 'pre-logical'. It is worth noting that Lévi-Bruhl rescinded before he died, declaring himself to have been wrong.

What then about African philosophy in taking the story on from there?

To Gain our African Soul we Must Lose it

African philosophical literature sometimes rests on a confusion between the popular (ideological) and strict (theoretical) use of the word philosophy. According to the first meaning, philosophy is any kind of wisdom, intended to govern the daily practices of a people; in the second sense philosophy is a discipline, like mathematics, with its own exigencies and rules. Hountondji of course favours the latter. As such, he reckons that ethno-philosophers, like Senegalese poet-statesman Leopold Senghor, have wasted their time with ready-constituted thought – whether Dogon, Yoruba or Rwandais – to justify themselves in European eyes. Instead, African philosophers should have thrown themselves into the fray in order to confront today's and tomorrow's problems.

In a completely sterile withdrawal, Hountondji laments, Africa goes on vindicating its cultures instead of transforming them. He who must gain his soul must lose it, which harks of our reformative process of emergence, prior to a newly normative navigation. *By dint of trying to defend African cultures, they have been mummified. Africa has betrayed its original cultures by showing them off for external consumption.* Such is the theoretical impasse into which such thinkers as Leopold Senghor, for Hountondji, have stumbled. Since then Africa's philosophical thinking has marked time, serving merely to reconstruct an African world-view as 'a mad and hopeless enterprise'. Such (phenomenologically based) 'ethno-philosophy' has got bogged down in an ideological discipline without recognizable status in the world of theory. People forget that 'African Studies' was invented in Europe.

Motivated by the genuine need for an African philosophy, ethno-philosophical predecessors have wrongly believed that it lies in the past, needing only to be exhumed and then brandished like a miraculous weapon in the astonished face of the colonialist European. They have not seen that African philosophy, like science or culture in general, lies before you and me, and must be created, albeit embracing the heritage of the past. Philosophy needs to be active, not passive, and, as for Popper and Soros an open system rather than a closed one:

> *we want the relentless questioning, the untiring dialectic that accidentally produces systems and then projects them towards horizons of fresh truths. African philosophers who think in terms of Plato and Marx and then transcend such are producing authentic African work.*[7]

The real problem is not to talk about Africa but to talk amongst Africans, or for that matter amongst Latin Americans, amongst Arabs, Chinese, Japanese or Indians, all of the latter being influenced by their Buddhist – amongst others – heritage. Europe is what she is today because she transformed the heritage of other peoples, including the ancient Egyptians, and conducted innumerable conversations across her diverse nationalities and peoples. Africa must liberate its thoughts from a previous ghetto, open up a breach in its closed space of its collectivist fantasies, so that theoretical issues will surge in, to be shared first of all with our immediate brothers, thus to steep them in the melting pot of African science.

The real problem is to liberate the theoretical creativity of African peoples or, indeed, in our programmes, of Arabs, or Muslims, or Chinese, or indeed Americans, which is the transformative orientation of our integral research. Everything else, including science, and in our terms social innovation, will come afterwards.

African Philosophy: Myth and Reality

Most African 'philosophers' in the first half of the 19th century have been men of the church, including Father Temples from Belgium, Alexis Kagame in Rwanda and Kenyan pastor John Mbiti. All have been preoccupied with finding a psychological and cultural basis for rooting the Christian message in the African's mind, without betraying either. Such philosophy is perceived as a stable system of beliefs. Other lay thinkers, such as Senghor in Senegal, and, for Hountondji, even Nkrumah in Ghana, were trying to identify a solid bedrock of African beliefs, a passionate search for the identity denied them by the colonizers. The idea was that every culture rests on a metaphysical substratum. Such 'philosophy' becomes a collective worldview, a collectively indigenous unanimity, rather than a specific discipline.

Such African philosophy, Hountondji asserts, does exist, but as a literature produced by Africans, dealing with philosophical problems. In other words, it exists as a body of literature, rather than as one prescribed text. This body of literature is written by Africans, thereby excluding Europeans like Placide Temples. Some of these African philosophers, including Hountondji himself, reject the exclusively ethno-philosophical approach; others, like Wiredu, wrote about subjects other than African ones. It is impossible to debate amongst the comparative merits of these approaches without freedom of expression and discussion. What then is the nature and scope of such a critical, written philosophy?

Philosophy and its Successive Revolutions

Philosophy is firstly a history and not merely a system. As such it is an open process, a restless unfinished quest, for us an ongoing research project, not closed knowledge. Second, this history does not move forward by continuous evolution but by leaps and bounds, by successive revolutions and consequently follows a dialectical path. Thirdly, African philosophy may be going through a decisive mutation, its outcome depending on contemporary philosophers today. Similarly, the same could apply for other transitional societies in that context. Czechoslovakia, as we saw in Chapter 5, could be seen as one such, until global market forces got in the way of 'living in truth' doctrine.

No philosophical doctrine, notwithstanding Havel's *Living in Truth*, can be regarded as the truth. The absolute is contained in the relative of an open-ended process, set within the context of an open society. In other words, truth is the process where we look for propositions, concepts, theories, more adequate than others. Truth lies in a journey that takes into account all prior doctrines and ideologies and then outdoes them. Traditional African systems of thought, but also traditional Islam or indeed Hinduism, limited for Hountondji as such, are not in themselves such a journey. There is no philosophy that would be an implicit system of propositions or beliefs to which all individuals of a society (past, present and future) would subscribe. The issue then is: why should such an 'African' philosophy have been sought after, by a European investigator like Temples, in the first instance? Each – European and African – in their own way needed something definite, that could be taken in at a glance, something they could hold onto, maintain and control. The same could apply today, if we are not careful, to the growing global interest in African *ubuntu* today, and in the 'real values' of Islam, rather than seeing both as dynamic, evolving belief systems.

A poem or a novel is valuable in itself. Philosophy, on the other hand, is only intelligible as a moment in a debate that sustains and transcends it. It always refers to antecedent positions, either to refute or to confirm and enrich them. It takes on meaning, only in relation to history, through which one generation questions the other. In the strictest sense, art has no history, though it unfolds in history. Every great philosophy, moreover, is a rebirth, a radical questioning, as Christianity and Islam both were at their formative stages. But the break occurs after the event, through a kind of recursion that is essential to all philosophy, as a necessary moment in the history of philosophy, a turning, a renascence, a revolution, a mutation taking place within history and not a suppression coming in from the outside. Every great philosophy, to establish itself, must ravage the existing theoretical space. The same applies to a great piece of research, which serves to make it a social innovation, as hopefully this integral research text may be!

True and False Pluralism

For Hountondji, European civilization is not a closed system of values, but a set of irreducible cultural products which have appeared on that great continent. Actually, our integral research approach is the same. At a deeper level, it is the set of these products and of the creative tensions which underlie them, the necessary infinite act of these products and tensions, in the forms they have assumed in the past and the yet unpredictable forms they will assume, that emerge out of that little strip of the world called Europe. Nor is African civilization, Arab civilization, Indian or Chinese – even American – civilization, a closed system. It is the unfinished history of a similarly contradictory debate.

We now retrace steps and revisit phenomenology through 'professional' philosophical eyes.

THE STRUGGLE FOR MEANING

The Phenomenology of Science

For Husserl – whom Hountondji actually studied under – science occupied the highest rung in the hierarchy of cultural practices. To him, no other form of thought, way of life, vocation, art or religion, appears nobler. This is not, Hountondji emphasizes, 'scientism': *science is not valued for itself, but for its human significance and meaning for life.* It is subordinated, like any other cultural production, to ethics; its exceptional value – far from its technical accomplishments – is that it is the bearer of norms and generative values. In our terms, and for Hountondji,[8] it emerges out of a particular and formative 'life world', African or Arab, Indian or Chinese, French or Japanese, subsequently reformed through exposure to other such worlds, and thereafter bears new norms and values.

Science, for Husserl, can either be defined pragmatically, as an experimental montage, a body of regulated material practices, or psychologically, as a linkage of acts of cognition. The term 'scientific rigour', usually associated with rigorous empiricism, is a total misnomer. Husserl mentions the 'science' only to annex it immediately to the 'acts of cognition'; instruments and apparatuses will never be anything but extrinsic tools linked to a unity of acts of thought. Hountondji's doctoral research, when he was based in France, was based on Husserl's philosophy. Interestingly, he deliberately held his research back until he had deepened and extended his critical and dialectical analysis, believing that such was required first, as a prelude to rationally based, scientific research. Whereas Africa was for him phenomenologically and interpretively richly endowed, it lacked critical rational thought where 'professional philosophy' came in.

Impoverished Science and Detached Philosophy

Methodology, for philosophy and research, for Hountondji as for us, must bring about the transformation of the world. In Africa, as everywhere else, theory has meaning only if it is organized and subordinated to practice, where it derives its legitimacy in relation to other practices. The myth of white supremacy, in that respect, cannot be dealt with by attachment to a counter myth of 'black supremacy' or 'yellow supremacy'. A simplistic comparison between a stereotyped North and South (or indeed East) will not do without due consideration of the interactions between them (also including the West).

The problem for Africa and many other transition countries today – which is all too evident in their business schools and universities – is that they have to a large extent internalized the discourse of their former masters in their research and educational activities, including their denigrating views on African (or Arab or Latino) ways of life and thought. At the same time Hountondji warns against the opposite danger, that of closing off Africa's or Islam's heritage without any critical approach, without any attempt to update and renew the intellectual legacy, in a way that allows a higher degree of rationality, and a steadier march towards efficiency and self-reliance. Things have to be considered afresh, at an equal distance from cultural alienation, which takes up the colonial masters' prejudices and any self-denigration, both of which results in a kind of intellectual self-imprisonment. Most transitional societies cultures are caught in between such closed traditions and a Westernized modernity.

Hence, in the process of scientific investigation in today's social sciences, the decisive stage is neither the collection of data, as fieldwork that so often starts the whole process off, nor the application of theoretical findings to practical issues, which is all too often the final stage. The decisive stage is what comes between them – the interpretation of raw information, the theoretical processing of the data collected and the production of those particular utterances which we call scientific statements, or indeed theory building. For Hountondji, the one essential shortcoming of scientific activity in the colonies was the lack of the intermediate stage. He claims, that the former colonies missed the central operation of theory building, then as now. They only had, and still have, the first and the third stages of the process:

- Stage 1: the data collection, the feverish gathering of all supposedly useful information;

- Stage 2: the intermediate theory-building then took place in the so-called 'mother country';
- Stage 3: the partial, occasional and limited application of the research outcomes to local issues

Thus, science in the former colonies was, and indeed still is, characterized by a theoretical vacuum – the lack of those intellectual and experimental procedures that, being at the heart of the entire enterprise, depended on infrastructure that existed only in the ruling countries. This theoretical vacuum (stage 2) was substantially the same as the industrial vacuum that used to, and still does, characterize economic activity. Universities today fall into the same trap, where the West and North lead, and the South and East follow; however, we are determined, with you, to get out of there.

Deprived of Theory-building

Modern science was introduced by the colonizer in the overseas territories in the form of an impoverished science, deprived of the theory-building activity that makes integral science. This was a side-effect of the same colonizers' launch of so-called 'modern', rational and pragmatic economies in these territories, devoid of holistic and humanistic underpinnings. The theoretical emptiness of scientific activity in the colony derives from the very nature of peripheral capitalism. For Hountondji, it is a mode of production based on the search for surplus, as in Europe, but deprived of the industrial activism. Such activism involves the will to transform rather than 'collect data', that is the creativity and inventiveness, the sense of initiative and propensity to risk, that makes capitalism productive in the colonizer's own country.

As a consequence of what Hountondji terms 'extroversion', local scholars tend to address issues that are primarily of interest to the Western public. The problem, however, is that this orientation indulges too often in some kind of imprisonment into the particular. In order to give a proper account of the local peculiarities of our culture, we first need to be aware of what is universal about them. You need to take that minimum theoretical distance that allows you to put things into perspective.

What is needed in Africa today is not just to apply traditional knowledge in agriculture or medicine, economics or management, while continuing to import from the West technologies that are poorly understood and mastered by the local users. What is needed, instead, is to help their people and their educated elite to capitalize and master existing indigenous knowledge and develop new knowledge in a continual process of uninterrupted creativity, while applying the findings in a systematic and responsible way to improve their own quality of life. Instead, for Hountondji, indigenous people have been serving as learned informants, for a theory-building activity located overseas and entirely controlled by the people there. Africa needs to invent ways in which knowledge can be better shared by the North, West and East, as well as the South, in all its phases, be it the phase of production, accumulation and capitalization, or of application. It needs to develop an ambitious strategy of knowledge appropriation that will allow Africans to freely and critically take up anything that can be useful for them in the intellectual heritage now available in the world.

The Liberation of the Future

The illusion of timelessness that is associated with any reductive reading of African civilizations, the tendency to mummify them, to empty them of their history, evolution, diversity and of their creative tensions, is therefore questioned by Hountondji. What is demanded instead is the internal dynamism of African cultures, the pluralism of beliefs transmitted by them. Individual speech must be liberated, and a multiplicity of speeches must be released and related to each other. African thought must be released from its local confines, and related for instance, as Nkrumah has done at least in part, to Plato or Aristotle, Plato or Marx. The great issue at stake, therefore, in Hountondji's critique of ethno-philosophy, is the liberation of the future. For the African intellectual, the burden of having to conform to a system of thought that had been worked out in advance had to be lifted. It had to be demonstrated that the freedom of the individual could not be restricted in advance. The horizon of possibilities had to be opened. In short, the over-determination of the concept of Africa is an obstacle to the freedom of Africans.

For the same reason the notion of philosophy (and research) has to be re-examined, to describe a history not a system, a discipline in which results matter more than reasoning, whose goals is to go beyond the results to achieve better ones. To liberate the future requires disentanglement from the collective 'us'. To liberate the future, the past has first to be liberated by restoring movement, contradiction and dynamism to it, in the same sense as Nkrumah[10] conceived of but did not apply. Real pluralism does not only consist in affirming – against the West's cultural hegemony – a plurality of cultures, but recognizing the complexity, diversity, tensions, contradictions, internal dynamics of each world, and seeing in that a source of richness.

The African philosopher should not be required to reflect on Africa alone. Hountondji's critique of ethnocentrism leads to a de-territorialization of cultural values. At a stroke this approach makes it possible for African science to claim to be universal. He deplores Africa's exclusion from science, the case for most of the developing world, and its remaining on the margins of the global production of knowledge, and he argues for constructing a new space of theoretical construction. He seeks to de-marginalize Africa, to place it firmly at the centre of its own history in a pluralized world whose unity needs to be periodically renegotiated. The reinsertion of thought in the real movement of history should enhance both a recognition of the specificity of works of speculative thought and their relationship to the social, political and economic context of different periods. It should find a pluralist vision of philosophy and African culture by sweeping away unanimist prejudice. It should see such critical rationalism in an integral research light. This brings us on to the practice of an open society.

11.5 Critical Rationalism in Practice: George Soros and the Open Society Foundation

THE MEANING OF OPEN SOCIETY

Open society is not an easy idea.[11] It resembles the concept of liberal democracy but there is an important difference: it is an epistemological concept, not a political one. It is based on the recognition of our imperfect understanding, not on a political theory.

Popper's book *The Open Society and its Enemies*[12] made a great impact on Soros in his youth. It threw a new light on the ideologies that had such a decisive influence on his life: fascism, national socialism and communism. Each asserted they were in possession of one valid interpretation of reality. But the ultimate truth is beyond reach; therefore these ideologies could only be imposed on society, and repression serves to bring about a closed society. In Popper's open society people of different views and interests live together in peace. Tribal morality, according to French philosopher Henri Bergson (who coined the term 'open society'), gave rise to closed society, whereas universal morality leads to an open one which recognizes fundamental human rights, irrespective of tribal, ethnic or religious affiliation.

For Soros, a traditional mode of thinking has only one task: to accept things as they are. This supreme simplicity extracts a heavy price; it generates beliefs that may be completely divorced from reality. Soros calls this the 'organic' society, a society in which individuals are organs of a social body. In a changing world, on the other hand, people are confronted by an infinite range of possibilities. The great merit of the critical process is that it can provide a better understanding of reality; its major drawback is that it does not satisfy the quest for certainty. The dogmatic mode, conversely, gives the illusion of certainty.

Free markets do offer economic choice, but they are not perfect, as market participants do not have perfect knowledge. Moreover, they are not designed to take care of social needs – such as the maintenance of law and order, social justice and stable markets – as distinct from the needs of individual participants. The satisfaction of social needs is the domain of politics. On their own, individuals provide an uncertain foundation for values sufficient to sustain a structure that will outlast them. Yet such a value system is needed to sustain society.

The conceptual model outlined above was developed in *The Burden of Consciousness*, which Soros completed at the age of 33, in 1963, and which he sent to Popper. Despite receiving some encouragement from him, Soros proceeded to get lost in philosophical abstractions, so he quit philosophy and decided to devote himself to making money. His success in the financial markets exceeded expectations, and by the time he was 50 the size of his hedge fund was approaching $100 billion. So he started wondering what to do with the money, and that process of reflection took him back to his framework of open and closed societies, and to the set-up of his Open Society Foundation.

THE OPEN SOCIETY FOUNDATION: OPERATING IN FAR-FROM-EQUILIBRIUM SITUATIONS

Soros' first major engagement was in South Africa, where he gave scholarships to African students attending the University of Cape Town. He was trying to use the system to undermine apartheid society from the inside, as the university involved proclaimed its commitment to the ideal of an open society. Unfortunately, the black students remained alienated and resentful, and Soros abandoned the scheme. He started supporting Charter 77 in Czechoslovakia, Solidarity in Poland, the Jewish Refuseniks in the Soviet Union. In Hungary, he supported experimental schools and libraries, artistic and cultural projects. Open Society Foundations were then set up in Hungary and in the Soviet Union. By 1991, there were Foundations in 20 countries, throughout Eastern Europe and the former Soviet Union, in South Africa and in America.

Soros, by then, considered himself a specialist in far-from-equilibrium situations, having learnt from his father that, at the height of a revolution, almost anything is possible. He had political convictions, financial means and an understanding of the importance of the moment. The Central European University was established in Budapest, as an intellectual resource centre for the foundation network. Annual expenditures jumped from $3 million to 300 million.

APPLYING THE FRAMEWORK

During all this time Soros was guided by the conceptual framework outlined, and in his book on *Opening the Soviet System*[13] he combined static models of open and closed societies with his theory of reflexivity to interpret the rise and fall of the Soviet system, his contention being that changelessness can initially be self-reinforcing but is ultimately self-defeating. In fact, reform accelerates the process of disintegration.

In an open society, every citizen is required to form his or her own view of the world, and society needs institutions that allow people with different views and interests to live together in peace. The task is so immense that it is impossible to make the transition from closed to open society without a helping hand from outside. Regrettably, in the case of the former Soviet Union, the West never rose to that occasion. Open society constitutes near-equilibrium conditions precariously poised between the static disequilibrium of closed society and the dynamic disequilibrium of chaos and disorientation.

THE NEXT CHALLENGE

The challenge that now preoccupies Soros is that of the US. Who would have thought that the most powerful open society in the world could pose a threat not only to open society at home but to the peace and stability of the world? The Bush agenda that has been set is the wrong agenda, Soros asserts, for the world. The survival of the fittest is a major theme, and competition rather than co-operation is supposed to determine who is fittest. Yet our globalized world is not a jungle ruled by naked power. In fact, globalization has made the world increasingly interdependent, and the challenges that mankind faces can be met only through increased co-operation. Little can be achieved without the US's leadership. Now that the United States has become an imperial power, it bears a unique responsibility for the future of the world.

In concluding, we retrace original steps, before distilling the rational ground we have now additionally covered, starting by reviewing Popper's contribution.

11.6 Conclusion

FROM LIFE WORLD TO OPEN SOCIETY

The 'swamp' that Popper has referred to is that prior phenomenological and interpretive ground. It is necessary, but all too blurred – though not the case for Hountondji – in the vision of the critical rationalist. Yet as conscious human beings, phenomenologically speaking, we always inhabit the life world; it is given in advance and experienced as a unity, as was the case for Popper himself, as Jew, in Nazi-infested Austria. The life world is the general and indeed questionable structure, which allows objectivity and thing-hood to emerge potentially as concepts, in Africa or in Europe, in the US or in the Middle East, in China or in India, in the different ways in which they do emerge in different cultures. In Popper's own case, his actual and horrific experience of fascism, mediated by the force of his own and others' imagination, ultimately gave rise to his philosophy of an 'open society'. There is not one single life world, but a set of overlapping worlds, beginning from the world, which is the indigenous 'home-world', and extending to other worlds farther away. For Popper, as for Soros, their horizons extended from central to Western Europe, from Austria and Hungary to Britain and America.

FROM POPPER TO HOUNTONDJI

Rootedness and Freedom

For Hountondji, you have to exist first, to take interpretive root in a tradition, but at the same time, you must be capable of keeping your rational distance from that cultural tradition. You must invent again and again, something with which Karl Popper would have much sympathy. In every society there exists a minimal consensus, a small common denominator, a spiritual cement that ensures the system's cohesion. But it must always be subject to critique. For us, the South has always to be re-viewed in terms of the other worlds, but for Hountondji such re-viewing has to always take place through African eyes, in other words, by African philosophers.

The term 'extraversion' has been used in contrasting a self-sustaining economy that is capable of counting on its own resources, and of being self-reliant by ensuring its own internal coherence, with the underdeveloped economy organized and subordinated to the needs of the ruling classes in the industrial capitals. Such an extraverted economy aims above all to furnish raw materials and outlets for the manufacturing industries located at the centre. Hountondji sees intellectual extraversion in the same light. One thing missing in each case is transformation, the transformation of raw materials into finished products in the one case, and the theoretical treatment of data in the other, the production of general statements from initial information; in other words an integral science.

Towards Reappropriation

Science is not reducible to one single methodology, that is the empirically based collection of information, and empirical observation, any more than it can be confused with a technical object that is only its technical by-product. *Science is an activity, for Hountondji, whose goal it is to produce true statements.* Such an activity was seriously lacking in the dominated territories. The colonies lacked laboratories as they lacked factories. Once this theoretical void – the equivalent of an industrial void – is acknowledged, you get a fairer picture of development. Decolonization did not put an end to this, with the former colonies remaining huge reservoirs of facts and raw data, and testing fields for the results of metropolitan inventions. The system has quite simply become more refined. The research institutions at the periphery are mere annexes of the mother institutions at the centre.

The theoretical demand like the economic one comes from the centre. In Africa, no effort was made to formulate new and original questions. To answer the questions of others seemed to be the continent's destiny. The international division of scientific labour freed Africa from thinking. To develop it had to apply the inventions of others, still the case today; social innovations like the Truth and Reconciliation Commission in South Africa are notable exceptions. The four weaknesses that Hountondji has specifically detected, that prevent African scientific practices from serving its peoples, are:

* financial dependence vis-à-vis the outside world;
* institutional dependence vis-à-vis the research centres of the North;
* primacy of North–South vertical scientific exchanges over South–South ones;
* intellectual subordination to the questions and expectations of the learned public in the West.

What we need, he says as a critical rationalist, is ultimately a 'radical appropriation of theory'.

PERIPHERY CUT OFF FROM THE CENTRE

Theory then, from a peripheral perspective, is always physically distant. The best universities, the best business schools, the best businesses, the best laboratories, the greatest libraries, the most credible publishing houses, the best researchers, are massively located in industrialized countries. The result is that the African or Arab or Chinese researcher in search of the sacred fire – the material and intellectual tools of knowledge – must move elsewhere. Just as integration into the world capitalist markets had resulted in the destruction of the equilibrium mechanisms of subsistence economies, without giving rise to industrial development in the periphery, so integration into world scientific research resulted in arresting the development of pre-existing forms of knowledge, all the while pushing the periphery into subaltern roles in relation to the global process of knowledge creation.

Research-wise, the periphery is shut off by the local and the particular, which becomes their research domain, at the expense of theory. Abstract universalism of course, as in the natural sciences, is no better, for it eliminates an essential question, that of the collective appropriation of the universal both as project and result. The African historian must be as interested in the process of industrialization in Japan as in the slave trade. Studying Japan or Finland or Ireland gives one an understanding, through contrast, of one's own society. As soon as it is produced, African knowledge is 'stolen' and integrated into the world system of knowledge administered from abroad.

To put an end to extraversion, to break with a marginalization that constantly siphons the results of their research, peripheral researchers need to be involved in what Thomas Kuhn called 'extraordinary' science,[14] to maintain a critical relationship with the paradigms in each discipline and to raise new problems that are linked to the preoccupations of their societies. The researcher at the periphery has to go back to the paradigms themselves and challenge them, developing his or her own basic research, promoting invention in all its forms. There is a great need for a sociology of science to be developed at the periphery.

PARTICIPATING IN THE CONSTRUCTION OF THE FUTURE

To participate in the construction of our future, in Africa as in the Middle East, in Latin America as in South-East Asia, we need a double movement, a critical appropriation of the scientific and technological heritage available globally, and, at the same time, a re-appropriation of indigenous local knowledge. In fact, the knowledge produced in the North has been produced over centuries. Rationality is therefore not appropriated in advance. It is still to be built. Hence the immense responsibility of contemporary generations: that of contributing together in a spirit of solidarity and sharing to the building of the common edifice, so that the germs of irrationality and progressively of ignorance and poverty will be eliminated forever from the planet earth.

We now turn from Hountondji, the professional philosopher, and Popper, the original critical rationalist, to the next critical step along the path of reason, from modernism to postmodernism, from rational debate to multiple discourses.

References

1. Popper, K. (1990). *On Problem Solving*. London: Routledge.
2. Popper, K. (2002). *Open Society and its Enemies*. London: Routledge.
3. Soros, G. (2000). *Open Society*. Boston, MA: Little Brown.
4. Hallen, B. (2002). *A Short History of African Philosophy*. Bloomington, IN: Indiana University Press.
5. Gyekye, K. (1997). *Tradition and Modernity*. Oxford and New York: Oxford University Press.
6. Hountondji, P. (1983). *African Philosophy*. Bloomington, IN: Indiana University Press.
7. *Ibid*.
8. Hountondji, P. (2002). *The Struggle for Meaning*. London, Thousand Oaks, CA, and New Delhi: Open University Press.
9. Serequeberhan, T. (2000). *Our Heritage*. Lanham, MD: Rowan and Littlefield.
10. Nkrumah, K. (1970). *Consciencism*. New York: Monthly Review Press.
11. Soros, G. (2006). *The Age of Fallibility*. London: Weidenfeld.
12. Popper, *Open Society and its Enemies*.
13. Soros, G. (1990). *Opening the Soviet System*. London: Weidenfeld.
14. Kuhn, T.S. (1996). *The Structure of Scientific Revolutions*. London, Chicago, IL: University of Chicago Press.

12 *From Critical Rationalism to Postmodernism*

Accommodate Multiple Discourses

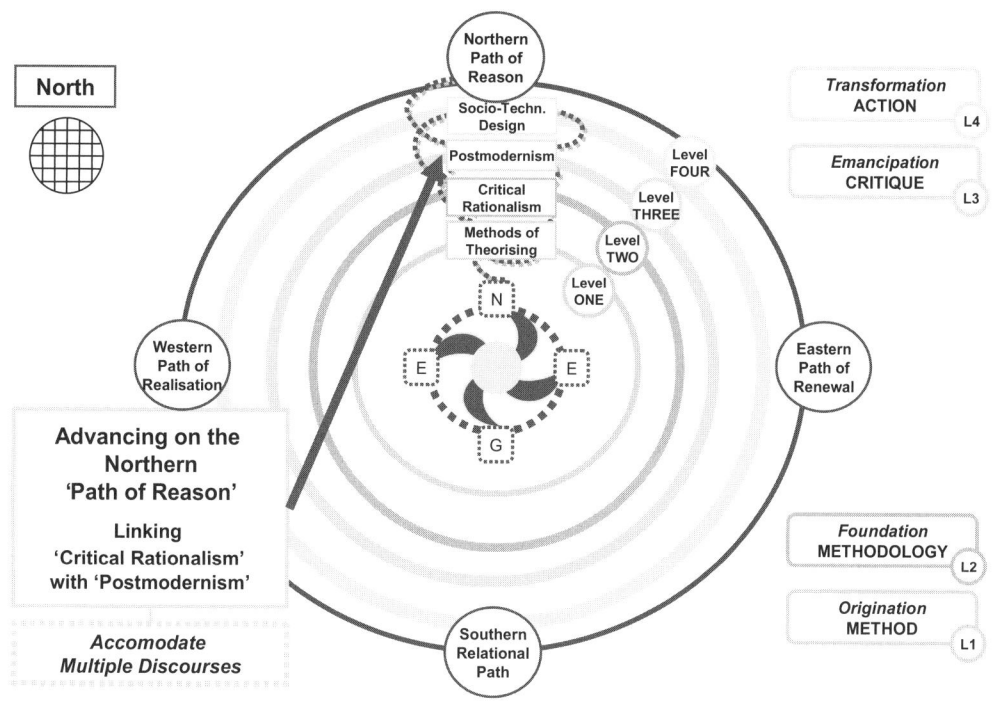

North

Figure 12.1 Overview Chapter 12 – Level 3/North

Summary: Postmodernism

- You are now entering the third level of the Northern path of reason. You have started out with the originating methods of theorizing (most likely via grounded theory) and have then worked yourself through Karl Popper's modernist approach to critical rationalism. We now turn from modernity to postmodernity.
- While modernist critical rationalism has Anglo-Austrian roots in Europe, and was picked up by the so-called 'professional philosophers' in an African context, postmodernism is strongly French in its original orientation.
- Modernism and thereby critical rationalism is oriented towards uncovering an 'objective truth'; postmodernism, however, argues that there are multiple truths, depending on the time and place, and that discontinuity rather than continuity is the order, or indeed disorder, of the postmodern day.
- The key tenets of postmodernism extend from the nature and scope of such multiple discourses, to the language that underlies such discourses, to the extent that it is subjectively constructed by the reader or interpreter, and cannot be taken as an objective given.
- The originators of postmodernism are primarily French philosophers, including Foucault, Derrida and Saussure, though Foucault remains the most prolific of these originators, and was himself a revolutionary in his own right, joining in with the French students who took to the streets against the status quo in the 1960s.
- The postmodernist perspective has spread from France to, in particular, the Muslim world, to the extent that the power of the 'other', the marginalized person, has been taken up vigorously by the Islamists, and philosophically by Karen Armstrong and academic, writer and philosopher Ziauddin Sardar. Sardar, one of the leading intellectuals in the Muslim world, is arguing for a transmodern approach to mutuality.
- It is Sardar's *Islamic Future Studies* that we have chosen as an illustration of a practical application of postmodernism. It shows the potential contribution of Islam, together with Christianity, for the building of an alternative more sustainable future, more precisely, a (global) open society.
- Such a postmodern reality, incorporating the emergence of multiple voices, has been turned, by American social philosopher Richard Tarnas, into the hallmark of our contemporary age. After postmodernism we shall come onto socio-technical design, and with that to the culminating social innovation along this Northern research path.

12.1 Orientation to Postmodernism

MODERNISM TO POSTMODERNISM

We now turn, in this chapter, from critical rationalism to postmodernism, its more recent and better-known counterpart. While the former had strong Anglo-Austrian roots, the latter is French in origin. While such a postmodern orientation toward the relativism of multiple discourses is a deliberate reaction against the modern notion of 'absolute' truth, both of these 'reasonable' research orientations are indeed 'rational'. Actually, the very fact that such French intellectuals as Foucault and Derrida have taken up the postmodern high ground, is a reflection of such ultra-rationality.

The evolution from so-called modernism to postmodernism, towards (in the late Peter Drucker's terms) the *Age of Discontinuity*,[1] and (UK's management guru Charles Handy's)

The Age of Unreason,[2] is perhaps the most distinctive overall movement of our times. For American social philosopher Richard Tarnas, what we can see in the 21st century, and which he anticipated in his *Passion of the Western Mind*, was a postmodernity that was reflected:

> in the widespread call for and practice of open 'conversation' between different understandings, different vocabularies, different cultural paradigms. Not only is the postmodern mind itself a maelstrom of unresolved diversity, but virtually every important element of the Western intellectual past is now present and active in one form or another, contributing to the variety and confusion of the contemporary Zeitgeist. Moreover, these in turn have been joined, and affected by a multitude of cultural perspectives from outside the West, such as the Buddhist and Hindu mystical traditions; by underground cultural streams from within the West itself; and by indigenous and archaic perspectives antedating Western civilization altogether – all gathering now on the intellectual stage as if for some kind of climactic synthesis. The postmodern collapse of meaning has been countered by an emerging awareness of the individual's self-responsibility and capacity for creative innovation and self-transformation in his or her existential and spiritual response to life. In virtually all contemporary disciplines it is recognized that the prestigious complexity, subtlety and multi-valence of reality far transcend the grasp of any one intellectual approach, and that only a committed openness to the interplay of many perspectives can meet the extra-ordinary challenges of the postmodern era.[3]

As we shall see later in this chapter, the Muslim voice has been vocally added to the others that Tarnas mentions. What is unique to postmodernism and makes it an excellent 'navigational vehicle' for our Northern research journey is that it has developed a distinctive method as well as methodology which, while rationally based, is much more discursive than analytically oriented towards building up an overall theory or hypotheses, and then seeking to debate such, with a view to getting closer to a universal truth.

POPPER TO FOUCAULT

In other words, Michel Foucault like Karl Popper is very much in favour of discussion, but such discussion is not aimed at revealing or falsifying a single truth, but rather at acknowledging a multiplicity of discourses.

Michel Foucault was a French philosopher and historian. He held a chair at the Collège de France, giving it the title *History of Systems of Thought* and taught at the University of California, Berkeley, from 1975 until his death in 1984. He is known for his critical studies of various social institutions, most notably psychiatry, medicine, the human sciences, and the prison system, as well as his work on the history of sexuality. His work concerning power, the relationship between power and knowledge and 'discourse' in relation to the history of Western thought, has been widely discussed and applied. His work is often described as postmodernist or post-structuralist by commentators and critics, although he was more often associated with the structuralist movement during the 1960s. He was initially happy with this description, but later vehemently distanced himself from structuralism and he always rejected the 'post-structuralist' and even 'postmodernist' labels, even though he has been the seminal influence on what has come to be known as 'postmodernism'.

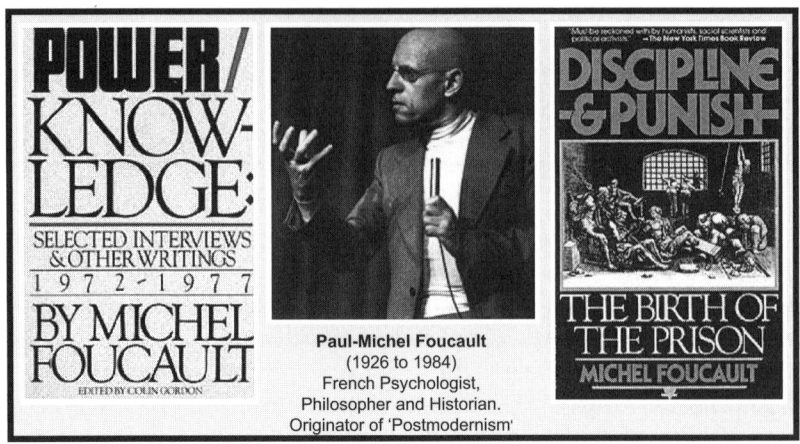

Figure 12.2 Postmodernism's Leading Thinker – Paul-Michel Foucault

Sources: Image 1: Amazon http://www.amazon.com/. Image 2: NNDB http://www.nndb.com/. Image 3: e-Clippings http://blogoehlert.typepad.com/

Foucault was born in 1926 in Poitiers as Paul-Michel Foucault to a notable provincial family. His father, Paul Foucault, was an eminent surgeon and hoped his son would join him in the profession. His early education was a mix of success and mediocrity until he attended the Jesuit Collège Saint-Stanislas, where he excelled. During this period, Poitiers was part of Vichy France and later came under German occupation. After World War II, Foucault gained entry to the prestigious École Normale Supérieure, the traditional gateway to an academic career in the humanities in France.

Foucault's personal life during the École Normale was difficult – he suffered from acute depression, even attempting suicide, and was subsequently taken to see a psychiatrist. Because of this, or perhaps in spite of it, Foucault became fascinated with psychology. He earned a degree in psychology, a very new qualification in France at the time, in addition to a degree in philosophy. He was involved in the clinical arm of psychology, which exposed him to thinkers such as the German psychoanalyst Ludwig Binswanger. Foucault joined the French Communist Party from 1950–1953. He was inducted into the party by his mentor Louis Althusser. He left due to concerns about what was happening in the Soviet Union under Stalin.

Foucault passed his agrégation in 1950. After a brief period lecturing at the École Normale, he took up a position at the University of Lille, where from 1953–1954 he taught psychology. In 1954 Foucault published his first book, *Maladie mentale et personnalité*, a work which he would later disavow. It soon became apparent that Foucault was not interested in a teaching career, and he undertook a lengthy exile from France. In 1954 Foucault served France as a cultural delegate to the University of Uppsala in Sweden (a position arranged for him by Georges Dumézil, who was to become a friend and mentor). In 1958 Foucault left Uppsala for briefly held positions at Warsaw University and at the University of Hamburg.

Foucault returned to France in 1960 to complete his doctorate and take up a post in philosophy at the University of Clermont-Ferrand. There he met Daniel Defert, with whom he lived in a non-monogamous partnership for the rest of his life. In 1961 he earned his doctorate by submitting two theses (as is customary in France): a 'major' thesis entitled 'Folie et déraison: Histoire de la folie à l'âge classique' and a 'secondary' thesis which involved a translation and commentary on Kant's *Anthropology from a Pragmatic Point of View*. *Folie et déraison* ('Madness and Insanity'; ironically published in English as *Madness and Civilization*) was extremely well received.

After Defert was posted to Tunisia for his military service, Foucault moved to a position at the University of Tunis in 1965. In 1966 he published *Les Mots et les Choses* ('The Order of Things'), which was enormously popular despite its length and difficulty. This was during the height of interest in structuralism and Foucault was quickly grouped with scholars such as Jacques Lacan, Claude Lévi-Strauss and Roland Barthes as the newest, latest wave of thinkers set to topple the existentialism popularized by Jean-Paul Sartre. Foucault made a number of sceptical comments about Marxism, which outraged a number of left-wing critics, but he quickly tired of being labelled a 'structuralist'. He was still in Tunis during the May 1968 student rebellions, where he was profoundly affected by a local student revolt earlier in the same year. In the autumn of 1968 he returned to France, where he published *L'archéologie du savoir* ('The Archaeology of Knowledge') – a methodological response to his critics – in 1969.

In the aftermath of 1968, the French government created a new experimental university at Vincennes. Foucault became the first head of its philosophy department in December of that year and appointed mostly young leftist academics whose radicalism provoked the Ministry of Education to withdraw the department's accreditation. Foucault notoriously also joined students in occupying administration buildings and fighting with police. Foucault's tenure at Vincennes was short-lived, as in 1970 he was elected to France's most prestigious academic body, the Collège de France, as Professor of the History of Systems of Thought. His political involvement now increased. Foucault helped found the Prison Information Group to provide a way for prisoners to voice their concerns. This fed into a marked politicization of Foucault's work, with a book, *Discipline and Punish*, which 'narrates' the micro-power structures that developed in Western societies since the 18th century, with a special focus on prisons and schools.

In the late 1970s, political activism in France tailed off with the disillusionment of many left-wing militants. A number of young Maoists abandoned their beliefs to become the so-called New Philosophers, often citing Foucault as their major influence, a status about which Foucault had mixed feelings. Foucault in this period embarked on a six-volume project on *The History of Sexuality*, which he was never to complete.

Foucault began to spend more time in the United States, at University at Buffalo (where he had lectured on his first ever visit to the United States in 1970) and especially at UC Berkeley. In 1979 Foucault made two tours of Iran, undertaking extensive interviews with political protagonists in support of the new interim government established soon after the Iranian Revolution. His many essays on Iran, published in the Italian newspaper *Corriere della Sera*, only appeared in French in 1994 and then in English in 2005. These essays caused some controversy, with some commentators arguing that Foucault was insufficiently critical of the new regime.

Foucault died of an AIDS-related illness in Paris in 1984. He was the first high-profile French personality who was reported to have had AIDS. His death marks the beginning of the post-AIDS era in France.

In our (Ronnie Lessem) own previous work *Business as a Learning Community*[4] and *European Management Systems*,[5] we not only introduced a multiplicity of worldly truths

– pragmatic and rational, holistic and humanistic – but also connected them explicitly with different orientations toward knowledge. In this book we have connected each one of these to diverse research paths: pragmatic to *realisable*, rational to *reasonable*, holistic to *renewal*, and humanistic to *relational*. Indeed postmodernism was specifically to herald a newly post-industrial, post-capitalist, knowledge-based society, which, for us, was built upon such multiple perspectives. We now turn to the key tenets of postmodernism.

12.2 Postmodernism – Key Tenets: Pursue Multiple Discourses, Review History as Transformative

Postmodernism – Key Tenets
① Pursue multiple discourses.
② Focus on meanings as multiple and shifting.
③ Socially construct meaning.
④ Engage in the art of thematic decomposition.
⑤ Use language as cultural representation.
⑥ Review history as transformative.

① PURSUE MULTIPLE DISCOURSES

A 'modern' approach to research sees useful knowledge as a hypothesis shaped (critical rational) or a mirror reflection (empirical) of things in the world. A postmodernist one, in contrast, involves constructing specific accounts of the world, through language and archive, discourse and culture, that form complex representations which have cultural significance.

Reality then is not a solid, monolithic and self-contained but a fluid, unfolding discursive process, an 'open universe', continually affected and moulded by a diversity of actions and beliefs. It is possibility that counts rather than fact. You cannot regard reality as a removed spectator against a fixed object; rather you are always and necessarily engaged in reality's multiplicity of forms and perspectives, thereby at once transforming them while being transformed yourself.

② FOCUS ON MEANINGS AS MULTIPLE AND SHIFTING

In their *Discourse Analytic Research*, Erica Burman and Ian Parker point to the way in which language organized into discourses, or interpretative repertoires, has an immense power to shape the way that people behave in the world.[6] Specifically they refer to the fact that, instead of studying the mind as if it were outside language, discourse analysts study spoken and written texts – that is conversations, debates and discussions – where images of the mind are produced and transformed. Such a 'discourse analysis' offers a social account of subjectivity by attending to the linguistic sources by which the socio-political, organizational and managerial realms are produced and reproduced. The overall implication is that meanings are multiple and shifting, rather than unitary and fixed. For such postmodernism or post-structuralism research involves a commitment to the socially constructed nature of reality; and a good way to examine such is through 'discourse analysis'.

For Potter and Wethereall[7] in Britain and Elliot Mishler[8] in America, conventional survey methods are flawed because they do not take into account the true variability of human thought and action, instead concentrating on the uniform, rational and classifiable. Finally, whereas modern attitudinal research sees language as an essentially colourless, transparent medium, unproblematically describing some underlying 'real' entity, discourse analysis takes language as actively constructing versions of the social world.

③ SOCIALLY CONSTRUCT MEANING

For discourse analysts, all forms of social reality have a peculiarly human and socially constructed nature. They share an assumption that 'knowledge of' can never be an objective fact, as all knowledge is produced, bounded and sustained by human beings and their constructions. This postmodernist constructivist and historicist commitment leads to a heightened emphasis on the means through which human meanings and experience are manufactured, that is through discourses. Such 'discourse' refers not only to observable linguistic activities, but also to the world of human signs, symbols, activities, texts that together comprise a particular worldview.

For environmentalist Philip Macnaghten,[9] 'nature', for example, can alternately be conceived of as 'wilderness', as 'harmony' and in terms of 'ecology'. The three statements below represent these respective discourses, as revealed in research public reactions to a local government's environmental orientation:

④ ENGAGE IN THE ART OF THEMATIC DECOMPOSITION

Discourses represent an amalgam of hypotheses, narratives and descriptions rolled up into one. We use narratives and discourses with themes that have already been socially arranged for us.[10] Such stories can be thought of as transindividual, historically localised, culturally specific formations of language-in-use.

For the French linguistic theorist Ferdinand de Saussure,[11] cultural representations are embodied in language. In contradiction to the positivist vision of scientific knowledge, his approach suggests there is no simple or neutral act of perception. Every word you use to understand natural things, for example in Sutu or Zulu, as opposed to English or French, is packed with meaning.

⑤ USE LANGUAGE AS CULTURAL REPRESENTATION

Another French postmodernist, Roland Barthes,[12] describes the way in which 'mythologies' are generated throughout culture. To denote something is to identify what is widely accepted as a descriptive and factual account, like 'this is an oak tree'. However, when we connote meaning to such, we recognize that, for instance in English culture, the 'oak tree' is understood as a symbol of cultural strength, of working within a cohesive social order with solid foundations. This is the difference between language (denotation) and meta-language (connotation).

In that context you, as an active reader, are a 'proactive' agent in the production of meaning through the text concerned. The idea of 'discourse', Foucault suggests, enables us to think about how language is situated and constructed through the cultural values of a particular historical and cultural context. By looking at the lived experiences of other cultures, their rituals, family structures, transitions through life, gift relationships and so on we can identify what is distinctive about our own culture.

⑥ REVIEW HISTORY AS TRANSFORMATIVE

An 'archive' can be both a vehicle for research and also a stimulus for transformation, as, for example, in the new South Africa, in the 1990s. For the French postmodernist and so-called 'deconstructionist', Jacques Derrida:

> The archive draws us forward in taking us back. Every beginning gathers energies from antecedent endings. All forgetting of the past is also a forgetting of the future. A focus on history as narrative and history writing as a charged political act has made the thinking about archives no longer the pedestrian pre-occupation of flat-footed archivists. The archive is not a library of events but a system of evocations.[13]

We now turn to a consideration of postmodernism in greater depth, most particularly to the work of Michel Foucault.

12.3 Postmodern Philosophy and Methodology in Depth

FOUCAULT'S NEW ORDER OF THINGS: THE FORCE OF DISCONTINUITY

The high priest of postmodernism, as we have seen, is the late Michel Foucault. For him, in the history of ideas, that is of thought in general and of the sciences in particular, the same mutation has broken up the long series formed by the progress of consciousness, or the teleology of reason, or the evolution of human thought. It has questioned the themes of convergence and culmination; it has doubted the possibility of creating totalities. It has led to the individualization of different series juxtaposed upon one another, overlapping and intersecting, without being able to reduce them to a linear schema.[14]

Thus in place of the continuous chronology of reason there have appeared periods that are sometimes very brief, distinct from one another, irreducible to a single law. These periods bear a kind of history peculiar to each one, and thereby cannot be reduced to the general model of a consciousness that acquires, progresses and remembers. It has now become one of the basic elements of historical analysis. As such the historian is trying to discover the limits of a process, the point of inflexion of a curve, the boundaries of an oscillation, the threshold of a function, the instant at which a circular causality breaks down. One of the most essential features of the new postmodern approach to history, for Foucault in his *Archaeology of Knowledge*[15] then, is this *focus on the discontinuous*, and as such:

- its integration into the discourse of the historian where it no longer plays the role of an external condition that must be reduced, but that of a working concept;
- and therefore the inversion of signs where it is no longer the negative of the historical reading, but the positive element that determines its object.

Globalization, in that postmodern light, is such a discontinuous element, a blip on the economic horizon, rather than part of an evolutionary trend. The parallel forces of Islamicism and environmentalism, therefore, are equally part of such emergent discourses.

The use of concepts of discontinuity, rupture, threshold, limit and transformation presents historical analysis with theoretical problems. These problems are analysed by Foucault in the context of the history of ideas, of science and of knowledge. There is first the negative work to be carried out: we must rid ourselves, he insists, of a whole mass of notions, each of which, in its own way, reinforces the theme of continuity. There are the notions of development and evolution: they make it possible to group a succession of dispersed events, to link them to one and the same organizing principle, to subject them to the exemplary power of life, to discover, already at work, a principle of coherence and the outline of a future unity. There is the notion of 'spirit', which enables us to establish between successive phenomena a community of meanings, allowing the sovereignty of collective consciousness to emerge as the principle of unity and explanation. As soon as one questions that unity, it becomes no longer self-evident; it indicates itself, constructs itself, only on the basis of a complex field of discourse.

DISCURSIVE EVENTS

Pre-existing forms of continuity, all these syntheses that are accepted without question, must, for Foucault, remain in suspense. They must not be rejected definitively of course, but the tranquillity with which they are accepted must be disturbed; we must show that they do not come about by themselves but are always the result of a construction the rules of which must be known. In short, they require a theory, and this theory cannot be constructed unless the field of the facts of discourse are built up as such. So globalization, for example in this postmodern context, has been uniformly thrust upon the world through the force of imposed capitalist circumstances, rather than naturally emerging out of the world's diversity.

In placing yourself in whatever unities are already given, such as psychology or economics, business or management, you need to question by what right they can claim a field that specifies them in space and time; according to what laws they are formed; against the background of what contexts they stand out; and whether or not they are ultimately the surface effect of more firmly grounded unities. You accept the groupings that history suggests only to break them up and then to see whether they can be legitimately reformed.

Once these immediate forms of continuity are suspended, an entire field is set free. One is led therefore to the project of a pure description of discursive events, or a multiplicity of discourses, as the horizon for the search for the unities that form within it. We must grasp the statement in the exact specificity of its occurrence; determine its conditions of existence, fix at least its limits, establish its correlations with another state that may be connected with it. Like every event it is subject to repetition, reactivation or transformation. By freeing it from pre-existing groupings, such as modernization and globalization, new unities can be perceived. It is not therefore an interpretation of the facts that might reveal them, but the analysis of their coexistence, their succession, their mutual functioning, their reciprocal determination and their independent or correlative transformation. In the final analysis, the chosen field cannot be regarded as definitive or absolutely valid; it is no more than an initial approximation that must allow relations to appear which may erase the limits of this initial outline: through discursive reality.

DISCURSIVE REALITY

The term 'discourse', according to Foucault's *Archaeology of Knowledge*, can be defined as the group of statements that belong to a single system of formation, such as clinical discourse, economic discourse, the discourse of natural history or psychiatric discourse. Discourse in this sense is not an ideal, timeless form. The problem therefore is not to ask oneself how and why it was able to emerge and become embodied at the present point in time. It is, from beginning to end, a fragment of history, a discontinuity in history itself, posing the problem of its own limits, its divisions, its transformations, the specific modes of its temporality. What Foucault has called 'discursive practice' is a body of anonymous, historical rules, always determined in time and space that have defined a given period, spanning a given social, economic, geographical or linguistic era. What does this more specifically imply?

Discourse, for Foucault, has not so much a meaning or a truth, but a history and indeed a specific history: it involves a type of history, a mode of succession, of stability and of reactivation, which belongs to it alone. It is caught up in the very things it connects; and if not modified by history it modifies it, and is transformed by it into certain decisive thresholds. It also ceases to appear as the inert, smooth and neutral element in which they arise, each according to its own movement, or driven by some obscure dynamics or themes, ideas or concepts. We are now dealing with a complex volume in which heterogeneous regions are differentiated. As such, we are not seeing, in the great mythical book of history, lines of words that translate into visible characters, thoughts that were formed in some other time and place. We have instead, in the density of discursive practices, systems that establish statements as events, with their own conditions and domains of appearance, and things with their own possibility and fields of use. The same is true for management.

POWER, CONSTRUCTION AND DECONSTRUCTION

A postmodernist approach would treat the constituent disciplines of management not as dealing with resources, connected to different aspects of reality, but as discourses, which socially construct and certify particular meaningful versions of reality. The manager is constituted and reconstituted through historically and socially contingent discourses. Any management discipline would hence be seen as a particular historical and social mode of engagement that restricts what is thinkable, knowable and doable. For Foucault, so-called 'genealogy' is the analysis of the conditions that make it possible for a particular discourse to develop, change and adapt.

In the construction and deconstruction of the taken-for-granteds that underlie a particular discipline, or indeed management in general, a key focus would be to analyse the socio-historical conditions that made it possible for a particular discourse to be developed and through which it might change. Moreover, central to a postmodern analysis, as for critical theory, would be power. Such power is seen to reside not in individuals as conscious agents but in the discourses themselves. For Foucault the exercise of power perpetually creates knowledge and, conversely, knowledge constantly induces effects of power. The deployment of any discourse is seen as empowering those people with the power to speak while subordinating others who are the object of the knowledge and disciplines produced by the discourse.

Meanwhile the disempowered collude in the relationship by accepting the authority of discourse speakers to analyse and categorize, thereby empowering them. Likewise those with privileged access to the relevant discourse gain a sense of meaning and identity from the practices it sanctions. In this manner individuals and collectives become constructed, classified, known and transformed into self-disciplining subjects through the power they don't possess. In this sense postmodernists see power as being everywhere but nowhere – as a relationship between subjects and yet independent of subjects – which in effect suppresses the articulation of alternative possible 'truth-effects'.

Research methodology is hence part of such a power structure, affecting the relationship between research student and supervisor, not to mention the relationship between the research subject and the people connected with it. Such an underlying power structure, in broader and much more poignant guise, underlies the relationship between fundamentalist Islam and the secular West in our day and age.

12.4 Global Variations of Postmodernism

MODERNISM, POSTMODERNISM AND FUNDAMENTALISM

Fundamentalism – Jewish, Christian, and Islamic – for former Catholic nun Karen Armstrong,[16] is a global fact and has surfaced in every major faith in response to the problems of modernity. At first religious people, Armstrong posits, try to reform their traditions and effect a marriage between them and modern culture, as many Islamic reformers in Egypt and Iran attempted (in the 1950s) to do. But when these moderate measures are seen to be of no avail, some people resort to more extreme measures and a fundamentalist movement is born. Of the three monotheistic religions, Islam was the last to develop a fundamentalist strain, when modern culture began to take root in the Muslim world in the 1960s and 1970s.

Such fundamentalist movements, which Armstrong sees as features of all faiths, share certain characteristics. They reveal a deep disappointment and disenchantment with the modern experiment, which has not fulfilled all that was promised. They also express real fear. Every single fundamentalist movement that she has studied is convinced that the secular establishment is determined to wipe it out. As such, fundamentalism is an essential part of the modern scene. The fundamentalist community can thus be seen as the shadow-side of modernity; it can also highlight some of the darker sides of the modern experiment. It therefore exists in a symbiotic relationship with a coercive secularism. Fundamentalism therefore reveals a fissure in society, which is polarized between those who enjoy secular culture and those who regard it with dread. Fundamentalists, moreover, have been successful to the extent that they have pushed religion from the sidelines back into centre stage.

Fundamentalism, for Armstrong, can be seen as a postmodern movement that rejects some of the tenets and enthusiasms of modernity, such as colonialism. Many Muslim women feel that veiling is a symbolic return to the pre-colonial period, before their society was disrupted and deflected from its true course. Yet they have not simply turned the clock back. A large proportion of veiled women hold progressive views on such matters as gender. They are coming to join the modern world but on their own terms and in an Islamic context that gives it sacred meaning. Uniformity of dress abolishes class differences and stresses the importance of community over Western individualism. Muslims then, Armstrong maintains, want modernity, but not one that has been imposed on them by America, Britain or France. For when Muslims look at Western society, they see no light, no heart, no spirituality.

Another contemporary Muslim scholar, Ziauddin Sardar, has a somewhat different perspective.

ISLAM, POSTMODERNISM AND TRANSMODERNISM

Sardar, a professor of cultural studies at City University in London, has placed himself on the side of the 'other', the dialectical opposite of the dominant mode of thought and action, whether in the West or internally within Islam. He is always on the side of the marginalized and the oppressed, always arguing for distributive justice, always trying to decentre the centre, always a radical. Islam, for Sardar, is a worldview, a vision of a just and equitable society and civilization, a holistic culture, an invitation to thought for discovering the way out of the current crisis of modernity and postmodernism. To reduce it to a recipe for dos and don'ts is a category mistake. For Sardar, Islam as such has to be reinterpreted in every era.

In sharp contrast to many modernists and secularists who believe that there is something culturally lacking in Muslim, Chinese, Indian and African cultures that keeps them in chains and underdeveloped, Sardar believes that cultural authenticity actually contains the seeds for the regeneration of these societies. But for this regeneration to occur, both tradition and culture must be seen in their dynamic forms:

Traditional pluralism is a mark of common respect we are called on to pay to each tradition in a world of diverse traditions; it is the basic idea that we might just know what is best for ourselves. It is the notion that inventiveness, ingenuity, enterprise and common sense are integral to all traditions; and that every traditions, if given the resources, opportunity, tolerance and freedom, can adapt to change and solve its own problems with their own traditions.[17]

In other words, while Sardar is a great believer, like the postmodernists, in pluralism, for him *traditional* pluralism is of the essence. Transmodernism, as opposed to both the modern and postmodern, for Sardar,[18] is a synthesis between life enhancing tradition, amenable to change and transition, and new forms of modernity shaped by traditional cultures themselves. In other words, it sees tradition as dynamic, and eager to change; and traditional cultures not as pre-modern but as communities with potential to transcend the dominant model of modernity. Transmodernism forces us to see non-Western cultures on their own terms, with their own eyes (ideas, concepts, notions), as part of a common future rather than as the past of humanity. A good example of such, according to Sardar, is contemporary Islam. The West has always seen Islam through the lens of modernity and concluded that is a negative, static, closed system. Yet from Morocco to Indonesia, Islam has changed profoundly in the last decade, particularly after the events of September 11, 2001. But to notice this change, Islam has to be seen from the perspective of transmodernism and understood through its own concepts and categories.

Transmodernism is all about listening, in the context of *mutually assured diversity*, to what we term diverse 'worlds'; and realizing that local identity as a cultural context is as much work in progress in traditional societies as in Western ones. In our terms, such local identity, in order to progressively actualize itself, needs to enter into dialogue with others such local identities, with a view to assuming a 'global integrity'. Indeed, this is what took place in the Arab world in the 9th to 13th centuries. And it is exactly that what Sardar calls for today, in the Muslim *ummah*, from Mali to Malaysia, from Guyana to the Gulf region, from Amman to America.

Such *mutually assured unity-in-diversity* is founded on the proposition that all identities have futures, and that their futures are most assured in mutual association. That local identity is then the cultural attitude to speak a better future, fashioned out of all the possibilities and predicaments offered by the contemporary times and circumstances, and in the light of histories that shape these circumstances. What is diverse is the means, institutions and social forms of delivering unifying values. To arrive at mutually assured unity-in-diversity requires, for Sardar, learning to see not only the debates, knowledge and distinctness of various different cultures, but to see how within them common values and commensurate ideas are enacted in radically different ways.

Mutually assured diversity, then, makes cultural relations part of the human condition and *opens the way to acculturation*, the multiple ways, or mutual processes of learning from, and exchanging ideas between different local identities. This is precisely where modernity and multiculturalism have failed. Acculturation is an adaptive process that domesticates influences, translates them into indigenous categories and applies them where they are of most benefit. Acculturation is not an imitative process; it is creative, innovative and endlessly diverse in its outcomes, ultimately building up integrity.

We now turn from postmodern philosophy and methodology to one of its effects, represented in Islamic future studies.

12.5 Postmodernism in Practice: Postmodernism as a Basis for Open Society

ISLAMIC FUTURE STUDIES (CHRISTIANITY AND ISLAM IN THE POSTMODERN AGE)

Human history has now reached a particularly interesting turning point – which gives Islamic futurist Ziauddin Sardar his main reason for hope. The grand narrative of secularism, as he sees it, has all but failed; under the passions, problems and predicaments of 20th century, the wishful intellectual structures of a narrow version of rationality, the dreams of the unchecked one-dimensional secular progress of the Enlightenment have collapsed. Philosophy is in disarray and science is in crisis. The changes of mind characteristic of the 17th century's turn from religion to rationalism are being reversed: from reduction to synthesis, from parts to whole, from structure to process, from clinical objectivity to epistemology, from building blocks to networks, and we are returning to tradition as the essence of meaning and identity.[18]

Modernity has been stripped naked of its pretensions: deconstructionists like Derrida and Foucault have shown how threadbare is the fabric of modernity. But as modernity self-destructs there is seemingly nothing to take its place. So the role is that of the believers to fill the moral and social vacuum with an ethical system that is both distinctively contemporary and deeply rooted in authentic religious traditions. As the grand narrative of secularism reaches its cul-de-sac, as the project of modernity loses its momentum, there is a dire need for a successor programme, a joint Christian-Muslim ethical enterprise.

For decades the church, Sardar maintains, has turned its back on the fight for real dignity and honour of humanity; the fight against a notion and practice of freedom that is divorced from responsibility, is based on self-indulgence and that tries to resolve moral and political problems with engines of self-enrichment, material expansion and economic manipulation. Muslims have been unwitting participants in this game; and where they have been aware of the true dangers of secular culture they have sought to resolve the problem through isolation, censorship, suppression of freedoms and by political violence. Yet only by making the ethical connections that are the true heritage of the Abrahamic faiths, and working together for the establishment of an objective moral order, can we make genuine progress toward the creation of true Christian and Muslim societies.

PROS AND CONS OF POSTMODERNISM

The transition from the modern to the postmodern worlds is based on a number of key developments that have jolted modern consciousness in the last two decades: Thomas Kuhn's demystification of 'scientific truth'; the emphasis on indeterminacy in quantum physics; Foucault's emphasis on discontinuity and difference in history; Bell's sociology of post-industrialism; and the newly discovered concern for the other in ethics, anthropology and politics. For American postmodern philosopher and guru, Richard Rorty, it is function rather than philosophy, narrative rather than theory, that provides a better perspective on human behaviour.

While, for Rorty, anything seemingly goes, he remains wedded to the values of liberalism. At the same time, Sardar suggests that postmodernism plunders history to render it meaningless. He argues that the reduction of history to instant consumerism leads to an instant loss of depth. For plurality in postmodernism serves as an end in itself. It is not the contents of other cultures that concern it, but merely the fact that they are different. In fact the new kind of postmodern assimilation of non-Western cultures is best seen in the marketplace where all the world's commodities are assembled under one roof for the consumer to experience 'different worlds'. In this banal plurality, Sardar maintains, with the confusion of the real and the artificial, meaning is sought by the purchase of the image.

THE END OF CIVILIZATION?

European ethnocentricism presents a conflict-ridden view of history, honed and sharpened by the techniques employed to effect change in European consciousness. Its rallying cries are familiar: liberty, individual conscience, equality, democratic freedom, justice, fraternity, liberality, tolerance, freedom of speech. All of these are noble qualities and enduring values. The distortion comes about in understanding them only as they have been defined and delivered within the context of a Western history of conflict.

In a world where domination is the rule, as well as the ruler, the distorted imagination has been appropriated within the traditional cultures through the colonization of the mind. The effect is the appearance of those who accept the logic and gratify the West, amplifying its prejudices and repudiating their own cultural heritage. That is not to say that the rest of the world has been an idyll, as the nostalgics today maintain. In fact, there is a growing understanding in the Muslim world, and elsewhere in non-Western civilizations, that nostalgics make good slogans but reify (reduce to a 'thing') a reductive vision of indigenous history. Both the dominance of the distorted imagination and the more visible opposing ranks of the nostalgics and the apologists are an impediment to the recovery of a genuine, autonomous history, a realistic perspective on what constitutes tradition and how that tradition can be employed today. Muslims must develop a new language of self-expression, for it is only by this means that they can address their own urgent agenda and continue the long war of attrition on the distorted imagination.

All this means that Islamic culture and other non-Western cultures have to be understood on their own terms, by their own inner dynamic, by how they see themselves, by what they think their sacred scriptures are saying – in other words, far above and beyond the distorted imagination, at the level of genuine authenticity. When Muslims look toward the Medina state of the Prophet Muhammad, they are not looking to go back to some medieval history; they are looking forward to capturing that sense of equality, freedom and justice which it represented.

THE COURSE OF FUTURES STUDIES

The Western Technological Imperative: Sardar posits that the future has already been colonized and its liberation is the most pressing challenge for the peoples of the non-West if they are to inherit a future made in their own likeness. The future, as it stands, is little more than the transformation of society by Western technologies. Thus there is an in-built momentum that seems to take us to a single, determined future. Technology is projected as an autonomous and desirable force. Its desirable products generate more desire. This trajectory is indeed an arch-ideology. The future, for Sardar, is thus waiting to explode. The process, which is transforming the world into a 'global village', is also shaping the world in the image of a single culture and civilization.

Globalization can then be identified with two elements. First, the economic wave of liberalization. Production is being replaced by consumption as the central economic activity, and privatization is becoming the norm. Secondly, the wide acceptance of liberal democracy is leading to a total embrace of Western culture. At the same time there is a total lack of future consciousness in most non-Western societies. Such a non-Western project should insist on exposing the political dimension of all knowledge related to the future, and cast it as a contested arena of conflictual practices, thereafter revealing the kind of alternative futures that might be shaped by the desires and vision of non-Western societies. However, a chasm has opened between the appreciation of tradition and the imaginative capacity to think traditions forward. If the future is a state of awareness then that awareness can only have genuine meaning if it emanates from the indigenous depths of a culture. The plurality of futures has to be reflected in the plurality of cultures.

Newly Contested Terrain: The power that Western civilization exercises over other cultures derives not from its military or technological might, nor even from its economic strength and political muscle and stability. The real might of the West resides in its power to define. The West defines everything – and the rest of the world is expected to embrace this. The West defines what is science, rationality, religion, civilization, freedom, democracy, human rights. Other cultures must accept these and the enslavement and cultural subservience that follow.

But definitions of what it means to be human and civilized will be a contested arena in the future. Asian civilizations (China, India, Islam), for example, have their own definitions of what is freedom, participatory governance, human rights, and so on, which differ from the Western notions. Western atomism is rejected by Asian civilizations, where communal harmony is preferred over individualism. Already, Asian societies are increasingly repudiating the idea of 'human rights' as just another tool of imperialism and have replaced it with their own notion of 'human dignity', which incorporates the rights not just to political dissent, but also the right of basic needs and freedom from exploitation and cultural imperialism.

Beyond Development – An Islamic Perspective: The basic assumption of development, no matter how it is defined, are always of a linear teleology vis-à-vis the standard yardstick of measurement: Western civilization. The Western traditions are thus the model of 'developed' states, with their industrial policies, free market economies, technological advancement, political, economic and social institutions. Within the framework of the Islamic way of development, material and spiritual aspects of life are complementary. To be able to live the good life of devotion to God, we have, therefore, to make the best use of the material resources of our world. Talking about development without considering the spiritual side of people is meaningless; development must preserve, for Sardar, the essence of our humanity. As such:

- The Islamic concept of development has a comprehensive character and includes moral, spiritual and material aspects.

- The focus for development effort and the heart of the development process is man; development therefore means development of man and his physical and socio-cultural environment.
- In an Islamic framework, development is nothing but a multidimensional activity, establishing a balance between different factors and forces.
- Economic development involves a number of changes, quantitative as well as qualitative.
- Among the dynamic principles of social life Islam has particularly emphasized two – firstly the optimal utilization of resources that God has endowed to man, and his physical environment; and secondly their equitable use and distribution and the promotion of all human relationships on the basis of rights and justice.

The idea of balance and harmony is deeply embedded in this concept. A development-free multi-civilizational world, then, could generate a more companionable concept of distributive well-being, of new kinds of growth that can be shared, or new alliances of interests and common aspirations that can collaborate across civilizational lines without demanding the denial of anyone's identity either in the non-West or the West. A development-free world of numerous big and small civilizations, each working out its distinctive way of knowing, doing and being, offers the prospect of discovering that the highest human aspirations are shared values, whose expression through difference makes their realization more attainable for all people – in the non-West as well as the West.

12.6 Conclusion

ALL IS A MATTER OF SUBJECTIVE INTERPRETATION

Out of this maelstrom of highly developed and often divergent impulses and tendencies within postmodernism, such as those manifested in today's Muslim world, a few widely shared working principles – according to Richard Tarnas[19] – have emerged.

The quest for knowledge, for you as a postmodernist, must be endlessly self-revising. You must try the new, experiment and explore, test against subjective and objective consequences, learn from your mistakes, take nothing for granted, treat all as provisional, assume no absolutes. The mind is not the passive reflector of an external world and its intrinsic order, but is active and creative in the process of perception and cognition. Reality is in some sense constructed by the mind, not simply perceived by it, and many such constructions are possible, none necessarily sovereign. There is no empirical 'fact' that is not already theory-laden, and there is no logical argument or formal principle that is *a priori* certain. All human understanding is interpretation, and no interpretation is final. Up until this last statement, there was much in common between critical rationalism and postmodernism, though, for the latter there is no objective truth, no universally falsifiable hypothesis. All is a matter of subjective interpretation.

KNOWLEDGE IS CONSTITUTED OF VARIABLE PREDISPOSITIONS

All human knowledge is mediated, for postmodernists, by signs and symbols of uncertain provenance, constituted by historically and culturally variable predispositions, and influenced by often unconscious human interests. Hence the nature of truth and reality, in science no less than in philosophy, religion or art, is radically ambiguous. The subject can never presume to transcend the manifold predispositions of his or her subjectivity. Postmodern philosophers, then, can compare and contrast, analyse and discuss the many sets of perspectives human beings have expressed, the diverse symbol systems, the various ways of making things hang together, but they cannot pretend to possess an extra-historical point from which to judge whether a given possibility validly represents the 'truth'. Postmodern thought has encouraged a vigorous rejection of the entire Western 'canon' as long defined and privileged by a more or less exclusively male, white, European elite. Received truths concerning 'man', 'reason', 'civilization', and 'progress' are indicated as intellectually and morally bankrupt.

Under the cloak of Western values, too many sins have been committed. Any alleged comprehensive, coherent outlook is at best no more than a temporary useful fiction, masking chaos, at worst an oppressive fiction masking relationships of power, violence and subordination. Not only, then, is the postmodern mind itself a maelstrom of unresolved diversity, but virtually every important element of the Western intellectual past is now present and active in one form or another, contributing to the variety and confusion of the contemporary Zeitgeist. Moreover, these in turn have been joined, and affected by a multitude of cultural perspectives from outside the West, such as the Buddhist and Hindu mystical traditions; by underground cultural streams from within the West itself; and by indigenous and archaic perspectives antedating Western civilization altogether – all gathering now on the intellectual stage for some kind of climactic synthesis.

WE ARE FREE TO CHOOSE OUR WORLD

The human predicament is here regarded as a human 'adventure', the challenge of being a radically self-defining entity. Human understanding is not unequivocally compelled by a set of data, to adopt one metaphysical position or another. The irreducible element of human choice intervenes. Hence there enters into the epistemological equation, in addition to intellectual rigour and socio-cultural context, other more open-ended factors such as will, imagination, faith, hope and empathy. The more complexly conscious and ideologically unconstrained the individual or society, the more free is the choice of worlds, the more profound their participation in reality. In the wake of such developments, the original project of Romanticism – the reconciliation of subject and object, human and nature, spirit and matter, conscious and unconscious, intellect and soul – has re-emerged anew.

EPOCHAL TRANSITION

For Tarnas, two antithetical impulses can thus be discerned in the contemporary intellectual situation, one pressing for a radical deconstruction and unmasking – of knowledge, beliefs, world views – and the other for a radical integration and reconciliation. The intellectual question that looms over our time is whether it is indeed the entropic prelude to some kind of apocalyptic denouement of history or whether it represents an epochal transition to another era altogether, bringing a new form of civilization and a new world view with principles and ideals fundamentally different from those that have impelled the modern world through its dramatic trajectory. Ironically, and at the time of writing in November 2007, the conflict being played out in Pakistan (where Sardar was born) between the secular and Islamist, democratic and militarist, Western and Middle Eastern, forces, is indicative of such.

It is our role, as social researchers and innovators in such a postmodern and also value-laden context, to help promote such an epochal transition. This brings us finally on the concluding step of the research path of reason, to so-called 'socio-technical design'.

References

1. Drucker, P. (1992). *The Age of Discontinuity*. New York: HarperCollins.
2. Handy, C. (1995). *The Age of Unreason*. New York: Random House.
3. Tarnas, R. (1991). *The Passion of the Western Mind*. New York: Ballantyne Books.
4. Lessem, R. (1993). *Business as a Learning Community*. London: McGraw Hill.
5. Lessem, R. and Neubauer, F. (1993). *European Management Systems*. London: McGraw Hill.
6. Burman E. (ed) (1993). *Discourse Analytic Research*. London: Routledge.
7. Potter, J. and Wetherell, M. (1987). *Discourse and Social Psychology*. London: Sage.
8. Mishler, E. (1986). *Research Interviewing: Context ad Narrative*. Cambridge, MA: Harvard University Press.
9. Macnaghten P. (1993). 'Discourses of Nature: Argumentation and Power.' In E. Burman and I. Parker (eds), *Discourse Analytic Research: Repertoires and Readings of Texts in Action*. London: Routledge.
10. Culler, J. (1987). *Ferdinand de Saussure*. Ithaca, NY: University of Cornell.
11. Barthes, R. (1993). *Mythologies*. London: Vintage Classic.
12. Hamilton, C. (ed.) (2002). *Re-figuring the Archive*. Cape Town: David Phillip.
13. Berger, P. and Luckman, T. (1967). *The Social Construction of Reality*. Harmondsworth: Penguin.
14. Foucault, M. (1989). *The Order of Things*. London: Routledge.
15. Foucault, M. (1984). *The Archaeology of Knowledge*. London: Routledge.
16. Armstrong, K. (2002). *A Short History of Islam*. London: Phoenix Press.
17. Inayatullah, S. and Boxwell, G. (2003) *Islam, Postmodernism and other Futures: A Ziauddin Sardar Reader*. London: Pluto Press.
18. Sardar, Z. (2006). *How Do You Know?* London: Pluto Press.
19. Inayatullah and Boxwell, *Islam, Postmodernism and other Futures*.
20. Tarnas, *The Passion of the Western Mind*.

13 *From Postmodernism to Socio-technical Design*

Evolve Democratic Processes

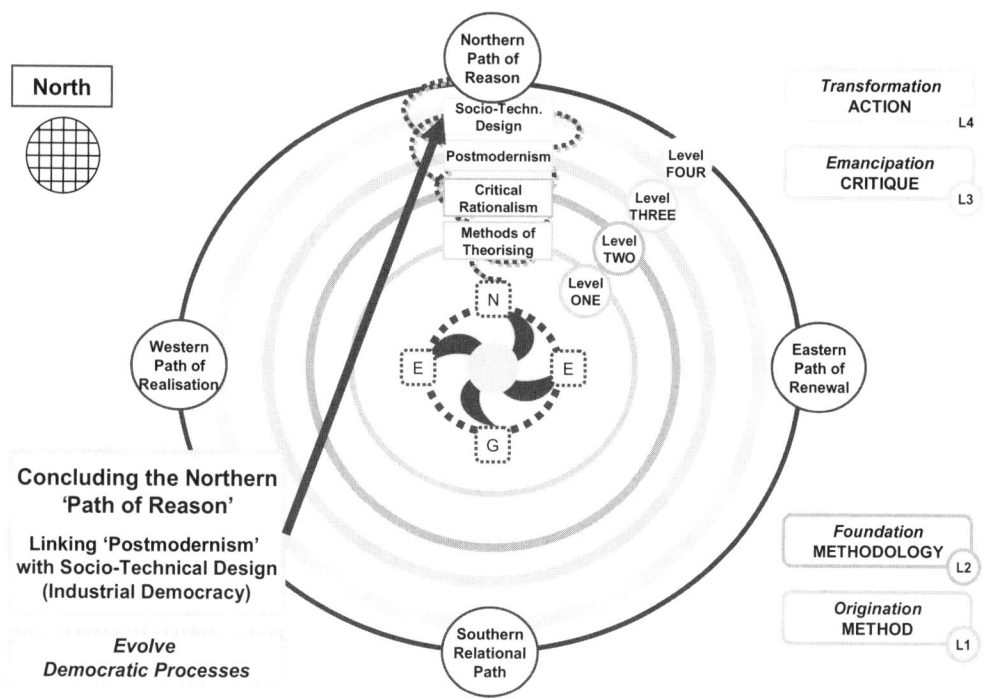

North

North

Northern
Path of
Reason

Socio-Techn.
Design

Postmodernism

Critical
Rationalism

Methods of
Theorising

Level
FOUR

Level
THREE

Level
TWO

Level
ONE

N

E

E

G

Western
Path of
Realisation

Eastern
Path of
Renewal

Southern
Relational
Path

Transformation
ACTION
L4

Emancipation
CRITIQUE
L3

Foundation
METHODOLOGY
L2

Origination
METHOD
L1

**Concluding the Northern
'Path of Reason'**

**Linking 'Postmodernism'
with Socio-Technical Design
(Industrial Democracy)**

*Evolve
Democratic Processes*

Figure 13.1 Overview Chapter 13 – Level 4/North

Summary: Socio-technical Design

- Socio-technical design is the culmination of our Northern research path of reason. It builds progressively on methods of theorizing, critical rationalism and postmodernism. In relation to postmodernism it builds particularly on the impulse of integration (rather than further fragmentation).
- Such integrated designs focus on the development of open socio-technical systems within institutions. In pursuit of organizational freedom, they are strongly rooted in industrial democracy. The close link to Popper's and Soros' shared concept of an open society becomes immediately evident, though the focus here is more strongly on the 'open' organization.
- The originators of such socio-technical design, from Europe and America, were Kurt Lewin and John Dewey, the one a social scientist and a refugee from Nazi Germany, the other an educator and philosopher with a passion for democracy in both educational and political institutions, both with an overall leaning towards action-oriented research.
- Socio-technical design is indeed an action research approach, which is both socio-politically and techno-economically integral and transformative. Why? Because it involves co-researchers working together, within democratic institutions, as fellow subjects rather than as researcher/subject and researched/object.
- This approach was most prolifically embodied in selective experiments in workplace democracy in the North and East; in the North it were Norway and Sweden that took the lead, in the East it was Japan, where it was combined with the evolving 'quality circles'.
- In the world at large, subsequent to such experimentation in the latter part of the 20th century, organizations have regressed, in the face of pressures from globalization and the financial markets, whereby economic fundamentals have superseded such social and technical experiments in democracy.
- To that extent Habermas' warning is notable: in the absence of a newly normative theory emerging at a macro level which could underpin them, these new formations could prove to be short-lived; in our own terms, resulting in a lack of thoroughgoing social innovation.
- However, examples of effective socio-technical design can be found. At the end of this chapter we introduce the Mondragon Co-operatives in Spain as a remarkable case in point for an industrial democracy, initiated, decades ago, by a Catholic priest, Father Arizmendiarrieta.

13.1 Orientation to Socio-technical Design

OVERVIEW

On the Northern research path of reason, you have now progressed through methods of theorizing onto the methodology of critical rationalism through emancipatory postmodernism. Altogether, you have progressively evolved towards the knowledge era (in such rational Northern terms), culminating in what has been termed 'socio-technical design'. Such socio-technical design is an overall manifestation of action research, duly incorporating industrial democracy.

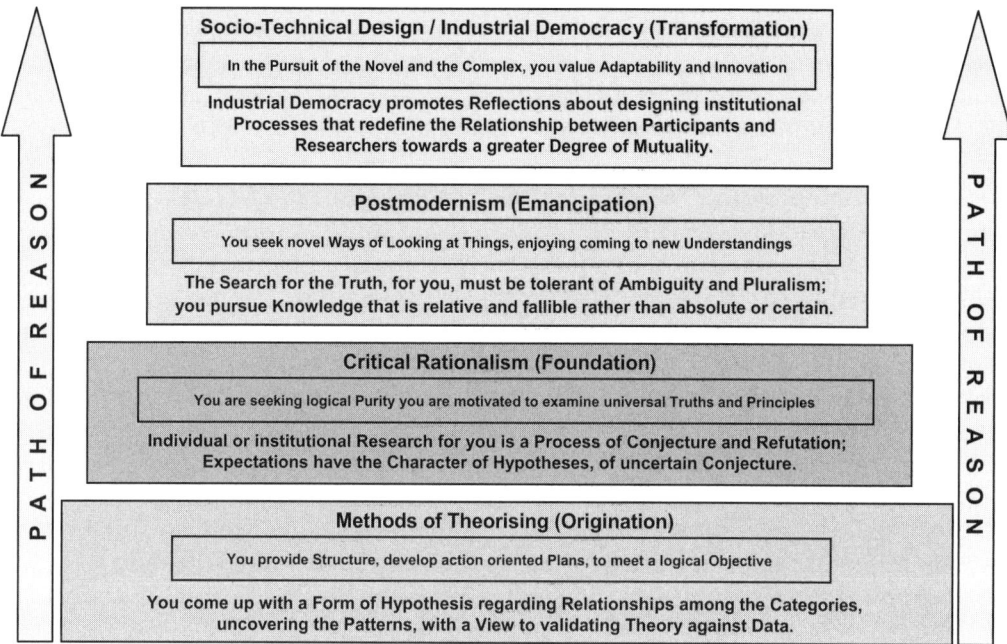

Figure 13.2 Towards Socio-technical Designs

Industrial democracy promotes reflections about designing institutional processes that redefine the relationship between participants and researchers towards a *greater degree of mutuality.*

Once again, though, one path overlaps to some extent with the others. In this culminating stage of the research path of reason, there is something of an overlap between realizability (West) and reasonability (North), as well as relationality (South) and renewal (East). In fact the two founding fathers of action research in general and of socio-technical design in particular were such typically rounded characters. Between them, Kurt Lewin and John Dewey spanned philosophy and psychology, biology and education.

THE FOUNDING FATHERS: LEWIN AND DEWEY

Kurt Lewin's work had a profound impact on social psychology as well as on experiential learning, group dynamics and action research. He was born in 1890 in Prussia (now part of Poland) as one of four children in a middle-class Jewish family. In 1909 Kurt Lewin entered the University of Freiburg to study medicine. He then transferred to the University of Munich to study biology. Around this time he became involved in the socialist movement. His particular concerns appear to have been the combating of anti-Semitism, the democratization of German institutions, and the need to improve the position of women. Along with other students he organized and taught an adult education programme for working-class women and men.

His doctorate was undertaken at the University of Berlin where he developed an interest in the philosophy of science and encountered gestalt psychology. In 1921 Kurt Lewin joined the Psychological Institute of the University of Berlin – where he was to lecture and offer seminars in both philosophy and psychology. His work became known in America and in 1930 he was invited to spend six months as a visiting professor at Stanford. With the political position worsening in Germany, he and his family settled 1933 in the USA. Kurt Lewin was first to work at the Cornell School of Home Economics, and then at the University of Iowa (this was also the year when his first collection of papers in English *A Dynamic Theory of Personality* was published).

The University of Iowa remained Kurt Lewin's base until 1944. There he continued to develop his interest in social processes. He also became involved in various applied research initiatives linked to the war effort. These included exploring the morale of the fighting troops, psychological warfare and reorienting food consumption away from foods in short supply. His social commitments were also still strong – and he was much in demand as a speaker on minority and inter-group relations. He wanted to establish a centre to research group dynamics – and in 1944 this dream was realized with the founding of the Research Center for Group Dynamics at MIT. At the same time Kurt Lewin was also engaged in a project for the American Jewish Congress in New York – the Commission of Community Interrelations. It made use of Lewin's model of action research (research directed towards the solving of social problems) in a number of significant studies into religious and racial prejudice. It was also out of some of this work in 1946 with community leaders and group facilitators that the notion of 'T' (for sensitivity) groups emerged. He and his associates were able to get funding from the Office of Naval Research to set up the National Training Laboratories in 1947 in Bethel, Maine. However, Lewin died of a heart attack in 1947, before the laboratories were established.

Lewin, along with John Collier, is generally accredited with the coining of the term 'action research':

> *The research needed for social practice can best be characterized as research for social management or social engineering. It is a type of action research, a comparative research on the conditions and effects of various forms of social action, and research leading to social action. Research that produces nothing but books will not suffice.*

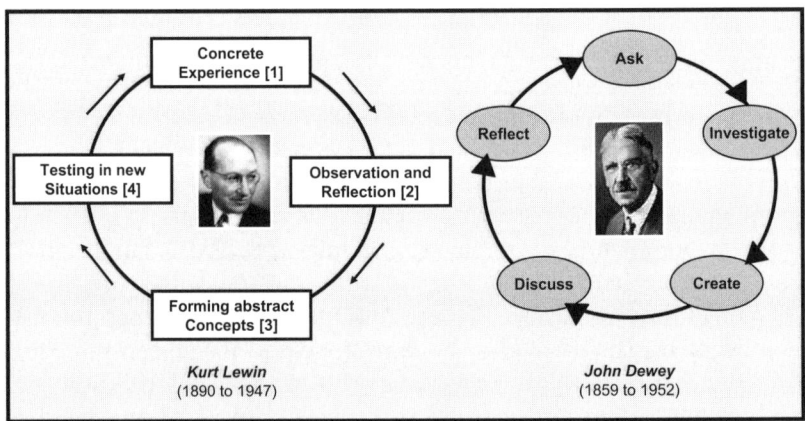

Figure 13.3 Socio-technical Design – Leading Thinkers

Sources: Image 1: Faxetteville State University http://www.uncfsu.edu/. Image 2: John Dewey, American Pragmatist http://dewey.pragmatism.org/

He was also closely aligned with the views of his compatriot John Dewey, both sharing the belief that democracy had to be continually invented anew.

John Dewey, the American philosopher on democracy and education, whose long life overlapped with that of Lewin, has made arguably the most significant contribution to the development of educational thinking in the 20th century. Dewey's philosophical pragmatism, concern with interaction, reflection and experience, and interest in community and democracy, were brought together to form a highly suggestive educative form. In many respects his work cannot be easily slotted into any one of the curriculum traditions that have dominated North American and UK schooling traditions over the last century.

John Dewey's significance for informal educators lies in a number of areas. First, his belief that education must engage with and enlarge experience has continued to be a significant strand in informal education practice. Second, and linked to this, Dewey's exploration of thinking and reflection – and the associated role of educators – has continued to be an inspiration. We can see it at work, for example, in the models developed by Kurt Lewin and the organizational psychologist Donald Schön at MIT. Third, his concern with interaction and environments for learning provides a continuing framework for practice. Last, his passion for democracy, for educating so that all may share in a common life, provides a strong rationale for practice in the associational settings in which informal educators work.

We now turn to the key tenets of socio-technical design.

13.2 Socio-technical Design – Key Tenets: Problem Solving, Organizational Development, Social Betterment

Socio-technical Design – Key Tenets
① You adopt a problem-solving orientation.
② Your research is inevitably linked to action.
③ Your research is geared towards social betterment.
④ You use a co-generative approach to organization development.
⑤ You act as a 'friendly outsider'.

① YOU ADOPT A PROBLEM-SOLVING ORIENTATION

Action research focuses on solving real-life problems. The focus of such institutionally based action research, for Greenwoord and Levin[1] is determined by what the organizational participants consider important, what affects their daily lives. The inquiry process is thus linked to actions taken to provide a solution to the problem being examined.

As such, the knowledge produced by the inquiry process must increase participants' control over their own situations, as well as being built on a critical understanding of the historical and political contexts within which the participants act. The participants must be able to use the knowledge that emerges, and this knowledge must support the enhancement of the participants' goals.

② YOUR RESEARCH IS INEVITABLY LINKED TO ACTION

In such action research insiders and outsiders join in a mutual learning process. The enabling mechanism for this is communication. New understandings are created through discourses between people engaged in the inquiry process.

The conventional social research community believes that credibility is created through generalizing and universalizing propositions, whereas action research believes that only knowledge generated and tested in practice is credible. Conventional social research assumes that only a community of similarly trained professionals is competent to decide issues of credibility, while action research places emphasis on the stakeholders' willingness to accept and act on the collectively arrived-at acts and the defining characteristic of credibility.

③ YOUR RESEARCH IS GEARED TOWARDS SOCIAL BETTERMENT

For the originator of action research, Kurt Lewin, 'nothing is as practical as a good theory', and 'the best way to understand something is to try to change it'. The social sciences themselves began as a form of engaged political economy, aimed at social betterment. Only as the social sciences were split out into the various existing conventional disciplines and subjected to harassment and purges because their social activism offended the rich and powerful, did the social sciences become separated from action. Greenwood and Levin (see Chapter 16) view such social sciences today as an impoverished derivative, albeit a methodologically and theoretically sophisticated one, of the original social sciences to which they see action as the natural heir.

In fact, the American social scientists who made up the so-called 'human relations' school in the middle of the last century, such as Mayo and Rothliesberger at Harvard, were much more radical in their overall, humanistic perspective, than their equivalents – management thinkers like America's Tom Peters and Britain's Charles Handy – today. The so-called 'co-generative' model underlying socio-technical design retains its wholesome link to social betterment, as well as to social science.

④ YOU USE A CO-GENERATIVE APPROACH TO ORGANIZATION DEVELOPMENT

Organizationally instigated action research can be thought of as a process consisting of at least two analytically distinct phases. The first involves the clarification of an initial research question, whereas the second involves the initiation and continuation of a 'social change and meaning construction process'. Both culminate in the creation of opportunities for learning and reflection in action (see Figure 13.4), within a co-generative process between insiders and outsiders.

Figure 13.4 Co-generative Approach to Organization Development

⑤ YOU ACT AS A 'FRIENDLY OUTSIDER'

A professional action researcher must know how to be a 'friendly outsider'. This role is vital in action research because the external perspective is a key element in opening up local group processes for change. But this outsider is 'friendly' in a special sense. He or she must be able to reflect back to the local groups things about them, including criticism of their own perspectives, in a way that is experienced as supportive rather than negatively critical or domineering.

The friendly outsider must also be expert at opening up lines of discussion, a kind of good Socratic teacher. Often local organizations or groups are either stuck in positions that have hardened or they have become pessimistic about the possibilities for change. Flexibility and opportunities for change are pointed out to local people, along with encouragement in the form of moral support, and information from other cases, where similar problems existed but change turned out to be possible. Another key role of the friendly outsider is to make evident the tacit knowledge that guides local conduct. This can be in the form of critical reflections or supportive comments about local capabilities.

13.3 Socio-technical Design in Depth

KNOWLEDGE GENERATION IN ACTION RESEARCH

The crux of the action-research-based knowledge-generation process is the encounter between local insights and the understanding that the outsider brings to the table and the fusion of these insights into a shared form of understanding that serves as the basis for solving practical problems. An affirmation or proposition from one of the parties (thesis) is brought forward and is met with demanding and challenging questions and counterpropositions (antithesis), and out of this friendly encounter of points of view an understanding (synthesis) will gradually evolve.

Such organizationally based action research is based on the affirmation that all human beings have detailed, complex and valuable knowledge about their lives, environments and goals. This knowledge is different from scholarly knowledge because everyday knowledge is embodied in people's actions, long histories in particular positions, and the way they reflect on them. This kind of knowing is different from much conventional scientific knowledge because practical wisdom, practical reasoning and tacit knowledge are its central characteristics. Action research then centres on a co-generatively structured encounter between the worlds of practical reasoning and those of scientifically constructed knowledge, integrating practitioners and professionals in the same knowledge generating process that it calls 'co-generative' learning.

Furthermore, a local theory is context bound and makes sense in the context of years of local processes matching interpretations with concrete experiences. In action research, the central intent is to generate knowledge that bridges these knowledge worlds. Conventional social researchers who have severed the connection between research and action rarely know whether they are right or not, as their findings are seldom acted upon and the practical results from their research rarely have direct consequences for them. Local knowledge belongs mainly to insiders, but outsiders can also develop varieties of local knowledge through ethnographic research based on local engagement over the long term. This conception of knowledge can be traced back to Aristotle's *phronesis*: the ability to spot the action called for in each situation.

Because action research privileges local knowledge, it necessarily works with the role of narrative in the research process, as well as in writing up the results. For most logical positivists (conventional social researchers), as well as those using formal qualitative techniques, the strong presence of narratives is taken to be hopelessly 'unscientific' and incapable of producing valid knowledge. In this respect, the rational-pragmatic bias of action research is combined with a holistic and also humanistic orientation.

THE KNOWLEDGE-GENERATION PROCESS

In organizationally based action research, *the research process must be democratic in the sense that it is open, participatory and fair to all the participants*. In addition, the outcome of action research should support the participants' interests, is was also the case for co-operative inquiry and indeed for participative research, so that the knowledge produced increases their ability to control their own situation. Action research, then, is a co-generative process through which professional researchers and interested members of a local organization, community or specially created organization collaborate to research, understand and resolve problems of mutual interest. Action research is therefore a social process in which professional knowledge, local knowledge, process skills, research skills and democratic values are the basis for co-generated knowledge and social change.

Conventional researchers view research techniques as important to the extent that they impart control, distance and objectivity to the researcher, so that any other similarly motivated researcher can reproduce the same results using the same techniques. Action researchers reject this view on a variety of grounds. They do not accept that it is possible to separate the research process from its human dimension or to separate the process from the results. Action research therefore seeks to bring the process and the results into the closest possible relationship and builds research upon fundamental respect for and trust in human capacities. Action research also emphasizes democratic values and processes by co-creating knowledge applicable by the local stakeholders in their efforts to increase control over their own situations.

In addition, action researchers aim to reopen the possibility for change, enhance a sense of responsibility for the direction of the future and emphasize that human agency, not impartial control systems, is the centrepiece of social change. One consequence of this perspective is that organizationally based action researchers do not 'apply' techniques to a situation. Rather they bring knowledge and skills to a group of people who collaboratively open up the possibility for self-managed social change.[2]

The more overtly political as well as rational and humanistic orientation (from an institutional as opposed to societal perspective) is the one to which we now turn, starting out with so-called socio-technical systems and ending up with industrial democracy, altogether born out of the initiating process of action research.

ACTION RESEARCH AND SOCIO-TECHNICAL SYSTEMS

Coining the term 'action research' was an honour that was held jointly by John Collier and the more famous Kurt Lewin. Collier, a commissioner for American Indian Affairs from 1933 to 1945, applied the term to his work in improving race relations, through a participative approach to collaborative research between whites and native Indians. Social scientist Lewin, as a refugee from Nazi Germany to the United States, held strong beliefs in democracy generally, and in action research specifically, as a tool that could advance science while dealing with practical societal concerns.

In Iowa, he worked with social psychologist Alex Bavelas to enhance productivity in a manufacturing company, by inviting workers to participate in experimental changes to work methods. They were encouraged to experiment, to discuss the results and to choose the most effective methods, anticipating the development of the learning organization today. Together with the American management philosopher Douglas McGregor, he experimented at a later stage with group dynamics, thereafter founding the Institute for Applied Behavioral Science in the United States.

Meanwhile psychologist Wilfrid Bion, at the Tavistock Institute in London, took on Lewin's collaborative approach to behavioural change to investigating the performance of small groups of people at work. His concern was to get them to deal with the problems they faced in their workplace, and to help them regain a sense of control over their lives. Democratic processes, in other words, were used to involve people in reconstructing their social arrangements.

After the war, another social psychologist, the Australian Eric Trist, took up the action-research cause at the Tavistock Institute, focusing his efforts on productivity in the coal mines. Workers in the more highly productive mines, he found, operated as self-managed groups. The miners themselves devised systems that allowed them to be multi-skilled and self-directing. He was able to demonstrate that the social and technical systems were interdependent: hence 'socio-technical systems'. In Norway, a series of efforts there became known as the Norwegian Industrial Democracy Project, whereby such socio-technical systems were diffused through action research, building upon an egalitarian culture. This 'social-democratic' process of progressively greater worker involvement spread from Norway to Sweden and Holland.

SOCIO-TECHNICAL SYSTEMS THEORY

Trist's colleague, the British social scientist Fred Emory, led the efforts to conceptualize these theories. Emory argued that because organizations employed whole persons, it was important to pay attention to human needs beyond those required for the regular performance of tasks dictated by technology. His paradigm, therefore, was directly in conflict with the master/servant relationship that characterized many workplaces.

In fact, Lewin as well as Trust and Emory, were committed to advancing scientific knowledge, particularly knowledge that could address practical problems of the day, and that would enable organizations and societies to better themselves. Each work group with which they were involved started with the premise that change begins with the involvement of those directly affected. Each believed that the predominant paradigm of the time, based on expert hierarchical control of social systems, would never prove adequate to face the challenges of a modern, post-industrial society. In Norway, as we have already intimated, action research was evolving to accommodate initial moves towards industrial democracy.

13.4 Global Variations of Socio-technical Design

TOWARDS INDUSTRIAL DEMOCRACY

Greenwood and Levin, drawing now upon Gustavsen's approach to action research in Norway, have documented his experience in arranging discourse 'conferences', within and across organizations, between management and unions. The core contribution of such action research in the 1960s and 1970s was to create relationships between actors, and arenas where they can meet in democratic dialogue. For Scandinavian Gustavsen, what made enlightenment possible was not the recognition that 'I think therefore I am', but the recognition that *unless people can relate in a democratic way to one another, no new ideas, no just causes or indeed any science, social or other, are possible.*

Gustavsen argued that a mediator was needed between one party and another, if purposeful thought and action was to be promoted, between them. Interestingly enough, and somewhat in contrast, the renowned German critical theorist, Jürgen Habermas, was of the view that the liberation of the oppressed from the prevailing powers that be had to start with new theory, and action, in the interim, was futile. In fact, from a 21st-century perspective, as market fundamentalism seemingly rides rampant over such experiments in industrial democracy, notwithstanding some distinctive exceptions like the Mondragon Co-operatives in Northern Spain, the John Lewis Partnership in the UK and (as we shall see in Chapter 16) Cashbuild in South Africa, Habermas may well have had a point.

FROM GERMANY TO THE US, FROM THE UK TO NORWAY TO JAPAN

That having been said, the emergence of what came to be called the 'industrial democracy' tradition or movement refers to the first systematic and reasonably large-scale action-research effort in Western industrialized countries. Its roots trace back to Kurt Lewin's early work in the United States – first at Cornell University and then at MIT. His ideas crossed back over the Atlantic, and he found fertile ground at the Tavistock Institute of

Human Relations in London. Though there were a number of action research related activities in Great Britain, most specifically related to the development of socio-technical systems, the major source of large-scale, institutionally oriented action-research projects, turned out to be in Norway in its Industrial Democracy Project. Many of these ideas were reinvented in the form of industrial management strategies in US and Swedish industrial firms; later, and in fact more prolifically, they reached Japan as well.

Lewin, as we learned earlier on, was trained as a social psychologist and his central interest was in social change, specifically questions about how to conceptualize social change and promote it. In action research, Lewin envisaged a process where one could construct an experiment in a rational and holistic social and material situation with the aim of achieving a certain goal. Lewin's thinking about experimentation in a natural setting became the main strategy for the Norwegian Industrial Democracy Project.

Two other strands of Lewin's thinking have an influence on the development of the industrial democracy tradition. First, Lewin conceptualized change as a three-stage process:

Second, his work on group dynamics, identifying factors and forces important for development, conflict and co-operation in groups, led to the concept of so-called T-groups, or sensitivity training, which have a rich subsequent history. In summary, the new paradigm that he and his colleagues brought to work and organization is the following:

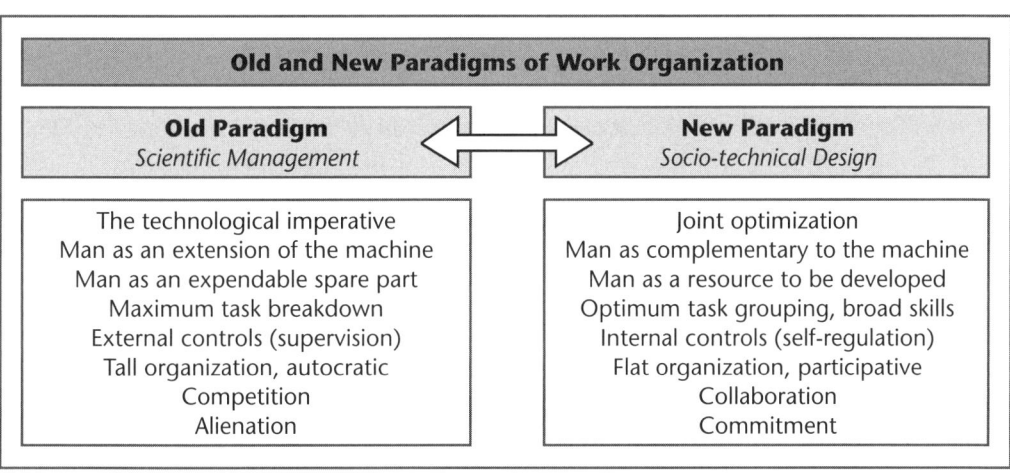

For Greenwood and Levin though, Lewin's specific orientation to managing change, related to unfreezing and re-freezing, is limiting. They argue in favour of action research as a continuous and participative learning process, not as a form of short-term intervention. For them, the change process has an open starting point and no absolute ending point.

However, Lewin's work remains a fundamental building block of what today is called 'action research' oriented towards organizational change. He set the stage for knowledge production based on solving real-life problems. From the outset he created a new role for researchers, and redefined criteria for judging the quality of the inquiry process. It was Lewin who shifted the researcher's role from being a distant observer to involvement in concrete problem solving. The quality criteria he developed for judging a good theory focus on its ability to support practical problem solving in real-life situations.

With a view to this, in Great Britain after World War II, rebuilding the industrial base was a major political goal. During the years of the war, this industrial base had been severely damaged and national efforts were launched immediately to revitalize the economy. The Tavistock Institute of Human Relations in London was therefore called upon by the British government to support various parts of this effort. No such organizational imperative in Britain if not elsewhere today parallels this. In fact, the recently proliferating impact of climate change on organizations has if anything further reinforced the emphasis upon technological or fiscal-economic fixes, rather than upon overall social innovation.

Yet, in the latter part of the last century, industrial democracy thinking also inspired other national movements. Japan was looking for ways to organize its industrial production that would secure both high productivity and excellent quality. Two US scholars who specialized in quality control, Juran and Deming, played an important role in the Japanese industrialization process. Their models for obtaining quality production were easily picked up by the Japanese companies. Actually, the Japanese were much more receptive to them than their US counterparts. The central themes of industrial democracy found fertile ground in Japan because collective work had a strong cultural base in the country. In Japan these activities appeared in the form of quality circles and problem-solving groups. In such an approach action learning emerged from an ongoing process of experimentation and reflection, in which mutual learning is the driving process for sustainable change and knowledge generation.

Industrial democracy in the West, though more in theory than in practice, was also the starting point for reflections about designing research processes that redefined the relationship between participants and researchers towards a much greater degree of mutuality. Carole Pateman, in her 1975 book *Participation and Democracy*,[3] drew a genealogy from Rousseau's and Mill's thinking to the modern debate on democracy at the shop-floor level. Despite this, the strongly idealistic-democratic content of this first decade of the industrial democracy tradition was gradually replaced by pragmatic arguments. The rhetoric shifted towards empowerment, from participation as the key to democracy to participation as a means to motivate workers to shape a more effective and profitable organization. For Greenwood and Morten, empowerment with its hierarchical connotations is an inevitable step backward.

LOOKING TOWARDS THE FUTURE

While action research continues to exist and to be widely practised in organizations and communities today, it remains an alternative paradigm. Human needs continue to be secondary to technical and economic advancement. The new paradigm required would, then as now:

Qualities of a New Research Paradigm

- Elevate the quality of the total human experience above measures of economic progress as the primary measure for the advancement of society.
- Devise ways of making expert knowledge readily available to those who need it.
- Place speed of learning and adaptation above costs and efficiencies.
- Elevate environmental and community issues above creation of wealth.
- Restore human dignity as underlying educational, organizational, political systems.
- Enhance diversity in scientific methods and ways of knowing.
- Locate control over systems to users rather than experts or designers.
- Develop ways for people to utilize diversity effectively, working together globally.
- Continue to explore ways for organizations and societies to develop, to realize and utilize the tremendous potential currently trapped in rigid structures.

We now turn to a case example of such a socio-technical design, that of Mondragon in Spain.

13.5 Socio-technical Design in Practice: The Making of Mondragon

Greenwood and Levin believe:

> *Institutionally based action research is framed as a democratic process supporting the creation of knowledge that potentially can be liberating. Obviously then, the inquiry process has to aim to solve problems important to the organizational participants, and the knowledge produced by the inquiry process must increase participants' control over their own situations. This is consistent with Freire's 'conscientization', which identifies the inquiry process as one shaping knowledge relevant to action, as well as being built on a critical understanding of the historical and political contexts within which the participants act.*[4]

A specific case in point is Mondragon in Spain's Basque country, which was been built as an industrial democracy by the remarkable Father Arizmendiarrieta.

CULTURE AND STRUCTURE OF MONDRAGON TODAY: COGNITIVE AND PROCEDURAL

The Mondragon Co-operatives Corporation (MCC) in the latter part of the 1990s was worth some $6 billion in sales, and had co-operatives ranging from construction to retailing, semi-conductors to household goods, banking to education. For its founder, the Catholic priest Father Don Jose Maria Arizmendiarrieta in the 1940s:

> *It is a social monstrosity that a system of social organization is tolerated in which some can take advantage of the work of others for their exclusive personal profit. The co-operatist distinguishes himself from the capitalist, simply in that the latter utilizes capital in order to make people serve him, while the former uses it to make more gratifying and uplifting the working life of the people.*[5]

In Arizmendiarrieta's library we find not only books of the key French Catholic philosophers (Jacques Maritain and Emmanuel Mounier) of his day, but also those of Karl Marx, Herbert Marcuse, Paulo Freire, J.K. Galbraith and the Yugoslav Vanek's *Self-management*. Maritain and Mounier in particular – both adherents of the so-called 'personalist' school of philosophy – saw capitalism as well as socialism as being incompatible with such personalist values. For Mounier, in his *Personalist Manifesto* of 1938, the point is not to attack capitalist society, but instead to 'implant in the vital organs, at present diseased, of our decadent civilization the seeds and the ferment of a new civilization.'

To understand Mondragon, we need to understand its organizational, as well as Basque societal, culture, including the support system that maintains that culture and influences its ability to change in adaptive ways. In their book on *Making Mondragon*,[6] William and Katherine Whyte think of the culture of the Mondragon co-operatives in terms of two categories of concepts: the cognitive framework and the shaping systems. The cognitive framework is the set of ideas and beliefs about basic values, organizational objectives, and guiding principles that form the foundation of any organization. *Shaping systems enable an organization to be maintained or to change.* A culture does not maintain itself but is shaped by forces such as major policies, structures and instruments of governance and management.

THE COGNITIVE FRAMEWORK OF MONDRAGON

The following 'cognitive framework', for the Whytes, characterizes the Mondagon co-operatives:

Basic Values

- *Equality:* All human beings, in the Mondragon context, are deemed to have been created equal, with equal rights and obligations.
- *Solidarity:* Members of a given co-operative should rise and fall together; this principle also applies to relationships between co-operatives, and between Mondragon and the Basque community.
- *Dignity of Labour:* There should be integrity to any labour, blue or white collar.
- *Participation:* Members have the right and obligation to participate as much as possible in shaping the decisions that affect them.

Objectives

- *Job Creation:* The creation of jobs was a primary objective from the very beginning, and the co-operatives retain a strong commitment to it.
- *Employment Security:* Every member in good standing should be able to expect continuous employment, but not a particular job, up to the age of retirement.
- *Human and Social Development:* Making the work itself humane and fostering the social development of the members.
- *Autonomy and Self-governance:* Developing autonomous and self-governing organizations that are linked together to help in coping with national and international economic conditions.
- *Economic Progress:* The generation of profits is viewed as a limiting condition (not the fundamental purpose) of the organizations.

Guiding Conditions

- *Balance:* Life in a co-operative should not be carried out as a zero-sum game where one gains and the other loses; there must be a balancing of interests and needs; the financial needs of the firm must be balanced with the economic needs of members; social and technical balance is also to be pursued.
- *Future Orientation:* Planning must be oriented towards a future well beyond the time when the immediate issue has to be resolved.
- *Organizational Self-evaluation:* What now exists must never be considered perfect and immutable; it is important to carry out frequent self-critical evaluations.
- *Openness:* Non-discriminatory in nature, the co-operatives are open to anyone with the requisite skills and training.
- *Pluralistic Political Orientation:* From the beginning, the leaders of the co-operatives avoided identification with any established political party or political ideology, in contrast to, for example, the situation with co-operatives in Italy, where they are affiliated with the unions or the communists.
- *Freedom of Information:* If members are to make intelligent decisions they have to have access to relevant information for decision-making.
- *Interco-operative Complementarity:* Individual co-operatives should buy from and sell to one another unless it is disadvantageous to one or the other.
- *Formation of Co-operative Groups:* To achieve economies of scale and strengthen solidarity with the movement, it is important for individual co-operatives to join together.
- *Size Limitation:* This principle is based on the assumption that it is difficult for an organization to remain flexible, democratic and efficient when it grows beyond a certain size.

We now turn from principles and guidelines to systems and structures. What about the systems that supported this cognitive framework?

SHAPING SYSTEMS TO MAINTAIN OR CHANGE THE ORGANIZATIONAL CULTURE

The forces shaping the organizational culture at Mondragon fall into three categories: major policies, structures and systems of governance and management. Some of these shaping systems attest to the extraordinary creativity of Mondragon on producing social inventions: new ideas put into place to meet important needs of the cooperatives.

- *Major Policies:* Membership is based on labour rather than capital; since 1965 all the surplus allocated to members has gone into their capital accounts rather than being distributed in cash. The policy has contributed enormously to the strength and stability of the co-operatives. Moreover, because the co-operatives are not free simply to lay off surplus workers they are driven to create new co-operatives and expand employment.
- *Structures and Systems for Governance and Management:* Mondragon has created both significant internal structures and a crucially important network of collaborating and supporting organizations. As well as providing for social security and unemployment compensation, the so-called Lagun-Aro plays an important role in placing members in other co-operatives when any one group is unable to provide jobs within its own group. The educational system, beginning with Escuela Politecnia, strengthened by the development of further research and educational institutes, provides members with knowledge and skills essential for Mondragon's future. Distinct social inventions include the financial institution, specifically designed to develop co-operatives, and the applied research institute, with its network of mutually supportive relations.

Mondragon also has several instruments of management systems and practices for shaping the work process. Some of these have been borrowed from abroad. For example, Mondragon modelled its initial management programme on the principles of scientific management propagated by F.W. Taylor. As they became increasingly aware of the limitations of these they reached out for guidance as to how to redesign work. They now speak of 'participatory management by objectives'.

13.6 Conclusion

HORIZONTAL AND VERTICAL SOCIAL INNOVATION NEEDS TO TAKE PLACE

What are the implications for our integral research, set here in the context of organizationally oriented action research generally, and socio-technical systems accompanied by industrial democracy specifically?

As we can see, *social innovation is an institutional, as well as a communal and a group process.* Specifically, the academic establishment hosting the research integrates it within its knowledge-creating and community-building orientation. In the process, a university as a public, private or civic enterprise is refocused on social innovation.

What is becoming ever more apparent, as we move from the humanistic (PAR) towards the more rationally based approaches to building socio-technical systems and industrial democracies, is that one requires the other, if a process of integral research with a view to social innovation is to take place. Moreover, the development of such democratic processes in the workplace, to accompany such evolving socio-technical systems, is likely to come to a halt if profounder shifts in the power balance, as the postmodernists would have called it, fail to come about. In other words, the formative build-up of new theories, for example ones dealing with enhanced participation, in the absence of a reformative approach to building open systems within and around organizations will fall on stony ground. Further, on a societal level, without the development of new postmodern norms around the power and participation of hitherto marginalised (race, class, and gender based) groups, actions on a group or organizational level are likely to fail. The kind of democratic and participative vision that the likes of Dewey and Lewin held will inevitably fail to materialise, unless horizontal and vertical social innovation takes place.

TOWARDS KNOWLEDGE CREATION AND OPEN SOCIETY

We have now completed the journey through the path of reason, towards the build-up of an open society. To that extent we have purposefully embarked, with the help of Popper and Hountondji, on theorizing, which for the latter is 'introverting theory', so that it is generated within rather than imposed upon a society. On a second level, through critical rationalism, we have built up, with the help of George Soros, an open society. Subsequently, with the support of Ziauddin Sardar, we have taken on board a Middle-Eastern, as well as a North-Western perspective. Finally, mediated through Arizmendi's Mondragon Co-operatives in the Spanish Basque country, as interpreted by American sociologist William Whyte, we have come up with a socio-technical design for corporate democracy.

After following progressively upon our research-to-innovation trajectory, your integral innovation should have come about, on an organizational and communal level, supporting knowledge creation (the Northern function of an enterprise or community) and, on a societal level, contributing to building open societies. The following table summarizes the entire Northern journey.

Northern Path of Reason *Knowledge Creation – Open Society*	
Theory *Originate*	*You categorize phenomena, breaking them into parts.* *You identify causal conditions,* events, incidents that led to them, using your head logically, always looking for connections.
Debate *Found*	You develop, scientifically, an organizing idea as *an opening hypothesis to bring some order to data,* quantitatively and qualitatively, proved or disproved through critical discussion.
Discourse *Emancipate*	No absolute ideology, social, political or technological system, governs your actions: you *pursue relative and fallible not absolute knowledge,* welcoming multiple discourses.
Design *Innovation*	You adopt a flexible, problem-solving orientation, aimed at social and technical betterment; you act as a friendly outsider, *using a co-generative approach to development.*

We would like to remind you, again, that while the four-level path to innovation may be presented here in linear form for ease of presentation, a full-fledged integral innovation is by no means a linear but rather a cycling, spiralling and iterating process. You could also call it an organic process, depicted in our integral innovation tree, with which we shall conclude this path. Note that, through the tree, we highlight here not only the particular path, but also the specific theme and social scientific disciplines that are most relevant for this Northern orientation.

Figure 13.5 The Integral Innovation Tree and the Northern Path of Reason

We now turn from the Northern path of reason to the Western path of realization.

References

1. Greenwood, D. and Levin, M. (2007). *Introduction to Action Research*. London: Sage.
2. Reason, P. and Bradbury, H. (2004). *Handbook of Action Research*. London: Sage.
3. Pateman, C. (1975). *Participation and Democracy*. Cambridge: Cambridge University Press.
4. Greenwood, D. and Levin, M. (2007). *Introduction to Action Research*. London: Sage.
5. Whyte, W. (1991). *Making Mondragon*. Ithaca, NY: Cornell University Press.
6. *Ibid.*

14 *From Experimental and Survey Methods to Empiricism*

Gather Relevant Data

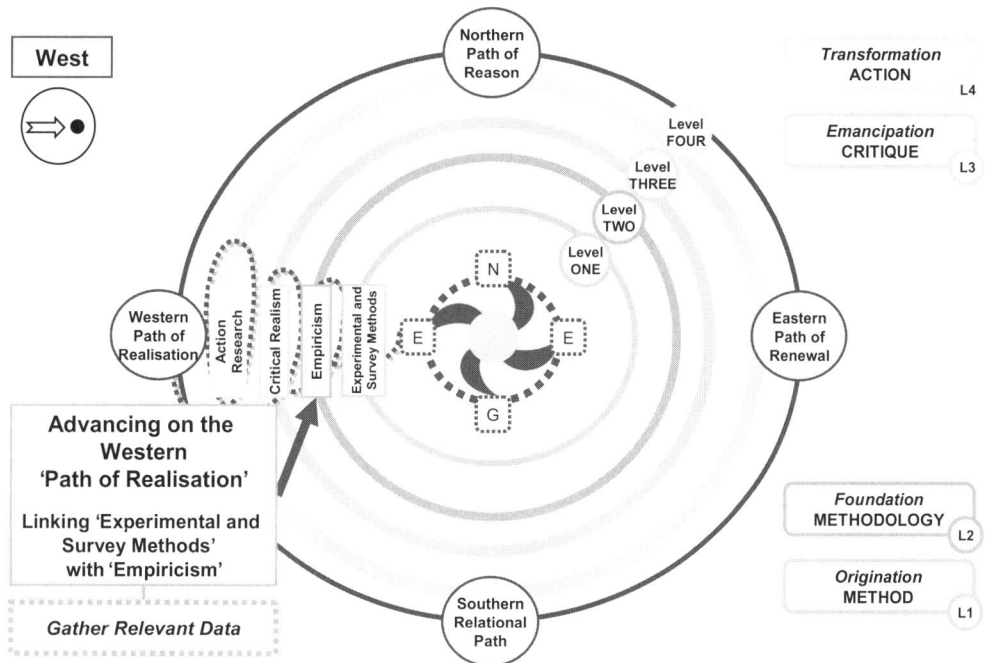

Figure 14.1 Overview Chapter 14 – Level 2/West

Summary: Empiricism

- We shall now immerse ourselves in the Western research path of realization. Building on the experimental and survey methods constituting the originating level one (method) of our Integral Research approach, we are now moving on to the foundational level 2 (methodology). Here we engage with empiricism.

- Empiricism is a theory of knowledge emphasizing the role of experience in the formation of ideas, while discounting the notion of innate ideas. Empiricism is closely related to positivism, seeking after the 'positive' facts rather than relying on pure faith or indeed dogma.

- Positivism incorporates a Western ontology of an ordered universe made up of atomistic, discrete and observable events, typified by the economic marketplace. Only that which can be observed, that is experienced by the senses, can be regarded as real. In such an epistemology, knowledge is seen to be derived from sensory experience by means of experimental or comparative analysis.

- Empiricism was spearheaded by such European luminaries as political scientists John Locke and David Hume, political economists Adam Smith and John Stuart Mill, and natural scientists Francis Bacon and Galileo Galilei. All together, these positivists were responsible for three of the major social innovations of the past 200 to 300 years: free markets, liberal democracy and classical scientific method itself in its classically Western vein.

- The success of the classical scientific 'method' is explained in terms of its ability to reveal the truth. Such a search for truth was assumed to be an intentional activity that reflected the needs of humanity and, as a consequence, secured human progress. In order to achieve progress, the researcher should deploy his capacity for reason within the methodological rules of scientific method.

- As the empiricist employs such 'scientific method' she searches for an assumed truth, seeks only for the 'positive' facts, distinguishes clearly between facts and values, collects observational data, builds theories and controls the research through 'closed systems'. The scientific experiment was Newton's way of artificially replicating the idea of a closed system, enabling researchers to isolate the objects they wish to investigate from all other objects, which would confuse the picture.

- Typical of such a 'closed' scientific orientation, especially in the 20th century, was the use of mechanical and experimental metaphors, along with a desire to emulate physics as the purest form of scientific activity. The idea of such 'closure' has been an important part of all scientific disciplines, which have sought to establish objective knowledge, including the social sciences.

- This metaphor of the 'closed system' becomes hugely problematic if it is accepted that social objects have an internal complexity and structure as a complex responsive open system. Yet the traditional 'quantitative' orientation, historically promoted by the physical sciences in the West, has reinforced the 'closed' nature of much research in the social sciences until this date.

- There is, however, hope. We shall illustrate, in the case presented in this chapter, the growing number of empirical economists worldwide, taking empiricist research out of its narrowly positivist perspective. Such empiricist research is then moving from a purely informative into a more reformative realm. Our example here is David McKibben's *Deep Economy*, which is providing 'empirical proof' of the dysfunctionality of the current economic growth paradigm, also laying the ground for the critical methodology introduced in the then following level 3: critical realism.

14.1 Orientation to Empiricism

Empiricism has certainly been the single most influential force in modern science. It is not only the core research orientation within the natural sciences, it has – until recently – also been the core research paradigm in the social sciences. We have highlighted various times in this book the danger and consequences of a predominating Western empiricist perspective and an isolated focus on such a methodology. However, empiricism, in our Integral Research framework, remains the foundation and an important ingredient of the Western path of realization, thereafter, as we shall see later, transcended by the emancipatory critique, that is critical realism (Chapter 15), and ultimately by an ultimately integral action research (Chapter 16).

Empiricism itself builds on experimental and survey methods, which have emerged out of the mode of 'doing'. Such 'doing' is not only the culmination of each of our research paths; it is also the particular emphasis of the Western path. The 'doing' hence is the crucial and ultimate culmination of our research; however, it needs to be an integral part of a whole. The Western perspective in isolation from the South, East and North has no sustainable ground to build on (as we can see from the desolate state of today's social sciences) and each path, without moving through its originating method, a foundational methodology and a substantive and emancipating critique, has little chance, so we argue, to build a sustainable, integral social innovation.

EMPIRICISM – A CONCEPTUAL OVERVIEW

Empiricism is a theory of knowledge emphasizing the role of experience in the formation of ideas, while discounting the notion of innate ideas. In the philosophy of science, empiricism is a theory of knowledge, which emphasizes those aspects of scientific knowledge that are closely related to experience, especially as formed through deliberate experimental arrangements.

Empiricism: The Term

The term 'empiricism' has a dual etymology. It comes from the Greek word εμπειρισμός, the Latin translation of which is *experientia*, from which we derive the word 'experience'. It also derives from a more specific classical Greek and Roman usage of 'empiric', referring to a physician whose skills derive from practical experience as opposed to instruction in theory. In fact, the term 'empirical' was originally used to refer to certain ancient Greek practitioners of medicine who rejected adherence to the dogmatic doctrines of the day, preferring instead to rely on the observation of phenomena as perceived in experience.

Empiricism is closely related to positivism, seeking after the 'positive' facts, rather than relying on pure faith or indeed dogma.

Positivism incorporates a Western ontology of an ordered universe made up of atomistic, discrete and observable events, typified by the economic marketplace. Only that which can be observed, that is experienced by the senses, can be regarded as real. In such an epistemology, knowledge is seen to be derived from sensory experience by means of experimental or comparative analysis.[1] Scientific theories are regarded as law-like statements, specifying simple relations or constant conjunctions between phenomena. Value judgements and normative statements require a separation of 'facts' and 'values'; furthermore values are denied the status of knowledge. The grounds for origination are lodged entirely and objectively in the external world 'out there', rather than in the internal and subjective world in yourself, as researcher and would-be social innovator. As a result, so-called objective-based survey methods, including questionnaires and structured interviews, incorporating also statistical controls, constitute the formative base to such.

Such scientific 'method' with its conventional procedure of observation, experimentation, and verification, emerged in the 17th century. It was forged out of a 'liberal' and reasoned Enlightenment reaction to the perceived dogmatism of religious orthodoxy in Europe. As such it was spearheaded by such European luminaries as political scientists John Locke and David Hume, political economists Adam Smith and John Stuart Mill, and natural scientists Francis Bacon and Galileo Galilei. These kindred spirits were the early advocates of democracy, free markets and the pursuit of the 'scientific' truth. In their day, they were all radical thinkers, staking their liberal claims – often risking their lives – against the conservative status quo. All together, these positivists were responsible for three of the major social innovations of the past 200 to 300 years: free markets and liberal democracy, and scientific method itself, in its classically Western vein.

EARLY FORMS OF EMPIRICISM

Early forms of empiricism include the epistemological works of Buddha,[2] Aristotle[3] and Church Father Thomas Aquinas. The first empiricists in Western philosophy were probably the Sophists (*ca.* 5th century BC), who rejected the rationalistic speculations about the nature of the world common among their predecessors, in favour of focusing 'on such relatively concrete entities as man and society'. The Sophists invoked sceptical semantic arguments, using examples that could be readily seen and observed by others, to undermine the claims of pure reason.

Among the medieval Scholastics, Thomas Aquinas derived from Aristotle the famous axiom: 'Nothing is in the intellect which was not first in the senses.' Aquinas argued that the existence of God could be proved by reasoning from sense data.[4] He used a variation on the Aristotelian notion of the 'active intellect', which he interpreted as the ability to abstract universal meanings from particular empirical data.

ORIGINS OF MODERN EMPIRICISM: LOCKE, HUME, BACON

The doctrine of empiricism was first explicitly formulated by John Locke in the 17th century. Locke argued that the mind is a *tabula rasa* ('clean slate' or 'blank tablet'; Locke used the words 'white paper') on which experiences leave their marks. Such empiricism denies that humans have innate ideas or that anything is knowable without reference to experience.

Locke made however an important exception: he, for his part, held that some knowledge (for example, knowledge of God's existence) could be arrived at through intuition and reasoning alone.

Earlier concepts of the existence of 'innate ideas' were the subject of debate between the Continental rationalists and the British empiricists in the 17th century to the late

18th century. John Locke, David Hume and Francis Bacon were among the primary exponents of empiricism.

Responding to the continental 'rationalism' most prominently defended by René Descartes, John Locke, writing in the late 17th century, in his *An Essay Concerning Human Understanding* (1689), proposed a new, and ultimately very influential view wherein the only knowledge humans can have is *a posteriori*, that is based upon experience.

Locke's ideas had enormous influence on the development of political philosophy, and he is widely regarded as one of the most influential Enlightenment thinkers and contributors to liberal theory. His writings influenced Voltaire and Rousseau, many Scottish Enlightenment thinkers, as well as the American revolutionaries. This influence is reflected in the American Declaration of Independence.

Locke's theory of mind is often cited as the origin for modern conceptions of identity and 'the self'; it figured prominently in the works of later philosophers such as David Hume, Jean-Jacques Rousseau and Immanuel Kant. Locke was the first philosopher to define the self through a continuity of 'consciousness.'

The Scottish philosopher David Hume added to the empiricist viewpoint an extreme scepticism. Via his sceptical arguments he maintained that all knowledge, even the most basic beliefs about the natural world, cannot be conclusively established by reason. Rather, he maintained, our beliefs are more a result of accumulated habits, developed in response

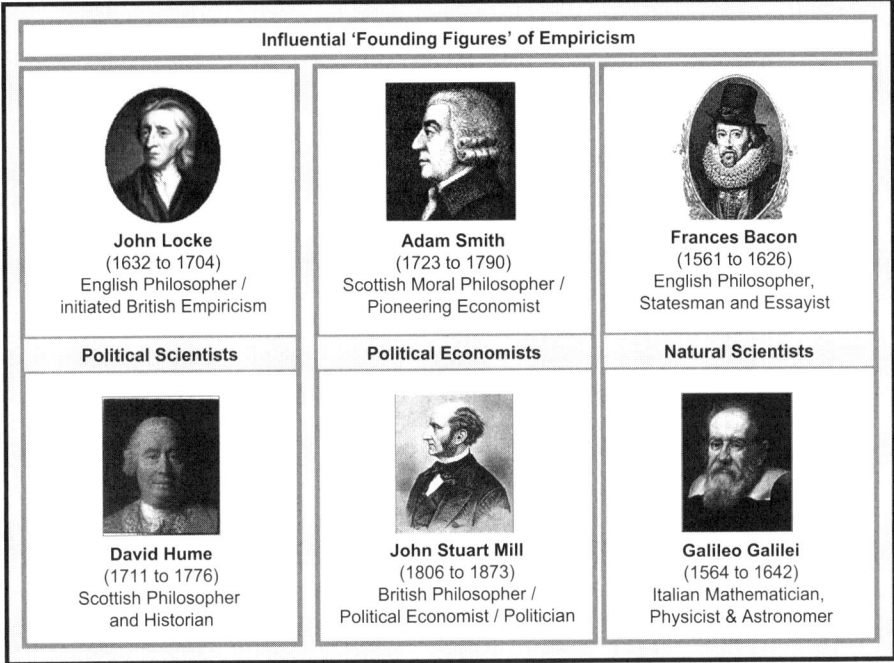

Figure 14.2 Empiricism – Core Thinkers

Sources: Image 1: OldCoyote http://oldcoyote.wordpress.com/. Image 2: Bluepete (Blog) http://www. blupete.com. Image 3: Jochen Ebmeier (Blog) http://ebmeierjochen.wordpress.com/. Image 4: Christers. net http://www.christers.net/philosophy. Image 5: University of York http://www.york.ac.uk/. Image 6: Solarnavigator http://www.solarnavigator.net/

to accumulated sense experiences.[5] Among his many arguments Hume also added another important slant to the debate about scientific method – that of the problem of induction. Hume argued that it requires inductive reasoning, that is generating theories from facts or data, rather than the other way around, to arrive at the premises for the principle of inductive reasoning, and therefore the justification for inductive reasoning is a circular argument. Among Hume's conclusions regarding the problem of induction is that there is no certainty that the future will resemble the past. Thus, as a simple instance posed by Hume, we cannot know with certainty by inductive reasoning that the sun will continue to rise in the east, but instead come to expect it to do so because it has repeatedly done so in the past.[6]

Hume concluded that such things as belief in an external world and belief in the existence of the self were not rationally justifiable. According to Hume these beliefs were to be accepted nonetheless because of their profound basis in instinct and custom. Hume's lasting legacy, however, was the doubt that his sceptical arguments cast on the legitimacy of inductive reasoning, allowing many sceptics who followed to cast similar doubt.[7]

Francis Bacon, who is best known as a philosophical advocate and defender of the scientific revolution, established and popularised the inductive methodology for scientific inquiry, often called the Baconian method or simply the scientific method. In the context of his time such methods were connected with the occult trends of hermeticism and alchemy, against which the empiricist Bacon reacted. His resultant demand for a planned procedure of investigating all things marked a new turn on the framework for science, much of which still surrounds conceptions of proper methodology today. His dedication to experimental science brought him however into a rare historical group of scientists who were killed by their own experiments.[8]

EMPIRICISM AND THE RISE OF ECONOMICS

Empiricism also gave rise to a new discipline called economics. The Scottish philosopher Adam Smith, who is depicted on the back of today's Bank of England £20 note, was probably the most pioneering thinker in this field. It was Smith's systematic studies of the historical development of industry and commerce in Europe that led to his famous treatises: *The Theory of Moral Sentiments* (1759),[9] and *An Inquiry into the Nature and Causes of the Wealth of Nations* (1776).[10] Smith's work helped to create the modern academic discipline of economics and provided one of the best-known intellectual rationales for free trade, capitalism and libertarianism. In the empirically laden process, of course, his latter book on the wealth of nations proceeded to eclipse the former, much less popular work.

Smith libertarian ideas were taken forward by John Stuart Mill whose early economic philosophy was one of free markets. Mill's *Principles of Political Economy*,[11] first published in 1848, was one of the most widely read of all books on economics in the period. As Adam Smith's *Wealth of Nations* had during an earlier period, Mill's *Principles* dominated economics teaching, in England then, and today in the wider world.

EMPIRICISM AND THE RISE OF A NEW NATURAL SCIENCE

The Italian physicist, mathematician and astronomer Galileo Galilei is also closely associated with the scientific revolution. His achievements include the first systematic studies of uniformly accelerated motion, improvements to the telescope, a variety of astronomical observations and support for Copernicanism. Galileo's experiment-based work is a significant break from the abstract approach of Aristotle.

Galileo is often referred to as the 'father of modern physics', and as the 'father of science'. The motion of uniformly accelerated objects, treated in nearly all high school and introductory college physics courses, was studied by Galileo as the subject of kinematics. Galileo pioneered the use of quantitative experiments whose results could be analysed with mathematical precision. He recognized that his experimental data would never agree exactly with any theoretical or mathematical form, because of the imprecision of measurement, irreducible friction and other factors.

Although he tried to remain loyal to the Catholic Church, Galileo's adherence to experimental results, and their most honest interpretation, led to his rejection of blind allegiance to authority, both philosophical and religious, in matters of science. In broader terms, this helped separate science from philosophy and religion, a major development in human thought. Albert Einstein, in appreciation, called Galileo the 'father of modern science'. According to Stephen Hawking, Galileo probably contributed more to the creation of the modern natural sciences than anybody else.

We now turn to the key tenets of empiricism.

14.2 Empiricism – Key Tenets: Searching for Truth in Closed Systems

Empiricism – Key Tenets
①   Search for truth.
②   Seek after the 'positive facts'.
③   Separate facts and values.
④   Collect observational data and build theories.
⑤   Control the research through 'closed systems'.

① SEARCH FOR TRUTH

The search for truth is assumed to be an intentional activity that reflects the needs of humanity and, as a consequence, secures human progress. In order to achieve scientific progress, you should deploy your capacity for reason within the methodological rules of scientific method. Scientific statements are seen as pictures or snapshots of the things they refer to. Reality for the empiricist is made up of atomistic, discrete and observable experiences and events. Hence, one of the core 'instruments' of the positivist is the method of induction. Such a method refers to a logical process of constructing knowledge about observed relationships between variables in particular instances.

② SEEK AFTER THE 'POSITIVE FACTS'

The empiricist seeks after the 'positive' facts, rather than relying on pure faith or indeed dogma. Only that which can be observed, that is experienced by the senses, can be regarded as real. Knowledge is seen to be derived from sensory experience by means of experimental or comparative analysis.

The logical positivist uses induction to collect observational data and build theories to explain the observations. Thus the method of induction involves two movements simultaneously: from the particular to the general, and from observed events to theoretical constructions.

③ SEPARATE FACTS AND VALUES

Value judgements and normative statements require a separation of 'facts' and 'values'; furthermore values are denied of having the status of knowledge. The grounds for origination are lodged entirely and objectively in the external world 'out there', rather than in the internal and subjective world, in yourself, as researcher and would-be social innovator. As a result, so-called objective-based survey methods, including questionnaires and structured interviews, also incorporating statistical controls, constitute the formative base to such.

④ COLLECT OBSERVATIONAL DATA AND BUILD THEORIES

The logical positivist uses induction to collect observational data and build theories to explain the observations. The method of induction refers to a logical process of constructing knowledge about observed relationships between variables in particular instances. This can be taken as a basis for making universal generalizations in as yet unobserved, particular instances. As a researcher you identify a limited number of variables and observe their behaviour and changes of one in relation with the other. Therefore, you identify factors which are significant so their effect can be observed and you pinpoint which factor actually causes the observed outcome to occur.

⑤ CONTROL THE RESEARCH THROUGH 'CLOSED SYSTEMS'

Research happens within 'closed systems', enabling you as a researcher to isolate the objects you wish to investigate from all other objects, which would confuse the picture. Such a 'closed system' research – means in addition to the identification of variables and the observation of their behaviour – that you avoid any interference from unexpected external forces. Exclusion clauses ensure that the mass of possible influences is screened out (*ceteris paribus*). It is you who controls the situation by manipulating variables.

We shall now have a close look at empiricism, a core expression of the positivist worldview, which has its purer pedigree in the natural sciences.

14.3 Empiricism in Depth

THE NATURE AND SCOPE OF CLASSICAL SCIENTIFIC METHOD

For Open University based social scientist Mark Smith in the UK, in his *Social Science in Question*,[12] the success of the scientific 'method' is specifically explained in terms of its ability to reveal the truth.

Such a search for truth was assumed to be an intentional activity that reflected the needs of humanity and, as a consequence, secured human progress. Each part of the circuit is defined through its relationship with the others. In order to achieve progress, we should deploy our capacity for reason within the methodological rules of scientific method, in order to establish the truth of a situation and use this as a means of serving the needs of humanity. These were the roots of so-called 'positivism', today seen in much more traditional, and now conservative guise in the social sciences than hitherto. However, in more recent years during the 20th century, the radical nature and scope of such theorists has been dissipated, and they have come to represent the status quo, at least in Western secular terms. Let us explore further the link between the empirical methods and the positivist philosophy underlying them, drawing upon the even more refined version of such empiricism: 'logical positivism'.

THE INDUCTIVELY BASED LOGICAL POSITIVIST APPROACH

Logical positivism placed an exceptional emphasis upon sensory perception and the role of observation in research as the foundation for knowledge. Scientific statements were seen as pictures or snapshots of the things they refer to. The more contemporary origins go back to England's Bertrand Russell and Austria's Ludwig Wittgenstein subsequently promoted by the Vienna Circle from the 1920s. To each object, they maintained, corresponds a definite statement. For Austrian Rudolf Carnap, an influential member of the circle, this approach was identified as 'physicalism'.

The logical positivist uses induction to collect observational data and build theories to explain the observations. Thus the method of induction involves two movements simultaneously: from the particular to the general, and from observed events to theoretical constructions. Such induction, with its focus on doing, can be compared with deduction (focus on knowing), retroduction (oriented towards becoming) and abduction (linked with being).

To summarize, the method of induction refers to a logical process of constructing knowledge about observed relationships between variables in particular instances. This can be taken as a basis for making universal generalizations in as yet unobserved, particular instances. The strength of induction lies in its appeal to data collected through human senses, rather than perceived intuitively or conceived abstractly, as a means of validating propositions. The explanatory power of this approach is said to rest upon its predictive uses. However, such prediction tends to be restricted to 'closed' systems.

CLOSED SYSTEMS TAKE PRECEDENCE OVER OPEN SYSTEMS

Typical of such a 'closed' scientific orientation, especially in the 20th century, was the use of mechanical and experimental metaphors, along with a desire to emulate physics as the purest form of scientific activity. Indeed, experimental method was correlated with scientific method. Newton (1642–1727), for example, in his study of matter, motion and light, was developing the method of induction by using observations of particular conditions – experimenting with light through the use of prisms and pieces of white card – as a foundation for constructing a general theoretical account of light. Within such a closed system it is possible to:

- identify a limited number of variables;
- observe their behaviour, the frequency of changes in one in relation to the other;
- account for or avoid any interference from unexpected external forces.

The scientific experiment was Newton's way of artificially replicating the idea of a closed system, enabling researchers to isolate the objects they wish to investigate from all other objects, which would confuse the picture. Identifying simple relations between discrete things would enable a scientist to understand and explain events beyond the experimental situation. The idea of such 'closure' has been an important part of all scientific disciplines which have sought to establish objective knowledge, including the social sciences. In psychology, for example, such experimental closure involves the physical separation of human beings from their normal context, and subjecting them to particular stimuli with a view to gauging their response.

Closed and Open Systems		
	Closed Systems	**Open Systems**
Simplicity and Complexity	A limited number of variables is involved to increase the possibility of identifying and predicting clear relationships.	A 'state of complexity' is acknowledged as the condition of one's object of analysis and the relation between them.
External Boundary	Exclusion clauses ensure that the mass of possible influences are screened out (ceteris paribus).	Each object can be part of multiple relationships and no outcome can be predicted.
Intrinsic Properties	All objects of analysis are taken at face value so that the intrinsic properties of an object are not taken into account.	It is recognized that all objects have intrinsic properties and structures affecting performance in different conditions.

Through theoretical closure, in econometric models for example, the economy is replicated as a series of variables and relationships through a computer programme, including growth measures, the money supply, manufacturing output, employment levels and prices. The relationships between the variables are conceived of in terms of the susceptibility of one variable to changes in the others. No model though, however elaborate, can mirror or replicate the uncertainties or complexities of the real economy. Furthermore, statistical closure involves a situation in which quantitative numerical data sets are processed to identify correlations, as for example with the study of voting behaviour. As soon as the complexity of social life is acknowledged in social research, though, these techniques for simulating closure are problematized and the status of causal laws produced in this way is dramatically altered. This problem is accentuated if it is accepted that social objects have an internal complexity and structure as a complex responsive open system (see table). Yet the traditional 'quantitative' orientation, historically promoted by the physical sciences in the West, has reinforced the 'closed' nature of such a 'positivist' epistemology. This applies as much to experimental research method as it does to positivist research methodology.

POSITIVIST EPISTEMOLOGY IN THE SOCIAL SCIENCES

Such positivist approaches to the social sciences often exclusively claim the label of 'scientific', for they assume things can be studied as hard facts, and the relationship between these facts established as solid, empirically based, scientific laws. For such positivists, these laws have the status of truth as social objects, and can be studied in much the same way as natural objects. Not surprisingly, classical economics, with its belief in 'market mechanisms' is heavily influenced by positivism.

The most influential early positivist in the social sciences was France's Auguste Comte (1798–1857). He brought together the search for the truth with his faith in progress. To replace 'divine truths', Comte looked to the natural sciences, calling his approach 'social physics'. Comte sought to identify the laws of social statics and social dynamics with a view to social engineering. The English utilitarian Jeremy Bentham, following in Comte's footsteps, characterized human beings as pleasure seeking or pain avoiding, based on their making rational choices. This approach treated aggregate bodies as the total of individual actors, with a view to gaining 'the greatest good for the greatest number'. The economy is thus an aggregate of individuals, firms and households; the political process is an aggregate of voters in elections and parties and pressure groups. We now turn, problematically as we shall see, to global variations.

14.4 Global Variations of Empiricism

THE LOCAL-GLOBAL EMPIRICAL CONUNDRUM

Unlike the other three classical methodologies of Integral Research's level 2 (that is phenomenology, hermeneutics and critical rationalism), each of which has been evolved and adapted in other parts of the world, empiricism remains a homegrown Western product. In other words, and because (at least in its pure form) it is alien to the North, East and South, if not also the Middle East, it has no explicitly global variations. Actually, in our own experience, working in such far-flung places as in China and India, Africa and South-East Asia, it tends to be misused, rather than evolved, in these places. In other words, research-wise, it became something like a lowest common denominator.

One of us will never forget an experience during the early stages of a doctoral thesis being undertaken by one of our Jordanian participants, Mohammad Al Zoubi, and author in our series, a civil servant and member of a prominent local family, in Jordan and Syria. Working on a topic connected with globalization and its economic impact on his society, he asked Ronnie Lessem, at their first session together, 'What do you think are my independent and dependent variables?'. Needless to say Ronnie's answer was 'I would not start from there.'

Although empiricism has not evolved geographically through global variations, over the course of time such an empirical-pragmatic course of evolution has taken place in the Anglo-Saxon world.

EMERGING PRAGMATISM

In the late 19th century and early 20th century several forms of pragmatic philosophy arose out of empiricism. The ideas of pragmatism developed mainly from discussions that took place while Charles Sanders Peirce and William James were both at Harvard in the 1870s. James popularized the term 'pragmatism', giving Peirce full credit for its patrimony, but Peirce later demurred from the tangents that the movement was taking, and redubbed what he regarded as the original idea with the name of 'pragmaticism'. Along with its pragmatic theory of truth, this perspective integrates the basic insights of empirical (experience-based) and rational (concept-based) thinking.

Charles Peirce (1839–1914) was highly influential in laying the groundwork for today's empirical scientific method. Although Peirce severely criticized many elements of Descartes' peculiar brand of rationalism, he did not reject rationalism outright. Indeed, he concurred with the main ideas of rationalism, most importantly the idea that rational concepts can be meaningful and the idea that rational concepts necessarily go beyond the data given by empirical observation. In later years he even emphasized the concept-driven side of the then ongoing debate between strict empiricism and strict rationalism, in part to counterbalance the excesses to which some of his cohorts had taken pragmatism under the 'data-driven' strict-empiricist view.

Among Peirce's major contributions was to place inductive reasoning (data come first) and deductive reasoning (theory comes first) in a complementary rather than competitive mode, the latter of which had been the primary trend among the educated since David Hume wrote a century before. To this, Peirce added the concept of abductive reasoning, evoked directly out of people's life worlds, which we have identified with our relational research path. The combined three forms of reasoning serve as a primary conceptual foundation for the empirically based scientific method today. Peirce's approach 'presupposes that firstly the objects of knowledge are real things, secondly the characters (properties) of real things do not depend on our perceptions of them, and thirdly everyone who has sufficient experience of real things will agree on the truth about them'. In his Harvard *Lectures on Pragmatism* (1903), Peirce enumerated what he called the 'three contrary propositions of pragmatism', saying that they 'put the edge on the maxim of pragmatism'.[13]

The renowned US social philosopher and educationalist John Dewey (1859–1952) who became one of the founding fathers of 'action research' (see Chapters 13 and 16), built on such theories on pragmatism to form a theory known as 'instrumentalism'. The role of sense experience in Dewey's theory is crucial, in that he saw experience as unified totality of things through which everything else is interrelated. Dewey's basic thought, in accordance with empiricism, was that reality is determined by past experience. Therefore, humans adapt their past experiences of things to perform experiments upon and test the pragmatic values of such experience. The value of such experience is measured by scientific instruments, and the results of such measurements generate ideas which serve as instruments for future experimentation. Thus, ideas in Dewey's system retain their empiricist flavour in that they are only known *a posteriori*.[14]

Finally, we can see today that a broadly based empiricism, and indeed pragmatism, can lead to factual observations that serve to transcend the conventional wisdom on free market economics (see 'deep economics' below).

14.5 Empiricism in Practice: The Wealth of Community

GROWING ECONOMIC INEQUALITY

Though the American economy in recent decades has been thriving, income inequality between rich and poor has been growing. The median wage in the US is the same as what it was 30 years ago. More than 80 countries have seen per capita incomes fall in the last decade. Basically almost all of the growing wealth accumulates in a few pockets. The 2006 tax cuts, for example, delivered 70 per cent of their benefits to the richest 5 per cent of Americans. Alongside the exhilaration of the flattening earth, celebrated by journalist Thomas Friedman, the plane is containing an increasing number of flattened people, flattened by the very forces that are making the few, for McKibben, wildly rich.[15]

When Thomas Newcomen launched the Industrial Revolution, he was using coal to pump water out of a coalmine. The birth of the Industrial Revolution was all about fossil fuel. We have learnt an enormous amount in the past two centuries through our ever-growing body of scientific knowledge, but coal and oil and natural gas are still at the bottom of it all. Now it is plausible, indeed likely, that if we run short of such; our lives may fundamentally change as scarcity of energy wreaks havoc. Moreover, even before we run short of energy we are running short of planet. If the Chinese, by 2030, are to become as rich as Americans are, they will consume 20 million more barrels of oil per day than the entire world consumption today.

Then There is Global Warming

Then there is global warming. All of those pools of oil and beds of coal beneath our feet are being drilled and dug. For a brief moment the resulting energy burns and does something useful: moves your car, heats you shower. But after that instant of combustion most of the carbon in the coal or oil mixes with oxygen in the air to form the gas carbon dioxide, which drifts into the atmosphere, creating almost a mirror image of the reservoir you drilled it from in the first place. The molecular structure of carbon dioxide than traps heat from the sun that would otherwise radiate back into space. That is what global warming is – the gaseous remains of all fields and coal beds acting like an insulating blanket. The year 2005 was the warmest on record, and nine of the ten hottest years were in the decade that preceded it. Indeed everything frozen on earth is now melting and melting fast. And climate change has only just begun! The WHO expects vast changes in mosquito-borne diseases, as just one result, warning that climate change could kill 184 million people in Africa alone before the century is out. Humans have never been responsible for anything potentially more destructive, not even the invention of nuclear weapons.

While American industry may be using less energy per dollar's worth of stuff it produces, as the knowledge-based economy takes hold, so much more stuff is produced per year that the carbon emission totals keep rising. Between 1990 and 2003, for example, annual emissions increased by 16 per cent.

The Advent of Ecological Economics

The creeping recognition that economics, even in its ever-growing mathematical sophistication, has become abstracted from the actual planet we inhabit, has spurred the steady development of an increasingly impressive new school of ecological economics. As far back as the 1960s economists like Kenneth Boulding were at work on what he termed 'the economics of the coming spaceship earth'. In the 1970s, a World Bank economist, Herman Daly, published a collection titled *Toward a Steady State Economy* that actually began to nose around the question whether perpetual growth was possible. And by the 1980s Daly, together with Bob Constanza, had formed the Society of Ecological Economics.

At the same time, the last decade has seen one effort after another to replace, or at least supplement, gross national product as the measure of our success. Under the current system, all we do is add together expenditures so that the most 'economically productive' citizen is a cancer patient who fills up his car with petrol on the way to meet his divorce lawyer. Instead many have proposed a 'green national product' or an 'index of sustainable economic welfare'.

Towards Happiness and Satisfaction

For McKibben, ideas like happiness and satisfaction have traditionally been waved aside by economists as poetic irrelevancies, when compared with 'utility maximization'. Such a conventional economic theory holds that every time a person buys something, sells something, quits a job or invests, he is making a rational decision about what will provide him 'maximum utility'. In recent years, however, something new has happened. In 2002, Daniel Kahneman, trained as a psychologist, won the Nobel Prize in economics. In his book *Well-Being* he announced the development of a new field called 'hedonics', defined as 'the study of what makes experience and life pleasant or unpleasant'.

The idea that there is a state called 'happiness', and that we can dependably figure out what it feels like and how to measure it, is extremely subversive. It would allow economists to start thinking about life in far richer terms, allow them to stop asking 'What did you buy?', and start asking 'Is your life good?' On average, all of us in the West are living lives materially more abundant than most people did a generation ago. What's odd is that is does not seem to have made us happier. In 1946, according to McKibben, the United States was the happiest country amongst four advanced economies; 30 years later it was eighth amongst the 11 most advanced; a decade later it ranked 10th among 23.

In the United Kingdom, for instance, gross national product per capita grew 66 per cent between 1973 and 2001, yet people's satisfaction with their lives changed not at all. Japan saw a fivefold increase between 1958 and 1986 without any reported increase in satisfaction. In one place after another, rates of alcoholism, suicide and depression have gone up dramatically, even as the amount of stuff has accumulated. If satisfaction was our goal, therefore, the vast expenditure of effort and resources since 1950 has been largely a waste. For the peasant farmer in China, for example and on the other hand, a boost in income brings tangible benefits. Up to a certain point, income-wise, more does certainly mean better. So China's relentless growth – 9 per cent per year for the last couple of decades – has indeed lifted lots of people out of poverty and made their lives happier. McKibben cites researchers as saying that up to $10,000 per annum money does buy happiness, and then the correlation disappears.

Where then did we go wrong? The answer is obvious! We kept doing something past the point where it worked. Since happiness had increased with income in the past we assumed it would continue to do so in the future. At the time of Adam Smith a concern with economic issues was understandably primary. Meeting simple human needs for food, shelter and clothing was not assured, and satisfying these needs moved lockstep with better economics. In 1820 the average American earned the equivalent, in current dollars, to the present African average. In what Richard Layard calls a 'cultural lag', market democracies continue to emphasize the themes that have brought them to the current position. As he says in the conclusion to his book *Happiness*: 'Utilitarianism is the guiding philosophy of our time, but theories of what produces happiness have changed since Bentham'. We need, in short, a new utilitarianism.

THE WEALTH OF COMMUNITIES

Starting with Energy

Perhaps we should start by thinking about energy in new ways. Instead of something that you buy from far away, energy becomes something you help make and distribute to your neighbours. By their very nature, fuels like solar and wind are diffuse and dispersed: instead of a few people digging them from the ground, a great many of us can harvest energy from the planet's surface. To make localized power generation work you need community. Ask yourself why Japan leads the world in building a decentralized solar-panel energy economy. Because it has so much sun (it does not)? Or because it has so much fellowship? People in Japan feel they are able to trust each other.

Consolidation or Localization

If our larger society, moreover, is running up against the realization that 'more is not necessarily better', then one of the alternatives is to think on a different scale. And, for McKibben, food may be the place to begin. A Harvard Business School professor recently reported that 'fifty per cent of the world's assets and consumer expenditure belong to food system'. Half the jobs too. The 'food system' in America has been made over in the name of efficiency and growth as much as any other: the average bite of food has travelled 1500 miles before it reaches our lips.

The self-sufficient all round farms with which the colonists covered the country have largely disappeared, at least outside Amish country. But there is now an exception to this trend: the quick spread in the last decade of 'community-supported agriculture' or the CSA farm. Consumers pay farmers a few hundred dollars apiece in midwinter and then are supplied with a weekly bin of incredibly diverse vegetables throughout the growing season and deep into autumn. Almost every corner of America now has a CSA nearby.

From America to Cuba – Semi-sustainable Agriculture

Surprisingly, in Cuba, new farming 'technologies' are emerging that are the most exciting inventions of our age, for McKibben perhaps more exciting than even the iPod or the Internet. The unlikely scene for a major such experiment is Havana. With the sudden collapse of the Soviet Union, Cuba fell off a cliff of its own and became the first place in the world to face peak oil. All those tractors and combines had been products of an insane 'economics' underwritten by the Eastern bloc for ideological purposes. Castro spent three decades growing sugar and shipping it to Russia and East Germany, both of which paid a price well above the world level, sending the ships back to Havana equipped with rice, wheat and oil, and more tractors. When all of that disappeared, virtually overnight, Cuba had nowhere to turn. In other words it became truly an island, not just a real one, but an island outside the international economic system.

During the Soviet era much of what Cubans ate came straight from Eastern Europe, and most of the rest was grown industrial style, on the big state farms. All those combines needed fuel and spare parts, and all those long rows of grain and vegetables needed pesticides and fertilizer, none of which were available any longer. What happened was simple, though unexpected. Cuba learned to stop exporting sugar and instead started raising its own food again, growing it on small private farms and in thousands of pocket-sized urban market gardens. Since the country lacked fertilizers the food became de facto organic. Cubans produce as much food today as they did before the collapse of the Soviet Union. In so doing, they have created what may be the world's largest working model of a semi-sustainable agriculture, which has benefited enormously from Castro's lavish spending on education, organic farming being no simple task. In fact, its new agricultural system is no less of an invention as the tractor farming it replaced. In the interim, back in the United States, the country had 340 farmers' markets in 1970, 1,700 in 1994, and 3,700 in 2004. CSA farms meanwhile have grown from just one in 1985 to 1500 today.

Changing Course

For McKibben, if the rich countries of the world cannot change course, then the poor countries will not. America's biggest exports are television programmes and movies – modelling its idea of the good life, wildly out of scale with the rest of the world and what it can deliver. If we continue to idolize the likes of a Donald Trump, the Chinese will create their own versions of him. If America cannot move away from the ideal of the hyper-individual, then much of the world will keep running in the same direction. So first-world countries must become less growth oriented and more locally rooted. What then should development in the future look like? It should look to the local far more than to the global. It should concentrate on creating and sustaining strong communities, not creating a culture of economic individualism. It should worry less about what is ideal from a classical economist's view of markets, and far more about what is ecologically possible. It should aim not at growth but at durability. It should avoid the romantic fantasies offered by the prophets of endless wealth in favour of the blunter realism of people holding out for each other, as they have done over millennia of human existence.

14.6 Conclusion

THE EMPIRICAL BEREFT OF THE INTEGRAL

We highlighted in this chapter the limitations of an empiricism, which acts in isolation and is bereft of an integral perspective. While the same applies to any one, single method or methodology, the fact that empiricism is the most commonplace one worldwide makes these limitations more marked. Indeed, it was this isolated and unrelated (to context) perspective that gave rise, in the 19th century, to phenomenology.

That having been said, there are a number of strengths that empiricism, well used, brings to the table in the social sciences. Specifically, it is overtly practical, seemingly evidence based and coherently argued. It clearly presents a particular perspective, argues its case demonstrably and incorporates many well-researched facts and figures to back up its overall argument.

However, its weakness often lies in its surface nature, unable to accommodate the depths of a particular nature and culture, as seen 'through local eyes'. Often, the actual faces or voices that (locally) belong to the researched context are not seen or heard. They remain silent.

Moreover, and historically, there is no acknowledgement, or indeed reporting, on what has come before. Empiricism, in most cases, does not embed the research in its larger historical or societal context. Its mode of comprehension, while full of facts and figures, is bereft of a particular life world; history or philosophy are often left out of empirical account.

Reformative and Transformative Left out of Account

In such a narrowly empirical form, there is no attempt to co-create a new world, simultaneous to investigating it. As a result, a purely empirically based research, lacking integral credentials, is unable to pave the way for any form of social innovation, or indeed social and economic transformation.

It is for that reason that we now turn from empiricism to critical realism, from what is observable and measurable to, in addition, the underlying, generative forces. It is hence time, to enter the third level of 'critique'. Here on our Western path of realization, critical realism will probe beyond the empirical surface, and take us a step further to innovation.

References

1. Markie, P. (2004). 'Rationalism versus Empiricism.' In Edward D. Zalta (ed.), *Stanford Encyclopedia of Philosophy* . Palo Alto, CA: Stanford University.
2. Kalupahana, D.J. (January 1969). *A Buddhist Tract on Empiricism*. Honolulu: University of Hawaii Press.
3. Aristotle (2007). *Posterior Analytics*. Translated by G.R.G. Mure. Adelaide: University of Adelaide.
4. *Macmillan Encyclopedia of Philosophy* (1969). Thomas Aquinas. Subsection on 'Theory of Knowledge'. Vol. 8, pp. 106–107. New York: Macmillan.

5. Hume, D. (1975). *A Treatise of Human Nature*. L.A. Selby-Bigge (ed.). London: Oxford University Press.

6. Hume, D. (1902). 'An Enquiry Concerning Human Understanding.' In L.A. Selby-Bigge (ed.) *Enquiries Concerning the Human Understanding and Concerning the Principles of Morals*, 2nd edition. Oxford: Oxford University Press.

7. Chisolm, R. (1948). 'The Problem of Empiricism.' *Journal of Philosophy* 45, 512–17.

8. Achinstein, P. and Barker, S.F. (1969). *The Legacy of Logical Positivism: Studies in the Philosophy of Science*. Baltimore, MD: Johns Hopkins University Press.

9. Smith, A. (1759). *The Theory of Moral Sentiments*. Oxford and New York: Oxford University Press.

10. Smith, A. (1759). *An Inquiry into the Nature and Causes of the Wealth of Nations*. Oxford and New York: Oxford University Press.

11. Mill, J.S. (1848). *Principles of Political Economy*. Oxford and New York: Oxford University Press.

12. Smith, M. (2000). *Social Science in Question*. London, Thousand Oaks, CA, and New Delhi: Open University Press.

13. Peirce, C.S. (March to May 1903). *Lectures on Pragmatism*. Cambridge. Reprinted in part, Collected Papers, CP 5.14–212. Reprinted with Introduction and Commentary: Turisi, P.A. (ed.) (1997). Pragmatism as a Principle and a Method of Right Thinking: The 1903 Harvard 'Lectures on Pragmatism'. Albany: State University of New York Press. Reprinted, pp. 133–241, Peirce Edition Project (eds), The Essential Peirce, Selected Philosophical Writings, Volume 2 (1893–1913), Bloomington: Indiana University Press, 1998 .

14. Dewey, J. (1906). *Studies in Logical Theory*. Chicago, IL: The University of Chicago Press.

15. McKibben, B. (2007). *Deep Economy: The Wealth of Communities and the Durable Future*. New York: Times Books.

15 *From Empiricism to Critical Realism*

Discover Underlying Reality

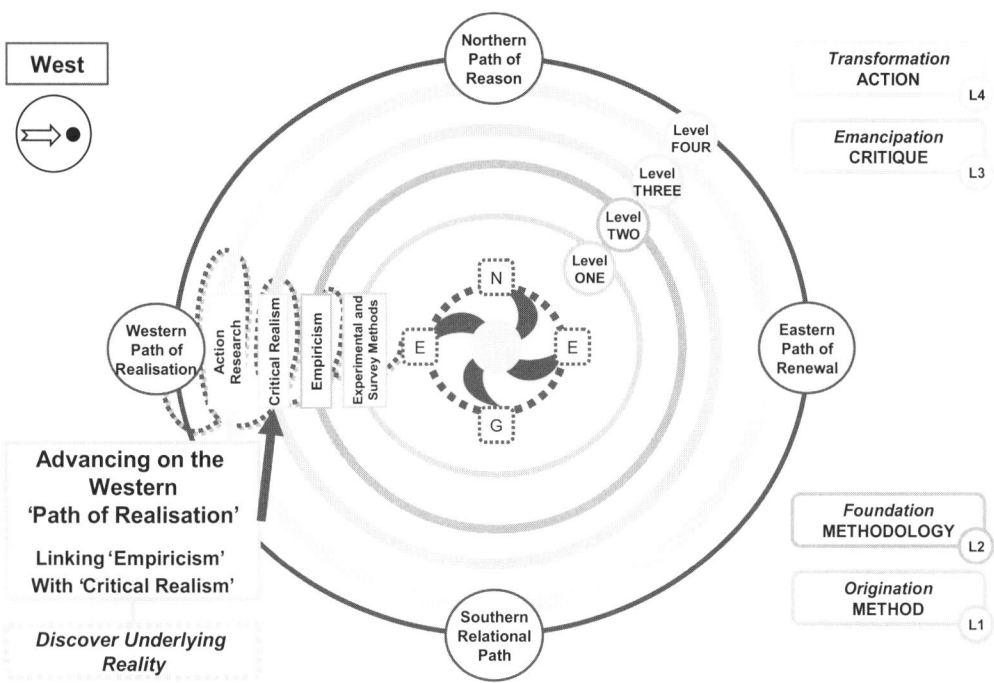

West

Northern
Path of
Reason

Transformation
ACTION
L4

Level
FOUR

Emancipation
CRITIQUE
L3

Level
THREE

Level
TWO

Level
ONE

Western
Path of
Realisation

Action Research

Critical Realism

Empiricism

Experimental and
Survey Methods

N

E

E

G

Eastern
Path of
Renewal

**Advancing on the
Western
'Path of Realisation'**

Linking 'Empiricism'
With 'Critical Realism'

*Discover Underlying
Reality*

Southern
Relational
Path

Foundation
METHODOLOGY
L2

Origination
METHOD
L1

Figure 15.1 Overview Chapter 15 – Level 3/West

Summary: Critical Realism

- Following the path of realization we now turn to critical realism (emancipation) as an evolution from experimental and survey methods (origination) and conventional empirical methodology (foundation).
- The originator of critical realism is the Anglo-Indian social philosopher Roy Bhaskar, who was influenced in turn by the New Zealander Rom Harre and the Argentine Mario Bunge.
- The key tenets of critical realism are its combined objective and subjective nature, its interpretive as well as explanatory orientation, its stratified nature, its recognition of human fallibility and its critical as well as emancipatory orientation.
- Explored in depth, it is characterized by a pragmatic orientation and a focus on abstraction, by a metaphysical orientation and a focus on different levels of theory, as well as by its explicitly scientific approach.
- In its more global reach it is associated with an Eastern turn, whereby its focus on 'meta-reality' explicitly brings in a spiritual dimension that was previously only implicit, and a dialectical orientation to supplement the pragmatic orientation.
- At the end of the chapter we offer Homer Dixon's work on *The Upside of Down: Catastrophe, Creativity and Renewal* as a practical application of critical realism. While this Canadian peace activist and environmentalist empirically engages with the downside of today's consumerism and growth paradigm, he also uncovers the deeper layers of stress underneath the surface of our societies.

15.1 Orientation to Critical Realism

With critical realism we enter the third level of the Western path of realization. While we have positioned critical realism on the Western path, it is a kind of a 'mixed breed'. It has Western (realistic) connotations, but it also carries a strong Eastern flavour, adding to the visible surface of the research object its more invisible ground of origin. In that sense it clearly transcends a purely positivist empiricism. Adding, critically, a deeper (subjective) experiential ground to the outer (objective) empirical surface, it enables the researcher to connect inner subject to outer reality. As such, it paves the way for the final innovatory level of the Western path, an integrated action research, which follows in Chapter 16.

THE ORIGINS OF CRITICAL REALISM

Roy Bhaskar is unique in having given birth, almost single-handedly, to a research philosophy, that is critical realism. Actually, when one of us began to first discover the profound difference between research method and methodology – or philosophy – it was the discovery of critical realism which first enabled Ronnie Lessem to come to such a conclusion. Soon after that, Ronnie met up with Bhaskar at a seminar in London, and was overwhelmed by his casual, offbeat appearance: a tall, long-haired man, shoddily dressed in jeans and sneakers. Immediately he began to speak, though, the attending participants became enthralled.

Bhaskar was born in London, to an Indian father and English mother, both of whom were theosophists, heavily influenced by Eastern philosophies, upon which, in his later years in particular, Roy Bhaskar would draw. As a young man in 1963 he went up to Baliol

College, Oxford, on a scholarship to read philosophy, politics and economics. Having graduated with first-class honours in 1966, he began to work on a PhD thesis dealing with the relevance of economic theory for under-developed countries. This research led him to the philosophy of social science and then the philosophy of science. In the course of this Rom Harre became his supervisor. Harre, of French Huguenot stock but born and bred in New Zealand, is a philosopher, psychologist and anthropologist who spent much of his adult years teaching philosophy at the University of Punjab in India.

Bhaskar was also influenced in his early thinking by the Argentinean philosopher Mario Bunge. Bunge set out his thinking systematically in his *Treatise on Basic Philosophy*, a monumental work in eight volumes, comprising semantics, ontology, epistemology, philosophy of science and ethics. In 40 books and some 400 papers, Bunge develops a comprehensive scientific outlook, which he then applies to the various natural and social sciences. Bunge was also a left-wing intellectual, and his interdisciplinary approach and political credentials appealed to the young Bhaskar.

Bhaskar's own consideration of the philosophies of science and social science resulted in the development of critical realism, an emancipatory body of thought that aspires to move beyond the Enlightenment, avoiding reductionist rationalism through enhanced historical self-awareness and use of dialectical thought. To achieve this, it draws on pre-modern spiritual traditions as well as on positive aspects of the Enlightenment: its commitment to scientific inquiry and to freedom.

It is interesting to note that Bhaskar has no fixed academic abode. He remains a truly free spirit, on the edges of academia, though he, with his close colleagues, has developed an International Association for Critical Realism.

In the year 2000, Bhaskar published his *From East to West: The Odyssey of a Soul*, in which he first expressed ideas related to spiritual values that came to be seen as the beginning of his so-called spiritual turn. This was initially very controversial, but has since won growing support after the publication in 2002 of his book on the radical development of critical realism which he called *The Philosophy of Meta-reality*. Here he made it clear that this latest phase of his thought applied to people of all faiths and no faith, that is, was susceptible to a purely secular interpretation.

What he refers to as meta-reality, however, may be seen as a different philosophy altogether. In *Reflections on Meta-reality*, he states:

> This book articulates the difference between critical realism in its development and a new philosophical standpoint which I am in the process of developing, which I have called the philosophy of Meta-Reality.

The main departure, it seems, is a shift away from Western dualism to a non-dual model in which emancipation entails 'a breakdown, an overcoming, of the duality and separateness between things'. In effect, in his midlife, Bhaskar has turned very explicitly back to his Eastern roots, and combined such with his Western realist approach, in a very distinctive way.

FROM EMPIRICISM TO CRITICAL REALISM

As in postmodernism, critical theory and feminism, so also in critical realism knowledge is socially constructed, but only in 'transitive' part. For, in critical realism unlike in postmodernism, an objectively based reality does exist, 'intransitively' so to speak. So reality is partly pre-existent and partly socially constructed. Insofar as reality is pre-existent, such a 'realist' approach shares with empiricism its grounding in an objectively definable world. However, for such critical realists, that is not the end of the story.

What is of profound importance for them is that ontology is stratified, with underlying reality constituting the generative depths. Our emancipation, hence, is preconditioned by our coming to understand and work with such 'real' depths. As a result:

Critical Realism – Core Assumptions

A purely empirically based truth is unattainable – all knowledge is socially constructed, while at the same time there is a pre-ordered external reality.

All human behaviour and knowledge occurs within and simultaneously reconstructs culturally derived meanings.

The purpose of social scientific inquiry is to produce causal explanations which can guide (and may be evaluated through) human interventions in our social world.

Pragmatic-critical realism demands a reflexive political axis, focused on the way in which knowledge shapes human activities.

Let us now investigate, more purposefully, the origins and scope of critical realism.

REALISM RATHER THAN EMPIRICISM

Roy Bhaskar's *Realist Theory of Science*[1] was strongly influenced by his doctoral supervisor Rom Harre who, in his book *The Method of Science*,[2] had laid early critical-realist foundations with his comprehensive criticism of positivism. Harre argued that *there had to be underlying generative mechanisms in order to analyse the world in terms of cause and effect.* For Mario Bunge,[3] moreover, *reality is arranged in levels; something qualitatively new can only emerge from a lower level.*

There is therefore a *distinction between a real world and a conceptual one, and empiricism is criticized for reducing reality to the observable.* Bhaskar then, took the realist story on from a newly critical-emancipatory perspective, building on the prior ground that his predecessors from their diverse cultural heritages had established.

FROM WEST TO EAST: REALISM TO META-REALITY

What then is this stratified, critical-emancipatory perspective? For Roy Bhaskar it seemed in fact, in the late 1960s when he was writing his doctoral thesis, that the most important problem facing mankind was that of overcoming world poverty. As such, and not unlike his kindred 'critical theory' spirits, he was tapping into his humanistic roots. Specifically then:

What is required is a revolutionary transformation far more profound than any of us can imagine. Unless capitalism is overturned, by a revolution, which will be at once much more peaceful and deeper than the one that overthrew socialism, that will draw on resources and aspects of our being that are at once spiritual and cultural, set in the context of a feasible transition, and done in a non-violent way – unless capitalism is overturned in that way, I can see very little prospect of humanity surviving much into the 21st century on this planet.

Human freedom, for Bhaskar, depends above all on understanding the truth about reality and acting toward it. The task of social innovation is thereby one, that his transformative approach to *Meta-Reality*[4] would take on, from where analytically based critical realism leaves off, the two together forming the emancipatory platform for such innovation.

So it is essential for the critical realists that science and philosophy should be explicitly concerned with human liberation. The key to such liberation, though, was to uncover the generative forces that underlay our economic and social, as well as our physical reality.

The further development of critical realism, what Bhaskar terms meta-reality, makes possible a re-evaluation of the old dispute between idealism and materialism. Capitalism at the moment is the dominant world order. It is, however, faced with two pressing contradictions. A rising organic composition of nature threatens to tear the world itself apart with ecological contradictions while, at the same time, a rising organic composition of ideas makes possible the notion of a new organization of the social world attuned to universal self-realization and harmony. A new synthesis is what is required between 'leftist' politics and 'new age' psychology. Such a synthesis, for Bhaskar, will need to be set in a context of a global philosophy, which resonates with themes traceable back to the dawn of the great world civilisations – such as Buddhism and Taoism – rather than only drawing upon modern Eurocentric times.

The philosophy of meta-reality describes the way in which this very world nevertheless depends on, is ultimately sustained by, and only exists in virtue of: the free, loving, creative and intelligent energy and activity of states of our 'real' being. In becoming aware

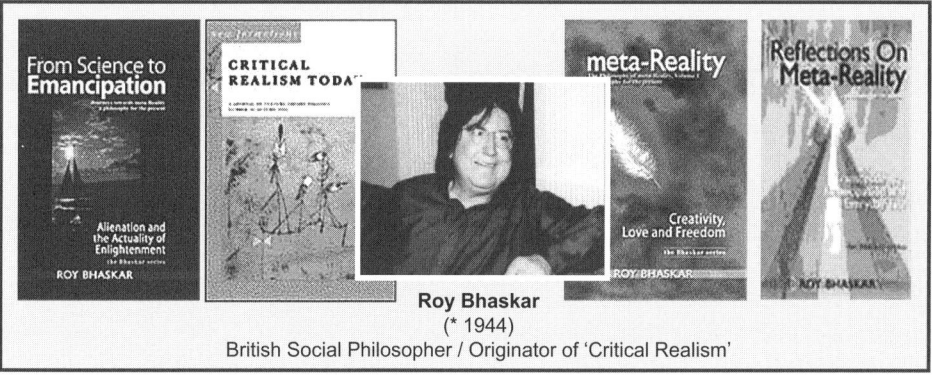

Roy Bhaskar
(* 1944)
British Social Philosopher / Originator of 'Critical Realism'

Figure 15.2 Critical Realism's Core Thinker – Roy Bhaskar

Sources: Image 1: Bagchee.com http://www.bagchee.com. Image 2: Lawrence & Wishart http://www.lwbooks.co.uk/. Image 3: Lancaster University http://www.lancs.ac.uk/. Image 4: Sage http://www.uk.sagepub.com. Image 5: All Time Books http://www.alltimebooks.com/

of this we begin the process of transforming and overthrowing the totality of structures of oppression, alienation and mystification and indeed misery which we have produced. Such a vision opens up a balanced world, of a society in which the free development and flourishing of each unique human being is understood to be the condition, as it is also the consequence, of the free development and flourishing of all.

In that sense Bhaskar is taking psychologically and spiritually on, from where Marx left economically and socially off. In that context he rubs shoulders with his critical-theory-oriented counterparts. However, unlike them, there is a strong pragmatic and Anglo-Saxon edge to his argument. Alongside such, we can see the influence of his Indian heritage, where the notion of 'levels of consciousness' (or indeed, for him and his Anglo-Saxon colleagues: the stratified nature of reality or ontology) predominates. We now turn to the key tenets of critical realism, starting with the notion that critical realism is indeed 'critical', and ending with the hermeneutic, as well as pragmatic, side to critical realism.

15.2 Critical Realism – Key Tenets: Critical of Status Quo, Involved with Layered Reality

Critical Realism – Key Tenets	
①	Critical realism is critical of the status quo.
②	You become involved with a stratified or layered reality.
③	You view such a layered perspective on reality as fallible.
④	You conceive reality as both transitive (subjective) and intransitive (objective).
⑤	There is a hermeneutic as well as an empirical side to critical realism.

① CRITICAL REALISM IS CRITICAL OF THE STATUS QUO

'Transcendental realism' signifies an ontology transcending the empirical level; in this sense relating to a critique of 'flat' empiricism. In being critical of the merging of structure and agency, Bhaskar transcends such through his transformational model of social action, culminating in his 'meta-reality'. Any universalist claims to truth need to be set, in addition to their objectively 'intransitive' reality, in the context of a subjectively 'transitive' character of science.

② YOU BECOME INVOLVED WITH A STRATIFIED OR LAYERED REALITY

The most fundamental enterprise in science is to find the inherent mechanisms that generate events; it is these inherent properties the critical realists call 'causal powers'. Critical realists distinguish three domains: the basic one is the domain of the 'real' – here we find the generative mechanisms, existing irrespective of whether they produce an event or not. When mechanisms produce a factual event it comes under the domain of the actual, whether we observe it or not; when an event is experienced, it becomes an empirical fact. Insofar as reality is stratified, what is important is that new mechanisms are created in their respective strata, through emergent powers.

③ YOU VIEW SUCH A LAYERED PERSPECTIVE ON REALITY AS FALLIBLE

All knowledge is socially produced, but not all is equally valuable; critical realism presents a 'third way' between empiricism/objectivism and relativism/idealism. In critiquing neutral empirical observations, critical realism assumes all knowledge is conceptually mediated and concept-dependent. There is, first, a real world independent of our knowledge of it, and second, it is possible to gain knowledge about this world; however, knowledge is always fallible.

④ YOU CONCEIVE REALITY AS BOTH TRANSITIVE (SUBJECTIVE) AND INTRANSITIVE (OBJECTIVE)

An external reality exists, independently of our conceptions of it. The purpose of science is to come as close to this reality as possible. It is such theories of reality (for example, the laws of gravity) that constitute objective knowledge of it, its intransitive object – the transitive dimension is socially determined, subjective and changeable. What makes social science special, compared to natural science, is that social scientists seek knowledge about a socially produced reality, not just a socially defined one.

⑤ THERE IS A HERMENEUTIC AS WELL AS AN EMPIRICAL SIDE TO CRITICAL REALISM

For critical realism, society is made up of thinking and reflective human beings who are capable of continually changing their perception of social reality. Hence, you as a researcher are supposed to study other people's interpretations of the social world – the object of study is therefore socially defined. It is important to note, that social systems are rather open than closed: we cannot just isolate social events in order to manipulate a situation, with the purpose of studying what happens.

We now turn to a consideration of critical realism in greater depth.

15.3 Critical Realism in Depth

REALiTY IS ULTIMATELY LAYERED

For Roy Bhaskar, the nature of reality, of 'what exists' and the 'essence of things', is intrinsically ontological (underlying the nature of reality) and must necessarily form the foundation for everything. This has been clearly spelt out by his fellow critical realists Berth Danermark and her Scandinavian colleagues in *Explaining Society*.[5] A distinction can therefore be made between three ontological domains:

Ontological Domains of Critical Realism
① Empirical
② Actual
③ Real

The observation of the 'real' domain of stratified reality, the deep dimension of so-called generative mechanisms, is thus what distinguishes critical realism. It is this deep dimension of reality, not immediately observable, that forces us to seek knowledge rather than just accumulate experiences and facts. Since reality is differentiated, structures are stratified and involve many different and sometimes conflicting practices and interests; there also exist several parallel conceptual frameworks and sometimes-competing interpretations. Knowledge, independently of what it is about, is always a social product. Facts are relative to the conceptions we initially form of the phenomena.

Natural and social science 'facts' therefore are theoretically and/or ideologically determined. Critical realists argue however that the fact that social phenomena are concept-dependent should under no circumstances be seen as if the social world only exists as a mental construction in people's minds. For the social structures that are reproduced or transformed, when members of society act in accordance with their concepts of reality, are real. They contain powers and mechanisms, which operate independently of the actions here and now.

Natural science, then, explores a basically value-neutral world, where the objects are neither good nor bad; they simply exist. Social science, on the other hand, investigates an inherently value-charged world of social phenomena, positions, roles, identities and relations. When social science brings into question and analyses everyday knowledge, it therefore not only risks getting into conflict with alternative experiences and concepts, but also with deeply felt issues and ethical guidelines. Thereby it also challenges vital power and dominance relationships. These relationships are invariably hidden from immediate view. They therefore need to be conceptualized, from a perspective of hidden depth, as they cannot be directly perceived, experientially, from an empirical surface.

CONCEPTUALIZATION AND ABSTRACTION ARE KEY

For the critical realists, conceptualization stands out as the most central social scientific activity. Vital here is the understanding that the critical realists have of the stratification of reality, of emergent powers, and of open and closed systems. A very common and important route to conceptualization is through abstraction. Everyday knowledge tends to oppose abstraction in the same way as theory is opposed to practice. It is associated with vagueness and distance from reality. The concrete, on the other hand, is what 'exists'. It is tangible, real and observable. Thus abstract knowledge is considered, by empiricists, to be 'out of touch with reality'. Critical realists take the opposite view.

Abstractions, hence, freeze the moment. If we wish to understand the dynamic dimensions of reality the abstract and structural analyses need to be supplemented by causal analysis, which deals with explaining why what happens, happens. Understanding such causal relations is central to science, connected to the fact that it is a practical activity we make use of to orient ourselves to life. If we know what underlies a certain course of events we can also intervene and direct future events. The predominant methods of empiricist social science, the study of empirical regularities or co-variation between standardised variables, cannot answer questions regarding causes. This is critical realism's fundamental, structure-changing departure from positivism, while retaining its practical orientation. To ask what has caused something, for Bhaskar, is to ask what makes it happen, what produces, generates, creates or determines it, enables or leads to it.

From a realist perspective, it is not a matter of a relation between events, separated and demarcated from each other. It is a matter of what causal powers or liabilities there are in a certain object or relation. Thus water has the causal power to quench fire; living creatures have the power to reproduce; human beings also have 'work power' and 'love power'. It is important to observe, moreover, that 'powers and liabilities' also include such properties as 'weakness' and 'vulnerability'. Water has the intrinsic liability to evaporate, living creatures have the similar liability to die, human beings to be dependent on others. It is critical therefore to recognize that powers and liabilities exist whether exercised or not. Water can quench fire irrespective of whether anyone uses it thus. People can work even when they are unemployed, and love whether or not they enter a love relation. The mainland Chinese generally have a subservient attitude to authority, whether or not it is immediately applied. On the other hand, the existence of causal powers is not an assumption about fixed, unchangeable, eternal essences. Things can and do change. China today is not what it was yesterday.

A THEORETICAL CONTINUUM FROM 'META' TO 'DESCRIPTIVE' EXISTS

Such causal powers are underpinned by three different kinds, or indeed levels, of theory: meta-theory, normative theory and descriptive theory. It is these levels of theory, which distinguishes critical realism from critical rationalism, where such stratification is absent.

1. Meta-theory is theory about the foundational assumptions and preconditions of natural or social science – critical theory, critical realism, feminism and postmodernism as well as phenomenology, hermeneutics, critical rationalism and empiricism – are all examples of such, each building upon alternative ontologies and epistemologies. They indeed provide the underlying foundations, or indeed research character, for the activity outlined here.
2. Normative theory refers to the theoretical language and argument, which examines as well as supports various ideas of how something might be, and is thereby incorporated into much of your mainstream literature search. It can be a theory focusing on moral, political, ideological or managerial issues.
3. By descriptive theories one means those able to describe and characterize more fundamental properties, structures, internal relations and mechanisms. Classical economic theory, for example, with its accompanying properties of demand and supply, price equilibrium and marginal utility, is an illustration of such a 'descriptive'

theory. Theories demarcated for specific objects of research, like unemployment, drug abuse, consumer debt,and managerial attitudes and behaviours are applicable here.

PRAGMATIC REALISM: THE ACTIVE ROLE OF THE HUMAN AGENT

Realists, and particularly critical realists, for Johnson and Duberley,[6] are united by a rejection of the view, held for example by the postmodernists, that the world is created by the minds of human observers. However, critical realists specifically reject a merely 'empirical realism', where the facts of a cognitively accessible reality supposedly speak for themselves. A central issue in critical realism is the active role of the human agent, particularly with reference to his or her interaction with an independent external reality, which can constrain or facilitate human action. So while – for the critical realists – so-called 'transitive' personalized explanations of events, change according to socio-cultural variations in human understanding, intransitive depersonalized, causal mechanisms located in external reality do not change, unless they are themselves dependent on human agency and intent.

Thus science is seen as the result of both social action and also nature's dynamics. Science is therefore construed as a social activity where people intervene and manipulate an 'intransitive' reality. As such they confront and change things on the basis of socially constructed 'transitive' theory, through practice. *The underlying theoretical schema is principally assessed through evaluating the effectiveness of an intervention in achieving particular ends.* So for critical realism, rather than rejecting experience and observation, in order to delve deeper and beyond the conceptual limitations they impose, any analysis should include both such surface features as well as unobservable structures and subjectively experienced social phenomena. Whereas management research is currently dominated by a particular form of positivist epistemology, which encourages an exclusive focus upon deductive and often quantitative methodologies, the pragmatic-critical realist position is more qualitatively variegated.

For critical realists, the context dependence of (in our case) business and management knowledge, necessitates the investigation of the socio-historical development of such social scientific recipes. This needs to involve a focus upon how they enable the interest-laden, but fallible, interaction of humans with their external worlds. Therefore *such knowledge must be conceptualized as a changeable cultural resource that influences, constrains and legitimizes particular social and organizational arrangements, relationships and practices.*

LANGUAGE, CONCEPTS AND REALITY

The predominant understanding of the concept of 'science' for Roy Bhaskar, in conclusion, has for a long time been the notion of an activity steadily accumulating general and objective knowledge of its object, by means of systematic and neutral empirical observations. This conventional scientific paradigm, which in its pure form may be called an empiricist/objectivist ideal, is still very influential all around the world as the 'traditional movement' in practical research activity. It also corresponds rather well with our everyday understanding of 'how we can know'.

Criticism of this ideal of science, this 'naïve objectivism', has called attention in particular to the complex relation between language/concepts and reality. If our different ways of seeing things, mediated by language, irretrievably determine what we see, for postmodernism for example, what then remains of the scientific project? In their more radical forms such relativists imply that we cannot uphold the existence of any reality. Critical realism, on the other hand, bears the criticism of naïve objectivism (empirically based) in mind, while trying to maintain the positive claims to a useful and liberating knowledge, which was the basic motivation for the Enlightenment project. Realism then holds to the view that reality does exist, independently of our knowledge of it.

We now turn to the more 'global' reach of critical realism, in fact now heralding its Eastern turn towards 'meta-reality'.

15.4 Global Variations of Critical Realism

ADULT ANGLO TO MIDLIFE INDIAN

Interestingly enough, the birth and growth of critical realism took place during the 1970s and 1980s when Roy Bhaskar was in his twenties and thirties, during and after his doctoral studies at Oxford, in England. It was as he approached his midlife, and was undergoing a midlife crisis and resolution in the 1990s and into the new millennium, that his original philosophy, critical realism, underwent a West–East metamorphosis. It evolved into his 'meta-reality'. In the same way as commentators refer to the early and late philosophical orientations of the great Austrian philosopher Ludwig Wittgenstein, the same can be said about the adulthood and midlife of Roy Bhaskar.

In his early adult writings on critical realism, Bhaskar remained closely wedded to Western pragmatism, though of course arguing against pure positivism and empiricism. While then, even at this initial stage of his philosophical analysis, he opposed a 'naïve objectivity' preoccupied with surface analysis, he retained a practical and rational orientation, and one causally oriented towards 'generative mechanisms' underlying events and experiences. In other words, while his underlying philosophy was critical of the purely empirically based Western mainstream, the overall rational-pragmatic language remained true to his Anglo-Saxon and indeed European heritage. Moreover his doctoral supervisor at Oxford, Rom Harre, though New Zealand born and bred, was of Northern French Huguenot origins.

Bhaskar's two seminal works in the 1970s, at this 'adult' stage of his philosophical and psychological development, were a *Realist Theory of Science*[7] aimed at the natural sciences, and *The Possibility of Naturalism*,[8] focused on the social sciences. The break then came, explicitly and publically at least, in the early 1990s when he published his *Dialectic – The Pulse of Freedom*.[9] At that point he turned from West to East (though still in a European context) serving to link Western European 'realism' with central and Eastern European 'idealism'. Here he was duly influenced by Germany's Hegel, alongside the Anglo-French Rom Harre. In the final analysis, though, Bhaskar retained his overwhelmingly realist orientation.

DIALECTICAL EMERGENCE

The first explicitly Eastern turn (albeit to begin with in European guise) was towards Hegel. The German 19th-century philosopher saw splits, dichotomies, disharmonies and fragmentations as calling for restoration or unity in diversity, in his absolute idealism.

Negation, as such, always calls for a new and richer determination. The mutual exclusion of opposites passes over into their reciprocal interdependence. For Hegel then the truth is a whole, and the whole is a process. Error lies in one-sidedness. Its symptom is the contradictions it generates and its remedy involves their incorporation into richer, more inclusive conceptual forms. Either the implicit is made explicit (telemony), or some want or inadequacy is repaired (teleology), both of which correspond with Bhaskar's notion of 'negation'. This is also picked by Nonaka and Takeuchi, in terms of their knowledge 'externalization'.[10]

'Dialectical' then, in contrast with the analytical and reflective, grasps concepts and forms in their systemic interconnections, not just their determinate differences. It considers each development as a product of a previous less developed phase, whose necessary truth or fulfilment it is. So there is always a tension between a latent form and what it is becoming. For Bhaskar this is the power of *emergence*, upon which we have also 'genetically' drawn. In short, Hegelian dialectic is the actualized entelechy of the present, comprehended as everything that has led up to it. It involves a transformation of the consciousness of the dialectical observer as well as the expansion of the existing conceptual field.

META-REALITY TO TRANSFORMATIVE AGENCY

The possibility of human emancipation, for the now Easterly-facing Bhaskar, depends not on Western democratic freedoms and free markets but on expanding the zone of 'non-duality' within our lives. That is the level of what Bhaskar calls a being's 'ground-state', which is its most essential level. It is the level upon which all other levels depend, which has much in common with a phenomenological 'essence'. It also serves to transcend his prior notion of an underlying, generative reality. Altogether, in this newly 'meta-real' case, every human situation, as such, must now be characterized by MELDA:

1. **M**: an element of potential, which corresponds to the critical realist domain of stratified ontology, grounded in Meta-reality (M).
2. **E**: creativity, that is the Emergence (E) of something new, even if this novelty is a repeat of the old, which would not otherwise have occurred.
3. **L**: any human situation must be characterized by that form of bonding, solidarity, compassion, care and consideration that Bhaskar calls, altogether, Love (L).
4. **D**: each agent in the situation needs to be capable of Doing (D) something, spontaneously and correctly in each situation, creating an effect.
5. **A**: the agent's intentionality will be in some manner fulfilled: Aah (A) – I see!

Bhaskar in his midlife then produced such books as *Meta-Reality: Creativity, Love and Freedom*,[11] *Reflections on Meta-Reality*,[12] as well as *From East to West – Odyssey of a Soul*,[13] taking forward this MELDA theme. In this last book, Bhaskar reviews several great world belief systems – including ancient Greek, Judaic, Essene and Christian, Hindi (Vedic), Buddhist, Confucian, Taoist, Zen, Islam (Sufi) and modern materialist thought. He uses such a retrospective to cast light on the contemporary crises in Western social and philosophical thought. These themselves reflect wider and deeper crises in society, which he relates to a dialectical chain of 'avidya' (ignorance), 'dualism' (split) and 'maya' (illusion), itself grounded in ontological (existential) 'insecurity'.

While on the one hand, Bhaskar's fellow critical realists (as Anglo-Saxon pragmatists) may consider that their founding father has become ever more 'esoteric' of late, for us, overall, the reverse is the case. For, in turning East, Bhaskar has become more practically transformative and indeed globally integral in his orientation. Indeed our own GENE effectively evolved out of Bhaskar's meta-reality.

We now turn to our critical reality 'case', that of the Canadian peace activist and environmentalist, Thomas Homer Dixon, whose work involved penetrating to the generative depths – so-called tectonic stresses – of the issues we face today, and positing theories underlying creativity, catastrophe and renewal.

15.5 Critical Realism in Practice: The Upside of Down

TECTONIC STRESSES

Stresses and Multipliers

The 21st century will be, for Homer Dixon at the Trudeau Center for Peace and Conflict Studies in Toronto, the *age of nature*.[14] We will learn, probably the hard way, that nature matters: we are not separate from it, we are dependent on it, and when there is trouble in nature there is trouble in society.

According to Homer Dixon, the following 'tectonic stresses' are accumulating deep underneath the surface of our societies:

* *Population Stress:* arising out of the differences in growth rates between rich and poor societies, and the spiralling growth of mega-cities in poor countries.
* *Energy Stress:* above all from oil scarcity.
* *Environmental Stress:* from increasing damage to land, water, forests, fisheries.
* *Climate Stress:* from changes in the make-up of our atmosphere.
* *Economic Stress:* from global financial instabilities and growing income gaps, which is our point of focus here, in relation to economic opportunity.

In addition to these five *stresses* are two *multipliers,* which combine with the stresses to make breakdown more likely, widespread and severe. The first is increasing speed and connectivity of activities, technologies and societies. The second is the escalating power of small groups to destroy things and people.

From Management to Catagenesis

Today most experts who take our global problems seriously advocate what Homer Dixon terms a 'management' response. While this may be better than denying our problems, it often does not help very much. For any management policies that really address the underlying causes of our hardest problems usually require big changes in the existing political and economic order. After all, that very order is the reason why our problems are so bad. Surprisingly too, there is no term in English for the commonplace occurrence of renewal through breakdown. So Homer Dixon calls it *catagenesis*, from the Greek for 'down', *cata*, and that for 'birth', which is *genesis*. Whether the breakdown in question is psychological, technological, economic, political or ecological – or some combination of these – catagenesis involves the reinvention of our future.

Complex systems adapt to their changing environment by going through a four-stage cycle of growth, breakdown, reorganization and renewal. Specialists have a term to describe complex systems; they call them *path dependent*. Here the system depends at any time on the tortuous, circuitous route by which it got there.

THE INCOME GAP AND THE GROWTH IMPERATIVE

What is the Way out of Constant Growth?

Homer Dixon posits that never in history have the differences between us, in terms of income and opportunity, been so great. Whereas in 1870 the average income of the world's richest country was about nine times that of the poorest, by 1990 it was 45 times greater. Meanwhile, even within a particular developed country, if material desires are not satisfied, and if significant numbers of workers cannot move smoothly to more high-skilled jobs, over time the economy's workforce will tend to polarize between, on the one hand, a shrinking but ever-richer elite of hyper-cognitively-adept workers who own and run the ferociously productive technologies of the economy, but who are unwilling to consume all its products, and on the other, an expanding mass of technologically displaced workers – who cannot generate enough demand to consume the boom.

What is the way out: constant economic growth? Growth creates the new industries and generates the new jobs needed to absorb technologically displaced workers. The American economy, for example, must expand 3–5 per cent annually – doubling its size every 15 to 25 years – just to keep unemployment from rising. And to get this growth – operating on the assumption that people can be inculcated with insatiable desires and ever rising expectations – encourage us to become relentless consumers. In essence, the logic of our economic behaviour works like this: if we are discontented with what we have, we buy stuff; if we buy enough stuff, the economy grows; if the economy grows enough, technologically displaced workers can find new jobs; and if they find new jobs there will be enough economic demand to keep the economy humming and to prevent wrenching political conflict. Modern capitalism's stability – and increasingly the global economy's stability – requires the cultivation of material discontent, endlessly rising personal consumption and the steady economic growth this consumption generates. Without this economic growth, rich and poor people would soon confront each other in a fierce zero-sum conflict, and over time the widening gap between rich and poor would tear our societies apart.

Our economic role in this culture of consumerism, Homer Dixon argues, is to be little more than walking appetites that serve the function of maintaining our economy's throughput. Our psychological state is analogous to that of drug addicts needing a fix: buying things does not really make us happy, except perhaps for a moment after the purchase. But we do it over and over anyway. Why? There are many reasons. Consumerism helps anaesthetize us against the dread produced by many empty lives. New technologies create constant economic upheaval, which means that an average person in the American economy, for instance, has to change jobs every four years or so. The chronic economic security cranks up stress in our lives, while the churning of our economy atomises society as a whole. Both of these trends shred the social fabric of trust, caring and reciprocity that is essential to our happiness. So in place of vital connections between people that come with strong communities, families and friendships, we substitute the transitory pleasures provided by newly bought things.

The flip side of such economic growth, meanwhile, include rich society's epidemic of eating disorders, like obesity and anorexia. Indeed, the number of overweight people in the world (about 1.2 billion) now matches those that are undernourished. Then there is the related and more general problem of depression, which has become three to ten times – depending on how it is measured – more common in the last 50 years. Explanations for all of these problems include the erosion of community and family, an economic culture that promotes chronic insecurity, and extreme individualism.

Winners and Losers Made Manifest

Today's global capitalism – which has linked the world together and subordinated people everywhere to its relentless energy as never before – is producing a stew of changes and stresses that is almost a perfect recipe for widespread and even violent resentment of the world's rich by the world's poor. Because capitalism cultivates material discontent, because we naturally compare ourselves with each other, and because comparisons are now so easy, through the Web and television, widening gulfs of wealth and opportunity cannot but encourage huge numbers of people to be chronically dissatisfied with their lot. We now live with an inescapable juxtaposition of winners and losers. Everyone knows who is ahead and who is behind.

At the same time, many people in poor societies feel that Western markets and cultures are submerging their local cultures and institutions. Combined, for Homer Dixon, these are astonishingly dangerous trends. If our global society is to be resilient and adaptable – and if it is to be peaceful – it must give its citizens roughly equal opportunities to advance their economic and political interests, and it must give them ways of expressing their diversity within a shared human identity. But instead it is giving people ever more unequal opportunity and ever-starker differences in their daily lives. Compare, for example, the day-to-day experiences of a bond trader in the City of London with those of a slum dweller in Sao Paulo or Karachi. These people have little in common on which to build a shared identity. At the same time capitalism is promoting a relentlessly homogenized, mass culture of consumerism. The question ultimately is, how much more unequal world income distribution can become before the resulting political instabilities and flows of migrants reach the point of directly harming the well-being of the citizens of the rich world and the stability of their states. To survive, let alone prosper, in our new and more dangerous world, however, we need to open our minds to change.

INTRODUCING PANARCHY

Ecological Economics

A noted proponent of such change, or indeed transformation, is the ecologist Crawford Holling. He argues that, during the early phase of growth, the forest ecosystem is steadily accumulating capital. As its total mass grows, so does its quantity of nutrients, along with the amount of information in the genes of its increasingly varied plants and animals. Over time, as the forest matures and passes into the late phase of growth, the mechanisms of self-regulation become highly diverse and finely tuned. Species and organisms are progressively more specialized and efficient in using energy and nutrients available in their niche. Indeed the whole forest becomes extremely efficient – in a sense it effectively adapts to maximize the production of biomass from the flows of sunlight, water and nutrients it gets from its environment. This phase cannot go on indefinitely. Its ever-greater connectedness and efficiency reduces its capacity to deal with severe external shocks. Eventually the ecosystem loses resilience, and its high degree of efficiency makes it harder to realize its potential for novelty. Overall it becomes 'an accident waiting to happen'. Actually, the collapse of the whole ecosystem liberates its potential for creativity and allows for novel and unpredictable recombination of elements. It is as if somebody threw the energy flows and genetic information, the plants and nutrients, into a gigantic mixing bowl and stirred. Once marginal species can now capture and exploit newly released nutrients, and genetic mutations, which were a bane, can now be a boon.

In these ways the forest ecosystem reorganizes and regenerates itself, quite possibly in a very new form. Put simply, the catastrophe of collapse allows for the birth of something new. And this cycle of growth, collapse, reorganization and rebirth allows for the forest to adapt over the long term to a constantly changing environment. The adaptive cycle embraces growth and stability, on the one hand, change and variety on the other. It is at once conserving and creating, a characteristic of adaptive systems. Moreover, no one adaptive cycle exists in isolation: it is usually sandwiched between lower and higher ones. Panarchy theory, then, helps us understand how complex systems of all kinds evolve and adapt. Its core idea – that systems naturally grow, become more brittle, collapse and then renew themselves – repeatedly recurs in literature, history, philosophy, religion, and the natural and social sciences. We are currently in a period of great volatility in the world system. Some kind of systemic breakdown, Homer Dixon believes, is inevitable, and we ought to do what we can to avoid deep collapse; rather to exploit the opportunity.

BEYOND CATAGENESIS

Breakdown tends to be disruptive to parts of the system, but it need not be, for it can produce exactly the conditions required for a burst of creativity, reorganization and renewal. A long view of human history reveals not regular change but spasmodic, catastrophic disruptions followed by long periods of reinvention and development. Breakdown is something that human social systems must go through to adapt successfully to changing conditions. In our communities, towns and cities, we can use small-scale experiments to see what kinds of technologies, organizations and procedures work best under different breakdown scenarios. Scientists moreover have found that complex systems that are highly adaptive – like markets and even the immune system of mammals – tend to share certain characteristics. First of all, the individual elements that make up the systems are extraordinarily diverse. Second, the power to make decisions is not centralized in one place. Thirdly and finally, highly adaptive systems are unstable enough to create unexpected innovations but orderly enough to learn from their successes and failures. We are all familiar with just such systems – the Internet, and the Worldwide Web. So far we have only tapped the surface of the potential for such adaptive systems.

15.6 Conclusion

Critical realism is the fourth of our critical emancipatory orientations to research (level 3). While on the one hand, it follows in the pragmatic footsteps of experimental and survey methods and empiricism, on the other hand, like the three others, it is both critical and emancipatory.

Along the research path of realization, critical realism has a pragmatic orientation, geared towards an ultimately transformative effect, as well as being grounded in an objective, as well as subjective reality. However, it is more broadly based then experimental method and empirical methodology in that it deals with an overtly stratified reality and it values abstraction. In other words, and like the other critical emancipatory approaches, it is more 'worldly' than its predecessors.

Secondly, in comparing and contrasting critical realism with the other three emancipatory orientations, we find that the realistic emphasis on stratification compares and contrasts with that of postmodernism (*reason*), critical theory (*renewal*) and feminism (*relational*).

As we evolve via this Western path of research towards an Integral Innovation, we now turn from critical realism to action research.

References

1. Bhaskar, R. (1977). *The Realist Theory of Science*. London: Verso Press.
2. Harre, R. (1970). *The Method of Science*. New York: Crane Russak and Co.
3. Bunge, M. (1973). *Methodological Unity of Science*. Dordrecht-Boston: Kluwer Academic Publishers.
4. Bhaskar, R. (2000). *Meta-Reality*. London: Sage.
5. Danermark, B. et al. (2002). *Explaining Society*. London: Routledge.
6. Johnson, P. and Duberley, J. (2000). *Understanding Management Research*. London: Sage.
7. Bhaskar, R. (1977). *The Realist Theory of Science*. London: Verso Press.
8. Bhaskar, R. (1979). *The Possibility of Naturalism*. New York: Harvester.
9. Bhaskar, R. (1993). *Dialectic – The Pulse of Freedom*. London: Verso Press.
10. Nonaka, I. and Takeuchi, H. (1995). *The Knowledge Creating Company*. Oxford: Oxford University Press.
11. Bhaskar, R. (2000). *Meta-Reality: Creativity, Love and Freedom*. London: Sage.
12. Bhaskar, R. (2002). *Reflections on Meta-Reality*. London: Sage.
13. Bhaskar, R. (2000). *From East to West – Odyssey of a Soul*. London: Sage.
14. Homer Dixon, T. (2007). *The Upside of Down: Catastrophe, Creativity and Renewal*. Toronto: Vintage Canada.

16 *From Critical Realism to Action Research*

Become a Scientist in Action

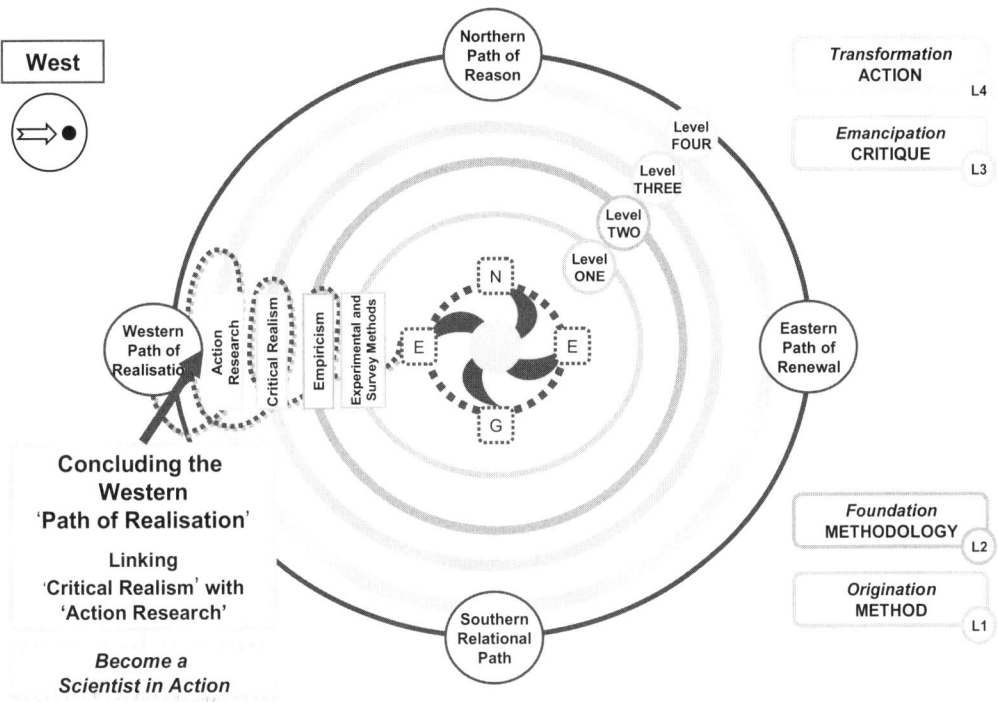

West

Northern
Path of
Reason

Level
FOUR

Level
THREE

Level
TWO

Level
ONE

N

E   E

G

Transformation
ACTION
L4

Emancipation
CRITIQUE
L3

Eastern
Path of
Renewal

Foundation
METHODOLOGY
L2

Origination
METHOD
L1

Western
Path of
Realisation

Action Research

Critical Realism

Empiricism

Experimental and
Survey Methods

**Concluding the
Western
'Path of Realisation'**

Linking
'Critical Realism' with
'Action Research'

*Become a
Scientist in Action*

Southern
Relational
Path

Figure 16.1 Overview Chapter 16 – Level 4/West

Summary: Action Research

- Finally we are concluding the Western research path of realization, by entering into its fourth and integral level: action research. In this particular case we speak of generic action research, as we also categorized PAR, co-operative inquiry and socio-technical design as articulations of action research.
- Action research, in its generic form, was originally developed by Kurt Lewin in the middle of the 20th century in the United States and has been taken forward in the 21st century by Peter Reason in the UK.
- Action research is a form of collective self-reflective inquiry undertaken by participants in social situations in order to improve the rationality and justice of their own social or educational practices, as well as their understanding of those practices and the situations in which the practices are carried out.
- Action research refers to the conjunction of three elements: action, research and participation. AR aims to increase the ability of the involved community or organization members to control their own destinies more effectively and to keep improving their capacity to do so within a more sustainable and just environment.
- Action research in depth involves a consideration of the management of change, alongside of learning from experience, individually and organizationally.
- In its global variations, the participatory dimension in action research takes pride of place, building up its political alongside its individual and organizational reach.
- An effective business case story in point is that of Cashbuild of South Africa and its social innovator Albert Koopman who, through an ongoing process of action and reflection, theory and practice, progressively turned the company into an industrial democracy.

16.1 Orientation to Generic Action Research

SOCIETAL TO INDIVIDUAL ORIENTATION

We begin in this culminating chapter on generic action research by retracing our steps. In the same way as action research, in terms of your research path of realization, builds upon experimental and survey methods, empirical methodology and a critical realist approach to emancipation, it is (via level 4) interconnected with participatory action research (in the South), co-operative inquiry (East) and socio-technical design (North). In the latter respect, it is individually, as opposed to communally (PAR), transpersonally (CI) and organizationally (socio-technical design) oriented.

Four Action Research Orientations
Integral Research Level 4: From South to West

Individual Orientation	Intensely practical, now culminating in composite Action, building on experimentation, empiricism and critical realism.
Organizational Orientation	Heavily conceptual, and as such explicitly combining knowledge-based socio-technical systems, drawing on hypothesis, rationality (critical rationalism) and postmodernism.

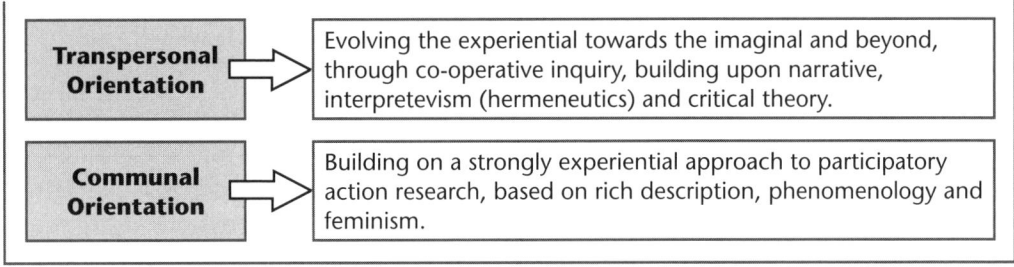

| Transpersonal Orientation | Evolving the experiential towards the imaginal and beyond, through co-operative inquiry, building upon narrative, interpretevism (hermeneutics) and critical theory. |
| Communal Orientation | Building on a strongly experiential approach to participatory action research, based on rich description, phenomenology and feminism. |

ORIGINS OF ACTION RESEARCH

Kurt Lewin and the Origins of Action Research

The origins of action research, as we indicated in Chapter 7, can be traced back to Kurt Lewin and to John Dewey. In a specifically 'action research' context, Lewin's approach can be articulated in terms of a series of steps, each of which is composed of a circle of planning, action and fact-finding about the result of the action.

The first step then is to examine the idea carefully in the light of the means available. Frequently more fact-finding about the situation is required. If this first period of planning is successful, two items emerge: namely, 'an overall plan' of how to reach the objective and secondly, a decision in regard to the first step of action. Usually this planning has also somewhat modified the original idea. The next step is composed of a circle of planning, executing and reconnaissance or fact-finding for the purpose of evaluating the results of the second step, and preparing the rational basis for planning the third step, and for perhaps modifying again the overall plan. What we can see here is an approach to research that is oriented to problem solving in social and organizational settings, and that has a form that parallels, as we shall see, Dewey's conception of learning from experience. The approach does take a fairly sequential form – and it is open to literal interpretation. Following it can lead to practice that is 'correct' rather than 'good'.

Action research, in the United States at least, did suffer a decline in favour during the 1960s because of its association with radical political activism. However, it has subsequently gained a significant foothold both within the realm of community-based and participatory action research, and as a form of practice oriented to the improvement of educative encounters. The use of action research to deepen and develop classroom practice has grown into a strong tradition of practice. For some there is an insistence that action research must be collaborative and entail groupwork.

Action research is a form of collective self-reflective inquiry undertaken by participants in social situations in order to improve the rationality and justice of their own social or educational practices, as well as their understanding of those practices and the situations in which the practices are carried out. The approach is only action research when it is collaborative, though it is important to realize that action research of the group is achieved through the critically examined action of individual group members. Finally, when set in historical context, while Lewin does talk about action research as a method; he is stressing a contrast between this form of interpretative practice and more traditional empirical-analytic research. The notion of a spiral may be a useful teaching device – but it is all too easily to slip into using it as *the* template for practice.

John Dewey and the Origins of Action Research

John Dewey, to whom we were first introduced in Chapter 7, moved to the University of Chicago at the turn of the 19th century to head the Department of Philosophy, Psychology and Pedagogy. It was at this time that Dewey began to consider the philosophy of education in a serious and systematic way. In 1896, he founded the University Laboratory School now better known as the 'Dewey School'. The Laboratory School was not a model institution; rather, it truly lived up to its name. It was a place for educational experiments in the genuine etymological sense of experiment, that is, to make a trial of something. Theories and practices were developed, tested, criticized, refined and tried again. Experimentalism became increasingly important as Dewey's philosophy matured. For him, not only were these experiments falsifiable, but in a contingent evolving world, their generalizability was always subject to revision. There is no end of inquiry for Dewey; nonetheless, he believed it the best way to render human experience intelligent.

The Laboratory School was not the only site for educational research in Chicago at that time. Jane Addams and her work at Hull House, for which she eventually received the Nobel Prize, greatly influenced Dewey. Rosalind Rosenberg writes that for Dewey, Hull House was a laboratory and an example of what he was trying to accomplish in education. Dewey visited Hull House even before moving to Chicago. Upon his arrival there, Dewey actively participated in the life of Hull House. There he met some of the most influential early feminists whose involvement in the political issues of the day caused by massive immigration, the social and economic effects of urbanization, and rapid technological advance exercised considerable influence. He also mixed with workers, trade unionists and political radicals. Some of his most influential educational works emerged out of these laboratories. These works not only set out Dewey's practical pedagogy, but they

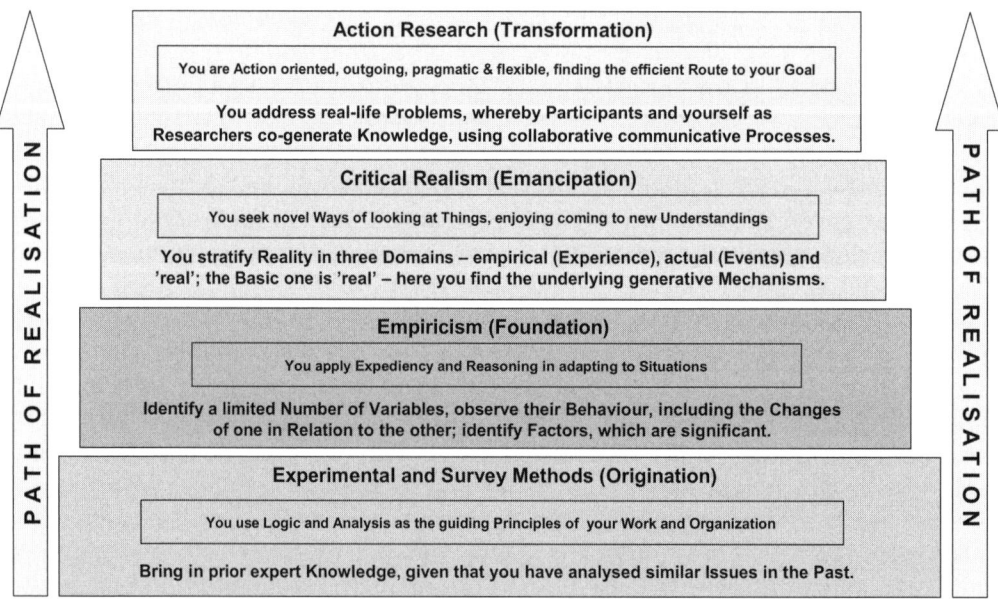

Figure 16.2 Towards Action Research

also outlined the psychological and philosophical principles upon which it relied. These principles devolved from the trial and error experiments that occurred within and without the walls of the Laboratory School.

FROM EXPERIMENTAL AND SURVEY METHODS TO ACTION RESEARCH

As we journey along the research path of realization, from experimental method to empirical methodology onto critical realism and ultimately action research, so we forge such a path to Western pragmatically based social innovation, in a way with which John Dewey would have felt very much at home.

We now turn to the key tenets of this generic form of action research.

16.2 Generic Action Research – Key Tenets: Action Learning, Social Change

Action Research – Key Tenets	
①	You start out with appreciative inquiry.
②	You challenge power relations.
③	You diverge and you converge.
④	You undertake social research for social change.
⑤	Knowing *how* is more important than knowing *that*.
⑥	Action research incorporates action learning.

① YOU START OUT WITH APPRECIATIVE INQUIRY

Peter Reason at the University of Bath in England and his colleague Hilary Bradbury have played a leading part in articulating[1] the wider reaches of action research. In so doing, they refer to refer to David Cooperider's *Appreciative Inquiry*, a noted communally based research method in its own right, as for them representative of a particpative approach to action research.

In their original formulation of appreciative inquiry Cooperider and Srivastva,[2] 20 years ago, argued that action research had largely failed as instruments for advancing socio-organizational transformation because of action research's preference for critique as opposed to appreciation. For if we devote our attention to what is wrong with organizations and communities, we lose the ability to sustain and enhance their life-giving potential:

> *More than a method or technique, the appreciative mode of inquiry ... engenders a reverence for life that draws the researcher to inquire beyond superficial appearances to deeper levels of the*

life-generating essentials and potentials of social existence. That is: '... the action researcher is drawn to affirm, and thereby illuminate, the factors and forces that serve to illuminate the human spirit.'[3]

② YOU CHALLENGE POWER RELATIONS

Action research, from the outset and symbolized by Kurt Lewin's status as a refuge from Nazi Germany, has always had a political dimension to it. Overlapping with both feminism and critical theory, action and participatory research are closely interconnected. To listen to people is to empower them. Before you can expect to hear anything worth hearing, you have to examine the power dynamics of the space and the social actors. For practitioner-researcher Susan Noffke:

we must see ourselves as part of the process of breaking apart the barriers for speakers and listeners, writers and readers, which are perpetuated through, and act to support our privileged positions.[4]

③ YOU DIVERGE AND YOU CONVERGE

John Heron compares and contrasts[5] a form of 'Apollonian inquiry', which takes a rational, linear, systematic, controlling and explicit approach to cycling between reflection and action, with a 'Dionysian inquiry' that takes a more imaginative, spiralling, diffuse, impromptu and tacit approach. Any effective process of action research requires both.

Specific skills are needed in the kind of action research, which overlaps with co-operative inquiry. They involve:

- *Being Present and Open*: empathy, resonance and attunement.
- *Bracketing and Reframing*: holding in abeyance the constructs we impose.
- *Radical Practice*: being aware of one's own underlying values and motives.
- *Non-attachment*: not investing one's own identity and security in an action.
- *Emotional Competence*: ability to identify and manage emotional states.

To ensure the overall validity of the inquiry process, there should be:

- *Research Cycling*: between action and reflection.
- *Divergence and Convergence*: looking several times at the same issue in ever more detail; looking at different issues in ever more variety.
- *Reflection and Action*: balancing between the two.
- *Chaos and Order*: interdependence of chaos and order.

④ YOU UNDERTAKE SOCIAL RESEARCH FOR SOCIAL CHANGE

Greenwood and Levin[6] argue that action research is a set of self-consciously collaborative and democratic strategies for generating knowledge and designing action in which trained experts in social and other forms of research and local stakeholders work together. The research focus is chosen collaboratively among the local stakeholders and the action researchers, and relationships amongst the participants are organized as joint learning processes. Action research centres on doing 'with' rather than doing 'for' stakeholders and credits these with the richness of experience and reflective possibilities that long experience living in complex situations brings with it.

Action research (AR) then is social research carried out by a team that encompasses a professional action researcher and the members of an organization, community or network who are seeking to improve the participants' situation. AR promotes broad participation in the research process and supports action leading to a more just, sustainable or satisfying situation for the stakeholders. The following table shows how action, research and participation interconnect:

Action, Research and Participation	
Action	AR is participatory because AR aims to alter the initial situation of the group, organization or community in the direction of a more self-managing, liberated and sustainable state.
Research	AR upholds research, the power and value of knowledge, theories, models, methods and analysis.
Participation	AR involves trained social researchers who serve as facilitators and teachers or members of local communities or organizations. Because these people together establish the AR agenda, generate the knowledge necessary to transform the situation and put the results to work, AR is a participatory process in which everyone involved takes some responsibility.

⑤ KNOWING HOW IS MORE IMPORTANT THAN KNOWING THAT

John Dewey believed that all humans are capable of scientific judgement and that society could be improved to the extent that these capacities are increased among all society's members. Consistent with this, he strongly opposed the division of public education into vocational and academic tracks, seeing this as the preservation of inequality and ultimately the weakening of democracy as a whole. Everyone could be a capable participant in experimental knowledge creation. He believed that limiting the learning of any individual ultimately limited society as a whole.

For Dewey, scientific research was not a process separate from democratic social action. Scientific knowing, like all other forms of knowledge, was a product of continuous cycles of action and reflection. The centre of gravity was always the learner's active pursuit of understanding through puzzle-solving activity with the materials at hand. The solutions achieved were only the best possible ones at that moment with the material at hand, hence the denomination of his philosophy as pragmatism.

⑥ ACTION RESEARCH INCORPORATES ACTION LEARNING

For Reg Revans, one of Britain's most creative management thinkers and originator of 'action learning',[7] the salvation of individual countries and their enterprises is not to be found by observers scouring the world in the hope of turning up some miracle there. Their salvation, their 'Kingdom of God', is rather to be found within their own shores, their local source, and within the wills of their own people. At the level of the individual enterprise, he further argues, it is not unreasonable to suggest that an essential part of any research and development policy is the study of the human effort, out of which the saleable products of the enterprise are largely created. Such a study involved 'scientific method' (survey, hypothesis, test, audit and control = the core elements of the action learning cycle).

Learning moreover must demand not only research and analysis. It must demand power to get the knowledge needed to see one's part in what is going on. In particular, one needs to know the effect of one's behaviour upon those with whom one works. For Revans, this is best achieved within small 'action learning' groups. In the Japanese context, he referred particularly to the establishment of small work groups, not only with a high degree of autonomy, but organized in a way that it gave people a continuing opportunity to develop. You learn with and from each other, in small groups or 'learning sets', by supportive attacks upon real and menacing problems, through:

- an exchange of information – ideas, advice, contacts, hunches, concepts;
- interaction between set members, offering each other support/challenge;
- behavioural change resulting more often from the re-interpretation of past experience than the acquisition of fresh knowledge.

We now turn from the key tenets of action research to a consideration of action research in depth, focusing on three key issues therein: the dimension of praxis, the dimension of science and the participatory dimension.

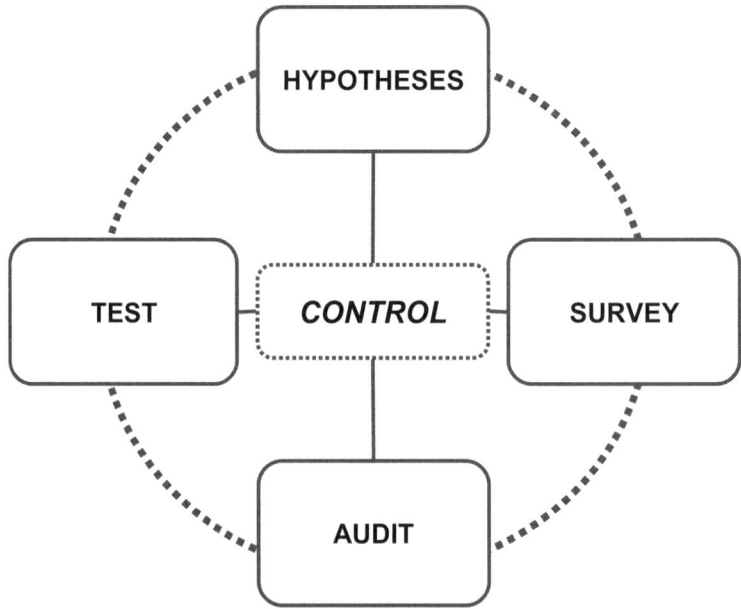

Figure 16.3 Action Learning Cycle

16.3 Generic Action Research in Depth

THE DIMENSION OF PRAXIS

AR focuses on specific contexts, demands that theory and practice are not separated and is committed to the idea that the test of any theory is its capacity to resolve a problem in a real-life situation. This focus on the world of experience, with its complexity, historicity and dynamism, means that AR distances itself from the then purified world of conventional, social research with its friction-free, perfect information and 'others being equal' assumptions that make being an academic easier though at the cost of being irrelevant. AR as a form of research has the following core characteristics:

- AR is context bound and addresses real-life problems holistically.
- AR is inquiry through which participants and researchers co-generate knowledge using collaborative communicative processes.
- AR treats the diversity of experiences and capacities within the local group as an opportunity for the enrichment of the research-action process.
- The meanings constructed in the inquiry process lead to social action or these reflections on actions lead to the construction of new meanings.
- The credibility-validity of AF knowledge is measured according to whether actions that arise from it solve problems (workability) and increase participants' control over their own situations.

The focus of the inquiry is determined by what the participants consider important, what affects their daily lives. The inquiry process is thus linked to actions taken to provide a solution to the problem being examined. This leads us onto so-called 'action learning' and indeed 'action science'.

THE SCIENTIFIC DIMENSION

Action Science and Organizational Learning

The Israeli organizational psychologist Victor Friedman provides three definitions of 'action science'[8] at the outset:

Action Science: Three Definitions

'The action scientist is an interventionist who seeks both to promote learning in the client system and to contribute to general knowledge.'
(Chris Argyris, 1985)

'An action science would concern itself with situations of uniqueness, uncertainty and instability which do not lend themselves to the application of theories and techniques derived for science in the mode of technical rationality. it would aim at developing themes from which, in these sorts of situations, practitioners may construct theories and methods of their own.'
(Donald Schon, 1988)

> 'Action science focuses on creating conditions of collaborative inquiry in which people in organizations function as co-researchers rather than as subjects.'
> (Argyris and Schon, 1996)

Action science (AS) attempts to address the widening gap between social science theory and research and social-science-based professional practice. Technical rationality and its positivist foundations, in requiring completeness and precision, produces theories that are too complex for practitioners working in real time. Moreover, phenomenological and interpretive research methods offer a useful approach to practitioners who require theories that explain problems in particular settings and systems of meaning.

The principal architects of AS and OL (organizational learning) are the American organizational psychologists Chris Argyris and Donald Schon.[9] *A key method in action science is confronting, a process whereby social actors are forced to come to terms explicitly with their own defensive reactions to changes and perceived threats by inquiring into the causes of these reactions and analysing the consequences of giving in to them.*

But the goals of action science are even more ambitious:

- inquiring into the variable embedded in the status quo that keep it there;
- inquiring into the variables involved in changing the status quo and moving towards liberating alternatives;
- inquiring into the variables in a science of intervention that will be required if the previous propositions are ever to be tested;
- inquiring into the research methodology that would make change possible and simultaneously produce new knowledge.

In the process 'espoused theory' refers to the account actors give for their actions. 'Theory-in-use' refers to observer-analyst's inferences about the theory that must underlie the observed actions. Secondly, and of particular relevance to Argyris, 'single-loop learning' refers to a situation where people or organizations alter their behaviour but do nothing to change the behavioural strategies that gave rise to the problems faced. By contrast, double-loop learning results from responding to a problem by stepping back and examining larger frames in which the problems could be put. The immediate problem is seen to be the result of a context, which needs to be altered. By altering this context a group can now move on to organizational learning. Action science, moreover, generally views the persistence of single-loop learning as the product of defensive reactions.

For Greenwood and Levin then, *action science takes a very narrow cut of the complexities of human psychology*, even though they welcome its analysis of motivation and behaviour. They criticize its reduction of human psychology, as relevant to action, to the production of defence routines leading to single-loop outcomes. The richness of human motivations, the complex interactions between cultural ideas and the economics and politics of certain situations, and the complex differences between all participants in a particular situation, are not explored if the analysis focuses only on defensiveness.

From Action Science to Communities of Inquiry

Action science involves research in practice rather than research on practice. This involves 'communities of practice', that is professionals who share a common 'language of practice': a set of values, knowledge and procedures. Science, as such, represents a 'community of inquiry', whose central activity is the creation of knowledge. Action science then assumes that human beings are theory builders who 'construct' theories of reality, which they constantly test through action.

Action science addresses the problem of multiple interpretations by requiring both practitioners and researchers to make their own interpretation processes explicit and open to public testing. Such explicit theories of action can be used to predict behaviour. Finally, action science takes a particular interest in intractable problems, helping practitioners to change systems and 'transform their world'.

We now turn to Peter Senge's community action research.

For Peter Senge and Claus-Otto Scharmer[10] of the 'Society for Organizational Learning' (SOL), industrial age institutions face extraordinary challenges to evolve which are unlikely to be met in isolation. Collaboration and joint knowledge building are vital. Competition, which fuelled the industrial era, must be now tempered by co-operation. Indeed the frenzy for optimal return on financial capital today threatens health and sustainability on all levels, not only of individual institutions but also of their members and indeed the larger social and natural systems in which they are embedded.

Community action research, then, represents an approach to collaborative knowledge creation with which Senge and Scharmer have been involved for a decade. Like action research, it confronts the challenges of producing practical knowledge that is useful to people in the everyday conduct of their lives. But unlike the traditional approach to such, it focuses on fostering relationships, creating settings and leveraging progress:

Community Action Research

- *Fostering relationships* and collaboration amongst diverse organizations.
- *Creating settings* for collective reflection that enable people from different organizations to 'see themselves in one another'.
- *Leveraging progress* in individual organizations through cross-institutional links to sustain transformative changes that would otherwise die out.

The purpose, building knowledge for institutional and social change, is why the community exists. Understanding the knowledge-creating process, something Nonaka and Takeuchi have investigated in depth[11] enables everyone to see how their efforts fit in a larger system, involving a continual cycle of creating theory, tools and practical knowhow. Especially in times of deep change, sustaining adaptive institutional responses requires better theory, method *and* practical knowhow.

We now turn to the participatory dimension, lodged more specifically in the Southern as opposed to Western, Northern or even Eastern, orientations of action research.

16.4 Global Variations of Generic Action Research

In turning towards the 'global variations' of action research, we actually revisist the Southern grounds of 'participatory action research'. Though this does obviously overlap with Chapter 7, this is the nature and scope of action research, in that its different manifestations (see conclusion to this chapter) are strongly interwoven.

DESTABILIZING POWER RELATIONS: FEMINISM TO CULTURAL STUDIES

Feminist and participative action research (PAR), particularly that in the South, both seek to unsettle and change the power relations, structures and mechanisms of the social world. Unsettling these is multifaceted, ranging from redefining power to rethinking the very purposes of knowledge creation. Turning the relationship inside out by promoting the approach of co-researchers in an effort to share or flatten power is at the heart of action research. Feminist scholars, at the same time, often disclose their biases, feelings, choices and multiple identities, clearly locating themselves within the research process. There we get glimpses of how we might each further transform ourselves as action researchers engaged in transforming the world. Finally, the research approach developed in the Black Liberation Movement includes:

- moving beyond traditional methods by;
- creating knowledge for the sake of economic, political and social change in the black community; and
- without forsaking rigorous social investigation.

PAR then, as we saw in Chapter 7, becomes a tool to dismantle the master's house, and to achieve social justice. It was also to be used as a building block to build 'black' social institutions. Under these circumstances, the role of the 'black' social scientist was to be both scholar and social activist. This stance of community members being responsible for building knowledge for the purposes of social equality and organizational change is one of the core values of action research. Co-inquiry emphasizes the research process as an elevating learning experience for all those involved in the research endeavour, stimulating dialogue between researcher and participant in the creation of new knowledge.

PROMOTING A LIBERATORY TRANSITION: TOWARDS VIVENCIA

The year 1970 was the first in a series of turning points for those (mostly in sociology, anthropology, education and theology) who were increasingly preoccupied with life conditions, which appeared unbearable in communities surrounding them. Fals Borda and his colleagues took for granted that these conditions were produced by the spread of capitalism and universalistic modernization which were seen to be destroying the cultural and biophysical texture of rich and diverse social structures dear and well known to them. They just could not be blind or silent when witnessing the collapse of positive values and attitudes towards humankind and nature. This seemed to require a radical critique and reorientation of social theory and practice. Conceptions of Cartesian rationality, dualism and 'normal' science were challenged, as they could not find answers from the universities that had formed them professionally. Many therefore broke shackles and left the academies. During the course of 1970 some began to formalize alternative institutions and processes for solving regional problems involving emancipatory educational, cultural and political processes.

Soon after 1970 it became clear that the PAR crowd were looking for a new conceptual element to guide fieldwork. They wanted to go beyond social psychology (Lewin), Marxism (Lukacs), anarchism (Kropotkin), phenomenology (Husserl) and classical theories of participation (Owen, Rousseau, Mill). They also wanted to respect the critical methodology they had inherited from the hermeneutic philosopher Gadamer, and to remain disciplined researchers. At the same time they wanted to link such thoughts with their experiences in the field. Recognizing that knowledge was socially constructed, rather than objective truth, they postulated that the main criterion should be to obtain knowledge that would be useful for dealing with worthy causes. As such, the rebel, the heretic, the indigenous and common folk may prove to be more significant than the PAR theorists themselves. Discussing then the evasive problem of purpose in science and knowledge, they went back to Newton's operational rationality and Descartes' instrumental reason, oriented towards controlling nature, since labelled 'scientism'. On the other hand, Bacon and Galileo were more ready to acknowledge the role of practice and community to explain the functions of everyday life. Indeed popular knowledge has always been a source of formal learning. Overall though, *it was felt that science was in need of a moral conscience, and reason needed to be enriched with sentiment and feeling.*

Rejecting the academic tradition of doing research to promote academic advancement, they had to 'de-colonize their minds'. Their praxis-inspired commitment sought after role models such as Paulo Freire, Mahatma Ghandi and Julius Nyerere, seeking to theorize and obtain knowledge enriched through direct involvement and social action. Moreover, they followed Francis Bacon's original guidelines (1607): 'truth is revealed and established more through the testimony of actions than through logic or even observation'. They had to consider, then, researcher and researched both as real 'thinking-feeling persons' whose diverse views on the shared life experience had to be taken into account. In fact, if applied in earnest, *such a participatory philosophy could produce social/collective transformations* between them. New 'reference groups' were formed with grassroots leaders. Hardcore data were combined with imaginative, literary and artistic interpretations.

In learning to develop an authentic attitude towards others, which was called *vivencia*, meaning entering into the other's life experience (Husserl's 'life world'), it became easy to listen to discourses coming from diverse origins. Participatory research, at an international conference in 1977, was defined as *vivencia* necessary for the achievement of progress and democracy, thereby becoming not only a research methodology but also a philosophy of life that would convert its practitioners into thinking-feeling-persons.

LIBERATIONIST PERSPECTIVES AND THE NEW PARADIGM

The overall objective then was to use the knowledge gained to understand better, change and re-enchant our plural world. For Immanuel Wallerstein – founder of the World Systems group in America – the 'two modernities' were those of technology and liberation, Fals Borda's orientation being towards the latter rather than the former. Thus to the Marxist orientation towards praxis is added the Aristotelean 'phonesis', that is the pursuit of judgement and wisdom for the achievement of the good life. The two-pronged *commitment to liberation and service* then undergirds PAR lifestyle and practice. *It is not only a quest for knowledge, but also a transformation of individual and communal attitudes and values, personality and culture, an altruistic process:* the construction of a practical and morally satisfying paradigm for the social sciences to make them congruent with the ideal of service, especially in the South of the world, combining ethics and praxis, academic knowledge and popular wisdom, the rational and existential.

For Fals Borda this is the most overarching challenge we face. We have moved together from 18th- and 19th-century participatory and utopian theories to the threshold of another set of theories on chaos, complexity and postmodern liberation. This has been done with guidance from intellectual and political giants. Now alert philosophers of action, eloquent postmodernists and critical theorists have taken this story on, with a view to liberating peoples who are under the heel of oppressive power systems. *The need now is to construct an altruistic ethos for heterogeneous forms of cultures, times, spaces and peoples; that however implies a worldwide effort to combine political, economic and intellectual resources from North and South, East and West.* For a while, our concern for knowledge, power and justice and their relationships grew independently in our respective regions. In the final analysis, the effect of PAR work carries a liberating, political accent worldwide. The rising universal brotherhood of critical intellectuals tends to construct open pluralist societies in which oppressive central powers, the economy of exploitation, monopolies and the unjust distribution of wealth, the reign of terror, the dominance of militarism and the abuse of the natural environment, as well as racism, is proscribed. As we arrive at a new millennium, it would be great to think, Fals Borda proclaims, *that PAR will be able to do its share to find better scientific, technical and social ways for improved living conditions, and for the enrichment of human cultures.*

We now turn to power and knowledge.

POWER AS A RELATION OF DOMINATION

The role of participatory action research is to empower people through the construction of their own knowledge, in a process of action and reflection, or 'conscientization', to use Freire's terms. Lack of empowerment occurs for several reasons. First there is the argument that the positivist methods distances those whose 'stuffy reality' (expertise) *is* disconnected from those who experience knowledge through their own lived subjectivity. Second there is the argument that traditional methods of research – especially surveys and questionnaires – may reinforce the passivity of powerless groups, quantitative forms of knowing, moreover, reducing the complexity of human experience. Third, there is the critique that dominant knowledge marginalizes other forms of knowing. PAR, on the other hand, recognizing that knowledge is socially constructed, allows for social, collective analysis of life experience. Participative research makes claims to challenge power relations in each of its dimensions through addressing the needs for knowledge, action and consciousness:

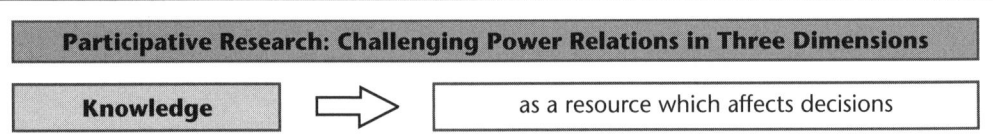

Participative Research: Challenging Power Relations in Three Dimensions

| Knowledge | ⟹ | as a resource which affects decisions |

Action	⇨	which looks at who is involved in the production of knowledge
Consciousness	⇨	how the production of knowledge changes the worldview of those involved

One of the most important contributions of PAR to empowerment and social change is in the knowledge dimension. Through a more open and democratic process, new categories of knowledge, based on local realities, are framed and given voice.

However, relatively powerless groups may merely speak in ways that echo the voices of the powerful. Treating situated representations as facts serves to characterize positivism. Actually, to fulfil its liberating potential, PAR must surface and reinforce alternative forms and categories of knowledge, which may not at first appear. Such knowledge must be embedded, moreover, in cycles of action and reflection. In other words, a process of critical consciousness needs to ensue. Ultimately, developing and using new forms of participatory knowledge on a large scale, as the World Bank has begun to do, thereby promoting and using new forms of participatory democracy, involves ordinary citizens in using their knowledge and experience to construct a more just and equitable society. At a time when inequality between rich and poor is greater than ever before, the challenges of going to broader scale with PAR are enormous, but so also are the risks of failing to do so.

RESEARCH OF THE PEOPLE, BY THE PEOPLE, FOR THE PEOPLE

PAR then is research of the people, by the people, for the people. The more obvious purpose of such is to bring about changes by improving the material circumstances of affected people. To this end, people engage in different kinds of activity: inquiring into the nature of a problem to solve it by understanding its causes and meanings, getting together by organizing themselves as community units and mobilizing themselves for action by raising their awareness of what should be done on moral and political grounds. For the first of these objectives, the inquiry makes use of conventional methods, additionally facilitated by art and theatre, oral history, music and dance, to reveal the more submerged and difficult-to-articulate aspects of the issues involved. In all cases, however, group processes play an important role. Dialogue, in particular, looms large, as a means whereby participants can share experiences and information, create common meanings and forge concerted actions together. Overall then, the kind of knowledge that the research generates needs to produce technically useful results while at the same time strengthening community ties and heightening transformational potential through critical consciousness.

To demonstrate the effect of action research, that is a continual cycling between action and reflection, between theory and practice, we introduce here the case story of Cashbuild. We will learn how through a painful and protracted, but ultimately fruitful and proactive, process of action research, Koopman and Cashbuild had been inching their way towards an industrial democracy. While such a focus on industrial democracy, as in the Mondragon case we discussed in Chapter 13, is a feature of socio-technical design, the pre-emphasis in the Cashbuild case is upon the successive processes of action and reflection, experimentation and observation, deployed 'scientifically' by Cashbuild's former chief executive officer Albert Koopman.

16.5 Generic Action Research in Practice: The Cashbuild Case

TOWARDS INDUSTRIAL DEMOCRACY

What happened at Cashbuild in South Africa resonates with the views of action researchers Greenwood and Levin:

> *Institutionally based action research is framed as a democratic process supporting the creation of knowledge that potentially can be liberating. Obviously then, the inquiry process has to aim to solve problems important to the organizational participants, and the knowledge produced by the inquiry process must increase participants' control over their own situations. This is consistent with Freire's 'conscientization', which identifies the inquiry process as one shaping knowledge relevant to action, as well as being built on a critical understanding of the historical and political contexts within which the participants act.*[12]

Cashbuild, the South African retailer of building material, was turned – at least for a period of two decades from the mid 1980s to the early part of the 21st century – into an African industrial democracy, as well into a successful business, by the redoubtable Albert Koopman.[13] All this happened in the most turbulent time in South Africa's recent history. We shall present Cashbuild's story in Koopman's own words.

THE CASHBUILD STORY

> *I was raised as a street fighter. My mother died when I was 13 and my father lived in Mozambique, 1,240 miles from me. Set free at a very early age I had to learn to survive. That meant dealing with people, including people who had hang-ups, and people who wanted to do me in for what I believed. The one thing that I learnt as a result was that I was going to enter my life as a clean, moral fighter, someone who sterilised his bicycle chains before he entered the fight of interpersonal relationships. Unlike the animals with claws and teeth, God gave me his supreme gifts; choice and intellect. Making use of these two gifts, I was able to meaningfully observe, and speculate in different ways, upon my fellow man going about his daily activities. From this I acquired my moral purpose. The story you are about to hear is one of my personal experience in an African context, through my involvement as the Chief Executive of a Cash and Carry Building Material Merchant in South Africa. It is a story of success and many failures, a story of victories and sadnesses in my attempt to create an excellent company, to put it mildly, in a somewhat turbulent society. It is the story of how a white (northern) man in Africa became a White African (southern). It is the story of how I combined the rationality of the First World with the humanity of the Third.*

Cashbuild was started as a wholesaler in 1978 and became a very successful business in a short space of time. Situated predominantly in the rural areas of South Africa and focusing on the black housing market, the staff complement consisted of 84 per cent black, 13 per cent white and 3 per cent Indian. However, by mid 1982, with 12 outlets, profits started sliding. Everything Northern was in place – systems, procedures, technology, combined with a booming market – but something was going wrong and Koopman did not know enough about the South, at that point, to recognize where to start looking.

> *We embraced our cardinal principles of giving value to our customers, being innovative, adaptable, and totally committed to the business as well as having efficient organizational structures, but obviously something was changing and we did not know what it was. Our hierarchy was well displayed on the walls of all our outlets, everyone was placed in neat little boxes with prescribed job descriptions and functions, and no one was achieving our objectives as had been laid out! I came to the conclusion that we had a lot of trained men but no actual committed soldiers.*

> *It was clear that our organizational structure was autocratic, as was my own personal management style. We had to change, but how? What if people started seeing me as soft, when I became more participative and democratic? What about the chaos that might occur during the period of transition? Well there was no other way to do it at the time but by MBFA – Managing by Fumbling Around. There was no alternative but to plunge in at the deep end and to risk my neck and possibly be forced to say 'I'm sorry' for my original way of doing things. I immediately commissioned an attitude survey and found that pro-company feelings, to the tune of 89 per cent in 1980, had slipped to 74 per cent in 1982.*[14]

Arising out of 3,000 issues that came to Cashbuild's attention through the brainstorming sessions, Koopman drew up a set of cardinal principles emerging out of the interdependent relationships that existed between customer, employee, company, competitor and motivation. He realized at the same time that the Northern principles would have to embrace the Southern spirit of every employee, so they were spelled out as follows:

- 'We recognize that the marketing process of getting goods from supplier to customer is the concern of every employee and that we have to liberate him/her to achieve this.'
- 'We want to strive for quality service through people and keep our system as balanced as possible through on-the-job training, motivation through better supervision, self measurement and statistical control rather than boss control, giving people a say over their workplace.'
- 'We recognize that quality service and total productivity will only come if we rediscover the spirit of man within the workplace, providing job enrichment by changing the work people do.'
- 'People need to belong to and identify with the company's cause; customers must be satisfied through committed people.'

No stone was left unturned and over a period of one year Koopman listened to why people worked, with whom they preferred to work, and what they saw would be the design of the perfect workplace. After spending extended periods of time living amongst his black employees, experiencing life within their communities, and consulting with them directly, he found he had to review his whole understanding of the people he employed, as well as how they saw their relationship with the business and with its philosophy. The degree to which aspects of indigenous Southern culture were to become 'spiritualized' in the workplace was to depend on the type of Northern organization imposed upon the individual, including the degree to which the organization would allow expression of these elements.

> We had to turn our thinking about people upside down and look at our business totally differently. The perception of capitalist exploitation at Cashbuild had to be changed. This change needed to be achieved not merely through some superficial 'western' programme of empowerment, but through an active 'northern' restructuring of the hierarchy, to liberate the work ethic. We had to design an organization that was truly free so that the co-operation between all individuals became its own sustainable social form.[15]

Koopman needed a social form that could accommodate the freedom to be enterprising, as well as harnessing the spiritual consciousness of all the employees. His CARE philosophy was 'Cashbuild's Aspirations with Regard to Excellence'. In essence the CARE philosophy sought to bring about a balancing of power within the organization. At that stage, in 1982, authority was vested with management (but no power) and power with the unions (but no authority). Firstly, he built in mechanisms for the protection of individual rights vis-à-vis the organization, through a Northern code of conduct. Secondly, CARE groups were formed to give expression to the Southern spiritual consciousness of individuals, serving as a vehicle for discussion of issues affecting their working life. Groups were formed at five levels – general labourers, semi-skilled personnel, junior, middle and senior managers – each with their own majority elected president. Thirdly, these groups were to engage with the economic process, sharing information about efficiency and productivity, and learning about as well as influencing the company's wealth-creating process. A CARE philosophy designed by the people for the people spelled out how the workplace should be regulated, and set out the rules of the business game. Some of the salient points were:

- a commitment to joint decision-making at all levels, with everyone playing their part in finding solutions to problems
- an open and free culture with everyone in the organization having access to any line manager
- a team consisting of different races, sexes and cultural creeds, none of which were to be discriminated against.

As such, Cashbuild became a fully fledged industrial democracy and remained such for some 15 years, till the first decade of the 21st century.

> This was our company. It was proposed that a governing body of five people be constituted to each outlet – the VENTURECOM – with each person being democratically elected to hold a portfolio, save for the manager who was appointed to the operations portfolio, based on his or her expertise. This portfolio was concerned with the 'hard' variables whereas the Safety, Labour, Merchandise and Quality of Work-Life portfolios were the 'soft' ones. Moreover, each of these managers was continually assessed by lower levels in the hierarchy. The subsequent newspaper headlines – 'Cashbuild – the company where workers have the right to dismiss their

managers' – frightened the hell out of the capitalist fraternity. Yet precisely because that right existed within the workforce we never needed to use it. In fact, this Cashbuild VENTURECOM system was socialistic in that it reinstated distributive justice and offered security against destitution. It was likewise capitalistic to the extent that individual expression was given its due reward, and group development its due recognition. Our system thus gave expression to the work ethic and also to the enterprising spirit of people.[16]

This process of action research took place through several years of trial and error, action and research; it remained in place for several years after Albert Koopman left the company, in the latter part of the 1990s, and when it was run by his own protégé. But when the protégé in turn left, that was the end of the democratic Cashbuild story, and since 2005 it has reverted to classically undemocratic business type. Agency and structure, leadership and organization, in other words, go hand in hand.

16.6 Conclusion

OVERLAPPING APPROACHES TO ACTION RESEARCH

We find it remarkable that action research, as a whole, while a strong research movement in its own right, is so often cut off from the mainstream of research method and methodology. Its limiting factor, perhaps, is that this Western approach to action research retains a somewhat analytic – albeit combined with action – orientation. In other words, it lacks some of the dynamic and transformative elements associated with innovation, and thereby needs to be supported by the origination, foundation and emancipation brought to bear upon the integral nature and scope of each research path. Actually, all too often, action research is considered in isolation of these. With Integral Research we sought to overcome exactly this isolation; indeed we have moved from isolation to integration.

Each of our four research paths, as we have now seen, has ended with its own particular variation of action research, illustrating a particular Southern, Eastern, Northern or Western flavour. Invariably though, the four approaches to action research overlap. In some respects, they are not easy to distinguish. Their closeness to each other underlines the 'integrated dimension' of level four of Integral Research. Not only needs, in our approach, level 4 to serve to integrate the three levels that came before (origination, foundation and emancipation), vertically as it were, it is also horizontally integrative so to speak, in that the four approaches to action research have close links to each other. That is also the reason why we re-introduced Southern PAR as a global variation in this Western chapter on action research. The following table gives a concluding overview on the action research territory:

SOCIAL INNOVATION TERRITORY					
Forms of Action Reseach	Core Exponents	Dimension	Type of Transformation	Contribution to Integral Social Innovation	
Participatory Action Research/ Appreciative Inquiry	Fals Borda (Colombia) /Cooperider (USA)	Communal	Social Transformation	Provides Underlying Grounds	SOUTH
Co-operative Inquiry/ Participative Spirituality	Heron (UK)	Transpersonal	Spiritual Growth	Source of Emergence	EAST
Knowledge Creation /Socio- Technical Design	Morten Levin (Norway)	Organizational	Industrial Democracy	Provides Navigation	NORTH
Action Science	Revans/ Argyris /Schon (USA)	Individual	Action Learning	Ultimate Transformative Effect	WEST

As we have seen and in very simplistic terms, action research is a very 'broad church'. In fact, it may even be considered too broad, as it incorporates:

- participative action research: our Southern *grounding*;
- co-operative inquiry: our Eastern *emergence*;
- socio-technical design: our Northern *navigation*;
- action learning and action science: our Western *effect*.

All under one 'action research' roof. However, we have chosen it as our penultimate chapter. Integrally crafted action research has a highly integrative and innovative nature and scope. To the extent that it serves to integrate the research levels that come vertically before and to the extent that it is open to the full span of action research, horizontally, it serves to release the full GENE-ius of social innovation. This is demonstrated by Figure 16.4.

Figure 16.4 Integral Action Research Leading to Social Innovation

TOWARDS SUSTAINABLE DEVELOPMENT AND ECONOMIC OPPORTUNITIES

We come to the end of the Western path of realization by revisiting once more the four levels along the research-to-innovation trajectory that you have, by now, progressively built upon. Through such, your Integral Innovation would have come about, on an organizational and communal level, supporting sustainable development (the Western function of an enterprise or community) and, on a societal level, contributing to the creation of economic opportunities. The following table summarizes the entire Western journey.

Western Path of Realization	
Sustainable Development – Economic Opportunity	
Experimentation *Originate*	*You manipulate and control variables, or experiments, as a scientist, politician, professional or business practitioner, making the most of a free market, democratic environment.*
Analysis *Found*	*Through classical scientific 'method' you observe, experiment, and verify; as such economic and security problems/situations are to be fixed, controlled, managed.*
Stratification *Emancipate*	*The 'reality' you face is stratified* – deep reality underlying observations/events is generative; economic emancipation requires in-depth management of physical/human nature.
Action *Transform*	As a pragmatic, life-giving social 'scientist' you pursue sustainable development, promoting ongoing economic opportunity, through *action, reflection, theory and practice*

We also conclude this final chapter of the fourth path with our Integral Innovation Tree, this time adapted to illustrate the particular characteristics of the Western path. The Western path is predominantely oriented towards the creation of economic opportunities. However, by now, you will have certainly recognized that the relation between a particular path and a particular domain of innovation is not that linear. Particularly the lines between neighbouring paths blur. We have had many cases in our research and innovation programmes where participants, who clearly connected with the relational path, pursued a path towards Integral Innovation, which was lodged in the adjacent Eastern domain of peaceful co-evolution.

That, however, never inhibited the research-to-innovation process. On the contrary, the overlapping of the various paths opened, in most cases, the horizon of the individual researcher and facilitated the interaction and cooperation between researchers. In other words, the tree has many roots. Actually, it has four (see Figure 16.5). And they all come together in the main stem, jointly supporting the evolution of the entire tree, altogether promoting Integral Innovation. The metaphor of the tree is particular useful in illustrating the importance of research communities in tackling the complex burning issues we face today, as organizations, communities, societies and in the world at large.

We are now ready to draw together the threads of our Integral Research-to-Innovation argument.

Figure 16.5 The Integral Innovation Tree and the Western Path of Realization

References

1. Reason, P. and Bradbury, H. (2004). *Handbook of Action Research*. London: Sage.
2. Cooperider, D. and Whitmore, D. (2005). *Appreciative Inquiry*. San Francisco, CA: Berrett Koehler.
3. Reason and Bradbury, *Handbook of Action Research*.
4. *Ibid.*
5. Heron, J. (2006). *Participative Research*. San Francisco, CA: Lulu Press.
6. Greenwood, D. and Levin, M. (eds) (2007). *Introduction to Action Research*. London: Sage.
7. Revans, R. (1999). *The ABC of Action Learning*. London: Mike Pedlar Library.
8. Reason and Bradbury, *Handbook of Action Research*.
9. Greenwood and Levin, *Introduction to Action Research*.
10. *Ibid.*
11. Nonaka, I. and Takeuchi, H. (1995). *The Knowledge Creating Company*. Oxford: Oxford University Press.
12. Greenwood and Levin, *Introduction to Action Research*.
13. Koopman, A. (1991). *Trans-cultural Management*. Oxford: Blackwell.
14. *Ibid.*
15. *Ibid.*
16. *Ibid.*

4 *Institutionalizing Social Innovation*

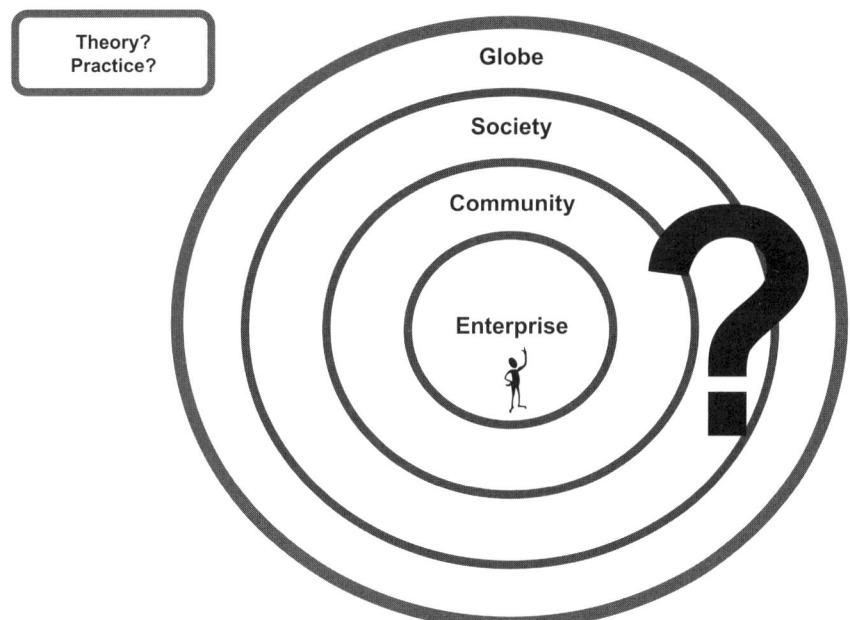

17 *Integral Research and Innovation*

Summing Up, Moving Forward

Figure 17.1 Four World Integral Innovation Tree

Summary: Integral Research and Innovation

- Integral Research and Innovation is an organic process that evolves from original research, aligned with research method, to transformative action, aligned with action research.
- In the process a burning issue is addressed which is simultaneously your burning issue, set within a particular social context; you select a specific research path, aligned with yourself and your culture; you interconnect the social sciences and the humanities; ultimately resolving, at least in part, the burning issue at hand.
- This process is altogether transformational, transcultural, transdiciplinary and transpersonal, involving the development of self, organization and society, each one in an integral direction.
- Each of the four paths – relational, renewal, reason and realization – of research-to-innovation has a double-layered trajectory, that is static – method, methodology, critique and action – and dynamic – origination, foundation, emancipation, transformation.
- You may alternately adopt 'path flexibility', as is exemplified by the case of Dr Sam Rima of Bethel University, where you mix paths or else pursue a coherent path, following the static (method to action) and dynamic (origination to transformation) layers of a single path.
- The 'paradigm shifts' with which we are involved are: from individual research to research communities; from social research to integral innovation; from method as isolated technique to method as an integral source of origination; from North-Western dominance to involving all worlds; and finally from separation to integration of the social sciences and the humanities.
- We see Integral Research as a step along the way towards an Integral University, standing on the shoulders of integral giants such as the original concept of the liberal arts university, the seminal Frankfurt School in Germany that gave rise to the New School of Research in New York, and the social and educational laboratories created by Lewin and Dewey in America.
- The four keynotes of such a prospectively Integral University, interacting with our integral enterprise, are: the transformational, building on nature and community; the transcultural, evolved out of a particular culture and spirit; the transdisciplinary, spanning the social sciences and the humanities of a specific society; and the transpersonal, involving self, organization and community/society.
- Dedicated to releasing full GENE-ius the Integral University promotes, for a particular self, organization and society (or community) four rhythms: (1) being (self), community building (enterprise) and healing the planet (society); (2) becoming (self), conscious evolution (enterprise) and peaceful co-evolution between peoples (society); (3) knowing (self), knowledge creation (enterprise), and open society (society); (4) doing (self), sustainable development (enterprise) and creating economic opportunity (society).

17.1 Integral Research-to-Innovation: Summary of the Theory

THE FOUR WORLD INTEGRAL INNOVATION TREE

We have now concluded all four research paths (Integral Research) and each of their trajectories (Integral Innovation). Each path of research to innovation, moreover, follows a double-layered analytical and transformative, four-fold trajectory. These two intertwined static and dynamic trajectories extend from method to action (analytical) and origination to transformation (transformative) respectively. The latter transformative trajectory is grounded in a burning issue, both subjectively and objectively, and infused with substance by one or more of the social sciences, if not also the humanities.

Analogous to a yin–yang rhythm, as we have indicated, the analytical trajectory embodies the more stabilizing research categories, while the transformative one embodies the more dynamic innovative force. Together, both trajectories, along each one of the four paths serve to build up Integral Research, analytically, and Integral Innovation, dynamically. That is why this book, in summary, is constituted of both Integral Research, via four paths, and also ultimately, of Integral Innovation, as the culmination of a fourfold and double-layered trajectory.

For you, the reader and would-be Integral Innovator, the challenge is, firstly, to uncover your own research path, a path which is authentic to yourself and to your culture and society, and thereafter to follow through a corresponding fourfold trajectory, analytically (method to action) and transformatively (origination to transformation).

Interestingly enough – and referring to the renowned American psychologist Daniel Levinson – this fourfold process can also be likened to the cycle of life, whereby you start out with origination (being); move on to develop an emerging foundation for your life, often adopting, or adapting to, a guiding philosophy in your community or society (becoming); then, at midlife, you develop a critical and emancipated perspective on life (knowing); until, in the final stage, which Levinson calls 'maturity', you are ready to ultimately bring to the world your fully actualized originality, the full fruits (doing) of your life. Of course, as Levinson emphasizes, such a life cycle often gets thwarted, for both internal and external reasons, never then even reaching the third stage (know thyself) of personal emancipation. In such a case your full GENE-ius, like that of an enterprise or community, remains inhibited.

The GENE then embodies the transformational flow, which we had, in our earlier work, identified as the 'life force' of each living system. We have described this 'natural flow' in detail in *Transformation Management*,[1] the companion volume to this book. There we illustrate how the GENE, if understood and consciously applied, serves to release the GENE-ius of the interconnected living systems of self, organization and society. Similarly the Four Worlds, our *transcultural forces,* underlie the four research-to-innovation paths.

Analogous to that, the GENE serves here to release the full GENE-ius of you, the Integral Innovator to be, and, of course, of your own Integral Innovation.

Integral Research and Innovation		
Transpersonal Transformation	Active engagement with a particular context; transformation of the burning issue at hand; transcending your personal perspective, towards organization, community and society; building on all that has come before.	**Branches**
Transdisciplinary Emancipation	Creative and critical interaction between different social disciplines; reconnecting the social sciences and humanities; building a new knowledge basis.	**Mainstem**
Transcultural Foundation	Research paths authentic to a particular culture; interaction of local and global philosophies and knowledge systems; evoking creative synthesis between cultures; building on local knowledge foundations and connecting with global knowledge.	**Roots**
Transformational Origination	Destined to transform a burning issue within a particular social context; evoking the transformational potential and originality of the particular culture by putting in touch with the richness of its soil (nature, religion, art, music, dance).	**Soil**

The entire process is designed to engage you in the full bandwidth from fundamental research, starting, if you like, with method and origination, to transformative action. We have further illustrated that this process is not only transformational but simultaneously, and by necessity, transcultural, transdisciplinary and transpersonal (applied to the development of self, organization and society). We summarize this once more in the above table where we, at the same time, link these four rhythms to the Integral Innovation Tree that is depicted in Figure 17.1.

RETRACING STEPS: THE FOUR RESEARCH-TO-INNOVATION PATHS

The full process from transformational origination to transpersonal transformation also alludes, again, to the fact that the seed for the final and Integral Innovation is already lodged in the very soil – individual and collective – from which the research to innovation starts. Let us, at this stage, once more retrace the steps of each of the four paths to innovation that we have introduced.

For each of the four levels of each path, that is for each double-layered trajectory, we have both developed a set of analytical tenets and also an overall, transformational teleology. You will find both of them summarized in the Annex to this book. Here we purely focus on the transformational teleology, which provides for the dynamic unfolding of each of the four paths.

You will notice that, in order to give you a more concrete 'touch and feel' for each path, we have departed somewhat from the slightly esoteric language embodied in 'research methodology' for each path. As such, for example, you move along the Southern relational path from *passion* (descriptive methods), to *engagement* (phenomenology), to *liberation* (feminism) to *participation* (participatory action research or PAR). We start with the Southern path, and then proceed onto the others. In each case, at the head of the Table, we also indicate the ultimate course you pursue.

Southern Relational Path to Integral Innovation	
Community Building – Healing the Planet	
Passion *Originate*	*You are passionately and concretely involved with a particular people and environment.* You portray them vitally and intimately, in rich colour and texture, rhythm and form.
Engagement *Found*	You enter philosophically *into the life world and spirit of a culture,* conceiving of their unique time and place as a local part of a larger story and a wider world.
Liberation *Emancipate*	You reflect critically and contextually on your self and others, via ecology, anthropology and sociology, using *such situated knowledge as a means for liberation.*
Participation *Transform*	Via discussion, consensus building, activity, using popular stories and oral traditions, *you heal environments and build communities,* enhancing human and more-than-human life.

The Eastern path of renewal begins with the story (narrative methods) of yourself and your particular social context. From there you move on to interpretation (hermeneutics and interpretivism), thereafter onto dialectical dialogue (critical theory) and finally to co-evolution (co-operative inquiry).

Eastern Path of Renewal to Integral Innovation	
Conscious Evolution – Peaceful Co-evolution of Peoples	
Story *Originate*	Each event in the grounding of self, organization and society is novel; no struggle, no story; no trouble, no tale. The overall plot in each case unfolds with a view to continuing development.
Interpretation *Found*	Through a fusion of horizons between tradition and modernity, matter and spirit, self and other, indigenous and exogenous, you *imaginatively reconceive of your world.*
Dialogue *Emancipate*	Such understanding and co-evolving of reality is dialogic and dialectical – via history, psychology, and spirituality – *promoting a progressively raised consciousness.*
Co-evolution *Transform*	Effectively engaging co-researchers as fellow subjects, you *consciously evolve* self/ others via experiential, imaginative, conceptual and practical modes of thought and activity.

We then come onto the Northern Path of Reason, where your journey follows a trajectory from *theory* (methods of theorizing), to *debate* (critical rationalism), to *discourse* (postmodernism) and, ultimately to a new *design* (socio-technical design).

Northern Path of Reason to Integral Innovation	
Knowledge Creation – Open Society	
Theory *Originate*	You categorize phenomena, breaking them into parts. You identify causal conditions, events, incidents that led to them, using your head logically, always looking for connections.
Debate *Found*	You develop, scientifically, an organizing idea as *an opening hypothesis to bring some order to data*, quantitatively and qualitatively, proved or disproved through critical discussion.
Discourse *Emancipate*	No absolute ideology, social, political or technological system, governs your actions: you *pursue relative and fallible not absolute knowledge*, welcoming multiple discourses.
Design *Innovation*	You adopt a flexible, problem-solving orientation, aimed at social and technical betterment; you act as a friendly outsider, *using a co-generative approach to development*.

Finally, through the Western path of realization, you take part in a journey from *experimentation* (experimental and survey methods) to *analysis* (empiricism). From there you emancipate yourself through *stratification,* discovering new layers of reality (critical realism), which then builds up the basis for your ultimate transformative *action* (generic action research).

Western Path of Realization to Integral Innovation	
Sustainable Development – Economic Opportunity	
Experimentation *Originate*	*You manipulate and control variables, or experiments*, as a scientist, politician, professional or business practitioner, making the most of a free-market, democratic environment.
Analysis *Found*	*Through classical scientific 'method' you observe, experiment, and verify;* as such economic and security problems/situations are to be fixed, controlled, managed.
Stratification *Emancipate*	The *'reality'* you face *is stratified* – deep reality underlying observations/events is generative; economic emancipation requires in-depth management of physical/human nature.
Action *Transform*	As a pragmatic, life-giving social 'scientist' you pursue sustainable development, promoting ongoing economic opportunity, through *action, reflection, theory and practice*.

The paths introduced are a reflection of the variety-in-unity and unity-in-variety embedded in our world. All of the paths are necessary and relevant in order to address the core issues of our time in a dynamically balanced way, including and building on the knowledge and wisdom of the four corners of our world. Moreover, and in each case, the transformative trajectory is underpinned, subjectively and objectively, by a burning issue, and builds substantively upon one or other of the social sciences, ranging from anthropology to economics.

We have then, once more, laid out the full map of the research to innovation journey. Again, it may look, as if the journey is a linear one. However, it is a stormy journey, full of pitfalls, iterations, spiralling and cycles. We shall now illustrate our work once more with some current examples within our research and innovation community.

17.2 Integral Research-to-Innovation in Practice

INTEGRAL RESEARCHERS IN ACTION

The research-to-innovation journey, as mentioned various times in this book is by no means as linear as it is projected here. For example, while, as Integral Researcher-and-Innovator, you may start with originating method, and from there move on to a foundational methodology, you may, after that, and before moving on to level 3, come back to method to revise the origination process. Indeed, in many cases, particularly at the beginning, the continuous revisiting of your own origins and of the originality of your own social and cultural context is the norm rather than the exception. We shall now introduce you to a small number of Integral Researchers from all over the worlds, all of them participants on our programmes. We start with Dr Sam Rima from the US. While we feature Sam's research in more detail, because of the significant role he and his Bethel University are playing with us, we also present the other members of our integral innovation community, albeit in less detail.

Sam Rima, USA

Sam is an American with Native Indian roots, who did his second part-time doctorate with us at the University of Buckingham. It took Sam about two years and many intensive interactions with us, to help him to get deeper to the root of the burning issue he was ultimately addressing and the integral innovation he intended to bring about. Having done previous research on *the dark side of leadership*, Sam, who himself is deeply steeped in Christianity but disenchanted with the increasing superficiality and commercialization of it, gradually moved towards the development of a theory on 'spiritual capital'. As a current title for his research journey, four years on, Sam chose 'From a Theory of Spiritual Capital to an Institute for Reconciliation and Social Innovation'. Note, moreover, as we take you through Sam's journey, that while he moved progressively through a fourfold trajectory, from origination to transformation, he actually crossed from one path to another in the evolving process. Sam's case is therefore a stimulating case of *path flexibility,* as we shall see.

Level 1 – Origination – Theorizing Method: Sam engaged to begin with in grounded theory method to develop a theory of Spiritual Capital that might be used as the foundation for a newly emerging form of economic practice. He chose seven interview subjects representing each of the Four Worlds, each of the world's major theistic religions, as well as the various sectors of society. After months of interviews, many pages of transcripts and many hours of coding the data, a coherent theory of spiritual capital emerged. Sam could not help, moreover, but interpret the data through the lens of himself, a Native American Christian, disenchanted with the focus of his own religion because it was deeply embedded in consumer culture, and also impassioned by his own beliefs in and previous work on the 'dark side of leadership'. Such personal convictions led him onto phenomenology.

Level 2 – Foundation – Phenomenological Methodology: Rather than conducting the interviews by phone or in some other non-personal way, Sam chose to immerse himself in the lived world of each of the interview subjects. Having immersed himself in Husserl's and Heidegger's work on phenomenology, he assimilated their unique approaches as well as witnessed the people who were being impacted by it. This involved spending a week in Egypt to absorb Egyptian culture and also a further couple of days experiencing the innovative work of one of the interview subjects before interviewing him on site. Sam spent another week in South Africa experiencing several manifestations of a second interviewee's activities and getting to know her personally in her own environment before conducting the interview. A similar process of immersion took place in Philadelphia, Pennsylvania, London, England, San Diego, California, Knoxville, Tennessee and St Paul, Minnesota. This combined exposure to the lived world of the seven interview subjects provided a rich perspective that was analysed in depth when Sam began processing the data, through grounded theory, and ultimately writing up his theory of spiritual capital. He was able to see and experience the high priority of personal relationships in each of the interviewees' work and how they saw what they were doing in a holistic context that impacted people and the world beyond their immediate context.

Level 3 – Emancipation – Critical Theory Critique: Even before the research began, as well as throughout it, it was Sam's critique of existing forms of neoliberal, advanced capitalism using the critical emancipatory lens of critical theory which enabled him to see how existing social, economic, political and even religious power structures were actually at work. Sam drew especially on the work of Habermas, Adorno, Marcuse and Fromm (*To Have or to Be*) in that respect. As the theory of spiritual capital then emerged from Sam's interpretation of the data and assimilation of the theory, it did so in sharp relief against the backdrop of the existing practice of advanced capitalism. Could this newly emerging theory of spiritual capital find its place and practice within the existing paradigm? How might this new theory gain purchase in the hardscrabble world of economics fuelled solely by self-interest and the increasingly deformed 'invisible hand'? It became clear that an intellectual revolution of sorts would need to take place to prepare the social soil before this newly minted theory of spiritual capital would be given the light of day and take life-giving root in a hostile economic environment.

Level 4 – Action – Action Research: In this final stage of his research to innovation journey, Sam envisioned a new academic programme,rather than the mindless research going on in his current doctoral programme at Bethel, which would begin to not only disseminate his theory of spiritual capital but actually equip others to challenge the socio-economic status quo and become social innovators in their own right. The initial form of this academic programme would be a Doctor of Ministry degree in Social and Economic Innovation, created and taught in partnership with TRANS4M. After the initial planning of the programme's curriculum (action), it was revisited and refined (research) a year later in the light of new developments and understandings, while Sam was in the final stages of his doctorate. Simultaneous to the second round of revisions for the Doctor of Ministry curriculum, Bethel and TRANS4M engaged in much more intense co-operation and co-creation.

Sam's case, though he engaged in various research paths, is ultimately a contribution to the core Western themes: 'sustainable development' and 'providing economic opportunities', the latter particularly through his theoretical work on alternative economics, infused by his core theory on spiritual capital.

We shall describe the further evolution of this process later in this chapter. For now, we introduce, in much shorter vein, a representative selection of Integral Researchers/ Innovators from all four corners of the world as well as from the centre.

Reza Moussavian, Iran/Germany

Reza Moussavian, a seasoned management consultant with Germany's leading telecommunication consultancy DETECON, was of Iranian descent and educated in Germany. His initial research interest was in analysing the potential of the Middle East to form a socioeconomical union, following in the footsteps of the EU, and to develop a coherent framework for this. However, though his consulting work was strongly focusing on the Middle East, he ultimately ended up with a research question much closer to home. Instead of engaging with the large-scale theme of economic union, he developed a theory of an integral investment as an evolution of corporate social responsibility. His approach involved directly building on our Four World approach.

In his consultancy-based application to companies in the Middle East and Africa, and due to his own pragmatic nature, Reza from the very beginning tested his evolving theory in practice. In our terms, he moved at a very early stage along the path of realization to an action-oriented, transformative stage of his Western and also somewhat Northern trajectory, albeit building on prior empirical foundations as well as critical realism, for his emancipatory critique of business in society. In Figure 18.2, we provide a first intimation of Reza's model of an integral business. Altogether it is a good example of, in fact, a new socio-technical design which, within our framework, incorporates the Northern research-to-innovation path of reason, alongside his Western one.

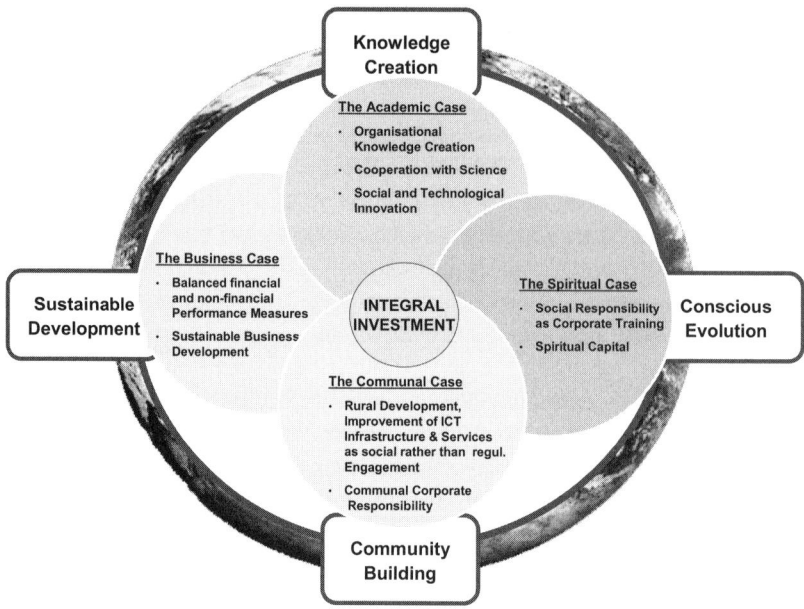

Figure 17.2 The Integral Business Case (based on the Research of Reza Moussavian)

Hanniah Tariq, Pakistan

Hanniah Tariq, a Pakistani by birth and initial education, pursued her Master's degree at the University of Warwick in the UK, as a development sociologist. In the process she was drawn towards a feminist orientation, consistent with the relational path, albeit from a critical emancipatory perspective. As a woman, a sociologist and a passionate advocate of a communally based approach to development, this was not surprising. She also, and from the outset, began to take an interest in Islamic economics, which was strongly oriented towards equity (relational) as well as efficiency (reason).

At the same time, and at the start of her doctorate, Hanniah was seconded to the International Business Leader's Forum and was immediately impelled towards a path of reason and realization, to complement the relational orientation towards which her culture and her personal vocation led her. Working on a project sponsored by the Aga Khan Foundation to promote corporate social responsibility in the Islamic world, she found herself combining her powers of description, which she encouraged in the project participants from the Islamic business world, with socio-technical design. In fact, with help from an old friend, who was a web designer in Pakistan, she developed an interactive self-assessment tool on corporate social responsibility in the first year of her doctorate, which she began to test out with the corporate participants.

Anisa Al Raisi, Oman

Anisa Al Raisi, a former participant on our Master's programme on social and economic transformation in Jordan, is herself a stunning embodiment of an integral innovator. Starting with an opening narrative, on her originative path of renewal, she told the story of how she came from a poor rural Omani family, growing up in a time when girls were not allowed to go to school. Having found a way to educate herself against all obstacles, thereby combining together her indigenous Omani knowledge with a Westernized school education, she later rose to become head of the Omani World Trade Centre. From there, and as part of the projects in her Master's programme, she set up the Arabian Foundation, by now a respected educational provider within Oman. Tapping deeply into her own story, as an Omani feminist Anisa could not help but to address the educational situation in Oman and, through that, become one of the key transformation agents of her country.

Paul Muchineripi and Steve Kada, Zimbabwe

Another interesting two cases in point are Paul 'Chidara' Muchineripi and Steve Kada from Zimbabwe who joined our Southern African Master's programme. It was only when both Chidara and Steve fully reconnected to their Southern African origins, individually and societally, that they were in a position to become Integral Innovators. Whereas Steve Kada followed a relational path, Chidara pursued a path of renewal.

Firstly, each became clear about the burning issue that they needed to address, which they described and narrated in terms of food security. Secondly, and revisiting their indigenous history, they found the very seeds to of a solution to rampant hunger in their villages. In other words, entering into the life worlds of their rural communities, they rediscovered, together, indigenous foods. Proceeding, in the process, to de-colonize people's minds from what they had been told to grow by the colonizer, a new relationship with nature and with indigenous foods was established. Chidara is the son of the local chief; Steve is the HR Director of Cairns Food. Together they combined indigenous (Chinyika village) and exogenous (Cairns Food Processing) forces to effectively feed five villages which had been on the verge of starvation. The ultimate means they used, communally, towards that productive end, was both co-operative inquiry between themselves and the village elders on the one hand, and Cairns senior management and food technologists on the other, and also participatory action research with local villagers.

The case of Steve and Chidara has by now won increasingly national and international recognition. Their work has not only been financially supported by Kellogg's Foundation, it is also about to be written up as a case study by the London-based Africa Research Centre. Under the title 'Together We Grow' Chidara's and Steve's story also been featured in *Forum CSR International*.[2] In addition, a client of ours, Virgin Money, part of the Virgin Group of Richard Branson, has agreed to sponsor Chidara's doctoral research with us. With a view to further developing Steve and Chidara's Integral Innovation, Chidara will, through his doctorate, promote cross-sector partnerships that foster sustainable economic approaches, rooted in African culture. At the same time Virgin, which is also active in Southern Africa, is keen to learn from and with Chidara, what kind of innovative financial infrastructure and products would need to be designed to build up meaningful financial services in the region. The Southern case of Chidara and Steve is altogether also an inspiring contribution to 'community building' and 'healing the planet'.

BUILDING A FOUR WORLD RESEARCH-TO-INNOVATION COMMUNITY

Developing a Research-to-Innovation Community

The development of such research-and-innovation communities is not easy. Not only are they virtually completely absent from the social sciences, but conventional doctoral and post-doctoral research in management, economics and other social sciences is largely an 'individual business'. Apart from occasional meetings, doctoral and post-doctoral researchers don't work purposefully together, which is indeed a catastrophe given the devastating (social) state of the world. In our case, however, and as you have seen, we start out by developing a profound awareness of burning issues and of personal and cultural context, and do what we can to encourage a more communal approach, notwithstanding the constraints of individual, academic accreditation.

Tapping into Society: Becoming Society Builders

In all the cases that we have introduced, from Sam to Reza, from Anisa to Chidara, the individual perspective of the researcher was transcended as they began to apply their particular innovatory impulse within relevant communities or organizations, including that of our own TRANS4M, and from there reached out into society. For example:

- Sam's development of a theory base for spiritual capital evolved into the development of a new doctoral programme at his own centre at Bethel University. Bethel as a whole is now engaging with TRANS4M to the set up of a new Institute for Reconciliation and Social Innovation (see below). The new programmes and the institute together are designed to make a transformative impact on society.
- Reza, as we have seen, translated his theoretical research base into a new conceptual and practical offering for his consultancy. Through his approach towards an integral business-societal offering, client companies of DETECON make a more holistic contribution to the societies in which they operate.

Furthermore, to a significant degree, the research undertaken has been interlinked with and communicated within our research community. The community has been particular helpful in challenging each researcher to develop the authenticity and originality of his or her social innovation. Having purposefully developed a transcultural research community, we continuously bring our participants into purposeful contact with their particular and diverse cultural roots, personal stories and belief systems. Moreover, by encouraging a 'getting into the skin of the other' we enable each to probe more deeply into their own origins and originality. At the same time, such intense personal and interpersonal experiences help the community to continuously evolve their capacity for communication, dialogue and co-creation.

It is worthy of note, that many of our co-creators are well into their 40s and 50s. Once a person is in and around midlife, there is an enormous transformational potential underpinned by significant life experience and knowledge. While many educationalists today speak of lifelong learning, the predominating educational focus, at least where degree programmes are concerned, is always on the so-called young leaders. As important as this age group is, we, however, see the urgent need to purposefully develop the research and innovation potential of the age group beyond 40 years of age alongside our young adults. It was, in our particular case, also this age group which was in a position to make significant steps towards promoting and implementing new educational, research and consulting institutes and centres, designed to take the research–to-innovation journey forward in their particular societies.

INCREASED IMPACT: TOGETHER WE GROW

This orientation, then, towards directly addressing the burning issues of our time, admittedly still on a modest scale, but with enormous potential for growth, gives our research community a unique kind of spirit. A central concern of TRANS4M, through our Geneva-based centre, has been to further evolve our catalysing role of building, hosting and stimulating such a growing research and innovation community. Furthermore, many of our doctoral students, hitherto on the Buckingham University programme, have evolved to some extent our existing knowledge base on transformation management, focusing on the development of an Integral Enterprise, alongside Integral Research and Innovation.

Together we are developing thereby a new knowledge base, which, as we see it, underlies the new disciplines of Integral Innovation (research based) and Integral Enterprise (practitioner based). The organic evolution of our research-to-innovation community, however, bears a number of further exciting fruits. Some of the participants of our programmes have taken the TRANS4M impulse into their own countries and, in close co-operation with our institute in Geneva, are building their own local centres, serving their particular communities and societies, differentiating and integrating into their work the local cultural context. Here are some of the current examples:

- *Sam Rima and Bethel University:* While Bethel intends to contribute the necessary infrastructure and its own particular intellectual capital, TRANS4M's knowledge base on Integral Research and Innovation was seen as the very DNA of the centre. At the time of our finishing this book, the process of setting up this new institute is still at an early stage; however, all parties involved are moving forward with commitment and speed. This includes the International Business Leaders Forum, primarily through its Director Asia Pacific, Peter Brew, a longstanding supporter of TRANS4M, and Ros Tennyson, IBLF's deputy chief executive officer and herself an international expert on cross-sector partnerships. At Bethel University, Dr Rima is joined by Curtiss de Young, who runs Bethel's unique programme in Reconciliation Studies: hence a prospective Institute for Reconciliation and Social Innovation.
- *Anisa Al Raisi and an emerging TRANS4M Oman:* Anisa Al Raisi has recently set up an educational institute in Muscat called TRANS4M Oman. It is closely linked with TRANS4M Geneva and committed, through educational programmes based on TRANS4M's knowledge and catalytic base, to take forward the impulse for renewal that she specifically, and Oman's Sultan Qaboos much more generally, has brought to the nation.
- *Mfuniselwa Bhengu and an emerging Africa TRANS4M Research Institute*: Bhengu, a South African Member of Parliament and social philosopher, was introduced to TRANS4M by Professor Lovemore Mbigi of Africa Intellectual Resources (AIR), with whom the University of Buckingham is running its Master's in social and economic

transformation. Together with Bhengu, we are developing a prospective African research institute that will serve to co-evolve indigenous African philosophy and our generic transcultural and transformational approaches.

TRANS4M then, together with its research community and emerging local applications, is moving increasingly into a position, where we can contribute to a paradigm shift in management research and education.

SHIFTING RESEARCH AND INNOVATION PARADIGMS: TRANS4MING RESEARCH

TRANS4M, through our Geneva-based institute and together with our partners across the Four Worlds and the centre, has a vision. We have set out to transform research and education in a way that it leads to Integral Innovation, and to the evolution of Integral Enterprises, set within an Integral Society. In so doing, we are contributing to a number of major paradigm shifts. As we see it, these shifts are necessary to address successfully and on a large scale, locally and globally, the burning social issues of our time. Given the importance of this matter, we summarize, once more the core paradigm shifts, with which we are here concerned.

Individual Research to Research Communities: Firstly then, the burning social issues we face today are far too complex to be addressed by an individual researcher alone. We need, therefore, to build up research communities. Doing this has been common currency in the natural and life sciences and in the domain of technological innovation for a long time, reflected in large research laboratories like CERN in Geneva, but it is still very much the exception in social science and social innovation.

From Social Research to Integral Innovation: We secondly argue (see Chapter 1) that while technological innovation is blossoming, social innovation has fallen far behind. We have illustrated, however, in this book, that social research if done in an *integral* way has an enormous potential to contribute to solving key social, economic and environmental issues. In that process, we have, for example, revealed, that all research methodologies are rooted in fundamental philosophical critiques of prevailing societies. By and large, however, most social science researchers are cut off from these very philosophies, having to comply to one or only a few methodologies favoured by the research context in which they are operating. Integral Research aims to restore that link to the philosophies, and to explicitly introduce such philosophies from North and South, East and West. In addition, it turns the research process on its head by starting with research method.

Recasting Method as Origination: A third paradigm shift, for us, is the new significance we attach to research method, when recast in integral terms. Method matters! It matters, particularly for us, as a tangible and original starting point for a social innovation. Method is, as we have shown, closely linked to the core of our humanity (being, becoming, knowing and doing), connected to the immediate experience of the life world and social context in which you are operating. Therefore, method becomes the starting point for your research to innovation journey and is used for you to get in touch with burning social issues within a particular context. At the same time, it can serve to connect you with the origins and originality of your particular cultural context and to an initial understanding of how this originality can contribute to the development of an integral innovation. That brings us to the third paradigm shift.

North-Western Domination to Four World Integration: Fourthly, we have described, how most of the current research methodologies have their origins in Europe, while research method has, by and large, been developed in the USA. The rest of the world, with the exception of critical realism (Anglo-Indian) and participatory action research (Latin American and South-East Asian) hardly gets a look-in. As a result, the South and East is failing to evolve its own knowledge base or research grounds. However, that is not the end of the story. While the South and the East remain inhibited, so the North and the West become restricted themselves. Northern and Western approaches to research have proven to be successful foundation for the technological (rationalism based) and economic development (pragmatism based) of societies, at least to a point. But, on their own they lack the capacity for social innovation, which is more a Southern (humanistic and relational) and Eastern (holistic and renewal) domain. In other words, the Four Worlds need each other if Integral Innovation is to take place. For that reason, we have scoured the world as a whole in this book to uncover Eastern and Southern philosophies that underpin our integral approach to research and innovation.

Reconnecting the Sciences and the Humanities: Finally, there has been an overall paradigm shift, in the natural sciences, from atomism to holism, from certainty and objectivity, to uncertainty and a blend of objectivity and subjectivity. To that extent we seek a new alliance between natural and social sciences in this newly integral (subjective-objective) guise. In addition and given the priority we attach to natural and cultural context, the humanities – art and literature, music and drama – need to be locally aligned with the more globally oriented social sciences.

So, where do we go from here? In our work with our research community, we notice, that we continuously, through working within a conventional university, transcend the limits of the traditional university approach. We recognize, that Integral Research and Innovation needs a totally transformed university format, a format, that enables the Integral Innovation Tree to fully flourish (see Figure 17.1). By now you, the reader, are fully aware, that we are already working towards such a new university, which we have termed an Integral University.

In the following section we therefore demonstrate, that, in our efforts to transform the conventional university design we are building on the shoulders of the giants who have come before us. Hence, before we outline the core design of such an Integral University, we shall provide an overview on a number of historically promising approaches towards a new university design.

17.3 Building the Integral University: Standing on the Shoulders of Giants

FROM IVORY TOWER TO INTEGRAL BRIDGE

For us, Integral Research and Innovation needs to pave the way for a new kind of Integral University, one to accompany the Integral Enterprise that serves as a culmination of our transformation (of) management.[3] Such a university would function as a bridge between indigenous and exogenous knowledge, between one civilization and another, between diverse social sciences, between thought, feeling and action, as well as, ultimately, between individual, organization and society. In other words such an *Integral University would transcend the proverbial image of a university as an ivory tower. Rather it would serve to reconcile different worlds*.

A FOUR WORLDS LIBERAL ARTS COLLEGE

Such a new kind of university would stand on the shoulders of giants who have come before; that is, a number of formative academic and research institutions which have preceded it. Firstly then, it would serve as a 21st century version of the original liberal arts college, which focused on the whole person over the course of the 19th and 20th centuries.

Our Integral University would simultaneously focus on the social sciences and on the humanities, though not in isolation of the natural sciences. Moreover, we would be drawing our knowledge from all four corners of the globe.

A KNOWLEDGE-CREATING RESEARCH UNIVERSITY

Secondly, such an integral academic institution would follow in the footsteps of the research university, founded originally in Germany in the 19th century, and exported to America in the 20th, with a contemporary knowledge-creating twist.

Actually, from our socially innovative perspective, the primary function of a university is to create new knowledge for the benefit of the society in which it is based, if not the whole world. Participating in such a knowledge-creating enterprise are the 'students', so-called, who are therefore seen, not as mere 'readers' of knowledge, but as potential social innovators in their own right. Where the Integral University of the 21st century parts company from the German or American research university of the 20th century is in its focus on the social as opposed the natural sciences. As such, it is explicitly involved in social as opposed to technological innovation.

FRANKFURT SCHOOL IN GERMANY TO NEW SCHOOL IN NEW YORK

The third giant shoulder on which we stand is the one whereby a research institute, and ultimately a whole university, has been built upon an emancipatory philosophy of humankind. Such an institute was the Frankfurt School in Germany in the 1930s, established almost exclusively by German Jews, the so-called critical theorists who had to flee from the Nazis to 'the land of the free'.

The New School for Social Research that was subsequently established in the USA provides an education grounded in history and informed by a legacy of critical thought and civic engagement. The school's dedication to academic freedom and intellectual inquiry reaches back to the university's founding as a home for progressive thinkers and the creation of the University in Exile in 1933 for scholars persecuted in Nazi Europe. The interdisciplinary education offered by the New School today explores and promotes global peace and justice as more than theoretical ideals.

ACTION RESEARCH FOR SOCIAL BETTERMENT

Fourthly, and now outside of a university context, an institution that also serves as an inspiration for us is the National Training Laboratories (NTL) established at Bethel, Maine, in the United States in 1947.

Its founder Kurt Lewin, as we saw earlier, was not only the inventor of action research on which the NTL was based, but also viewed the social sciences as a whole as a means of social betterment. The research laboratories that he established were a means towards that end. In fact, his predecessor John Dewey also established a laboratory with a similar aim in mind, early in the 20th century, in his case focusing on the spread of democratization, both in government and in the workplace.

THE NEW SCIENCES OF COMPLEXITY

Fifthly, a contemporary version of such a research institute, in this case focusing on so-called 'chaos and complexity theory', serves to connect the life sciences with social science. This Santa Fe Institute founded in the 1980s in New Mexico shares with the Institute for Noetic Sciences in San Francisco, a focus on 'integral science'.

Both institutes link recent, evolutionary developments in the natural sciences, especially in physics, biology and ecology, with those in the social sciences, particularly in-depth psychology and systems sciences. Finally, the contemporary integral philosopher Ken Wilber, based in Colorado in the US, has established an Integral Institute, operating virtually across the globe, to promote the unification of knowledge.

BUSINESS SCHOOLS ATTACKING THE SOCIAL PROBLEMS INCIDENT TO CIVILIZATION

The final shoulder we stand on, ironically in the light of recent business and economic developments, is the original American Business School. For Quaker Joseph Wharton, founder of Wharton Business School at the turn of the last century, it seemed self-evident that those of 'inherited wealth and capacity' must dedicate themselves to the needs of the community and to attacking 'the social problems incident to our civilisation'.

If they did not discharge this responsibility via the established professions, they must do so via 'careers of unselfish administration'. Wharton clearly desired to elevate not only the competence but also the social consciousness and moral character of those who chose to devote themselves to what the 19th century gentlemen of businessman called business 'affairs'. Unfortunately business schools today are a far cry from such original ideals and bear at least part of the responsibility, as we shall see, for the 2008 financial crisis, if not the energy crisis as well.

This is a point made very poignantly by Rakesh Khuranain his book with the evocative title *From Higher Aims to Hired Hands: The Social Transformation of the American Business Schools and the unfulfilled Promise of Management as a Profession.*[4] As Harold Bloom also pointed out in his *Closing of the American Mind*,[5] gradually the humanities and the more philosophically based social sciences, from the 1970s onwards, became eclipsed by the more practical, professional-based courses.

These impulses are very promising. In fact, while many of the giants we have cited are based in America, a land of experimentation, there and several others now emerging around the world, in India and in the Philippines, in Egypt and elsewhere, which we hope will soon be the subject of another book. While most of these forerunners of our Integral University focus on a particular gap left by the conventional university, we can summarize these altogether, as below:

Core Reform Impulses with Respect to the Conventional University Design

- Focus on the whole person.
- Students/participants are not mere 'readers' of knowledge, but potential innovators in their own right.
- Purposeful engagement in Integral Innovation.
- Linking of research, education and action.
- Building on emancipatory philosophies of humankind.
- Informed by critical thought and civic engagement.
- Dedication to academic freedom and intellectual inquiry.
- Interdisciplinary education.
- Exploring and promoting global peace and justice.
- Regard social science as a means of social betterment.
- Spread of democratization, both in government and in the workplace.
- Building on evolutionary developments in the natural sciences, especially in physics, biology and ecology, with those in the social sciences, particularly in-depth psychology and systems sciences.

We now turn more specifically towards the prospective Integral University.

17.4 Towards an Integral University

KEYNOTES OF THE INTEGRAL UNIVERSITY: TRANSFORMATIONAL TO TRANSPERSONAL

It is interesting to note that all the giants' shoulders upon which we have so far stood are American ones, even if the idea of the research university, and the Frankfurt School, originally came from Germany. This of course is not altogether surprising given the overall climate of innovation in 'the land of the free'. However, there is more than a little irony in that fact, given the situation in the US today, economically if not also politically and environmentally. For us, what underlies this US paradox is the very nature and scope of the American 'melting pot'. For while it promotes in many instances significant innovation arising out of the fusion of cultures, in more conventional cases Middle America melts things down to their lowest common denominator. In the October 2008 US presidential campaign this was symbolized by the now immortalized 'Joe the Plumber'.

The twist in the American tale then – and that's where 'the giants fall short' – is in its insularity and parochialism, if not also in its individualism and materialism. In fact, all the seminal institutions to which we have referred have operated exclusively and physically within America, even if they have drawn faculty and inspiration from diverse parts of the globe. In other words, our newly envisaged Integral University has to break new worldly ground, geographically as well as philosophically, albeit building on established foundations. Given our own integral orientation the four *keynotes*, to use a musical metaphor, of our Integral University are the transformational, the transcultural, the transdisciplinary and the transpersonal. We start with the Southern keynote, the transformational.

TRANSFORMATIONAL KEYNOTE: ADDRESS BURNING ISSUES – RELEASING GENE-IUS

The first unique attribute of our Integral University is its transformational *natural* keynote. For us this means two things. Firstly, a new metaphorical basis for scientific investigations needs to be established, rooted in the natural organism as opposed to physical mechanism. Here we are building on developments in the new sciences, as has been the case at Santa Fe Institute, most especially in biology and ecology. Such a natural orientation to self-organizing, life-giving processes transcends the metaphor of the self-made man. It also serves to take us back to our indigenous soils, in North and South America, in Africa and in Europe, in Asia and in Australasia, so as to re-align ourselves with 'Mother Nature', from whom modern man has become so ruinously disconnected. In that overall context, then, we build on the transformational flows of nature, which we have translated into our GENE rhythm: starting from the Ground-up, and thereafter engage in Emerging, Navigating, Effecting.

Secondly, in the course of such a re-alignment, we seek to overcome the economic pre-emphasis today of societies generally, and of universities and business schools specifically, by building upon nature and then culture prior to politics and economics.

TRANSCULTURAL KEYNOTE: DIFFERENTIATING AND INTEGRATING WORLDS

In all subjects of concern, ranging from ecology to economics, religious to business studies, our focus is upon both the local (indigenous) and also the global (exogenous). For example, and in relation to religious studies in America or in Africa, the indigenous focus would be on native religions, and the exogenous orientation would be towards the monotheic as well as polytheic ones. Interestingly enough, such a transcultural orientation would have served to overcome the anomaly, as we perceive it, of Barack Obama being identified as a 'black' American. He is patently not 'black', but rather a fusion of peoples, something with which 'melting pot' America is largely unable to identify. Indeed, global America has never come to terms with its indigenous, local origins, which is why our integral approach is needed.

Though universities and research institutes are to be found throughout the world, the content of the research and education in most subject areas will be dictated by Europe (North) and America (West). There are, of course, exceptions. Languages are indigenous, albeit that English has become the world's lingua franca. In the arts and humanities, including visual art and sculpture, music and dance, literature and drama, there is likely to be significant local influence. That said, even in the humanities, Spanish (in Latin America) and English (in Africa, the Indian subcontinent and much of the Middle East) will be the languages of overall instruction, thereby distorting the acquired knowledge in an exogenous direction.

When it comes to the sciences, both natural and social, and to the applied professions, course content will be almost entirely European and American in origin. Additionally, research – if it at all exists within the South and within much of the East – will be dominated by Western empirical methods rather than by an integral approach such as ours. Our starting point, wherever possible, will be to incorporate research and educational content from all four corners of the globe, as well as from as the centre: we would start then with the rich vein of comparative philosophy and religion, of the East and West, North and South, as well as from the Middle East.

Whereas courses and research in such areas as Oriental studies, African studies, Latin American studies and of course European studies, as well as English, French, German or Italian literature are commonplace, these are restricted to their particular subject areas, without serving to bring out the worldview of one or other particular culture. Whereas many would argue against the very notion of such a culturally specific worldview, there is no doubt that in some areas – most especially in the natural sciences, in business and economics, as well as in sociology and psychology – a North-Western worldview predominates. In our Integral University we would do our level best to counteract such a 'mono' or 'duo' cultural tendency in all major subjects of concern, by incorporating, at least, a 'quaternity' of worlds.

In the African South, for example, philosophy is very strong and distinctive. In the Near and Far East, including India and Pakistan, China and Japan, spirituality is well articulated, and again distinctively so. In Europe, if you take the time and trouble to look for it, philosophy and the humanities, the natural sciences, as well as economics, are clearly differentiated within and between at least the major European countries: the UK and France, Germany and Italy. Such realms of clear-cut cultural differentiation will both be taken into integral account, in both research and education.

Moreover, to the extent that such areas of integration are overshadowed by their opposite, that is disintegration and the proverbial 'clash of civilizations', so reconciliation studies would be a key part of such a transcultural offering. This would include research in social justice, conflict resolution and peace building alongside the study of comparative cultures and civilizations. In fact, and in the light of today's energy and financial crises in the West, a review of the economic activities in traditional societies, informed by cultural anthropology, would be a good place to start.

Moving from economic to business studies, we discover that Japanese *kaizen* emerged as an integration of Zen Buddhism from the East and statistical quality control from the West. In fact, most great artists, whether for example a Gauguin (French/Polynesian) or a Picasso (Spanish/African) were such 'integral masters'. Another example is modern global and rational chemistry, which emerged in its original form out of indigenous and magical alchemy. For Jean Gebser, the Austrian social philosopher, the ultimately integral society emerges out of what he terms ever-present origins; such an integral perspective, however, progressively builds on the magical, the mythical and the mental.[6]

Finally, and to the extent that the indigenous continually invites us to return to our origins – so, for example, the American Indians and the Australian aborigines, the African bushmen and the Nordic eskimos, as well as the indigenous peoples of China, India and Indonesia – indigenous cultures assume greater importance in the overall scheme of things, notably for their art, religion and their philosophies. To that extent these 'forgotten' peoples begin to come into their own. The South and the East gain more importance vis-à-vis the North and the West.

Our pre-emphasis, from an *integral*, and in this initial case, *transcultural* perspective, is with the differentiation and integration of the local (indigenous) and the global (exogenous). To that extent, for example, the European Renaissance in the 15th to 18th centuries, the Japanese economic miracle in the 20th century, South Africa's social and political emergence in our day and age and innumerable more specific examples from art and religion would be particular cases in point of local identity evolving towards global integrity. Ultimately, our Integral University transcends the very idea of *universality*, which is to be found within the conventional 'university'. Why? Because our 'integral' combines global text with local context; indeed, it starts out the other way around.

We now turn from the transformational and the transcultural to the transdisciplinary keynote of the Integral University.

TRANSDISCIPLINARY KEYNOTE: RECONNECTING SOCIAL SCIENCES AND HUMANITIES

The British academic and humanist, C.P. Snow, notably declared in the middle of the last century how tragic the separation between 'two cultures', for him the sciences and the humanities, had become. In contrast, the American liberal arts college as well as such contemporary research institutes as the New School for Social Research and the Santa Fe Institute, pride themselves on their interdisciplinary nature and scope, the former lodged in the social sciences and the latter in the life sciences. Moreover, the original American business schools, as Harvard's Rakesh Khurana identified, were as much concerned with law and political science, sociology and psychology, as they were with economics and more conventional business and management studies. Our Integral University, then, would follow in those illustrious footsteps, albeit that the humanities, except in the liberal arts case, tend still to be left behind in such places. The major vehicle for such a transdisciplinary approach will be our so-called Integral Research and Innovation, an area where even the 'giants' cited fall short.

For whereas the natural and life sciences (including those at Santa Fe) and the humanities (including those taught at liberal arts colleges) lack the ontological and methodological research versatility of the social sciences, the New School for Social Research, for example, is primarily rooted in critical theory, inherited from Germany's Frankfurt School. Similarly, in social science departments – particularly in sociology, which is the most prolifically methodologically endowed – one or other such ontology, epistemology and methodology tends to predominate. Whether it is feminism or postmodernism, critical realism or critical theory, one tends to preclude the other.

Moreover, in the developing world, Western empiricism rides roughshod over all other research methodologies. Our Integral Research approach then is somewhat unique in that, firstly, it differentiates between four major research paths, each of which has an integrating trajectory. The wide range of methodologies incorporated within our Integral

Research span the global social sciences, from anthropology to economics, from political science to behavioural psychology, as well as at least touching on the local humanities, from history and geography to philosophy and theology.

A second feature of our approach is the connection it makes between research and innovation, or between what we term 'fundamental research' and 'transformative action'. While such an interconnection is second nature to the natural sciences, resulting in technological innovation, it is virtually non-existent in the social sciences. In fact major social and economic breakthroughs, ranging from psychoanalysis (Sigmund Freud) to management (Peter Drucker), from liberal democracy (John Locke) to capitalism (Adam Smith) as well as communism (Karl Marx), are usually not acknowledged as social innovations.

Few have taken the time and trouble, for example in the case of democracy, to study the full nature and scope of such a 'social innovation'. The case may stretch back to the time of Socrates and the ancient Greeks, onto Locke and Montesquieu in the modern era, subsequently incorporated into the original American constitution. It may also include its further amplification through industrial democracy, via the thought and action, for example, of Robert Owen of Lanark Mills in Scotland and Father Arizmendiarrieta of Mondragon in Spain's Basque county. Moreover, to bring another example, there has been no similar study of the democratic traditions inherited from matriarchal communities of West Africa, and how they might have been drawn upon in modern times. Whereas such research may exist in political science, it is not reviewed as a past or future social innovation.

In the integral approach to research and innovation then, not only are such social innovations studied retrospectively, but also they are contextualized within particular cultures and societies. Further, they are reviewed from different ontological and methodological perspectives. More importantly, moreover, because such innovations have predominantly occurred in Western Europe and America, at least in the modern era, specific attention is given to all Four Worlds. This brings us onto the penultimate, and perhaps most far-reaching feature of an Integral University, embodied in what we term its 'transpersonal' functioning.

TRANSPERSONAL KEYNOTE: EDUCATION FOR COMMUNITY BUILDING TO SUSTAINABLE DEVELOPMENT – SERVING SELF, ORGANIZATION AND SOCIETY

Universities since their inception have been involved in the education of individual students, albeit that the best of them have been also engaged in research and knowledge creation. Overall, the primary focus has been on the individual. From an *integral* point of view this is a functional anomaly, because societies are made up, yes, of individuals, but also of organizations and communities. To the extent that our ultimate and integral focus is on social innovation, then the development of individual, organization and community are altogether involved. Moreover, we are talking of *particular* individuals, institutions and societies. To the extent that such is the case, we envision the following process to release individual, organizational and societal GENE-ius:

- *Grounding:* Each person, organization or community has its own context or grounds; each has its own development trajectory.

- *Emerging:* Having reviewed the grounds, and engaging in the developmental trajectory, the shared local and global issues of self/organization/society emerge synergistically through dialogue and through recognition of shared patterns (emerging).
- *Navigating:* In the process each living system has its own means of navigation and knowledge generation around the emerged burning issues; such emergence is channelled towards systematic conceptualization and knowledge creation ...
- *Effecting:* ... and each self/organization/society in combination has its own way of effecting innovation.

Dedicated to releasing the full GENE-ius the Integral University promotes, for a particular self, organization and society (or community) the following interconnected rhythm:

- being (self), community building (enterprise) and healing the planet (society);
- becoming (self), conscious evolution (enterprise) and peaceful co-evolution between peoples (society);
- knowing (self), knowledge creation (enterprise), and open society (society);
- doing (self), sustainable development (enterprise) and creating economic opportunity (society).

The role of the Integral University is to facilitate all of these. Of course this is a tall order, which the university cannot fulfil in isolation. If, however, embedded in a community of organizations from all sectors of societies, to which the university serves as a hub for Integral Innovation, then, in co-creation with others, it can live up to this challenge. While the university would retain its primary function, that of research, education and knowledge creation, by combining with these other entities, such an Integral University is in a position to pursue Integral Innovation. Figure 17.3 illustrates the overall orientation of the Integral University, interconnecting, in its pursuit to address burning issues, self, organization and society.

An Integral University, building up overall unity-in-variety, through its transformational, transcultural, transdisciplinary and transpersonal keynotes, is, like the Integral Enterprise that we have introduced in our work *Transformation Management*, an ultimate society builder. Indeed, enterprise and academe need each other. The Integral Enterprise needs the Integral University for the Integral Innovation the latter serves to bring about, enabling the enterprise to continuously evolve. Interestingly enough this is already, by and large, the case for technology-based companies like a Google or a Microsoft, which have their own 'in-house' universities. As such the Integral University is dependent on the wider community of Integral Enterprises, which it serves. Together, Integral University and Integral Enterprise are the foundations to renew, on an ongoing basis, the particular society, be it Jordan or Jamaica, Argentina or America, in which we live in.

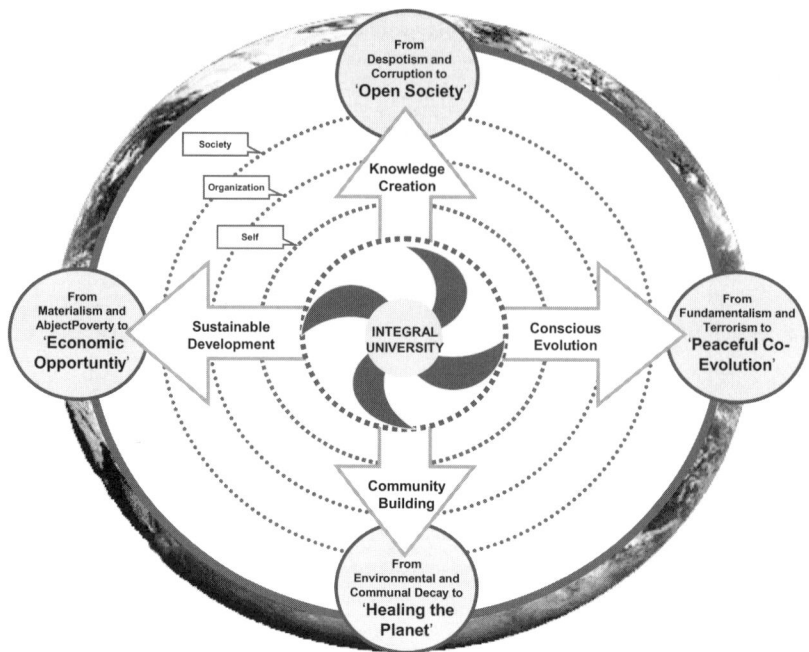

Figure 17.3 A Hub for Integral Innovation – Orientation of the Integral University

17.5 Conclusion: Integral University and Integral Society

The overall paths of Integral Innovation, accommodated by our Integral University, extend from nature, through culture, onto social (as well as natural) science, and ultimately onto management. Overall, such an Integral University serves to build up an Integral Society. Deeply embedded in one particular world, alongside others, it is working towards healing the planet, promoting co-evolution between peoples, building up open societies and creating economic opportunities integrally, that is promoting unity-in-variety and variety-in-unity.

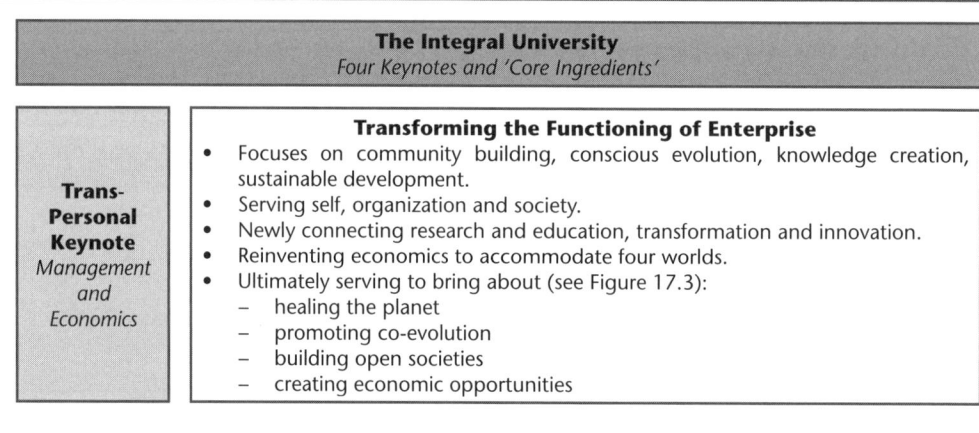

The Integral University	
Four Keynotes and 'Core Ingredients'	
Trans-Personal Keynote *Management and Economics*	**Transforming the Functioning of Enterprise** • Focuses on community building, conscious evolution, knowledge creation, sustainable development. • Serving self, organization and society. • Newly connecting research and education, transformation and innovation. • Reinventing economics to accommodate four worlds. • Ultimately serving to bring about (see Figure 17.3): – healing the planet – promoting co-evolution – building open societies – creating economic opportunities

Trans Disciplinary Keynote *Science and Technology*	**Orchestrating Transdisciplinary Dialogue** • Reconnects social sciences and humanities. • Evolving integral research and innovation. • Promoting integration of research, action and innovation across disciplines. • Building transcultural, transdisciplinary research communities. • Contextualized within particular cultures and societies. • Faculty from all disciplines of social sciences and humanities/co-researching and co-education 'beyond departmental borders'.
Trans- Cultural Keynote *Culture and Spirituality*	**Evolving Cultural Dynamics** • Integrates all Four Worlds (and the centre), promoting unity in variety. • Promotes creative synthesis between cultures and between local (indigenous) wisdom and global (exogenous) knowledge. • Incorporates research and educational content from all four worlds, as well as from the centre. • Engages in comparative civilizations, cultures, philosophies and religions. • Research and education in social justice, conflict resolution, peace building. • University as a place where the Four Worlds come alive through the arts, music, dance and other forms of expression. • University has interconnected cells all over the world.
Trans- Formational Keynote *Nature and Community*	**Engaging in Societal Renewal** • Addresses burning issues – releases GENE-ius. • Natural orientation to self-organizing, life-giving and life-affirming processes. • Building on latest developments in ecology, biology, neurobiology with respect to the design of sustainable living systems. • Re-aligned with 'Mother Nature'. • University embedded in nature; nature integrated in learning processes.

The four keynotes are each distinct and altogether integral, building on each other sequentially and also cyclically, just like in a melody or indeed a whole symphony. The conventional divisions between university departments, as such, are superseded. Nature and culture, science and management each have their complementary role to play. Furthermore, our respectively transformational and transcultural, as well as transdisplinary and transpersonal emphases, serve to ensure that there is not one path to salvation, but the universal and the particular, the global and the local, are continually interwoven.

An Integral University would require a combination of academics and practitioners from the realms of anthropology and ecology (nature and community), the humanities including religious studies (culture and spirituality), the social sciences (science) and public, private and civic praxis (management).

Ultimately, moreover, it goes without saying that such a university would need to be lodged within and across the Four Worlds, both physically and virtually, in order to become authentically integral. Figure 17.4 illustrates the core elements of the Integral University. With this figure we end, as we started: with the Tree of Innovation. Now it is embedded in the Integral University within a supportive and sustaining ecosystem.

We fully acknowledge that Rome was not built in a day. Our Integral University will not be established in one fell swoop. But we need to start to build different kinds of universities that reassume their role as innovation hubs within a particular community or society.

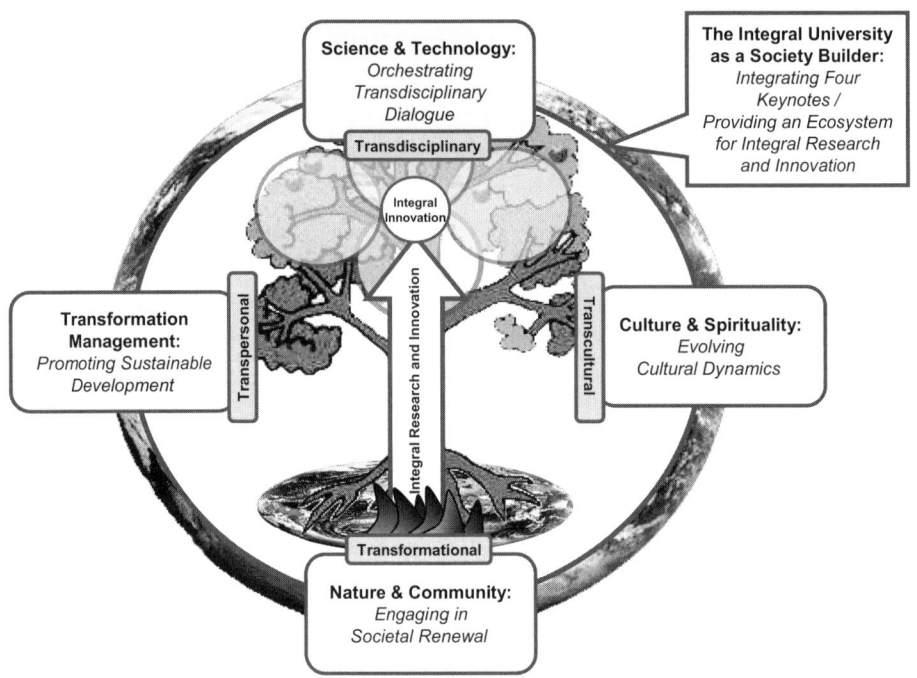

Figure 17.4 The Integral University

It is the role of universities to provide the relevant ecosystem for research and innovation to flourish. In this book we have introduced a newly integral approach to such. Such an approach spans the full trajectory from original research to transformative action. It is an approach that empowers social scientists, together with practitioners, from all Four Worlds to become Integral Innovators in their own right. The next step, as we have begun to do is to build a 'home' in which these can come together, interact and flourish. A home for transformation. A home for Integral Innovation.

Such a home is the Integral University. The time to build it is now!

References

1. Lessem, R. and Schieffer, A. (2009). *Transformation Management: Towards the Integral Enterprise*. Farnham: Gower.
2. Muchineripi, P. and Kada, S. (2008). 'Together We Grow: A Transformative Approach to Food Security in Africa.' *Forum CSR International*, February.
3. Lessem and Schieffer, *Transformation Management: Towards the Integral Enterprise*.
4. Khurana, R. (2007). *From Higher Aims to Hired Hands: The Social Transformation of the American Business Schools and the Unfulfilled Promise of Management as a Profession*. Princeton, NJ: Princeton University Press.
5. Bloom, A. (1988). *Closing of the American Mind*. Chicago, IL: University of Chicago Press.
6. Gebser, J. (1985). *The Ever-Present Origin*. Athens, OH: Ohio University Press.

The Analytical Trajectory of Integral Research and Innovation

Analytical Tenets of the Four Innovation Paths

The Southern Relational Path
Analytical Tenets

Origination
METHOD

Descriptive Methods (Origination)

- You seek to reveal more fully the essences and origins of human experience.
- You uncovering qualitative and quantitative factors in such.
- Engage your total self as participant, in a state of passionate involvement.
- You do not seek to predict or to determine causal relationships.
- You rather illuminate them through careful, comprehensive descriptions, vivid and accurate renderings of experience, rather than measurements or ratings.

Foundation
METHODOLOGY

Phenomenology (Foundation)

- Engage in a process of radical inquiry.
- Immerse yourself in a life world of immediately lived experiences.
- Concentrate on illuminating the nature of the 'inner self'.
- Focus on the subjective view of experience.
- Locate every unique cultural history as an episode in the larger story.
- Go beyond reductive positivism and naïve empiricism.

Emancipation
CRITIQUE

Feminism (Emancipation)

- You aim to create social change.
- You see knowledge as a tool for liberation not domination.
- Feminist research strives to represent human diversity.
- Feminist research complements the androcentric (masculine) perspective.
- As a researcher you as a person are included …
- … and so is nature.

Transformation
ACTION

Participatory Action Research (Transformation)

- The problem is defined, analysed and solved by the community.
- As a scientific methodology, PAR facilitates an authentic analysis of social reality.
- PAR involves the full and active participation of the community.
- PAR is aimed at the exploited, the poor, the oppressed, the marginal.
- PAR creates awareness of the people's own resources, mobilizing for self-reliant development.
- The ultimate goal of the research-and-innovation is the radical transformation of social reality.
- You as researcher/innovator are a committed participant, facilitator and learner in this process.

The Eastern Path of Renewal
Analytical Tenets

Origination METHOD

Narrative Methods (Origination)

- Your individual and communal stories are still unfolding.
- Each one of you, personally and collectively, is legendary.
- Each event in your individual and communal lives is therefore novel.
- The narrative mode leads to gripping drama and to creative origination.
- You are tying together potentials and possibilities of your respective beginnings.
- No struggle, no story; no trouble, no tale; no ill, no thrill!
- A plot shaped by many of the larger strategy-stories in which it is set.

Foundation METHODOLOGY

Hermeneutics (Foundation)

- Understand how the world is 'constructed'.
- Give 'the other' a voice.
- Interpret reality indirectly.
- Reconstruct self and society.
- Move from spectator to active agent.
- Evolve from interpretive to transformative.
- Reconnect with the source.

Emancipation CRITIQUE

Critical Theory (Emancipation)

- As a critical theorist, your research is rooted in concrete experience.
- It arises out of the problems of everyday life.
- Critical theory is strongly emancipatory in orientation.
- Critical theory uncovers power relations.
- You analyse specifically the suffering of people.
- Reality is regarded as socially constructed and multiple interconnections exist.
- Critical theory is explicitly focused on promoting 'liberation'.

Transformation ACTION

Co-operative Inquiry (Transformation)

- You engage in a politically oriented process, in a participative form of inquiry.
- You are involved in a knowledge-oriented process – epistemic in nature and scope.
- You engage in an alternating current of informative and transformative inquiry.
- You undertake your research in successive action-reflection cycles.
- The validity you seek for your research is goodness, trustworthiness and authenticity.

The Northern Path of Reason
Analytical Tenets

Origination
METHOD

Methods of Theorizing (Origination)

- Nature and social life consist of essential uniformities – patterns of events.
- It is the aim of science to discover these uniformities to find universal statements, which are true because they correspond to the forces of nature.
- Sensory experience is rejected as a secure foundation for scientific theories.
- Observations do not make much sense until they have been organized by some 'conception', an organizing idea; hypotheses formulated bring order to data.
- As a process of conjecture and refutation, we can never hope to actually establish a truth; we can only eliminate those theories, which are false.

Foundation
METHODOLOGY

Critical Rationalism (Foundation)

- Empirical science has nothing absolute about it.
- Derive theories from tentative conjectures.
- Falsify rather than verify.
- Strong theory drives out the weak.
- Natural and social science are value neutral.
- You ultimately formulate an overall deductive strategy.

Emancipation
CRITIQUE

Postmodernism (Emancipation)

- Pursue multiple discourses.
- Focus on meanings as multiple and shifting.
- You socially construct meaning.
- Engage in the art of thematic decomposition.
- Use language as cultural representation.
- Review history as transformative.

Transformation
ACTION

Socio-technical Design (Transformation)

- You adopt a problem-solving orientation.
- Your research is inevitably linked to action.
- Your research is geared towards social betterment.
- You use a co-generative approach to organization development.
- You act as a 'friendly outsider'.

The Western Path of Realization
Analytical Tenets

Origination METHOD	**Experimental and Survey Methods (Origination)**

- You are able to ask good questions – and to interpret the answers.
- You are a good listener – not trapped by your own ideologies and preconceptions.
- You are adaptable so that new situations can be seen as opportunities.
- You have a firm grasp of issues being studied, theoretically or policy oriented.
- You are unbiased by preconceived notions, responsive to contradictory evidence.

Foundation METHODOLOGY	**Empiricism (Foundation)**

- Search for truth.
- Seek after the 'positive facts'.
- Separate facts and values.
- Collect observational data and build theories.
- Control the research through 'closed systems'.

Emancipation CRITIQUE	**Critical Realism (Emancipation)**

- Critical realism is critical of the status quo.
- You become involved with a stratified or layered reality.
- You view such a layered perspective on reality as fallible.
- You conceive reality as both transitive (subjective) and intransitive (objective).
- There is a hermeneutic as well as an empirical side to critical realism.

Transformation ACTION	**Action Research (Transformation)**

- You start out with appreciative inquiry.
- You challenge power relations.
- You diverge and you converge.
- You undertake social research for social change.
- Knowing how is more important than knowing that.
- Action research incorporates action learning.

2 *The Transformative Trajectory of Integral Research and Innovation*

Transformational Teleology of the Four Innovation Paths

The Southern Relational Path
Transformational Teleology

Origination METHOD

Origination (Descriptive Methods)

Engage your total self, in passionate involvement with the phenomenon, undertaking careful, comprehensive descriptions, vivid and accurate renderings of your and others experiences, rather than conducting measurements or ratings.

Foundation METHODOLOGY

Foundation (Phenomenology)

Immerse yourself in a life world of immediately lived experiences, concentrating on illuminating the nature of the 'inner self', of self and other, locating every unique personal, communal and natural history as an episode in a larger societal story.

Emancipation CRITIQUE

Emancipation (Feminism)

Aiming to create social change, you see such knowledge as a means of liberation not domination, of physical and human nature, you strive to represent diversity.

Transformation ACTION

Transformation (Participatory Action Research)

This level involves the full and active participation of the community, aimed at the exploited, the poor, the oppressed, the marginal, serving to create awareness of the people's own resources, mobilizing for self-reliant development with you as committed participant.

The Eastern Path of Renewal
Transformational Teleology

Origination
METHOD

Origination (Narrative Methods)

Tying together potentials and possibilities of individual, organizational or societal beginnings; no struggle, no story, no trouble, no tale, no ill, no thrill. The narrative is like a plot shaped by many of the larger stories in which it is set.

Foundation
METHODOLOGY

Foundation (Hermeneutics)

Reconnect with the historical cultural and spiritual source; understand how the world with which you are dealing, including yours, is constructed; give relevant others a voice in the process.

Emancipation
CRITIQUE

Emancipation (Critical Theory)

Your social construction arises out of the problems of everyday life; critical theory uncovers power relations; you analyse specifically the suffering of people; you are explicitly focused on promoting liberation of self and others.

Transformation
ACTION

Transformation (Co-operative Inquiry)

You engage in a politically oriented process, in a participative form of inquiry, also involved in a Four-World knowledge-oriented process; engaging in an alternating current of informative and transformative inquiry, in action-reflection cycles.
The validity you seek for your research-and-transformation is goodness, trustworthiness and authenticity.

The Northern Path of Reason
Transformational Teleology

Origination
METHOD

Origination (Methods of Theorizing)

Observations you undertake make sense when organized by some 'conception', an organizing idea; you apply hypotheses (theories) to bring some order to data; in your search for the truth, you cannot establish it, only eliminate what is false.

Foundation
METHODOLOGY

Foundation (Critical Rationalism)

Deriving theories from tentative conjectures, you falsify rather than verify; strong theory drives out the weak; the natural and, more especially, social science you engage with – sociology or psychology, political science or economic – is value neutral.

Emancipation
CRITIQUE

Emancipation (Postmodernism)

You pursue multiple discourses, or worldviews, focusing on meanings as multiple and shifting, constructing your own unfolding meaning, using language purposefully as a means of cultural representation, reviewing history as potentially transformative.

Transformation
ACTION

Transformation (Socio-Technical Design)

You adopt a problem-solving orientation, your research being inevitably linked to action, geared towards social betterment; you use a co-generative approach to organization development, acting as a 'friendly outsider'.

The Western Path of Realization
Transformational Teleology

Origination METHOD

Origination (Survey and Experiment)

Able to ask good questions, you are a good listener – not trapped by your own ideologies and preconceptions; you are adaptable so that newly encountered situations can be seen as opportunities; unbiased by preconceived notions, you're responsive to contradictory evidence.

Foundation METHODOLOGY

Foundation (Empiricism)

In the search for the truth you seek after the 'positive facts', separating facts from values; you collect observational data and build theories from them; you control the results of any experimental research through 'closed systems', excluding unwanted variables.

Emancipation CRITIQUE

Emancipation (Critical Realism)

Critical of the status quo, you become involved with a stratified or layered reality; you view such a layered perspective on reality as fallible, knowing that there is an interpretive as well as an empirical side to critical realism.

Transformation ACTION

Transformation (Action Research)

Starting out, transformatively, with appreciative inquiry, you also challenge power relations; diverging and also converging, undertaking social research for social change; knowing how is more important than knowing that; action research incorporates action learning.

Index